THE INSIDERS' GUIDE ®

TO

North Carolina's OUTER BANKS

THE INSIDERS' GUIDE® TO

North Carolina's OUTER BANKS

by
Jayne DePanfilis
and
Nancy McWilliams

THE INSIDERS' GUIDE®

Insiders' Guides®, Inc.

Published and Distributed by:
The Insiders' Guides®, Inc.
P.O. Box 2057 • Highway 64
Manteo, NC 27954
(919) 473-6100

•

FIFTEENTH EDITION
1st printing

•

Copyright © 1994
by David Poyer and
The Insiders' Guides®, Inc.

•

Printed in the United States of
America

•

•

ISBN 0-912367-61-X

The Insiders' Guides®, Inc.

Publisher/Managing Editor
Beth P. Storie

President/General Manager
Michael McOwen

Creative Services Director
Michael Lay

Project Editor
Theresa Shea

Partnership Services Director
Giles Bissonnette

Fulfillment Director
Gina Twiford

Distribution Manager
Julie Ross

Advertising Sales Manager
Georgia Beach

Controller
Claudette Forney

Preface

In this, our 15th year, *The Insiders' Guide to the Outer Banks* continues a tradition of acting as your local information source, your friend and host, providing you with detailed information, extensive historical perspectives, thoughtful commentaries and interviews. In addition, there are updated descriptions of attractions, restaurants, accommodations, recreation and shopping. *The Insiders' Guide* includes important, otherwise difficult to find, information on medical services, camping, real estate and vacation rentals, annual events, fishing and ferry schedules.

Our maps assist readers in visual journeys to the towns and villages of the Outer Banks. Valuable information about the National Park Service and visitors' centers is included. Making park interpretive exhibits and programs a part of your journey is sure to enrich your Outer Banks experience. Remember to bring your binoculars, camera and adventurous enthusiasm to explore these island habitats.

Whether you're an armchair traveler or a hands-on visitor, *The Insiders' Guide* will serve as a handy reference for all aspects of life on the Outer Banks. For many years the wide, desolate beaches were an adventure in themselves. As growth occurs, the experiences change, yet the adventure continues. In an environment that is beyond the ordinary, you'll meet nature face to face and run into warm and friendly people.

Whether you're looking for big fish or to try your wings in flight, you'll find excitement. If it's peace and quiet you're after, you'll find that too. If history fascinates you, you'll confront it everywhere you go. This, after all, is the land of beginnings, the site of the first English explorations in the new world. (Sir Walter Raleigh must have known what a jewel lay waiting here for the English to enjoy!)

This 15th edition of *The Insiders' Guide to the Outer Banks* has been prepared by Jayne DePanfilis and Nancy McWilliams. It still carries some of the flavor of original writer Dave Poyer, who started the book back in 1979. Some of his priceless historical interviews have remained a part of the book, while McWilliams has added several fresh, new writing perspectives this year.

Of course the success of a serious guidebook is measured not by its first reception, but by its continued service, dependability and acceptance by the traveling public over a period of years. Since we will see more than 180,000 books in print with this edition, we feel justifiably proud that our readers continue to find this book helpful, and obviously invite others to use it too.

From the beginning, the book was designed to be a daily, in-hand piece, (a constant companion, if you will) fitting the needs of both visitors and residents. Even a glance will show you the time and effort that have gone into it.

Through the years, people have told us we didn't need to be so thorough. We could reprint press releases instead of doing our own research, or update less often; we didn't have to improve and expand every year. Wrong! We have an old-fashioned mind set: that painstaking research and careful writing, that solid value rather than glossy paper and bathing beauties, would pay off in repeat sales. Time has proven us right.

We as authors certainly don't deserve all the credit. This book would not be possible without the cooperation received so widely from our information sources, including the National Park Service and the hundreds of local business people and their staffs who cooperated so readily to make sure we got the best information possible. In a seasonal environment where everything seems to change constantly, it can be difficult to provide up-to-the-minute reports in an annual book, but we think you won't find better information anywhere, definitely not in one handy and complete source.

Since this book's first edition, the Banks have changed immensely — miles of open beach have become populated areas; the islands themselves have moved slightly closer to the mainland. The northern Banks have opened to widespread settlement. Ocracoke has condominiums and is immersed in popularity rather than seclusion. Hatteras Island is going strong, even after the huge blow dealt by Hurricane Emily in 1993. The central Banks of Nags Head, Kitty Hawk and Kill Devil Hills are busier than ever, with new shops, restaurants and cottages. Manteo continues its downtown face-lift and forever offers its special presence to this area.

Some things haven't changed. The Outer Banks remains a vacationer's paradise. It's still home to old residents and thousands of new ones. It's still a daughter of the sea, tumultuous with storm in February and placid and glittering in July. It is still dunes and wild ponies, sea oats and yaupon. It's still fun in the sun at the beach, from lazy days to entertainment-filled nights. It's a place to escape to as well as a world of fun and activity. We have had many wonderful times here and hope you will too.

Thank you for your support. We've done everything we can to make your time on the Banks happy. That has, quite simply, been our goal all along.

— Jayne and Nancy

About the Authors

Jayne DePanfilis is a native of St. Mary's, Pennsylvania and has resided in a number of states from Maine to North Carolina. Until relocating to the Outer Banks, most of her time was spent up north (in Massachusetts, if you should know) during which time she received her bachelor's degree from Bates College, Lewiston, Maine, where she majored in Political Science and French. Her command of the French language really came in handy during her travels to Europe.

She came to the Outer Banks after receiving her master's degree in business from Old Dominion University in Norfolk, Virginia. Jayne intended to enjoy her "last summer of freedom" and then move on to seek her fortune but discovered, as many of us have, that the Outer Banks has a subtle charm and a way of "capturing" people who believe themselves to be just passing through.

Jayne is director of marketing, advertising and sales for Kitty Hawk Kites, Inc., the world's largest hang gliding school, where she has been challenged to new heights, especially while she pursues hang gliding. Along with enjoying freelance writing for the past several years, Jayne has an extensive background in

marketing and real estate. Much of her time since coming to this area was devoted to market research and feasibility analysis until she served as managing editor for another Outer Banks publication. This is Jayne's second year with *The Insiders' Guide*. She is excited about this year's edition and hopes her knowledge of the area will benefit everyone who is interested in the Outer Banks.

Nancy McWilliams, born in Bristow, Oklahoma, and raised in the "Heart of Dixie" (south Alabama), swept onto the shores of Nags Head in 1988 after spending an exciting decade in the West, writing for community newspapers in Wyoming, Colorado and Montana. A graduate of Auburn University's school of journalism, Nancy feels her destiny is to use her writing skills to portray the positive, uplifting, challenging aspects of people, art and life.

She has been a columnist and feature writer for the *Virginian-Pilot's* "Carolina Coast" section for more than four years, and her work has been published in a variety of other publications, including *Hang Gliding Magazine, Windsurfer, Paragliding Magazine, Carolina Style, Go (AAA) Magazine* and many others. She also writes brochures and publicity for local tourism-related businesses.

She writes the newsletter and does public relations for First Flight Society, the nonprofit organization that commemorates the achievements of the Wright brothers, and has been publicity director for North Banks Rotary Club for five years.

Nancy enjoys cooking, traveling, reading and learning. Definitely not a desk-bound writer, Nancy has rafted the Colorado River and other western whitewater numerous times, been an avid cross-country skier, tried skydiving, hang gliding and paragliding, taught canoeing in an Adirondack Mountain camp and rounded up cattle on the open range of Montana. She has lived on cattle ranches and at ski areas. At the age of 37, her quest for adventure continues. Right now, the fun and challenge of raising a son is more exciting than she had ever dreamed.

Nancy is glad to have been a part of *The Insiders' Guide.* As she frequently uses guidebooks in her own travels, she knows the value of accurate and up-to-date information, and has tried to offer those qualities to *Insiders' Guide* readers.

Acknowledgments

It was great fun compiling the latest information about the Outer Banks for the 1994 *Insiders' Guide*. It wouldn't have been possible without the kind cooperation of the hundreds of business and restaurant owners, attraction managers and government employees who took time from their hectic schedules to answer my questions. Thank you for helping me obtain accurate, up-to-the-minute reports.

A special thanks to resources such as the National Park Service staff, especially Bob and Bebe Woody at headquarters in Manteo. Thanks also to Suzanne Wrenn for her birding knowledge, Tony Beugless for his surfing expertise, Damon Tatem for his excellent fishing comments, Sam McGann of the Outer Banks Culinary Association, Tim Caferty of the Dare County Board of Realtors, Wynne Dough of the Outer Banks History Center, Elizabeth Evans of the Lost Colony, friends Glenn and Pat Eure and John Harris for listening when I needed to be heard and to my cowriter and friend Jayne DePanfilis. Also to be thanked are the Dare County Tourist Bureau, Dare County Library and the Outer Banks Chamber of Commerce, always helpful and knowledgeable.

Last, but never least, much gratitude goes to my son Ethan for his patience when I was on the telephone or at the computer and when I hauled him along on research trips.

I look forward to next year!

— Nancy

I would like to thank everyone who shares our interest in making *The Insiders' Guide to the Outer Banks* the best, most comprehensive and up-to-date source of information about this unique and ever changing place I call home.

The search for a single phone number or an out-of-the-way address would be impossible without your help. It's not unusual that we would drive from one end of the Banks to the other to talk with any of you, and we thank you for being there to meet with us and share your insights, historical perspectives and information about the Outer Banks.

I would like to recognize the editorial staff for "true" attention to detail and for once again guiding me through this process.

This year, in particular, I would also like to indulge myself and thank my father who is forever insisting that I "dig in" and rise above challenging circumstances.

— Jayne

Table of Contents

Directory of Maps

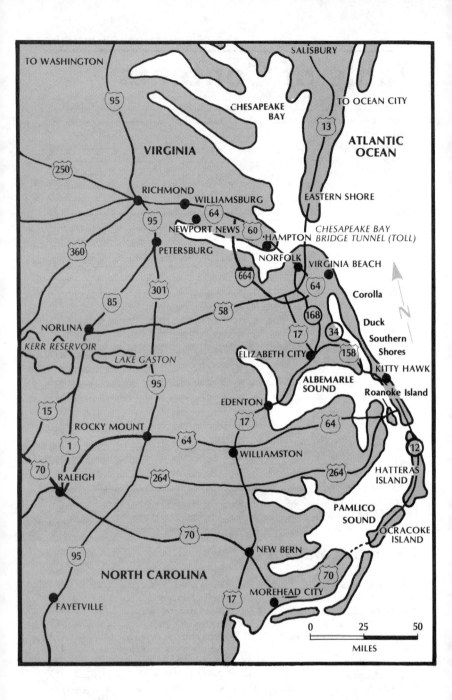

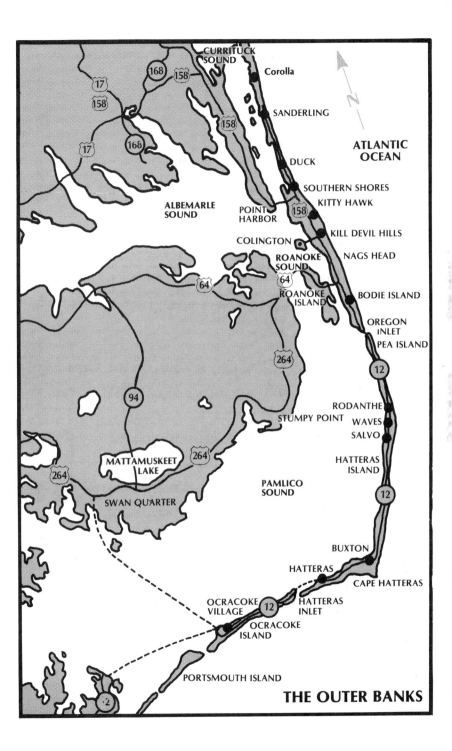

THE OUTER BANKS

THE ONLY COUNTRY ON THE BEACH
CAROLINA 92 FM

WNHW, the only station on the Outer Banks offering a mix of modern, traditional and cross-over country music, with CNN and local news, sports, weather, fishing information, beach conditions, community promotions, tourist information, and daily updates of what's happening on the Outer Banks and surrounding areas. Located at 92.5 on the FM dial, Carolina Ninety-Two serves Northeastern North Carolina with offices in Nags Head. Stay informed and entertained with the only country at the beach, WNHW, Carolina Ninety-Two!

Inside
The Outer Banks

Although it is well known through recounting the lives of the Native Americans and the early English colonists in plays, books and historical sites, the geological interpretation of these islands warrants reflection.

"Barrier island" is the term used to describe a land form made up entirely of sand and without the keel of rock that normally anchors most islands to the earth. This fascinating phenomenon of a constantly changing land form is not so difficult to understand once you realize that such a land mass is subjected to the process of change by the wind and the sea.

The level of the ocean has changed as a result of water released or stored in great polar ice caps. A lowering sea and extended sandy coastline that are illustrated in these island lands were consequences of great amounts of water that were not circulated during the ice ages. As the last great ice age ended, approximately 20,000 years ago, the seas began to fill. Slowly, the sea has risen some 400 feet. North Carolina's Outer Banks, authorities agree, were formed in this process. The Banks were a mixture of maritime forests and sparsely vegetated sand dunes. Perhaps, silt from inland rivers con-

tributed to the buildup of sand as well as the wash of the ocean. Shifting sandbars, raging winds and lofty breezes somewhat artistically formed high and low areas of land separated by water, thus the string of islands.

In times of wild, wind-driven storms, sections of small islands were over-washed by the oceans. This created what we refer to as sounds. Differing from bays, the waters of the sound are trapped waters, not essentially bodies of water created by rivers emptying into them, which correctly describes the Chesapeake Bay, for example. Sounds in this eastern region of North Carolina — Roanoke, Currituck, Pamlico and Albemarle sounds — were formed by such an over-wash of land mass. Some areas became completely covered by water, thus creating inlets where sand again accumulates and often closes an inlet to navigation. These islands today are separated by inlets and sounds, and in more recent times the waters have been spanned by bridges or connected by ferry service.

Prior to recent times, however, ships at sea were subjected to shifting sand and the variations of the North American Continental Shelf. More than 500 shipwrecks attest to the difficulty of navigation around these shores. Once a ship navigated the coast, inlets or sounds and arrived in an open harbor, there were no assurances that the same passage would be open on recurring journeys to these barrier islands. The history of English expeditions sent by Sir Walter Raleigh to these shores is filled with agonizing tales of hardship in seafaring exploits, as well as those about establishing land settlements.

The change in the shorelines and land masses of the Outer Banks has occurred over hundreds of years, so don't cancel your reservations yet. It will be thousands of years before these barrier islands rejoin the North Carolina mainland. But it's fascinating to understand how dynamic, moving, living these Banks are.

Today we observe this string of barrier islands, measuring from about seven to 12 feet above sea level and stretching from a few hundred feet to several miles across, in a fascinating shift or movement. For example, as you cross Oregon Inlet, your drive on the Herbert Bonner Bridge will expose a view across an expanse of low, flat land under the northern piers of the bridge. A marshland area of numerous waterfowl and wildlife, it was not there when the bridge was built in 1964. This indicates the islands are moving south since sand and vegetation are accumulating here.

Oyster and water-snail shells found on the beach in the areas of Nags Head, Coquina Beach or on Hatteras Island, and some large chunks of peat formed in freshwater bogs are indications of how the sand-islands have changed. These shells have been washed from interior regions or shellfish beds toward the ocean, perhaps during high winds from the west, which push water in an easterly flow. Ancient tree stumps protruding from the ocean at various places along the Outer Banks reveal the existence of maritime forests along the once-extended coastline. The islands are moving west.

The movement occurs slowly, and for those who inhabited the islands years ago, the history of Kinnakeet on Hatteras Island reveals large forested areas and wild grapes that grew in abundance. Ships left for points north loaded with lumber from large oak trees that grew in these forests. In more recent times, the Outer Banks terrain exposes wide expanses of open, flat beach with some maritime forests farther inland on the west side of the islands.

Bridges and roads have been built and subsequently maintained at great costs to keep the islands connected. During the fall of 1990, a section of the Bonner Bridge was knocked out by a major storm that drove a barge into the pilings. Prior to this, constant windblown sand created the necessity of building a portion of the highway farther to the west on a narrow stretch of Hatteras Island in Rodanthe.

During the Halloween storms of 1991, portions of the National Seashore highway south of the Bonner Bridge experienced ocean overwash. Huge sandbags are being used to build a "wall" against the surge of the ocean. During storms or exceptionally high, full-moon tides, water continues to wash over the road. Salt water intrusion into the marshlands poses a threat to waterfowl and wildlife. The water tables or aquifer providing drinking water are threatened by saltwater intrusion, which in turn threatens the habitability of the land. While we are focusing on a very small area of the Outer Banks by comparison, this natural occurrence of ocean over-wash is of some concern. Similarly, there is concern from the rise of the sound waters during storms with high westerly winds, as was the case with the March 1993 storm. Areas of Roanoke Island, Rodanthe and the other beaches were devastated by sound over-wash that flooded houses, ruined cars and polluted water tables.

The most recent devastation was caused by Hurricane Emily on August 31, 1993. The name Emily will long be remembered on the lower end of Hatteras Island, where 115 mobile homes and 58 houses were destroyed, and hundreds more were damaged.

The events or results of storms have been separated by time in such a manner that continuing development of the Outer Banks has been possible. Wildlife on the islands is abundant and in some areas is increasing. The soundside of the Outer Banks is home to thousands of birds, deer, fox and rabbits. The oceanside habitat reveals a large variety of marine animals, such as ghost crabs,

clams and skates. The present-day Outer Banks offers extraordinary adventure and exploration.

It was the same to explorers more than 400 years ago. To go back in history, it is possible that Italian Giovanni Verrazano sailed and mapped these coasts as early as 1524. Others may have learned to use Cape Hatteras as a navigable area or a short-cut from the West Indies back to Spain.

If these lands were discovered in seafaring days of Spanish and Italian explorers, it wasn't until the English, determined to establish colonies on the new land, discovered and settled on the islands off the coast of North America and later the area that was to become the coast of North Carolina. The first recorded community was on Roanoke Island, near the current site of Fort Raleigh National Historic Site. This community failed, but the English kept trying, and a few years later John Smith succeeded at Jamestown where John White had failed on Roanoke Island.

The Banks were permanently settled by second-generation English who trickled down from the Virginia settlements of Jamestown, Williamsburg and Norfolk, leavened by fugitives from the King's justice and shipwrecked mariners. These early settlers were the direct ancestors of today's numerous Midgetts, Austins, Baums, Grays, Ethridges, Burruses,

Take a slow-paced stroll around Manteo to look at the historic houses and pretty gardens.

Insiders' Tips

Photo: Mike Booher/DCTB

You know the old line, "Leave only your footprints."

Tilletts, Manns, Twifords and other old and famous families of the Banks. They settled at the islands' widest points — Kitty Hawk, parts of Hatteras and Ocracoke, as well as Roanoke and Colington Islands — where forests offered shelter and the land mass provided the opportunity to raise cattle and crops to sustain life. It was not an easy existence, but it was a free one, and healthier than the cramped and plague-haunted cities of Olde England.

There was one part of the Banks that flourished in those early days, and that was Ocracoke. The inlet, deeper then, was an important place of entry for ocean-going vessels. But Ocracoke was also attractive to another sort of seagoing entrepreneur: the pirate, especially the infamous Blackbeard. The story of Captain Edward Teach's (his real name) "war" with the law-abiding citizens of these shores is told in the Ocracoke Island section of this book.

Another war, this one the War between the States, left its mark along the Outer Banks with battles at Hatteras Inlet (August 1861), Chicamacomico (October 1861) and Roanoke Island (February 1862). The Federalists won victories in early skirmishes and established control of an area that geographically would seem to have been influenced by Southern causes. At that time, however, the inhabitants were not strongly attached to that point of view and many took an oath of allegiance to the United States.

As if to reward them, the postwar era saw a steady flow of federal dollars to the Banks, and they were spared Reconstruction. Navigational improvements had become unavoidable, and three fine lighthouses, at Corolla, Bodie Island and Hatteras, were built in the years between 1870 and 1875. The U.S. Lifesaving Service — the forerunner to the Coast Guard — was also established and lifesaving stations were built along the Banks. These stations and the service provided residents with jobs, and the accompanying cash that employment brought.

Changes were taking place in the Banks' internal economy as well. Nags Head was becoming the area's first and finest summer resort. Commercial fishing and wildfowl hunting were replacing wrecking and whale oil as sources of income.

The 20th century, destined finally to end the fabled isolation of these low, remote islands, began with a symbolic event: the arrival of the Wright brothers. The history of their failures and their final success at man's first powered, controlled flight is probably the best-known story of the Outer Banks, though the story of the lost colony must run a close second.

The Banks' boom years began in 1930-31. The rest of the country was in the Great Depression, true, but these years marked the completion of the first road accesses to the "beach," the Wright Memorial Bridge across Currituck Sound to Kitty Hawk and the Washington Baum Bridge from Roanoke Island to Nags Head. Paved roads down the islands followed, and development began.

Another milestone was passed in the late 1930s, when the federal government set up six camps for its Civilian Conservation Corps, and millions of dollars were spent erecting sand fences and planting vegetation along 115 miles of shoreline — all designed to "save" the Outer Banks. Man-made dunes as high as 14 feet in many areas were built. The Cape Hatteras National Seashore was officially established in 1953. The major section of land controlled by the National Park Service arm of the Department of the Interior is the area between Whalebone Junction (at South Nags Head) and Ocracoke Inlet. There are villages established in exempted portions, such as Waves, Rodanthe, Salvo, Avon, Buxton, Frisco, Hatteras Village and Ocracoke Village. Fort Raleigh on Roanoke Island and the Wright Memorial in Kill Devil Hills are also maintained by the National Park Service.

Surprising to more recent residents and visitors, many World War II confrontations at sea took place on the coastline of North Carolina. In 1942, Hitler's U-boats struck at American merchant ships. A look at a *National Geographic* map of shipwrecks and battles reveals a number of these confrontations. In fact, the first U-Boat sunk by Americans lies a few miles off the beach of Bodie Island.

One of the reasons that the northern beach communities were not developed as early as those farther south in the Nags Head area was their close proximity to the military bases in Norfolk, Virginia. Lifelong residents of the tiny village of Duck recall the days when bombing tests were conducted along the shores north of the village.

The permanent population of the area has grown from approximately 7,000 in 1970 to approximately 25,000 today. Many derive their income from businesses that provide services to visitors. Commercial fishing is alive in the villages of Hatteras, Wanchese and Colington. Real estate has provided employment opportunities for many since the early 1980s.

As more people discover the unpolluted environment and the more casual lifestyle (in spite of certain hardships that come with island living), communities have grown, and the permanent residents are called on to support adequate services, schools, medical facilities, churches and other community needs. Mayors, planners, civic groups and others are giving careful attention to growth. There is a need for better access and egress to the communities and resorts of the Outer Banks. Roads are being widened and bridges are being planned. A new two-lane bridge is being built parallel to the present Wright Memorial Bridge, which connects Point Harbor (on the mainland) with Kitty Hawk and other villages of the Outer Banks. Another bridge connecting the Currituck County mainland to Corolla has recently received wide support. Local government officials have been working with a lobbying group to request federal funding for this span, and a toll fee has been discussed for funding purposes. If successful, the northern Outer Banks could see this new bridge early in the next century.

Regardless of the changes taking place, the way of life is extraordinary in many ways. The residents know they're onto something precious: a land of beginnings not to be taken lightly. All its treasures — the waters, maritime forests, beaches, and small, quaint towns — are worth exploring, whether as a one-time visitor or as a lifelong lover of the Outer Banks.

Photo: Mary Ellen Riddle

The boatbuilding industry still thrives in Wanchese.

The Outer Banks
Getting Here, Getting Around

Arrival on the Banks is an adventure in itself. Most will come by car, though many choose to arrive by light plane, boat or even bicycle. Which mode of transportation you choose depends on how much of a hurry you are in to get here — and how fit you are.

The popularity of the Outer Banks has no limit, especially for those in the northeastern regions of the country, and it's easy to get here by car. North of Richmond you'll take I-295 toward Norfolk and Williamsburg and then I-64 eastbound to the Norfolk-Hampton Roads area. Alternate Route 664 is a great enhancement to the trip, and you pick it up between Hampton and Newport News. From Route 664 you can take Route 17 South in Deep Creek, then Highway 343 in Camden continuing on to Route 158, which leads to the Outer Banks. Or, from Alternate Route 664 you can pick up Route 168 in Great Bridge and head south. The highway becomes Route 158 about 30 miles from the beach. Stay on Route 158, and when you cross the Wright Memorial Bridge you're on the Outer Banks. This way will probably be more congested, as Route 168 is only two lanes wide, but insiders still prefer this route.

If you're a resident of North Carolina you'll more than likely arrive via Route 64 East onto Roanoke Island and then to the beaches of the Outer Banks. Visitors from other southern routes can travel the same route, or perhaps arrive by toll ferry from Swan Quarter and Cedar Island onto Ocracoke Island where NC 12 actually begins. Of course, another ferry ride, this one free, from Ocracoke to Hatteras Island is in store for you on such a journey.

The ferry rides are fun, and we recommend one in the early morning if you're here during the summer months. The departures are frequent from Hatteras to Ocracoke — every 15 minutes during the busy time of day during high season, but the lines are often long during the middle of the day. A complete ferry schedule is listed in the Ferry section.

Air service to the Outer Banks is available via Southeast Airlines' scheduled flights from Norfolk International Airport or through charters with Outer Banks Airways. Arrival at Dare County Regional Airport in Manteo or First Flight Airstrip in Kill Devil Hills by private plane is also an option. (Information on the airport is found in the Roanoke Island section and in the Kill Devil Hills section for the airstrip.) Car rentals are listed in the Service & Information Directory.

Once you're here, you'll definitely need a car, even though there is a new form of public transportation on the Outer Banks. You won't be able to miss The Beach Bus, 255-0550. These authentic English double-decker buses (eight in all) are candy-apple red. Three of the buses will be topless — perfect for evening rides under the stars. The buses will travel along the Outer Banks on a designated route. Customers will be able to pay one fare and ride all day to such places as the Wright Brothers National Monument in Kill Devil Hills, the North Carolina Aquarium in Manteo and shopping destinations including Kitty Hawk Connection in Nags Head. The Beach Bus will also offer a Pub Ride during the evenings and transportation to The Lost Colony performances. It will be very convenient for hotel and motel guests all over the Outer Banks to ride the bus to your favorite night entertainment destination. Look for the new beach buses this summer. We think they'll be a lot of fun for everybody, and they'll help fill a public transportation void.

Also, there are several dependable cab companies. One caveat: The Dare County police and sheriff forces are quite large (per capita) in order to handle the load that thousands of summer visitors create. This means that in the off season, there are six cops per driver (an exaggeration, but it sure *seems* that way). They also are extra watchful for drunk drivers, which we applaud. So, consider yourself warned.

The islands are strung out for over 100 miles and it's an impossible walk . . . though we know by saying that, we'll probably hear from some of you who have proved us wrong! Some villages and towns are conducive to "pleasure" walking, however, Ocracoke and Manteo being two.

Biking is popular along Route 158 where bike lanes are well-marked. A stretch of NC 12 north of Southern Shores also has bike lanes, and other towns have marked bike paths. There are plenty of places in the area to rent bicycles if you don't want to lug yours along.

It's possible to visit the Outer Banks and just enjoy the beach where you're staying. But there's so much to see that we recommend a car tour or a combination of car, bike and walking. You know your preferences and capabilities; you're in charge of how you get around to see everything, we're in charge of bringing them to your attention!

As you can see from the map at the beginning of this section, the barrier islands don't leave much room to roam from east to west. But, those areas included in a north to south exploration, from Corolla to Ocracoke, will provide many adventures. Enjoy!

Insiders' Tips

Speeding on the Outer Banks will probably get you a ticket.

Photo: Mike Maher/DCTB

Piers are enjoyed all along the Outer Banks.

Public Access Areas

Public access on the northern beaches from Southern Shores to Corolla is not allowed except when you are renting a cottage — in other words, there's no parking, and only those who own property or lease through a property management company have access to the beach. (The four-wheel drive or off road areas north of Corolla are open to bathing and fishing within the limits of posted regulations at the beach access ramp north of Corolla.)

Public access to the beach is marked along Route 158 and the Beach Road from Kitty Hawk to Nags Head. Along the highway you'll notice large green signs with white lettering noting the distance to public access and parking. As you travel the Beach Road, the signs are orange and blue. Some access points have parking lots, others are walking paths to the beach.

Along the Cape Hatteras National Seashore, parking lots provide ample parking for visitors who want to get out beyond the dunes and explore the uninhabited beaches of the south shores. (Shell picking is different here, so if that's a hobby, you might not want to miss an afternoon walk in this area.) Some folks like to run off the side of the road, park their cars and hike over the dunes. We don't recommend it. If you're unaccustomed to driving on soft shoulders, and if you don't happen to be driving a four-wheel drive vehicle, you could encounter some difficulty — sandy shoulders are softer than soft. And, once you're stuck, you probably won't get "unstuck" until you're pulled out, either by a good samaritan for free, or by a tow service . . . not for free. Besides, walking over the dunes creates breaks in the vegetation and promotes erosion during winter storms, heavy rains and winds. The National Park Service maintains many public parking areas, and the walkways to the beach are easier to "navigate" for walkers of all ages.

We're not encouraging additional driving for visitors who come here on a vacation, but most visitors are unable to check into their cottage or motel until around 4 PM. The traffic is heaviest during the hours around noon, and it can sometimes be exasperating to try to just drive around and kill time. So, if you want to come early in the day and have no place to go, hit the beach. It's here — just beyond the public access areas — and there are small public bathhouses along the Beach Road in Kitty Hawk, Kill Devil Hills and Nags Head so you can conveniently shower before putting back on your "street clothes." We know a family that traveled at night and arrived on the Outer Banks at daybreak. Their check-in time was 4 PM, but with a little early planning for getting to those chairs and towels, they drove to a public parking area and hit the beach in time to see the sunrise! They grabbed some extra beach time and less time in traffic. After a light lunch and some leg-stretching through a grocery store, they were ready to check into their cottage at the appointed time and were rested, happy and already ahead on their tans!

Photo: Mary Ellen Riddle

The red brick Currituck Beach Light was built and first lighted in 1875.

Inside
The Northern Banks

It used to be that visitors to the Outer Banks considered Kitty Hawk the "beginning" of the beach area. There were, after all, few if any rental cottages farther north than Kitty Hawk. But, as the Outer Banks as a whole became more popular, expansion flung its arms both north and south. In the northerly direction, Duck, once a sleepy little bend in the road with only a few stores, started to attract visitors, thus development. Then, the community of Sanderling, with its beautiful homes and exemplary landscaping, showed up. But, there was still that elusive land in the far northern regions of the Outer Banks that beckoned. It wasn't until October 1984 that most of us could even enter this extreme area of the northern Banks. There was a guarded gate until then blocking access to Currituck County on NC 12, so access to this private northern frontier was confined to property owners, friends of property owners and those who had a four-wheel-drive vehicle that could traverse the beach.

Well, dramatic changes have occurred on these upper northern beaches since 1984. The guard gate came down, and with that the public was able to enjoy the vast expanses

of scenic, undeveloped land north of Sanderling, including viewing wildlife refuges and sanctuary lands. But there's no denying it, and no way around it; the biggest changes of all resulted from major real estate development in these northern beaches. Interestingly enough, planned unit developments (PUDs) did not begin to occur in the immediate area where the guard gate once stood. Instead, they began to spring up farther north in the areas of Corolla and Whalehead. Planned unit developments combine residential building with desirable amenities and, more recently, with commercial development. You can now take advantage of nearby services on the northern banks, like grocery shopping, hardware stores and restaurants, that you used to have to drive 10 miles or more south to find.

The past five to seven years have seen a proliferation of developments of this sort. And developers have successfully imposed strict architectural guidelines within these resort communities. They've preserved natural landscapes as much as possible with low density development and have provided the northern Outer Banks with first rate, family-oriented resorts like Corolla Light,

NORTHERN BANKS

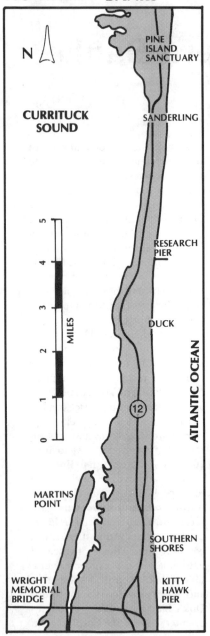

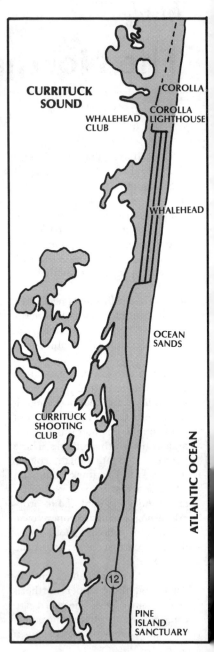

Monteray Shores, Ocean Sands, Buck Island and, most recently, Pine Island.

Therefore, it is safe to say that the northern Outer Banks, that area from the town of Southern Shores to where the paved road ends north of Corolla Light, has become a destination all its own. This area includes the beaches and resorts (in addition to those mentioned above) of Southern Shores, Duck, Barrier Island, Ships Watch, Whalehead Beach, Ocean Hill and the off-road developments of Seagull, Swan Beach, North Swan Beach and the northernmost development of Carova Beach, bordering Virginia's False Cape State Park.

Residential neighborhoods and one-road (dead end) subdivisions with names such as Nantucket, Bias Shores, The Tides, Tuckahoe, Sea Hawk, Sand Dollar Shores, Georgetown Sands, Duck Blind Villas, Sea Pines, Ocean Pines, Poteskeet and Saltaire line the road from Southern Shores to Duck along both sides of NC 12.

North of the village of Duck, you'll pass by residential communities, large and small, such as Sea Ridge, Osprey, Snow Geese Dunes, Carolina Dunes, Wild Duck Dunes, North Point, Port Trinitie, Caffey's Inlet Hamlet, Gull's Flight, Spindrift and Crown Point.

If you arrive in Southern Shores (and Kitty Hawk) from the north, you'll cross the Wright Memorial Bridge over Currituck Sound. Barges and other equipment now line Currituck Sound, signaling that work is well underway on the new bridge. Pilings have been built and will be tested; and more pilings will be poured. The new span is scheduled for completion in 1995. Once completed, the two bridges together will allow two lanes of traffic to flow in each direction, making it much easier to enter and to leave Dare County during peak season vacation time. And for safety purposes, more efficient hurricane evacuation will be possible.

Southern Shores is one of the oldest planned developments on the Outer Banks, located on the north side of Croatan Highway. The town of Kitty Hawk begins on the south side of this road. Southern Shores was part of Kitty Hawk for many years, and both towns share shopping facilities and conveniences. But, as you will see, Southern Shores remains a more private area; the private beaches are designated for property owners and renters only.

Southern Shores was first developed by Frank Stick, the well-known outdoorsman and artist. He purchased 26,000 acres of ocean-to-sound property for a reported

Avoid grocery shopping on Saturday.

Insiders' Tips

$25,000 in the late 1940s. As an environmentalist before his time, he envisioned careful development, and this is evident throughout this town. Southern Shores offers visitors and residents two vastly different but complementary environments. Year-round homes nestle under the canopies of wooded areas on the edge of the maritime forest surrounding Duck Woods Country Club and the Marketplace Shopping Center. Here, landscapes roll with mature greenery, and no two yards are alike. Or, if you prefer the wide open skies over your part of the beach, the oceanside and dune area along NC 12 promises a grand vacation. Older fishing cottages, mostly of block construction from times gone by, are becoming extinct as newer larger beach homes are built. Homes here sit right out in the open sand; you can feel the wind on your cheeks and taste the salt air on your tongue — you're that close to the beach.

To discover the newer, rapidly growing areas located between Duck and Carova Beach, first find Route 12, Duck Road. This winding scenic two-laner curves left (north) at the stoplight in front of the Aycock Brown Welcome Center, located on the northern edge of Kitty Hawk. As you drive north along the seaside route of NC 12, through Southern Shores, you'll see dunes covered with low, scrub woods and private roads leading off to the right and left to expensive cottages in the many private, one-road subdivisions. Despite the growth, this area seems less populated than elsewhere on the Banks, testimony to the stricter building

codes established by the original developer and maintained by the city council. It's worth your time for an afternoon drive to just meander through these areas before heading up to Duck.

Duck, a village that used to be strongly reminiscent of the village of Hatteras, also changed with 1980s development. It's a popular place. The village is nestled along the sound on the curves of a shopping mecca. Today's visitor finds remaining old-line residents earning their living either owning or working in dozens of retail shops, real estate agencies, sailing centers, sandwich shops, restaurants and other service-oriented businesses formed in recent years. Retail development was especially astounding in the late 1980s. Duck boasts a wide variety of unique boutique-style shops located at shopping areas such as Scarborough Faire, Osprey Landing, Loblolly Pines, Duck Waterfront Shops, Wee Winks Square and most recently, Duck Village Square. Water sports such as windsurfing, sailing, jet skiing, canoeing and sea kayaking are enjoyed by the beach-going public here.

Still, as you continue north, there are two things time hasn't changed. The sea is quite close to Duck; the village has even been referred to as a "ribbon of sand." A turn right almost anywhere near the village will bring you to a short walk over the dunes where nature abounds. There are sea oats and wild beans and peas. A variety of shore birds, including loons, cormorants, gannet and flocks of terns and gulls soak up the sun's warmth near the water's edge. If you

Photo: Mary Ellen Riddle

The Northern Banks' wild ponies are fun to watch, but don't get too close.

find yourself lingering (and you will), look out to sea to the horizon's edge; there's no telling what you may see . . . perhaps a school of bottle-nosed dolphins, common in these fish-rich waters.

Moving north, just on the periphery of the village of Duck, you'll pass Barrier Island Station, one of the largest and most successful timeshare resorts on the Outer Banks, and Ship's Watch, a first-rate, luxurious, year-round community of seaside homes with impeccably-manicured landscaping along the edges of NC 12.

Wide open spaces and high dunes dot the landscape as you leave Duck. You'll pass a sign for the U.S. Army Coastal Engineering Research Facility, an 1,800-foot-long, reinforced-concrete coastal engineering research pier used by the Corps of Engineers to investigate the forces that create and destroy

beaches. Sorry, the Army doesn't encourage casual visitors here.

As you continue your drive, you'll be sure to notice some of the finest homes on the Outer Banks in the partially hidden community of Sanderling. Privacy, exclusivity and integrity best describe this resort development. Surrounded by the thick growth of live oaks and pines, Sanderling has also become known for impressive landscapes filled with flowers and greenery indigenous to the Outer Banks.

In 1985, the Sanderling Inn and Restaurant opened. Though both are profiled later, each deserves special mention here for their architectural and historic significance. The Inn has the southern charm that characterized the old Nags Head resorts at the turn of the century. It's large and airy, with wide porches that provide room for conversation and drinks. Note the cedar shake siding, natural wood interiors and English country antiques. Expansion at the Sanderling Inn means there will be even more guest accommodations for visitors to enjoy. These will be some of the most luxurious accommodations on the Outer Banks. Guest rooms will feature even more amenities including central sound systems.

The restaurant is housed in an Historic Landmark, Caffey's Inlet Station. Designated U.S. Lifesaving Station Number Five, it was built on its present site in 1899, when, along with two at Corolla, one at Ocean Sands, and others dotting the shore every seven miles, it served as home to the men who patrolled the beaches searching for signs of shipwrecks. Though abandoned and deteriorating for a number of years, the Station was given a new lease on life with a thorough renovation, serving first as the Sanderling office, then, in 1985, as the restaurant.

Just north of the Inn on the east side of NC 12, you won't miss the majestic million-dollar homes of the Palmer's Island Club of Sanderling. A few hundred yards farther north, a sign informs you that you've left Dare County and are now entering Currituck County. To the west is approximately 5,000 acres of marsh, islands, and uplands preserved as the National Audubon Society Pine Island Sanctuary. To the east for the next 3½ miles will be the planned unit community of Pine Island, covering about 385 acres when completed. There will be 300 single-family homesites, oceanside and oceanfront. Property owners will have access to jogging trails, swimming pools, tennis courts and a private

landing strip for touchdowns. As a property owner you will also have access to the Pine Island Indoor Racquet Club located west of NC 12. An 80-room hotel, beach club with an indoor swimming pool and a 200-seat restaurant are also planned. Development is well under way at Pine Island.

Ocean Sands is located nine miles north of Duck. There are about 450 oceanside and oceanfront residences in this family-oriented resort community.

Just 11 miles north of Duck lies the exclusive oceanside and oceanfront resort development of Buck Island. Developer Buck Thornton decided to break new ground with Buck Island and offer the buying public another unique, full-service resort maintaining the same standards of excellence as his other seaside development, Ship's Watch. Reminiscent of nautical seaside villages, Buck Island offers 78 single-family homesites and 41 townhome sites. Construction is now under way on Phase II of the TimBuck II Shopping Village. Signature architecture consistent with that of the residential development best describes the appearance of this plaza boasting 12 merchants who are going into their second season. The plaza includes a Brew-Thru, video store, realty office, covered parking and public rest room facilities. Construction is underway on a second building that will house 12 additional merchants. The outparcels are being developed at the same time adding even more shopping, recreational and dining opportunities. Great efforts were made to maintain the area's natural landscape, preserving live oaks whenever possible.

Of course there's the Monteray Shores resort, located just north of Buck Island on the sound side of the northern banks. The magnificent homes here come complete with Caribbean-style red tile roofs and arched verandas. But if traditional Nags Head style is what you're after, they have that too. This resort offers an impressive clubhouse, recreational amenities and the Monteray Shopping Plaza. You won't be able to miss the new ACE Hardware building and the Monteray Professional Center.

Probably the best all-round resort in this area is Corolla Light, located in the heart of Corolla. Richard A. Brindley, the developer, has created a multifaceted year-round resort on the northern banks. His idea that everyone deserves a piece of the beach is reflected in the resort's layout. Oceanfront and oceanside homes are situated along the dunes and back a few rows but are separated by a huge oceanfront complex, accessible to all who own property or vacation here. The clubhouse, swimming pools, tennis courts, indoor sports center and soundfront activity center make Corolla Light Resort very popular with owners and vacationers.

The Whalehead Club is located soundside in Corolla, north of Corolla Light, and in November 1992, Currituck County Commissioners signed documents preserving this historic landmark for the public as a wildlife museum. The property is also to be used as a destination beach, grandly accomplishing Currituck's longtime goal of providing adequate water access for the beach-going public.

The old village of Corolla is tucked in between the resort, Currituck Beach Lighthouse and the end of the paved road. There is one-stop shopping at a Wink's grocery complete with a few gas pumps. At the end of the paved road you'll discover The Villages at Ocean Hill. This resort covers 153 acres with 300 single-family homesites and some of the widest-looking, white, sandy beaches anywhere.

The growing non-road-accessible communities between Corolla and the Virginia border are reachable only by four-wheel-drive along the beach. They've been the subject of intense speculation as discussion concerning the MidCounty Bridge continues. The state Transportation Improvement Program determined that construction would begin sometime after the year 2000. It seems we'll just have to wait until the first piling is driven before we know for sure if there's going to be a bridge.

As we've seen, the northern Outer Banks beaches have experienced incredible growth in recent years, growth dictating that these areas will be some of the most exclusive ones to visit or own. But despite intensive development, the northern Banks retain a certain remoteness. And make no mistake, there is an abundance of gorgeous white sandy beaches here. Families gather on these wide beaches for day-long volleyball, complete with picnics, beach gear and awnings. The overall attitude here encourages a relaxed lifestyle not often found on beaches along the East Coast. Adults and children are welcome to spend their dream vacations here, and that means a real change of pace. Remember, getting into life at the beach is an unforgettable experience on the northern Outer Banks.

Attractions

PINE ISLAND SANCTUARY

Situated on both sides of Ocean Trail, or NC 12, as you head north past Sanderling, this 5,000-acre wildlife sanctuary is home to ducks, geese, sanderlings and many other species of the bird population as well as deer, rabbits, foxes and other animals that inhabit the wilderness. Low-growing live oaks, bayberry, inkberry, pine, yaupon, holly and many varieties of sea grass distinguish the area. It looks primitive and weatherbeaten and holds our attention. There are very few places like this in the world. If you're a member of the Audubon Society, tours are available; if not, then there's no trespassing. The drive is enjoyable, and during the off season, the quietness of the area is intense.

COROLLA WILD HORSE FUND, COROLLA WILD HORSE SANCTUARY AND THE SANCTUARY PROGRAM

The wild horses that thrive on the Outer Banks are descendents of the Spanish mustang and were here long before the Outer Banks became a popular place to hunt, fish or vacation.

In 1523, Spanish expeditions brought the horses here and, when colonization was unsuccessful, they were left behind. In the years between 1584 and 1589 the English settlers purchased horses from the Spaniards and brought them, along with other livestock, to Sir Walter Raleigh's colony on Roanoke Island. When the Outer Banks began to attract settlers, the horses provided transportation, rounded up livestock and pulled fishing nets. During the 1800s, some of the horses were used for the beach patrol by the U.S. Life Saving Service. Many of the horses were sold during the Depression.

As the local population began to settle in Nags Head, the wild horses began to limit their range to areas north and south of Nags Head, thereby splitting the horses' population into two groups. Settlement of Kill Devil Hills and Kitty Hawk caused the northern group to continue migrating north to Corolla. Today, the wild horses are almost exclusively in the northernmost areas of Currituck County. The larger herd tends to range around the Corolla Light area and north of it, while the shunned colts range from Whalehead Beach to Pine Island. But the shunned colts have even frequented the Sanderling area (farther south) at different times during the past year.

The many homes and vacationers on the northern beaches could potentially threaten the horses' existence, yet there have been incredible efforts to protect these last remaining ones from extinction. The majority of the citizens of the Outer Banks are intent on protecting the herds and their ability to roam free and continue to exist in spite of increased development. To this end, the Corolla Wild Horse Fund on the Currituck Beach has been established and through their efforts a Wild Horse Sanctuary and Sanctuary Program have been established as well.

The Corolla Wild Horse Fund was established in 1989 to help involve and educate the public about the wild ponies. The numbers of ponies have dwindled due to their tendency to inhabit areas of development that contain lush vegetation rather than to remain in the remote off-road areas of the northern Outer Banks where food is not as plentiful.

Sadly, 13 ponies have died as a result of car accidents since 1989, and three horses were hit in 1992 but survived. With their migration to "civilization," the horses encounter automobiles. Motorists are cautioned by a number of signs, but it is impossible to predict the movement of these ponies who graze alongside the road and are prone to walk right out into the path of oncoming vehicles. **Please drive carefully!**

Thanks to the efforts of the Wild Horse Fund, the Wild Horse Sanctuary was established, and now it is unlawful to attempt to approach, touch, feed, harass, harm or kill the Corolla wild horses. For your safety, stay back 50 yards from the horses.

The Sanctuary Program was established in early spring of 1992. Uniformed officers accompany the herds in an effort to inform the public of dangers regarding physical proximity. They also hand out literature, prevent human contact and feeding, slow or stop traffic when horses are on the roads, assist the vet when needed and answer questions. The officers maintain radio contact with the Sheriff's department and/or veterinarian when necessary. The Sanctuary Officers have been working with the Corolla Wild Horse Fund to determine how best to accomplish herding of the horses north, where they will be out of harm's way. This continues to be the goal of the CWHF. Sanctuary officers work long hours each week and can be contacted at the Currituck Beach Lighthouse during the summer months.

More recently, in October 1993, a meeting was held at the Currituck County Satellite Office concerning the plight of Corolla's Wild Horses. Senator Marc Basnight, Representative Vernon James, State and County government officials, U.S. Park Service Managers, Estuarine Reserve Managers and Corolla Wild Horse Fund members attended this meeting. For the first time in more than four years, officials agreed on the protection and preservation of Corolla's special horses. A sound/sea barrier will be erected to steer the Mustangs away from new developments and heavily-travelled roads.

A county plan of placing a fence from within the Currituck Sound to within the Atlantic Ocean was approved by the state. Access to the northern beaches will remain the same for motorists. At the north beach access will be a livestock grate, which some feel will deter the horses from crossing back into the developed area. Grazing is plentiful on the 15,000 acres of unpaved land that will be home to the horses.

Donations for the preservation of these animals may be made to the Corolla Wild Horse Fund, P.O. Box 361, Corolla, NC 27927.

KILL DEVIL HILLS
LIFESAVING STATION
Corolla

This lifesaving station, built in 1878, is now the property of Twiddy Realty in Corolla. Lifesaving stations were built along the Outer Banks for the purpose of rescue operations when powerful storms hit the coastal areas. This is the lifesaving station that was located in Kill Devil Hills and assisted the Wright brothers during their glider and plane experiments. It was moved to Corolla in 1986 and became a realty office after considerable restoration. It is open for interested viewers, and there is a collection of memorabilia used by the lifesaving service and the Wrights. This unique building is on the west side of Ocean Trail in the village of Corolla.

WHALEHEAD CLUB
Corolla

This grand old hunting mansion is now the property of Currituck County, and plans for a wildlife museum are underway. The purchase of the Whalehead Club by Currituck County in 1992 also means the public has access to the sound; in the north beaches this is sorely needed. As "privatization" of the north beaches continues, developers will not be able to prevent the public from enjoying the sound at the Whalehead Club.

There's a lot of history attached to the club, which dates back to 1874. Back then, hunting clubs were a popular gathering place for sportsmen from New York. These men formed a club known as the Lighthouse Club of Currituck Sound. The first building was situated on 2,800 acres of the best duck hunting area on the east coast. Up to 300 birds a day were brought down by expert marksmen, including President Teddy Roosevelt. One of these hunters, Mr. Edward Collins Knight, wanted to bring his wife to the Lighthouse Club to hunt. Mrs. Knight was of French descent and an excellent markswoman, but she was discouraged from coming to the all-male Lighthouse Club hunting parties. So, Mr. Knight bought some of the land and built this grand mansion for his wife and their friends.

The mansion was built in 1922 for approximately $380,000, and construction is said to have taken three years. On the outside, the five chimneys and copper-clad roof have been two of its most distinguishing characteristics. On the inside, walls that are 18 inches thick, Tiffany light fixtures and fine home furnishings gave the mansion a sense of splendor. The Knights called their mansion, the "Castle." The house also has a basement — which is unusual so near sea level — that contains 16 rooms used for storage, wine cellars, food cellars, offices and the like.

The Knights passed away within months of each other in 1936, and the mansion was subsequently purchased in 1940 by Mr. and Mrs. Ray Adams of Washington, D.C. The Adamses named their new home the Whalehead Club. Mr. Adams was a wholesale meat broker in Washington and used the mansion to entertain business associates and friends. It was Adams who leased the property to the U.S. Coast Guard during WWII.

The mansion next became the property of George T. McLean and W.I. Witt of the Virginia Beach and Portsmouth areas. Under their ownership it was once used as a boys school, Corolla Academy.

Through the years, the once grand mansion suffered from lack of maintenance and use. Vandals removed many of its furnishings and fixtures. The proposed development of the late 1980s failed to give it a proper place in a resort community, and during the fall of 1991 negotiations got underway for its restoration and eventual use as a wildlife museum.

CURRITUCK BEACH LIGHTHOUSE, KEEPER'S HOUSE AND OUTER BANKS CONSERVATIONISTS, INC.

Corolla Village   453-4939

The northernmost lighthouse on the Outer Banks is this red-brick Currituck Beach Light that was built and first lighted in 1875. At night, it still flashes its warning signal with 50,000 candlepower every 20 seconds to ships hugging the coastal chain of barrier islands.

The Lighthouse Keeper's House, a Victorian "stick style" dwelling, was constructed from pre-cut, labeled materials, shipped by the U.S. Light House Board on a barge and then assembled on site. Since 1876, when the Keeper's House was completed, two keepers and their families shared the duplex in the isolated seaside setting. When the Lighthouse was automated, keepers were no longer needed to continually clean the lenses, trim the wicks, fuel the lamp and wind the clockwork mechanism that rotated the beacon. At that point, the Keepers' House was abandoned.

In the 1950s, even though falling into disrepair, the Keepers' House won recognition for its architectural significance and historic value when it was placed on the National Register of Historic Places. Despite the fact that states are required by executive order to protect their National Register listed holdings, the Keepers' House became more dilapidated with each passing year.

By 1980, the Keepers' House stood open to the elements with no windows or doors; porches had fallen, and vines had invaded the north side. Much of the inside had been vandalized. In that same year, Outer Banks Conservationists, Inc., a private nonprofit organization dedicated to the conservation of the character of the Outer Banks of North Carolina, became concerned with the preservation of the historic property and signed a lease with the state of North Carolina. The lease charges the conservation group with the responsibility of restoring the Keeper's House.

While the foremost task of exterior restoration is complete, the rehabilitation of the interior remains a mammoth undertaking. Plaster walls and pine floors must be repaired, vandalized wainscotting replaced and the mahogany balustrades, which were stolen from both sets of stairs, exactly replicated and installed. Happily, Outer Banks Conservationists worked with N.C. Cultural Resources to stabilize the smaller (and possibly older) dwelling to the north, which was moved here around 1920 to house a third keeper and his family. The Keepers' House is closed to the public at this time, but it is hoped that the house will soon be open, allowing us to recall the lifestyle of another era when faithful keepers kept the light burning to provide safe passage for those sailing on dark seas.

You'll notice the lighthouse when you arrive on the northern Outer Banks. The approach is along Ocean Trail (NC 12) through Corolla Light Resort and into Corolla Village. Actually, when you pass the famous Whalehead Club, the sandy lane to the left is the one leading to the parking area of the lighthouse grounds. The Currituck Beach Lighthouse is open to the public — it's 214 steps to the top! (There's a landing every 25 steps so you can catch your breath, but check your own mobility before getting underway on this climb.)

The lighthouse is open Easter through Thanksgiving, 10 AM until 6 PM, seven days a week during most of the year. High winds or thunderstorms may make climbing dangerous; the lighthouse will be closed during those times. Call for winter hours before you drive all the way to Corolla and find that the lighthouse may be closed that day. The cost is $3 per person. Half this amount is dedicated to restoration of the lighthouse, while the other half is dedicated to restoration of the compound. Annual memberships are invited to further support restoration of the Keeper's House.

Recreation

The northern Outer Banks beaches, stretching from Southern Shores to Corolla, offer a wide range of recreational possibilities and sports facilities. When the beach itself isn't enough, and you're anxious to catch a movie or get out on the sound to sail, windsurf, kayak or play tennis or miniature golf, a number of places come to mind. Let's take a look at what's available.

Southern Shores

Southern Shores has some of the most private beaches along the coast. There are several parking lots for access to the beaches for property owners or renters, but these may not be used by the public in general. In addition, the streets that run perpendicular to the ocean are off limits for public parking. In other words, if you live in Southern Shores, whether you are a property owner or temporary guest renting a cottage, you have beach access (by permit) and can park in marked areas.

WE CAN HELP YOU FORGET WHAT YOU DO THE OTHER 50 WEEKS OF THE YEAR.

Jet Skis, Parasailing, Windsurfing, Sailing, Pontoon Boats
Lessons • Rentals • Sales • Sea plane tours new for '94

North Beach Sailing

3 convenient locations: at Barrier Island Sailing Center 261-7100
(Toll free from Corolla 417-4414) • at The Promenade Recreation
Village 261-4400 • at The Waterfront Shops 261-6262

If not, access is not permitted. This appeals to many who are truly getting away from it all! Therefore, there is little public recreation, per se, in Southern Shores.

Duck Woods Country Club, 261-2744, is located at MP 1 in Southern Shores. Located just over the bridge, Duck Woods is a private club with golf, tennis and swimming. Contact the membership chairman through the club number for information about fees and dues. It's the only private club on the beach, but they are open to the public after Labor Day until sometime in June. It's for members only and their guests during July and August. Their snack bar, The Grill Room, is located in the clubhouse along with the Pro Shop.

Colony Cinema, 261-7949, is also located at MP 1 in Southern Shores at the Marketplace Shopping Center just past Duck Woods Country Club. The twin theaters offer first-run movies and attractive matinee prices.

Duck

As you head into Duck Village, along Duck Road (NC 12), you'll see **WaterWorks Too, Sailing Site**, 261-7245, at Wee Winks Square. The wide open waters of the Currituck Sound await your pleasure. Take off on your sailboard or sailboat, or rent jet skis, boogie boards and surf boards for an afternoon of fun. Parasailing is once again on the agenda for the '94 season. They're open 9 AM until 6 PM daily during the summer season.

Kitty Hawk Kites, 261-4450, is adjacent to Waterworks in Duck and will be offering a sea kayak program of their own this year. The new program will consist of a 2½ hour combined lesson/tour. No prior experience is required. Advance reservations are required, and the class will be limited to 12 students. Inquire about group rates. Rollerblades can be rented in Corolla. Join Kitty Hawk Kites for Roll Patrol. (Corolla is a great place to learn how to rollerblade or to refine your skills.) Kitty Hawk Kites is also the world's largest hang gliding school, and lessons are offered daily at their Nags Head location.

Kitty Hawk Sports, 261-8770, is a water-sports legend on the Outer Banks. The challenge is all yours if you have your sights set on water sports lessons. Kayaking, windsurfing and sailing lessons are booked here, but you'll need to visit their locations in Nags Head, 441-6800, and Avon, 995-5000, for windsurfing equipment or rentals. Boogie boards, surf boards and skim boards are available for rent, and you'll find a good selection of sports-wear and accessories here.

Before you leave Duck Village heading north on Duck Road you'll see **Barrier Island Sailing Center**, 261-7100 or toll free in Corolla, 453-4414. It's a large facility; many windsocks and flags will attract your attention. The Sailing Center is operated by Bill Miles, an experienced sailing and windsurfing enthusiast. There's a wide range of water activities here that includes windsurfing, jet skis, parasail flights, pontoon boats, sailboats, Island Motor Boats, kayaks, canoes, paddle boats, Waverunners and water bogans. Reservations are recommended for high performance and beginner windsurfing lessons, parasailing flights and Waverunners. Fishing and environmental tours are also being offered this year. You'll enjoy hanging out at the gazebo, which offers a nice vantage point while you're waiting for your turn, the right conditions or to talk with the experts and novices.

Farther north on Duck Road, you'll find **Nor' Banks Sailing Center**, 261-2900 or toll free in Corolla, 453-8191. It is located on the sound, a short distance past the Duck Fire Department. It's the oldest sailing school on the north beaches and offers instruction in sailing and windsurfing. Jon Britt really loves teaching, and he has something for everyone. A wide variety of equipment is available for family water recreation. He has small motor boats built in Wanchese, and classic sailboats — Flying Scots, Waverunners and other fun stuff including Hobie Cats, Sea Ray Jet Boats and TIGA sailboards and Neilpryde sails. Families take note, this is a large site with picnic tables, outdoor showers and rest room facilities. There's plenty of space to relax, so bring your lunch and spend the day. You won't find anything here but water sports! Well,

he does sell some T-shirts.

North Duck Water Sports, 261-4200, is located on Currituck Sound at Sound Sea Village near Sanderling. This venture is the former site of Outer Banks Cruising and features Waverunners, small boats and a pontoon cruising boat. Private boats are allowed to launch from here as well.

PINE ISLAND
North of Sanderling

Once you're in Currituck County north of Sanderling, Duck Road becomes Ocean Trail (NC 12). You'll discover the **Pine Island Indoor Racquet Club**, 441-5888, part of the development of Pine Island that is located approximately three miles north of the county line. It is open to the public and has three tennis courts, one squash court, one racquetball court and an outdoor platform tennis court. Call for court times and availability.

Corolla

You'll drive to Corolla via Ocean Trail and into Corolla Light Resort Village. If you're a guest of Corolla Light Resort you'll have access to the **Sports Center at Corolla Light**, 453-4565, which opened in 1991. This facility features indoor tennis, racquetball, swimming and a spa.

The Outer Banks is a fragile place. Respect and care for it.

Insiders' Tips

The Clubhouse Cafe and Lounge, located within the facility, offers guests a light fare menu including sandwiches, subs and ice-cold beer. It is the only sports center of its kind on the Outer Banks. In addition to the recreational options available inside the sports center, you'll also find three outdoor clay tennis courts, four outdoor hard tennis courts, basketball courts, shuffleboard and volleyball. Children's activities are scheduled throughout the summer.

Hang gliding, soundside sailing and windsurfing are available in Corolla, too. **Corolla Flight**, 261-6166, sets you free to fly over the Currituck beaches. Owner Greg DeWolf recommends reservations by phone or at his retail store located at **Whalehead Landing Shops** just north of Winks in Corolla Village. Tandem hang gliding over the northern Currituck beaches is an experience you won't want to miss. Flights are $69 for individuals, and discounts are available for groups of eight or more. Weather variations dictate whether or not you can fly, but every perfect day from April through September is fly-time with Corolla Flight. Transportation for tandem hang gliding is provided from their shop at Whalehead Landing. Clothing, T-shirts and items with an aviation theme can be purchased here.

You will have lots of fun playing with **Seabreeze Wave Runners**, 473-5715 year round or 453-0833 during the season. Anita Fobbe and company will be more than happy to deliver the Waverunners and jet skis you rent to your beach location as long as it's north of the four-wheel drive access in Corolla. (Regulations require that activities such as parasailing, waverunning and jet skiing occur only north of this access area in Corolla. This actually makes for more fun for you since you have, for the most part, an empty, wide-open ocean to cruise around on . . . no having to watch out for surfacing swimmers and boogie boarders.) You're going to need to check in and do your paper work first at their location next behind the Twiddy Realty Building on Second Street in Corolla. Currituck County has a law that no business transactions are to take place on the beach. Reservations are recommended for this wet, wild adventure. The cost is $65 per hour, and you must be at least 16 to ride by yourself. Half-day rentals may be available depending upon demand. Credit cards are not accepted, but traveler's checks and cash are welcome.

You'll also find **Tackle N' Tours**, 453-4266, at Whalehead Landing. Besides being a salt and fresh water fish tackle shop and providing rod and reel rentals and repairs, these folks supply information on offshore charters. They also provide a bass guide service for up to four people, a hunting guide service and guided tours of the northern beaches. You might ask them about boat rentals for fishing trips on the sound, for groups of up to four. Ron and Jody will tell you everything you need to know.

Cap'n Woody's Fun Camp, 453-2129, is an area information and booking service located in Corolla at the Village Toy Store in the TimBuck II Shopping Village. Cap'n Woody and

his crew will book beach horseback rides, carriage rides, full water sports, offshore fishing, *Lost Colony* and almost any activity an individual or group desires. If you want to have fun . . . the Cap'n is wait'n for ya.

Corolla Outback Adventures, 453-4484, rents ATVs and provides a complete booking service for parasailing, windsurfing, Waverun-ners, fishing trips and more.

If you have your own board and sail, take off from the **Bell Tower Station** (near the Sport Center) launch area for a day on the beautiful waters of Currituck Sound. Or, take the family for a challenge on The **Grass Course and Garden Golf**,

also a part of Corolla Light Resort Village. Garden golf is traditional miniature golf on a PGA-approved putting surface, and the grass course is an 18-hole course with a par 72. These two miniature golf courses are open to the public from 10 AM until 11:30 PM, with the last tee time at 11 PM. The cost for one 18-hole game is $7 for adults and $5 for children under 12. For more information, call Bell Tower Station, 261-4650. A snack bar is also located here in case you work up an appetite.

OFF ROAD BEACHES
North of Corolla, Four-wheel-drive access

Recreation of a different style

awaits those who have a four-wheel drive vehicle. At the end of the paved road, just north of Corolla, is a point of access. The "rules of the road" are posted. If you'll stop and take time to read, it'll save you a lot of trouble. The posted regulations are strictly enforced. The speed limit and description of the areas where you are actually permitted to drive are two of the most important things to observe in this area. Four-wheeling is not a sport, but a different way to enjoy beach activities such as fishing, volleyball, family picnics and swimming. The beaches are wide and flat and conducive to driving here, but you should not take this privilege lightly. It's 12 miles to the Virginia state line, but since you would have to travel through Back Bay Wildlife Refuge to get all the way to Virginia, access is restricted for the casual visitor.

This area of beach is not for racing or recklessly cruising along. During summer months, families use the beach for sunbathing; kids run into the water just like they would on any other beach; and the surf-fishing is some of the best on the Outer Banks. So there are lots of fisher-folks to look out for. There's room to play volleyball and launch your sailboard or boat. Spending an entire day "off the road" in this northern paradise sure clears the cobwebs.

Shopping

The shops along the 20-mile stretch of the northern Outer Banks begin with the Marketplace in Southern Shores and end in Corolla at

Whalehead Landing. The north beaches are booming, and there's no mistaking a proliferation of retail shopping options. You'll find most anything and everything up this way. As development tends to be upscale, so do the shops. The newest shopping centers in the north beach area are TimBuck II Shopping Village located on the west side of Highway 12, across the street from Buck Island and Duck Village Square, located on the southside of Kellogg's True Value in Duck. Phase I of TimBuck II Shopping Village is complete with development of Phase II well under way while construction on Duck Village Square is still in progress at the time of this writing.

Most beach shops are open for extended hours during the summer months, but during the off season some have early closings, some are open only on weekends until Thanksgiving, and some close during the winter and reopen in March. Telephone numbers are provided so you can call ahead and check the hours. Shopping on the northern beaches is a pleasant experience. Whether you're looking for the ordinary or the unusual—you'll find them both here.

Southern Shores

The Marketplace Shopping Center is easily discovered on the wide stretch of Route 158 on your way into town. This shopping center is adjacent to the west side of Southern Shores and the edge of Kitty Hawk. This destination provides a mix of medical and shopping opportunities. Medical offices include **Professional Opticians**, 261-8777;

DUCK ❦ VILLAGE ❦ WATERFRONT ❦ SHOPS

Wellness Center of the Outer Banks, 261-5424; and **Coastal Rehabilitation**, 261-1556. Services located here include the **Dry Cleaners**, the **Travel Connection**, 261-2848, **Adam's Needle Flower Shop**, 261-8917; and **Wachovia Bank**, 261-6688.

Food Lion is where you may stop for the week's groceries, but there are other specialty shops here as well. **Daniel's**, 261-8200, a locally-owned specialty department store, offers quality, affordable clothing for the family, home furnishings, an expanded gift department, housewares and shoes. This is a great place to purchase a unique gift for any occasion. The **Mule Shed**, 261-4703, features a top line of women's wear, sportswear and lingerie. **Carolina Christmas**, 261-7518, offers gifts and decoys. **Good Vibes Video**, 261-8006, is conveniently located for all you folks in Kitty Hawk and Southern Shores.

Paige Harrell, the owner of **Paige's**, 261-1777, set out to make women's dressing an event. This she has achieved in her shop that features one-of-a-kind garments, and, you'll be delightfully surprised to discover **Robin's Fine Jewelry**, 261-4020, in the same store. Robin offers an extensive line of high-quality jewelry including one-of-a-kind pieces. Robin's jewelry and accessories provide just the right finishing touches. Look for Robin's new store in the TimBuck II Shopping Village in Corolla

The Marketplace also provides a drug store for the northern beaches. **Revco**, 261-5777, is a general store of sorts, but a full-time pharmacist can assist with prescriptions while you're at the beach.

Duck

When Duck was discovered in the early '80s by families on vacation, the Wee Winks general store, Duck Blind Art Gallery and Bob's Bait and Tackle joined the Duck Methodist Church as places to see other folks at the beach. All that has changed, and if you're inclined to shop-til-you-drop, you won't be disappointed. Duck Village has a personality of its own, as a tour of the many shops will show.

As you drive into Duck Village, do stop in and browse at **Duck Blind Limited Art Gallery**, 261-2009. The unique collection of fine art, crafts, jewelry and carvings at this contemporary gallery is one of the best on the Outer Banks. You'll learn about local artists here too — they're featured in special exhibits and shows throughout the year.

Across the road soundside, you'll discover **Duck Soundside Shoppes**. The entire family will enjoy many interesting treasures at the **Sea Shell**

Insiders' Tips

Shop, 261-7828. For fine women's apparel, unique jewelry and accessories stop in at **La Rive Boutique**, 261-7197. Everything you need for a country home can be found at **The Farmer's Daughter**, 261-4828. T-shirts, decoys, crafts, Christmas decorations and gift items can also be found here. If you're looking for advice on where to catch that "really big one," stop in at **Bob's Bait & Tackle**, 261-8589. This store is an original building from the old days when a soundside dock out back served as a port to ship fresh fish from the ocean to points north and west. **Surfside Casuals**, 261-7264, features an extensive line of women's swimwear for just about everyone. Men and women enjoy shopping for fashionable beachwear here too.

Scarborough Faire is one of the most carefully developed shopping centers in this area, and it offers a variety of shops featuring everything from art and clothing to videos and flags. Entertainment is featured during the evening in the summer be-

ginning at 7 P.M. You can enjoy jazz music while you shop. There are 23 shops here including **Elizabeth's Cafe and Winery**, 261-6145 (see Restaurants) and **Waldt Construction,** 261-3721.

On a visit to this collection of shops, you'll discover **Morales Art Gallery**, 261-7190. Morales offers you original art works by local and regional artists in many different subjects and styles. In addition to the main gallery you will enjoy **The Print Shop**, 261-7190, which features a large selection of limited edition prints, sculptures, nautical art, beach scenes, wildlife art and the largest selection of Duck Stamp prints on the Outer Banks. The Print shop also offers fine art reproductions in a variety of subjects.

The Flag Stand II, 261-2837, offers state flags, decorative flags and just about any kind of flag you could hope for. **Elegance-of-the-Sea**, 261-7872, specializes in oil lamps, shells, collector's dolls, baskets, carved items and custom-designed wreaths and arrangements. **The Christmas Duck** is a part of this shop offering unique Christmas decorations and gifts.

Being at the beach is a time for fun, and you'll discover some great toys and hand-dipped ice cream at **Floats, Flippers & Flyers and Little Dipper**, 261-3939. Owners Cheryl and Woodie West pride themselves on their selection of educational toys. You'll also find lots of other items the children will enjoy at the beach. **Gourmet Kitchen Emporium**, 261-8174, has every kitchen gadget imaginable plus gift baskets, gourmet foods, condiments and more — all with a kitchen theme.

Motifs, 261-6335, is a great place for women's apparel, accessories and finely-crafted jewelry. **Kids Kloset**, 261-4845, carries an assortment of play and dress clothes for the little ones who like to have something new at the beach too! Sizes range from infants to preteens. **Island Bookstore**, 261-8981, is one of the best bookstores on the Outer Banks. Owners Martha and David Monroe constantly add new titles to their collection of unusual books. Of course you can find all of the best sellers here too. While browsing, we enjoyed the extensive selection of Southern literature, children's books and books on tape. New York Times best selling hardbacks are discounted daily. Island Bookstore has also become the northern beach headquarters for your favorite blues and jazz, tapes and CDs.

Ocean Annie's, 261-3290, an Outer Banks tradition in pottery, jewelry and fine wood carvings, tempts you with a special piece to take home from the beach or to give a loved one. You won't be able to forget their gourmet coffee because it smells so good. **Solitary Swan**, 261-7676, is a quaint antique shop with unique gifts for your home, and **Lion's Paw**, 261-5575, is a unique ladies apparel shop featuring linen and silk clothing and art jewelry. **Smash Hit**, 261-1138, is a great place to shop for women's and men's tennis and golf clothing, shoes, equipment and gifts. Owner Sally Dowdy, keeps her shop open year round and has some of the most fashionable selections on the East Coast. **Island Dyes,** 261-1008, features a wide selection of tie-dye clothing.

If you are a repeat visitor to the Outer Banks, and many of you are, we're sure you have come to recognize Gray's family department stores. **Gray's Department Store**, 261-3514, is located at Scarborough Faire. They offer a complete selection of quality clothing for the entire family. You'll feel at home in Duck when you see their famous Duck T-shirts and sweatshirts looking at you as you come in the door! **Ocean Atlantic Rentals**, 261-4346, has everything you need for the beach, and they rent videos too. **Impromptu**, 255-0633, is a gift shop with unique items including recycled Mexican glassware, cobalt and turquoise cards, Chinese pottery and shard boxes. **Rainbow Harvest**, 261-6796, provides handcrafted items from across the country. You'll find contemporary home accessories, functional and decorative handcrafted jewelry — from kick-around to sophisticated, wall hangings, hand-painted baskets and flower pots and clocks

made out of handmade paper. The fine handcrafted jewelry of **Sara DeSpain**, 261-4047, is something you shouldn't miss. Sara DeSpain and Impromptu share the same retail location.

Out of the Woods Sign Makers, 261-2940, is located at the top of the stairs leading near the entrance to the Kid's Kloset. This wood boutique is one-of-a-kind on the Outer Banks. Tricia Rivera has been on the Outer Banks for quite some time and finally found a craft that no one else was doing — personalized wooden signs for all occasions. They're neat and colorful, and there are more than 130 designs to choose from. Your sign is personalized while you watch or while you shop. "Fall leaves" is a popular design. The signs can be used outdoors with a coat of polyurethane, and they're very reasonably priced. Mail order is available too. Ask for a new color catalog. They make neat gifts for the folks back home. Look for their second location at the Outer Banks Mall.

Head to Toe, 261-5602, carries lots and lots of souvenir T-shirts. No shopping center on the Outer Banks seems complete without a fudge shop, and this one is no exception; try **The Fudgery**, 261-8283.

Osprey Landing is a smaller shopping area overlooking the sound as you continue north through the village. **Carolina Moon Gallery**, 261-7199, is the place to go if you're looking for the unique and unusual. Collections of crystals, jewelry, cards and gifts are interestingly displayed, and the music played while you shop is usually so wonderful you'll want to stay a little longer. (Featured tapes are always available for sale.) **Birthday Suits**, 261-7297, is a boutique of relaxed California and New York fashions for men and women. They have one of the best collections of bathing suits anywhere — for variety and size — including toddler, D-DD cup suits, masectomy and maternity suits, men's suits and suits for literally every body. The entire family can be outfitted here, and the staff is great

at helping you find one that actually fits. **Osprey Gourmet**, 261-7133, is a delightful cafe for takeout or for eating right there on the waterfront deck. Daily luncheon specials are featured. **Books 'N Things**, 261-2413 carries books and gifts and **The Board Room**, 255-0939, features intellectual and challenging games. **Local Color T's**, 261-7873, sells souvenir T-shirts and lots of them.

Loblolly Pines Shopping Center provides an assortment of shops and eateries. The **Duck Duck Shop and Post Office**, 261-8555, features every wood-carved duck imaginable, and **Yesterday's Jewels**, 261-4869, carries an interesting collection of old but fashionable jewelry. **The Phoenix**, 261-8900, offers eclectic clothing, jewelry and accessories for shoppers with discriminating taste. This boutique boasts a strong repeat business year after year. Items can be "pricey" but you'll appreciate the high quality, fashionable merchandise. The hand-sewn hats are beautiful, and you will find one-of-a-kind

items in this store that you won't find anywhere else on the Outer Banks. **TW's Bait & Tackle Shop**, 261-8300, is probably the first door that opens every morning in Duck to provide all those necessary fishing supplies... (the early bird really does catch the worm at TW's). **Just for the Beach**, 261-7831, comes close to being a general store for beach stuff and casual clothing. **Candy Cone Creations**, 261-8055, has scrumptious treats including homemade, hand-dipped ice cream and waffle cones and candy gift items. **Pizzazz Pizzeria and Sub Shop**, 261-8822, cooks up great pizza and subs to go. You can buy their pizza by the pie or the slice.

Jan Chappell has four locations on the Outer Banks now for her swimwear and sportswear boutique, Ocean Threads. **Ocean Threads** in Duck, 255-0443, is located just north of the Loblolly Pines Shopping Center across the street from the sound. Look for Ocean Threads and Jan's new shop the, Gourmet Garage, in a

Don't Miss Out Why Everybody Is Flocking To The Lucky Duck

Many years ago a legend stated that "much happiness and good luck will come to those whose home shelters a duck." Our little duck offers a legend of happiness to the home in which it lives. May this happiness be yours.

Season Hours
9am-9pm

Winter Hours
10am-6pm

THE LUCKY DUCK
EST. 1984

Located in the Village of Duck

quaint cottage on the hill with an aqua stairway leading to the front door. Shoppers will find swimwear and sportswear for the entire family, sunglasses, hats and just about any other clothing item your family will need for a trip to the beach. Jan will have plenty of Duck and Corolla T-shirts in all sizes too. Look for other **Ocean Threads** locations at Corolla Light Village Shops in Corolla, in Kill Devil Hills at the 8 MP on the Beach Road and in Nags Head at the Outer Banks Mall.

The **Gourmet Garage**, 261-0353, features gourmet baskets, wine, bathsalts, lotions, potpourri and everything you'll need to create your own special gift basket. Gift basket ideas will be in abundance at this specialty shop. We like the basket idea with wine, cheese, crackers and pâté, mm, mm, good!

Herron's Deli, 261-3224, is right up the road and they serve lunch and breakfast and dinner during the summer season. You can eat in or take out. Either way, the Philly steak and cheese sub is the best we've ever had.

The newest north beach shopping destination is **Duck Village Square** located on the southside of Kellogg's True Value in the heart of Duck. Duck Village Square will be home to four specialty shops. **Duck Donut and Bakery**, 255-0014, is a full-service bakery and donut shop with three other locations on the Outer Banks including one in Corolla at TimBuck II Shopping Village, Three Winks Shoppes in Kitty Hawk and the Island Donut and Bakery on Roanoke Island. This is a family-owned and -operated bakery,

and the staff is very friendly. Ice cream will be served at the Duck and Corolla locations. **Mustang Sally's**, 261-0600, specialty clothing shop will feature outerwear for men and women and women's fashions and accessories. Look for Mustang Sally's other north beach location in Corolla at the Corolla Light Village Shops. **Glitz** will feature jewelry and **The Village Wine Shop and Deli**, 261-8646, will offer an extensive variety of affordable wines and beers from all over the world, homemade breads, cheeses and specialty food items including custom cut steaks and homemade desserts. This specialty food shop also will offer a deli featuring deli sandwiches with gusto and capuccino and gourmet coffee.

Kellogg's True Value, 261-8121, is much more than a hardware store. You'll find a garden center, outdoor furniture and lots of other items especially for folks who enjoy working inside their house and outside in their yard. **Centura Bank**, 261-2975, is located in Duck Village for your vacation banking convenience.

Farther along Duck Road you'll find **Schooner Plaza**; it's the place with an extraordinary perennial garden. This is where you'll find **Confetti**, 261-5444, a boutique specializing in designer clothing for work or play. Bright colors abound here, and you'll also find apparel appropriate for the office on the Outer Banks. This is a fun store offering its own fashion designs. Their clothing can't be found in any other shop on the Outer Banks except at their other location in Monteray Shores. **Nalani Designs**, 261-1788, provides shoppers with unique home accents,

Original Creations In Wearable Art By Donna

One of a kind, one at a time.

Kitty Hawk Connection, MP 13 1/2 across from Jockey's Ridge, Nags Head • 441-6232
Waterfront Shops, just north of the watertower on the Sound, Duck • 261-6868

decorative art, area rugs, home furnishings and accessories. Nalani Designs operates a lot like a home planning center. **Changes**, 255-0504, is a full-service hair salon for north beach visitors and residents.

Along the narrow winding road into the heart of Duck Village you'll find **Wee Winks Square**. **Kitty Hawk Sports**, 261-8770, invites you to shop for clothing selections in name brands along with their full selections of boogie boards, accessories and sunglasses. Don't forget to visit "Sports" at their main location in Nags Head across the street from Jockey's Ridge at MP 13. Kitty Hawk Sports offers windsurfing lessons and camps, sea kayak lessons and special events during the summer including their famous Wacky Watermelon Weekend.

The Lucky Duck, 261-7800, offers a wide selection of accessories for the home and local arts and crafts. This store started out in a smaller location several years ago and became so popular that they

had to find a much bigger space to accommodate the demand . . . a clue to how appealing their merchandise is. **Beach Essentials**, 261-1250, carries virtually everything that is essential for the beach including boogie boards, lotions, rafts and lots more. The children are always fascinated by hermit crabs, so gather the family and take a look for yourselves. In its second season **Artisans Boutique**, 261-5445, offers an eclectic combination of ladies' apparel, jewelry and accessories for the home. The boutique is filled with items that bring to mind the artist's touch. For the best seafood in town, visit **Dockside 'n Duck**, 261-8687. They also carry steamers, condiments, sauces and the finishing touches for the gourmet chef on vacation. **Lady Victorian**, 261-1654, is a stylish women's boutique. This shop is filled with quality dresses, evening wear, intimate apparel, travel accessories and personal items including bath products, soaps, powders and fabric clothes hangers. "Outfits" and suits are the emphasis, and you'll find lots of cotton, silk and linen. Everything is nicely merchandised. For your convenience, an **ABC** store, 261-6981, is also located at Wee Winks Square.

Wee Winks Market, 261-2937, has been remodeled — including new gas pumps — and getting in and out for those last minute food purchases or grabbing a newspaper is easier than ever. **Green Acres Produce** stand is open during the summer season, and their fresh-from-the-farm vegetables and fruits are the best in the village. **Kitty Hawk Kites**, 261-4450, is next door. We think that this is one of the most colorful shops on the Outer Banks with kites displayed throughout the store. You can find just about any kite imaginable at this shop. Kitty Hawk Kites is ready to supply you with everything you may need for a great vacation on the Outer Banks. You can find anything from roller blades to kites. Their selection of clothing includes quality men's and women's sportswear and outerwear, sandals, Duck T-shirts and sweatshirts. Look for free daily workshops at this location during the summer including kite workshops and kid's day. Kitty Hawk Kites will also be offering kayak lessons/ tours at their Duck location.

Their main location in Nags Head offers hang gliding lessons on the dunes across the street at Jockey's Ridge State Park. Children of all ages enjoy wall climbing, tandem hang gliding, paragliding and rollerblading.

Tommy's Market, 261-8990, is a place to pick up delicious, fresh baked goods in the early morning. Pastries, turnovers, breads, bagels and donuts are waiting for you. You'll also find a complete deli featuring roast ham and chickens, ready-to-eat spiced shrimp, sandwiches, fresh salads, fresh-baked pies and daily luncheon specials. Tommy's maintains an extensive wine selection and lots of imported beers in addition to a full range of groceries.

Pizza Dude, 261-3901, delivers hot, handmade pizzas with all the toppings to your door during the summer months. This main location delivers from Southern Shores to Corolla. For delivery to Kitty Hawk and northern Kill Devil Hills, call 261-5005. For delivery from southern Kill Devil Hills to Nags Head, call 441-6633.

Duck Waterfront Shops provide all kinds of great shopping opportunities. Stop in **Duck's General Store**, 261-5579, and you'll find unique and interesting selections of cards, Outer Banks books, fine crafted jewelry, ironwood sculptures, photography and candles. Popular items include Audubon Series books and environmental gifts such as endangered species books and T-shirts, bird feeders and bird houses. The T-shirt manufacturing companies donate part of their proceeds from purchases to environmental causes including the Nature Conservancy, Friends of the Earth and the Dolphin Fund. So help yourself and the earth at the same time! We were happy to see binoculars for bird watching and wind instruments for gauging the wind. Look for specialty food items this year too.

Islands, 261-5164, will tempt you with all kinds of merchandise that you would ordinarily have to go to

the "islands" to find. We know you will enjoy the rain forest murals and bamboo fixtures accenting this boutique along with the African folk music that plays while you shop. The owners of this boutique are certainly hoping you will experience a "total island feel." Unique gift items include coconut picture frames, metal art, (hammered metal designs), custom scenting lotions and natural hair products you can scent yourself. Custom-scented gift baskets and natural Batik quilts are great finds too. Women's fashions include resortwear for the beach or out to dinner. The wrap skirts in Batik prints are perfect for beach life on the Outer Banks. We know you will have fun shopping here.

Barr-EE-Station Catalog Outlet, 261-1650, features some unbelievably low prices on name brand clothing and shoes, and they're always well-stocked. We saw lots of 100-percent cotton, seersucker, linen and great outerwear, workwear, casualwear and dresses. One of the best-dressed people we know buys most of her clothes here, at a fraction of the cost she'd typically pay for the brands elsewhere . . . who says you need big city shopping!

Barr-EE-Station Swimwear Outlet, 255-0300, will make you happy with discounted name brand swimwear selling at up to 50 percent off. This outlet will also carry beach accessories, flip flops, espadrilles, straw bags, hats and more.

Donna Designs, 261-6868, is a unique shop featuring airbrush designed clothing for women and children. These are one-of-a-kind handmade designs — crabs, fish, turtles,

flowers and pelicans are some of the elements you'll find in her work. By airbrushing color onto the fish itself, Donna is able to bring out many of the details in the fins and scales. Designs are available on 100-percent-cotton T-shirts, sweatshirts, sundresses and French terry. The children's outfits are adorable, and the matching hand-painted sneakers are a hit. She has another retail location at Kitty Hawk Connection in Nags Head across from Jockey's Ridge State Park.

North Beach Sailing, 261-6262, has expanded and offers even more of the latest in windsurfing and sailing gear, equipment and accessories. You will also find a good selection of quality T-shirts, sandals and shorts. The boogie boards and rollerblades are lots of fun. Look for kayak sales too. **The Kid's Store,** 261-3553, has toys for kids of all ages. Their selection includes toys for the beach, craft kits, wildlife and museum replicas and infants and children's T-shirts in sizes ranging to preteens. Cool treats are also available at the Waterfront Shops ice cream shop, **Sunset Ice Cream**.

TimBuck II
Shopping Village

This is one of the newest and most visible commercial retail ventures on the northern banks. Twelve merchants were located in this shopping village last year, and Phase II is now underway, adding 12 more shops directly across the parking lot and even more shops around the perimeter. TimBuck II is a unique commercial development combining quality shopping with dining, recreation and entertainment opportunities. Plans for entertainment include live music on select evenings during the week. Folks will enjoy eating out at **Mane Street Eatery**, **Steamer's Restaurant and Raw Bar** and **Finely Ron's Grille**. Plans for family recreation include canoeing and kayaking on the "pond" in TimBuck II.

This shopping village offers ground-level covered parking, covered staircases leading up to the shopping level, covered walkways and public rest room facilities. We consider it to be one of the premier shopping destinations on the Outer Banks. Those of you who visited TimBuck II last year will no doubt remember some of the fine shops listed below. For those of you who will be visiting the north beach shopping village for the first time, here's an idea of what you can expect to find at TimBuck II.

You may have already visited Kitty Hawk Sports in Nags Head or Duck, and you are sure to find more of the same here. **Kitty Hawk Sports**, 453-4999, offers a wide selection of quality T-shirts and clothing at their Corolla location. You can also book windsurfing, sailing and kayaking lessons here (lessons are given in Nags Head), and you will also be able to rent boogie boards, skim boards and surf boards. **Gray's Specialty Department Store**, 453-4994, offers high quality swimwear for the entire family. We would be remiss if we didn't mention their line of Duck T-shirts and sweatshirts, (and don't forget that Gray's is the home of the "Big Duck" T-shirt). Joan Estes of **Interior Techniques**, 453-8844,

moved her interior design and furnishing services to this location from Kitty Hawk. This design boutique features exclusive "Weekend Retreat" furnishings and an eclectic line of accessories for the home. Home owners in the north beaches will appreciate the convenience of Joan's new location for her design services.

Surfside Casuals, 453-8181, offers an extensive line of swimwear, while **Tar Heel Trading**, 453-3132, carries American handcrafted decorator items and designer jewelry. **The Salt Marsh**, 453-8383, provides shoppers with an extensive line of more than 200 designs of wildlife/nature and conservation T-shirts. The gifts, toys and games are educational. Shoppers and collectors can also purchase products from the rain forests of Central and South America that support indigenous tribes. Look for Talbot, Brandenburg and Lassen prints.'

Corolla Book 'N Card, 453-4444, will keep you busy with plenty of great reading choices. You may find a neat gift here too for the folks back home. Corolla Book 'N Card carries a large selection of local books, bestsellers in hard cover and paperbacks. The store also offers a variety of unique gifts such as posters, Corolla souvenirs, Mickey Mouse and Looney Tunes shirts, hats and toys. Most of us are already familiar with **The Cotton Gin**, 453-4446. Their primary location is in Currituck on the mainland. If you arrived on the Outer Banks via Route 158 South, we're sure you saw this store complete with its "countryesque" gifts. The Cotton Gin also features quality name brand clothing including Pendleton and a unique selection of fine bedding, bath and kitchen supplies.

Just for the Beach, 453-4505, resembles a general store supplying you with just about everything you will need to enjoy a great day at the beach. You will find casual clothing here too. Look for their other location in Duck. **Sea Images**, 453-8999, is also located at Sea Holly Square Shopping Center in Kill Devil Hills on the Beach Road. This nautical boutique tempted us with some truly unique nautical finds. You will find everything you'd expect to find at a nautical store and more. **Beach Realty and Kitty Hawk Rentals**, 453-4141, can help you find a great place to stay during your vacation on the northern beaches, and if you're hoping to make your trips to the Outer Banks a more permanent arrangement, they can also help you with the purchase or the construction of your dream house. And, as we've observed before, no shopping destination on the Outer Banks seems to be complete without a fudge shop and TimBuck II is no exception, so visit **The Fudgery,** 453-8882, if you have a hankering for mouth-watering fudge.

New merchants at TimBuck II include: **Kitty Hawk Kites**, 453-8845; **Earth Art**, 453-0944; **"The Summer House"** by Surfside Casuals, 453-8860; **Island Tobacco**, 453-8163; **Island Gear**, 453-4816; **Dolphin Dreaming**, 453-0840; **Michael's Gems and Glass**, 453-4310; **Nags Head Hammocks**, 453-0844; **Horse Play**, by Gayle, 453-4315; **The Soot Slayer,** providing appliances and propane service; **Seaside Art Gal-**lery; **Beach Bites Bakery**; **Big Buck's Ice Cream**, 453-8016; and **Steamer's Restaurant and Raw Bar**, 453-3344.

Additional shopping opportunities, (as if that's not enough already), include **Gourmet Kitchen Emporium**, 261-1609, **Jeanine's Cat House**, **Village Toy Store**, 453-2129, where you can book all kinds of activities through Cap'n Woody's Fun Camp, **Robin's Fine Jewelry**, **Wild Horses**, 261-3803, **Match Point Golf and Tennis Shop** and one of our personal favorites, **Duck Donut and Bakery**, 453-0920. This is one of four locations on the Outer Banks for this donut and bake shop. In addition to homemade and freshly-baked donuts, bagels, breads and muffins, Duck Donut and Bakery will also serve cool ice cream at this location. This family owned and operated bakery delivers great customer service too. You will probably find yourself chatting with the proprietors while waiting for your first cup of hot coffee in the morning.

Other services located here for your convenience include **Brew Thru**, 453-2878, **Video Vibes** and **BP Fuel Station**.

Monteray Plaza
10 miles north of Duck

Out there in the wide open spaces of Whalehead Beach and about 10 miles north of Duck, a new convenience awaits those who come to this area of the northern Outer Banks.

Monteray Plaza, which opened in 1991, brought a major supermarket within easy reach of families vacationing on the northern Currituck Beaches: **Food Lion**. Other businesses opened as well to make Monteray Plaza a nice shopping destination. There's a **Gray's Department Store**, 453-4711, continuing their Outer Banks clothing tradition, with quality name brands of clothing for men and women. Gray's provides shoppers with a nice assortment of gift items too. Debbie Pelley and Howard Goldstein opened two women's boutiques in 1991, one here and the other in Duck. **Con-**

fetti, 453-8888, features clothing for adults and kids. We saw bright, stylish clothes for work and play at the beach. The fish T-shirts are beautiful, and the tropical fish designs on the wall are great to look at too. They also have fun things, like dress-up fashions that are a little girl's dream — feather boas, sequined shoes, tiaras, magic wands, fairy dresses and other theme costumes. **Ocean Annie's**, 453-4102, is another

fine shop with attractive collections of handcrafted pottery, jewelry, fine gifts and gourmet coffee. The ceramics are decorative and functional and originate from across the country. Blown-glass items are featured at this location, and the extensive wind chime collection was singing in the wind when we visited. You'll find horse related themes are more predominant in shops on the northern beaches because the wild horses are near and dear to just about everyone who lives in Corolla, and visitors to this area love to learn more about the wild horses too.

Kitty Hawk Kites, 453-8845, opened another colorful shop of unique games on the Outer Banks, and they offer an extensive assortment of kites, windsocks and banners — just the things for those wide-open skies of the northern beaches. Lots of unique gift items are yours for the choosing, and the Gilligan hats and pith helmets intrigued us. Fine outerwear by Columbia is also available here along with clothing by Gear and sandals by TEVA. The entire family will want to try rollerblading. Rentals are available for a half day, full day, overnight or on a weekly basis. Look for the "Roll Patrol" during the summer and rollerblade through Corolla with an instructor; skates are available for a small fee. Stunt kite clinics and demos by professional pilots are also scheduled. Don't forget to try hang gliding lessons at their Nags Head location across the street from Jockey's Ridge State Park, after all, Kitty Hawk Kites is the world's largest hang gliding school, so let your dreams fly . . .

Birthday Suits, 453-4862, features an extensive line of swimwear for the entire family at all of their Outer Banks locations. Shoppers will appreciate mix and match separates that are often hard to find at most swimwear stores. Customers will enjoy relaxed California and New York fashions in addition to sunglasses, shoes, accessories, swim goggles, "Big Mig" socks and Fresh Produce T-shirts.

Try **Susan's Calypso Cafe**, 453-8833, for food prepared island style, and **Smokey's Restaurant, 453-4050,** serves great barbecue ribs and other good barbecue items.

The Bank of Currituck, 453-4900, is located just up the road from Monteray Plaza and **Cooperative Saving and Loan,** 453-4111, is located in the new **Monteray Professional Center** along with attorneys Kellogg, White, Evans and Gray and Bob DeGabrielle and Associates. The new **ACE Hardware**, 453-8456, building is located just north of the Professional Center, and it is a welcome sight for all those who visit and live on the northern banks.

Corolla

Driving north on Ocean Trail and into Corolla Light Resort Village, you'll find the soundside shops of the **Bell Tower Station**, 453-3987 or 261-4650. Nestled among the trees and overlooking Currituck Sound the resort wear shop **Corolla Collectibles**, 453-4731, features casual attire for women and children. **Chauncey's Porch**, 453-3133, offers hot dogs, hamburgers, sandwiches and seafood. This is the place to cure your sweet-tooth with an array of pastries and ice cream. You can order your food to go or enjoy it seated on their screened-in porch overlooking the sound. It's a popular spot during the summer for families grabbing a bite to eat during the day. We noticed that the standard attire here is bathing suits and cover ups. That tells you something about what it means to relax on the northern banks.

Corolla Light Village Shops offers a good mix of shopping destinations, in fact the best yet for this retail center. **Ocean Threads**, 453-8967, specializes in swimwear for the entire family including maternity, masectomy and long torso suits. This shop is also packed with lots of sportswear for men and women including a good selection of tennis clothes and accessories. You won't be able to miss the great selection of Corolla and Duck T-shirts, sweatshirts, sunglasses and hats. We noticed a great supply of T-shirts to fit the entire family. Ocean Threads is open seven days a week during the season. Look for Ocean Threads in Duck, Kill Devil Hills on the Beach Road and at the Outer Banks Mall. After shopping stop for a bite to eat at **Cosmos's** or the **Horseshoe Cafe**.

Owner Debbie Ferrell Moore's life experiences and travels abroad provide the inspiration for her shop, **Izit Emporium**, 453-3302. Debbie was born in Currituck County and traveled for 10 years after she graduated from college. Her travel destinations included Southeast Asia and South Africa, where she lived for five years. The bright orange and purple colors in her store reflect Debbie's desire to create a distinct mind-set. Debbie discovered Zulu baskets while she was in South Africa. Zulu baskets are traditional, decorative and functional. They are used for making African beer, and they are a part of at least one African ceremony. Americans don't use Zulu baskets for making beer but they are beautiful to display. We also enjoyed the cactus rain sticks and Balsa wood carvings from Equador. All of Debbie's jewelry is handcrafted, and ladies, you will appreciate the good selection of Batik clothing and accessories.

Dolphin Watch Gallery, 453-2592, features the works of owner/artist, Mary Kaye Umberger. Mary Kaye moved to the Outer Banks from Tennessee because she knew she wanted to call the Outer Banks home for at least part of the year. We were struck by Mary Kaye's hand-colored etchings on handmade paper. Her themes include scenes indigenous to the Corolla area including wildlife, ducks and waterfowl, seascapes and lighthouses. Etchings are images created on a copper plate and reproduced. No two etchings are exactly the same. Shoppers will also enjoy many other art pieces here including pottery, stoneware and sculptures out of wax. These candle sculptures are shaped entirely by hand, and the flower petal sculptures are molded by the artist's fingertips. We were interested in the dulcimer, bowed psaltery and lap harps. These musical instruments are functional and beautiful to look at.

Mustang Sally's, 453-4749, opened during the spring of '93.

Casualwear, dresses and outerwear are featured for both men and women. There was no shortage of bags, accessories and cotton sweaters either. **Ocean Atlantic Rentals**, 453-2440, has everything your family needs for a more enjoyable vacation at the beach. You can call them at (800) 635-9559 to reserve necessary items for your vacation that you'd rather not haul in the car. The **Silk Gardenia**, 453-8863, offers fresh and lovely silk flowers and wreaths for every occasion. Owners Ed and Ruby Cox have been in the flower business here since the Corolla Light Village Shops first opened. It would seem terribly strange to visit the shops and not see the bicycle and flower display placed in front of their shop indicating that shoppers are welcome.

This is the third season for **Duck-In Donuts**, 453-4513, at Corolla Light Village Shops. The owners here are constantly finding new ways to tantalize the taste buds of their customers. Paul has been in the retail bakery business for 11 years, and his expertise produces tasty results. Breakfast includes orange juice, coffee, homemade donuts, cinnamon rolls, sticky buns, muffins and croissants. Choose from Corolla chips, brownies, doggy cupcakes, horse shoe cookies or wild tie-dyed cookies for an afternoon snack, and the desserts... well, they're too sinful to mention. Oh, alright, maybe just a few... cream horns, peanut butter baskets, cannoli, chocolate eclairs and more. The decorator cakes and fresh-baked breads are special too.

Duck-In Donuts also offers cappuccino and gourmet flavored coffee. Pasta lovers will enjoy great homemade pastas including spinach and tomato pasta. This shop is open daily during the summer; you can take out or relax underneath the green awning outside.

Corolla Landscaping, 453-4255, wants to help you preserve and beautify your home and the surrounding landscape. This retail location was opened in 1992 and is designed for the "do-it-yourself" gardener. A complete line of outdoor plants, house plants, decorative planters, pottery, potting soil, fertilizer and more is offered. Landscape timbers, hardwood bark, mulch, topsoil, pea gravel and river rock are stocked in large or small quantities.

Beach Cove, 453-8016, carries an extensive line of T-shirts for infants up to size XXXL including Corolla Lighthouse and Whalehead Club T-shirts. You can also customize your own shirt by selecting the decal of your choice and transferring it to the shirt. There's something for everyone and just about everything you will need for the beach. We saw children's games, aqua socks, jewelry, souvenirs, film and pottery. **Seasons Grocery**, 453-8016, is a mini market carrying those items you may need to round out your meal plans for the day. You'll find wine, beer, soft drinks, dry goods, snacks, toiletries, detergents and loose shrimp by the pound. **Something Cool Ice Cream**, 453-8016, offers hand-dipped ice cream, loose taffy and all kinds of novelty candies.

The **Winks** store with a few gas pumps and the **Corolla Post Office** occupy a small strip north of the Currituck Beach Lighthouse. For many years, it was the center of activity and the only place to buy groceries in Corolla. **Winks**, 453-8166, is a general store and with an adjacent shop and office is often referred to as "the mall" by those who live and work there. We were surprised to find that there is an **ABC** Package store, 453-2895, in Corolla now too. It is located across the street from the Winks shops and next to the new Sun Realty Building.

Things have changed in Corolla, and just north of the Winks store is a row of shops and businesses known as **Whalehead Landing Station**. You'll find several shops and offices here. **Tackle 'n Tours**, 453-4266, has everything for the fisherperson including equipment, rod and reel repairs, rental boats for sound fishing trips and information on off shore charters. If you would like to try tandem hang gliding on the northern beaches, try **Corolla Flight**, 453-4800.

John de la Vega Gallery, 261-4964, features works by John de la Vega and seven other artists. Mediums include oils, which Mr. de la Vega is known for, watercolors, ceramics, sculpture and photography. The Gallery's regular hours are Monday through Saturday from 1 to 5 PM during the summer and fall months. It is open anytime by appointment; just call first.

Again, we've provided telephone numbers and suggest you call before you go for an off season shopping excursion. Merchants open early for business in season, but in the fall and early spring, some have irregular hours during the week or open only on weekends.

Happy Shopping!

A Life on the Northern Banks:
Maggie Mae Twiford

The late November sunlight glints off the Nags Head dunes outside the window, and glints again off Maggie Twiford's snow-white hair. Her hair is cut short and pinned up with a brown barrette. Her tiny hands lie softly together in the colorful Afghan that covers her lap, except when they twist at the plastic band at her wrist. Outside in the corridor there is the hiss of wheelchairs on tile, the chatter of nurses.

"It was all dirt roads in them days. All such as that. And I remember a lot about it. My mother and my father have been dead for years, and my sisters and my brothers too. And I've got three relatives here, and all my other kinfolks are dead. I've got children — three, two boys and a girl. And today's my youngest son's birthday, he's 62 years old today.

"I was born in 1900. Our closest doctor was at Poplar Branch, Dr. Griggs. Had to go by water to get him, wa'n't no bridges, you see. Sometimes you died fore the doctor got there. My mother had a doctor, Dr. Newburn. He lived at Jarvisburg. And both of them was with my mother when I was born.

"Most all my people were Service people. My father was in the Coast Guard — it was the Lifesaving Service, years ago. He was a surfman. I heard him say that his mother died when he was 13 years old, and he couldn't go to school. He had to go out and work to take care of his mother; his daddy was dead. He had it pretty hard. I never heard him say what he did when he was a boy. I imagine he fished. T'weren't nothing else much to do here. He didn't have no education, that was the reason he couldn't get rated, couldn't get up. Well, he was a big stout man, and he had a red complexion. Oh, he was a wonderful father. And he didn't live too long after he was retired. But he was in the Service 37 years. I heard him say that when he went in the service it was at Number Nine station. That was Poyner's Hill. Then he was transferred to Paul Gamiels. Don't imagine there's anything left there now, they've had so many storms.

"My people come from Kitty Hawk. My people were Beals. B-E-A-L. Some B-E-A-L-E. We call ours B-E-A-L-S. Now my father I don't know where really he come from. Up in the hills . . . seems to me I've heard him say that his mother was from Columbia or somewhere over that way. Uh huh. My mother's family name is Perry. She was a Kitty Hawk Perry. They have a lot of Perrys in Kitty Hawk. Used to. There's a few still living but not as many as there was years ago. And my mother's mother, she was a Fisher. I think there were four of them, Fisher girls. My grandmother Betty, and Thanny, Amy and Lebarcia. I didn't know them, that was before I was born. I didn't have no grandparents when I was small.

"My mother died having my sister, when I wasn't quite 3 years old. I don't remember what she looked like. I wish I had some faint remembrance of her, but I don't. She's buried in Kitty Hawk. All my people are buried in Austin's Cemetery there.

"But my little sister lived to be grown and married. And she died the same way my mother died. And she had typhoid fever along with it, and of course the baby didn't live. There wasn't time for it to be borned. And my sister Martha, she died about the same way my mother died. In childbirth. And then my oldest sister died in 1919 of the flu, when it was raging, you know, so bad? She didn't live but one week from the time she was taken, went into pneumonia and died.

"My daddy was a hard workin' man. And he raised a big family. I had three sisters, and I had one, two, three — four brothers. There was eight of we children to raise up, and he in the service. He had to have a housekeeper to take care of us. No, not colored, elderly white women mostly. And I'm telling you he had a hard time of it.

"But he was a good father. Didn't make much money, but there was a lot of people didn't make as much as he did. We had something to eat and a place to stay in. He always worshipped we four girls.

"I was a little barefooted girl. In the summer I went barefoot. We had a little one-room schoolhouse in Duck. You wouldn't believe it to go up there now. There's a art gallery there now. And it was history, geography, arithmetic, things like that.

"We had ball games. We had a game we called 50-oh. And ring around the roses. And a game we called sheepie. You'd be surprised at the silly things we had them days. How do you play 50-oh? Some would go off and hide, and we'd try to find them. And if you found them and could make the home run before they did we'd win the game. Yes, hide and seek was what it was, and they called it 50-oh then. We played cat, sure did. It's been so long ago I nearly forgot. And we had a croquet set, young people used to come to our lawn and play.

"And on Sunday afternoon we'd go to this big hill north of Duck. It wasn't as big as Jockey's Ridge, but it didn't lack much. And we'd run up and down it and play until we were so tired we couldn't hardly get back.

"We had one teacher that rang a bell — it was a hand bell. The teacher would stand in the door and ring, ring, when we children would be playing, for us to come in. And we had to stay in at recess a lot, we'd misbehave and done something we shouldn't. Whisperin' in school or laughing. There was a lot of laughing. And certain ones had to stay and sweep the schoolroom and put things in order for next day. Went to school in the summertime, hot weather, barefoot — we didn't have to wear shoes, no.

"The Wright brothers? They flew in 1903. I was born in 1900. Oh, yes, they came back in 1908. I remember that. But there was always something going on that I didn't know about. I didn't really live that close to Kill Devil. I saw them flying around. It looked different from planes they have now. We thought it was something scary, flying around up there.

"My daddy had a horse that he used at the station and then on his liberty at home. He'd bring the horse home. He didn't have but one day liberty a week, one day and one night. He come home at 12 and left next day at 11 to get back to the station. It was about an hour's ride on the horse because it was sand, it took longer to go. He had to be on time, they were strict them days. The horse was named Fanny. That horse ran away with him. I think he was on patrol and the horse got frightened, something happened that he just ran. And throwed him out of the cart and hurt him pretty bad. Throwed him out on his head. Doctor had to tend him.

"Sometimes he patrolled with the horse, but most times he walked. He had what they call a lay-house on each end. Between the two stations, you know. And most times he had to walk the night. He had a north patrol, sometimes he had a south patrol. If it was a stormy night he'd patrol twice a night. And again he'd just have one patrol a night. He'd walk up and down the beach — that ocean had to be watched for ships, y'know. And I can remember all the ships come ashore when he was in there, and I used to worry when I was a kid when I'd hear talk — we'd get word from the station there was a shipwreck on the beach, and I knew my daddy had to go. I remember how I used to worry about it, thought maybe he wouldn't make it back. Because then they said go, you didn't have to come back. It was the rule. If it was possible to get to the ship, to get the men off, they had to go. And sometimes you didn't come back. You got drowned. I remember seein' em come ashore. Ships from different countries. Some men got lost, some got saved. Some ships was torn to pieces. I've seen men washed ashore on the beach drowned. That's when I was a little girl.

"There wasn't very much. The houses weren't very well kept up. There weren't very many big homes. There were some hunting lodges, one or two. The people who weren't in the service depended on fishing.

"I'm telling you we had a rough time of it, but them were the happy days. Happier than they are in this day and time. We didn't have a lot, but what we had we enjoyed. And we didn't look for a whole lot. If I got a rag doll at Christmas, and a stocking full of nuts and candy and all that, I was happy with it. Now little children gets everything and in no time it's tore up and gone. We took care of our little things that we got.

"But we were happy people them days. It was almost like one big family. Some of them was poorer than others. And them that had a little bit more they'd always divide. I know my daddy did.

"My daddy never had much money, but he always raised a lot of stuff to eat around him. Even guineas. And hogs. He had a lot of hogs. We didn't have to buy no meat, no lard. The hogs went free till the new law, the fence law come in, and he had to get rid of them. The woods used to be full of hogs and cattle. Always had a plenty to eat on Christmas. Wasn't like it is now — all beefsteak. We raised chickens and raised geese and ducks; we had fowls of all kinds. And then gunnin', you know, you killed wild ducks and geese. No problem 'bout eating. We had a garden and grew beans, and collards, and cabbage, sweet potatoes and horse potatoes, cucumbers, tomatoes, most every kind of vegetable you could raise around here. It wasn't the kind of food people eats this day and time. It was good food, it sure was.

"No, you wouldn't hardly believe how people lived them days. We only went to the city once a year. Elizabeth City, that was the closest city. That wasn't very big but to us it was a big one. It was like goin' to New York. Nobody got nowhere much — I think I did go to Norfolk once or twice when I was growin' up. Went on a steamboat.

"I moved to Chesapeake in 1918. We didn't have no high school. I went there to take a business course. It was in Norfolk, on Main Street. Mr. Wresler's college. He died, and Mr. Keyes took it over.

"No, I didn't get a job then. I married William Twiford, in 1918, and he wouldn't let me go to work. He was from Princess Anne, there's where his people was from. He lived down Corolla. But we lived in Norfolk for right many years. My oldest son was born in South Norfolk, and my daughter was born in South Norfolk.

"Then we moved from Norfolk to Church's Island. He was a guide, for two lodges. White's, and for Hampton. Duck hunting lodges. Oh, yes, I know that's a unpleasant job — he complained about it. I think we were there a couple, three year he worked for the lodge. From there he put in for the Coast Guard. He decided he'd better when he was younger go in the service.

"And we were stationed in Dam Neck. And we lived there I think two year. From there we moved from one station to the other. And finally settled down in Duck, where I was born. And he was in Caffey's Inlet, and then in Kitty Hawk. And I think in Nags Head too. He was all over. And he went to Florida too, was there a whole winter. But I didn't go, the children was small. And he got transferred back. We were in Wash Woods I think six years. That's up above Corolla. And Caffey's Inlet. I think he retired out of Kitty Hawk. He's been dead — buried him close to 20 year.

"I remember the worst hurricane up there was in 1933. You can't imagine what a hurricane sounds like. It's terrible — Whoooo. The water came up and flooded us out of our house. Everybody had to leave their home. First we went to the garage, on a hill, and there was lots of women and children in there. The ocean was between us and the station, and the surf had bursted their lifeboat all to pieces. So the men couldn't come and help us. We were helpless. And the water was rising. There was this old lady who had a big house, and she would take people in. The children wanted to go there. So to please the children I left the garage and was trying to get to it. Wading. But the water was too deep, and it was coming in, and I had to try to get up to the top of a hill. And it was sand, and I had the children by both my hands, trying to get up to the top of that sand hill. And I couldn't do it, and the water was rising. But just then the eye of the storm came, and we was able to get to safety at the house.

"Some of the houses was took away — the ocean just took them away. I was lucky. The sand was hilled up as high as the eaves of my house. The wind was so strong it blew the winter lights and the curtains and the shades and the glass out, and blew some of the roof off. And the sea had eat under my kitchen. But I had my house. That's the reason I don't think much of the beach. I just look on that water and walk away. And I think that was why when I was growing up, my father kept us so far from the shore.

"Oh, yes, I really feel lucky to have my children. I got five or six grandchildren. There's more than grandchildren, of great ones. I don't know how many I got, haven't counted them up lately. And I love the great ones just as good as I do the grandchildren.

"I've been in here for two years now. I'm not getting much better, but my mind seems to be clearer. But I'm a lot better than some of them in here. I'll tell you, this is a pitiful place. You go around and see the sufferin' and the sick people. I'm not bodily sick, but I broke my hip a couple of year ago, and something happened that the leg got twisted. They did try to straighten it out, but I think they waited too long. It can't never be back right. And this wheelchair . . . I'm still not well. And I don't think I've got enough time for this hip to ever heal.

"This is a wonderful place to be. They have helicopters here, they take you to hospitals, to the doctors. I haven't been on them. We have everything here that's needed for this kind of home. And my children take care of me pretty good, they do all they can for me. But I'll be glad if I can get out.

"I've had a lot of trouble in my life, yes I have. I think the unhappiest time was when the children left home. I had two in the war. Clyde was in Germany, right in the midst of the battle there. He got his feet froze there. He still has trouble with his legs. And Tom was in the Navy, on the high seas the times when ships were getting sunk down here. You never knew when word was coming that he was drowned. I had a lot of worry on to me. You're bound to worry about them when they're facing danger every minute of their life. And Tom got rheumatic fever in England, and it still bothers him.

"The happiest time was when I was young — getting married, I reckon.

"The best way I'm happiest is when I know the Lord's going to take care of me. I know I've got to die. But while I'm living I feel like if I live the right life, which I try my best, then he'll take care of me. Although I'm suffering, that'll be over after a while. I want to be prepared to not have none of these aches and things. No, I'm not afraid, not a bit. I want to live as long as the Lord sees fit for me to live, then when it's time I got no dread. No worry about my soul. I know the Bible tells us a lot, but I still think we got to die and go on to find out really what it's all about. Maybe I'm wrong, but if I am it's ignorance, the Lord will forgive me."

Maggie Twiford sits facing the window, immobile in the waning sunlight, watching as the wind ruffles the beach grass at the top of a dune. If you were 8 years old, barefoot, you could scramble to the top in a minute. And see for a long, long ways.

The northeast wind blows for an odd number of days.

Insiders' Tips

Inside
Kitty Hawk

If you arrive in Kitty Hawk from the north you'll cross the Wright Memorial Bridge over Currituck Sound on Route 158. Travelers from southern parts of the country or western North Carolina will probably arrive in Kitty Hawk from the west end of the Outer Banks through Manteo. From the west end of the Banks, you'll continue north through the towns of Nags Head and Kill Devil Hills until you reach your destination: Kitty Hawk.

Once you've crossed the bridge, it's time to slow down and remember that you are on a mission here. Your mission may include getting the best suntan you've had in years, surfing some of the best waves on the East Coast, relaxing and unwinding on some of North Carolina's finest beaches, or getting your fill of great seafood caught fresh from the ocean waters surrounding the Outer Banks. The choices for outdoor recreation are countless, and they include swimming, surfing, bicycling, hiking and golfing, windsurfing, parasailing, kayaking, hang gliding and paragliding. You need to get accustomed to doing things differently now. You need to put the fun and relaxation of you and your family before all else. We guarantee this will be easy to do here on the Outer Banks.

Our journey through Kitty Hawk will provide you with a visual guide through the town as though you have just crossed the Wright Memorial Bridge and entered Kitty Hawk from the north end of the Banks. Our highway system may seem a little different for newcomers to the area. It's wide and looks like a place to drive fast, but wait! The outside lane has many access and egress points, and the inside lane serves as an exit to the turn lane, which runs down the middle, so be safe and drive with care.

The threat of suddenly finding yourself right behind a car that has discovered at the last moment that it's time to turn is reason enough to travel within the speed limits here. Or, you may experience the "Carolina pullout," you know, when that car traveling at 15 mph pulls out in front of you at the corner!

Milepost markers will give travelers hints about where they are. Most rental cottages, shops, restaurants, attractions and resorts located north, south, east and west of the Wright Memorial Bridge will be noted by milepost indicators along Route 158 and the Beach Road — the two roads running parallel to the beach. The first milepost marker is located in Kitty Hawk.

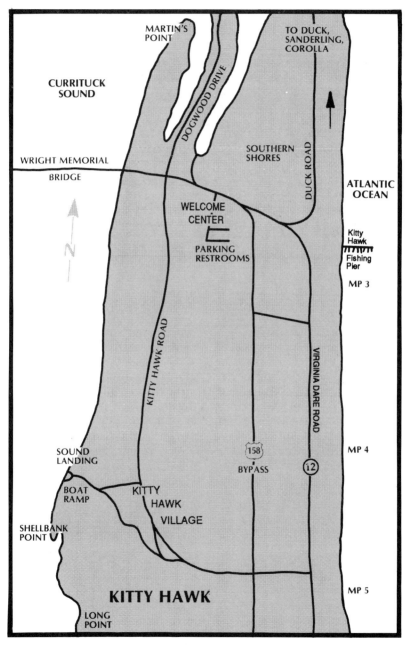

CURRITUCK
SOUND

MARTIN'S
POINT

TO DUCK,
SANDERLING,
COROLLA

DOGWOOD DRIVE

SOUTHERN
SHORES

DUCK ROAD

WRIGHT MEMORIAL
BRIDGE

ATLANTIC
OCEAN

N

WELCOME
CENTER

PARKING
RESTROOMS

Kitty
Hawk
Fishing
Pier

MP 3

KITTY HAWK ROAD

VIRGINIA DARE ROAD

SOUND
LANDING

MP 4

BOAT
RAMP

KITTY
HAWK
VILLAGE

158
BYPASS

12

SHELLBANK
POINT

KITTY HAWK

MP 5

LONG
POINT

There's no finer way to spend the day.

The maritime forest of Kitty Hawk Woods seen on the west side of the island surprises the first-time visitor. After all, typically the beach is supposed to be flat, and forests belong on higher ground. Not so, here on the Outer Banks. These forests are important ecosystems, and they are beautiful to look at too. Spanish moss drapes over trees in what appears to be in random fashion, and lush green ground cover creates a path as far as the eye can see. The maritime forest provides a strikingly beautiful contrast to the wide open, expansive, golden-sunlit areas surrounding the sandy beach area of the Banks.

As noted above, two roads run parallel through the easterly portions of Kitty Hawk, the old two-lane Beach Road, aka NC 12, and the newer dual lane Route 158. A drive on the Beach Road shows original and more weather-beaten beach cottages contrasting the newer and more modern beach homes. In many cases, older cottages are not suitable for year-round living because they lack the necessary insulation needed to endure the winter months on the Outer Banks. Owners didn't have it in their minds "back then" to relocate to "Nags Head" on a more permanent basis, or let's say, "year round." In most cases, newer and more modern beach cottages are suitable for year-round living.

A drive along the Beach Road will give you an idea of how harsh life by the sea can really be. The winter storms of 1991 and 1992 hit the beaches of Kitty Hawk with a vengeance. This town was one of the first popular beach settlements on the Outer Banks, but the deep erosion along this portion of the Banks has given way to a narrower, unprotected beach. Even Old Station, a popular ex-lifesaving station landmark, has been moved to a more

protected location west of the Beach Road. Newer businesses and homes built along here tend to be on higher ground, helping to protect them from the elements. Areas between the highways and along the Beach Road primarily contain second homes and rental cottages.

Year-round residences in Kitty Hawk are concentrated in soundside areas west of Route 158 in neighborhoods with names like Kitty Hawk Woods, Kitty Hawk Estates and Kitty Hawk Landing. Sandpiper Cay Condominiums and Seascape also are year-round resort communities that offer a variety of amenities.

The Regional Medical Center is conveniently located next to the Aycock Brown Welcome Center at MP 1½ A new post office was opened in Kitty Hawk last year, and it's located between the highways at MP 4.

The first families of Kitty Hawk were named Twiford, Baum, Etheridge, Perry and Hill. Many descendants of these first families live on the west side of Kitty Hawk, and a drive on Kitty Hawk Road will lead you to other roads with such names as Elijah Baum Road, Herbert Perry Road and Moore Shore Road. Along the latter is a monument that designates the spot where Orville and Wilbur Wright assembled their plane before their historic flight a few miles away in 1903. More on this part of Outer Banks history is found in the chapter on Kill Devil Hills.

Attractions

THE AYCOCK BROWN WELCOME CENTER

Rt. 158 , MP 1½　　　　261-4644

It's just what it says it is — a welcome center — and you'll enjoy a stop here. Information on the Outer Banks is abundant. Free community newspapers offer good reading and a flavor of what constitutes important news in this part of the world. Maps, flyers, motel and hotel information, cottage rental books, community events and information about the prospects of good fishing can be obtained from the friendly people who work here. The Welcome Center is open 9 AM until 5 PM all year, with extended hours during the spring, summer and fall to accommodate visitors. The building is handicapped accessible and has public rest rooms. The picnic area is a welcome sight for those who have been riding for a while.

It is worthwhile to note that the Dare County Tourist Bureau can be contacted at (800) 446-6262 for free information to be mailed to visitors planning a trip to the Outer Banks. The Dare County Tourist Bureau will be happy to answer all of your questions regarding the Outer Banks.

KITTY HAWK PUBLIC BEACH & BATH HOUSE

Beach Rd., MP 4½

Located across the road from the ocean, a bathhouse and small parking area offer visitors a place to go on the beach as soon as they arrive on the Outer Banks. If you arrive too early for check-in, you can change into bathing suits here and enjoy a few hours on the beach until it's time to head to the hotel or the property management company for keys to your beach retreat.

Recreation

THE PROMENADE

MP ¼
West side of Rt. 158　　　　261-3844

Located near the Wright Memorial Bridge, this area on Currituck Sound is home to a beautiful maritime forest and even more fun and family recreation than last year. The Promenade is open year round. All of the activities are available 8 AM until midnight, May through September. (It's best to call ahead for hours during the off season.) Activities for the entire family include: **Waterfall Greens**, an 18-hole miniature theme golf course; putting greens, a separate 27-hole putting course on natural grass; target driving range; **Watersports Center**, The SandTrap, a gourmet coffee and draft house with an adult arcade and Smilin' Island, an innovative children's playground for kids ages 1 to 12.

Theme miniature golf with waterfalls appeals to children and young adults. Prices are $4 per game or $5 to play all day. Skilled golfing enthusiasts will enjoy the putting greens with 27 longer holes covering three acres in a maritime forest setting. Here, the cost for 18 holes, one-time play, day or night, is $7.

The Promenade also offers the only full-size public target driving range on the Outer Banks; it's lighted, and clubs and balls are available for your use. The cost for a small bucket of golf balls is $5, and a large bucket costs $10.

As if that's not enough, you can enjoy the wetter side of life at the Watersports Center. **North Beach Sailing**, 261-4400, provides rentals of sailboats, fishing boats, pontoon boats, jet skis, waverunners, canoes, kayaks, paddle boats, windsurfing equipment and more. High performance and beginner windsurfing lessons, sailing lessons and parasailing are provided soundfront near the bridge by certified instructors. Reservations are recommended. The Watersports Center also features a small retail store, called North Beach Sailing, with windsurfing equipment, T-shirts, sunglasses, cameras and other necessities.

In addition to all of this, kids will certainly enjoy the two arcades, and you'll find a snack bar, picnic area and public rest rooms so you can spend the day. We think this is a good recreational choice for the entire family.

KITTY HAWK FISHING PIER
Beach Rd., MP 1   261-2772

Once you cross the bridge, count the traffic lights and at the third light, turn east towards the beach road. You'll see the Kitty Hawk Fishing Pier straight ahead. Built in the mid-'50s, the pier is privately owned and operated by friendly experts. It stretches 714 feet into the ocean, has a nice bait and tackle shop and

has a good restaurant. Fishing is good for all the inshore species normally caught. Some record-holding catches have been landed here, and it is a very popular, easy-to-reach pier when the blues are blitzin'. Kitty Hawk Pier is open April through Thanksgiving. Daily admission is $5 for adults and $3 for children. A weekly pass is $25, and season passes are $125. Handicapped persons are admitted free.

BERMUDA GREENS
Rt. 158, MP 1½   261-0101

Miniature golf on real Bermuda grass is offered at Bermuda Greens. The two 18-hole courses are sure to bring out the best in every player who golfs here. In addition to miniature golf, you will also enjoy a video arcade and TCBY yogurt in their yogurt shop. Tables with umbrellas are available for your convenience in the pavilion area. The cost to play 18 holes of golf is $7 for adults and $4 for children 10 and under. Bermuda Greens will be open Easter through Thanksgiving, and hours during the summer will be 10 AM until midnight.

SEA SCAPE GOLF CLUB
Rt. 158, MP 2½   261-2158

After you pass the Aycock Brown Welcome Center, you'll see the fairways of Sea Scape golf course to the west. This is a Scottish-type golf course without trees or water hazards, but the sand traps are as big a challenge as anywhere. The course boasts top-notch greens—as smooth as any in the state. There are 18 holes on the par 72, 6,200-yard long course.

Cart rental is required. The bar and grill at the 19th hole will help you relax after the game. Sea Scape is open 7 AM until dark every day of the year.

COLONY CINEMAS

Rt.158, MP 4½   *261-7949*

Colony Cinemas is located at Kitty Hawk Plaza on the west side of Route 158 and offers twin theaters for family entertainment. The phone number above carries a recorded announcement for showings at all Colony Cinemas on the Outer Banks.

Shopping

A garden center, custom flag shop, seafood store, tackle shop, eateries and three surf shops join the usual run of banks, department stores, hardware stores, lumber yards and grocery stores that serve most year-round resort communities. **Central Garden & Nursery**, 261-7195, is located at the ¼ MP. This is a family-owned and -operated garden center that has been serving the Albemarle area for 28 years. The garden center features foliage (inside) plants, shrubs and trees, and a landscape architect is available to assist you with landscape planning. They have a good reputation, and they're open year round, 9 AM until 5 PM. The Garden Center is open six days a week and part of the day on Sunday during the planting season. It's open six days a week during the summer and closed on Sundays. **Islander Flags of Kitty Hawk**, 261-6266, is also located at the ¼ MP just before The Promenade. They are the only flag makers on the beach. All of their flags are appliqued, and you'll find custom flags, state flags, U.S. and foreign flags, decorative banners, windsocks and flag poles and accessories.

The Shoreside Center shopping center is across the street from The Market Place Shopping Center in Southern shores and it is home to **Wal-Mart**, 261-6011. For those of you who thought you could shop only at locally owned "moms and pops" and other small chains on the Outer Banks — Surprise! (KMart is also located down the road in Kill Devil Hills.)

The Shoreside Center also includes, **Seamark Foods**, 261-2220, an upscale grocery store complete with a bakery, deli, salad bar and an extensive selection of cheese and wines. This Seamark location also offers a large selection of fresh fish and everything you need to prepare your fresh seafood Outer Banks style. (Seamark Foods can also be found at The Outer Banks Mall in Nags Head.) **Cato's**, 261-1974, a new boutique-style shop, offers women's fashions, sportswear and career wear and clothing for larger sizes too. Cato's also offers a complete line of shoes and accessories. **The Dollar Tree**, 255-0320, is a great place to shop for incidentals. You never know what you'll take home from a dollar store! **Carolina Video**, 255-0821, is a full-service video store and **Radio Shack**, 261-6334, moved from The Market Place Shopping Center to Shoreside Center. We know you'll be hungry after all of this shopping so you can grab a sandwich at **Subway**, 255-0539, or a hamburger under the golden arches of McDonald's.

Remember your neighborhood hardware store? Well, this one is just like it. For those wanting to pick up household supplies, art supplies, or items needed for home improvement in a small hardware store, the kind folks at **Virginia Dare Hardware**, 261-2660, on the Beach Road, MP 2½, will have what you need. Don't be surprised if you find some off-the-wall items here too.

Carawan Seafood Company, 261-2120, is ready and willing to provide you with the fish you didn't catch for dinner. Take time to consider their selection of wines, spices and sauces. They will gladly pack your fish on ice to go.

Three Winks Shops is home to an ABC store, Teed Off, Duck Donut Company and Bakery and North China Express. For discount golf and tennis equipment, visit **Teed Off**, 261-Golf. This shop carries only new, first quality merchandise at discount prices. Custom built golf clubs are also available here. For great Chinese food, available at a fast pace, try **North China Express**, 261-5511.

A lot has happened to the **Duck Donut and Bakery**, 255-0038, during the past year. Their original location at Three Winks Shop is thriving, and the owners from Indiana have opened three other locations on the Outer Banks. (And they

thought they were going to take it easy.) The other locations include Tim Buck II Shopping Village in Corolla, 453-0920, Duck Village Square in Duck, 255-0014 and Island Donut and Bakery, 473-6166, on Roanoke Island. You will still find the same great home-baked goods and treats in Kitty Hawk including donuts (of course), homemade breads, bagels, muffins and other specialty items. Their special-order cakes and cookies for all occasions will tempt you too. And expect nothing less from their other locations either — including friendly service for you early risers.

Duck Donut and Bakery resulted from a dream about a hot dog stand. The story goes on from there including the part where only one year ago, George and Mary Gavalas and Bob and Althea Weimer, moved to the Outer Banks for a more relaxing lifestyle. These grandparents were only too happy to give up the interstate for a calmer way of life. Now they have 15 employees during the summer and four bakery locations — all in one year, need we say more?

Located farther south in Kitty Hawk, past the Welcome Center, at the 2½ MP is **Ambrose Furniture**, 261-4836. This family-owned and operated furnishings showroom has been in business for 47 years, and they're open year round. A qualified staff will assist you with your selection of furniture, blinds and houseware packages — and the design service is free of charge.

When one surf shop opens, others are sure to follow. **Whalebone Surf Shop**, 261-8737, built its own establishment at MP 2½ on Route 158. Whalebone offers what's hot in the line of beach fashions, swimwear and surfwear. This is a real surf shop, and owner Jim Vaughn is very popular with the locals. Surfboards, surfing supplies, skate boarding supplies, travel gear — you can get it all here including Whalebone T-shirts and sweatshirts for the whole family. Hawaiian Island Creations is another cool line of clothing and surfboards that can be found at this shop. (Don't forget to check out their other location in Nags Head in front of the Food Lion Plaza for more cool stuff.)

Adjacent to Whalebone Surf Shop, you'll find the bike shop, **Cactus Tire**, 261-FLAT. The managers of this new bike shop toured the East Coast a few years ago on bikes to determine if the Outer Banks was as great a place to live as they thought it might be. Their journey began in Key West, Florida and continued north to Montreal, Canada. Of course they discovered what most of us who live here know already know — that there is no place quite like the Outer Banks. Cactus Tire offers bike sales, rentals and repairs. These two guys, Mike Stainback and Robert Patterson Wells, will also provide a delivery and pickup service for bike rentals during the season. Mountain bike video rentals are available. Summer hours are 9 AM until 6 PM, seven days a week.

And the next thing you know, **Wave Riding Vehicles**, 261-7952, at MP 2 3/4 has enlarged their shop to become the largest surf shop on the Outer Banks. Wave Riding has everything you need to satisfy your surfing desires. This is a very popular destination for surfers and serious shoppers alike. Surfers everywhere know "WRV."

Practically neighbors, **Bert's Surf Shop**, 261-7584, famous in Nags Head, built another shop in Kitty Hawk at MP 3½ on Route 158. All these stores have great clothes in addition to what they're in business for — surfing and surf boards! And, luckily, the chase for the perfect wave often ends right here in the Outer Banks.

Open your eyes wide. What do you see before you but a bright pink building and a bright pink delivery van at MP 3½! Well that's, **Seabreeze Florist**, 261-4247 or (800) 435-5881. Seabreeze isn't your typical florist; their creative abilities are almost beyond compare. They specialize in fresh flowers and floral souvenirs with an emphasis on custom designs. Shells and flowers are used together to create tasteful beach mementos. Nautical baskets and gifts baskets from the area are very popular, and, of course, they offer balloons, plants and flowers for all occasions.

For all you homeowners and dream home owners, **Ace Hardware**, 261-4211, is also located at 3½ MP. We know they can help you with your hardware needs. **A & B Carpets**, 261-8106, is practically next door to assist you with your carpet, tile, vinyl floors and custom window

treatments. They've been in business since 1974, and you'll see their brand new building on Route 158; it's white with aqua-teal trim. **Pella Window & Door**, 261-7811, is a full-service window and door company. They share the building with A & B Carpets. **COECO** office furniture and supplies, 261-2400, is a full-service office supply store and can help you with all of your business needs while you're on the Outer Banks. (Of course we hope there won't be many.)

Just about every store on the Outer Banks carries fishing gear, but you really can't beat **TW's Bait & Tackle**, 261-7848, next to the 7-11 at MP 4. Stop in for the best gear and info on what's biting. Owner, Terry "T.W." Stewart has been in business for more than 10 years and can sell you what you need, including ice and live bait.

Kitty Hawk Plaza is located at the 4 ½ MP, and you'll find some great shops here. **Gray's Specialty Department Store**, 261-1776, is an Outer Banks legend. Top name brands and friendly service are featured at this family owned and operated retail shop. They specialize in men's and women's clothing and swimwear for the whole family. Their shoe department is very popular with locals and visitors alike. Women will enjoy tasteful accessories, jewelry, belts and handbags. Gray's department store is home of the official "Big Duck" T-shirt — everyone in your family will probably want one. Next door is **Decor by the Shore**, 261-6222, featuring complete home furnishing packages. Designers will assist you with all of your decorating decisions.

Crafter's Gallery, 261-3036, is a spacious crafter's marketplace featuring only handmade one-of-a-kind crafts, pottery, jewelry and fine art. Most of the crafters are local folks, so your purchases help support the local crafters population. Crafter's Gallery is open year round offering craft shows during Easter, Thanksgiving and Christmas. We purchased some truly unique ornaments for Christmas last year; it's a fun place to shop or browse during the holidays.

You'll find **Phelps Drapery & Interiors**, 261-6644, and the new **Designer's Market**, 261-6090, located at **The Dunes Professional Center**, MP 5 in Kitty Hawk. Phelps has been in business since 1978, and they offer a complete home-fashion center. They can assist you with carpet, furnishings, accessories, window treatments, wall coverings and more. Accessories are featured in the store, not furniture. There is a wide selection of fabrics available for custom work.

Designer's Market, 261-6090, specializes in distinctive home furnishings, decorative accessories and interior design from selection of that perfect picture to decoration of an entire home or cottage package. Unique offerings include reproduction furniture, porcelainware, hand-carved shore birds and fish, mirrors, chandeliers and lots more. This store has a small showroom but it is packed with very interesting and tasteful furniture, furnishings and gift items.

A couple of supermarkets added to the first Kitty Hawk grocery store will have all the food you need for your vacation. For big shopping trips, **The Marketplace Shopping Center** (see the description under Northern Beaches Shopping), MP 1, has a **Food Lion** supermarket, and across the street you'll find **Seamark Foods** (next to Wal-Mart). **Food-A-Rama** at the Kitty Hawk Plaza, MP 4, can supply you with most of your grocery needs as well. **Billy's Seafood**, 261-7946, in Kitty Hawk on Route 158, offers the same fine quality Outer Banks seafood found at their Colington location. **Winks Grocery,** 261-2555, is on the Beach Road at MP 2½. Miles Davis, Margaret, Janice and all the others will welcome you to the beach. Shopping here is what it is supposed to be like at a beach store, with their sometimes-sandy floors and laid-back atmosphere. You'll find all the reality-soaked newspapers you thought you'd left behind and everything else you'll need for the beach. A deli and butcher shop provide you with another shopping convenience. The radio and speakers hanging inside the door on the wall grabbed our attention one day with some good beach music, not often found while shopping. Get to know the folks at Winks; they're open year round.

Inside
Kill Devil Hills

Kill Devil Hills is situated in the middle of the barrier islands and is the only town on the beach where you can get just about everything you need within the town limits.

Today, the Outer Banks' first beach town is Dare County's population center. More than 4,200 permanent residents call Kill Devil Hills home, compared to the 250 permanent residents back in 1953. In a *Coastland Times* article commemorating the 40th anniversary, former Town Commissioner, Richard Baer, who began visiting Kill Devil Hills during the summer of 1948, observes, "there were three stores — one of which sold gasoline. And there weren't any trees or shrubs on the beach because the animals grazed them all down. For fun, we begged our parents to take us to Leary's Bingo and the merry-go-round in Nags Head. It was where the Wharf restaurant is now. And when we got older, we took our dates to Norfolk. The only thing to do around here was stop by my parents' store and chat with the neighbors. The only movie and bar were in Manteo then."

The barren dunes and sandy pathways that once existed here have been claimed by more than 41 miles of paved roads. Beach cottages, con-dominiums, franchise hotels and "moms and pops" now dot the five miles of once-barren, wide-open dunes. Fast food signs have sprung up along the four-lane Route 158, forming the island's commercial hub.

There's something here for everyone including lots of public beach and sound access (and more traffic lights than in most other areas of the beach). Yet, Kill Devil Hills remains a popular beach destination for visitors and permanent residents because all that the town has to offer is accessible to the public, and it is definitely family oriented.

New schools for children on the Outer Banks are centrally located in Kill Devil Hills. The Dare County Reverse Osmosis Water Treatment Plant (tours conducted every day), a new public library and the Thomas A. Baum Center (for senior adult activities) are located in this mid-beach town. The Outer Banks Chamber of Commerce offices, a Welcome Center and Dare County satellite offices are here too. The Dare Center shopping center opened several years ago, and one of the largest Kmart stores on the East Coast opened in Kill Devil Hills in 1992. This town also has its own pier, the Avalon Fishing Pier.

Regardless of the trend toward bigger and better resort homes and amenities elsewhere on the Outer Banks, Kill Devil Hills remains attached to its place in history as a family-oriented beach for visitors and a centrally located town of moderately-priced housing for the permanent population. Fishing, crabbing, kite flying, sea kayaking, windsurfing, sunbathing, surfing, air tours, shopping, restaurants, motels, churches, libraries, schools and close proximity to Kitty Hawk's Regional Medical Center or Nags Head's Medical Center, churches, libraries and schools make this town a choice for many.

Legends about how Kill Devil Hills got its name are as numerous as those who speculate about it. Some of these explanations bear repeating. The most popular account says that the town was named after a Jamaican rum called "Kill Devil." After a trip to the barrier islands in 1728, William Byrd returned to Virginia and reported drinking rum that was strong enough to kill the devil. A less popular version of the tale suggests a ship carrying a cargo of the liquor wrecked offshore and a resident nicknamed "Devil Ike" volunteered to guard the rum. Neighbors reportedly stole the cargo and Devil Ike, not wanting to snitch on neighbors, explained that the devil stole the goods, but he had caught and killed the devil by the sand hills. Another explanation reports a possible connection to the name of a once-common shore bird, the "Kill Dee" or "Killdeer." We're not sure when Kill Devil added the "s" to become Kill Devil Hills.

Famous Outer Banks historian and author, David Stick, discusses these legends and others in his book, *The Outer Banks, 1584-1958*, published by UNC Press. Most who have studied possible origins of the name agree it probably originated in association with the drinking of Jamaican rum. Other possible sources of origination are considered to be much less plausible. Let's not forget that as Kill Devil Hills celebrated its 40th anniversary last year, this town is also the site of the Wright brothers' first flight. At the turn of the century we directed our attention to a sandy hill — west of the ocean — that captured the drama of the first flight. This story has been told and retold many times.

The Wright Brothers

The Wright brothers from Ohio first built bicycles, then gliders and airplanes. They began to track weather conditions to determine the best place to test their heavier-than-air machine. Ideal conditions were located in Kitty Hawk, North Carolina. Constant winds and soft hills of sand met their requirements. Responding to their inquiry, Capt. Bill Tate of the Kitty Hawk Weather Station wrote to the Wright brothers encouraging them to come here and try their machine. He promised to do everything possible to assure a successful venture in a convenient location among friendly people.

Wilbur Wright arrived on September 13, 1900, after a dismal two-week schooner trip from Elizabeth City. He set up camp near Capt. Tate's home, in Kitty Hawk Village about four miles north of Kill Devil

Plan now for vacation fun!

*S*un Realty has over 900 choices of vacation homes to help make your Outer Banks vacation a memorable one for you and your family. Call our 800 number or complete the coupon below to receive our free vacation home rental brochure and start planning your vacation today!

1·800·334·4745

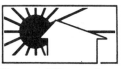

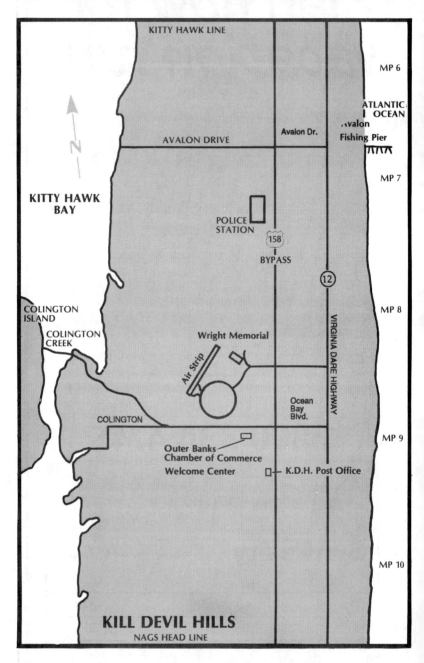

Photo: N.C. Travel and Tourism

Shipwrecks are scattered up and down the Banks.

Hills. Orville Wright arrived two weeks later, and they began assembling their first glider. They first experimented with tie-lines as though they were flying a kite. Later, they carried it four miles to a 90-foot high sand hill and made about a dozen glides, taking turns piloting it. Their total time aloft was about 15 seconds.

The gliding season for 1900 was over, and although their time in the air had been short, they made some important observations. The lifting power of the wings was less than they had expected, but the wing warping system they had invented to enable them to turn the machine worked well. They left for Dayton, Ohio, resolving to return the following year.

By the summer of 1901, they had completed a second glider. This model had wings 22 feet wide and seven-foot chord, with increased cur-

vature to conform to Otto Lilienthal's aerodynamic theories. They arrived at Kill Devil Hill with this new glider on July 10 and put in a few days building a large shed and drilling a well. Between July 27 and August 20 they made several dozen flights. These flights proved Lilienthal's figures inaccurate. They decided a vertical surface was needed at the tail. But they still succeeded in gliding farther and more skillfully than anyone had before.

They returned to Dayton that winter and continued in the bicycle business. They also built the first scientifically accurate wind tunnel to carry out their own calculations of wing curvature and lift. By September 19, 1902, they were back on the Outer Banks, in Kill Devil Hills. They brought a new glider with a tail and designed it with new knowledge of aerodynamic principles and theories. During September and October that year, tests proved they were very near the 'secret' of flying. The glider soared, remaining aloft for more than a minute and going more than 600 feet. When they added a movable rudder to the vertical tail, the basic idea of the airplane was complete.

Back in Dayton they built their own engine. A four-cylinder, aluminum block gasoline engine that delivered between nine and 12 horsepower was completed according to the Wrights' demanding specifications. Then they built a complete new plane. No one had ever built propellers, so they designed and built one for their new plane. The final result produced all the elements of today's aircraft, if not in appearance, in theory. A 40-foot span of double wings with aileron control interacting with a movable rudder provides a description of their machine, which also had a gasoline engine placed alongside the prone pilot on the lower wing, driving two counter-rotating pusher props. The launching system consisted of a rail down which the plane could roll before dropping off.

Their fourth trip to Kill Devil Hills came in September 1903. They stayed busy building another shed, repaired a number of breakdowns and ground-tested the machine. The Wright brothers' work had aroused the interest of the press. By December 14 they were ready to fly. Men from the lifesaving station were signalled to come and help. The launch rail was set up near the top of the hill. Wilbur won the toss, the engine was warmed up and the flying-machine slid down the rail. Wilbur en-

thusiastically brought the nose up too fast, stalled the plane and dropped it into the sand at the foot of the hill.

Repairs were made and on December 17 with cold 21-mph winds blowing, the brothers pulled out the machine again and called the men from the lifesaving station for help. With such strong winds they decided to fly from a level track and set up the launching apparatus near the sheds. At 10:35 AM, Orville climbed aboard and started the engine. The propellers began to turn. Facing a brisk wind, the machine started very slowly when Orville released the hold-down wire. Wilbur ran alongside. The flier, in Orville's words later:

". . . lifted from the track just as it was entering on the fourth rail. Mr. Daniels took a picture just as it left the tracks. I found the control of the front rudder quite difficult on account of its being balanced too near the center and thus had a tendency to turn itself when started so that the rudder was turned too far on one side and then too far on the other. As a result the machine would rise suddenly to about 10 feet and then as suddenly, on turning the rudder, tip towards the ground. A sudden drop, when out about 100 feet from the end of the tracks, ended the flight . . . "

He had been in the air only 12 seconds. Other attempts went like this:

At 11:20 AM on the second flight, Wilbur piloted. The wind dropped for a time and the machine flew faster, going 175 feet in 12 seconds.

At 11:40 AM on the third flight,

Orville piloted the plane for a distance of 200 feet in 15 seconds.

At noon a fourth and last flight with Wilbur flying went 852 feet in 59 seconds.

The brothers planned to go for distance on the next flight, perhaps as far as the lifesaving station in Kitty Hawk, but a few minutes later, as the flier was sitting on the sand, a gust of wind struck. The machine rolled over and over. It was destroyed. The 1903 flying season was at an end.

That afternoon, after eating lunch and washing their dishes, the Wright brothers walked to the Kitty Hawk weather station, which had a telegraph connection. Orville wrote the famous message:

"Success Four Flights Thursday Morning All Against Twenty-One Mile Wind Started From Level With Engine Power Alone Average Speed Through Air Thirty-One Miles Longest 50 Seconds Inform Press Home Christmas. Orville Wright."

In 1904, the Wrights shifted their experiments to a field near Dayton, extending their flights to 24 miles in 38 minutes by the end of 1905. Incredibly, they attracted very little attention, even in Dayton. In 1908, they returned to Kill Devil Hills to test new aircraft, engines and control arrangements. The press discovered them around this time, and history was recorded.

Kill Devil Hills' population grew with the construction of bridges spanning Roanoke and Currituck sounds between 1920 and 1930. The famous hill had been stabilized with grass in 1928 and was capped with the Wright Brothers Memorial, a granite monument, in 1932. In 1938 a post office opened in Kill Devil Hills, and in 1953 the town became incorporated.

Colington Island

Big Colington Island on the western perimeter of Kill Devil Hills offers some history of its own. The island is known for its rugged maritime forest and marshlands and is home to abundant wildlife, plants and trees draped in Spanish moss. Back in the mid-1600s, Sir John Colleton, an English gentleman, was granted this small island in Roanoke Sound. Original inhabitants of this island lived a hard existence farming and raising livestock. In more recent years, Colington was home to large numbers of families who lived on the water. Some older areas of Colington Island are still inhabited by seafaring families. There are small restaurants and seafood businesses lining the narrow curving road on Colington Island. During the month of May when soft-crabs are plentiful, a drive down this road in the wee hours of the morning or late at night will reveal people at work in the shedding troughs along the water. Newer communities are being developed in this attractive island setting, beyond the small bridges spanning creeks and waterways, where the evening sun quietly melts into Roanoke Sound. Take time to drive out Colington Road and experience something of a bygone era.

Attractions

WRIGHT BROTHERS MEMORIAL
Rt. 158, MP 8　　　　　441-7430

The monument to Orville and Wilbur Wright sits majestically on a high grassy dune to the west of Route 158. This high dune was the site of the first flight in December 1903. The granite monument was established in 1932, and when seen during evening hours, presents an imposing silhouette against a fading sunset or a softly lit reminder of the creativity and innovation of two men from Ohio.

The low, domed building on the right of the main drive provides interpretive exhibits of man's first flight and of those that came later. These explanations of the Wright brothers' struggle to fly include parts of their planes, engines and notes. Reproductions of their gliders are located here. A short walk outside the exhibit center reveals the reconstructed wooden sheds of the Wrights' 1903 camp. These sheds are furnished with tools and equipment like those used by Orville and Wilbur Wright.

It's a bit of a walk from the Visitor Center to the Memorial. If you're not feeling up to it, parking is available closer to the base of the hill where the monument is located. Paved walkways make access easier, yet a number of things discourage walking: rainwater doesn't run off quickly in the low-lying areas at the base of the dune, and there are pesky little sand spurs and cactus hiding in the grass awaiting an errant bare foot! In fact, one *real* insiders' tip is to be sure you're wearing shoes — not flip flops — when you visit this attraction since those sticky beasts are everywhere.

The Exhibit Center is open for summer programs and kite flying demonstrations. The grounds are definitely open to vehicles from 9 AM until 5 PM, and hours may be extended during the summer. You can walk the grounds any time.

The cost for entry at the guard gate is $2 per person or $4 per car.

KITTY HAWK AERO TOURS
Wright Memorial　　　　441-4460

To experience the thrill of flying over the Outer Banks, take a 30-minute tour from the flight booth a short distance from the parking lot at the west side of the Memorial. A flight from here takes you out over the water, beyond the pines and roof tops to a new adventure. Believe us, it's a thrill! Pilots know the history of the area and the location of sunken ships in the ocean. The views are breathtaking and evoke a sense of wonder about who we are and how we live. Rates are: $19 per person for a parties of three, five and six, $24 per person for a party of two and $22 per person for parties of four.

WRIGHT BROTHERS NATIONAL MEMORIAL

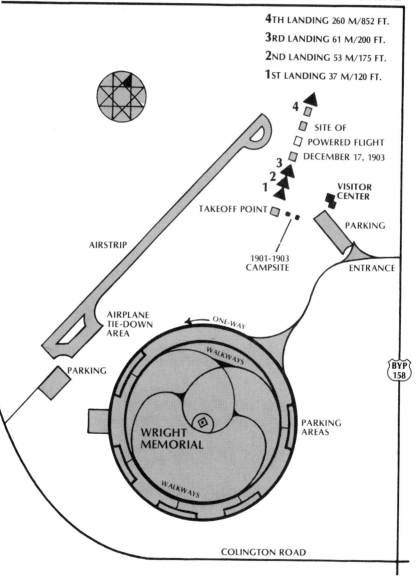

4TH LANDING 260 M/852 FT.

3RD LANDING 61 M/200 FT.

2ND LANDING 53 M/175 FT.

1ST LANDING 37 M/120 FT.

4

SITE OF

POWERED FLIGHT

DECEMBER 17, 1903

3

2

1

VISITOR
CENTER

TAKEOFF POINT

PARKING

AIRSTRIP

1901-1903
CAMPSITE

ENTRANCE

AIRPLANE
TIE-DOWN
AREA

ONE-WAY

WALKWAYS

PARKING

BYP
158

WRIGHT
MEMORIAL

PARKING
AREAS

WALKWAYS

COLINGTON ROAD

Biplane flights are also available on a 1941 Waco. These are 15-minute flights where you head south to Jockey's Ridge State Park and back again to the Wright Brothers Monument. Starting around Easter the booth is open daily and flights are scheduled every day except when weather conditions aren't favorable. Call ahead for reservations.

COLINGTON ISLAND
Colington Rd., MP 8 1/2
West of Rt. 158

A winding road takes you away from today's world to the world of those who earn their livelihood in the commercial fishing industry. There are campgrounds, seafood packers, bait and tackle stores, small cafes and restaurants and the almost-world-famous Billy's Seafood, which doubles as the island's general store. While you're driving, look beyond the mobile homes and small bungalows to the magnificent marshlands and maritime forests. Huge live oaks draped in Spanish moss, flowering dogwoods and a multitude of ferns, holly and pine grow here. Bring your camera, and if you plan to go crabbing or be near the marshgrass along the road or waterways, don't forget the insect repellant!

OUTER BANKS CHAMBER OF
COMMERCE WELCOME CENTER
Colington Rd. and Mustian St.
MP 8   *441-8144*

A new building houses the Chamber's Welcome Center in Kill Devil Hills. This center has tons of information for the visitor or resident. It's a nice place to stop if you missed the Aycock Brown Welcome

Center in Kitty Hawk. It is a clearinghouse for written and telephone inquiries, and the friendly staff can assist in relaying information about activities, accommodations and the like. Its mailing address is: P.O. Box 1757, Kill Devil Hills, NC 27948. The center is open year round from 9 AM to 5 PM, Monday through Friday.

DARE COUNTY LIBRARY
KILL DEVIL HILLS BRANCH
Mustian St. and St. Clair St.   *441-4331*
West of Rt. 158, MP 8

The new library offers books, tapes and videos and a meeting room for small groups. If you have books you'd like to donate, they're much appreciated. Children's programs are provided on Thursdays and Fridays at all branch locations. Their hours are Monday through Friday, 9:30 AM to 6:30 PM, Saturday, 10 AM to 4 PM and closed Sundays.

NAGS HEAD WOODS
ECOLOGICAL PRESERVE
Ocean Acres Dr.   *441-2525*
West of Rt. 158

Nags Head Woods Ecological Preserve is a very special place. If you've had a little too much sun, or if you'd just like to spend time observing a part of the unique environment of the Outer Banks, you'll find it here. The Nature Conservancy, a privately-funded organization dedicated to preserving a barrier island ecosystem, oversees the land making up this Outer Banks maritime forest. It is private property, not a park, but it is open to visitors Tuesday through Saturday, 10 AM until 3 PM during the summer (1994) and Monday through Friday, 10 AM un-

til 3 PM during the winter months.
During the spring, it's open Tuesday through Thursday. Two loop trails begin at the center and wind through forest, dune, swamp and pond habitats. Organized groups may arrange for further use of the center by calling the staff.

No camping, loitering, bicycling, firearms, alcoholic beverages, picnicking, or pets are allowed. The maritime forest itself is well-hidden on the west side of the Outer Banks, and many wonders of nature are hidden within this environment. Canoe trips are available during the summer. There is a small exhibit center, and new exhibits will be in place by June of this year. A staff member or volunteer can provide information on how to join the Friends of Nags Head Woods. Write: 701 W. Ocean Acres Drive, Kill Devil Hills, NC 27948. All donations are welcome, and memberships start at $25. Monies support the preserve's environmental education and research programs.

Recreation

AVALON FISHING PIER
Beach Rd., MP 6   441-7494

Avalon Pier was built in 1960 and is 705 feet long. The pier was refurbished in 1990-'91, has lights for night fishing, a snack bar, bait and tackle shop, ice, video games and rental fishing gear. A popular place in season, the pier is open 24 hours a day. The pier house is open from 5 AM until 2 AM. The pier is closed December through February. Admission prices are: $5 for adults and $2.75 for children under 12. A weekly pass costs $28. A weekend pass is $13, while a season pass is $100. Handicapped persons are admitted without charge.

OUTER BANKS
NAUTILUS ATHLETIC CLUB
Beach Rd., MP 7   441-7001

This athletic center is located on the lower level of Sea Ranch II and has a full line of Nautilus and Para-

Seniors enjoy themselves at the Baum Center in Kill Devil Hills.

Photo: Baum Center

mount exercise equipment. They also offer a full free weight center and aerobic equipment including exercise bikes, Life Fitness and Life Steps. Nancy and Stu Golliday are in charge and want to assist you in developing a program suited to your needs. Whirlpool, sauna and locker rooms are available, and juices, supplements and T-shirts can be purchased. It's open year round, Monday through Friday 7:30 AM to 9 PM and Saturday, 10 AM to 7 PM. It's closed on Sunday. Daily, weekly, monthly and annual memberships are available.

GRASS COURSE OF KILL DEVIL HILLS
Rt. 158, MP 5½   *441-7626*

Miniature golf is a popular pastime for visitors. There's a new grass course near the Kill Devil Hills/Kitty Hawk town line. It's the second such course for developer Rick Willis. His popular Grass Course in Corolla Light Resort Village prompted this one. It is a 36 hole, par 72 course on

each side. The average length for holes is 110 feet on these 328 Bermuda greens. In season hours are 9 AM until 1 AM, but the last tee time is midnight to allow time for you to finish 18 holes. The cost for one, 18-hole game is $7 for adults and $5 for children under 10. A discount is available for the second 18 holes played in succession. A snack bar and pro shop are located on the premises.

FRONTIER GOLF
Rt. 158, MP 7   *441-3281*

This place is a favorite of visitors and locals alike. The entire family can enjoy frontier miniature golf, batting cages and video games. You can cool off at the ice cream shop after you've finished. The cost for 18 holes of miniature golf is $4 per person, and the batting cage will challenge you for $2 per 21 balls. Their hours during the season are 10 AM to midnight, Monday through

Saturday and 1 PM to midnight on Sundays.

DIAMOND SHOALS FAMILY ENTERTAINMENT PARK
Rt. 158, MP 8½   480-3553

Diamond Shoals provides fun for the entire family. Activities include two, 18-hole miniature golf courses on real grass, three, state-of-the-art waterslides and a batting stadium. Diamond Shoals also offers a snack bar complete with hamburgers, hot dogs, French fries, beverages and picnic tables. This fun destination will be open seven days a week during the season, 9 AM until midnight.

Shopping

Shopping is something to look forward to along Route 158 and the Beach Road in Kill Devil Hills — there's a little bit of everything along this stretch of the beach. So, when you've had enough sun, or you're just in the mood for leisurely browsing or shopping, begin at the north end of Kill Devil Hills at **Seagate North Shopping Center**, MP 6 on Route 158. You'll find a good variety of shops here. **T.J.'s Hobbies and Sports Cards**, 441-3667, has hobby and craft materials, model cars, airplanes and boats, Radio Control supplies for models, railroading supplies, and collectibles including cards, Fenton glass and Hudson pewter. They have metal detectors too. **Sea Birds**, 441-5223, stocks religious cards and gift items. **Mom's Sweet Shop and Beach Emporium**, 441-2829, reminds you of an old-fashioned ice cream parlor, and they have everything for your sweet tooth including 24 delicious flavors of ice cream and yogurt; they even make their own fudge. While you're enjoying that cool treat, you can browse around Mom's Beach Emporium for a special souvenir for the folks back home. It's open year round.

Charlotte's Web Exotic Pets and Supplies, 480-1799, is a pet shop, of course. **Movies, Movies**, 441-2377, rents videos and provides all of the services you would expect from a video store. You'll find a large selection of shirts and prints at **T-shirt Whirl**, 441-1414, and all kinds of themes are available. **The Wooden Feather**, 480-3066, presents a gallery of award-winning, hand-carved decoys and shore birds. More than 60 carvers are exhibited here, including Dr. Couch, one of the owners. I guess you could say he has a passion for decoys and decoy carving. The driftwood sculptures are interesting, and they also have a good collection of original watercolor paintings of waterfowl. Owner and goldsmith, Martin Tyson, does custom casting at his shop, **Pearl Factory**, 441-7722. All of the gold work is done on the premises, and nautical marine themes are emphasized. Beach charms such as lighthouses, pelicans, sea gulls, seashells and more are very popular. Martin also provides a jewelry repair service, but you won't find stone cutting here. Most items are moderately priced, and you will find specialty pieces too.

Hatteras Swimwear, 480-1580, has custom-made swimsuits for our custom-made bodies. After you've been on the beach all day or played 18 holes of golf, check out **East Coast Softspa**, 480-0220, for a downright relaxing and hydrotherapeutic way to end the day. Softubs and portable hot tubs are sold and rented here. They set up easily, indoors or out, and three sizes are available. Country gifts, crafts and wood working can be found at, **I Love Country**, 441-1675. Shirl Caleo, owner of **Shirl's Gift Shop**, 441-6776, designs her own silk flower arrangements on driftwood and in baskets. **Lenscape Photos**, 441-2280, is a full service photography shop. **Nostalgia Gallery**, 441-1881, specializes in antiques while **Rock N' Roll Rarities** offers imports, CDs and LPs. **The Shoe Dock** is just opening at Seagate North with shoes for the entire family.

Vitamin Sea Surf Shop, 441-7512, is located south of the Seagate Shops on Route 158. This shop is more of a stylish boutique for men's and women's fashion beachwear and casual wear than it is a serious surf shop. But serious and not-so-serious-surfers have been coming here for years for Vitamin Sea surfboards and all of their surfing supplies including wetsuits, leashes—you name it. You'll also find a good assortment of quality boogie boards and skim boards. This shop offers an extensive line of sunglasses and unique women's clothing that can't be found anywhere else on the beach, including Betsey Johnson dresses. Because it's a small shop, customer service is a priority for owner Lisa Noonan.

Here's the place for shoppers and "would be shoppers": **Second Hand Rose Thrift Shop**, 441-0352, located at the 5½ MP, Route 158.

This is a thrift, antique and consignment store of mostly old—but some new — items. There's something for everyone including a nice selection of jewelry, decorative items with stories behind them and clothing for the entire family. Prices range from 10 cents to $1,200. It's open 10:30 AM until 5 PM Monday through Saturday. Located right across the street is the **Donut Factorie**, 441-6219, a family-owned and operated donut shop that originally opened at that same location in 1972. They're open Memorial Day through September, seven days a week, 7 AM until 12 PM.

The Dare Center shopping center in Kill Devil Hills is located on the west side of Route 158 at MP 7. **Belk** department store, 480-2355 and **Food Lion** are the anchor tenants. For good eats, try **Little Caesars Pizza**, 480-1354, **NY Bagels**, 480-0990, **Subway**, 441-2824, **Morgan's** yogurt and sandwich shop and **Petrozza's Deli**. Petrozza's, 441-1642, features fresh Italian breads, great lunch or dinner entrees, daily specials, super sandwiches, outstanding homemade desserts, Boar's Head deli selections and, of course, freshly made pastas and sauces. Petrozza's caters, and they are open most of the year. The food here is great, but you may want to call ahead for daily specials and place your order over the phone because they get very busy. Lunch specials may take extra time to prepare.

Team Kitty Hawk Sports, 480-3444, specializes in (what else?) team sporting goods and active wear including Champion, Nike, Starter and Russell. They can also help your team

or group with silk screening for uniforms and what not. Are you looking to leave the Outer Banks? We wouldn't know why, but **The Travel Agency**, 441-1501, can help you with your travel arrangements. **Clothing Liquidators** has gobs of clothes from everywhere at very reasonable prices, and **Shoe Liquidators** has gobs of shoes at very reasonable prices. If it has been a while since you played a game of darts or shot a game of pool, try **Paradise Billiards**, 441-9225.

Shops located at the **Sea Ranch** on the Beach Road at MP 7 include a full-service hair salon, **Shear Genius**, 441-3571. This salon, under the ownership of Linda Porter, has an excellent reputation. Color and

highlighting are their specialty, but of course they offer perms and super hair cuts too. The salon carries natural shampoos and other products, and they also offer full body massages. **Alice's Looking Glass**, 441-7126, is a fine apparel shop for women.

North Carolina Books, 441-2141, is located at MP 7½, in the Times Printing building on Route 158. Thousands of secondhand paperback books are stocked here along with some reduced hardcover books. You can bring in your old paperbacks and apply them as credit toward the purchase of other secondhand books from the store. They have also added new books and tapes

Photo: Mary Ellen Riddle

Yes, it is possible to fish and take care of your child simultaneously!

to their stock this year.

If you have a hankering for pizza cooked in a stone oven, you need to try **Stone Oven Pizza**, 441-3339. This new pizza takeout is located on the west side of Route 158 on Colington Road next to Metro Rentals. They offer scratch recipes for all of their pizzas including gourmet and specialty ones. You can choose from spinach pizza, BLT pizza, Philly steak pizza, Taco pizza, Hawaiian pizza and more. Subs and pizza-by-the-slice are also available. They're open 11 AM until 11 PM. Look for their second location at Soundings Factory Stores in Nags Head on Route 158.

Carolina Connections, 441-4023, is located behind the Kill Devil Hills post office on the west side of Route 158. This multifaceted business offers business support services that are available to visitors as well. They can help you with all of your packaging and shipping needs, and they offer incoming and outgoing fax services too. They will even print files from your floppies on a laser printer if you have information the folks back at the office are expecting. If you visit the Outer Banks during the holidays and you're interested in exquisite gift wrapping for your purchases, well they do that too — anytime. The Carolina Connections Catalogue is a full-color, 30-page compilation of gifts and other craft items sold on the Outer Banks; call (800) 553-5424 for a free catalogue, or stop by their shop where these items are sold. And, if you're in need of creative design services, they do that too with a full-time artist on staff.

KIEKO, 441-6626, is located just past the Kill Devil Hills' post office. You won't miss the Bermuda green color of this shop. Kieko's features island wear, recycled clothing and fine sterling silver jewelry. Indian and Guatemalan apparel is also on hand for both men and women. There's also a good selection of accessories including sunglasses, hats, belts, bags and scarves.

The Seafood Store, 441-2348, is located on the west side of Route 158 just past the KDH post office. They carry a complete line of fresh seafood and cooked and microwaveable items. During the season, you can also purchase locally-grown produce and basic grocery items.

The Bird Store, 480-2951, is located in a free standing building on Route 158 and carries a complete line of decoys. **17th Street Surf Shop**, 441-1797, is a Virginia-based shop carrying everything you'd expect a surf shop to have.

Sea Holly Hooked Rugs, 441-8961, is open year round, and we hope you find them at their new location this year, in the Shore Realty building, across from the Towel Outlet on Route 158. Traditional rug hooking is featured here, not latch hooking. Finished pieces include small rugs, chair pads, coasters, seat cushions and more. All-wool fabrics are used. Rug hooking kits are designed and put together by owner Jean Edmonds. This craft is true American Folk Art, and summer workshops are offered on Wednesday afternoons beginning in June from 1 PM to 4 PM.

Much more than just a pet shop,

the **Pet Gallery**, 441-1852, is located at MP 9 on the west side of Route 158. They carry a complete supply of birds, reptiles, salt and fresh water fish and small animals as well as everything you need to care for your pet. We found the reptile exhibits fascinating, especially "Worm," a 33 foot-long python. You can also see iguanas, alligators, lizards, crocodiles, turtles and African clawed frogs. Children will really enjoy these displays. Aquariums house a large supply of pet fish, and there are plenty of animal theme gifts and bird feeders to go around.

Jim's Camera House, 441-6528, is right down the street, and it is a popular place. Jim and Hattie Lee have a full-service photography store. If you have a question, have film to be developed or need to purchase film or camera equipment, you can do it all here. Jim likes to talk about lighting and subjects; he has interesting stories to tell about his adventures all over the world on the sight-side of a camera. Family vacation portraits, weddings, passport photos, you name it — call Jim Lee for experienced photography and advice.

If you like salt water taffy, try **Forbes**, 441-2122. **Pigman's Barbecue**, 441-6803, is right next door. **The Laughing Mermaid Gift Shop**, 441-3722, is on the west side of Route 158, and they specialize in fire, police and Emergency Medical Service novelty gift items. For quality, traditional hammocks, a trip to **Nags Head Hammocks**, 441-6115, is a must. Rocking chairs, rope foot stools, two-seated porch swings and single hanging swings are featured. All of the featured items have rope seats. These are very durable products, and they can also be purchased through mail order year round by calling (800) 344-6433. You can't miss this shop on Route 158; their landscaping has a tropical look with palm trees and hammocks. Look for their new location in Corolla at the Tim Buck II Shopping Village. **Viking Furniture**, 441-6444, is family owned and operated, and they specialize in rattan, wicker and casual furniture. They also have bedding, lamps, pictures and accessories. The furnishings in this shop are geared more toward resort properties and rentals.

Ocean Threads third location on the Outer Banks is at MP 8½ on the Beach Road just north of the Outer Banks Beach Club. **Ocean Threads**, 480-0888, specializes in swimwear for the entire family including maternity, masectomy and long torso suits. You will also find quality sportswear for men and women and a great selection of Outer Banks T-shirts in all sizes.

Photo: Baum Center

The Thomas A. Baum Center is a vibrant place for senior adult activities.

A good general store for a day at the beach, **The Trading Post**, 441-8205, is located at the 8½ MP on the Beach Road. T-shirts, souvenirs, swimwear and convenience grocery items can be purchased here. The Trading Post is also a branch post office.

The Bike Barn, 441-3786, is located behind Taco Bell on Wrightsville Avenue at the 9½ MP. They offer sales, repairs and carry a full line of parts and accessories. Serious bikers will appreciate specialized equipment including Caloi, Jamis, Giant, Trek and more. Quality mechanics are on duty. The shop is open seven days a week in season and weekends during the winter.

The Beach Barn Shops are located at MP 10 in the building that looks like a red barn on the west side of Route 158. These shops are a nice change of pace. **Carolina Moon**, 441-4000, is a favorite place for finding unusual gifts, pottery, cards and tapes. They also have an outstanding line of jewelry — all kinds of jewelry — but mostly pieces you've never seen before. The shop has a New Age ambiance and offers a fine collection of esoteric gifts. **Birthday Suits**, 441-5338, is a boutique of relaxed California and New York fashions for men and women. Owners Gregg and Jill Bennett are pretty hip. They keep up with the times, and their shops reflect their desire to provide an extensive array of tasteful swimwear and casualwear. A full line of accessories is also available including sunglasses, jewelry, belts, hats and lots more. Carolina Moon and Birthday Suits can also be found in Duck Village.

Roanoke Press and Croatan Bookery, 480-1890, is also located at the 9½ MP on Route 158, and it's owned by the same folks who own the *Coastland Times* newspaper and **North Carolina Books**. Secondhand books can be found here, not new books. Both book stores carry an extensive line of books about North Carolina and the Outer Banks.

Seashore Shops are located at

the 9½ MP on the Beach Road. A longtime tenant, **Sea Isle Gifts and Lamp Shop**, 441-7206, carries lamps, repair kits, shells galore, jewelry and an assortment of small gifts. **Ivey's Beachwear**, 441-4272, specializes in swimwear and casualwear for the entire family. Rafts, toys, boogie boards, T-shirts and other beach supplies can also be found here. A picture frame shop and gallery, **Frames at Large**, 441-5120, is open year round. Ready-made frames are available, and you'll find a large number of framing accessories to choose from for your custom framing needs. They provide custom framing services. The gallery displays prints, watercolors, etchings and posters of seascapes. Civil War engravings are featured items as well. **Dip-N-Deli**, 441-4412, is also open year round. Let them tempt you with Breyer's hand-dipped cones, ice cream sundaes and homemade soups, salads and sandwiches, eat-in or takeout. Fresh tuna salad will be featured as well as other daily lunch specials. We highly recommend the sandwiches and luncheon specials at this deli; they are mouthwatering.

Located at the 9½ MP just a bit south of Seashore Shops is **Sea Holly Square** shopping center offering a wide variety of places to shop. **Beach Boys and Girls**, 441-7176, specializes in quality men's and women's swimwear and sportswear. **Tar Heel Trading Company**, 441-5278, is filled with quality American crafts, many of which are Carolina crafted. If you're looking for a special col-

lection of serving pieces, accessories, and the like, Mary Ames' shop will have it. **Beach Bikes and Blades**, 441-1212, offers rentals, sales and service of bikes and inline skates. **NRG Surf Shop**, 480-1006, is new this year. **Rhetty Made, The Country Store**, 480-2207, is a family-owned and operated craft shop. There is really only one way to describe what we saw here, "countryesque." We adored the handmade, life size dolls, "Granny" and "Gramps." Loretta, or "Rhetty" as she is affectionately known, paints the woodworking that the members of her family do so well. We really enjoyed this country store and Rhetty will be adding a country candy counter this year.

Other shops you'll find at this shopping center include **Pottery by Sunny Fletcher**; **The Fudgery, Sea Images**, 441-4779, offering shell lamps and nautical gifts; **Michael's Gems and Glass Gift Shop**, 441-1011; **Wright Kite Company**, 480-2855; **Card King**, 480-2393, featuring sports collectibles; **Creative T's**, 441-5944; **The Rain Forest**, 441-5547; **Hair Design Studio**, 441-1790, which is open year round; and **Blue and Grey**, 441-5311, specializing in Civil War memorabilia.

Argyle Bake Shop, 441-7710, is located just south of Sea Holly Square on the Beach Road. Fresh-baked breads, cakes, cookies, pastries, scones and new this year — ice cream cakes — are only some of the tempting treats found here. Special orders are welcome.

Inside
Nags Head

Nags Head is the destination for many who come to the Outer Banks. And, while the modern-day town is the focus for most visitors, the historical background of the area holds interest for many. Legends concerning how the town got its name, pirates and local lore are plentiful.

One legend explains how in early times the inhabitants tied lanterns around horses' (nags) necks and led the animals up and down the beach signalling merchant ships at sea so that perhaps they would think these lights meant other ships were safely in the harbor. The legend continues that when these ships ran aground, the natives salvaged the cargo to supplement their own needs.

Other strange goings-on are recorded from the early 1800s. There were tales of ships missing at sea and of a 29-year-old woman named Theodosia Burr Alison, the daughter of adventurer, duelist and former vice-president Aaron Burr, who was lost at sea when her New York-bound ship, the *Patriot*, disappeared in late 1812. Later on, a portrait bearing a startling resemblance to Theodosia was discovered in a cottage in Nags Head by its owner, who said that it had been taken from aboard a deserted schooner around 1813. Other stories capture the confessions of former pirates during their final hours; their tales are of murdering all hands on ocean-going vessels and seizing the goods for their own use or for trading.

Nevertheless, Nags Head was becoming a summer resort even during the mid-1850s. Only the wealthy could manage the trip here aboard ships crossing the waters separating the Outer Banks from the mainland to the west and north. Summer cottages began to appear, and the first hotel was built in 1838. A grand structure, the Nags Head Hotel attracted many who wanted to enjoy a vacation here. Fishing, sea-bathing, dancing, bowling and gambling in the hotel's casino kept the visitors busy while the natives remained in the soundside village in Nags Head Woods. In 1851, the hotel was enlarged, and a half mile of mule-drawn railway was laid to make the journey to the ocean less troublesome. During the Civil War the Nags Head Hotel was burned by retreating Confederates, but it was rebuilt in the early 1870s.

During this time, Nags Head was not only vulnerable to pirate ships and war, but the rugged coastline also became a burial ground for ships and crews during massive storms.

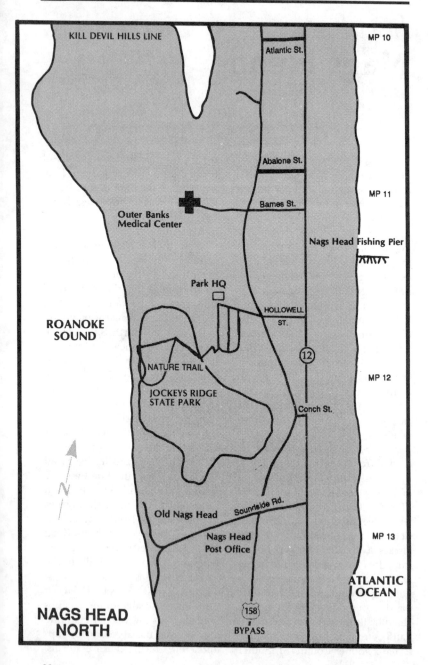

KILL DEVIL HILLS LINE

MP 10

Atlantic St.

Abalone St.

Barnes St.

MP 11

Outer Banks
Medical Center

Nags Head Fishing Pier

Park HQ

ROANOKE
SOUND

HOLLOWELL
ST.

(12)

NATURE TRAIL

MP 12

JOCKEYS RIDGE
STATE PARK

Conch St.

N

Old Nags Head

Sounriside Rd.

MP 13

Nags Head
Post Office

ATLANTIC
OCEAN

NAGS HEAD
NORTH

158
BYPASS

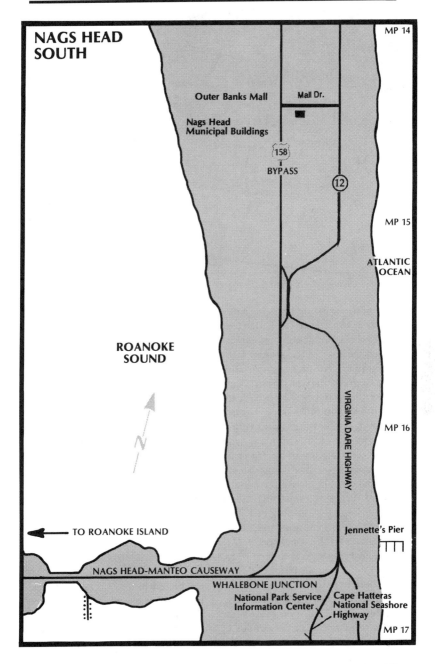

Photo: Dare County Tourist Bureau

Hang gliders often fly from Jockey's Ridge during good weather.

One of the worst disasters in Outer Banks history happened here in 1877, when the 541-ton barkentine-rigged steamer, USS *Huron*, went aground in a November storm. Due to Congressional cutbacks, Nags Head Lifesaving Station No. 7, located only two miles away, was unmanned at the time. Local fishermen helped those who made it to shore. The remains of the *Huron* lie on the bottom of the Atlantic Ocean, straight out between mile-markers 11 and 12, almost even with the end of the Nags Head Fishing Pier. Diving enthusiasts continue to explore artifacts from the wreckage.

Nags Head-style architecture refers to the simple cottage design first built here by a Dr. Pool of Elizabeth City in the early 1880s. The cottage was set on pilings to allow the stormy ocean to flow under it. Most of the timber used to build his

and other cottages came from wood washed ashore after shipwrecks. The homes included two or three rooms with lots of windows, all of which were closed in during winter months by heavy wooden shutters. Large porches adorned the homes, which were left unpainted.

In the period after World War I, local builder S.J. Twine modified the design into what today is recognized as a classic architectural form. Many older cottages have been renovated; other much larger homes were built of a similar style and are some of today's most popularly-designed beach homes.

In the early '30s, the Outer Banks' peaceful atmosphere began to attract many more visitors. It became the summer place for the wealthy of the Albemarle region of the state (the mainland area across the waters of Albemarle Sound and inclusive of towns such as Elizabeth City and Edenton). Leroy's Seaside Inn was built on the oceanfront, slightly north of Jockey's Ridge to accommodate these guests. Today, that old hotel, moved off the oceanfront and completely refurbished as a bed and breakfast known as the First Colony Inn, is a romantic spot where the sweeping roof and wide porches charm visitors. (Further description of First Colony Inn is noted in the chapter on Accommodations.)

Newman's Shell Shop, noted in the Attractions chapter, was the first store on the beach. Sam & Omie's, noted in the Restaurants chapter, located at Whalebone Junction, was opened around the same time. Both are more than 50 years old.

Nags Head became an incorporated town in 1961, and by this time it was also a well-known fishing and vacation destination for people from North Carolina and beyond. Whether folks came to stay at places in Nags Head or Kitty Hawk, the phrase, "we're going to Nags Head" often referred to any of the towns or villages on the Outer Banks — and still does. Hotels, motels, fishing piers, restaurants, kite-flying, hang gliding, surfing, windsurfing, dancing, artistry and many other forms of water sports and recreation became and remain popular here.

Businesses opened, small communities were built, and folks who were once just loyal visitors began to come here to live year round. Native families were generally engaged in fishing as a livelihood, later opening restaurants and other seafood businesses. As commercial development continued, the Outer Banks were connected to the mainland by bridges across Roanoke and Currituck Sounds, providing easier access and thus making necessary the development and construction that have transformed the area into the popular destination it is today. The Village at Nags Head, with its magnificent soundfront golf course, is one of the most recently developed resort communities on the beach. The golf course opened in 1988, and since then hundreds of homes have been built. Most of the homes, as you will see, are variations of the Nags Head style, mentioned earlier. The newest homes in this subdivision are those on the oceanfront.

The primary reason the Outer Banks has retained its low-rise development is that most folks want to keep it as close to the way it was as possible. There are no high-rise buildings here on the oceanfront to block out the sun or restrict the view. Growth is managed to allow resorts to be developed, yet the fragile ecology of the barrier islands and the threat of hurricanes and nor'easters help keep a sense of natural order about development here.

Attractions

JOCKEY'S RIDGE STATE PARK
Rt. 158, MP 12   441-7132

Jockey's Ridge has been a tourist attraction since 1851 and was established as a state park in 1965. There is a legend that "... the lady who may accompany you to its summit, if not already a wife, will shortly become yours." Whether or not the legend is believable shrinks in importance when you're standing at the top of the ridge. When you're at the top (or at the bottom!) questions about how this 410-acre hill was formed or about its unique ecosystem of shifting sand ridges, dense shrub thickets, temporary pools and soundside habitats boggle the mind.

It is a mile long, up to 4,000 feet wide and rises to 140 feet above sea level. The ridge forms the tallest "medano" (the geological word for a large isolated hill of sand, also called a "transverse dune") on the East Coast. Once thought to be caused by the early colonists destroying the natural cover of the banks with logging and stock grazing, it now seems certain that these huge bare sand hills have been here for thousands of years. Actually, there are two great dunes, one lower on the east and a higher one beyond.

From the top of the ridge, you can see both ocean and sound. The homes along the beach look like tiny huts. Kite-flying and hang-gliding enthusiasts hike to the top of the dunes to catch the breezes that flow constantly, shifting the sands in all directions. The desert-like appearance of the sand dunes reveals strange but artistic patterns of those winds and of the footprints made by people who climb the hills. The climb is a test of stamina on hot

sunny days, but the view is definitely worth it. It's more manageable after a stabilizing rainfall.

Park headquarters is located near the northern end of a parking lot to the west of the main highway. You'll notice an entrance sign at MP 12, Carolista Drive in Nags Head. Maps are available from the park ranger that will indicate walking areas. There are natural history programs and sheltered picnic areas for a leisurely lunch. Call 441-7132 for program schedules. A self-guided 1½ mile nature trail was dedicated in 1989. It starts from the southwest corner of the parking lot and proceeds towards Roanoke Sound. The trail is marked by plant identification — persimmon, bayberry, Virginia creeper, wild grapes and black cherry. Animal tracks are identified as well, among them fox, raccoon, white-tailed deer, racerunner lizard, antlions, opossums and hognosed snakes. It takes about 1½ hours to walk at a leisurely pace. Wear shoes, as there are sand spurs. There's a special 360-foot boardwalk if your mobility is impaired.

For the visually handicapped, there are audio guides at the park office. Pick up a brochure at the visitor center that will explain and illustrate the trails.

A traffic light was installed by the Department of Transportation at the

crosswalk on the highway, farther south in front of Kitty Hawk Connection. The colorful flags and kites of Kitty Hawk Connection attract visitors. You can enter the park from Kitty Hawk Connection or park your car at the state park.

NEWMAN'S SHELL SHOP
Beach Rd., MP 13½   441-5791

Newman's Shell Shop is an Outer Banks attraction as well as a shopping destination. The bright pink establishment qualifies as an Outer Banks museum. This was the first store on the beach, and it opened in 1939. It has remained a family-owned business through the years and carries shells from all over the world. Owner Susie Stoutenberg displays a labeled shell collection with shells from places such as India and Peru — those faraway beaches that most of us can only imagine. A large variety of gifts and accessories spill from attractive displays. Sea shells are hanging all over the place in an assortment of mobiles and wind chimes. Newman's is an important stop on the tour, not just a place to browse or make a purchase. Woodcrafted birds and fish hang from the ceiling; accessories include napkins, cards, placemats, mugs, crystals and Christmas ornaments. Millions of shells are for sale. An enormous variety of shell jewelry, jewelry made from stones and various metals will surely amaze you.

There's even a collection of antique guns, pistols and swords on display which have been in the family for many years. The building is at least 55 years old, and we can only imagine the stories that have been

traded here as well as the millions of people who have visited and made a purchase. Susie notes that many of their shell crafts are made on site, and visitors can watch the creations as they're made. Fresh flower arrangements are also available here in the summer. And, of course, hermit crabs are a most popular item with the younger set. There's even a Hermit Crab Race, held on the last Saturday in July.

OLD NAGS HEAD
Rt. 158, MP 12

Most of the villages on the Outer Banks began as small soundside communities. Just south of Jockey's Ridge you'll notice a narrow road leading toward the sound. Here are some of the original, old-style Outer Banks homes. Some properties have been lost due to the shifting sands of Jockey's Ridge. It is an interesting section of the Outer Banks.

On the oceanfront, older houses reflect their age in the dark brown color of shake-siding and wooden shutters propped open with poles during the summer and closed during the winter. Some were built low, tucked behind the dunes for protection, but now sit vulnerable and open to storms that cause erosion of the dunes. Nevertheless, these older homes have a lot of character and attest to the harshness of the elements over time.

OUTER BANKS MEDICAL CENTER
W. Barnes, west of Rt. 158
MP 11   441-7111

Not necessarily an attraction but worth mentioning here, the Outer Banks Medical Center is a family

NAGS HEAD GOLF LINKS

A CAROLINAS GOLF GROUP FACILITY

- **Open to the public.**
- Corporate & private golf tournaments/outings with reduced rates.
- True Scottish Links style course.
- 18 holes / par 71, 4 soundside holes.
- Longest 6126 yards you'll ever play!
- Wind blown fairways.
- Best bent grass greens on the East Coast.
- Beautiful clubhouse.
- Driving range.
- Rental clubs.
- Weekly shootouts.
- Golf clinics and private lessons.
- All golf clubs sold at wholesale plus 10%.
- MasterCard, VISA accepted.

> "At Nags Head Golf Links the holes along the sound are among the most beautiful in the Eastern United States."
> *Jim Moriarty*
> Golf Digest, 4/91

LINKS GRILLE ROOM
on the Roanoke Sound
(919) 441-8076
Delicious lunch and appetizer menu, fabulous sunsets.

BEACH CLUB & CAFE
(919) 480-2222
Tennis courts, swimming pool, private parties, corporate outings, wedding receptions

---

Call **1-800-851-9404** for Starting Times, Golf Packages & Golf Information.

or (919) 441-8073 locally

Nags Head Golf Links

Hwy. 158 Bypass • Milepost 15 • The Village at Nags Head

and emergency medical center. It is a nonprofit branch of Chesapeake General Hospital of Virginia. Appointments can be made between 9 AM and 5 PM, seven days a week, year round. Emergency care is available 24 hours a day, and Dare County Emergency Services has a helicopter pad for transportation to nearby hospitals. Laboratory services and X-ray facilities are available as well. Hospital signs are noted on Route 158.

GALLERY ROW
Driftwood St., MP 10 ½

The Outer Banks is home to many artists and the galleries located on this street and along Gallery Row were established some years ago. We've included a complete list of the art galleries at the end of the Arts section of this book for easy reference, but some of the galleries bear mentioning here.

Glenn Eure's Ghost Fleet Gallery, 441-6584, is open all year and is one of the most popular galleries displaying local art. Each year in February, the Frank Stick Memorial Art Show is held here. It is a juried exhibit and a popular cultural addition to life on the Outer Banks. The literary artists also hold readings of original work as a part of the Frank Stick show, and poetry readings held in the gallery are quite popular during the off season.

Glenn is at home here with his own artistic creations. You might find him sketching or carving an ice sculpture in the parking lot. He's an interesting person. He's had many adventures in his life; plus he's an artist. **The Ghost Fleet Gallery** comes

alive in its own structure of planks and boards. Glenn and Pat, his wife, who works magic with framing and matting artwork and photography, support the art community with numerous exhibits in the main gallery, and they are often there to provide interesting commentary. Stop by and meet them. Off-season hours are posted, but in season hours are 10 AM until 5:30 PM, Tuesday through Saturday and noon until 4 PM on Sundays.

Across the street, **Jewelry by Gail**, 441-5387, is an interesting place. Gail Kowalski is a designer-goldsmith who has won national recognition for her creations in precious metals and stones.

An unusual amethyst crystal chandelier created by Pennsylvania artist Michael Fornadley is hung in the shop and is definitely worth a look. Most of the jewelry created here falls into the "wearable art" category.

Gail's newest addition, **Selections by Gail**, 441-1547, is a department of very high quality but moderately priced handmade jewelry from all over the world. Gail personally selects each piece exhibited here. The two departments complement each other nicely.

Open year round at the south end of Gallery Row is the **Morales Art Galleries**, 441-6484. In the main gallery, which was established in 1978, you'll find original artwork in many different mediums with an emphasis on the work of local artists. Next door to the main gallery is the **Morales Art Gallery of Fine Art Prints**, 480-3900. This gallery specializes in collectible fine art limited edition prints with an emphasis on quality. The Fine Art Print Shop is the exclusive representative on the Outer Banks for marine artist John Barber, Amish artist Lynn Graebner, the outstanding Greenwich Workshop Collection, Hadley House Prints, Somerset Prints and the internationally renown Mill Pond Press. They also offer a very large collection of wildlife art and Duck Stamp prints. Professional custom picture framing is also available by framers who are members of the Professional Picture Framers Association. The Morales Gallery can be contacted nationally at (800) 635-6035 or at their Duck location, 261-7190.

Along Gallery Row, you'll also see **Ipso Facto Gallery**, 480-2793, where antiques, curios and objects of art from all over the world are displayed. You won't find any theme collections here. The merchandise is quite eclectic; and it's reasonably priced too. Ipso is really more of an antique shop than a gift shop. It's a great place to browse, ooh and aah and, of course, find a treasure to take home. Ipso Facto Gallery is closed on Sunday.

Down the Beach Road to MP 10½, you'll discover Anna Gartrell's **Gallery By the Sea**, 480-0578. Anna's artistry is discovered in an exceptional display of watercolors, acrylics and photography. She grew up in D.C., and the Smithsonian was her playground. Anna pursued fine arts and photography. You can expect to find a very unusual and highly original photography series, crystal lace art, Dec-art, ocean creations, landscapes and more at the gallery.

Recreation

HANG GLIDING

This sport has become increasingly popular through the years. If you want to try flying like the gulls, you can sign up for lessons. Hang gliding's roots stretch beyond the Wright brothers' flight. Lilienthal, one of the original designers of the hang glider wing, was killed while flying a glider. Francis M. Rogallo, a retired NASA engineer now living in Southern Shores, developed the flexible Rogallo Wing in order to bring down space capsules. Though the parachute finally won out for this endeavor, the light, Mylar and aluminum gliders began to appear in the hands of sport fliers about 20 years ago, and now the sport has caught on in a big way, especially here on the Outer Banks.

John Harris, president of Kitty Hawk Kites, says, "It's as close as you can get to flying as the birds do." The novice hang glider begins with basic instruction to glide from a high elevation to a lower one. Gradually you learn to make use of the same thermals and ridge-lift air currents that birds use in order to extend their powerless flights.

The Rogallo Foundation has been established in Kitty Hawk. The goal of the foundation is to support education, research and literary pursuit of the science of gliding and soaring flight. A museum of interpretive exhibits is planned in the future to assist the public in understanding the contributions gliding and low-speed aerodynamics have made to society. Rogallo, now 82,

Art By the Sea

By Nancy McWilliams

Like magnets to metal, artists are drawn to life at the seashore.

Subject matter is one reason they come, paintbrushes in hand, ready to capture the gorgeous expanse of sand, sky, water, sea oats, vacationers with their brightly colored umbrellas and nature — always nature in all her glory. They arrive in search of freedom, seeking alternative lifestyles, promising themselves a relaxed pace of life.

The Outer Banks is host to a refined art community, one that grows, bends, stretches, changes, yet one that is surprisingly sophisticated. Some excellent artists call these islands home and find here a supportive community of fellow artists, art lovers and patrons who encourage creative efforts.

They gather at the water's edge, writers, painters, poets, photographers, potters, crafters, jewelers, designers, actors, dancers and musicians. Their souls have need of the sea; the way the siren calls makes one think the ocean has need of them too.

The local artist community stretches from Corolla to Ocracoke and consists of men, women and children whose call is to create. Some seek publicity and get it; others shy away, isolating themselves from the public eye. Some make the Banks their year-round residence; others use this as a base to travel from, or as a home away from home, a place of renewal and refreshment. Some portray the Outer Banks in all their work; others never do.

At the core of this art colony are several "old timers," artists who have

Photo: Mike Booher/DCTB

The Outer Banks offer a multitude of natural wonders to captivate an artist's senses.

been here for decades and have heavily influenced the artistic climate. Glenn Eure and Rick Tupper, fine area artists for nearly 25 years and gallery owners, are included. Eure, a retired U.S. Army major, has made a double "second career," one in creating art and the other volunteering to promote the arts. His Ghost Fleet Gallery in Nags Head is unofficial art headquarters, home to the annual Frank Stick Memorial Art Show, many other special shows by guest artists, numerous poetry readings and other cultural happenings. Eure's early work was heavily influenced by local pirate legends. Today, he creates a wide range of work, from nautical to abstract. With astounding versatility, he turned to contemporary abstracts and collagraphs, even creating three-dimensional canvases that burst out of their frames. Boisterous and jolly, Eure basks in the attention he commands at the helm of his gallery.

Tupper, painter of exquisite, nationally known work, owns Greenleaf Gallery. Fish, flowers and hearts are favorite themes for Tupper. A Rhode Island School of Design graduate, Tupper has earned a solid reputation in the art world with his outstanding acrylics. Yet Tupper prefers the quiet life, attracted to the Outer Banks for the surfing, fishing and time he shares with his family here.

Painter John de la Vega, a native Argentine, visited the area 15 years before moving here. "Here I would most likely have the desire to paint above all else," he said. "Being here is like being high all the time." Primarily a portrait artist, de la Vega found himself painting more nature scenes because of life at the coast. "I want to study nature as I've never been able to do it before," he said.

Painter Denver Lindley relocated to the Duck area from Pennsylvania, bringing tremendous talent with him. Expect the unusual from Lindley, who likes to try new methods and often portrays life's more commonplace, everyday items in most uncommon ways.

Lee Knotts, who came to Manteo from Richmond, Va., said living here is "like taking a sabbatical." It was the environment that brought him; most of his seascapes and landscapes are painted on site, often traveling the back canals in his boat to get the right perspective.

Don Bryan, a well-known oil painter, retired from a military career and picked Nags Head as home in 1972 after vacationing here for many years. Coastal scenes, including fishing villages, ducks flying over the sound, boats and beach cottages, are his forté, but he also does wonderful still life scenes and cityscapes.

Former nurse Cecelia Anne Hill uses Nags Head as home base, traveling the world in search of artistic subject matter. Her acrylics capture a variety of colorful settings, from tobacco fields to hang gliders to foreign open-air markets.

James Melvin, known for his illustrations of children's books, also does outstanding portraits, landscapes, seascapes, and teaches art classes. When he decided to pursue art full time, Nags Head was the right place. "It seemed inspirational," he said. "It was a good step. It helped me grow in great depth."

Watercolorist and collage artist Pat Monahan of Kill Devil Hills moved here and built a light-filled, spacious studio where she works and teaches art classes. An Art Students' League pupil, the outspoken and witty Monahan has definitely been a positive force in the Outer Banks art world.

For watercolorist Tom Hughes of Nags Head, coming here was returning home. The Elizabeth City native loves his oceanfront cottage, located on the same beach where he spent many happy childhood days.

Variety is the key word for artist Jill Bartel, who alternately lives in Minneapolis and on the Outer Banks. Working in oil, etchings, monotypes, screenprints, charcoals, collages, plaster, Bartel presents very finished work. "It's a privilege to be in a spot like this," she said. Living near the ocean motivates Bartel, not so much to paint the sea, but for the knowledge that she's "not in charge" that comes to her from walking on the beach. "There is a strength in nature, a range of beauty and power."

Former New Yorker Ginger Carslake shifted gears from package design when she came to Kill Devil Hills. "I'd always wanted to live by the ocean," the young and energetic Carslake said. "I fell in love with this place. It feels like home." Working in oils, acrylics or photography, Carslake is inspired by the ocean, but admits it can be a distraction — when the waves are good she's tempted to surf.

Painter Pat Williams came to Nags Head in retirement after vacationing here all her life. "You get addicted to this place," she said. With oil as her favorite medium, Williams presents seascapes with lighthouses, dunes and water. Her current trend is capturing scenes, such as old-time gas stations or vegetable stands, before they disappear.

Up and coming painter Susan Vaughan of Kill Devil Hills paints with a folk-art style, putting local scenes on canvas with her detailed style. For Vaughan, every painting tells a story, particularly a recent work of downtown Manteo that captured the very essence of the waterfront town.

Kerry Oaksmith-Sanders, a silk dye artist living in Nags Head, relocated here from Los Angeles because it was an attractive place to raise children. The former television set designer is producing beautiful work using a unique method of painting stretched silk, then dying the fabric to give it a washed, soft watercolor look.

Colored pencil artist Linda Ritchie Crassons was drawn to the Outer Banks by the ocean, the quiet and the serenity. Living on Roanoke Island suits Crassons fine, where she creates detailed nature studies with a somewhat whimsical touch.

Stephen Sneed of Nags Head creates ink line drawings of trawlers and peaceful harbors. After vacationing here for 12 years, he made the move. "I liked the wide open spaces. I'll always be drawn to the place."

Avon artist Gretchen Kreitler draws striking sharks, rattlesnakes, turtles, bats and swans with pen and ink. She relocated here after studying the area on a map for years, and is quite happy with life on Hatteras Island "where the weather keeps everyone excited."

Corolla's Michael Riggs is known for pen and ink renditions of local lighthouses. "This area is made for artists," he stated. "It's quiet, and there is subject matter everywhere."

Two Roanoke Island potters, Jim Fineman and Bonnie Morrill, have made their separate distinctions on the local art scene. Fineman came to the area intending to spend one summer; that was more than 20 years ago. Morrill, who lives in Wanchese and has a pottery shop and studio in Manteo, came here following a stint with the Peace Corps. Both produce excellent utilitarian pottery.

True locals may be hard to find in this area, but they are here, and there are some fine creative spirits among them. Roanoke Island's Tony Edens' pencil work captures the past exquisitely — scenes such as "Frisco Village 1936" will stop you in your tracks.

Manteo native Hubby Bliven says his favorite art subject is Dare County. "There's so much to choose from," he said. "History, waterfowl, wildlife, sand, sun, wind — there's no end to the subjects."

Native Wanchese poet Wayne Gray said he tries to stay away from being a regional poet, but can't seem to stay away from local subjects. "I love the Outer Banks," he professed.

Mashoes resident Julia McPherson, lifelong local, weaves and creates soft sculptures, often inspired by the natural world outside her windows. "A lot of what I do I get from nature," she said

Photographers find the Outer Banks to be a treasure trove of subject matter. Walter Gresham, Ray Matthews, J. Aaron Trotman, Henry Applewhite and Michael Halminski have all made names for themselves locally in the photography field. Each has caught the essence of place in his own unique way. Two famed photographers made their names long before coming here, but continue to make a splash today — Richard Darcey of Hatteras Island and Frank Christopher of Duck. New work continually appears too; the haunting black and whites of Mary Ellen Riddle are remembered long after viewing them. And, the photography and poetry of Steven Lautermilch are unforgettable. This Greensboro professor is drawn to this area immensely, spending every free moment at his Colington vacation home. "I'm exploring new kinds of feelings and voices here," Lautermilch said. "There is a clarity next to the ocean."

The Outer Banks is a popular area for retirement, and many outstanding local artists have come here at the conclusion of other careers.

Watercolorist Carol Trotman of Kill Devil Hills came here after a teaching career. Working exclusively with flowers, Trotman has created a truly excellent series that exlpodes with color. "There's so much beauty around us," she said. "I have a natural sensitivity to beauty, and I enjoy creating it."

Southern Shores artist Helen Borne left behind a banking career to become an Outer Banks artist, specializing in pencil portraits. This is "absolutely a dream come true," she says. "I hope I have enough time in my life to make a meaningful impression on the artistic world of the Outer Banks."

When Ellie Grumiaux retired from commercial art, he came to Southern Shores after vacationing here for more than 20 years. His watercolors present lovely images of boats, beach scenes and old NagsHead cottages.

Nancy and Chris Nolan of Frisco became full-time artists after retiring on Hatteras Island. At their home studio, they create lifelike wooden herons, willets and piping plovers. They had camped on Hatteras Island for 20 years before moving here.

While the art scene is as changeable as the patterns in the sand brought by the tide, one thing remains constant — amazingly talented artists continue to desire to live by the sea — particularly the shores of the Outer Banks of North Carolina.

(To view work of the artists mentioned in this story, visit any local art gallery and request a pamphlet that will guide you to the many fantastic galleries of the Outer Banks. An excellent representation of hundreds of local artists' creations is presented every February during the Frank Stick Memorial Art Show at Glenn Eure's Ghost Fleet Gallery in Nags Head. Contact the Dare County Arts Council at 261-5868 for more information.)

and his wife serve on the board of this foundation. Tax deductible donations can be sent to: Rogallo Foundation, P.O. Box 1839, Nags Head, N.C. 27959.

For those of you who like to read up on a sport before asking your body to do it, a brief description of hang gliding follows. The flier is attached at the waist to the center of gravity of the wing. In front of the flier is a triangular metal control bar. After a good run downhill, against the wind while gathering speed, the glider will begin to lift and leave the ground. From there on, altitude and direction are controlled by the pilot. Shifting body weight will turn the glider right or left. Moving the control bar forward or back with the hands causes the center of gravity to move and the kite's nose to pitch up or down. When the pilot runs out of hill or wind, a soft landing is managed by pushing the control bar out, causing the glider to stall. Several practice landings are the norm for soft, ideal landings.

Lessons are definitely suggested. Sign up at Kitty Hawk Kites, across the road from Jockey's Ridge in Kitty Hawk Connection. Kitty Hawk Kites offers two kinds of lessons, foot launched lessons on the dune and tandem hang gliding lessons with a certified instructor.

Truck-towing, or tandem hang gliding, along the open beach areas north of Corolla or at the Currituck County airport is a great way to lift off. Tandem hang gliding requires no prior experience, and it's a great way to get a good overall perspective on the sport. The tandem lesson lets you experience flight at higher altitudes of 1,000 feet or more.

No extra physical conditioning is required to take hang gliding lessons at Kitty Hawk Kites. Participants enjoy this sport almost year round but are most frequently airborne during warm days when the winds are east.

KITTY HAWK CONNECTION
Rt. 158, MP 13

The attractive, two-story wooden structure across the road from Jockey's Ridge is called Kitty Hawk Connection. It is a conglomeration of shops. You can see for miles from the towering observation deck located on top of Kitty Hawk Kites.

Land and Sky Sports

If hang gliding is your desire, the instructors at **Kitty Hawk Kites**, 441-4124 or (800) 334-4777, will put you through the drills and lessons so vital to learning about the sport. This is the home of the largest hang gliding school in the world, teaching flight adventure since 1974. All the gear you need is provided for your first foot launched flight. Beginner lessons require a three-hour commitment including classroom time, ground school and five flights on the sand dunes. Advanced clinics are also available.

In addition to the foot launched lessons on Jockey's Ridge, try flying at 1,000 feet or more with your instructor beside you. In its fourth year, tandem towing is becoming more popular, and if that's not enough, tandem paragliding will take you to even higher heights. All instructors are USHGA-rated pilots. There are lots of options for flying enthusiasts: beginner classes, advanced clinics, camps, vacation packages and more. Reservations are required.

For more fast fun and adventure, try rollerblading. Rentals and lessons are available. In-line skating is a great way to enjoy the great outdoors and get some aerobic conditioning at the same time. Entire families will enjoy Kitty Hawk Kites. There is even a climbing wall located inside the Nags Head store, and Wednesday is kid's day during the summer. Free workshops are always going on for things like juggling, Roll Patrol for rollerblades, boomerangs and stunt kites. (For a schedule of events throughout the year, refer to the chapter on annual events.) Hours during the season are 7:30 AM until 10:30 PM, seven days a week. If it's kite flying or hobby crafts, Kitty Hawk Kites has some of the most beautiful and unusual kites, flight toys and games found anywhere in the world and they carry the latest outdoor wear for the whole family.

And new this year at Kitty Hawk Kites is sea kayaking. **Kitty Hawk Kites and Outer Banks Outdoors**, 441-4124, will offer a combined lesson/tour for sea kayaking. Lessons will take two to three hours. Students can sign up for the lesson/tours at any of their five locations on the Outer Banks. Scheduled lessons will take place at their Duck and Avon locations and other designated locations for tours will be available too. No prior experience is required. Class size will be limited to 12 students. Advance reservations are recommended.

Water Sports

If water sports are your thing, **Kitty Hawk Sports**, 441-6800, is the place to be. The Outer Banks has become an international windsurfing center and Kitty Hawk Sports is making it their business to expose as many people as possible to this exhilarating recreational activity. Beginner windsurfing classes require a three hour commitment

and all of the necessary gear is provided. Advanced classes and camps are also available. Their teaching location is just on the south side of Miller's Restaurant in Nags Head. This is a great place to learn because the wind is steady, the water is shallow and the area is protected.

Beginner sailing lessons are another option. This program is designed for catamaran sailors. Maybe you just want to take a leisurely sailing tour around Roanoke Sound. You can do that, too, with an experienced instructor on board.

Kitty Hawk Sports/Kitty Hawk Kayaks now offers a full kayaking program. Beginners can have lessons in sound paddling, guided tours are available and you can rent boats; experienced paddlers are introduced to the Outer Banks paddling specialties and steered to longer cruises.

Learning to paddle a kayak on the Outer Banks is easy for the average person. After a few minutes of instruction a beginner can balance the kayak and learn efficient paddling strokes. A lifetime experience for the get-away-from-it-all visitor lies just minutes from Roanoke Island in the Alligator River Wildlife Refuge. Kitty Hawk Sports and Kitty Hawk Kayaks people have completed a kayak trail through the winding lakes and forested channels of the refuge; it's open now to all paddlers. Maps are available at the Fish and Wildlife Service office in Manteo and at Kitty Hawk Sports.

In addition to the water sports lessons, excellent equipment and all the accessories that go along with them, Kitty Hawk Sports also features a great collection of sports clothes for men and women. Summer hours are 8:30 AM until 10:30 PM.

KITTY HAWK SPORTS SAILING CENTER

Rt. 158   441-6800
MP 16½   441-2756

Kitty Hawk Sports operates their new waterfront recreation center just south of Miller's Restaurant. From May through September, 9 AM until 6 PM, those who enjoy water sports will find a haven here. Instruction is offered in windsurfing and sailing. Windsurfing, sailing and kayaking equipment is available for sale and rent. This is an internationally recognized high wind test center for Bic, F2 and North High Wind windsurfing products. Plenty of colorful activity can be seen here, especially when the spring regattas get under way drawing windsurfers from all over the country. (For a schedule of events, see the chapter on Annual Events.)

NAGS HEAD PRO DIVE CENTER

Kitty Hawk Connection   441-7594
Rt. 158, MP 13

Nags Head Pro Dive Center is also located here at the Kitty Hawk Connection. This is a full-service dive center specializing in scuba sales, service, rentals, repairs and instruction. Dive travel, commercial diving, open-water certification and offshore boat charters are also available. Charters take place on their privately owned 50-foot custom dive boat, the Sea Fox.

Beach diving is offered at MP 7 and MP 11. Two shipwrecks are located at MP 7, Kyzickes, a tanker and,

Carl Gerhard, a freighter. These two wrecks are more commonly recognized as the Triangle wrecks. They are located about 100 yards off of the beach. The U.S.S. Huron, a federal gun ship, is located 200 yards off of the beach at MP 11. This ship went down during a hurricane in 1877, and 95 hands were lost. A tug boat, The Explorer, is also located about 200 yards off of the beach, at MP 11.

SEA SCAN DIVE CENTER

Beach Rd., MP 10½   480-3467
For Boat Charters 480-2628

Sea Scan is a full service dive center and a NAUI Pro facility. Scuba sales, rentals, repairs, instruction and dive trips are offered here. For a fee, you can also have your own personal guide service to the wrecks. Near shore and offshore trips are provided. Charters are available on the boat, Diving Blues Make It So. Snorkeling lessons are a lot of fun too.

NAGS HEAD WATERSPORTS

Nags Head-Manteo Causeway   480-2034
                               480-2236

This watersports business is going into its fifth year and is a good destination for family water recreation. Although you won't find windsurfing here, you will find plenty of other ways to enjoy a day in the water at this soundfront location. Waverunners, jet boats, sailboats and paddle equipment are available on a first-come basis. Equipment includes such favorites as Waverunners III, Yamaha VXR, Kawasaki Sport Cruisers, side by side and Kawasaki Tandem Sport. Reservations are required for pontoon boats and fish-

ing boats; 24-hours advance notice is recommended. There are designated areas for the use of sport vehicles, and you can cruise the Roanoke Sound in the jet boats and sport cruisers. Nice sandy beaches are available for swimming and a picnic area is the perfect place for lunch — there's even shade for folks who prefer a break from the sun.

WATERWORKS
Rt. 158, MP 16½   *441-8875*

The two-story soundside building is the place to buy or rent equipment for a day on the water. They offer windsurfing, parasailing and sea kayaking lessons at this location and have a retail shop featuring Yamaha and Sea Doo equipment, T-shirts, wet suits, surfwear and other accessories. You can buy or rent boards and sails as well. Airboat rides, dolphin tours and kayak tours are available at their location on the Nags Head-Manteo Causeway; for information call 441-6822. Waterworks is also located near the water

tower in Duck Village at Wee Winks Square, 261-7245. You can rent surf boards, boogie boards and check out their line of beach supplies for a perfect day at the beach and in the water. They're open mid-April to mid-October, depending on the weather.

NAGS HEAD FISHING PIER
On the Atlantic Ocean
MP 12   *441-5141*

This is one of the most popular fishing piers on the Outer Banks. It is 750 feet long and has its own bait and tackle shop. There is night fishing, game tables for the kids and a restaurant. The Pier House Restaurant features fresh seafood and wonderful views of the ocean. The restaurant serves breakfast, lunch and dinner, and summer hours are 6 AM until 10 PM. The pier is closed December and March and reopens in April. It is open 24 hours during the season. Admission is $5 per day for adults, $12 for a three-day pass and $30 for an eight-day pass. Season rates are $135 for singles and $225 for couples. Kids between the ages of 6 and 12 are always half price. Inquire about cottage rentals near the pier; weekly and nightly rentals are available. These are one to four bedroom cottages.

JENNETTE'S PIER
On The Atlantic Ocean
at Whalebone Jct.   *441-6116*

This popular fishing pier is the largest on the Outer Banks — 1,000 feet. It's also the oldest pier, and friends have been gathering here for more than 60 years. About 400 feet of brand new decking opened for fishing Easter weekend of '94, and construction will continue on the other 600 feet. The current rates are $5 per day, $12.50 for a three-day pass, $25 for a weekly pass, and children 11 and under are free. You can walk out on the pier for $1 per person.

This pier is usually crawling with people who fish. (We're told that the activity here is not putting a damper on the fish being caught.) It's located in the heart of Whalebone Junction — along the hotbed of big catches and tall stories. Rest assured, the pier, a very popular place at anytime, will be even more so by late spring and summer. The pier opens Easter Weekend each year and closes December 15. Hours do vary, but their schedule is 6 AM until 10 PM Easter through Memorial Day Weekend. The pier is open 24 hours between Memorial Day Weekend and Labor Day Weekend. You won't find a snack bar but, snacks are available for sale.

OUTER BANKS FISHING PIER
On the Atlantic Ocean
MP 18½   *441-5740*

This 650-foot pier was originally built in 1959 and rebuilt in 1962 after the Ash Wednesday storm. Owner Garry Oliver has all you need in the bait and tackle shop for a day of fishing along this somewhat remote stretch of beach. The pier is open 24 hours a day from Memorial Day until mid-October and closes during the winter. It reopens in late March. Rates are $5 per day, $12.50 for three days, $25 per week, $90 per season for one person and $150 per season for a couple. Drinks and snacks are available, but you won't find a snack bar.

NAGS HEAD GOLF LINKS
AND LINKS GRILLE
Rt. 158, MP 15   *441-8073*
Village at Nags Head   *(800) 851-9404*

Nags Head Golf Links is an 18-hole soundfront and soundside course, resembling those of Scotland with few trees but with wind-blown, open fairways and well-tended, bent grass greens. A par 71 course, its overall length is 6,126 yards, and conditions are excellent. It was voted again this year as one of the top 50 courses in the southeastern region by *Golf Week* magazine. Call for green fees, cart information and starting times. It's open to the public all year. Inquire about discounted green fees during the off season. Golf club rentals are available throughout the year. Summer hours are 6 AM until 6:30 PM.

The **Links Grille**, overlooking Albemarle Sound, is one of the best kept secrets on the Outer Banks.

The combined dining and lounge area offers a spectacular sound view, and a continental breakfast is served for golfers. Lunch and light fare menus appeal to everyone. You can enjoy appetizers such as fried onions, homemade chips and salsa, spicy Buffalo wings, daily seafood specials and lots more. Sunsets here are incredible too, especially after a round of golf. You can also enjoy cocktails and heavy hors d'oeuvres as the sun sinks. The Links Grille is open to the public and available for small parties in the evenings and during the off season. This Carolinas Golf Group facility welcomes you.

VILLAGE AT NAGS HEAD BEACH CLUB

On the Atlantic Ocean, MP 15   *480-2222*

This beautiful, oceanfront Carolinas Golf Group facility is part of the Village at Nags Head development and, as such, is *basically* private. We say basically, because it is available to the public for rent for special events such as wedding receptions, corporate outings and private parties. Catering is available through the Village's catering service. Call for information or reservations.

DOWDY'S AMUSEMENT PARK

Rt. 158, MP 11   *441-5122*

This park features fast-moving rides like the scrambler and the tilt-a-whirl and evokes memories of childhood with its carnival atmosphere. Adults and children alike enjoy the Ferris wheel. There's just enough to whet your appetite for this kind of fun, and the kids will probably take the upper hand on what's fun and what's not. It's open evenings from sometime in the spring until Labor Day.

FAMILY LIFE CENTER

Rt. 158, MP 11½   *441-4941*

At the Ark on the west side of the highway in Nags Head, there's a low-key Christian atmosphere available for young people. Indoor games such as Ping Pong, basketball, video games and roller skating are available on Friday and Saturday evenings. Thursday night is adult basketball night.

Other Things To Do

Nags Head is the activity center of the Outer Banks when it comes to variety. While some other towns and villages feature plenty of water sports, Nags Head offers other activities, as well.

The **Beach Bowling Center**, 441-7077, is located at MP 10, on the west side of Route 158, just south of the Food Lion Shopping Plaza. **Sea Fit Aerobics and Dance Studio,** 441-0600, is located at Pirate's Quay Shopping Center and offers aerobics classes daily along with step classes, yoga and more at scheduled times. Walk-ins are welcome. Weekly and monthly memberships are available. **Surf Slide,** 441-5755, is an outdoor adventure on the west side of Route 158 at MP 11, open summers only 10 AM until midnight. **Colony Cinema's** new location in Nags Head, 441-5630, on the east side of Route 158 at MP 10½, is convenient for vacationers and locals who live on the south end of the beach. **Nags Head Raceway**, 480-4639 is a go-cart track located in Nags Head at the 16½ MP. Kids must be 13 years of age and meet certain size requirements to drive by themselves. Two-seater carts are available for younger folks and their parents. Summer hours are 9 AM until 11 PM, seven days a week.

The land available for full-sized golf courses on the Outer Banks is scarce. But there are a number of miniature golf courses in the Nags Head area, and they provide recreation for everyone. **Pink Elephant Mini Golf** has 36 lighted holes with an African jungle motif. It's located at MP 11½on the Beach Road and is open summers from 10 AM until midnight. **Forbes Candies and Mini Golf**, 441-7293, is also a favorite gathering place for family activity on the Beach Road. They're open 9 AM until 11 PM during the season. **Soundside Golf**, 441-6841, is located on the west side of Route 158. **Blackbeard's Miniature Golf Park and Arcade**, 441-4541, is a lot of fun for the entire family.

Shopping

Nags Head claims the bulk of Outer Banks shopping, including small boutiques along the Beach Road and Route 158 as well as large shopping centers such as the Outer Banks Mall and Soundings Factory Stores. You'll definitely need to drive along Route 158 and the Beach Road to cover the entire array of shopping options here.

Ben Franklin, 441-7571, is located across the street from the Food Lion Plaza in Nags Head, and they carry everything you need for the beach, just like their store in Kitty Hawk. **Nags Head News**, 480-6397, is a great bookstore and news stand located at the Food Lion Plaza. For an outstanding deli sandwich you can't beat, **Mrs. T's Deli**, 441-1220. They have great desserts too.

You can't miss the surf shops and **Whalebone Surf Shop**, 441-6747, at MP 10, is a great place to shop for

neat clothes and, of course, surfwear and gear. This shop is located in front of the Food Lion Plaza. Don't forget their other location in Kitty Hawk!

Art work, jewelry, fine crafts and lots more are available along Driftwood Street and **Gallery Row**, as we mentioned in the section on Attractions.

At MP 10½ **The Christmas Mouse**, 441-8111, is open all year and is a delightful store. You'll find Christmas collectibles, Cairn Gnomes, papier mâché Santas, porcelain dolls, unique ornaments, nautical trees and rooms. There's definitely something here for everyone. They're open seven days a week throughout the year. **Nags Head Hammocks**, 441-6115, has two locations, one on the Beach Road at 10½ MP and another on Route 158 at MP 9½. They not only feature the famous hammocks made right here in Nags Head, but they also have beautifully landscaped, award-winning grounds,

vastly different from the Outer Banks *au naturale* landscaping style. Look for their third location in Corolla at the TimBuck II Shopping Village.

Seaside Art Gallery, 441-5418, is located at MP 11 on the Beach Road and features more than 2,000 original works of art including sculptures, paintings, drawings, Indian pottery, fine porcelains, seascapes and animation art from Disney. Artists include Picasso, Whistler and Renoir. They're open seven days a week all year. Hours are 10 AM to 9 PM, Monday through Saturday and 10 AM to 2 PM on Sunday. Look for their second location at TimBuck II Shopping Village.

Yellowhouse Gallery and **Annex**, 441-6928, at MP 11 houses one of the largest collections of antique prints and maps in North Carolina. Thousands of old etchings, lithographs and engravings are organized for convenient browsing in several rooms of one of Nags Head's older beach cottages. Established in 1969,

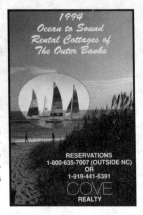
the gallery features Civil War prints and maps, botanicals, fish, shells. Thomas Nast cartoons and antique maps and charts of the Outer Banks.

The Yellowhouse Annex next door offers a wide variety of Outer Banks souvenir pictures and maps, hundreds of decorative prints and posters and fast, expert, custom framing. Yellowhouse Gallery and Annex are open all year.

The **Secret Spot Surf Shop**, 441-4030, is located at MP 11½ on Route 158. Owner Steve Hess has been in business since 1977 and is unusually helpful to the youngsters who aspire to be surfers. This is a good place for beginners and longtime enthusiasts. The surfwear is pretty cool too.

For neat and unusual finds, shop at **Vintage Wave Clothing**, 480-9283. They do a great job of merchandising here. We especially like the pink porcelain freezer used for displays. Expect to find vintage beaded wear, vintage Levi's, estate jewelry, all kinds of hats, vintage glasses, purses and more. This shop is located across

from the Colonial Inn Motel at MP 11½ on the Beach Road.

Twila Zone, 480-0399, is located across from the Nags Head Fishing Pier at MP 12 on the Beach Road. It is also a wonderful shop of vintage clothing for the entire family. Owner Jo Ruth Patterson has a nice selection of hats, accessories and costume jewelry as well as dolls, doll houses and other fine quality vintage furnishings.

Pirate's Quay, a shopping center located at MP 11½ on Route 158 is home to several nice shops and larger stores. **Island Magic**, 441-5692, features contemporary fashions and wood crafts from Bali. You'll enjoy these creations, especially the colorful wood masks. **Rollin' in the Dough**, 441-6042, caters to those who love freshly baked breads and pastries, as well as salads and made-to-order sandwiches. They offer daily lunch specials and full scale catering too. Hours are 8 AM to 6 PM, Monday through Saturday and 10 AM to 4 PM on Sunday during the season **Cloud**

Nine, 441-2992, is an adventure in clothing, accessories and other discoveries from around the world. There are beads and lots of them. Other finds include recycled glass, Grateful Dead merchandise, T-shirts, beautiful batiks and Guatemalan finds. Plan on spending some time here. In its second season, **The Quacker Connection**, 441-2811, features decoys, country crafts and collectibles. The owners relocated here from Pennsylvania and brought some of their special finds with them. Doug is the resident carver, so you can expect to see him carving and painting decoys. Old and new decoys will be available. Country crafts include Redwear pottery, indigenous to areas in and around Lancaster, Pennsylvania, baskets and hand-stenciled lamp shades. Merchandise is not limited to what's found in Pennsylvania however. Enamelware from Colorado will also be available, including popcorn bowls and colanders. Seashell bowls glazed in mother-of-pearl and edged with 18-karat gold

are from Maryland. Expect to find gifts and furnishings here with a country and beach appeal.

Across from Jockey's Ridge at MP 12½, **Kitty Hawk Kites** and **Kitty Hawk Sports** are located at opposite ends of the complex known as Kitty Hawk Connection, also described in our attractions section of this chapter. There's a big play area for the kids, the playport, which makes shopping more fun. You'll enjoy a stop at the ice cream and candy shops as well as a shopping spree in **Donna Designs,** 441-6232. It's a store of one-of-a-kind sportswear with air-brush designs. There's everything from children's shoes and shirts to adult sportswear. All have been designed and painted with soft subtle colors of the beach, fish and birds, by the artist-owner. **Salt Marsh**, 480-1116, is an environmental and educational store filled with gifts, T-shirts, jewelry, books and toys. The T-shirts are especially nice, and everything in the store relates to nature. A percentage of every sale is donated to wildlife preservation groups. Look for Salt Marsh at the TimBuck II Shopping village. **The Stadium**, 441-8535, offers nostalgic clothing from your favorite sports teams. **How Sweet It Is**, 441-4485, offers homemade ice cream and tasty deli sandwiches. Don't forget **Nags Head Pro Dive Center**, 441-7594, previously discussed in Attractions. You will enjoy homemade fudge from **The Fudgery**, 480-0163.

At MP 13 you'll find the **Surfside Plaza** has numerous shops featuring everything from fishing tackle to contemporary clothing and crafts. **Surfside Casuals**, 441-7449, has more swimsuits than any store on the beach. This shop also carries an extensive line of casual wear for both men and women. Surfside Casuals is also located in Avon, Duck and Corolla. **Suits Galore**, 441-5192, offers a great selection of full and larger size bathing suits for women. **Beach Peddler**, 441-5408, "peddles" everything you'd need at the beach and then some. **Darnell's Gifts**, 441-5687, stocks souvenirs, T-shirts, homemade fudge, hermit crabs, homemade chocolates and seashells. Try the **Fishing Hook**, 441-6661, for fishing and camping supplies.

The **Outer Banks Mall** is located at MP 15 on Route 158, and it is open year round. Shops in the mall are spread out between **Seamark**

Foods and **Roses Discount Department Store,** and the north wing is home to a mixture of shopping and service destinations. **Colony House Cinema**, 441-5630, is the place for moviegoers while **Outer Banks Cleaners**, 441-3354, is the neighborhood dry cleaner and **P & G Laundromat** offers laundry convenience for visitors. For good eats there's **New York Bagels**, 480-0106, where we recommend the "Everything" bagel. **Sesame Seed Natural Foods**, 441-5030, carries healthful snacks and sodas, vitamins and herbs, low-salt, low-fat and sugar-free products, body building supplements and body care products. Be forewarned that children are not allowed in the store. Early risers will appreciate **Mister Donut**, 480-1987, and for good Chinese cooking, try **North China Restaurant**, 441-3454. After you've had dinner you'll be ready for a movie, and you'll find a good selection of video rentals at **Video Andy's Movie Rentals**, 441-2666. Finally, after that movie you'll be ready for a stroll on the beach and **Soundfeet Shoes**, 441-8954, can help you with the proper footwear. Speaking of feet, **Outer Banks Podiatry**, 480-1194, can take care of any of the problems that may arise if you don't wear the proper footwear — those new sneakers you bought just for your Outer Banks vacation

Here you may find the perfect waves.

could cause blisters, you know! It is important to note that **Outer Banks Animal Hospital**, 441-2776, is also located here in case your pet is feeling a little under the weather from the long car ride to this beach destination. **United States Cellular**, 441-3377, will be more than happy to help you with all of your portable phone needs. **New Image Hair Salon**, 441-2700, will be only too happy to help. **Peggy's Next to New Consignment Shop**, 441-1655, features household goods, whatnots, jewelry, shoes and a good selections of clothing for women and children.

Inside Outer Banks Mall you'll find the **Mule Shed**, 441-4115, is a popular clothing store for local women. They carry quality brand clothing and stay open most all year. **Ocean Annie's Jewelry and Handcrafted Pottery**, 441-4500, offers a large assortment of gifts from all over the country, with strong emphasis on pottery and jewelry. They also sell gourmet, ground-to-order coffee. **Lady Dare**, 441-7461, is a clothing store for the fuller figured woman. This boutique offers a very nice selection of fashions and accessories for the office and the beach. Lady Dare also offers the largest selection of swimwear and sportswear for the fuller-figured woman. Mothers of brides will like this store too. Their styles appeal to women of all ages, and the sales staff is especially helpful in selecting and coordinating outfits. **Waters Edge Books and Gifts**, 441-1118, is a full service bookstore stocking greeting cards, baseball cards, stationery, framed and unframed prints and more.

If you have an interest in endangered species, **Sea Witch Gifts**, 441-5442, specializes in that sort of thing along with nautical gifts, pewter and stone critters, lanterns, wind chimes

An early morning ride by the sea stays with you for a long time.

and a lot more. **Irish Imports**, 480-0055, features Irish clothing and gifts — everything in the store carries an Irish theme. For NASCAR Winston Cup souvenirs visit **T-Tops and NASCAR Souvenirs**, 441-8867. Shirts, collectibles, jewelry, country artist shirts, Harley Davidson shirts and Outer Banks souvenirs will interest you. **Big Dipper Ice Cream**, 441-4757, offers tempting cool treats and hand-dipped cones; and **Yellow Submarine Restaurant**, 441-3511, is a good place to grab a bite while you're shopping. **Island Tobacco**, 441-1392, is the only tobacco shop on the Outer Banks. They stock 14 blends of bulk tobacco and offer a full range of smoking accessories including imported pipes and pipe lighters. They also sell darts and dart boards. **Professional Opticians**, 441-6353, carries the latest in eyeglasses and sunglasses — just in case you forgot those all-too-important accessories at home. **The Habitat Earth**

Nature Store, 480-0015, maintains an extensive line of earth-theme products and science and nature-oriented toys. The artwork featuring Aboriginal and rain forest themes is interesting, and they have a good supply of Native American music. You can also find large fossil replications, binoculars, birdhouses, unusual gift items and astronomy aids. Are you planning a family reunion or get together on the Outer Banks? No mall is complete without, **Everything's a Dollar**, 441-0275. **Peg's Hallmark**, 441-7015 will help you keep in touch with the folks back home. If you forget your tunes — try **Radio Shack**, 441-2581. For that special something for that special someone while you're away, visit **Riddick Jewelers**, 441-3653. And finally, if you're tired of mall walking and shopping, **Games People Play Arcade**, 441-6713, can be a lot of fun. **Ocean Threads Surf Shop**, 441-8967, is also located in Kill Devil

Hills on the Beach Road at MP 8, in the village of Duck and in Corolla at Corolla Light Village Shops. Ocean Threads offers swimwear for the entire family and has a good selection of maternity and long torso swimsuits. You will be sure to find your favorite Outer Banks T-shirts here too. They have a size to fit everyone in your family. You will enjoy shopping at any of their four locations. **Out of the Woods SignMakers,** 441-4971, had such a great first year in Duck at the Scarborough Faire Shops that they decided to open a second location in the mall. Out of the Woods offers at least 130 designs of personalized wooden signs for all occasions. We recommend a visit to either of their shops locations. You won't be able to miss their shop in the mall, just look for the fiberglass replica of a nag in the mall side window, her name is Precious. When you see her, we think you will know why she was named this way. Once inside the mall, you will see their sign with a fluffy pink flamingo that reads, "please don't feed the lifeguards." The owners of Out of the Woods do not lack a sense of humor. Ask for a new color catalog. Mail order is available from both locations.

The Farmer's Daughter, 441-3977, is located at MP 16 on Route 158. It's a delightful place to browse and find a special gift or handcrafted

Photo: Mary Ellen Riddle

Waves constantly wear on ocean pier pilings.

accessory for your own home — this is country craft and folk art heaven. The **Chalet Gift Shop**, 441-6402, is located at MP 15½ on the Beach Road. It's one of the nicest stores on the beach and features exquisite gifts and collectibles. You'll find Lladro and other porcelains, dolls and jewelry here. Just to balance things out, there is another side to the store, one where you can find just about anything and everything for the beach. **Sea Shore Stuff**, 441-8446, is located in the long yellow building on the east side of Route 158 at the 15½ MP. They carry everything from A to Z, including suntan lotions, rafts, seashore oriented gifts, homemade fudge, nautical sterling silver

jewelry, figurines, T-shirts, note cards, limited edition prints, wooden lighthouses, pewter — you name it, even salt and pepper shakers. They even have hermit crabs in season.

Greenleaf Gallery, 480-3555, is located at MP 16 on Route 158 and is a contemporary multimedia art gallery showcasing only American arts and crafts. Approximately 150 artists and craftspeople are represented offering a good geographic variation. The emphasis is on one-of-a-kind pieces including jewelry, stoneware, furnishings, sculpture, acrylic and watercolor paintings, etchings, lithographs, mixed media pieces and more. Wonderful handmade collectibles are found here. We highly recommend a visit to this gallery.

At MP 16 on the Beach Road, you'll see **Souvenir City**, 441-7452. They probably have the largest collection of souvenirs on the beach. You'll want to take something home from here, and the kids will almost certainly push for a hermit crab — they're for sale, and the folks here will instruct you on how to care for it. There's also a great collection of miniature lighthouses and miles of T-shirts. **The Dare Shops**, 441-1112, at MP 16½ on the Beach Road has been in business for 36 years. It's a store that carries a nice selection of men's and women's sportswear, sweaters and other items as well as beautiful gold and silver jewelry.

Soundings Factory Stores, 441-7395, is a discount outlet mall with numerous shops carrying all sorts of things from clothes to dishes. It's located at MP 16½ on Route 158. Some of our favorites here are **Westport** and **Westport Woman**, 441-1568, for stylish and affordable clothing and accessories; a **Pfaltzgraff Collector's Center**, 441-1800; a **London Fog** outlet, 441-6409, with a vast selection of coats; and a **Rack Room Shoes**, 441-9288, which carries all the styles you expect to find with prices you can afford. **Publisher's Warehouse**, 441-5106, is a warehouse bookstore offering thousands of books and computer software at discount prices. **Cabin Creek**, 441-4040,

features Americana gifts, crafts and accessories while **Jerzees**, 480-2569, specializes in American sportswear and heat transfer printing. Rock and glass collectors will be interested in **Michael's Gems**, 441-4449, and one of our personal favorites is the **Corning/Revere Ware Store**, 480-0005. **Bugle Boy**, 441-8669, offers great prices on sportswear for the whole family and hardly anyone just walks by the **Bass** outlet, 441-8553. You'll find other name brand discount stores here as well including: **Benetton**, 441-7816; **Polo Factory Store**, 480-0661; **Arrow**, 441-0899; **Nine West Outlet**, 441-8488; **Van Heusen**, 441-8553; **Leggs-Hanes-Bali**, 441-9136; and **Jones of New York**, 480-0311.

If you're looking for grocery stores in Nags Head, **Food Lion** is located at MP 10 on Route 158 Bypass, and **Seamark Foods** is located at the Outer Banks Mall. Seamark stocks more specialty items than any other grocery store on the Outer Banks. Look for their new location in Kitty Hawk next to Wal-Mart.

Cahoon's on the Beach Road is a large variety store, and it's located at MP 16½. Dorothy and Ray Cahoon bought their store shortly before the Ash Wednesday Storm of 1962 and, despite what must have been a rather wild start, have had great success for the past 30 years. Everything you need for your visit to the beach is here, plus good meats that butcher Robert Heroux cuts to perfection. They're convenient to Jennette's Pier and nearby motels and cottages. You'll find this family-owned store a nice change of pace from the large city-size supermarkets.

There are several seafood stores in Nags Head. **Austin Fish Co.**, 441-7412, is located at MP 12½ near Jockey's Ridge. They've been here for years. This store also serves as a gas station. Watch the signs. **Whalebone Seafood**, 441-8808, is run by the Daniels family at MP 16½. The fish is always fresh, and they'll know how to cook every fish they sell.

If you follow Route 158 to its end, you'll see the highway signs designating Highway 64 to Manteo. You're still in Nags Head as you cross the causeway, and a few stores are worth mentioning here. **Blackbeard's Treasure Chest**, 441-5772, is one of those places the whole family will enjoy. They carry seashells, beachwear, jewelry, local crafts, and they even have an indoor flea market in one room of the shop. There's no telling what you'll find here, but we know you'll find Blackbeard theme gifts somewhere along the way. Farther along this road is **Shipwreck**, 441-5739, which you won't want to miss. It has driftwood, nets, shells and other nautical treasures piled everywhere.

Another store along the causeway will delight all who love fresh steamed crabs. **Daniels Crab House**, 441-5027, is the place to go. There's a picking room and large steamers in the back. You get only the freshest steamed crabs here.

Inside
Roanoke Island

Before we get into the history of Roanoke Island, the town of Manteo deserves a review. Manteo is the county seat of Dare County, which includes most of the Outer Banks except for Ocracoke Island and the very northern beaches.

As you drive into Manteo from Nags Head or from the western village of Manns Harbor, you'll notice an abundance of trees. Tall pines and live oaks reach for the sky here, and in summer the crepe myrtles bloom profusely along the streets. If it's a breezy day, pull off the road into a parking lot and stand there and listen for a few minutes; the melody played by the wind in the trees is worth a quiet moment or two. The area just beyond the fringes of the business section is the best place for listening — near the Elizabethan Gardens and Fort Raleigh Historic Site.

A sense of history abounds in this small, comfortable town. You have to stretch your imagination to consider the hardships of discovery 400 years ago, since this island is the site of the first attempt at permanent settlement by the English in the 1500s—more about that in a minute. Everything appears to be in place, comfortable and easygoing.

The Waterfront provides a place to ponder the days of the first landing and the immense beauty of the water just beyond the shores of Roanoke Island. Geographically, the island seems protected from the ocean by other land — across the sound is Nags Head—a slim strip of protection in times of angry storms. And, the picturesque, open waterfront and the tall pines of the main highway evoke a slower pace, a relaxed feeling.

Part of the business area is scattered along U.S. 64. Everything from car dealerships, marinas, flower shops, eateries, gas stations, the library, an auto body shop, a tire shop, schools, banks, motels and restaurants, to the Art Deco Ace Hardware store, optician, seafood shop and drug stores dredges up memories of those times when all the businesses necessary for day-to-day comfort were within walking distance in many towns all over the country. There are even a few cattle grazing along the roadside not far from the ABC Store — funny juxtaposition — but representative of the interesting diversity offered by this gem of a small town.

Roanoke Island is steeped in the history of exploration and discovery. In the late 1500s the English colonization of America began.

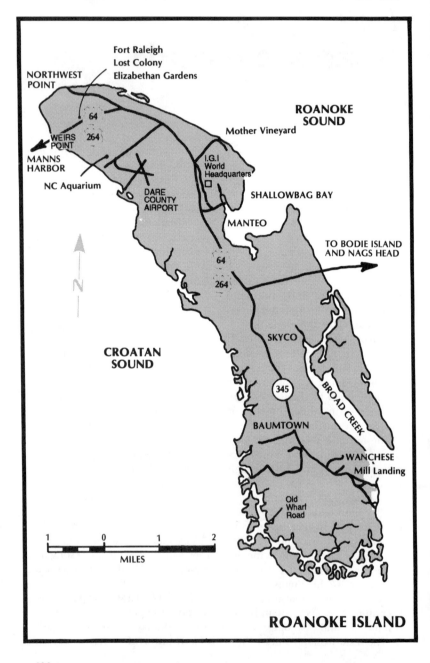

Fort Raleigh
Lost Colony
Elizabethan Gardens

NORTHWEST
POINT

64

**ROANOKE
SOUND**

Mother Vineyard

WEIRS
POINT

264

MANNS
HARBOR

I.G.I
World
Headquarters

NC Aquarium

DARE
COUNTY
AIRPORT

SHALLOWBAG BAY

MANTEO

TO BODIE ISLAND
AND NAGS HEAD

64

264

**CROATAN
SOUND**

SKYCO

345

BROAD CREEK

BAUMTOWN

WANCHESE
Mill Landing

Old
Wharf
Road

1   0   1   2

MILES

ROANOKE ISLAND

Photo: Mary Ellen Riddle

Captain Willie Etheridge is a long-time leader in the local fishing industry.

Spain ruled the oceans in those days and had made historical discoveries of treasure in the New World nearly 100 years earlier. Their plundering of South America's Native American empires had left that area devastated. Other than a small settlement at St. Augustine, Florida, North America was left untouched. Then, the French explored the southeastern part of North America and Canada. It was inevitable that England's growing naval expeditions would reach these shores. They were looking for an advanced base of operations against the Spanish and for new land for permanent settlement.

Sir Walter Raleigh's expedition to the new land in 1584 followed that of Humphrey Gilbert in 1583, during which Gilbert himself was lost. Raleigh caught the "fever" of colonization of America, and he was determined that the English would be the first to settle the area.

On July 4 — a date later to be commemorated throughout the land for different reasons — Captains Arthur Barlowe and Philip Amadas arrived off the Banks and began their explorations. They landed north of Kitty Hawk to take formal possession and were astounded at the profusion of cedar, deer, wildfowl and wild grapes (see "Mother Vineyard"). They met the local Native Americans, who had a village on the northwest end of Roanoke Island, and found them friendly. They left after a month, taking along two Native Americans named Manteo and Wanchese, and their reports caused a stir in England. In fact, by the very next spring Raleigh had outfitted seven ships and 600 men, getting them to sea in April. Again, Raleigh himself could not go; Elizabeth wanted him in England in case of Spanish attack.

Sir Richard Grenville was placed in charge of the fleet, with Ralph Lane as lieutenant governor.

Grenville had a little trouble at Ocracoke Inlet — his flagship *Tiger* went aground and was almost lost — but he freed and floated her and pushed on, into the sound.

He took a week to explore the mainland within the sounds. The English visited several Native American villages and were well received at most. After a visit to one named Aquascococke, however, Grenville found himself missing a silver cup (it is possible there was a misunderstanding about an exchange of gifts.) Unable to regain it, he had his men burn the town, then proceeded on his explorations.

At last he pushed on up the sound to Roanoke and after some time decided that this would be the site for the first settlement.

Why did Grenville and Lane choose Roanoke? There were better sites for a colony already known — the Chesapeake Bay area, farther north, had much better soil, deep rivers and better harbors. They may have chosen Roanoke because it was inaccessible to large ships — Spanish ships. Or it may have been a simple miscalculation.

The 600 men spent the summer building a small earthwork fort, Fort Raleigh, and a few houses. In August Grenville sailed with his ships, leaving Governor Lane in charge of 107 men.

The winter was not easy, but more ominous than the weather was the worsening of relations with the Native Americans. Lane and some of his men explored up the rivers of the Albemarle, following rumors of cities of gold, but their methods of obtaining food and information quickly turned the inhabitants against them. When he returned, the governor, alleging conspiracy, then led an attack on the village of the Roanoke weroance (king), Wingina, killing the chief and his advisors. Afterward he tried to set up Manteo, who remained pro-English to the end, as the new king, but it was evident that the English and the Native Americans were beginning to regard each other as enemies.

Perhaps that was why, when Grenville was late in returning, Lane decided to pull out when Sir Francis Drake stopped by in the spring. Grenville's relief fleet arrived just a few weeks later, and he was surprised to find the island deserted. Unwilling to abandon the fort, he left 15 soldiers there to spend the winter before sailing again for home.

High dreams were dreamed that winter of 1586-87 in England, for Raleigh was pulling together, at long last, his colonizing expedition. Led by John White, three ships left Plymouth, carrying 120 men, women and children.

The first mystery met them when they landed. The 15 men Grenville had left were gone; only one skeleton was found, decaying beside the demolished fort.

The new colonists shook their heads, doubtless prayed, but pitched in to clear land and build homes, guarding always against the hostile and shadowy figures in the forest. On August 18 a child was born, Virginia Dare, the first English child

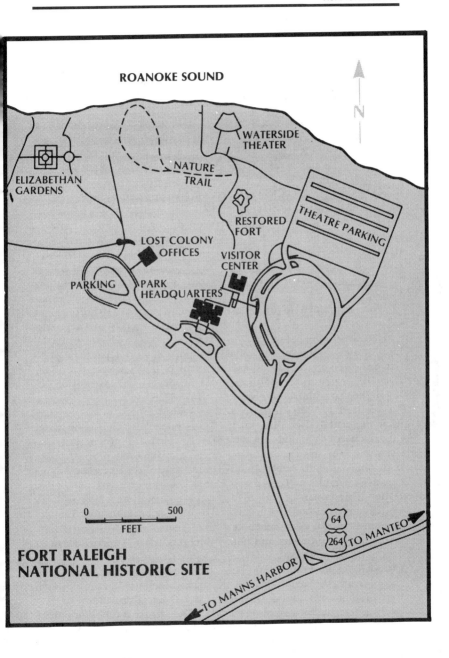

ROANOKE SOUND

WATERSIDE THEATER

NATURE TRAIL

ELIZABETHAN GARDENS

RESTORED FORT

THEATRE PARKING

LOST COLONY OFFICES

VISITOR CENTER

PARKING

PARK HEADQUARTERS

0   500
FEET

64
264 TO MANTEO

FORT RALEIGH
NATIONAL HISTORIC SITE

TO MANNS HARBOR

born in the New World (though let us not forget that the Spanish had been around, farther south, for almost a century). Governor White, her grandfather, left with the autumn for England to organize more supplies and colonists.

But war with Spain intervened and, with Philip's Armada menacing England, Elizabeth had no ships to spare for Raleigh's dream colonies. It was not until 1590 that White was able to return, and when at last he landed again on Roanoke, the village had been evacuated, and the colonists had gone — where? On trees nearby were carved the words: CROATOAN; CRO. But on Croatan Island no traces have ever been found.

What happened to the "Lost Colony"?

Paul Green, in the last scene of his historical drama of the same name, suggests that they abandoned Roanoke because of a Spanish threat, hoping to stay with friendly Native Americans of Manteo's tribe. As to what happened after that, many theories have been advanced over the years. One was that the main body found friendly Native Americans at Croatan Island (now part of Hatteras), intermarried with them as they wandered about North Carolina and survived until modern times in the English surnames and blue eyes of the Lumbee Native Americans of Robeson County. Another theory is that the main body went north rather than south, arriving safely at the southern coast of the Chesapeake Bay. They lived with the Native Americans there peacefully but were massacred by Powhatan

when the Jamestown expedition arrived in 1607. Other possibilities include death by starvation or the Spaniards; the colonists attempted to sail back to England and sank; or a hurricane wiped them out. No one will ever know for sure.

One thing for sure, though, is the fact that historians and a certain element of the public remain fascinated with the fate of the colonists. In the spring of 1993, the world's most noted Roanoke scholars gathered in Manteo for "Roanoke Decoded," a symposium that offered the authorities a chance to discuss every facet of that first English settlement, from archaeological studies to Native American lore. Resulting from the workshops was the establishment of a research office at East Carolina University in Greenville. Dr. E. Thomson Shields Jr. of the school's English department is director of this new research office. Write him c/o ECU, Greenville, NC 27858-4353.

With the departure of the colonists, Roanoke was left to the Native Americans for a long time. But eventually, c. 1655, the press of whites southward out of Tidewater Virginia reached the northern Outer Banks, and some of those families still are seen today on the island. Families with names such as Gallop, Baum, Meekins, Tillett, Daniels and Midgett settled down to stay. The small population was supported by stock raising and small-scale farming through the 17th and 18th centuries.

The island's location prompted its use during the Civil War as a military bastion to control the sounds and rivers of northeast North Caro-

lina. At 10:30 AM, February 7, 1862, a gigantic shallow-draft Federal fleet, with 12,000 troops aboard, began a bombardment of Confederate shore batteries on the northern end of the island (an overlook at Northwest Point today commemorates this battle). That evening 7,500 Federals disembarked at Ashby's Landing (now Skyco). The next morning they moved north, opposed bitterly every step of the way up the island, until a final charge routed the Rebels, who surrendered. Union forces held the area for the duration of the war.

After Union forces gained control of Roanoke Island, black refugees arrived by the thousands hoping for a new beginning. A freedmen's camp was established on the northern end of the island (west of where the Elizabethan Motel now stands). Here 3,000 slaves lived in a village of nearly 600 houses, with a steam saw and grist mill, schools, stores and a hospital. After the war, the federal government restored the land to the original landowners; the camp was abandoned in 1866.

As the population increased after 1865, homes clustered around the two harbors at Shallowbag Bay and at Mill Landing. These areas were referred to respectively as the "Upper End" and "Lower End" of the island. Around 1886 the "Lower Enders" grew understandably tired

Photo: Mary Ellen Riddle

All kinds of entertainment await you on Roanoke Island.

of being called that and chose the name of Wanchese for their town; Manteo followed suit, incorporating in 1899, shortly after being named seat of newly formed Dare County. Since then both towns have grown slowly but steadily.

In 1902, Reginald Fessenden, a pioneer in the development of radio, transmitted signals from an apparatus on Roanoke Island to one on Hatteras.

In 1900 to 1903, the brothers Wright took a ship from Roanoke for Kitty Hawk.

In 1928, a privately constructed bridge first connected the island with the beach at Nags Head, opening the outer islands to development.

In 1937, "The Lost Colony" was performed for the first time.

After World War II, the stabilization of the Banks and the construction of roads and bridges, along with the creation of the National Park, brought modern tourism and real-estate development to the island.

Today Roanoke Island is characterized two ways. For much of the year it is a quiet, low-key area where most of the permanent residents know one another by name or at least by face, and the principal commercial activities are fishing at Mill Landing and service-related businesses. All this begins to change round about May, when the golden tide of tourists begins; the months of summer are full of activity, especially at Fort Raleigh, the North Carolina Aquarium, The Waterside Theater where performances of "The Lost Colony" take place, *Elizabeth II* and in the shops and stores of downtown Manteo and along Route 64/

264. Still, though activity is brisk, Roanokers have not yet succumbed to full-scale commercialism. Much of the island remains wild, with forests and marshes covering the land outside the town. The people are friendly, and beauty still lies on the land during the long humming evenings of summer. As Amadas and Barlowe found in 1584, this might still be ". . . the goodliest land under the cope of heaven."

Attractions

THE ELIZABETHAN GARDENS
Manteo   473-3234

Located in Manteo off Main Highway (Route 64) on the north end of Roanoke Island, the Elizabethan Gardens are open all year from 9 AM to dusk. However, the gardens are closed Saturday and Sunday during December, January and February. They are adjacent to Ft. Raleigh and the Waterside Theatre, where "The Lost Colony" is performed. When "The Lost Colony" is playing during the summer months, the gardens are open later; however, all guests are asked to leave by 8 PM so that the grounds may be cleared. There is a small admission ($2.50 per adult). Children younger than 12 are admitted free if accompanied by an adult (non-applicable to groups). Group rates are available upon request. Annual passes are $5 each, allowing unlimited visits (a nice bargain and a chance to support the beautiful work accomplished here).

These magnificent gardens, created by the Garden Club of North

Carolina, Inc. in 1951, are a most delightful environment at any time of year. Visitors enter at the Great Gate into formal gardens containing trees, flowers and statuary amidst curving walkways of brick and sand. Horticulturists, nature lovers, history buffs and culturalists will find these classical gardens a sensual escape from the anxiety of 20th-century living.

There is a great deal more than meets the casual eye in these gardens. The bricks used throughout are handmade from the Silas Lucas Kiln, in operation during the 1890s in Wilson, North Carolina. The famous Virginia Dare statue located here was conceived after a Native American legend that said Virginia grew up in their midst and became a beautiful woman. The statue was sculpted by Maria Louisa Lander in Italy in 1859, affirming the Graeco-Roman influence of its appearance. Prior to being situated in these gardens, the statue was reportedly lost at sea for some years, recovered, then displayed in the North Carolina State House before being given to Paul Green to take back to Roanoke Island. (Paul Green wrote the historical drama, *The Lost Colony*, previewed later in this section.)

Spring in the gardens is breathtaking. Azalea, dogwood, pansies, wisteria and tulips are in full bloom. During May, rhododendron, roses, lacecap and hydrangea appear. Summer brings fragrant gardenias, colorful annuals and perennials, magnolia, crepe myrtle, Oriental lilies and herbs. Autumn begins its show with chrysanthemums and the changing colors of trees. Camellias

bloom from late fall through the winter. Many brides and grooms have chosen this lovely setting for their weddings.

Herbs, bedding plants, vines, ivy and other plants are for sale in the gift shop.

A visit to the gardens is a time for quiet reflection and appreciation of nature. A small plaque at the entry notes that the gardens are a living memorial to the English colonists who came here in the 1500s — cause for reflection in itself.

FORT RALEIGH

Three miles north of Manteo
Off Hwy. 64/264   473-5772

Located on the north end of Roanoke Island (Route 64) in Manteo, the center of history on the Outer Banks begins here. Fort Raleigh was designated as a National Historic Site in 1941. Its 500-acre expanse of woods and beach includes the location of the settlement sites by English colonies of 1585 and 1587, a visitor center, a restored fort and nature trail. The Elizabethan Gardens, the Waterside Theatre and National Park Service Headquarters for the Outer Banks are also located here.

Stop at the Visitor Center where interpretive exhibits in the small museum and a 17-minute video will introduce you to this historic place.

There is a 400-year-old Elizabethan Room from Heronden Hall in Kent, England. The furnishings, carved mantelpiece, paneling, stone fireplace and the blown glass in the leaded windows are interesting to note.

Self-guided tours or tours led by the Park Service are optional. Inter-

pretive exhibits and living history programs are an important part of Fort Raleigh's attraction. The program varies depending on the time of day and year.

The Thomas Hariot Nature Trail is a short self-guided trail with soft pine-needle paths that lead to the sandy shores of Roanoke Sound, near the spot where it is thought that Sir Richard Grenville first stepped ashore on Roanoke Island.

Before you leave the area, drop by the Lost Colony Craft Shop.

The Fort Raleigh National Historic Site is open year round. From mid-June until late August its hours are from 9 AM until 8 PM Monday through Saturday; Sunday from 9 AM until 6 PM; and from September through mid-June the site is open from 9 AM until 5 PM seven days a week; it's closed Christmas Day. There may be shorter hours of operation this year due to budget considerations, so it's best to call ahead for an accurate schedule.

THE LOST COLONY
Near Fort Raleigh   473-3414
Waterside Theatre   (800)488-5012

This historical outdoor drama was the first such work ever produced. Pulitzer Prize-winning author Paul Green brought the history of English colonization to this outdoor theatre in 1937. It is a wonderful experience to learn the story of the Lost Colony, that first English settlement on Roanoke Island, through drama. The choir, costumes and reenactments are exciting and well-performed by the Lost Colony troupe.

The play is presented in two acts. Act I opens with a prologue by the choir and the historian, a sort of narrator who provides for unity in the drama. Subsequent scenes are set in a 1584 Native American village on Roanoke, in England, in the court of Elizabeth, again in Roanoke a year later and on a street in Plymouth, England, as the colonists embark, filled with fear and hope. Act II is set, for the most part, in the

'Cittie of Raleigh' on Roanoke, which was somewhere within 1/4 mile of where the Waterside Theatre now stands, and follows the web of circumstance that led to the final tragedy: the disappearance of the colonists, into . . . legend.

The Waterside Theatre is the semicircular bowl where the play is presented. It's just north of Fort Raleigh; bear to the right as you enter from Route 64 to reach the large parking area. As you walk in you can see the waters of the sound over the backdrop.

For your comfort, here are a couple of noteworthy suggestions: the wooden seats are *not* padded, so bring stadium cushions! Pillows can also be rented at the theatre. It can get chilly in the evenings, when the wind blows off the sound, so bring sweaters even in July and August. Finally, mosquitoes can be vicious, especially when it has rained recently. The woods nearby are sprayed, but this is only partially effective; bring repellent. The theatre is now wheelchair accessible, and the staff is glad to accommodate special customers. If calling ahead for reservations, be sure to note any needs for the handicapped.

With all the creature comforts taken care of, settle back and enjoy a thoroughly professional, well-rehearsed, technically outstanding show. The leads are played by professional actors. Most of the backstage personnel are pros too, and it shows. Supporting actors are often local people, and some island residents pass from part to part as they grow up. The colorful costumes, the choir and the tension inherent in the play itself make it a combination of delights that you won't soon forget.

Now, about the tickets: All shows start at 8:30 PM. The show season runs from mid-June to late August and is presented nightly, except Sunday. Adult tickets are $12, children under 12, $6, active military and senior citizens $10. Accompanied children are admitted half price for Monday night performances. Those over 65 are admitted for $8 on Fridays. Groups of 15 or more can call for a discount.

This is probably the most popular event on the Banks in the summer, and we recommend you make reservations, though you can try your luck at the door if you care to. You can make paid mail reservations by writing The Lost Colony, 1409 Highway 64/264, Manteo, NC 27954; or make phone reservations starting in early June by calling (919) 473-3414 locally and the toll free line, (800) 488-5012 for out-of-area customers. Reservations will be held at the box office for pickup until 7:30 PM.

Insiders' Tips

The beach by the bridge at the north end of Roanoke Island is full of treasures when a wet west wind blows hard.

Photo: N.C. Travel and Tourism

The North Carolina Aquarium on Roanoke Island has many secrets to share.

NORTH CAROLINA AQUARIUM
Airport Road   473-3493

Tucked away northwest of Manteo on Route 64, by Manteo Airport, is a surprising place called the North Carolina Aquarium. It's one place you won't want to miss if you have the slightest interest in the sea, the Banks, or the life that thrives in this unique chain of barrier islands.

The aquarium contains labs used by marine scientists and a reference library on marine-related topics. But these aren't what attract visitors. The display section and aquarium — that's what you'll want to see.

You'll walk among changing displays on such topics as underwater archaeology and marine ecosystems. Children love the shallow observation tank with live marine creatures you can actually touch. The aquarium is beautiful. Set like jewels in a long, darkened corridor, the lighted tanks display sea turtles,

longnosed gar, ugly burrfish and sea robin, lobster and octopi. The aquaria start out with fresh water species, shading through brackish to salt water. The biggest is a new 8,400-gallon shark tank. A special room exhibits information on sharks — kids marvel at the open shark jaws showing rows and rows of pointy teeth. A wetlands exhibit features fresh water turtles and amphibians. Feature films on marine and biological topics are shown, and there are daytime programs for all age groups, including field trips, bird walks through Pea Island, and more. Check at the desk for a current schedule. The aquarium caters to groups of any kind and can even supply meeting facilities in its conference room, seminar room or 240-seat auditorium. You'll also find a great gift shop with marine-related gifts, books and T-shirts.

To reach the aquarium, drive

The Lost Colony Roots
Run Deep on Roanoke Island

By Nancy McWilliams

When The Lost Colony's general manager, Jon Summerton, stated recently that the famous outdoor drama "is and always has been a product of the Outer Banks community," he hit the mark.

While today's theatergoer sees The Lost Colony as a professional symphonic play that runs smoothly with paid performers, elaborate costumes and a splendid outdoor amphitheater, a look at the play's origin brings simpler, much more rustic images to mind.

That Roanoke Islanders would choose to commemorate their special place in history is natural. After all, this tiny island hosted one of history's great moments. This is the spot where English explorers came to in 1584 and the first English settlers tried to tame as their new home in 1587. While the fate of the "lost" colonists remains a mystery, local residents hold dear the unique history of their island, remembering those brave souls who wandered mysteriously into the pages of nearly forgotten history. They've kept that story alive through The Lost Colony, touching millions with its bittersweet tragedy.

Those 117 men, women and children who sailed from Plymouth, England, to Roanoke Island (calling their new home Virginia in honor of Elizabeth, their virgin queen) were worthy of remembrance, for they paved the way for permanent habitation by the English in this "new" continent. Their experiment seems to have miserably failed, yet, the successful ones who followed them, settling farther north, may not have achieved their goals without those other colonists' brave first attempt.

While history books projected Jamestown into star status, they relegated the Roanoke Island settlement into relative obscurity. Feeling that their heritage deserved to be more widely known, the people of Manteo had, as early as 1880, paid tribute to this heritage by organizing programs to recognize Fort Raleigh and the historic happenings here. By the early part of the 20th century, the local folks had begun staging a yearly celebration, featuring a drama that told the colonists' story. Amateur actors reenacted the highlights of history on the north end of the island. August 18 was the date chosen for these community pageants, the birthday of Virginia Dare (the first English child born in the new world).

As social occasions, the annual pageants presented an opportunity to visit with friends and neighbors, as well as pay tribute to the colonists. Most of the audience brought picnics and enjoyed "dinner on the ground."

Billed as "homecoming celebrations in honor of the English settlers," these events attracted thousands. Colorful, elaborate speeches were made

Source: Lost Colony

at the annual celebrations hosted by the Roanoke Colony Memorial Association. In 1926 during Virginia Dare Day, Lt. Governor Lindsay Warren remarked, "You are here today in a state that cherishes its old traditions." How true, and perhaps nowhere in the state were those traditions treasured as much as they were on Roanoke Island.

In 1921, the pageant took a giant step when resident Mabel Evans Jones got the idea that it was worthy of a silent film production, a major accomplishment for such a small town. *The Lost Colony Film* depicts the Manteo folk dressed in colonial costumes. Far from a Hollywood production, the movie was made by the people of Manteo and nearby communities. Bear in mind the year — in 1921 the movie industry was only 10 years old, yet in this isolated corner of the state, citizens with no experience in filmmaking endeavored to produce a film. At that time, the Outer Banks was an isolated, fairly rugged place, accessible only by water. Yet the hardy locals were determined to tell their story on film. Mabel Evans, the superintendent of schools for Dare County, wrote the script and took it to Raleigh, where she obtained $3,000 in funding from the State Historical Commission. A professional crew of three (including a female director from the New York School of Theater) worked with 200 volunteers organized by Evans. Nearly everyone in Manteo was involved in the film in some manner, making costumes, constructing the boat and set and acting. Filmed on the exact location of the original Fort Raleigh, the movie was shown across the state, bringing attention to Manteo.

After this brief brush with stardom, the islanders continued their efforts. Many members of the film cast continued to give live performances and pageants. Records indicate that in 1926, the homecoming attendance was 5,000 and in 1931, 8,000. A three-day celebration in 1934, called the Pageant of Roanoke, took the play a step further along its progression and brought in a professional festival company from Asheville to take charge of the production. Thousands attended these performances, in which, again, most of the actors and technicians were locals. *State* magazine in August 1934, declared "big doings down in Dare County with hundreds of residents and thousands of visitors gathering on Roanoke Island for a full week's celebration . . . "

As the 350th anniversary of the 1587 settlement approached in 1937, locals decided to turn their little pageant drama into a full-fledged symphonic drama and hired professional writer Paul Green to pen a script. The rest, as they say, is history. "To pull a drama of that proportion together during the height of the Depression on a remote island was an amazing feat," said Elizabeth Evans, public relations director for *The Lost Colony*. The play was planned for just one season, but was such a big hit that it continues to this day. "It blossomed," Evans, herself a former Lost Colony dancer, said. "It struck an emotional chord with people." From the start, the play consisted of about 60 percent local talent; as the years went by it came to rely less on island residents and more on professional actors and acting students from outside the area. In many families, *The Lost Colony* was tradition, and locals took a lot of pride in their involvement. Commitment was required; actors had to dedicate their entire summer, six nights a week, to performances. Yet, the tradition and pride continue, even today. Many children from the nearby area are cast in the play, and one local teacher, Robert Midgette, has been playing the role of Chief Manteo for 15 years. Midgette has been in the play for 23 years. Manteo resident Cora Mae Basnight, who portrayed the Indian maid Agona for 25 years, is practically a local legend. And, to this day, each August 18 you'll see local babies cast in the role of Virginia Dare.

It's safe to say that the play we know and love today would not have developed to this point without the efforts of Roanoke Islanders, who faithfully performed their pageant, insisting stubbornly on keeping alive the memory of the colonists. They brought history to life with love and passion by refusing to forget and by giving with all their hearts.

north from Manteo on Route 64. Turn left on Airport Road, following signs to airport; the aquarium will be on your right. It's open from 9 AM to 5 PM, Monday through Saturday and 1 PM to 5 PM on Sunday. Admission is $3 for adults, $2 for senior citizens and active military, $1 for children 6 to 17, and free for children younger than 6. (Aquarium Society members are admitted free.)

WEIRS POINT AND FORT HUGER
N. end of Roanoke Island

Weirs Point, at the northwest corner of the island, where the Route 64/264 bridge arrives from Manns Harbor, is an interesting place to visit. Consisting of empty shoreline as recently as fall of '83, it is now a pretty, easily-accessible public beach. Parking is available at the first turn-off after the bridge.

About 300 yards out (the island has migrated quite a bit in 120 years), in six feet of water, lie the remains of Fort Huger, the largest Confederate fort on the island during the Union invasion of 1862.

A few years later, from a hut on this beach, one of the unsung geniuses of the electrical age began

investigating what was then called "wireless telegraphy." Reginald Fessenden held hundreds of patents on radiotelephony and electronics, but died without credit for many of them.

For most people, swimming and fishing in the sound will take precedence over vanished forts and disappointed inventors. The beach is sandy and shallow, and shoals very gradually, except under the bridge, where currents scour a bit deeper. If you approach in a boat, watch carefully for stumps and old pilings. Picnic benches, a Dare County information kiosk and rest rooms are also available at Weirs.

DARE COUNTY REGIONAL AIRPORT
410 Airport Rd.   *473-2600*
next to the N.C. Aquarium

Dare County (formerly Manteo) is the major airfield serving the Outer Banks and the only one with fuel and services (the others, at Kitty Hawk, Hatteras and Ocracoke are paved strips only). Manteo has two runways, both asphalt-surfaced. Runways 16 to 34 measure 3,290 feet, and runways 4 to 22 measure 3,300 feet, with 500-foot stopways. (Runways 10 through 28 were closed permanently in 1986.) Twenty-four-hour self-service aircraft refueling for 100 LL and autos is available for those with MasterCard or Visa. Jet A and 100 LL fuel is available from a truck during operating hours. Equipment: VOR and DME, NDB, VASI, REILS, Unicom 122.8. Automated Weather Observation System, (AW0S) is provided at a frequency of 128.725 or by phone at 473-2826. Runway lights are activated at night by keying the Unicom frequency three, five or seven times within five seconds.

Dare County is the point of arrival for most of those who come to the Banks by air. You can grab a hot sandwich and drinks from machines, and rest rooms are available. Rental cars are available through **B & R Rent-A-Car**, 473-2600, a local company offering pickup and dropoff service in the terminal at the Airport. They offer compacts, mid and full size cars and vans seating up to 12 people. Call for daily and weekly rates, MC, VISA, AMEX, Disc and Phillips 66 are accepted. Taxi and limousine services are also available.

Dare County Airport is operated by the Dare County Airport Authority. It provides light aircraft rentals, flight instruction, sightseeing tours and charter services out of Dare County. Dare County Airport provides service and minor maintenance from 8 AM until 7 PM all year.

Southeast Airlines, 473-3222, has regularly scheduled flights to and from Norfolk International Airport as well as to and from Raleigh-Durham and other airports on the east coast. They also offer air tours from the airport and touchdown

flight service to Pine Island.

Outer Banks Airways provides daily on-demand charter flights to Norfolk International from Dare County. This company books charters "anywhere." Call 441-7677 for reservations and information.

Kitty Hawk Air Tours provides air tours and aircraft maintenance. Call 473-3014 for additional information.

MOTHER VINEYARD
Manteo

Mother Vineyard Scuppernong, the Original American Wine, is still produced by a company in Petersburg, Virginia. Old-timers in town say the wine once produced in Manteo was far superior, but the Petersburg product did not taste bad when we sampled a couple of bottles. It is a pink wine, quite sweet. If you like white port or Mogen David you will take to scuppernong wine. You can find it in many of the Banks groceries.

All this is a roundabout way of getting to the fact that the oldest known grapevine in the U.S. is in Manteo. That's right: the oldest. You see, when the first settlers arrived here, the Banks were covered with wild grapes. Arthur Barlowe wrote to Sir Walter Raleigh in 1584:

". . . being where we first landed very sandy and low toward the water side, but so full of grapes as the very beating and surge of the sea overflowed them, of which we found such plenty, as well there as in all places else, both on the sand and on the green soil, on the hills as in the plains, as well on every little shrub, as also climbing toward the tops of high cedars, that I think in all the

PROFESSIONAL PROFILE

MARY ELLEN RIDDLE

Mary Ellen Riddle specializes in black-and-white photography; her work has received regional and local recognition. While she shoots a wide variety of subjects, her primary interest lies in social challenge. Mary Ellen has been honored by North Carolina's former Governor James Martin, the North Carolina Women's Press Club and the National Women's Press Club for her radio public-affairs programs on social and environmental issues. As a Dare County Arts Council board member, she is working to establish a middle-school program on the "Creative Process." Mary Ellen is the feature writer for *The Sportfishing Report* and covers marine life, sea captains and the environment in which they thrive. A Roanoke Island resident, Ms. Riddle says there is no place she would rather live and raise her children Chris, 11, and Zoe, 3. The beautiful environment, peaceful community, and fabulous "old-time" Pioneer movie theater make Dare County home.

world the like abundance is not to be found."

The Mother Vine is one of those ancient grapevines, so old that it may have been planted even before whites arrived in the New World. Certainly it was already old in the 1750s, as records attest, and scuppernong grape vines do not grow swiftly. Another story is that this vine was transplanted to Roanoke Island by some among the Fort Raleigh settlers. Whichever story is true, whoever planted the Mother Vine, it is ancient — most likely more than 400 years old, and it's still producing fine fat, tasty grapes. In fact, for many years a small winery, owned by the Etheridge family, cultivated the vine on Baum's Point, making the original Mother Vineyard wine until the late '50s.

Despite its history, the Mother Vine doesn't offer much to the eye, nor is it easy to find. To try, drive north out of Manteo on Route 64. About 3/4 mile past the city limits, turn right on Mother Vineyard Road. Go about ½ mile, to where the road makes a sharp turn to the right at the sound. The patient old vine crouches beneath a canopy of leaves, twisted and gnarled, ancient and enduring, about 300 feet on the left past the turn. It's private property — so please stay on the road.

DARE COUNTY LIBRARY
Manteo 473-2372

Sometimes there's nothing for it but to curl up with a good book. From a location on Highway 64, about ½ mile north of downtown Manteo, Librarian Melinda Creef runs a 40,000-volume library with recordings, video tapes, slides, books-on-tape, meeting facilities and a local history room that's invaluable for probing deeply into the lore of the Banks. Hours are: Monday, 8:30 AM to 7 PM; Tuesday through Friday, 8:30 AM to 5:30 PM; Saturday, 10 AM to 4 PM; closed Sunday. See the Service Directory for Kill Devil Hills and Hatteras branch information.

DARE COUNTY TOURIST BUREAU
Hwy. 64 473-2138
Manteo (800)446-6262

Do you have a question? The Dare County Tourist Bureau is set up to help, with a large collection of brochures, maps and the latest data on hand available to the visitor. The summer of '94 will find the Tourist Bureau housed in larger, newer surroundings, but still on Highway 64. This site (formerly Nations Bank) offers lots more space, ample parking and handicapped accessibility. Drive-up service is even a possibility ... what a great idea! It's open year round Monday through Friday, 8:30 AM to 5 PM, and Saturdays and holidays, as well during the summer season, 10 AM to 3 PM.

For specific information and a free detailed Vacation Guide, write to Dare County Tourist Bureau, P.O. Box 399, Manteo, NC 27954.

THE ISLAND GALLERY AND CHRISTMAS SHOP
Manteo 473-2838

There is only one word for the Christmas Shop and Island Gallery: fascinating. From hundreds of miles away people travel to the Banks for the (nearly) sole purpose of visiting Edward Greene's burgeoning world of fantasy, which opened its doors on June 1, 1967.

Basically, you might say that this establishment is a store ... because things are sold here. There, all resemblance to conventional stores ends. There are seven rambling, multilevel buildings in the shop, but there's not a single counter, display rack, or glass case. Instead there are rooms, room after room, furnished with antique furniture (not for sale), and each is filled with wonder.

"We stock a minimum of about 50,000 different items, from 200 companies, 150 artists and craftspeople and 35 countries," says Greene, formerly an actor in New York City. "And there isn't a thing in the building anybody *needs* to have. So we have to let each product tell us

We Know All About Keeping In Touch.

We go out of our way to make sure our customers keep in touch with their business, family and friends by providing quality cellular service. No matter where you travel, count on United States Cellular to keep in touch.

UNITED STATES
CELLULAR
MOBILE TELEPHONE NETWORK®

Suite N-7 Outer Banks Mall, Nags Head, NC 27959 (919) 441-3377

Take Home Som

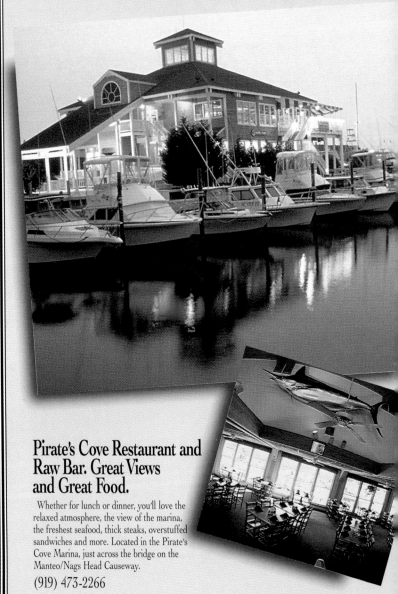

Pirate's Cove Restaurant and Raw Bar. Great Views and Great Food.

Whether for lunch or dinner, you'll love the relaxed atmosphere, the view of the marina, the freshest seafood, thick steaks, overstuffed sandwiches and more. Located in the Pirate's Cove Marina, just across the bridge on the Manteo/Nags Head Causeway.

(919) 473-2266

sland Memories

Thrill to the excitement of deep sea fishing. The crew does all the work, you just catch the fish and have fun. If you can't go fishing, join us on the dock at 4:30pm as the boats deliver their catch. It is a sight to see. If you miss a visit to the Ship's Store, you have missed a chance to view the nicest line of sportswear along with gifts and jewelry unequaled anywhere in the area. Reservations required for Charters. Call **(919) 473-3906** or **1-800-367-4728.** MasterCard and Visa accepted.

ate's Cove Marina and Yacht Club. arter Boats and Ship's Store

(919) 473-1451
1-800-762-0245
Located on Roanoke Island
Manteo/Nags Head Causeway
Pirate's Cove

ijoy Our Summer Sunset Festivals.

n us on the docks for great parties during the fishing tournaments.
every Wednesday night from June 15–August 31 (except August 17),
e's the food, fun, arts, music, and more of our Summer Sunset
ivals from 4pm–8pm. It's fun for the whole family.
you at the Docks.

Dockominiums • Priced from the $50's to the $500's.

how it wants to be displayed."

The result is mind-boggling . . . like a child's dream of everything you ever wanted in the world gathered in one place and displayed artfully. Whole walls are filled with toys, pottery and handcrafts. Some rooms feature nothing but porcelain eggs; others are filled with baskets, carvings, miniatures, handmade jewelry, ornaments, seashells, candles and Christmas cards. One hundred and twenty-five switches light innumerable atmosphere lights that give everything a magic glow. Imagine, added to all this, scores of decorated Christmas trees. There is even a year-round Halloween room, possibly a first, according to Greene. You'll have to see it before you realize what a fantastic place this is. Bring plenty of money or your credit cards, because, believe us, you won't be able to resist purchases. You'll also find an old-fashioned candy store, a card and stationery shop, a basket shop, suncatchers and fun things for kids.

You'll find a delightful collection of art in the Island Gallery, featuring the work of 100 artists. Stroll through the rooms, and enjoy these fine seascapes and Outer Banks scenes.

The Shop and Gallery is located about ½ a mile south of Manteo, on the sea (east) side of Route 64/264. Hours are: Memorial Day through mid-October, daily 9:30 AM to 9:30 PM, Sunday 9:30 AM to 6:00 PM; mid-October through mid-June, 9:30 AM to 6:00 PM, Sunday 9:30 AM to 5:30 PM. It's closed Christmas Day.

THE WEEPING RADISH BREWERY

Manteo   *473-1157*

Did you know that the first beer brewed in America was right here on Roanoke Island? It's true. History tells us that when Lane's exploratory colony was here in 1585, they made a batch — to befriend the Native Americans or maybe to keep their nerves calm while waiting for the next encounter with the new world they had come upon. In any event, Roanoke Island again is the home of its own brewery at the Weeping Radish. A brewmaster makes both light and dark lager beers to be sipped on-site at the restaurant of the same name. But five-liter minikegs and one-liter refillable bottles are sold to take home. New this year are 22-ounce bottles of Weeping Radish beer (check out the artistic labels of local landmarks) available for sale at area retailers. You can take it with you!

Curious beer lovers can actually see the brew being made — there are daily tours — and, afterwards, sit and have a mug or two. We found it to be especially tasty — richer than the six-pack variety.

Annual SpringFest (Easter weekend) and OktoberFest (Labor Day weekend) events are held at the Weeping Radish, complete with oompah bands and German folk dancers. Check the Annual Events chapter for a schedule of events.

Locals find this a favorite evening spot in the off season, when the draw — other than, of course, the beer — is seeing friends and savoring a Weeping Radish hamburger (delicious) or other special pub menu items. Visitors will feel at home, too, if they happen upon it on a chilly autumn night.

ANDREW CARTWRIGHT PARK
Manteo

This small state park commemorates the Outer Banks' African American community. Born in northeastern North Carolina in 1835, Andrew Cartwright devoted his life to spreading the Gospel among his brethren. After organizing 12 A.M.E. Zion churches on or near Roanoke Island after the Civil War, he founded the first Zion Church in Liberia and worked on in Africa until his death in 1903. Plaques recount the history of the Freedman's Colony on Roanoke Island, the Pea Island Crew and the African Methodist Episcopal Zion Church. To reach it, turn west off Highway 64 at Sir Walter Raleigh Street and go 3/10 mile. The park is on the right.

WANCHESE AND MILL LANDING
Wanchese

Don't look for downtown Wanchese — you won't find it anywhere. This quintessential small town is miles of winding country roads, lined with white-clapboard 1920s-style homes, each with a boat in either the front or the back yard. Girls riding bareback on horses clop along the roads, and the people (almost all year-round residents — Wanchese is no summer community) are North Carolina at its best, honest, hard working and friendly. Small shops selling shells, curio and handicrafts are open in the summer, and if you're after sand-cast pewter, decoy carvings, patchwork tablecloths, rusty old trawler anchors or handmade shell goods, you can easily spend a day just wandering, looking and buying.

At the very end of Route 345 (Mill Landing Road), you'll find one of the most picturesque, and also most overlooked, parts of the entire Outer Banks — Mill Landing. Painters, photographers, those who love the sea and just plain tourists shouldn't miss it.

Mill Landing is a ¼ mile of crowded soundfront that is home port for a small but highly productive fleet of oceangoing fishing trawlers. These sea-battered ships spend most of their lives off Cape May and Hatteras, 50 miles out at sea, bringing in the seafood that appears in a day or two in restaurants all along the East Coast. Mill Landing is fish companies: Wanchese Fish Co., Etheridge's, Jaws Seafood, Quality Seafood, Moon Tillett's and King Crab Seafood. In the middle of it all, perched above the booms and nets, is the Fisherman's Wharf Restaurant. Mill Landing is hardly a touristy place, but it has its appeal. It's a real work-intensive fishing village, and if you want to lay in a stock of fresh fish, shrimp or scallops, stop at the Wanchese Fish Co., or Etheridge's Retail. Fisherman's Wharf is the tall wooden building with the stairway. Just past it is a free boat ramp, and beyond that, if you like to sketch or photograph half-sunken trawlers and minesweepers, you're in for a treat.

Out beyond the inlet, you'll see the concrete bulkhead built by the State of North Carolina as part of their effort to develop the fishing industry. It was designed to bring the really big companies in to pack fish right here in Wanchese. The

Photo: N.C. Travel and Tourism

The Elizabeth II is the only traveling historic site in the state.

current difficulty is the shoaling that Oregon Inlet (under the bridge to Hatteras Island) is experiencing; several trawlers have gone aground there, and many are avoiding it by using other, less convenient, means of getting to the open sea. Large-scale dredging is necessary, and even this might not work. It has the local trawler operators worried (see Oregon Inlet). Meanwhile, though, the visitor can enjoy the photo and painting opportunities. Wanchese Marina, 473-3247, hosts trawlers and drop-netters with fuel and a small, homey store.

On the east side of Wanchese Harbor, things get less picturesque and more productive. Here the Wanchese Seafood Industrial Park hosts the Marine Maintenance Center, Coastal Engine and Propeller, Harbor Welding, Wanchese Trawl and Supply, TopFin Inc., Bimini Marine and the state Department of Marine Fisheries oyster cultch planting operation. Owned by the State of North Carolina, the park leases property for use of seafood or marine-related industries. Rodney Perry, director, says visitors are welcome to watch boats being hauled. Call Perry at 473-5867 for information. The park is the site of the annual Wanchese Seafood Festival, held the last Saturday in June.

Residents of Wanchese generally welcome visitors, but there are a few common-sense things to keep in mind. The trawlers are working boats, and the fishermen are not enthusiastic about having uninvited visitors aboard. The fish processors and boatyards are also industrial enterprises, presenting special hazards to the unwary, so don't go bumbling around; sketch and photograph as much as you like, but please don't interfere with work.

PIRATE'S COVE

Manteo-Nags Head Causeway   473-1451
Sales (800)762-0245

MARINA

473-3906
Ship's Store   (800)367-4728

There have been a lot of changes recently at Pirate's Cove, and more are on the way. The marina now has 119 wet slips for 25-foot outboards to 75-foot yachts, with plans for 200 in total. A quickly-growing number of charter boats run Gulf Stream fishing trips out of here to where the big ones roam; full day trips cost about $800 for six people paying cash ($850 to charge), half day in the inlet and sound, $275 cash or $285 credit. There is also a half day, intermediate trip, 10 to 15 miles off the beach for king mackerel and blues at a cost of $375 cash or $387.50 credit. These are live bait trips. Other types of charters, both inshore and sound, can be arranged individually at this full-service marina. Allen Foreman's perennially popular head boat, *Crystal Dawn*, operates out of here. Allen now books cruises from his office at the Ships Store, or you can call, 473-5577. June through August he runs two trips a day at a cost of $25 per adult and $20 per child. Plus he offers all-day bottom fishing on his boat *Country Girl* for a cost of $60 per person. You can also experience an enjoyable evening cruise, six days a week for $6 per adult and $3 per child (age 10 and younger). He takes a break on Sundays. During the off season he runs one trip a day and one cruise.

For those who want to learn more about fishing, Pirate's Cove offers a fishing school each March and October. Pirate's Cove now offers the area's only handicapped-accessible charter boat. Captain Bob Sumners has specially rigged his boat *For Play'n* so that the handicapped can enjoy a fishing trip too.

The marina has a Ships Store that's a must for shopping for active sportswear, T-shirts, marina supplies and groceries. The 11th year for the growing Annual Billfish Tournament, run here in mid-August, is 1994. Other fishing tournaments are set for kids, small boats, etc. from June through November. Check the Annual Events chapter for a schedule of events. You can also write: P.O. Box 1879, Manteo, NC 27954. Pirate's Cove Restaurant and Raw Bar serves fresh seafood and great steamers and is located on the second floor above the Ships Store.

Perhaps the biggest news is Pirate's Cove's growing, residential-marina-resort community. Of the 600-odd acres on the north side of the causeway, 500 are being left as untouched marsh preserves, and the remaining 100 acres are being turned into 627 residential units over the next five years — single-family, townhomes and condominiums. All have deep-water dockage. A clubhouse, pool, tennis courts and boardwalk surrounding the entire community are amenities that make this an attractive place.

Watch for summer sunset festivals held Wednesday afternoons (4 PM to 8 PM) from mid-June to the end of August. Crafts, food, live bands, Lost Colony actors, pirates, puppets and free beer make these lively afternoons on the waterside

Photo: Mary Ellen Riddle

Several festivals are held throughout the year on the Manteo waterfront.

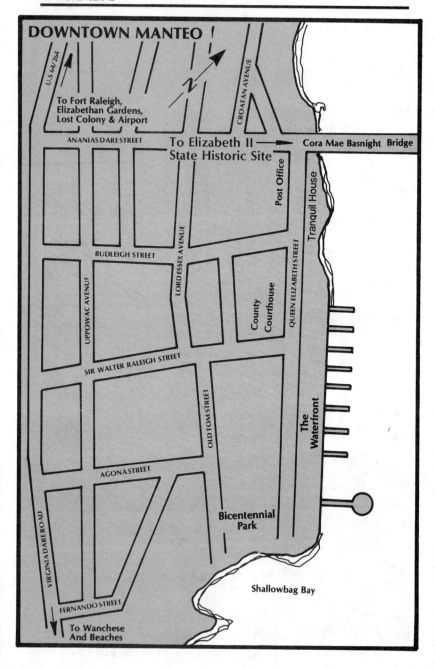

DOWNTOWN MANTEO

U.S. 64/264

To Fort Raleigh,
Elizabethan Gardens,
Lost Colony & Airport

ANANIAS DARE STREET

To Elizabeth II →
State Historic Site

CROATAN AVENUE

Cora Mae Basnight Bridge

Post Office

Tranquil House

BUDLEIGH STREET

LORD ESSEX AVENUE

UPPOWAC AVENUE

County
Courthouse

QUEEN ELIZABETH STREET

SIR WALTER RALEIGH STREET

OLD TOM STREET

The Waterfront

AGONA STREET

VIRGINIA DARE ROAD

Bicentennial
Park

FERNANDO STREET

Shallowbag Bay

To Wanchese
And Beaches

lots of fun. Donations go to a local cancer support group.

Downtown Manteo

Despite its indirect "Cittie of Ralegh" antecedents, Manteo, as a town, is not all that old. There were only a few houses on Shallowbag Bay, on the eastern coast of the island, when Dare County was formed in 1870 and the town designated as the county seat. (Manteo was one of the two Roanoke Native Americans who accompanied the explorers back to England after the first expedition.) Today, though, after more than a century of slow growth, Manteo is a year-round, comfortable, diversified community with the feel of small-town America that has been lost in so many communities.

The downtown area, fronting directly on the bay, has undergone intensive redevelopment in the last few years. The Waterfront, provides a combination of residential and commercial development including the Tranquil House, built after the style of an inn of the same name that stood nearby early in the century. Specialty shops, residential condominiums and several good restaurants are also located within the three-story, courtyard of the Waterfront. The breezeways, water views and exceptional landscaping that surround this area provide a relaxing, cool alternative to the busier shopping available in the beach area. More information on The Tranquil House and its new restaurant, 1587 can be found in the Accommodations and Restaurants chapters. There are also 53 modern docks

with 110 and 220 hookups and a comfort station for boaters with rest rooms, showers, washers and dryers.

Across the street from the Waterfront, in the center of the downtown area, are other shops well worth your visit. Establishments such as Wanchese Pottery on Fernando Street, across the street from the waterfront, and Manteo Furniture, the Green Dolphin Pub, Manteo Booksellers, Accent on Flowers, the Duchess of Dare Restaurant, the Pioneer Theatre, the Pig & Phoenix Cafe and Gift Shop and almost 40 other small-to-medium-sized businesses and offices are packed into a four-square-block area, just like the center of every small town used to be before Henry Ford came up with his infernal carriage. (There's plenty of parking across the street from Manteo Booksellers.) Watch the time limits for curb-side parking during the season, you will be ticketed!

There's more to do here than shop and eat. Around the southeast point of the waterfront stands the town's American Bicentennial Park. Read the inscription under the cross . . . and shudder at its relevance today. There are picnic benches and comfortable places nearby for you to sit and enjoy the view.

Turning north, you will find the docking of the waterfront a pleasant place to stroll, sit on weathered benches and take pictures. The 400th anniversary of the Roanoke Voyages brought the *Elizabeth II* to her mooring across Dough's Creek; more about her in a moment. A bit farther north is the municipal parking lot, a public boat ramp and the Manteo Post Office.

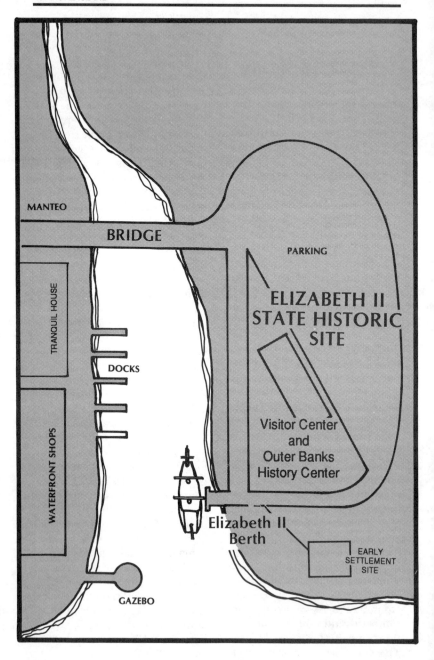

MANTEO

BRIDGE

PARKING

TRANQUIL HOUSE

ELIZABETH II
STATE HISTORIC
SITE

DOCKS

WATERFRONT SHOPS

Visitor Center
and
Outer Banks
History Center

Elizabeth II
Berth

EARLY
SETTLEMENT
SITE

GAZEBO

Many visitors find that a walk or bike ride around town is relaxing and provides a chance to see some of the nice, older homes and talk with the locals. Complimentary bikes are provided for guests of the Tranquil House Inn.

The relaxed, small-town atmosphere typical of Manteo in the years we have known it picked up during Dare County's four-year-long commemoration of the Roanoke voyages. During these celebration years, visitors to the island found a lot of new construction and a lot of things to do, and the pace never really has slowed down since. Several downtown streets were resurfaced with river rock. A boat construction facility was built at the end of Sir Walter Street, and the *Elizabeth II*, a full-size reproduction of a 16th-century English sailing ship, was launched there in 1983; it is moored at The Elizabeth II State Historic Site (see "Elizabeth II"). Be sure and head across the bridge and take in the Visitor's Center, History Center and beach there. The latest project is a new $4.5 million sewage treatment plant that will remove the unsightly old tank from the waterfront.

If, as most visitors do, you reach the Banks via Route 158, you can find Manteo by continuing south until you reach Whalebone Junction. Turn right there on Route 64/264. Be alert for a revision of the traffic patterns at the junction. They're widening 64/264 on the causeway to five lanes to include a turn lane. And they're constructing a new bridge next to the Melvin Daniel's Bridge, (or the "Little Bridge"). The new span will allow two lanes of traffic to travel in each direction. These two improvements together should help significantly reduce the bottleneck that used to occur along the causeway. Continue across the high rise bridge and the newly widened road past Pirate's Cove, and bear right at the Y. Then, turn right at either of the town's first two stoplights to go downtown.

We think you'll like Manteo and make friends there. We certainly have, and now that we've improved our access, there's no reason not to check out this town that's unlike any other located on the beach!

THE WATERFRONT
Manteo Docks   473-2188

The Waterfront is a 34-unit condominium and marketplace at the head of downtown Manteo overlooking Shallowbag Bay. The four-story architectural style is Old World, and its scale complements the small-town feel of Manteo. With its festive shops that open onto a breezy courtyard, it is one of the cornerstones of the revitalized downtown area. The first level of the development is reserved for private parking. Level two contains some 20,000 square feet of retail space. The third and fourth levels are entirely residential. Residents get to keep their "yachts" at the backdoor docks on the Manteo harbor. A ship's store, shower facilities and washer and dryers are available for boaters' use. The north and south channels and Shallowbag Bay were dredged in 1989.

Visitors can enjoy the public areas of The Waterfront, which include a dockside walkway, two restaurants and a variety of shops, in-

Tips from Outer Banks Teens

•Go to Hatteras for nice surfing waves.

•The Soundside Market Place has great video games.

•The sound is a great place to swim because there are no rough waves or strong currents.

•We have a lot of storms, like nor'easters, on the Outer Banks.

•Go to Joe Dowdy's for fun games and rides, but beware of the prices.

•Fresh steamed crabs are great to eat.

•Go to the North Carolina Aquarium to see all kinds of fish.

•Nags Head Dairy Queen has great ice cream and lots of video games.

•Daredevils can leap into bungee jumping at Rodanthe.

•Charter boats are a big attraction — not only can you fish, but you can see all kinds of mammals like whales and porpoises.

•A great place to jetski is Willetts Wetsports on the beach in Nags Head.

•A great thing to do on a calm summer day is to sit in the backwash at the sound and try to catch minnows.

•If you're visiting the Outer Banks in June, be sure to go to the Seafood Festival in Wanchese.

•Parents can take their children to the Dare Days festival in downtown Manteo; it's held the first Saturday in June.

Special thanks to the 1993-94 Manteo Middle School
Creativity Class: Jermaine Bell, Carolia Hollis, Steven Ruhle,
Michael Brodie, Raymond V. Thomas, Jr., Jessica Meekins,
Jessica Sadler, Andy Hatzigeorgiou, Charlie Midgett
and Adrian Hoy.

TEENS!

What's Up?

It's Smooth
It's Bad
It's Cool
It's Hot

What you'll find if you **DON'T** come to the beach

What you'll find if you **DO**

For a good time that you won't forget, **come to the Outer Banks**

cluding a discount clothing store for women, a fashionable woman's boutique, a hair salon, gift shops, a unique candle store and a jewelry store. (See the Roanoke Island shopping section for more details.)

THE ELIZABETH II

Elizabeth II   473-1144
State Historic Site

The centerpiece of the quadricentennial, moored in the harbor of downtown Manteo, is one of the most characteristic artifacts of English pre-industrial civilization — a wooden sailing ship. This year marks its 10th anniversary.

And a beautiful sight she is. Unexpectedly colorful in bright blue, red and yellow, with a hull of nut-brown gradually-weathering wood, she lifts her foremast, mainmast and lateen mizzen sharply toward the sky. Her rigging is a hempen web of tackle, so complex as to confuse the eye. Her high-sided hull and sloped stern and foredeck lend her the awkward grace of a newly hatched duckling.

Elizabeth II's story properly begins in 1584, when Thomas Cavendish mortgaged his estates to build the *Elizabeth* for the second expedition to Roanoke Island. With six other vessels, she took the first colonizing expedition to the New World. Four hundred years later, galvanized by the approaching quadricentennial of that faraway beginning, private and governmental entities in North Carolina began planning for an ambitious commemorative project: an authentic reproduction of an Elizabethan ship, a living and sailing link to the past.

After thorough research of available plans and histories, the American Quadricentennial Corporation, the organization funding and directing the construction, concluded that there wasn't enough information today to faithfully reconstruct one of Sir Walter's original vessels. But there was, fortunately, some data available for one of the ships in Sir Richard Grenville's 1585 expedition. With this as a guide, William Avery Baker and Stanley Potter, probably America's foremost experts on Elizabethan-era sailing ships, designed the *Elizabeth II*.

The construction contract was let in 1982 to O. Lie-Nielsen, a shipbuilder in Rockland, Maine, and construction began at a for-the-purpose boatyard on the Manteo waterfront. The completed 50-foot, twin-decked ship — all 70 feet of her — slid smoothly down hand-greased ways into Manteo Harbor in late 1983. She is as authentic as love and research could make her. Built largely by hand, her frames, keel, planking and decks are fastened with 7,000 trunnels (pegs) of locust wood. Every baulk and spar, every block and lift, are as close as achievable to the original, with only two exceptions: a wider upper-deck hatch, for easier visitor access, and a vertical hatch in the afterdeck to make steering easier for the helmsman.

In July 1984, the official opening of the quadricentennial, *Elizabeth II* was turned over to the state of North Carolina for berthing and display at a brand-new visitor's center and dock, across a bridge east of downtown Manteo. She leaves the island in spring and fall for trips to nearby towns, making her the only traveling historic site in the state.

To reach the ship, you can park in downtown Manteo and walk across, or drive over the arched bridge and park on the island (on the whole, we recommend the latter). Once there, you'll find the visitor's center and the Outer Banks History Center. The center is built after the style of the classic old Nags Head cottages, with cedar shake roofing and wide porches. Inside, you'll find an exhibit area, a gift shop, auditorium and rest rooms. Behind the center a raked path leads to the ship and to another summer event, the Early Settlement Site. *Elizabeth II* is to the right, and the settlement to the left. The site is an eternally frozen August 17, 1585, with soldier's tents, a general's tent and living history demonstrations of woodworking, ninepins and cooking.

Admission is $3 for adults; $2 for senior citizens; $1.50 for students; free for children under 6. Groups of 10 or more receive 50 cents off the admission price. The price of admission includes the 20-minute presentation, which is held every 30 minutes in the auditorium, a tour of the ship and the settlement site. Costumed sailors and soldiers explain how the ships of Elizabethan England were built and sailed (explanations are given in Elizabethan dialect). Hours of operation are: November 1 through March 31, 10 AM to 4 PM Tuesday through Sunday; closed Mondays. April 1 through Oct. 31, 10 AM to 6 PM daily. (The costume presentation is Tuesday through Saturday in the summer only, from early June through August.) Note: the last tickets are sold at 3 PM from November 1 through March 31 and at 5 PM from April 1 through October 31, to allow time for a complete tour.

OUTER BANKS HISTORY CENTER
Ice Plant Island   473-2655

As you cross the bridge onto Ice Plant Island from the Manteo Waterfront, the Outer Banks History Center is located in the building on the right. Adjoining it is the Elizabeth II Visitor Center. There is plenty of parking for a day of exploring history. You'll find here 25,000 books, 4,500 official documents of the U.S. Coast Guard and the U.S. Life Saving Service, more than 3,000 photographs, 1,000 periodicals, 700 maps and audio and video recordings. Special collections include the David Stick Papers, the Frank Stick Collection, the Cape Hatteras National Seashore Library, the Cape Lookout National Seashore Oral History Collection, the Aycock Brown Tourist Bureau Collection (17,000 photographs) and numerous other collections.

The Outer Banks History Center opened in 1988. Natives of the state can take time to explore a bit of their own history here. Visitors might find traces of their ancestors and other interesting facts. The collection of North Carolina history found here is second only to that located at the University of North Carolina in Chapel Hill. The History Center, a repository of writings, maps, photographs, books and pamphlets, houses the enormous collection of well-known author David Stick. Due in large part to his dedication and

Photo: N.C. Travel and Toursim

TheTranquil House Inn on the Manteo Waterfront is a favorite
place to stay for many visitors.

hard work, the History Center became a reality and is now seen as an important facility for the area.

Stick, local historian and author of many books on the Outer Banks, collected these works during his years of research and writing. Untold hours were spent categorizing and cataloguing this collection. He continues to write narratives to assist others in finding documents, which makes the collection one of the most extensive and accurately detailed found anywhere. After some inquiries about what he planned to do with his papers, maps and documents, Stick saw the importance of keeping all of them in one place rather than dispatching parts to the various repositories requesting them.

In 1984 he began working with the North Carolina Division of Archives and History to establish a private library. He requested two conditions for his sizeable collection: one was that the library be maintained as a research facility. The other was that it have proper security. When assured of these things, Stick worked with others to obtain the necessary funding for the facility. Although many people supported the David Stick Library as a name for the facility, he preferred it to be known as the Outer Banks History Center. He credits strong interest and support from many, including local resident and television actor Andy Griffith and State Senator Marc Basnight, for the project's realization.

The staff at the center is very knowledgeable of the material and its whereabouts and have proven most helpful in a variety of research undertaken there. They are happy to be of assistance to those using the facility. The research library entices journalists, history professors, students, poets, painters, photographers, musicians, novelists, genealogists, real-estate dealers, archaeologists, relic hunters, sociologists and politicians. There is also an exhibit gallery where History Center holdings and visiting exhibits are displayed. Among the primary exhibits has been the artwork of Frank Stick, David's father.

The Frank Stick Collection consists of more than 325 paintings of fish and wildlife and lends an important dimension to the written documents of Outer Banks and North Carolina history. The art exhibits change from time to time. Historical flats, documentary pieces and other interesting works are displayed. The reading room is open 9 AM until 5 PM Monday through Friday and 10 AM until 3 PM Saturday all year. Gallery hours are 10 AM to 4 PM Monday through Friday and 10 AM to 3 PM on Saturday all year.

Recreation

Fishing Charters

Half-day and all day trips are available for fishing and for scenic cruises. Take your pick: trolling for blues, Spanish mackerel, king mackerel, speckled trout, red fish, or bottom fishing for flounder, spot and trout. Also, offshore fishing for tuna, dolphin, blue marlin, sail fish and more is available.

Reservations for offshore and inshore charters can be made by calling the **Pirate's Cove Booking Desk**, 473-3906 or (800)367-4728. For headboat information, call Allen Foreman at 473-5577. MC and VISA are accepted at Pirate's Cove. There are lots of charters and captains available at Pirate's Cove but be sure to inquire early for reservations.

Rick Caton, captain of the *Sow Trout* and owner of **Custom Sound Charters**, 473-1209 at home or 473-8432 on his boat, will be offering six unique package charters for visitors who want to fish, shrimp, crab and explore the waters around Oregon Inlet and the Albemarle Sound. The *Sow Trout* is a bright yellow—and we mean *bright* yellow — 42-foot workboat that has been well maintained. Charter packages include evening shark trips, inlet trips, light tackle tarpon trips, birdwatching trips and trips to the towers offshore for sea bass, king mackeral and amberjack. Rick also offers a trip for those of you who want to live a day in the life of a waterman, which includes pulling shrimp nets in the Albemarle Sound, pulling crab pots and exploring the sandy islands around Oregon Inlet. This half-day trip costs $300, maximum six people, and you get to keep your entire catch. Something new this year is a twilight champagne cruise, for those with romantic, rather than fishing, interests. No credit cards are accepted. For a free brochure, write: Route 1, Box 745 A, Manteo, North Carolina 27954.

Land, Air and Water Sports

BICYCLE PATH
Hwy. 64/264

A first for the Outer Banks is scheduled to be ready for summer use — a bicycle path along the Roanoke Voyages Corridor. The six-foot wide path runs parallel to Highway 64/264 from the Washington Baum Bridge over Roanoke Sound to the William B. Umstead Bridge over Croatan Sound. In most cases, the path will run on the east side of the crepe myrtles and live oaks near Fort Raleigh. This should be a wonderful addition to the island way of life and will make joggers, bicyclists, parents with baby strollers and in-line skaters very happy. Hurray to Senator Marc Basnight for his efforts in bringing this much-needed recreational addition to Roanoke Island.

Adjacent to Manteo Marine on Highway 64, you'll find **Shoreline Recreation**, 473-1231. They sell recreational vehicles, All-Terrain vehicles, motorcycles, go carts, dune buggies, canoes and water scooters. There can't be a better way to explore Dough's Creek or Shallow Bag Bay. **Darwin's Cafe** on the Manteo Waterfront rents canoes. For information call 473-6113.

NAUTICS HALL
HEALTH & FITNESS COMPLEX
U.S. 64   *473-1191*
The Elizabethan Inn

Nautics Hall facilities are open all year long from 6:30 AM to 9 PM, Mondays through Fridays and 9 AM to 9 PM Saturdays and Sundays, for exercise, fitness, aerobics, yoga, swimming, racquetball and weight training by the year, month or day. A friendly, fully qualified and certified staff is there to help you. Facilities include a competition-size indoor, heated pool, an outdoor pool, racquetball court, sun decks, tanning bed, whirlpool, sauna, aerobicycles, a full line of Nautilus equipment, free weights, Stairmaster and dressing/shower/locker rooms.

You can work out solo or participate in a variety or classes such as low-impact aerobics, step aerobics, water aerobics, dance and yoga. You can even sign up for full body or neck massage therapy. Call for special class times and nursery hours.

ALBEMARLE AVIATION

Dare County Airport　　　　441-1503

For those looking for a thrill, acrobatic flights are now offered at the Dare County Airport in a 1943 Stearman airplane. You and the pilot fly in an open cockpit, performing loops, rolls and other stunts. We enjoyed this type of flight twice last summer, and found it to be an exhilarating way to see the Outer Banks!

Entertainment

PIONEER THEATRE

113 Budleigh St.　　　　473-2216

This is one of the best-kept entertainment secrets on the Outer Banks. The Pioneer Theatre is a bargain for family outings, since adult admission to first-run films here is only $3, and the popcorn, drinks and candy inside will only set you back a buck

or two. But, it's more than affordable entertainment; it's living history. The original theatre, built in 1918, burned. The theatre in use today opened for business in 1934, back when movie admission was 10 cents. The projector that has been in use since 1947 is an open carbon-arc — of real interest to old movie buffs. This is the oldest theater operated continuously by one family in the United States. George Washington Creef was the founder, and today, his grandson, H.A. Creef, can be found at the ticket booth or the popcorn counter. Check it out; you'll find many Manteo locals there happily enjoying "their" movie theatre.

ELIZABETH R LIVE
THEATRE MATINEE

The Pioneer Theatre will be the setting for an excellent one-woman play called *Elizabeth R* each Wednesday afternoon at 2:30 from June 15 to August 24. For $3, theater-goers can see this quality drama about the life of Queen Elizabeth. Presented last summer at Fort Raleigh, the show met with outstanding success, so much so that it outgrew the space there. Barbara Hird, who has played Queen Elizabeth in *The Lost Colony* for nearly 10 years, takes on with great relish, this new role written expressly for her. Audiences love her presentation of a queen alive with emotion. In *Elizabeth R*, we learn accurate history in an entertaining way, laughing, crying and celebrating the life of this remarkable woman. Tickets for the 45-minute performance are available at the Pioneer Theatre or by calling 473-1144. The play's writer, Lebame Houston, calls *Elizabeth R* "the perfect companion to *The Lost Colony.*"

CYPRESS COVE CAMPGROUND

U.S. 64   *473-5231*
Manteo   *MC, VISA, DISC*

An in-town campground, Cypress Cove has conveniently shaded sites bordering the town of Manteo and is located behind Hardee's fast food restaurant. Rates begin at $17 per night for one or two occupants of RV/Campers and $15 per night for one or two in tents. They are also offering furnished camper cabins and mobile home efficiencies. In season rates begin at $35 per night for two people for the cabins and $65 per night for up to six people in the efficiencies. Pets are allowed in the campground provided they are quiet and on a leash. Cypress Cove is family oriented and open year round. See the Camping chapter for additional information.

Shopping

Manteo

Shopping on Roanoke Island runs the gamut from small shopping centers and businesses along Main Highway (Route 64) to a collection of shops on and near the waterfront.

Pirate's Cove Ships Store on the Manteo-Nags Head Causeway, 473-3906, has a nice selection of active sportswear, T-shirts, marina supplies and groceries. They also have impressive 14K gold jewelry.

Island Produce stand on Hwy. 64 offers fresh vegetables and fruits in season.

We covered the **Island Art Gallery and Christmas Shop,** 621 S. US 64, in the section on Attractions — you'll notice the lovely flower beds along Main Highway. There's plenty of parking in lots on both sides of the road. Plan enough time to enjoy the array of fine art and crafts.

Garden Pizzeria, 473-6888, a small eatery known for its mouthwatering, hand-tossed White Pizza, subs and salads, is located on U.S. 64 across the street from McDonald's. You can eat inside or on their front porch, or call for take-out. Locals flock to this spot because of and the super friendly service.

Shoreline Recreation & Wetsports, 473-1231, is located adjacent to Manteo Marine on U.S. 64. They specialize in the sales of sailboats and water skis.

The **Chesley Mall** and **Food-A-Rama** shopping center includes **Davis Clothing Store**, 473-2951, which carries jewelry, shoes and clothing for the whole family. There's a **Revco Drug Store**, 473-5056, to fill your prescription drugs and sundries needs. **Qwik Shot** and **J. Aaron Trotman Photographs**, 473-5598, can provide a fast turnaround on your vacation film; one hour photo processing for 3 1/2 by 5 up to 8 by 10. J. Aaron Trotman Photographs provides photography services for family reunions, weddings, portraits and commercial. The photos can be taken in their studio or a location of your choice — even the beach? Next door, **The Video Store**, 473-3278, rents to visitors and has a huge array of first-rate movies. It also rents VCRs, 220 Nintendo and

Nintendo games. **Susan's Hallmark**, 473-5141, carries a wide variety of party supplies, religious products, candy, bakery items and cards. **Mr. Clean**, a coin-operated laundromat, is also located at the Chesley Mall.

Just up Highway 64/264 **The Card Shed**, 473-3459, a sports fanatic's dream. They have collectible sports cards — football, baseball, basketball, hockey, golf — along with hats with sports logos and pennants. They also carry Marvel cards and have a big selection of those great old comic books you loved as a kid.

Across the street is **Crockett's Seafood Market**, 473-2912, selling right-off-the-boat fresh seafood and all the accompaniments. Adjacent to Crockett's is **The Crab Dock Restaurant**, 473-6845. This establishment features a steam bar," soups and sandwiches and a children's menu. You can enjoy dining on the deck out back overlooking the sound.

Next door is **Judy's Thrift Shop** and **Island Donuts & Bakery**, 473-6166. The bakery was a welcome addition to Roanoke Island this year, and it has become a popular spot to stop by for fresh baked variety breads, bagels, donuts and special order cakes for all occasions. This is operated by the folks at Duck Donut and Bakery.

Island Pharmacy, 473-5801, is located right down from the Chesley Mall. Pharmacist Roy Phillips will be more than happy to fill your prescription needs. They also offer film developing, shipping, UPS and Airborne Express. **Doug Saul's BBQ**, 473-6464, is right behind the pharmacy. Some say the barbecue here is the best on the whole Outer Banks.

Pizza Hut, 473-1945, offers dine-in and carry-out service just a little farther down the road.

At **Burnside Books**, 473-3311, you'll find office and art supplies and a good selection of historical and children's books. A good selection of used hardback and paperback books can be found upstairs.

There's an abundance of clothing and household items at the **Hotline Thrift Shop**, 473-3127, located on U.S. 64, past the Dare County Public Library. This is a fundraising shop for the benefit of the Outer Banks Hotline, a crisis intervention service with a shelter for battered women and their children. The inventory includes good used furniture, toys, books.

Wanchese Pottery, 473-2099, is a small shop opposite the waterfront on Fernando Street, featuring a studio where customers can watch local potter Bonnie Morrill at work. A display explains the stages of pottery-making, and there's a small gallery of finished work. Bonnie's husband, Bob, helps with the trimming and glazing. This shop is well-known locally for its beautiful, useful art — dinnerware, oil lamps, tumblers, lotion dispensers, hummingbird feeders, mirrors, soup mugs, pitchers, and canisters in colors of mauve, sea green and Williamsburg blue. Her most popular design features sea oats and a gull on a creamy background. All of her stoneware is toxic-free and oven and microwave safe. The shop also features handmade baskets and fresh cooking herbs. Summer hours are Monday through Saturday, 10 AM until 5 PM. During the winter, call for hours or to re-

SHOP DOWN

𝕬anchese ℭottery

107 Fernando St.
Manteo, NC 27954

Mon.-Sat.   10 a.m. - 5 p.m.

*Bonnie and
Bob Morrill*

473-2099

quest an appointment. And don't forget to sign the guest register!

Located on Sir Walter Raleigh Street is **Manteo Furniture**, 473-2131, offering a large, in-stock selection of home and cottage furnishings ranging from traditional to contemporary. They have been in operation for nearly 50 years, and you can expect down-home friendly service. You'll need plenty of time to browse through the many rooms of furnishings found in this 48,000-square-foot warehouse/showroom. **Accent on Flowers**, 473-6810, is located in the Evans Building across the street from the Green Dolphin Pub. This is a full-service florist wiring anywhere in the world. They also have beautiful silk and dried arrangements and welcome specialized custom orders.

Our favorite bookstore in the region (we'd even say the world, but we haven't been to *every* bookstore yet,) sits on Sir Walter Raleigh Street. **Manteo Booksellers**, 473-1221, housed in charming quarters, is a must-see for every reader. There are several rooms packed with books covering everything from the literary classics to delightful children's stories. Their short story collection is excellent, as are the historical, self-help, Civil War and Southern fiction areas. Plan on giving yourself a *long* time to browse; there are comfortable chairs for sitting, coffee and cookies on a nearby table, and several literary cats giving the place a comfortable air about it. If you don't know what you want, manager Steve Brumfield or his staff (sister and aunt), will assist you. The bookstore has a busy calendar filled with au-

thor signings and free readings by authors, poets and storytellers. This is definitely worth the trip to Manteo! Next door is a quaint antique shop.

For the perfect gift for yourself or someone else, stop by **My Secret Garden**, by Plantiques, Inc., 473-6880, next door to Manteo Booksellers. The Tiffany-style lamps, silk flowers you'd swear are real, unique garden accessories, Mary Engelbreit cards and gifts and much more will charm you. Those of you from Newport News might recognize owner Jerri Hopkins of Plantiques, Inc., so drop by and say hello.

Across the way are **The Waterfront Shops** that were referred to briefly in the section about Attractions. **Shallowbags, Ltd.,** 473-3078, is a quality women's boutique. Contemporary fine clothing, accessories and gifts are offered, and the attentive help by the staff is professional and appropriate. **Donetta Donetta**, 473-5323, is a full-service beauty salon for men and women situated on the waterfront side of this shopping arcade. They pamper you from head to toe and have a sun tanning bed if you feel you need to augment your summer color.

Island Trading Company, 473-3365, features antiques, original art, greeting cards and finewares. Owners Jack and Marilyn Hughes also own **Island Nautical**, 473-1411, where you'll find an interesting array of gifts and accessories. Ken Kelley and Eileen Alexanian are the owners of a jewelry shop, **Diamonds and Dunes**, 473-1002, and work as a designing couple to produce fine, handcrafted designs. With more than 20 years of experience in the jewelry business, this is a great shop to come to for professional work — everything from setting a stone or sizing a ring to creating a one-of-a-kind keepsake. There's something for everyone here, from Outer Banks-oriented charms to one-of-a-kind custom pieces. Roger and Cheryl Hannant opened **The Candle Factory**, 473-3813, in December of '92. They have 14 years of experience making candles from molds. The candles are art forms created on site. Roger and Cheryl may let you observe this time-consuming process if you're interested — and you *will* be interested! We saw beautifully colored candles molded to look like turtles, frogs, snails and starfish. The starfish were our favorite. Stop by and give them a look. **Darwin's Cafe**, 473-6113, is a favorite small cafe on the waterfront side with a large menu and daily specials worth fighting over they're so good. Menu items include ethnic foods such as hummus and tabouli, salads, homemade soups and deli sandwiches. Wine and beer are served, and the view is wonderful. **Clara's Steam Bar & Seafood Grill**, 473-1727, is also located here, serving wonderfully-prepared lunches and dinners. Clara's continues to be a local favorite, and the view of Shallowbag Bay can't be beat. Both of these restaurants are described in more detail in the Restaurant section.

Look to **Butch's Hotdogs**, 473-3663, for the best dogs on Roanoke Island and to **Poor Richard's**, 473-3333, for a delicious deli sandwich or homemade soup. Both these shops are located on the Manteo waterfront.

On Budleigh Street, you'll find the **Pig and Phoenix Cafe, Soda Fountain and Gift Shop**, 473-2149, located in the old Fearing building, which has been a downtown Manteo institution for more than 60 years. Enjoy lunch or an ice cream treat while you watch the downtown passersby coming and going to the courthouse and other offices on Budleigh. You'll almost feel like you're in Mayberry! Owner Pat Fearing also caters at your place or hers.

Venture out onto U.S. 64 again, and head northeast to Etheridge Road. Turn left on Etheridge Road and visit **The Cloth Barn**, 473-2795, a store packed with everything for sewing — lots of fabrics, motions and patterns.

For travellers heading west from the Outer Banks on Highway 64, Manns Harbor has two nurseries you won't want to miss. **Caimen Gardens**, 473-6343, boasts the largest selection of top quality plants in Dare County. It's one mile from Manns Harbor Bridge on Ina Waterfield Road. Also stop by **Nature's Harmony**, 473-3556. Nature's Harmony, a full-scale nursery, has three greenhouses and specializes in herbs, perennials and wildflowers. It's located three miles from Manns Harbor Bridge on Shipyard Road.

Wanchese

After your trip across Roanoke Sound on the Nags Head-Manteo Causeway Bridge, a left turn at the intersection will take you to the village of Wanchese. Large areas of marshland and tall stands of pine trees create a beautiful scene as you drive along this road. You'll discover **Added Touch**, 473-2972, a craft shop opened 14 years ago by Maxine Daniels, a friendly local resident. Her shop is located in one of the family's residences, therefore Maxine tries to keep the home atmosphere as much as possible. Needlework supplies and hand-knitted and hand-crocheted baby items are featured along with machine-washable children's books. You can also find baskets, seasonal decorations, wall hangings and specialty items, darning net and weaving placemats. "This type of weaving is possibly the oldest form of lacemaking and almost a lost art," says Maxine. She has her shop open 10 AM until 5 PM daily and closed Wednesday and Sunday during most of the year. Maxine closes for a few weeks after Christmas to catch her breath. Then she resumes her normal schedule.

At the end of the road, you'll come to a conglomeration of seafood businesses and a restaurant that we've covered in the section on Roanoke Island Restaurants. After coming this far, it's easy to see that the seafood industry has put Wanchese on the map!

After you've turned around at the end of the road, return to Old Wharf Road and go left for an excursion off the beaten path. **Nick-E**, 473-5036, is a stained glass wonderland, with original creations by Ellinor and Robert Nick. This couple "live their work" here in this shop and studio. They teach classes through the College of the Albemarle and give private instructions as well. They've had people come from as far away as Pennsylvania to learn the art of stained glass. In addition to the fine crafts on display, they sell supplies and tools. They get lots of requests for their hand-painted, customized switch plates. The Nicks are happy to explain the process of their work.

Queen Anne's Lace, 473-5466, is a gift shop of local crafts and art. It is situated on the grounds of Queen Anne's Revenge, noted in the section on Restaurants. The gifts here are displayed in a renovated house that originally sat on Jigsaw Road in Nags Head, near Jockey's Ridge. The Ash Wednesday Storm of 1962 washed it off its pilings and sat in disrepair for years before Wayne Gray had it moved to Wanchese. The shop features pottery and other local crafts. It caters to those who come for dinner and want to browse for a gift or a purchase of unique crafts to take home. It's open from 6 until 9:30 PM during the season.

Inside
Bodie Island

Bodie Island (pronounced "body") begins where the Cape Hatteras National Seashore begins. In early times, livestock roamed freely on Bodie, and there were a number of gun clubs built here in the 1800s, when sportsmen were able to take advantage of the vast marshes and migratory waterfowl. As commercial fishing boats began to come through Oregon Inlet, it became the location of a lighthouse.

Bodie Island is not an island as it was long ago. Storms and shifting sands have closed inlets at a northern area known as Whalebone Junction. This junction occurs where Routes 158 and 64 intersect. Today, Bodie Island is a preserved marshland, a place where birds and wildlife claim a portion of the barrier islands for themselves with a lighthouse of their own.

Attractions

BODIE ISLAND LIGHTHOUSE
AND KEEPER'S QUARTERS
Bodie Island   441-5711
Bodie Island Light, one of the four famous lighthouses of the Outer Banks, is at the end of a road, west of NC 12, about six miles south of Whalebone Junction and opposite Coquina Beach.

Built in 1872, the 150-foot brick structure is identified by its horizontal black and white stripes. It was the only light between Cape Henry, Virginia, and Cape Hatteras when it was built. Over this 120-mile shoreline, Bodie Island Light provided important warnings for mariners coming too close to the Graveyard of the Atlantic.

It is the third lighthouse to stand at or near Oregon Inlet since the inlet opened in a hurricane in 1846. The first developed cracks and had to be destroyed; the second was destroyed by the Confederates to confuse the Federals in their shipping. The current one is located a little more inland than you might expect, as nature has built up the southern end of the island. The wide expanses of marshland behind the lighthouse are perfect for a short walk. You'll see cattails, yaupon, wax myrtle, bayberry and other vegetation. You'll find a short path to walk along, complete with overlooks for your viewing pleasure.

The double-keeper's quarters have been completely restored. On the outside, the building has been restored to its original look (it looks very much as it did in an 1893 photograph). The interior of the keeper's

From the top of the Bodie Island Lighthouse, the stairwell looks like a work of art.

quarters has also been restored to its original state, with adaptations that provide for its use as a Visitor Center. Renovations were time-consuming, but a significant pencil-drawing was recovered from inside the plaster walls helping recapture its original look. The artist, John B. Etheridge, was a carpenter who helped in a former remodeling of the building back in 1955. That was the year the Park Service took over the building from the Coast Guard. Etheridge was a descendant of the family that sold 15 acres to the government in 1870 (for $150) as the site of the Bodie Island Lighthouse and keeper's quarters.

John Gaskill, 77, of Wanchese, the son of Vernon Gaskill, served as the last civilian keeper at Bodie Island Lighthouse. He recalls the days when the lighthouse was the only thing between the area just north of Jockey's Ridge and Oregon Inlet — between 1919 and 1940. He cut the grass around the lighthouse with a push mower and helped his father strain the kerosene before it was poured into the lighthouse lanterns. This prevented particles from clogging the vaporizer that kept the light burning.

You may contact the visitor center at the above listed phone number during the season, Memorial Day Weekend through Labor Day Weekend, seven days a week. Opening and closing dates and daily schedules vary from year to year, so it's best to call before venturing their way. The Park Service tries to keep the visitor's center open as long as possible during the year, but funding can sometimes be a problem.

COQUINA BEACH

Bodie Island   441-7425

This wonderful, wide, desolate beach is one of the best swimming beaches on the Outer Banks. The sand is fine and almost white; the beach is flat. The name comes from the little shells, " Coquinas," which are found underfoot in the surf and resemble millions of tiny bronze coins.

The National Park Service has added public restrooms and showers; otherwise, it's as natural as it was long ago. This beach has been a guarded area in the past, but unfortunately a lack of funding prevents this beach and all other beaches on the Cape Hatteras National Seashore under the jurisdiction of the National Park Service from being guarded in 1994. At the time of this writing, the day use area of Coquina Beach remains closed. Storms during the past two years wreaked havoc on this area, and the parking lot was completely torn apart. Plans are being executed to redesign the Coquina Beach complex that includes parking for visitors. The park service hopes to be open for the 1994 summer season, but the opening could be delayed. It is best to check with them for information concerning the day-use area.

Coquina Beach is family-oriented and peaceful, the way many of us expect beaches to be. Children can be heard playing hide-and-seek around the base of the dunes where the wind has sculpted nooks and crannies. (Climbing on the dunes is discouraged by Park officials and all who are environmentally aware of this fragile area where sea oats and

other beach grasses grow.) Bodie Island and Coquina Beach are a part of the National Seashore and will remain protected from development. The area provides a sense of change or a place of transition from the towns-gone-commercial on the northern portions of the barrier islands to the villages struggling to retain their remoteness on the southern end — Bodie Island Lighthouse keeps a watchful pose over it all.

The phone number we've listed for Coquina Beach will put you in touch with the Park Ranger's office. It is open year round should you need to contact them for any reason.

OREGON INLET COAST GUARD STATION
Coquina Beach

Much of the history of the Outer Banks centers around the lighthouses and the lifesaving stations. The United States Lifesaving Service was the forerunner to the U.S. Coast Guard. It was in 1873 that Congress allocated funds to establish lifesaving stations for the east coast. Of the 29 stations planned, all but four were to be located on the North Carolina coast. There were two lifesaving stations built in the area. One was Bodie Island Station on the north side of Oregon Inlet, the other, Oregon Inlet station, was

When the water temperature hits 50 degrees, cruise Oregon Inlet beaches and search for bluefish blitzes.

Insiders' Tips

located on the south side of the inlet.

Violent, storm-tossed seas played havoc with the lifesaving stations as much as delays or poor construction practices. Other lifesaving stations were built and faced the same conditions. A government report, issued in late 1888, states that four stations, including Caffey's Inlet Station and Oregon Inlet Station, were under reconstruction. (The other two were Dam Neck Mills and False Cape lifesaving stations in Virginia.) Less than a decade later, disaster struck again at the Oregon Inlet Station. But, just before the turn of the century, the station had been reconstructed and Keeper M.W. Etheridge was assigned there.

Again in 1933-34, modernization took place, and a new four-story lookout tower was added. The tower had a catwalk displaying the coat-of-arms of the U.S. Coast Guard, which the lifesaving service had become by then.

In 1972, a new extension was added. Recently, this station was abandoned when the southward migration of the Oregon Inlet threatened everything in its path. However, a stone groin built by the state of North Carolina to protect the Bonner Bridge from the drifting inlet also saved the lifesaving station. Such is the fickleness of the sea. A brand new station is now operating behind the Oregon Inlet Fishing Center.

OREGON INLET MULTI-MISSION COAST GUARD STATION
Oregon Inlet　　　*987-2311, 441-1685*

The new Multi-Mission Oregon Inlet Station, completed in August

1991, is home base to Coast Guard operation in this area now. The 10,000-square-foot building features traditional cedar shake siding and houses a communications room, maintenance shop, administrative center and berthing areas. The Coast Guard bases all their boats, up to 40 foot cutters, here; there are two piers to handle the vessels. An organized tour program is not provided, but a visit may be possible after hours.

LAURA A. BARNES
Coquina Beach

As you enter the southern end of Coquina Beach, you'll notice the remains of a shipwreck on the dunes. The *Laura A. Barnes* was one of the last coastal schooners built in America. Built at Camden, Maine, in 1918, it was under sail from New York to South Carolina in 1921 when the 120-foot ship ran into a nor'easter that drove it onto the beach, just north of where it now lies. The entire crew survived. It was in 1973 that the National Park Service moved the remains to Coquina Beach for safekeeping. During the storms of 1991, it resisted the surge of the ocean, but it now appears to be settling because less of the boat is visible. The *Laura A. Barnes* serves as a startling reminder of the closeness of the ocean to the land.

OREGON INLET FISHING CENTER
Bodie Island　　　*441-6301*
(800)272-5199, FAX: 441-7385

Oregon Inlet is one of the centers of sport fishing activity on the Banks — especially deep-sea Gulf Stream fishing. From this National Park Service-leased marina, dozens

PHILIP S. RUCKLE, JR.
CUSTOM PHOTOGRAPHER

WEDDING SPECIALIST • LOCATION & ENVIRONMENTAL
PORTRAITS • FAMILY REUNIONS
BY APPOINTMENT ONLY

RT. 1, BOX 25-A
SCARBOROUGH SQUARE
MANTEO, NORTH CAROLINA 27954
(919) 473-1301

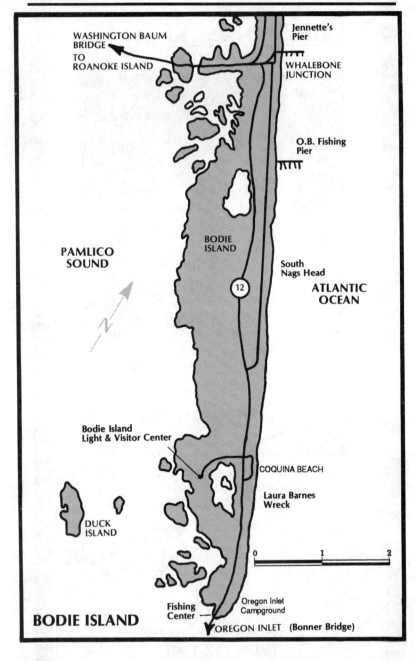

WASHINGTON BAUM
BRIDGE
TO
ROANOKE ISLAND

Jennette's
Pier

WHALEBONE
JUNCTION

O.B. Fishing
Pier

PAMLICO
SOUND

BODIE
ISLAND

12

South
Nags Head

ATLANTIC
OCEAN

Bodie Island
Light & Visitor Center

COQUINA BEACH

Laura Barnes
Wreck

DUCK
ISLAND

0   1   2

BODIE ISLAND

Fishing
Center

Oregon Inlet
Campground

OREGON INLET (Bonner Bridge)

of charter boats operate, catching thousands of dolphin, wahoo, marlin, sailfish, tuna and other sport fish every year.

Since they are concessionaires of the Park Service, the more than 30 charter boats that operate from here all charge the same prices. You can reserve a full day offshore, including bait and tackle; full day trips in the inlet and the sound; and half days in the inlet and sound (see The Outer Banks Fishing Guide section for what you can expect to catch.) You can make reservations at the Booking Desk (the number above) or with the captains themselves . . . and we recommend you make them well in advance during the summer because Oregon Inlet is one of the busiest places on the Banks come June.

Don't feel quite up to catching an 1,100-lb. blue marlin? A less demanding sport is head boat fishing, aboard *Miss Oregon Inlet,* a sleek 65-foot diesel boat out of Oregon Inlet Fishing Center. It carries up to 49 fisherpersons on half day inlet and sound bottom fishing cruises, catching spot, croakers, gray trout, bluefish, mullet, sea bass, etc. Bait and tackle are included in the price. Schedule: Early spring and late fall, one trip daily, departing at 8 AM and returning at 12:30 PM. During the season (Memorial to Labor Day) there are two trips daily, 7 AM to 11:30 AM and 12 Noon to 4:30 PM, at a cost of $25 per person. A non-fishing Twilight Cruise is offered Tuesday, Thursday, Friday and Saturday at 5:30 PM, at a cost of $6. If you've not fished the salt sea before, a head boat is a rewarding and much

less expensive way to start.

Aside from charter and head boats, the center also supplies a fish-cleaning service, restrooms and five boat ramps into the sound. The marina restaurant is open from 5 AM to 9 AM for breakfast and also offers a box lunch service upon request. The tackle shop carries a complete line of surf and deep-sea fishing equipment, as well as basic snacks, drinks and camping consumables.

Everything at Oregon Inlet is organized around the angler; the fish-cleaning service will take your fish right off the boat to a truck; mounting services are available to do your lifetime trophy up proud. Don't miss the outdoor display of mounted deep sea game fish, including a World's Record 1,142-lb. Atlantic Blue Marlin caught off the Inlet in 1974.

Finally at the south end of the piers, a scenic overlook displays the bronze prop of SS *Dionysus,* a Liberty ship sunk offshore as part of the state's artificial reef program.

The Oregon Inlet Fishing Center is eight miles south of Whalebone Junction, west of Highway 12 on the turnoff to the right just before the bridge. Prices for fuel are competitive. MasterCard and VISA are accepted, cash discounts may apply. For a free brochure, including reservation information, write: P.O. Box 2089, Manteo, NC 27954. But even if you're not fishing, it can be a lot of fun just to watch the charter boats return from their day of fishing, something the whole family will enjoy.

Photo: J. Foster Scott/DCTB

Herbert C. Bonner Bridge connects Hatteras Island to Bodie Island.

OREGON INLET
Between Hatteras and Bodie Island

Driving south from Nags Head, through Bodie Island, you'll soon find yourself lifted skyward on an immense concrete bridge. From 100 feet in the air you can see for miles — seaward, over Atlantic swells, soundward, over the vast calm sheet of the Pamlico.

This is Oregon Inlet, which has been the Banks' major avenue for trade and fishing for more than 100 years and is still the major outlet for today's heavy commercial and recreational traffic. Oregon Inlet opened during a hurricane in 1846 and was named, as was the custom in those days, after the first ship to make it through. Its opening brought shoaling to Ocracoke Inlet and economic ruin to the once-flourishing town of Portsmouth. Today it too is shoaling, and its consequences may be just as dramatic.

The Herbert C. Bonner Bridge, built in 1964 to provide access to the southern Banks, may have hastened this process by impeding the free tidal flow through the inlet. (Note, as you pass over it, the mile or more of new land under the bridge supports to the north.) But, it is more likely that simple beach migration, the eonslong march of the Banks to the south and west, is the real cause. Whatever the causative factors, the inlet has required nearly round-the-clock dredging for the last few years, and now the silting is overtaking the Corps of Engineers' ability to dredge; in fact Oregon has been completely closed for days at a time in recent years. In 1989 erosion at the southern side of the inlet accelerated dramatically, threatening much of the former Coast Guard station and requiring emergency repairs to the bridge.

The controversy over clearing or

Photo: Dare County Tourist Bureau

People have been enjoying the Outer Banks for many years.

stabilizing the inlet, or whether it can be stabilized at all, has been going on for some years now. A long rip rap jetty might keep the channel open, at great expense, but it, too, would have to be dredged, and there is no guarantee that it would work for more than a few years. The Oregon Inlet jetty project was approved by Congress in 1972, but permits for the rubble structures have never been granted. Since then, more than 200 acres of North Point have been lost to the sea. Jetty opponents have argued that jetties would accelerate erosion south of the inlet; they proposed letting nature take its course.

Meanwhile, the boatbuilders and trawling companies of Wanchese, have been hit with skyrocketing insurance rates. Many of them have moved south, to the Morehead City area. It is too soon to write Wanchese off as a fishing port, but there is no doubt that the situation there is serious. The four-day March, 1989, nor'easter and the damage it caused to the bridge supports spurred renewed efforts to get a project started, and a $20 million revetment and groin was completed in 1991.

The potential closing of the inlet also leads to the question: where will the next inlet be? Historically, the closing of an inlet has seemed to portend the opening of a new one somewhere else. All that water in the sound has to go somewhere. We don't know, and no one can really predict, where an inlet will open. But, it can happen pretty quickly when those winter waves come crashing over the barrier dunes.

Another sobering reminder of the precarious nature of human "mastery" over nature occurred in October of 1990, when hurricane-force winds blew a dredging barge into the Bonner bridge, stranding 5,000 tourists and residents. It took four months to repair the 370 feet of damaged bridge. This incident led to new studies of alternatives to the bridge, including tunnels and a return to ferries, but as of this writing the Bonner seems to be the only feasible means of access, given the nature of the bottom in this area and the heavy traffic demands during the summer months.

U-85

By David Poyer

Off Bodie Island

As you stand on Coquina Beach, the sun bright overhead, look straight out to sea. If you could take your car and drive outward for 15 minutes, you would be over one of the strangest yet least known attractions of the Outer Banks. Only 15 miles straight out, over 100 feet beneath the glittering sea, the first Nazi submarine destroyed by Americans in World War II lies motionless in the murky waters of Hatteras.

Almost undamaged, except for rust and the encroaching coral, it lies on its side, bow planes jammed forever on hard dive. Its hatches gape open to the dark interior, where silt swirls slowly between dead gauges and twisted air lines. Its cannon points upward, toward the dim glow that is all that remains of the sun at 18 fathoms. Its conning tower, flaked with corrosion, lies frozen in a roll to starboard that will last until its steel dissolves in the all-devouring sea.

Here, at 35 55' N, 75 18' W, it is still World War II. Here, and all along the coasts of the Outer Banks, dozens of wrecks lie half-buried in the sea bed. It is from here, from the silent hull of a 750-ton Type VIIb U-boat, that we can begin a journey back to the months when the Outer Banks was a battle line, when the German Navy patrolled and ruled our shores.

To Spring, 1942.

Adolf Hitler declared war on the United States on December 11, 1941, four days after Pearl Harbor.

In Europe the war was 2½ years old. Deep in the Soviet Union, Nazi and Red forces churned the mud in a precarious balance outside the city of Moscow. In the West the British, in from the first, had come close to strangling in the noose the U-boats had drawn around their island. German submarines had sunk over 1,000 ships, over a million tons of material and food; but as 1941 ended, quickly built escorts, ASDIC, and a convoy system were loosening the knot. In his operations room at Kerneval, Occupied France, Admiral Karl Doenitz wondered: where, now, would he find easy sinkings for his thinly stretched submarines?

On the 11th of December, he knew.

Operation *Paukenschlag* (Drumroll) began on the 18th of January, when the Esso tanker *Allen Jackson* exploded a few miles off Diamond Shoals Light.

Within weeks, the entire East Coast was under siege, and it was almost defenseless. Most of our ships had been sent to the Pacific, or to the North Atlantic run, where two of them, *Reuben James* and *Kearny,* were torpedoed even before war officially began. Aircraft? Almost none. To defend the east coast of the United States in spring 1942, there was a total of 10 World War I wooden subchasers, three converted yachts, four blimps and six Army bombers.

When the U-boats arrived, it was slaughter. They struck on the surface, at night, often not even bothering to dive. The stretch of coast off the Banks was their favorite hunting ground. Armed with both deck guns and torpedoes, they would lie in wait at night, silhouette the passing coasters against the glow of lights ashore, and attack unseen by the men aboard. Ship after ship went down in January, February, and March: *Rochester; Ocean Venture; Norvana; Trepca; City of Atlanta; Oakmar; Tiger;* and scores of others. Oil and debris washed up on the beaches, and residents watched the night sky flame as tankers burned just over the horizon.

The "Arsenal of Democracy" was under blockade; and from the protected pens at Lorient and St. Nazaire more raiders, fresh from refit and training, sailed to attack a coast where in three months of war not one German submarine had yet been the target of an effective attack.

One of them was the U-85.

U-85 was a Type VIIb, specially modified for the Atlantic war. A little over 700 tons displacement, 220 feet long, it was a little larger than a harbor tugboat, or the *Calypso*. It had been built in northern Germany in early 1941, the second year of the war. Its commander was Kapitan-leutnant Eberhard Greger, Class of 1935.

Greger and U-85 spent its first summer working up in the deep fiords of occupied Norway. On August 28 it left Trondheim for its first wartime cruise. On September 10, the wolf tasted blood for the first time. Greger latched on to a Britain-bound convoy. U-85's first five torpedoes ran wild. Throughout that day and the next he ran eastward, staying with the convoy on the surface, just over the horizon. The diesels hammered as U-85 slashed through heavy seas. The convoy's escorts, American destroyers, tried repeatedly to drive it off with gunfire and depth charges. Each time, it submerged and evaded, then came back up and hammered ahead again, rolling viciously, but gradually drawing ahead to position for a new attack.

The next afternoon it reached it, and Greger sent U-85 dashing in on the surface. Boldness was rewarded: at 1642 he made a solid hit on a 6,000-ton steamer, and, in the next half hour, struck at two more of the heavily laden merchantmen. Then the destroyers closed in for a close depth- charge counterattack. At a little past midnight, September 11, Greger brought it up slowly and then crept toward home for repairs.

U-85's second war cruise was less dramatic. Battered by heavy weather off Newfoundland, shrouded by fog, it never made contact with its prey, and engine trouble eventually sent it back to St. Nazaire.

For its third war cruise, a new man came aboard. He sounds like a sailor Goebbels would have exulted over; young (26), tall (six feet), blond and well built; but this German must have been different from the Nazi stereotype. For one thing, he kept a diary; and it is thanks to Erich Degenkolb that we know as much as we do about his ship's last cruises.

According to Degenkolb — we can imagine him wedged into his cramped leather bunk, diary on his stomach, listening to the waves crash against the outside of the hull — U-85's third war cruise was the most rewarding, both to Doenitz and to its crew.

Operation Drumroll had begun, and U-85 was one of the first reliefs to be thrown into the battle. On the way across it sank a 10,000-ton steamer and took a near miss from a plane off Newfoundland. "Off New York," as Degenkolb wrote in his diary in February, it sank another steamer after a seven-hour surface chase. It chased convoys throughout the month, probably in the Western Atlantic approaches to New York, till its fuel tanks sloshed near-empty, and then set course for home, crossing the Bay of Biscay submerged and arriving in St. Nazaire again on the twenty-third of February.

A month's refit and leave, and it was time to sail again. At 1800 on March 21, 1942, with a brass band on the pier, with a blooded crew, a confident captain, and a well-tried ship, U-85 set out once more for "Amerika."

The drumbeat of the U-boats had grown louder through February and March. No censorship could conceal the fact that ships were being lost. The explosions on the horizon, the oil on the beaches, the boatloads of huddled men being debarked at every seaport told the story too plainly for anyone to deny.

The Navy and Coast Guard, along with civilian authorities, were struggling with this new meaning of the once-remote war. Vice-Admiral Adolphus Andrews, directing the East Coast antisubmarine effort, found that aside from the lack of ships and planes, he had inadequate operational plans and even less clout. He couldn't even get the use of the destroyers and planes already in Norfolk assigned to the Atlantic Fleet.

One of the results of this unfortunate combination of censorship and unpreparedness was, typically, rumor. U-boats were refuelling, people whispered, in isolated inlets along the coast, and they had been seen in Chesapeake Bay itself. Citizens reported odd lights along the shore at night . . . obvious signals to someone out at sea.

One of the most persistent rumors concerned landings along the Outer Banks. German sailors, it was said, had actually slipped ashore, were mingling with the locals and even seeing movies, as ticket stubs supposedly recovered from sunken U-boats proved. Alas, a good story, but probably untrue. The Germans did land specially trained spies later in the war in Quebec and at Narragansett, Long Island; but according to the Coast Guard, Navy, and FBI, that was it in World War II. No U-boat captain must have had much desire to hazard his craft close inshore, or risk losing a skilled *obermachinist* so that he could report on the latest Errol Flynn epic. All that *can* be proven is that where news does not exist, gossip and invention will swiftly take its place.

And in March and April 1942, reality was bad enough. Eight ships had gone down off North Carolina alone in January; two in February, as the first team of submarines headed back across the Atlantic; and then 14 in March, as they were relieved. Once the "pipeline" of the 18-day cruise out of France was full, there would be eight boats on station all the time.

The Outer Banks were suddenly the focus of world war.

Cape Hatteras was dreaded by every merchant seaman on the East Coast. The "Graveyard of the Atlantic" was earning its name anew in the age of steam, and a new cognomen besides — "Torpedo Junction." On March 18, for example, the U-boats met an unescorted "convoy" of five tankers, and torpedoed three, plus a Greek freighter that stopped to rescue crewmen from a black sea filled with blazing oil.

This was how it was: in March 1942, three ships were going down every day, one every eight hours. But even worse was the closely guarded secret that the "exchange rate" — the magic number in antisubmarine warfare — was zero. Not one U-boat had yet been sunk off America.

It could not continue this way. Either the U-boats would be driven under, or all coastwise shipping would have to stop. America, the Allies, could not afford losses on this scale much longer.

It might not be too much to say, as Churchill later did, that it was the war itself that hung in the balance.

USS *Roper*, DD-147, was a fairly old ship in 1942, as warships go. At a little under 1,200 tons, it wasn't all that much larger than U-85.

It had been born in Philadelphia, at William Cramp & Sons, in 1918. *Roper* evacuated refugees from Constantinople in 1919 and then spent a few years in the Pacific before being laid up in San Diego in 1922. Recommissioned in 1930, it spent the slow years of the Depression on reserve maneuvers and patrol duty in Hawaii, Panama, and the Caribbean. In 1937 it was transferred to the Atlantic Fleet.

When war began in Europe, the pace picked up. The old four-piper rolled from Key West to Yucatan, and then north in 1940 to the coast of New England. In early 1942, it ran a convoy to Londonderry, passing the U-85, then on its third war patrol; they may have crossed each other's paths for the first time then, somewhere in the empty spaces of the North Atlantic.

In March, the rigorous glamor of convoy duty ended; it was ordered back to the coast for more patrol. Patrol — steaming endlessly through fog, storm, calm, night. Its crew carried out innumerable late-night actions: radar contact, a breakneck steam to intercept, the depth-charging that was always futile. Whales? Escaping U-boats? The crew never knew. Perhaps some day, in a war that everyone knew now would last a long time, they would have their chance to fight. But for now, it was more of the same, everlasting patrol.

Kapitan-leutnant Eberhard Greger sailed U-85 on its fourth sortie on March 21, beginning the long transit submerged. In a few days, though, he was able to bring it up, and dieseled west through seas "as smooth as a table," as Degenkolb, relaxing belowdecks, jotted in his journal. They took some damage from a storm on March 30 but repaired it and continued the cruise.

At this stage of the war, Germany's submariners were confident men — especially off America.

By early April it was on station, ranging the coast from New York to Washington. On the tenth, Greger took his boat below to sink a steamer with a spread of two torpedoes. But targets were scarce.

He decided to head south, toward the easy pickings off the Outer Banks.

On the night of April 13, as U-85 hammered through calm seas at 16 knots, Degenkolb made his last entry: "American beacons and searchlights visible at night."

Lieutenant-commander Hamilton W. Howe, captain of the *Roper*, was tired. His crew was tired. The ship itself, 24 years old, was tired. But they were alert. The old four-piper did not yet have the new gear Allied scientists were racing to produce. But it had enough. A primitive radar and sonar. Depth charges. And plenty of guns — nice to have, if only a U-boat would play the game for once and surface, instead of skulking away underwater while the horizon crackled with flame from dying ships.

At midnight on the 13th, *Roper* was running southward off Bodie Island. The lighthouse, still operating, was plainly visible to starboard. The night was clear and starry, and at 18 knots the knife bow of the old DD pared phosphorescence from the smooth water. Most of the crew was asleep below.

On the bridge as Officer of the Deck, Ensign Ken Tebo was awake and alert. At six minutes past midnight, the radar suddenly showed a small pip a mile and a half ahead. The ship had been plagued with these small contacts all night. Another small boat, Tebo thought; probably a Coast Guard craft, on the same mission as the destroyer — patrol. But he felt immediately that there was something strange, something different, about this one.

He ordered an eight degree change of course, to close slowly, and to present the smallest possible target — just in case. In seconds — the captain always slept in full uniform at sea — Howe was on the bridge.

Tebo explained the situation quickly. He still had that strange feeling. *Roper* was overhauling, but too slowly. At 2,100 yards range the two men saw the wake of whatever it was up ahead. White, narrow, it glowed in the starlit seas. Howe ordered an increase in speed to 20 knots. It still might be a Coast Guard boat. But Howe made his decision. At the clang of General Quarters, seamen rolled from their bunks and ran to man their guns, the torpedo batteries, the depth charge racks astern, and the K-guns, weapons that threw the drums of explosive far out over the ship's side, widening the carpet of concussion that could crush the hull of any submerged enemy.

Aboard the speeding U-boat, most of the crew was asleep. Degenkolb had thrust his diary into his pocket and turned in. On the darkened conning tower, only a few feet above the sea, an officer and two lookouts stared ahead. They anticipated no trouble. A U-boat had a tiny silhouette, almost impossible to see from a ship's deck at night.

After a time, one of the lookouts turned 'round and tapped the officer on the shoulder. There seemed to be something astern. A target? The submarine's rudders swung, and it began to creep to the right.

Below, the men slept on.

Aboard the *Roper*, now only a few hundred yards astern, Lt. William Vanous, the executive officer, stood panting atop the flying bridge. Commander S.C. Norton was beside him. Below them the two men could hear the pounding of feet on metal as the bridge team manned up. The starlight showed more men on the forecastle, running toward the three-inch guns. Beside them, the searchlight operator was swinging his lamp around, and they heard the clang as BMC Jack Wright charged the No. 1. 50-caliber machine gun.

Vanous strained his eyes ahead. At the end of a white ribbon of wake a black object was slowly drawing into view. Could it really be a submarine? It was awfully small. He noted happily that the men on the bridge below were keeping the ship a trifle to the side of the wake; most U-boats carried torpedo tubes in their pointed sterns as well as in the bow.

Yes, thought the German officer ahead of him, there is something back there. And it was very close. He reached for the alarm toggle, and below him, under the waterline, Degenkolb suddenly awoke.

The two ships were turning. The submarine was slipping to starboard. In a few moments its stern tubes would point directly at its pursuer. Howe ordered the helm hard right, and called into the voice tube, "Illuminate!" Above him, with a sputtering hiss, the searchlight ignited. Vanous coached it out into the darkness, and caught his breath. The beam had swept across the conning tower of a submarine with five men running along the half-submerged deck toward its gun.

Someone shouted to Wright, and with an ear-battering roar the chief began firing. The machine gun tracers swept forward, hung over the black boat, then descended, dancing along the thin-skinned ballast tanks, then reaching up the deck toward the frantically working gun crew. Forward, a second machine gun opened up. The glare of the searchlight wavered, but held. In its weird light men began to fall.

At almost the same moment, crewmen along the destroyer's side pointed and shouted at a sparkling trail in the water: a torpedo!

Inside the hull of the U-85, other men heard the clang of machine gun bullets on metal. They ran for their stations, forty men in a hull no wider than a railway car. The ship shuddered as a torpedo went out astern. Erich Degenkolb swung a locker open and pulled out his yellow escape lung. Could Kapitan Greger submerge and escape? He hoped so, desperately. But from the sounds that came through the steel around him into what the U-boat men called the "iron coffin," it seemed that U-85's luck had finally run out.

On the *Roper's* bridge, Howe had no time for thoughts and no time for feelings. It was a U-boat, and it was *surfaced*. The ship was still shuddering around in its turn. "Open fire!" he shouted.

On the exposed forecastle, in the mounts on deck aft, the three-inchers began to fire. Their target was only 300 yards away now, almost point-blank range. But it seemed smaller. It was submerging. In a moment it would be gone.

The *Roper's* men thought they saw their last round hit just at the base of the conning tower, where it joined the U-boat's pressure hull.

With the sound of a solid hit in their ears, the *Unterseeboot*-men knew their battle was lost. The ballast tanks were already filling, and the machine gun and shell fire must have holed them too. U-85 was on its last dive. There was only one way for its men to live now, and that was to get out of the narrow hull before it slipped forever under the icy sea.

Erich Degenkolb joined the crowd struggling under the ladder. Seconds later he found himself topside. The deck was familiar, but fire was still drumming on the sinking boat. A blinding shaft of light picked out every splinter, every weldment of the hull. He stumbled from the blaze of fire and sound over the side. The water was freezing cold. Gasping, he came up, stuck the mouthpiece of the lung between his teeth, and tried to inflate it. His heavy clothes were dragging him down.

Suddenly the firing stopped. The light went out. He drifted, seemingly alone, for a few minutes, feeling the cold of the sea gnaw into his bare hands, into his face.

Then, all at once, a string of deeper detonations brought his attention up, into the night.

The last thing he saw was the American ship. Immense, black, blazing, it loomed over the sinking shell that had been his home, over the struggling men in the water who had been his friends. And from its sides, in brief bursts of reddish light, he saw the depth charges leap into the night and splash on either side, amid the waving, screaming men.

When the black ship slid under, Howe doused the light. He was suddenly conscious of how conspicuous he was. Lights, shooting . . . the killers, it was common talk among destroyermen, often operated in pairs.

A few minutes later, the sonar operator reported contact. The destroyer, darkened and silent now, wheeled and headed toward it.

"Prepare for depth charge attack," said Howe.

"Men in the water ahead, captain."

"All stop."

Its screws slowing, *Roper* coasted forward. From the bridge he could see them now. One of them was even shouting up at him... *"Heil Hitler."* But he was thinking. He held course. He knew they were there. But the contact was solid. It might be another sub.

"Fire depth charges," said Howe.

Astern, from the fantail, the launchers exploded. The charges arched out, hit, and sank, and seconds later 3,300 pounds of TNT went off in the midst of forty swimming men. *Roper* made no more attacks that night, but lingered in the area of the sinking, echo-ranging and with every lookout alert. At about six the sun rose, lighting the scene of recent battle. Oil slicked the low waves; life jackets and motionless bodies drifted in slow eddies as the destroyer nosed back and forth, sniffing for the vanished enemy. At 0850, obtaining a ping on a bottomed object, it made a straight run and dropped four more depth charges. A great gush of air and a little oil came up when the foam subsided astern. At 0957, Howe dropped two more depth charges over the largest bubbles. At last he concluded that it was over. The U-boat was still down there, but it was dead. Coached from aircraft from shore, still watching for that constantly-feared other sub, the *Roper* lowered a boat, and began dragging bodies aboard.

One of them, his face and body swollen and discolored from the depth charging that had killed him, was Erich Degenkolb.

The first U-boat! The news was electrifying. At long last one of them had been destroyed, by an American ship, and in the very area where for four months now the wolves had hunted with impunity. The story was immediately released to the press. But this was not the end. *Roper* continued south on its patrol, but the remains of U-85 were far too valuable to be left undisturbed.

Over the next weeks, divers explored the shattered boat. A hundred feet down, clumsily-suited Navy men clambered over torn metal, pried open hatches, traced fuel and air lines and manifolds, and tried unsuccessfully to raise the hull with compressed air. They were unable to get inside and it was impossible to raise the wreck without a major salvage effort — not an easy option off Cape Hatteras in April.

In the end, they left it there, possibly with some of its crew still inside the now-silent hull, under the canted conning tower, with its painted device of a wild boar, rampant, with a rose in its mouth. The divers, the ships were needed elsewhere. There were valuable cargoes to be recovered. And from now on, there would be casualties from the other side as well — U-352, sunk off Morehead City in May; U-576; U-701; dozens of others. And, last of all, U-548, sent down a 100 miles east of the Chesapeake Bay entrances three years later, in April, 1945.

The U-boat threat was anything but over, but on the Atlantic horizon more light was dawning than that of burning tankers. In the months after April, 1942, American strength increased steadily in our home waters. The threat was overcome, this time; the enemy was steadily shoved back, first to the center of the ocean, then to his home waters. Finally, with the loss of France in 1944, he could deploy only the few war-worn boats that could slip out from Germany itself past close blockade into the North Sea.

Lieutenant-commander Hamilton Howe retired as a rear admiral in 1956. He lives in Winston-Salem, North Carolina. Captain Kenneth Tebo retired in 1961, and lives in Falls Church, Virginia. Captain William Tanous died the same year in a naval hospital in Annapolis. Erich Degenkolb, N 11662/41, lies in Hampton, Virginia, in plot #694 of the National Cemetery.

Kapitan-leutnant Eberhard Greger's body was not recovered.

U-85 lies rusting on a white, sandy bottom, 15 miles east of where Bodie Island light still glitters out over the troubled seas of Hatteras.

Inside
Hatteras Island

For many, the southern leg of the Outer Banks, Hatteras Island National Seashore and its small villages, is the grandest of places. Its natural beauty, remoteness, migratory waterfowl, expansive beaches and dunes provide a startling contrast to other more developed areas farther north on the barrier islands.

This portion of the Outer Banks begins just south of Bodie Island. The seashore highway lays a ribbon-like path into silence where water and sky meet and acres of marshland reveal a captive yet protective habitat for waterfowl and wildlife. Stalks of seasoned vegetation, wild flowers, beach grasses and wind-blown trees provide shelter from scorching summer sunlight and often-blustery winter winds for the variety of small creatures that live here.

When you can hear only the roll and hiss of the sea and the chatter of wildlife, you begin to appreciate what preservation means. Farther along the highway, you get a glimpse of how life for humans is more seasonal or, at best, rugged in most every way.

The Pea Island National Wildlife Refuge separates the towns of the north and central barrier islands from those small towns and villages

farther south and Cape Hatteras, the "elbow" that turns west almost in retreat from the wild Atlantic. Pea Island, administered by the U.S. Fish and Wildlife Service, provides miles of unspoiled beauty and, if you're inclined, several overlooks and nature trails give closer looks.

The National Park Service campground at Oregon Inlet is available for those who prefer life under the stars or out there on the beaches where fishing and swimming provide the only activity for campers during the day (see chapter on Campgrounds.) The Oregon Inlet Fishing Center on the west side tempts you to a day at sea on charter boat trips from the marina.

An occasional village appears as the drive south continues. Each year brings more businesses and services to these remote areas, where people come to get away from more populated ones. Shops, restaurants, cafes, motels and cottages line the short lanes from the highway to the ocean and sound. Nevertheless, recent storms, which created ocean and sound overwash along portions of the highway have slowed down future growth and have reminded residents of how unpredictable mother nature can be.

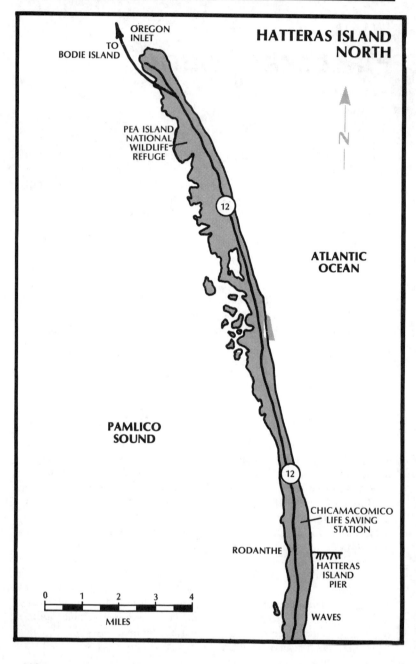

HATTERAS ISLAND NORTH

OREGON INLET

TO BODIE ISLAND

PEA ISLAND NATIONAL WILDLIFE REFUGE

N

12

ATLANTIC OCEAN

PAMLICO SOUND

12

CHICAMACOMICO LIFE SAVING STATION

RODANTHE

HATTERAS ISLAND PIER

0 1 2 3 4

MILES

WAVES

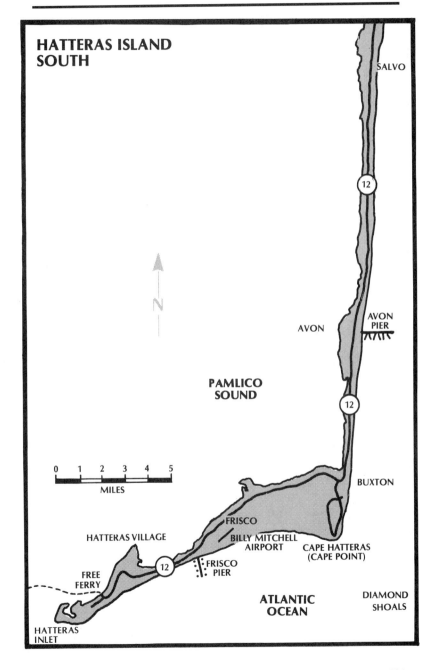

HATTERAS ISLAND
SOUTH

SALVO

12

AVON

AVON
PIER

PAMLICO
SOUND

12

BUXTON

0 1 2 3 4 5
MILES

FRISCO

BILLY MITCHELL
AIRPORT

HATTERAS VILLAGE

CAPE HATTERAS
(CAPE POINT)

12

FRISCO
PIER

FREE
FERRY

DIAMOND
SHOALS

ATLANTIC
OCEAN

HATTERAS
INLET

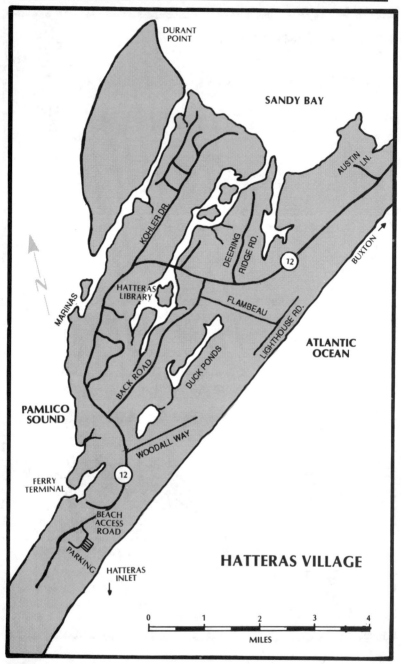

DURANT
POINT

SANDY BAY

AUSTIN LN.

KOHLER DR.

DEERING RIDGE RD.

12

BUXTON →

MARINAS

HATTERAS
LIBRARY

FLAMBEAU

LIGHTHOUSE RD.

ATLANTIC
OCEAN

PAMLICO
SOUND

BACK ROAD

DUCK PONDS

WOODALL WAY

FERRY
TERMINAL

12

BEACH
ACCESS
ROAD

PARKING

HATTERAS
INLET

HATTERAS VILLAGE

0   1   2   3   4
MILES

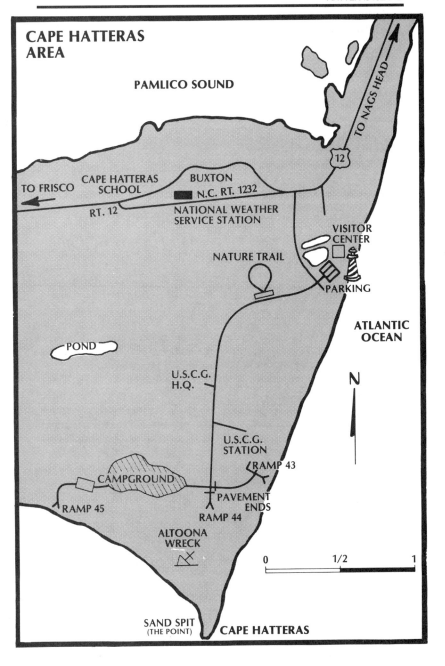

CAPE HATTERAS
AREA

PAMLICO SOUND

TO NAGS HEAD

12

TO FRISCO

CAPE HATTERAS
SCHOOL

BUXTON

N.C. RT. 1232

RT. 12

NATIONAL WEATHER
SERVICE STATION

VISITOR
CENTER

NATURE TRAIL

PARKING

ATLANTIC
OCEAN

POND

N

U.S.C.G.
H.Q.

U.S.C.G.
STATION

RAMP 43

CAMPGROUND

PAVEMENT
ENDS

RAMP 45

RAMP 44

ALTOONA
WRECK

0   1/2   1

SAND SPIT
(THE POINT)   CAPE HATTERAS

Rodanthe, Waves, Salvo

These three villages are scattered along the road toward Buxton and Hatteras. Each community has its own business area, composed mainly of bait and tackle shops, grocery stores, small restaurants and gift shops. Visitors will find something different and should take time to explore these small towns rather than passing them quickly by for the more storied Hatteras Village or Ocracoke. Many come here for fishing, surfing or windsurfing. There are fishing piers scattered throughout these villages, and the wide, open sound is a haven for water sports enthusiasts.

Rodanthe, Salvo and Waves were hard-hit by the "storm of the century" experienced on the Outer Banks in March 1993. Some of the local businesses display pictures of what the area looked like during peak sound flooding. Luckily, there were no fatalities on Hatteras Island as a result of the storm, but residents did fear for their lives. Soundside businesses and residences were hardest hit. No doubt, some of you will notice that the Rodanthe Post Office burned to the ground. The fire occurred during the storm, and fire fighters were unable to get to the building due to severe flooding of Highway 12. Now Pamlico Station in Rodanthe houses the post office for Rodanthe, Waves and Salvo.

Avon

Avon is primarily a summer community, but it has experienced more growth than the other villages as a result of the amount of developable land located here. A large shopping center is anchored by Food Lion and includes other small shops for convenience foods, clothes and water-sports gear. Several restaurants add to visitors' enjoyment of the area. Larger and newer homes are being built and resort developments like Kinnakeet Shores are selling lots with amenities including pools and clubhouses.

Buxton, Frisco and Hatteras Village

The southern "arm" of Hatteras Island — from the elbow at the Cape west and south, toward Ocracoke — took a hard hit from Hurricane Emily in August 1993. Signs of damage are still evident here. Emily will long be remembered by local residents, who say they'll be telling stories of this hurricane for generations to come. The hardy survivors of these three villages lasted through Emily's force and have worked hard all winter to try to recuperate. One shopkeeper said the area was "like a war zone" after the wrath of Emily swept through and that for months afterward the lower end of the island looked like "white trash America" with damaged furniture and appliances piled along the roadways in heaps. With the coming of spring, the villagers prepared for a new season with remodeling projects and fresh hopes. New carpet and fresh paint won't deter these strong people from pointing out to visitors their "high tide lines." Most are prominently marked for all to see by

signs that prove the water was there; the damage was done; and yet life goes on.

This area is more populated and more habitable than the open land to the north. More of it is privately owned, in contrast to the overwhelming proportion of National Seashore land on the rest of the island. Higher and more stable geologically, the southern arm is primarily a maritime forest habitat, thick with live oak and red bay, dogwood and loblolly pine. It offers more shelter from wind and storm and has borne a small and hardy population from the earliest Native American times. Historically, the people made their living from the sea. Many locals still fish commercially, at least part time.

Buxton, just inland from Cape Hatteras itself, is a rapidly growing town. The fishing flavor is strong here during the spring and fall seasons. Buxton is a mecca for sports fishermen and Atlantic Coast surfers. Canadian Hole, located just outside of Buxton, draws windsurfers in droves from all over the country, and, of course, from Canada. A winding, pleasant road runs west from Buxton toward Frisco. On the way you will pass several campgrounds and many roads leading back into new real estate developments, both on the ocean side and on the higher land overlooking the sound. Previously forested, this road is taking on

Rany Jennette

Keeper of The Light . . . and Its Stories

By Nancy McWilliams

When visitors at Cape Hatteras Lighthouse gather around National Park Service Ranger Rany Jennette to hear old tales, they are shocked to learn that Jennette's personal history is intertwined very closely with that of the 208-foot spiral-striped structure. Born and raised on the spot from which his talks are given, Jennette is the son of the last lighthouse keeper, Unaka Jennette, and was raised in the shadow of the light.

"That gets their attention," Jennette said with a chuckle. At 73, you can

Over the course of his career, Rany Jennette has entertained and informed thousands of youngsters.

tell he likes waking tourists up.

Marcia Lyons, park naturalist, called Jennette an "irreplaceable resource" and "the star" of interpretive talks. "It's wonderful to see the public's reaction when they find out he grew up here," Lyons said. "He represents those romantic days gone by. People can really see someone who was in the era of the care of the lighthouse."

That era began when lighthouse land was purchased from four Jennette orphans for construction of the original 1803 tower. The four acres were purchased for $50 by the U.S. Treasury Department. The current light was rebuilt in 1870, after the original was damaged in the Civil War. In addition to his father, Jennette also had two uncles who were principal keepers. The Jennette name goes back in lighthouse keeper history to 1842.

Jennette's father Unaka was born in Buxton in 1882. Unaka sailed the nearby seas from a young age; at 22, he joined the lighthouse service as a deck hand. He rapidly advanced, becoming a first-class pilot for Chesapeake Bay and its tributaries, with a home port in Baltimore. Unaka's dream came true in 1919 when he was transferred to Cape Hatteras Lighthouse as principal keeper; he was back home.

Unaka took his responsibilities for the lighthouse seriously, Jennette recalled. "His fearless dedication to painting it compelled him to rig a ladder from the upper deck of the light tower, lasso the lightning rod and pull himself up so he could paint the very top." As principal keeper, Unaka earned $157 a month, not a bad salary during the Depression, Jennette noted. He pulled 24-hour duty every 72 hours, with two assistant keepers to help him watch the light and bear the heavy burden of making sure the beacon burned brightly so that ships at sea could get their bearings and steer to safety.

Capt. Unaka devoted 20 years of his life to Cape Hatteras Lighthouse, until the U.S. Coast Guard took over in 1939. Jennette remembers his father as a mild-mannered man, firm and fair in his leadership skills. "He was highly respected by coworkers and island people," Jennette said. He was a loyal husband to his wife Jenny Luanna and father to seven children. He was also an excellent horseman who could bring a wild pony to its knees or throw a steer.

"Growing up at the lighthouse provided me with many good childhood memories," Jennette said. During that time, the beach at the lighthouse was flat, without the dunes that were constructed in the 1930s by the Civilian Conservation Corp. The land wasn't forested, either, he said, just flat and open. During that time, a sandy, twisting car track led to the village of Buxton.

He grew up drinking rain water, using outhouses for rest rooms, raising vegetables and animals for food and making monthly trips to Buxton for staples. Journeys to the mainland were rare and filled with excitement.

Keeping the light involved rituals that Jennette fondly recalls today. The kerosene-burning mantle lamp was always lit a half hour before sunset and extinguished at sunrise. The fuel was carried to the top of the lighthouse in five-gallon cans. Clockworks had to be oiled, and lenses inspected for smudges or spots. Touching the lens with fingers was never allowed, Jennette said. The light was visible 20 to 25 miles at sea, giving its unique pattern of a 1½ second flash and six seconds darkness. "Close up, its 24 sheets of light were visible at the same time and gave the appearance of a giant lighted fan revolving slowly from the top of the tower," Jennette said.

While the historic image may be that lighthouse keepers and their families lived lonely lives, Jennette said that wasn't so for him. The keeper's and two assistant keepers' families were large, and four or five other families lived about a mile away. There was much visiting back and forth. "The lighthouse has always been a favorite place to visit by the village folk," Jennette said. "We had lots of company, especially on Sunday afternoons and in the evenings." Swimming, baseball games, croquet, beachcombing, chasing wild horses and climbing the lighthouse were the fun activities. "Life was never dull at the

My Father The Keeper

By the edge of the sea
'Neath the sweep of the light
At the top of a spiral-striped tower
A family of seven — Unaka's delight,
Grew in wisdom and stature
To her e'er watchful eye.

The beach was our playground,
The woods a corral,
And the cattle and horses,
The goats and the pigs,
Had a run of the land
Until round-up time came.

Croquet on the lawn,
And visits from friends,
A trip into Buxton,
A climb to the top,
To peer through the spyglass
Or help clean the lens.

Small squares of sheeting,
Four strings to a weight.
A small boy could watch them
When tossed from up high.
They floated so gently
far below to the ground.

But the magical time
Was to be there at night.
The beauty of prisms,
Each spotless and shining,
Cast rainbow-hued diamonds
To dance 'round the deck.

The silence is broken
By only those sounds
Of the light at work
On its nightly rounds.
The mantle-lamp hisses.
(Can you still smell the oil?)

lighthouse," he said.

One of his favorite stories is how, at the age of 8, he painted the base of the light with black tar, thinking he was doing a big favor, but instead was making a huge mess. His untimely attempt at sprucing up came just before a federal agent inspected the premises. He eventually received a whipping with his father's razor strap, something his dad promised he would remember the rest of his life. "It has been more than 60 years, and I still remember," Jennette said. "But a spot or two of the tar is still there, and I did leave my mark on the Cape Hatteras Lighthouse for a long time."

Jennette said his childhood memories take him back in a way that could only be true for someone growing up under the shadow of "such a magnificent and well-known guardian of seamen everywhere." The freedom afforded by the beach and ocean is appreciated heartily as Jennette looks back. He recalls that stormy weather was a joy to the young folks, with beach walks resulting in rewarding scavenger hunts. Climbing the lighthouse at every opportunity and sliding down the rails on the lower levels are cherished memories, along with floating small homemade parachutes from the top deck.

That's the governor whirring
To control the weight's fall.
It's all like a clock, you know.
Turning the lens
And keeping it going
Is a big daily chore.

And who was in charge
Of the light's nightly glow?
Some knew him as Captain,
As friend or co-worker.
But I called him "Father,"
The best of them all.
　　　　—by Mary Dickens

"I enjoyed my young life at the Cape Hatteras Lighthouse," Jennette stated. That era ended in September 1933 when a severe storm hit the coast. As a warning came, the keepers sent their families to Buxton and stayed at their station, as lighthouse keepers were not allowed to leave for any reason. The damage was extensive, and the Jennettes never returned to the lighthouse quarters again. "But to each of us it was always home and still is to this day," Jennette said.

After leaving the Outer Banks for work in a Pennsylvania steel mill and service in the Coast Guard, Jennette finally returned, to operate an Esso service center, bait shop and Jeep rental service in Buxton. He left, again lured by the sea, rejoined the Coast Guard, this time on an oceanographic ship traveling the world, visiting Puerto Rico, Brazil, Argentina, England and Monaco. He returned home again in 1970, to become manager of the Cape Hatteras Water Association for the next 13 years. Not long after retirement, Jennette began working for the National Park Service as a seasonal maintenance worker. By 1986, he was officially an interpreter, telling stories as no one else could, because he had lived them. His very first presentation occurred at the dedication of the visitor center, the building that had been his childhood home.

"I enjoy what I'm doing," the soft-spoken and thoughtful Jennette said. "I plan to stay."

the look familiar along the rest of the developed areas of the Banks.

Hatteras Village, at the western tip of the island, is second only to Wanchese as the Banks' center of commercial fishing activity. We have seen upwards of 60 drop-netters (gill netters) run out from there during the late fall and early spring. At the docks, during this time of year, you can see all the activity of a busy fishing port, tons of trout coming in under the watchful eyes of wharf cats and gill nets being dried. Trout, croakers, big blues and king mackerel are packed in shaved ice, trucked out in 5,000-pound lots, ending up in fish markets in New York City within 24 hours. Most of these boats come from other towns and spend the season out of Hatteras, fishing in the neighborhood of the light. Do you feel like taking a different kind of vacation? If you're young and hearty, you might talk yourself into a billet aboard one of these hard working craft.

Sport fishing, for marlin and other big sport fish, is another Hatteras specialty. The Hatteras Marlin Tournament is perhaps the biggest single week in Hatteras Village. Up to 60 private boats, carrying some of the East Coast's leading politicians and business people, attend this invitation-only championship, one of the most prestigious in the country. The tournament is hosted by the Hatteras Marlin Club, in the village, and takes place the second week in June.

Attractions

PEA ISLAND
NATIONAL WILDLIFE REFUGE
N. end of Hatteras Island   *987-2394*

Once you cross Oregon Inlet, leaving the Herbert C. Bonner Bridge behind, you're on Pea Island. To your left is the surf, to your right the marsh. And everywhere, everywhere are birds.

Pea Island was founded on April 12, 1938, when Congress provided that Pea Island be preserved as a haven for wildlife, specifically as a wintering area for the greater snow goose. Roosevelt's CCC was put to work stabilizing the dunes with bulldozers and sea oats; sand fences were built; dikes

were constructed to form ponds and freshwater marshes; and fields were planted to provide food for wildfowl. The refuge was seldom visited by tourists until the Oregon Inlet bridge was constructed in 1964. Now Pea Island is one of the most popular spots on the island for naturalists, bird watchers and wildlife lovers. The name comes from "dune peas" that wintering geese fed on. The peas are found in a plant with tiny pink and lavender flowers, which at one time grew abundantly in the dunes.

Both bird watchers and wreck lovers will want to stop at the rest area some 4½ miles south of the Bonner Bridge. If you walk over the dunes toward the ocean you will be able to see the remains of the Federal transport *Oriental*. The black mass is thought to be her steel boiler, all that remains of the ship that went ashore in May 1862. A short walk toward the sound leads to an overlook of North Pond and New Field, where special crops are sown each year to be eaten by the waterfowl that remain on the Outer Banks during the relatively mild winter months (see North Pond Trail).

The 5,915 acres of the refuge are an important wintering ground for whistling swans, snow geese, Canada geese and 25 species of ducks. Many other interesting species, such as Savannah (Ipswich) sparrows, migrant warblers, shorebirds, gulls, terns, herons and egrets can be found here during the winter months and during spring and fall migrations. During the summer months, herons, egrets, terns, American avocets, willets, black-necked stilts and a few species of ducks can be found nesting at the refuge. Oceanic species can be expected during most any season but are most common during late summer and fall months and can be seen through the winter months too. Many species not usually seen on the Outer Banks have also been observed following storms. In all, more than 265 species of birds have been identified repeatedly at the refuge and over the ocean nearby. Another 50 species of accidental or rare occurrences have also been identified. We recommend you use mosquito repellent from March through October. Ticks may also cause problems; you may want to refer to the section on ticks in the Service Directory for some help.

The Refuge Headquarters is located some 7¼ miles south of Oregon Inlet.

Volunteers patrol from Memorial Day to Labor Day looking for Loggerhead turtle nests, relocating them if necessary and guarding hatchlings on their way to the sea. To volunteer, contact the Outdoor Recreation Planner at Alligator River, 473-1131.

NORTH POND TRAIL
Pea Island

This self-guided nature trail is a favorite of birdwatchers. It begins five miles south of Oregon Inlet Bridge or 2½ miles north of the Pea Island Refuge Headquarters. The parking area and rest rooms mark the beginning of the trail. It is roughly one mile long, taking you about 30 minutes to walk briskly to the sound and back.

The trail itself is on top of a dike between two artificially-made ponds, (Though interrupted by two stepped-viewing platforms, the trail, platforms and mounted binoculars are totally handicapped accessible.) The ponds and dike were constructed in the 1930s and early '40s by the CCC. Wax myrtles and live oaks stabilize the dike and provide shelter for songbirds. Warblers, yellowthroats, cardinals and seaside sparrows rest here during their spring and fall migrations.

On either side of the trail you'll look out over a closely managed ecosystem. The fields are planted with such bird goodies as rye grass and fescue. During the winter, hundreds of snow geese and Canada geese can be seen resting and eating in this area, and cattle egrets can be seen here during the summer. Pheasants, muskrats and nutria live here year round. The diketop view is ideal for birdwatchers. Bring a tripod-mounted scope of at least 15x. Probably 25x would be better. The ranges are long over the pond. However, this trail isn't just for birdwatchers; it's perfect for everyone who wants to escape to a quiet, scenic place.

PEA ISLAND REFUGE HEADQUARTERS
Hwy. 12 987-2394

Located on the sound side, 7¼ miles south of Oregon Inlet, is the refuge headquarters building.

There are a small parking area and a Visitor Contact Station staffed by refuge volunteers (Monday through Friday, April through November, 9 AM to 4 PM). Though visitor services are limited, you may want to stop in for information on bird watching and the use of the nature trails. Special public programs are offered during the summer months.

Discussions with refuge personnel about rules for visitation lead to the following list of things to do and not to do while you're on refuge land. You're not allowed to hunt. Camping is not permitted, and open fires are not allowed. Dogs must be on a leash and are allowed only on the beach and dunes, not on the west side of the highway in the ponds, marsh and salt flats. Four-wheel drive vehicles are not permitted on the beach. Firearms are not permitted within the confines of the refuge. Headquarters personnel say that shotguns and such must be stowed out of sight even if you are on the road just driving straight through. Those hunting farther south on Hatteras are advised not to flaunt their equipment on the refuge.

Beach fishing is permitted. Fishing, crabbing, boating, etc. are allowed on the ocean or soundside but not in refuge ponds.

We might suggest one side trip from the headquarters building. It's only a few hundred feet, but it takes you back a century in time. Walk east of the building, across the highway and over the dunes, in the surf or on the beach, and you'll find a few remnants of concrete foundation. Those bare chunks are the remnants of Pea Island Station, the only U.S.

Lifesaving Service station to be manned entirely by African-Americans. How it came to be so, and what they accomplished, is a little-known story that deserves to be told here.

Established with the rest of the stations in 1879, Pea Island was at first, like the others, manned entirely by white crews. Like the other crews, it had black personnel, but they were confined to such menial tasks as caring for the tough little ponies that dragged the surfboats through the sand. The first white crew let the Lifesaving Service down. They were dismissed in 1880, after only one year, for negligence in the handling of the Henderson disaster. The authorities then collected the black personnel from the other stations, placed them under the charge of Richard Etheridge, who was part black and part Indian, and set them to their duty.

The new crew carried out their duties magnificently. The Pea Island Crew risked life and health rescuing the crews and passengers of vessels that came driving ashore in northeasters and hurricanes. Etheridge became known as one of the best prepared, most professional, and most daring leaders in a service where professionalism and selflessness were a matter of course. The *E. S. Newman* was probably the most famous of their rescues. That story is recounted in the dry summary prose of The Annual Report of the Operations of the United States Life Saving Service for the Fiscal Year Ending June 30, 1897:

"Oct. 11 (1896), American Schooner *E. S. Newman*, Pea Island, North Carolina.

Photo: Mary Ellen Riddle

Buxton Books is a great place to select some good summer reading.

"Sails blown away and master obliged to beach her during hurricane two miles below station at 7 PM. Signal of distress was immediately answered by patrolman's Coston light. Keeper and crew quickly started for the wreck with beach apparatus. The sea was sweeping over the beach and threatened to prevent reaching scene of disaster, but they finally gained a point near the wreck. It was found to be impossible to bury the sand anchor, as the tide was rushing over the entire beach, and they decided to tie a large-sized shot line around two surfmen and send them down through the surf as near the vessel as practicable. These men waded in and succeeded in throwing a line on board with the heaving stick. It was made fast to the master's three-year-old child, who was then hauled off by the surfmen and carried ashore. In like manner his wife and the seven men composing the crew were rescued under great difficulties and with imminent peril to the lifesavers. They were all taken to station and furnished with food and clothing, and during next three days the surfmen aided in saving baggage and stores from wreck. On the 14th three of the crew left for Norfolk, and on the 21st the remainder departed for their homes, the vessel having proved a total loss."

CHICAMACOMICO
LIFE SAVING STATION

Rodanthe   987-1552

The buildings, once boarded up, with broken windows and rusted padlocks, are now restored to their stately beauty, thanks to a group of dedicated citizens who refused to see this historic attraction fade into oblivion. Chicamacomico was one of the most famous Life Saving Stations on the Outer Banks. In 1874, Chicamacomico Station was part of a daring new concept in lifesaving. During that year the U.S. Life Saving Service was building a chain of seven stations along the Banks, at the points of greatest danger for oceangoing vessels. (See The U.S. Life Saving Service for their story.) Chicamacomico Station at Rodanthe, Number 179, was foremost. Under three Keepers — Captain Little Bannister Midgett III (Ban), Captain John Allan Midgett, Jr., and Captain Levene Westcott Midgett — it guarded the sea along the northern coast of Hatteras for 70 years. Number 179 Station and the Midgetts are still legends in the Coast Guard today. Since 1876 seven Midgetts have been awarded the Gold Life Saving Award and three have won silver; six worked or lived at Chicamacomico.

The Station was active through World War II, until the Coast Guard closed it down in 1954. It languished unused for some years thereafter, and many readers will remember its sagging, rotting roof and its boarded-up windows. Today, like so many previously unappreciated reminders of the Banks' seagoing heritage, it is being restored. The Chicamacomico Historical Association, Inc., a nonprofit organization established for the station's preservation, has cleaned up the interior, restored the exterior and has opened displays in the main station building. They've received some federal

Photo: N.C. Travel and Tourist Division

*Built in 1870, the Cape Hatteras Lighthouse is one of the most famous landmarks
on the North Carolina coast.*

and state grants, but only on a matching fund basis. You can help doubly with a check to the association at P.O. Box 140, Rodanthe, N.C. 27968. Be a lifesaver!

During past summers, Chicamacomico has been the site for one of the best historical interpretations we've seen. Sadly, these commemorative life saving drills held by the National Park Service on Thursdays, from mid-June to the end of August, are not scheduled this year due to National Park Service budget cuts. Before driving to Rodanthe for this purpose, check with the park service, 473-2111, or look for a complete schedule in the "In the Park" newsletter — it's chock full of information about programs.

CANADIAN HOLE
1½ miles south of Avon

If the wind is right, you can't miss this spectacular attraction. Stop in the parking lot on the west side of the highway, and watch the windsurfers sail the sound in their brightly colored rigs. Kids can play in the shallow water while everyone enjoys the sight of hundreds of windsurfers in action. You never know who'll be on site, but some of the country's top windsurfers have been known to frequent it.

THE WRECKS OF NORTHERN HATTERAS

One of our nicest memories is the sunny, still day of late winter when we scrambled over the dunes of northern Hatteras with two friends after a storm. On the bare beach we found a freshly-uncovered wreck. We were able to date it to the mid-19th century by the method of fastening sheathing to ribs. We searched the sand in the still silence and found mementoes: a tiny bottle that might have held opium or perfume, a spar with emaciated iron fittings still attached, a broken teacup and a quaintly shaped whiskey bottle with the rotting remains of a cork. No treasure chest — not that time.

Yes, literally hundreds of ships have gone ashore on these beaches in 400 years. And most of them are still here. Wood, buried in sand along the Banks, holds up surprisingly well. The continual wrestle of beach and sea yields them up from time to time. Michael McOwen, who flies a light plane out of Manteo, made out the ribs of an old sailing ship one day in about 30 feet of water off the beach; he snorkeled out as soon as it got warm enough and had himself some fine tautog and porkfish. And there are more modern ships as well. In February 1948, while being towed to Charleston, LST 471 parted its lines and drifted ashore at Rodanthe.

Insiders' Tips

Wear shoes from your car to the beach, especially in midsummer.

Personnel from the then-still-active Chicamacomico Coast Guard Station rescued three of the crew with beach apparatus. Previous visitors will remember that the pilothouse was visible for some years, up till 1985, when a storm tore it apart and sent part of the hull crashing into the fishing pier. The remainder of it is (at least at time of writing) buried by sea and sand. But it will be back one day, like all the other ghost ships of the Outer Banks.

Find an established entry onto the beach then begin your search. Wrecks, like gold, are where you find them.

U.S. COAST GUARD FACILITY
Buxton   *995-5881*

Formerly the Naval facility at Buxton, the grounds and buildings were turned over to the Coast Guard in June 1982. It's not normally open for visitors, but retired military, dependents, and military personnel may use the few remaining facilities. There's a limited commissary, a small exchange, small mess hall, recreational facilities (tennis, basketball, and beach swimming) and a small dispensary. The hours, at all military bases and stations, are subject to change, but don't plan on anything being open after 5 PM.

THE ALTOONA WRECK
Cape Point

After driving to the end of Cape Point Way, you will see Ramp 44 straight ahead. Don't try to drive over, or even up to, this ramp in a regular car. A four-wheel-drive vehicle will make it over the soft sand between the road and the ramp; a

two-wheel-drive vehicle will not. We speak from experience, as we tried it and lost . . . and towing fees in Buxton are, to say the least, not competitive. Instead, leave your car on the solid ground near the road and walk over the ramp and continue on the foot trail that veers off at a 45-degree angle at the base of the dune. At the edge of the seawater pond, about a 10 minute walk from where you parked your car, you'll find all that remains of the sea-savaged *Altoona.*

The *Altoona* was a cargo ship, a two-masted, 100-foot-long schooner out of Boston. It was built in Maine in 1869. In 1878 it left Haiti with a load of dyewood bound for New York and was driven ashore on the Cape by a storm on October 22, 1878. Its crew of seven was rescued, the deck cargo lost, but the cargo in the hold was salvaged. A few years sufficed for the shifting sands to bury it. It reemerged in 1962 in a storm, and was quickly broken apart by the sea. The bow and part of the hull, still with greenish copper teredo sheathing on it, lie pointing south. A few odd pieces of ribs and beams lie scattered between it and the Atlantic.

DIAMOND SHOALS LIGHT
Off Cape Point

From the lighthouse, or even from the eastern shore of Cape Point, you may be able to see on a clear night a sudden white flash of light from far out at sea. Time it; if the flashes come every 2½ seconds, you are looking at the Diamond Shoals Light, some 12 miles out at sea southeast of the lighthouse, marking the end of the shoals that have claimed so many ships.

Through the years, there have been numerous attempts to build lighthouses out there on the shifting sandbars; all have failed. Three lightships have been on station there since 1824. The first was sunk in a gale in 1827; the second lasted from 1897 until 1918, when it was sunk by the German submarine U-140; and the third remained in service until 1967, when it was replaced with the present steel structure.

How long will it last?

THE MONITOR
Off Cape Hatteras

Every American knows the story of the *Monitor* from schoolbooks. How, during the Civil War, the Confederates built the first ironclad warship from the hulk of the Union frigate *Merrimac*, renaming it the *Virginia*. How, in the early hours of March 8, 1862, the tent-shaped ship steamed out of Norfolk to challenge a Union blockading force of six wooden ships — and how, by the end of the day, she had sunk two of them and damaged another, broken the blockade and written a new chapter in naval history.

The *Monitor* was an even more daring innovation. Built by John Ericsson, a Swedish-American engineer, the "Cheesebox on a raft" was a low-slung ironclad whose main battery was carried in a futuristic revolving turret. Arriving in Norfolk in the nick of time — the next day — the *Monitor* battled her adversary throughout the night, and finally, the fight at a draw, the *Virginia* retreated back under the guns of Norfolk. Neither of these first ironclads

lived very long. The *Virginia* was destroyed by retreating Confederates; the *Monitor*, ordered south, foundered off Cape Hatteras during a New Years' Eve storm in 1862. And there it lay for 120 years, unseen by human eye, even its location unknown.

It was rediscovered in 1973, resting quietly upside down, just as it sank, in 200 feet of water 25 kilometers south-southeast of Cape Hatteras.

Since then, the *Monitor* has been designated the first National Underwater Marine Sanctuary, and has been the object of repeated dives and evaluations by government agencies and underwater archaeologists. A few small artifacts — bottles, silverware, that sort of thing — have been recovered, and in 1983 the ship's distinctive four-bladed anchor was located and raised by a NOAA/ East Carolina University expedition.

So far, aside from a collection of artifacts at the Visitor Center, there's nothing to actually see of the *Monitor*. But someday there might be. NOAA is considering the feasibility of raising the turret, which is relatively complete, and other parts of the ship's hull for preservation and eventual display.

CAPE POINT,
CAPE HATTERAS NATIONAL SEASHORE
Buxton

As you continue that leisurely drive south along the length of Hatteras Island, you will come to the sharp elbow in the road that leads into Buxton. To your left, beyond a small cluster of motels, you can hear the surf booming; to the right are

Birding on Pea Island

Pea Island has earned a reputation as a birder's paradise because it's an outstanding birding area year round (the birds discovered the joys of the off season Outer Banks long before human visitors did.) An abundant variety of bird life passes through the "Atlantic flyway" over Pea Island. This flyway is one of several air routes migrating birds use regularly during their semiannual trips north and south.

The beginning birder should be armed with a good field guidebook and a pair of decent seven-to-ten-power binoculars. Of the several excellent field guides on the market, the most familiar is Roger Tory Peterson's *A Field Guide to the Birds* (Houghton Mifflin Co., Boston). This guide and others are available at any good bookstore. In this area, the National Park Service sells them at the Wright Brothers National Memorial in Kill Devil Hills. There are excellent free brochures about bird species available at the refuge headquarters and at the trailhead. One is published by Coastal Wildlife Refuge Society, a group of volunteers that maintains trails in the refuge. (If interested in helping this organization, write P.O. Box 1808, Manteo N.C. 27954.) An observation record sheet at the refuge headquarters allows visitors to record rare and unusual sightings. Many avid birders check this sheet before venturing onto trails or the beach.

In the spring the males of most species are more vividly colored during the mating season than at other times during the year. Passerines (perching birds) can be located at times, though spotting them is difficult. They are identified by a particular song sung by the males to mark their territory during nesting season. Pick a warm, dry day during the early morning, when birds are feeding (woodland birds tend to take a siesta during the hot midday). Dress in drab clothing that doesn't rustle so that you can hear the birds without startling them. Move slowly and quietly, listening and watching for movement in the trees or bushes. When you see movement, don't take your eyes off the spot, and raise your binoculars to locate its source.

In the summertime, you're more likely to see wading birds such as herons, egrets, ibises, terns, gulls black skimmers, willets. If lucky, you'll see a blacknecked stilt. Some have seen peregrine falcons, piping plovers and bald eagles, all endangered species. In the winter, snow geese, tundra swans and 25 different species of ducks make their home at the refuge, and can also be spotted during spring and fall migrations.

Here are some helpful hints for beginners trying to identify birds: first of all, determine the size of the bird, and then compare your bird to one you are already familiar with, a robin or a bluejay, say, or even a pigeon. Note the dominant color, and then note the color of its beak, throat, breast, wings, back and tail. Pay close attention to the beak shape as well as color. Seed-eating birds such as cardinals or sparrows, for instance, have relatively large, conical-shaped beaks suitable for cracking seeds, while flycatchers, which actually catch insects on the wing and thus have no need for this less aerodynamic appendage, have a slender bill.

Notice whether the bird has wing bars and, if so, how many. Does the tail have a band across it? Is there a different color under the tail? What shape is it? Finally, pay attention to what the bird is doing. A flycatcher won't scratch around on the ground like a towhee, and you won't find a woodpecker sucking pollen like a hummingbird or probing in shallow water like a dunlin.

Don't be discouraged if you can't identify everything right away. Starting a life list will increase your pleasure in birding enormously. You will probably find that even if you are a rank beginner, you can probably list a dozen birds that you already know. Note the date, the species and the location where you first identified the bird. You'll enjoy looking back over this list, and you will find you are eager to add to it. Good birding!

the trees of a small forest — here, on the Banks! As Highway 12 curves to the right, signs point to the left, toward the Lighthouse and the Coast Guard Facility. Resist your first impulse to turn, continue about 200 yards past the turn for the Facility, and turn left there to the Cape Point area of the Cape Hatteras National Seashore.

The approach is beautiful, a winding drive between brush-covered dunes with the white and black striped lighthouse looming on your left. There's a nice photograph on your left, about halfway there, where the lighthouse is reflected in pond water. The Cape Point area contains a number of attractions and recreational opportunities: the visitor center, the lighthouse (which you now are allowed to climb — a real treat for the fit!), a shipwreck, a nature trail and a campground. Surfing and surf-fishing are permitted year round.

HATTERAS ISLAND VISITOR CENTER
Near Hatteras Lighthouse   995-4474

Built in 1854, this two-story frame house was for many years the home of the assistant keepers of the light (the smaller home just to the east was the quarters of the keeper himself). Today it's a National Park Service Visitor Center. Extensive historical renovation was completed in 1986 to restore the building to its original condition. The Principal Keepers' Quarters has been restored too.

Along with a helpful ranger at the information desk, it now houses a well-kept museum devoted to Man and the Sea at Hatteras. The exhibits and displays focus on shipping, the Cape at War, Making the Cape Safe, the lighthouses themselves and the heroes of the Life Saving Service (later to become the Coast Guard). There's information on the rescue of passengers from stranded ships in storms, and a small, but well-stocked, bookstore carries books on related subjects. Last but not least, clean public rest rooms are located here.

You can also obtain a schedule of activities conducted by the Park Service on Hatteras Island daily during the summer. Schedules are available for spring and fall activities too. Activities and programs change each season, of course. The Center is open 9 AM to 5 PM daily, September through mid-June, and 9 AM to 6 PM from mid-June until Labor Day. (Hours are subject to change.) It's closed on Christmas Day.

CAPE HATTERAS LIGHTHOUSE

Cape Point   995-4474

For more than 175 years, mariners rounding stormy, dangerous Cape Hatteras have searched for the glimmer of Cape Hatteras Light to assure them of their safety. Sometimes they found it in time; sometimes, as the bare-boned wrecks on the point testify, they didn't.

Hatteras has been a place of danger for ships since the Europeans first began crossing the Atlantic. Its typically turbulent weather is caused by the confluence of two currents: the warm, northward-flowing Gulf Stream and the southbound, inshore Labrador Current. An eight-mile finger of shoal water, the Diamond Shoals, and the low, featureless nature of the Banks coastline conspired

to lure hundreds of ships to rest in the 'Graveyard of the Atlantic'.

The first lighthouse at Hatteras Point was raised in 1802. Not so many years ago, its sandstone ruin was still visible about 300 yards south of the present lighthouse. A blizzard in March 1980, finally took it, so utterly that you can now search the beach for a single piece of crumbling sandstone. It was 90 feet high, with a feeble whale oil light and proved inadequate. Also, as the century progressed, it became evident that erosion would soon overtake it. It was heightened and improved, but as the years went by, erosion weakened it, and by the late 1860s it had to be replaced. The War between the States left its mark, too; the Confederates, retreating in 1861, took the light's lens with them.

The new lighthouse was built in 1869-70, of 1.25 million Philadelphia-baked bricks, at a cost of $150,000. It's built on a crisscross of heavy pine beams, with its foundation eight feet deep in the sand. A granite base sits atop that, and then the brick begins, carrying the lighthouse up to the light at 180 feet, and from there to the very tip of the lightning rod 208 feet above the foundation. The first light installed was whale oil, with a special Fresnel lens to flash its beam far out to sea. The eye-catching spiral paint job was added to make the lighthouse visible far out at sea during the day, so that ships could determine their position by taking bearings from a known point. When it was completed, the old lighthouse was dynamited. The new lighthouse was in service from 1870 to 1935, when it was abandoned due to beach erosion. The erosion halted, and in 1950 the lighthouse was reactivated by the Coast Guard. Today, its 800,000 candlepower electric light rotates every 7½ seconds, reaching out more than 20 miles to sea.

From the Visitor Center you can walk across to the lighthouse. As you can see, the beach migration that destroyed the first beacon is seriously threatening the second. The sea seems to hate lighthouses; it either strands them inland, as it did at Bodie Island, or it eats them, as it does lighthouses on the French side of the English Channel — and as it ate the great Pharos of Alexandria, the first lighthouse ever. Perhaps it is in revenge for the ships these lights have cheated them of.... This threat became critical in December 1980, when the high tide came within 50 feet of the structure's base. There were intense efforts to save it, including sandbagging and the dumping of rubble; but most geologists now agree that the beach built back naturally — at least for a time.

As a result of this serious threat to the lighthouse, the Save the Lighthouse Foundation and the National Park Service mounted an intensive effort to thwart the Atlantic Ocean and save the structure. The National Park Service turned to the National Academy of Sciences for help determining the most appropriate alternative for saving the lighthouse. The academy proposed that the lighthouse be moved ½ mile from its present location — placing it approximately 1,500 feet from the ocean. It is interesting to note that when the lighthouse was originally built, it was located approximately 1,500 feet from the ocean.

It has also been proposed that the two Keepers' Quarters and the generator house be moved as well to keep the entire complex within its historic placement. In February 1992 the National Park Service awarded a two-year contract to an engineering firm to design the site plan for the relocation. The contract for the actual relocation has not yet been awarded. There is no specific time planned for relocation, but the plan itself indicates that the lighthouse will be moved when the risk of leaving the structure where it is outweighs the risk of moving it. (And, of course, Congress must appropriate the funds.)

Meanwhile, thanks to the efforts of Hatteras Islanders, the lighthouse is open for climbing for all who are physically able. If you're up to scaling the 268 steps, you'll find a fantastic view of beaches and the island — like looking down from a 20-story building. We heartily recommend this adventure, but be aware that you cannot carry children in your arms or in a carrier of any type, so parents of little tykes may have to take turns. Climbing times are 9:30 AM to 4 PM May 27 through Labor Day and 10 AM to 2 PM from Sept. 6 through Columbus Day. This free experience would not be possible without the local volunteers who man the station, so to speak, so be sure to thank them as you leave.

Nothing is permanent on the Banks, but one thing is certain: this striking structure is one of the quintessential symbols of Hatteras. It symbolizes the men, who for centuries

Photo: Mary Ellen Riddle

To get away from it all, take a walk in Buxton Woods.

have battled the seas and the women who battled to build their lives and families waiting at home. We hope it can be saved for generations to come.

BUXTON WOODS NATURE TRAIL
Cape Point

The Nature Trail is 3/4 mile long, leading from the road through the wooded dunes, vine jungles and freshwater marshes of Buxton Woods. It's one of the best nature trails on the Banks. It is a must . . . don't miss it.

Beginning on the right side of the road south of the lighthouse and heading to the Point, the trail winds at first among low sand hills and then into the maritime microforest that has gradually established itself on this broadest part of the island. Its natural beauty is enhanced by small plaques, masterfully written, explaining the changing surroundings of the closed, fragile ecosystems of the Banks: the water table; the role of beach grass and sea oats in stabilizing the dunes; the beach microforest and its stages of development; and the harshness of the wind, sand and salt in this Banks environment.

There are cottonmouths on this trail, unmistakably fat-bodied, rough-scaled snakes in various dull colors (brownish, yellowish, grayish, varying almost to black), though they are rare. Don't stick your hands or feet where you can't see. If you encounter a snake, allow it time to get away; generally it will retreat. The local people advise extra caution when encountering a cottonmouth during chill weather, in spring or fall. During this period, they say, the snakes are less confident of their ability to get away from you, since they're rather sluggish in cool weather, and they're more likely to attack. In midsummer they will often scurry off quickly. If they stand their ground, though, we advise retreat!

It might also be a good idea to glance over the section on ticks and chiggers in the Directory before starting out. We don't recommend this trail for handicapped or very small children, but for everyone else, it's a must. Bring a picnic. Tables and charcoal grills are located just south of the trail.

BILLY MITCHELL AIR FIELD
Frisco

This is a small no-frills landing strip located about a mile south of Highway 12 just west of Frisco. Named after the controversial Army aviator who conducted some of his bombing tests near here in 1921, the strip is 3,000 feet long, 75 feet wide, oriented NE/SW and asphalt paved. An exhibit at the pilot's shed provides a history lesson.

FRISCO NATIVE AMERICAN MUSEUM
Frisco   995-4440

From the outside this building may not look like a museum, but inside, we were taken aback to find rooms of Joyce and Carl Bornfriend's personal 15-year collection of Native American artifacts. The Bornfriends are very serious about their study of Native American History and very knowledgeable as well. Hopi drums, pottery, kachinas, weapons, jewelry — it's real. When you stop here and wander through rooms of history, remember two people have dedicated themselves to the study of our history and have made their personal collection of artifacts available to the public. It's pretty amazing. Lectures to school groups, etc., can be arranged through a nonprofit educational foundation. It's open daily except Monday. Call for an appointment for groups. Be sure to check out the nice little nature trails out back, especially nice for those traveling with children.

THE GRAVEYARD OF
THE ATLANTIC MUSEUM
Hatteras Village

This planned museum is to be located on seven acres of Park Service land at the south end of Hatteras Village adjacent to the ferry docks and the Coast Guard Station. We're providing you with advance notice because the Graveyard of the Atlantic Museum Committee is still plugging away at fund raising efforts, and we think this is a very worthwhile cause. The Federal Government has proven to be the biggest supporter of this project. The Reauthorization of the Marine Sanctuary Act (bill) included a provision for $800,000 for the construction of the museum. For more information or to make a contribution, write to the Graveyard of the Atlantic Museum, P.O. Box 191, Hatteras Village, N.C. 27943.

THE U.S. LIFESAVING SERVICE

In 1874, the U. S. Life Saving Service was a daring new concept. In that year the federal government began building a chain of seven stations along the Banks, at the points of greatest danger for oceangoing vessels. Each station was supervised by a keeper and had permanent winter crews of six skilled, strong and brave surfmen. They quickly proved their worth in an area known to all seamen as the "Graveyard of the Atlantic." Ships had a habit of coming ashore on the Banks in storms; the strong northeast winds and seas that developed during winter storms drove them helpless into shoal waters where pounding surf soon broke them up. Those who tried to swim ashore or row in life boats usually perished, battered to death in the icy water by waves and debris, or — even if they made it ashore safely — they froze slowly on a deserted coast.

The mission of the Life Saving Service was to rescue those on grounded ships . . . and a demanding, often suicidal mission it was. The surfmen stood watch all along the coast, in the worst winter weather. Once a wreck was spotted, they had to return to the station, get boats, rescue gear and the rest of the crew, and then drag everything in heavy carts through the soft sand to where the stricken vessel lay. There they might go out to it by boat, driven not by engines but by strong arms on the oars; might attempt to swim out; and might fire a line with a Lyle gun and pull the shipwrecked mariners and passengers to safety one by one by breeches buoy high above the deadly surf. In the wrecks of the *Metropolis* (1878), *A.B. Goodman* (1881), and dozens of others, these hardy men, for the most part native Bankers, distinguished themselves in courage and seamanship.

Some flavor of what they went through is preserved between the faded blue covers of the Annual Reports of the Operations of the U.S. Life Saving Service. A century old now, with pages fragile as old iron found in the surf, their laborious prose still evokes the terror of gigantic, freezing surf and the incredible heroism of these common men. Here, shortened a bit and paragraphed more closely to modern tastes, but otherwise unchanged, is the story they tell of one day in the Life Saving Service: the disastrous 24th of October, 1889.

WRECK OF THE SCHOONER HENRY P. SIMMONS

"October, 1889, was in general a very tempestuous month, but there can be little doubt that the most destructive storm experienced on the Middle Atlantic coast of the United States during the month was that which reached the coasts of Virginia and North Carolina on the afternoon of the 23rd, and raged with great violence and with but slight intermission until the evening of the 27th. The easterly wind blew at times with the violence of a hurricane, and drove the sea into mountainous billows which endangered all craft so unfortunate as to be within its influence. The low beaches of Virginia and North Carolina were literally strewn with wrecks, and the hardy crews of the Sixth District were kept exceedingly busy saving life and property. The storm had come with such suddenness that many coasters were unable to reach a harbor, and this will account for the great number of casualties . . . . In three instances . . . there was lamentable loss of life, the particulars of which are here given.

"The vessels involved were the schooners *Henry P. Simmons*, *Francis E. Waters*, and *Lizzie S. Haynes*; all three being wrecked within a few miles of each other, the first two in the night of the 23rd and the Haynes on the following day. The case of the Simmons was a particularly harrowing one, as, owing to the long duration of the storm and the great distance from the shore at which she sunk, it was not until the morning of the 28th that anything could be done by the crews of the neighboring stations . . . .

"The *Henry P. Simmons* was a fine, staunch three-masted schooner of about six hundred and fifty tons, hailing from Philadelphia, Pennsylvania. She carried a crew of eight men all told, and was commanded by Robert C. Grace, who owned an interest in her. She had sailed from Charleston,

South Carolina, on or about October 17th, on her way to Baltimore, Maryland, deeply laden with a cargo of phosphate rock for use in the manufacture of fertilizers. The place where she sunk is a mile and a half to the northward and eastward of the Wash Woods Station. . . .

"The voyage was without special incident until the afternoon of the 23rd, when the gale set in from the northeast and with it a high and dangerous sea, which caused the vessel to plunge deeply and ship a great deal of water. The sole survivor, Robert Lee Garnett, a colored man, says that the deck was so constantly deluged by the seas that at 8 o'clock, when the fury of the storm made it necessary to take in the already close-reefed mainsail, the men were unable to handle it for fear of being washed overboard; and all hands were driven to the rigging for safety. The helm was lashed amidships, and with no one to guide her the schooner was thus practically helpless, and drifted completely at the mercy of the wind and waves. Rain was also falling in torrents, so that it was impossible to see anything around them, and the poor fellows were quite ignorant of their distance from the shore, knowing only that they must be in the vicinity of False Cape, Virginia. The laboring of the vessel had also caused her to spring a leak, and this added to the peril of the situation, for she was liable to sink at any moment.

"In the midst of these dangers the men, by watching their opportunity, would descend to the deck and work the pumps until again driven to the rigging by the seas. At half past 10 o'clock that night the schooner struck with a crash on what is known as Pebble Shoal . . . and there she bilged and quickly filled with water. The top of the cabin was almost immediately swept away, and the vessel settled into the sand until the hull was wholly submerged, leaving nothing but the masts above water. What passed during the remaining hours of that dreadful night is a blank, beyond the statement of Garnett that at 3 o'clock in the morning (24th) the steward, a colored man, unable to hold on any longer, fell into the storm-lashed sea and was lost. This greatly shocked the rest.

"When day dawned the scene from the rigging of the wreck was a wild and terrifying one. The wind still raged and the waves broke into surf as far offshore as the eye could see through the pelting rain and spoon drift, while to the leeward lay the low sand hills, which ever and anon came into sight and were then hidden by the towering billows that madly chased one another shoreward, and were there scattered with thunderous roar into a smother of foam and spray upon the desolate beach.

"The first intimation the Wash Woods crew had of there being a craft in the offing was after midnight, when the incoming patrolman from the north beat reported a faint white light, apparently some distance off. This he had answered with his Coston danger-signal. It should be stated here that the storm tide had risen so high that it swept completely across the low parts of the beach, the water in some localities being over the lower floors of the stations. Under these conditions patrol duty was attended with the greatest difficulty and danger, the men having in places to wade hip-deep and being frequently driven to the knolls for safety.

"The next patrol upon returning at daylight brought news that a vessel had sunk during the night well off shore; the masts at that time showing above water about two-thirds of their length, while the end of the jib boom was just visible between the seas. The vessel lay with her head shoreward. And it was scarcely light when the patrolman passed her, he saw nothing of the crew. Another surfman was at once dispatched up the beach to obtain more definite information, and returned with the report that he could see several men in the rigging. It was impossible to handle the beach apparatus just then, by reason of the condition of the beach, but as soon as the water fell off on the ebb tide the men set out with the long-range gear and after a hard tug reached the scene at about 10 o'clock in the forenoon.

"In the meantime . . . the second mate had been swept from the rigging and another man shared a like fate an hour or so later. Thus but five men were in the rigging when the station crew arrived, and shortly afterwards another fell into the sea.

"An attempt to reach the craft with a line thrown from the wreck-gun failed utterly, the shot dropping into the water about half way. It was thus demonstrated that, owing to the great distance, the beach apparatus was practically useless . . .

the schooner was at least one thousand yards off. Indeed the purpose of the keeper in firing the gun was more to reassure and encourage the poor fellows than from any hope of reaching them with the line. At the same time the surf was so high and dangerous that no human power could have forced a boat through it. The hands of the beachmen were practically tied. They could do nothing but watch and wait for the storm to abate and the sea to run down, and the outlook for this was not promising. Here, on the one hand, was a sunken vessel with her crew in the rigging, looking imploringly to the shore for help, and, on the other, a band of sturdy men skilled in the handling of boats in the surf and equipped with the most approved appliances for the saving of human life from the perils of the sea, but withal powerless to save. Yet this was the exact situation.

"At noon the party on the beach was reinforced by the arrival of the False Cape crew from the north . . . but their coming did no good, since the storm continued with unabated violence all day, and absolutely nothing could be done. With the approach of darkness driftwood fires were lighted and kept blazing all night to encourage the hapless sailors on the wreck. On the following day (25th) at 8 o'clock, the tide being low, an effort was made with a picked crew to launch the boat, but although the gale had slackened a little, the surf was still tremendously high and the attempt failed. The agony of suspense the poor fellows suffered must have been terrible, as cold, wet, and hungry they clung with the desperation of despair to the dripping shrouds, watching for the relief which could not reach them, waiting for their awful doom. Towards noon one more unfortunate fell exhausted from the rigging and disappeared. This left but three remaining alive . . ."

"The beach was vigilantly patrolled that night, an extra force of men being out watching for a lull . . . Three attempts were made (on the 26th) to reach the *Simmons*, but every time the boat was driven back full of water, the wind having changed to the southeast and set in more fiercely than before, with, if possible, a higher sea. Two of the remaining men were washed out of the rigging during the day in plain view of the people on the beach, and the day closed with but one man left on the wreck. The weather on the morning of the 27th was no more favorable, the wind falling in torrents, with a continuance of the southeasterly gale. Towards evening, however, the storm had nearly spent itself, and there was promise of a shift of wind to the westward. This was what the lifesavers had been hoping for and it gave them encouragement, though there must necessarily be one more night of horror for the sufferer in the rigging before the sea could run down sufficiently for him to be reached. If he could hold on a few hours longer he would be saved.

"By midnight the wind had canted to the southwest and subsided to a moderate breeze. The sea also fell rapidly, so that at 5 o'clock in the morning of the 28th, before daylight, the surfboat was again moved

down to the edge of the water in readiness for a launch. Life belts were then strapped on by the picked crew of oarsmen from the Wash Woods and False Cape crews, including Keeper O'Neal of the last-named station, and with the veteran keeper, Malachi Corbel, at the steering oar, a bold and successful dash was made through the heavy line of breakers at the bar. Once through these the boat was not long in reaching the sunken wreck, which, in the darkness, had to be approached with some caution to avoid entanglement in the cordage hanging from the spars. To the great relief of every man in the boat a faint response came to the keeper's hail, and presently there crept out into view the form of the sole survivor of the dreadful tragedy. He had been ensconced within the sheltering folds of the mizzen gaff-topsail, and this protection, with the aid of a splendid physique, had enabled him to withstand the great hardships to which he had been exposed. He had been without food of any kind for over four days, his only sustenance having been rainwater caught in the sail, and his survival was simply marvelous. Once in the boat no time was lost in transferring him to the shore, where restoratives from the medicine chest were quickly administered, and he was then conducted to the station, comfortably clad in warm garments from the supply box of the Women's National Relief Association, and otherwise cared for.

". . . Five of the bodies of the drowned seamen were subsequently recovered at various points along the shore, that of the captain being found on November 19th, nearly four weeks after death. All were given decent burial, the body of Captain Grace being afterward claimed and removed by relatives. . . ."

WRECK OF THE SCHOONER
FRANCIS E. WATERS

"Next in order is the wreck of the schooner *Francis E. Waters*, of Baltimore, Maryland, which was capsized and driven on the coast of North Carolina about two and three-quarter miles north of the Nag's Head Station, (Sixth District,) the same night that the *Henry P. Simmons* stranded, October 23, 1889. The entire crew perished. As shown in the preceding account, a furious storm raged all that night. Nothing was known of the disaster on shore until the next morning, when the schooner was discovered bottom up in the breakers. The story is necessarily brief. It appears that the *Francis E. Waters* left Georgetown, South Carolina, with a cargo of lumber and shingles for Philadelphia, Pennsylvania, on or about October 20th, her crew consisting of six men. The much-dreaded Frying Pan and Hatteras Shoals had been safely passed and the prospects seemed good for a quick voyage up the coast when, in the afternoon of the 23rd, the freshening easterly wind and the gathering clouds gave portent of the coming storm. By sundown the wind backed to the northeast and increased to a gale of terrific violence, the night becoming, in nautical phrase 'as dark as a pocket.' This, together with a tempest of driving rain and the blinding spray flying shoreward from the crests of the

breakers, produced atmospheric conditions upon the shore absolutely impenetrable to human vision. There was also an extraordinarily high tide, so that after midnight almost the entire expanse of low beach was submerged, compelling the patrolmen for their own safety to take to the higher and remote parts of the shore, thus increasing the distance between themselves and the outer line of the breakers on the bar, where vessels might be expected to fetch up. This distance was fully from one-half to three-quarters of a mile, and in some places probably greater. The patrols of the Nag's Head and Kill Devil Hills Stations, between which the unfortunate craft stranded, met regularly and exchanged checks up to the time stated, but after that the surf and rising tide swept over the beach in greater volume, and cut such deep gullies in the sand that the man who took the north beat from Nags Head at 3 o'clock in the morning of the 24th was unable to get nearer than within half a mile of the point where he should have met the south patrol from Kill Devil Hills.

"Therefore, after peering as far as was possible through the storm towards the end of his beat, he turned back, reporting upon reaching the station that he had been unable to get through, and that he had seen objects which he took to be lumber or wreckage of some kind floating in the swash of the surf. This it should be remarked is not an unusual occurrence. . . . The patrol from the Kill Devil Hills Station, who should have met the patrol from Nag's Head, upon arriving at the

Day's End on Cape Hatteras

Night comes gently to the Outer Banks,
where warm soothing breezes
mingle with sharp salty spray, kissing the lips of beach walkers
playing on the edge of
the darkening pebbled shore
while the tide's foam like fingers
caresses their toes.

The fiery sun softly sets
on waves rocking back and forth
and then disappears below the ocean,
leaving the faint moon to light
the vast blackness over the sea
as bonfires lit by onlookers
glow on the pulsating waters.

The old striped lighthouse winks relentlessly
at this changing of the guard —
The seashore's rendition of
day turning into night.

— Rosalie Koslof

halfway place and not finding anyone, pushed on south to ascertain the cause of the man's nonappearance. He had not gone more than a quarter of a mile beyond his own beat when, in the early gray of the morning, for it was now about 6 o'clock, he was startled by the discovery through the rain and mist of a vessel half submerged and bottom up in the breakers out on the bar. His first thought was for the crew, but there was not a soul to be seen on the ill-fated craft, so after satisfying himself on that point, and taking a long and searching look in every direction as far as the weather would permit, he retraced his steps to the station and reported his grim discovery to the keeper. The latter (Keeper Partridge,) at once telephoned the news to Keeper Van Buren Etheridge at Nag's Head; the wreck lying within the latter's patrol limits. Etheridge immediately turned out his men, and as the launching of a boat was out of the question, proceeded with such appliances as he thought might be needed to the locality of the wreck, the party arriving there at about half-past 8 o'clock. It was plainly to be seen that there could be no one on the half-buried hull against and over which the surf was dashing incessantly. A man could not have maintained himself there for a moment. The surfmen were therefore deployed along the beach in quest of bodies, and before long the search resulted in finding one corpse, that of a Negro, entangled in a part of the rigging attached to a broken mast which had washed up some distance from the wreck, and been left by the now receding tide. This body was decently interred later in the day, there being no marks upon it which might lead to its identification.

" . . . A second body, that of a white man, was cast ashore nearly two weeks afterwards at a point at least thirty miles to the southward, and recovered by the crew of the Gull Shoal Station. It was identified as the body of R. W. Lecompte, of Cambridge, Maryland, one of the schooner's crew, and relatives came and removed it. . . .

"It is therefore supposed that, losing her canvas or springing a leak and becoming water-logged and unmanageable, she let go her anchors to avoid drifting into the breakers, when, the ground tackle failing to hold her, she fell off into the trough of the sea, rolled over on her beam ends, and in that condition drifted ashore before the gale and sea. This view is supported by the fact that after the subsidence of the gale, and the sea had gone down sufficiently to permit the launching of the surfboat . . . the crew found a quantity of wreckage outside the bar about a quarter of a mile from the shore, and this was attached in some way to the anchors on the bottom. Or it is possible that she capsized under too great a press of sail in the effort to work away from the treacherous sands under her lee. . . ."

WRECK OF THE SCHOONER LIZZIE S. HAYNES

"The third of the group of three disasters in the Sixth District attended with fatal results during the great October storm was that of the *Lizzie S. Haynes*, a three-masted schooner owned in Bath, Maine, which was wrecked between the Oregon Inlet and Pea Island Stations, on the coast of North Carolina, in the forenoon of October 24, 1889.

"The northeast storm was then raging in all its fury, and there was a frightful sea. Her crew numbered seven men, and of these all but two perished. She was a vessel of four hundred and thirty-seven tons and was bound from Savannah, Georgia, to Baltimore, Maryland, with a cargo of yellow-pine lumber. From the accounts received it appears that she was first sighted by the crew of the Oregon Inlet Station at about half past 8 o'clock, a mile or two distant to the northward and eastward, and could just be dimly made out through the blinding rain, as she plunged and rolled in the turbulent waters under scant canvas and with her head pointed offshore. It was soon evident that she was making no headway, but, on the contrary, was drifting to the leeward toward the land very fast. As she came nearer it was noticed that her crew had taken refuge in the rigging, a sure sign of her helpless condition. Two men could be seen in the fore shrouds, three in the main, and two in the mizzen. Keeper Paine, anticipating difficulty in rescuing them while such a high surf was tumbling in upon the beach, telephoned the news at once to Keeper Etheridge of the next station south (Pea Island), and asked his aid.

"By 9 o'clock, when the schooner was nearly abreast of Oregon Inlet, Paine and his men had set out with the breeches-buoy apparatus to follow her down the shore, but she drifted so rapidly before the gale, and the beach was so deeply flooded in places that it was found impossible to keep up with her. She struck at twenty minutes to 10 o'clock, three hundred yards from the beach, at a point three and three-quarter miles below Oregon Inlet and a little less than two miles north of the Pea Island Station. She was thus within Etheridge's beat. The latter, as requested by Paine, had promptly left his station with a spare shot-line, (a No. 7,) the medicine chest, and a bag of blankets, and being therefore lightly burdened and having the shorter distance to travel, he and his crew reached the scene first. Thinking that the sea would force the schooner along the bar still further south, and nearer to his station, Etheridge dispatched his men back with the horses for his own beach apparatus, while he proceeded on north to meet the Oregon Inlet crew to lend them a hand, and at the same time consult with his brother keeper. The latter arrived abreast of the vessel at 10 o'clock, before the Pea Island crew could return.

"In the meantime a distressing and terrible accident had befallen the hapless people on the schooner, which practically sealed the fate of all but two of their number. It happened about five minutes before the Oregon Inlet crew arrived. The two crews were at this moment hurrying to the scene from opposite directions with their life-saving appliances, when . . . the Oregon Inlet crew, then but a short distance away, were horrified by the sight of all three of the schooner's masts breaking off by the board, leaving nothing standing above the deck but a stump of about twenty feet of the mizzenmast. The masts fell toward the stern and carried all but one of the crew to the deck, that one falling overboard and being immediately swept out of sight.

"This appalling and exciting incident infused fresh energy into the little band of jaded life-savers as they pressed forward, and within five minutes of the time of their arrival the Oregon Inlet crew had thrown a line over the wreck. The line landed near the stump of the mizzenmast. This was not more than ten minutes after the spars fell. The lumber of the deck load was already coming ashore on every sea, and this, with the broken spars, the sails, and the rigging, formed quite an entanglement between the vessel and the beach.

"Only two men could be seen on board, the rest either having been severely injured or killed outright by their fall. These two were the captain and the steward. The latter caught the shot-line as it came near him, and both men began hauling it off in order to get the whip or larger line which would follow, but before they could gather much of it in the shot-line fouled the wreckage, and in the effort to free it, it was broken or cut in twain. A second line was

Wildflowers

Driving south of Oregon Inlet, roadsides afford a mixed wildflower population most of the year. The nearness of the warm Gulf Stream tends to prevent extreme changes in temperatures. Late autumn blooming plants such as the Goldenrods (*Solidago*) sometimes bloom well into January during a mild winter. Early Cresses (*Barbarea*) and Chickweeds (*Stellaria*) begin their flowering in February, so there are almost always a few wildflowers on hand.

If you have chosen a late spring visit, roadside plants may include Blue-eyed Grasses (*Sisyrinchium*). This small, lily-like plant is in the Iris family and is recognized by its startling bright blue color. It grows in large colonies that create carpets of blue in wet ditches and other damp places along the highway. Avon is a good place to see these and Spring Ladies' Tresses (*Spiranthes vernalis*), which are tiny, white orchids. Their leaves resemble grass, and the flowers are borne pole-style on a single twisted stem.

Groups of Yuccas are also fairly common; they are huge and tough with long, dangerously pointed, fibrous evergreen leaves encircling the thick, trunk-like stem. Fat, cream, bell-shaped flowers bloom in a large cluster that rises above the plant's leafy parts. The hairy, prickly Yellow Thistle (*Cirsium horridulum*) blooms during the late Spring too. Its hefty size makes it easy to spot, and its large, fluffy-looking flower is the palest of yellows. A couple of high climbing vines are worth looking for, like the Yellow Jessamine (*Gelsemium sempervirens*), which has a thick trumpet-shaped flower of brilliant yellow; it blooms in April. The Coral Honeysuckle (*Lonicera sempervirens*) has smaller, narrower flowers of a similar design and is a fiery orange-red. Both are evergreen.

Summer brings quantities of Gaillardias (*Gaillardia pulchella*) or Jo Bells, as they are known locally. Introduced here years ago, these low growing, hardy plants are so salt resistant that you may see them near your oceanfront cottage. They look a lot like daisies and come in mixtures of reds and yellows. You'll find a lot of them along sandy roadsides. Both the Yellow and the White Sweet Clovers (*Melilotus officinalis* and *Melilotus alba*) are common, especially near the villages of Avon and Buxton. Seaside Croton (*Croton punctatus*), in the same family as the Poinsettias of Christmas fame, bloom near the ferry docks in Hatteras Village and near the beach. Roadside lawn mowers generally make their appearance by the end of June and from then on, staying ahead of them can be difficult. Everything looks like a short lawn after their passage.

From late summer through early winter, Goldenrods (*Solidago*), Asters and Bonesets (*eupatorium*) can all be seen along most roadsides. Bushes with berries become colorful at this time. Yaupon Holly (*Ilex vomitoria*), from which the old timers made tea, shows red berries beginning in November. Bayberry bushes (*Myrica pensylvanica*) on the north end of the island bear clusters of silver-covered, waxy berries. The foliage smells spicy. Flowering Water Bushes (*Baccharis halimifolia*) resemble clouds of white feathers, and the Beauty Berry Bushes (*Callicarpa americana*) produce dense clusters of intensely fuschia berries along their branches. Patches of Hairawn Muhly (*Muhlenbergia capillaris*), a highly salt resistant grass, look like purple or pink fog banks on the ocean side of the highway near Salvo.

Cape Hatteras, like much of the rest of the Outer Banks, is home to many other salt-resistant wildflowers and weeds. Buxton Woods is a genuine maritime forest of some 3,000 acres located on the widest part of the island near the Cape. Its dense canopy provides good protection from salt spray, and a variety of plants flourishes within its borders. The forest covers a series of ridges, which are old or relic dunes and low, wet, freshwater valleys called swales. There are also a number of shallow ponds called sedges and a few somewhat deeper ponds.

The best viewing of forest plants is along the Buxton Woods Nature Trail, built and maintained by the National Park Service. The trail is near the Cape Hatteras Lighthouse, but you need to make a right turn instead of the left you would normally make to enter the lighthouse grounds. A clearly visible sign on the right marks the trail's beginning. Small, well-placed plaques provide good information about plants and other items of interest found on the looped path. Since its length is only 3/4 mile, it's a pleasant walk.

A late summer little mint named Blue Curls (*Trichostema dichotomum*) may be found at the trail's entrance as may Golden Aster or Silkgrass (*Chrysopsis graminifolia*) with its dusty-looking, grasslike leaves. In the waters of Jennette's Sedge there is Common Bladderwort (*Utricularia vulgaris*), which runs along the edge of the trail's right fork. The thready underwater leaves of this meat-eating, freshwater plant have small bladders that entrap tiny water-dwelling animals that the plant then uses as food.

You will encounter many more plants than have been mentioned here. If we've peaked your curiosity, book stores offer some good basic wildflower guides. Barbara Midgette's excellent *Cape Hatteras Wildflowers* contains color photographs and complete descriptions of flowering plants found locally on the Outer Banks.

quickly fired from the shore as successfully as the first, but the current setting along the beach was so swift and strong, and there were so many other difficulties to contend with, the principal of which was the inability of the two men to haul off the line through the wreckage, that notwithstanding the most persistent effort it was nearly 4 o'clock in the afternoon before the poor fellows on the wreck, weakened and exhausted by exposure, could complete the rigging of the apparatus to the stump of the mast a few feet above the deck.

"When this was at last done the two men turned their attention to the mate, the only other member of the crew remaining alive, and made strenuous exertions to place him in the buoy first. But, injured as he was and suffering also from exposure, he had become delirious and resisted the efforts for his removal to the shore. The captain and steward were unable to manage him either by persuasion or force, and as night was nearly upon them, they reluctantly abandoned him to his fate and resolved to look out for themselves. The captain therefore got into the breeches buoy and was drawn safely to the beach, the steward following him just as darkness closed upon the scene. . . .

"The two rescued men, thoroughly used up, were conducted to the Pea Island Station as quickly as possible and properly cared for. As the tremendous surf on the rising tide had gradually pushed the schooner farther onto the shore, the crews of the two stations . . . returned to the beach and waited for an opportunity to board the wreck, hoping from what the captain had told them to be able yet to save the mate.

"The opportunity . . . came with the ebb of the tide, which about midnight left her in such a position that the men were enabled to wade out to her. Quickly climbing on board they found two bodies, one the mate's, the other that of a seaman, the rest having been washed away. Both bodies appeared to be dead, but as the mate's was still supple, though cold, it was landed without delay and carried to a house on the beach, where, with restoratives from the medicine chest, all possible means were resorted to for its resus-

citation. These efforts were kept up for two hours, until the stiffening muscles gave indubitable proof that life was beyond recall. Thus five of the little band of seven men composing the schooner's crew, who but a few hours before were in the full flower and promise of manhood, became the victims of the storm.

". . . The two bodies recovered from the wreck were provided with decent burial near the life-saving station. The rescued men remained at the station for a week, until able to travel to their homes, and during this period the crews of the two stations were engaged whenever opportunity offered — for as shown in the account of the loss of the *Henry P. Simmons* the bad weather lasted for several days — in recovering such articles as it was possible to save from the wreck."

The U.S. Life Saving Service was merged with the older Revenue Cutter Service in 1915 to form the U.S. Coast Guard. Its aircraft, surface craft and support personnel, from stations at Coquina Beach (Oregon Inlet), Buxton and Ocracoke, still guard the Banks and their offshore waters today.

Recreation

WATERFALL PARK
Rodanthe   987-2213

As you travel south on Hatteras Island, you'll find the only water slide and go-cart track south of Oregon Inlet. A 36-hole miniature golf course is also located here for those who prefer a quieter activity. The

motorized cars and boats are lots of fun too, and the cars perform just like regular automobiles, thrilling the most experienced driver — but watch out — competition for the road is tricky. This amusement park is open Memorial Day through Labor Day from 10 AM until 10 PM every day.

BUXTON STABLES
Buxton   995-4659

How many of us have dreamed of racing down an empty beach on the back of a sleek horse? Well, you can do just that at Buxton Stables. The basic charge is $25 per hour per person and three-hour beach rides are offered for $60 per person. Call

anytime between 7 AM and 8 PM daily for reservations; they are required. The stables are open year round, but call for schedule information during the off season. And remember, weather does affect the horses, so rides may not be available on certain days.

WINDSURFING HATTERAS
Avon   995-4970

This facility just keeps getting better and is a popular place for lessons, rentals and clinics. A complete line of surfwear, swimwear, surfing and windsurfing necessities and equipment is for sale here, and their site for windsurfing and sailing in Pamlico Sound is one of the best.

Windsurfing gear, catamarans, jet skis, boogie boards, soft boards and roller blades can be rented. Parasailing and kayaking lessons are available too. They're open from 8:30 AM until 9 PM every day during the season. Check for winter hours; they close only in January. Reservations are recommended for lessons. Many special events are held just over the soundside bridge out back of the shop. Call for a schedule.

AVON WINDSURF COMPANY
Avon   995-5441

This shop specializes almost exclusively in windsurfing equipment and is located not too far north from the famed windsurfing spot, Canadian Hole. Windsurfing lessons are available on a private sailing site just north of Avon during June, July and August. Lessons are three to four hours long with certified instructors. Small classes are the norm, and the cost is $39 for each lesson. All you need to bring with you is a swimsuit, sunscreen and your sense of humor — remember, this is supposed to be fun so don't try to take it too seriously! Avon Windsurf even offers their own line of sails in addition to equipment from Europe and other parts of the world. The shop opens February 1 and closes December 15.

KITTY HAWK KITES
Avon   995-6060

Kitty Hawk Kites' Avon location offers kayak lessons and tours on the sound. No experience is necessary, but reservations are required. Call 441-4124. This location also sponsors free daily workshops on kite flying and sport climbing. Call for a schedule of events.

PARADISE WATERSPORTS
Buxton   995-6979
Avon   995-4970

This water sports business is located in Avon at Windsurfing Hatteras and at a second location in Buxton on Highway 12 on the sound. Paradise Watersports offers rentals of sailboats, waverunners, outboard skiffs and sailing lessons at both locations. Rentals and lessons in Avon are handled inside Windsurfing Hatteras, and the sailing site is located behind the shop on the sound. For rentals and lessons at the Buxton site you must either call their Buxton number or stop by the site. Personal watercraft repairs and equipment maintenance including battery and spark plug changes are offered in Buxton along with sailboat maintenance. Power equipment rents hourly, and the skiffs and sailboats rent for a half or full day.

FOX WATER SPORTS
Buxton   995-4102

Ted James originally came here from Florida to make boards. He now has a retail shop where he sells surfwear, offers windsurfing lessons and provides equipment rentals, including boogie boards and surf boards. He has been teaching windsurfing for years, and word has it there's almost no one he can't get sailing. Two or three consecutive hours of lessons are recommended for beginners and lessons cost $35 per hour. This windsurfing shop is located about five miles south of one of the best windsurfing locations on the east coast, Canadian

Hole. The shop closes before Christmas and reopens mid-March. Hours are 9 AM to 9 PM during the season. Check for off season hours.

OCEAN EDGE GOLF COURSE
Frisco 995-4100

Located in the heart of fishing territory, this nine-hole golf course covers 23 acres of dunes just off the main highway. The golf course offers a popular alternative to fishing, and many have found its three par-four holes and six par-three holes a good challenge. A full clubhouse facility is planned. Golf carts, club rentals and Ocean Edge logo items are available. Inquire about weekly rates for vacationers. It's open year round and the public is welcome.

TRENT WOODS GOLF CENTER
Frisco 995-6325

Situated in Trent Woods among tall pines, live oaks and fresh water ponds, the 18-hole championship miniature golf course is a perfect choice for family recreation after a day on the beach or on an overcast day. You're in the heart of nature in this well-planned facility, and it's a great place for a birthday party or other special occasions.

COOL WAVE ICE CREAM SHOP AND MINIATURE GOLF
Buxton 995-6366

Cool Wave features a nine-hole miniature golf course with moving obstacles. Hours are 12 PM until 10 PM, seven days a week during the season. The cost for play is $2 for nine holes and $2.75 for 18 holes (or around the course two times). Cool Wave is open between Easter

and Thanksgiving. And, of course, there's always ice cream for after the game!

AVON FISHING PIER
Avon 995-5480

This 471-foot-long pier has undergone extensive renovations. It's open from Easter until Thanksgiving, 24 hours a day. Pier fees are $6 a day for adults, $4.50 a day for children under 12 and $1 for sightseeing. Many species of fish are hauled in from this pier according to local anglers; you might catch flounder, trout, sea mullet, king mackerel and red drum.

Albert Mosley, pier manager, is very proud of the renovated pier house. Oh sure, the tackle shop is still there, but you can't miss the new two-story decking for the Pier Bar and Grill overlooking the ocean. The restaurant is open from 6 AM until 10 PM daily for breakfast, lunch and dinner and a children's menu is available. (See our chapter on Restaurants.) And, if you haven't already noticed, there's an 18-hole natural grass putting course, Avon Golf, in front of the pier. The golf house contains a large arcade game room, ice cream and snacks. The cost to play 18 holes is $5 during the day until 5 PM and $6 from 5 PM until closing (1 AM in season).

CAPE HATTERAS PIER
Frisco 986-2533

Also known as Frisco Pier, this pier is privately owned and is situated on National Park Service land in Frisco. It's located between Frisco Shopping Center and Burrus' Red and White. The pier points south into the ocean and is closest to the Gulf Stream. It's 480 feet long, and many species of fish are caught here night and day. There's a snack bar in addition to the bait and tackle shop. Rates on the pier are: $5 per day, $25 per week, $100 per season for individuals, $150 for a family and $135 per couple. The cost for sight-seeing is $1. Pier hours are 6 AM until 11 PM Sunday through Thursday, and it's open until midnight Friday and Saturday during the season. Check for off season hours; it's open from April through November.

HATTERAS ISLAND FISHING PIER
Rodanthe   987-2323

This is a privately-owned fishing pier located on National Park Service land in the small village of Rodanthe (the northernmost village of the Hatteras Seashore as you drive south). The pier opens in April and closes after Thanksgiving. Louise Twiner is the pier manager, and the pier shop provides bait, tackle, ice, rental equipment and everything you need to fish. The pier is handicapped accessible, and there's plenty of parking. We've been told that large channel bass are plentiful here. The cost for fishing is $5 a day, $25 a week, and children younger than 12 are $3. Sight-seeing will cost you $1.

For your convenience, you'll also find a 44-room motel, Hatteras Island Resort, located here. The motel opens and closes according to the pier schedule during the year but the motel-style rooms and efficiencies are available for nightly and weekly rentals. Cottages are available for weekly rentals. Down Under

Restaurant and Lounge, 987-2277, is right next door, and the moderately priced food here is very good.

TEACH'S LAIR MARINA
Hatteras Village   986-2460

This is the largest marina in the Hatteras Village. It has 92 slips and accommodates boats between 10 feet and 53 feet long, all with full hookups except sewage. There's a boat ramp and a tackle shop with a wide range of fishing gear, ice and bait. You'll also find a dive boat and dry storage for boats and campers. Charter boats operate from here. Rates for Gulf Stream charters run from $550 to $700 for a day. All this is conveniently located near the ferry terminal.

HATTERAS HARBOR MARINA AND GIFT STORE
Hatteras Village   986-2166
Charter reservations   (800)676-4939

Located on the soundside just over a mile north from the ferry terminal, this charter boat marina boasts some of the most modern accommodations for the big fishing boats available on the Outer Banks. As many as two dozen boats operate from here, and charter reservations for 18 different boats are easily made by calling the numbers listed above. There are 46 slips with 110/220V power, accommodating boats up to 60 feet long. The rate for docking is $.75 per day, and there's no time limit. Prices for full day Gulf Stream charters range from $600 to $800. Half day inshore charters are available for around $300. Diesel fuel is available.

This is the place for big boats, as the basin is dredged to seven feet at

Photo: Mary Ellen Riddle

Children love to play in the sand along the Hatteras beaches.

mean low water. Don't forget the annual Blue Water Open Billfish Tournament held here every year in June. The marina store carries everything you need and the gift shop is filled with interesting items including fishing supplies and better quality sportswear. In season hours are 6 AM until 8 PM.

Harbor Seafood Deli, 986-2331, is located adjacent to the marina store. Hours are 6 AM until 7 PM during the season, and breakfast and lunch are served. There are always daily seafood specials, and Ricki's shrimp pasta salad is a popular item. Beer and wine are sold here along with hand-dipped ice cream. Steamed shrimp to order is a great idea for the late afternoon while you're watching the boats come in with the daily catch. The screened-in deck area overlooks the marina. The deli will even pack a lunch for your charter trip if you notify them a day ahead of time.

ODEN'S DOCK
Hatteras Village   986-2555

Oden's is one of the oldest family-owned boat docks in Hatteras Village. There are a full line of supplies, a repair shop and Texaco marine products available here. *Miss Hatteras*, can be booked here too. Call 986-2365 to join a Wednesday night seafood dinner cruise ($20 per person) or a Friday night history cruise ($7). Birdwatching cruises are also available.

BURRUS FLYING SERVICE
Frisco   986-2679, 995-6671

Bring your adventurous spirit and camera for a flight-seeing tour. You can pick from three tours. You'll take off at Billy Mitchell Airstsrip in Frisco. There's a ticket office near the post office. Flights over Cape Hatteras Lighthouse, Diamond Shoals, Hatteras Inlet, Ocracoke and Portsmouth Island provide a thrill you won't forget. Rates are $25 per person for a party of two and $20 per person for party of three on the 30-minute cape tour over Pamlico Sound to Canadian Hole and Avon, and $32.50 per person for a party of two and $25 per person for a party of three for the 45-minute north or south tours. Flights are available 10 AM until sunset. On Sundays, flying times are from 2 to 6 PM.

LEE ROBINSON GENERAL STORE
Hatteras Village   986-2381

Bicycle rentals are very popular at this general store. Rates are $2 per hour, $10 per day and $35 per week.

HATTERAS LIBRARY
Hatteras Village   986-2385

The village has a rather large library of 10,000 or more books. It's located across from Burrus' Red & White, in the Civic Building. Hours are from 10 AM to 6 PM, Monday, Tuesday and Thursday and 1 PM to 7 PM on Wednesday. The library is closed Friday, Saturday and Sunday.

HATTERAS INLET FERRY
TO OCRACOKE
Hatteras Village

The ferry trip is free and links Hatteras with Ocracoke Island on an enjoyable 45-minute trip. The ferries accommodate cars, large camping vehicles and some trucks.

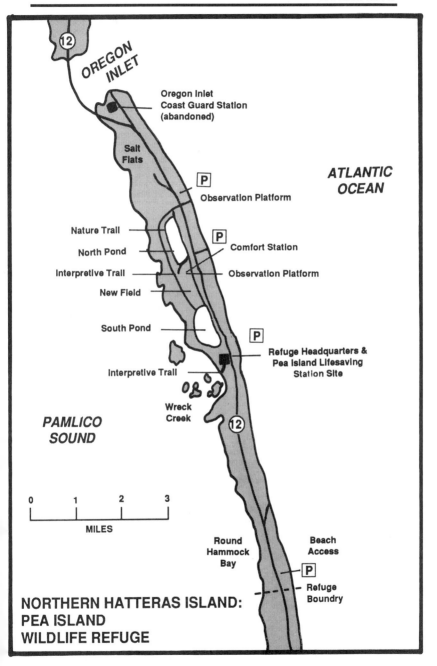

Oregon Inlet Coast Guard Station (abandoned)

Salt Flats

P Observation Platform

ATLANTIC OCEAN

Nature Trail

North Pond

Interpretive Trail

New Field

South Pond

Interpretive Trail

P Comfort Station

Observation Platform

P Refuge Headquarters & Pea Island Lifesaving Station Site

Wreck Creek

PAMLICO SOUND

0 1 2 3

MILES

Round Hammock Bay

Beach Access

P

Refuge Boundry

NORTHERN HATTERAS ISLAND: PEA ISLAND WILDLIFE REFUGE

The frequency of trips makes your wait bearable, but do expect a line during summer months. Reservations are not required.

For a full schedule, see the Ferry chapter of this book.

Shopping

Every year there are more shops on Hatteras Island. While the explosive pace of residential and commercial development has slowed down, there are still a few more new spots each time we give ourselves the pleasure of a trip "down south." With the growth, more shops on Hatteras Island are adopting the year-round schedule of their neighbors to the north, but most shops still close for at least a month or two during the winter.

Even though you may not find a huge variety of shops like you'd find in Nags Head, Kill Devil Hills or Duck, the ones you do find in the Hatteras area are interesting and carry fine quality items. We love the selection of handmade and handcrafted goods along with the usual array of souvenir and gift items found all along the Outer Banks. We'll begin our shopping excursion on the north end of Hatteras Island in the village of Rodanthe, located about 15 miles south of the Oregon Inlet Bridge.

Rodanthe

The **Island Convenience Store**, 987-2239, is a one-stop shopping place recently relocated to a spiffy new building just south of the old one. This move was prompted after

storm damage from the March 1993 high water. They have groceries, bait and tackle, gasoline and a small deli featuring breakfast foods, sandwiches, pizza and fried chicken dinners. Debbie Bell and Randy Hall, both NC natives, have lived in Rodanthe for 10 years and opened **Rodanthe Surf Shop**, 987-2412, five years ago. This surf shop is located in a bigger, new building this year too, due to the storm. This growing hard core surf shop carries men's and women's swimwear, surfwear, bodyboards, boogie boards and surfboards. Randy manufactures Hatteras Glass Surfboards in the back yard. You'll find everything you need here for a day in the Hatteras surf. The **Waterfowl Shop**, 986-2626, is a sports photography gallery featuring the work of Richard Darcey. You'll find other gifts here as well including new and used working decoys, tide clocks and wind speed indicators. **The Sea Chest**, 987-2303, has a wide variety of antiques and gifts. Myrna Peters opened this shop more than 20 years ago. She's a collector, and you'll spend a lot of time inspecting, browsing and talking about everything from antique dolls to hand carved decoys. Baseball memorabilia will be of interest to you baseball fans — you know who you are. **North Beach General Store**, 987-2378, is just that — a general store. You'll also find a good assortment of general merchandise at **Jo Bob's**, 987-2201. Stop in the **Olde Christmas at Rodanthe Gift Shop**, 987-2116, for the most complete cross stitch department on the Outer Banks. Unusual gift items are featured along with a good assort-

ment of nautical Christmas ornaments.

Next, you'll come to Pamlico Station, a two-story shopping center located on the east side of Highway 12 in Rodanthe. This is where you'll find the Rodanthe, Salvo and Waves Post Office. **Village Video**, 987-2988, is also located here. This is the first of their four locations as you head south on Hatteras Island. They offer rentals of televisions, VCRs, Nintendos, camcorders and movies. Also available are blank VHS tapes, head cleaners, rewinders, 8 MM film and VHS-C audio tapes. They're open year round. At **Lee's Collectibles**, 987-2144, you'll find T-shirts, beach supplies, gifts, jewelry, mugs, cards and antique bottles. The suncatchers are nice too. Hungry for fudge anyone? **The Fudgery** can fix you up with assorted flavors of yummy homemade fudge. The friendly folks at **Crafts Etc. Etc.**, 987-2435, are happy to answer any questions about their selection of North Carolina crafts. They know most of the crafters personally and offer a fine selection of dolls, ceramics, wood, Afghans. Also in this center are the **Casual Clam** raw bar, 987-2700; **Island Trader** gift shop, 987-2801; **Hatteras T-Shirt Outlet**, 987-1404; and **Surfside Casuals**, 987-1414, which features swimwear and clothing.

Down the road, **Bill Sawyer's Place**, 987-2214, has an assortment of "general store" items too. You'll find the woodcrafts especially interesting. He also rents boogie boards. **Ocean Atlantic Rentals**, 987-2492, is located in Waves and this is their first location as you head south on the island. They have everything you need for the beach. (For more information, see the chapter on Rentals.)

Michael Halminski Studio and Gallery, 987-2401, is a very interesting place to shop or visit. His gallery is located on the west side of Highway 12. Michael is a well-known Outer Banks photographer, with work that includes Outer Banks seascapes and landscapes. In Waves, **Peach Blossoms By The Sea** florist shop, 987-1404, provides locals and travelers with fresh flowers.

Avon

A small shopping center new in 1993 is the Island Shoppes, located soundside in Avon. Here you'll find delightful gifts and fun things to do. **Kitty Hawk Kites**, 995-6060, has a colorful store featuring a 23-foot indoor climbing wall — great fun for kids on a rainy day or adults who want to stretch their physical skills. There are free workshops throughout the summer in kitemaking, juggling, boomerangs and stunt kites. Of course, there's an excellent selection of kites, flags, windsocks, toys, T-shirts and clothing. This year Kitty Hawk Kites will offer kayak lessons and tours. It's open March to December. Next door, the folks from Windsurfing Hatteras have **Gearworks**, 995-6090, a consignment shop for windsurfing equipment. T-shirts are also available. **Ocean Annies** craft gallery, 995-4644, has an exquisite selection of pottery, jewelry, chimes and other gifts.

Windsurfing Hatteras, Sea Robin Restaurant, Dolphin Realty and

Home Port Gifts are all located at Avon Waterside Shops on the west side of Highway 12 in Avon just south of the Island Shoppes. **Home Port Gifts**, 995-4334, is one of the nicest gift shops on the Outer Banks. This shop opened seven years ago and features the works of many local crafts people. There is an abundance of fine wares, nautical jewelry, accessories for the home and all sorts of other gifts. We especially enjoy the custom-stained glass pieces, nautical sculptures and decoys, terra cotta sculptures and sea candles by Sally Knuckles. Ila's prints of sea turtles, pelicans and sandpipers are amazing. Each original work requires at least 500 hours of painting. The gourmet chocolates and truffles are wonderful too. Home Port is open 11 months of the year. **Windsurfing Hatteras**, 995-4970, has everything you need for windsurfing including equipment sales, rentals and lessons. You'll also find a great selection of T-shirts and men's and women's swimwear and casualwear.

The **Fisherman's Daughter**, 995-6148, features pottery from all over the United States and Wanchese — we're speaking of Bonnie Morrill's pottery of course. Local art and photography are also available in the upstairs room. Gift items include brass nautical items and furnishings, Christmas ornaments, Barely People bears and a large line of Department 56 Christmas. Woodcarvings by California artist George Edenfield are also featured along with lots of gold and silver jewelry. Then there's **Dairy Queen**, 995-5624, down the road a piece, offering cool treats for the whole family.

Hatteras Wind, 995-6055, has a good collection of handcrafted wooden gifts. This is not a retail store; it is a mail order catalogue business. So, you can write and order these great wooden items at: P.O. Box 521, Avon, N.C. 27915. Richard Landis is very busy so patience is a must when ordering handmade items. The **Wood Butcher**, 995-5227, offers quality, handmade deck furniture.

Kitty Hawk Sports, 995-5000, has another great location here in Avon on the west side of Highway 12. Their main store is in Nags Head across from the dunes at Jockey's Ridge State Park. They specialize in water sports lessons and rentals, including windsurfing and parasailing. Lots of T-shirts and clothing are available here too.

Avon Shopping Center, 995-5362, is a local's favorite for freshly cut meats, but they also have most everything else you'd expect from a general store including souvenirs, hardware, beachwear, groceries, all kinds of fishing supplies, lawn and garden supplies and quick serve foods. Amoco gas is sold on the premises too.

Carol's Seafood, 995-6132, is a retail seafood store offering some of the best local seafood around. Besides fresh local seafood you'll enjoy daily lunch specials like fresh tuna salad sandwiches, steamed and spiced shrimp and crabs when available. Carol's also carries T-shirts, hats, coolers, charcoal, beer and soda, grocery items, ice, wine and hot dogs and self-serve coffee. This store is located just west of the stoplight in Avon.

If you turn right at the stoplight in Avon (the only stoplight on the entire island so far) onto Harbor Road, you'll come across **Country Elegance**, 995-6269. Owned and operated by Lois and Dallas Miller, Country Elegance features wearable art, country collars, bonnets, hand painted shirts, antique quilted heirlooms, whimsical art, designer dolls and Southwestern decor. The Sportsman's Corner offers mallards painted on magazine racks, hat and coat racks and saws. Ask about the "original Kinnakeet Yaupon tea."

The Outer Beaches Realty Building is home to the Gaskins Gallery and Hair by the Sea. **Hair by the Sea**, 995-6754, offers family hair care; walk-ins are welcome. Denise Gaskins also owns the **Gaskins Gallery**, 995-6617, right next door — as a matter of fact you can enter the gallery from her hair salon. Original local art is available along with custom framing. The Gaskins Gallery exclusively features original family art. Denise's 80-year-old grandmother began painting with watercolors three years ago. Denise also paints with watercolors. Decorator prints and posters can also be purchased here and both shops are open year round.

Ocean Atlantic Rentals, 995-5868, has chairs, umbrellas, strollers, cribs, bicycles, movies, VCRs — you name it. Whatever you forgot or didn't have room to bring along, they will have. Next door **T-Shirt Whirl**, 995-4111, has one of the largest selections of T's on the Outer Banks. Both shops are located on the east side of Highway 12.

For great tasting, hand tossed pizza try **Nino's Pizza**, 995-5358. Homemade calzones, lasagna, spaghetti and subs are available for dining in or carry out. Pizza delivery service is offered for Avon from this location and for Buxton at their Light Keeper's Station location, 995-6364. They open daily at 4 PM during the season, but their hours are seasonal. Next, we come to **Village Video's** second location, 995-5138, in case you missed them in Waves. They're open year round.

Surfside Casuals/Suits Galore, 995-5577, in the Sun Realty Building, features a mixture of juniors and missy swimwear, sportswear, men's sportswear and T-shirts.

The Hatteras Island Plaza in Avon is anchored by Food Lion and offers other shops as well. **Bubba's Too Bar-B-Q**, 995-4385, is an all-time favorite. Don't expect to travel past without noticing the smoked ribs aroma, which will make you hungry even if you just finished eating. Sandwiches and plates are available along with good French fries, homemade cole slaw and delicious homemade pies too. **Beach Bites**, 995-6683, is a great deli and bakery. Daily specials are always offered, and the deli meats and gourmet cheeses are sliced to order. This place is home to the Outer Banks Elephant Ear, a large, sugar-dusted light pastry. They have homemade everything, like eight-grain bread, sourdough bread, bagels, muffins, decorated cakes and soups. Ask about the "pizza kit," a package of dough, homemade sauce, freshly grated cheeses and toppings. You bake it at home! **Baggies Surf Shop**, 995-6722, is next door with a good selection of men and women's swimwear, casual wear, windsurfing gear, body boards, wetsuits and accessories. They carry a small line of surfboards too. This is not a hard core surf shop, but you'll find just about everything you need for a day of surf on the Banks. The Dawsons also own Daydreams in Buxton, another great shop featuring high quality, stylish dresses and casualwear for the entire family.

Buxton

A five-mile drive south of Avon brings you to the village of Buxton. Here you'll discover the shops are more spread out and range from the general store, bait and tackle shops to specialty shops. **Daydreams**, 995-5548, has earned a reputation for having exceptionally stylish clothes, with name brands not usually found in the area. Clothes for men, women and children are offered, along with accessories and jewelry. You'll find names like Patagonia and Birkenstock; we think this is one of the nicest clothing stores you'll find on the Outer Banks. The store is smaller now, having remodeled and made room for two adjoining specialty shops next door. **Hatteras Outdoors**, 995-5815, adjoins Daydreams and has all the clothes for surfing enthusiasts. They rent and sell surfboards and boogie boards and provide surfing accessories too. You can also find Cape Hatteras T-shirts, sweats and just about everything you need for the beach including umbrella rentals and children's games and toys. **Cape Sandwich Co.**, 995-6140, offers daily

lunch specials, homemade soups and desserts, burgers, barbecue, crabcake sandwiches and ice cream. They also sell beer and wine to go. There is plenty of deck seating where you can enjoy beer, wine or cappuccino with your meal.

Dillon's Corner, 995-5083, started as a bait and tackle store, but has expanded into a complete fishing center downstairs that includes custom-built fishing rods and other items such as T-shirts, souvenirs and postcards. It's owned by Ollie and Kathy Jarvis. She has expanded the store to include a gift shop upstairs, **The Fisherman's Daughter**, which specializes in local crafts, pottery, dishware, wind chimes, Afghans, jewelry, Christmas ornaments and decorations and works of art by California artist George Edenfield.

Red Drum Tackle Shop, 995-5414, is a place you'll enjoy. Get the latest in fishing information and select gear from their complete line of custom rods, bait and tackle. A fish mounting service is also available. **Fox Water Sports**, 995-4102, features custom surf boards and sail boards. They specialize in windsurfing equipment including boards, booms, sails, harnesses and more. Windsurfing lessons are also available. This shop also offers lots of T-shirts and swimwear. You'll find just about everything you need for surfing, but the focus here is really on windsurfing. **Cape Yogurt Company**, 995-4018, serves ice cream, yogurt and the best shaved ice around, guaranteed to be enjoyed by the entire family. **Moonshine Florist and Hallmark Shop**, 995-5536, can help you celebrate special occasions while

you're away from home. Next door are **Hurricane Harry's T-Shirt Shop** and **Everything's A $.** You'll find all kinds of things at **Buxton Under the Sun Supply Store**, 995-6047. We noticed movie rentals, jewelry, Nintendo rentals, clam rakes, fishing supplies, even 4WD vehicles. Just south of Centura Bank, located on Buxton Back Road, you'll find **Village Video**, 995-6227. Remember them? They have two other locations north of Buxton and another location in Hatteras Village. Rent your favorite movies here.

Orange Blossom Pastry Shop, 995-4109, is loaded with delicious home-baked pastries, muffins, breakfast biscuits and breads. They have giant apple fritters, referred to as Apple Uglies, that we definitely don't pass up, regardless of any diet. Mexican dinners are now being featured too.

Natural Art Surf Shop, 995-5682, is owned by Scott and Carol Busbey. The phone number for their surf report is 995-4646. Scott and Carol are both serious surfers — they love

the sport and enjoy the lifestyle. The shop has been around for a long time and has the reputation for being "the surfer's surf shop," meaning they specialize in surfing rather than all water board sports. Surfers from everywhere and from all walks of life have been coming here for years. Sometimes they only see friends once a year, but they're never forgotten. Scott, who has his own line of boards called In The Eye, manufactures custom boards and does repairs while Carol makes clothes and tries to find time to surf. You can rent surfboards, boogie boards, swim fins, wetsuits and surf videos here. They carry all the necessary surfing gear, great T-shirts and Escher designs too. We've found some great cards here. Carol's handsewn clothing, including women's tops and children's shirts and dresses, is original, colorful and priced very reasonably.

Osprey Shopping Center is located behind Natural Art Surf Shop and the Great Salt Marsh Restaurant. There's an **ABC store**, 995-5532, located here for your convenience. **Lighthouse Pizza**, 995-4005, offers carry out, delivery service and outside dining on the porch. They deliver their special three-blend cheese pizzas with the Neapolitan crusts from Avon to Hatteras Village. You can also order Italian hoagies, Italian meatball sandwiches and salads. They're open 11 AM until 12 AM seven days a week during the season and 4 PM until 10 PM during the off season. Also, **Nino's Pizza** delivers from this location. Call 995-6364. You'll find a little bit of everything at **Ocean Notions Gift Shop**, 995-4335. They offer beach goods, gold and silver jewelry, nautical gifts, beachwear, casualwear, T-shirts and more. **Mane Attraction**, 995-5226, offers family hair care.

Seaside Garden Center, 995-4801, is located behind Natural Art Surf Shop next to the Osprey shops. This complete garden center specializes in coastal plants, landscaping, baskets, garden gifts and supplies. The staff is very knowledgeable and eager to help you with your planting needs.

Buxton's supermarket **Conner's Cape Hatteras Market**, 995-5711, carries everything you need in the line of groceries and basic supplies. Your alternative to Conner's Market for groceries is **Food Lion** located in Avon five miles north of Buxton.

Turn toward the ocean on Light Plant Road to find **The Old Gray House** gift shop, where you'll find baskets, woodwork, stitchery, miniatures, dolls, shells, potpourri, etc. The house is maintained as it must have looked at the turn of the cen-

tury. The owners say this place has "lots of stories to tell," and it's fun to speculate about what they might be.

Ormond's, 995-5012, is probably the oldest department store in Buxton. It specializes in apparel for the entire family including dresses, swimwear and casualwear. You'll also find a selection of shoes, socks, accessories, hats and a small gift section.

The Other Banks Antiques is a fun place to browse. **Beach Pharmacy II**, 995-4450, can help with prescription needs and sundries.

Buxton Village Books, 995-4240, in its 11th year, is packed with fiction, nonfiction, best-sellers, seafaring tales — in other words, lots of good books. Hard-to-find Southern fiction and saltwater fly fishing books are here, along with some used paperbacks, too. Owner Gee Gee Rosell has a great selection of cards, some office supplies and a FAX service. She writes a column for the local newspaper and is definitely at home in her delightful book shop. Her charm and wit are a pleasure to all of her customers. A second generation of cats accompany Gee Gee in the shop. Stop by and meet Siamese cats Mr. Mitchell and Moondoggie.

Cactus Flower Gallery is right next door to Buxton Books. Owner Mac Marrow has lived on Hatteras Island for a long time and was formerly in the landscaping business. He began handcast plastering as a hobby. He now makes his own molds and does an excellent job of recreating marble, granite and wooden artifacts. All of this work is done on the premises, and he will be happy to discuss this art form with you. Pieces

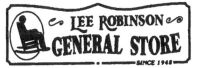
Hatteras Island · Hatteras Island · Hatteras Island

include sconces, brackets and decorative wall hangings. We saw pieces with mythological themes — cherubs and gargoyles. Also on display were human hands, angels, fish and lions. Colors include terra cotta, ecru, white, butternut washes, pinks and yellows. This is an interesting art form, and we suggest you take a look at these decorative pieces.

Buttons N Bows, 995-4285, is located just off Highway 12. Owner Laurie Farrow enjoys talking crafts with anyone stopping by. This cute little shop is open year round and offers crochet, knitting and cross-stitch classes. Laurie sells Outer Banks cross-stitch designs that feature beach scenes, Outer Banks maps and local birds. Fabric paints, yarn, notions and patterns are also available. **A-1 Rentals**, 995-6363, has jet ski, boogie boards, bike and 4WD rentals.

Frisco

The **Frisco Sandwich Shop**, 995-5535, has great sandwiches, homemade soups and salads and the best burgers on the island. Breakfast, lunch and dinner are served here. (See the chapter on Restaurants for more information.)

Scotch Bonnet Marina Gift Shop, 995-4242, has great fudge, custom and silk-screen T-shirts, hermit crabs and other gifts. **Times Past Antiques**, 995-4022, next to Arlyne's Hair Care, features antiques, with "new" items on hand each time you stop by. **Pirates Chest Gifts and T-Shirts**, 995-5118, is the oldest gift shop on Hatteras Island, having opened in 1953. Stop in to appreciate the amount of merchandise carried here — scrimshaw, coral, lots of jewelry, nautical items and gifts from far away places. We also saw a good selection of local shells, Outer Banks books, souvenirs, wooden lighthouses, baskets, craft supplies, a nice cookbook selection, toys (lots of pirate-type items) and handmade Christmas ornaments. The works of local artists are featured including Ila's prints of sandpipers and turtles, and you'll also find John Perry's sculptures on driftwood here. They even sell hermit crabs! They have another location in Ocracoke.

The **Gingerbread House**, 995-5204, is a delightful shop for early-morning baked goods. They also have fabulous pizza and sandwiches. You can eat-in or take out. Barbecue lovers will insist on a stop at **Bubba's in Frisco**, 995-5421, for a hearty meal.

Browning Artworks, 995-5538, is celebrating its 10th year. This fine art and craft gallery features the work of North Carolina artists exclusively. You'll be impressed by the creations of some 200 crafters who make blown-glass, porcelains, pottery, baskets, stoneware, fiber art, carved birds and jewelry; the works are very attractively displayed. New this year is a collection of 1940s black and white photographs of Hatteras Island. These vintage scenes are stunning. Other excellent photography by Ray Matthews and Michael Halminski is available. Antique tribal weavings by Majid are a beautiful attraction here, as are the watercolor originals of Dixie Browning. Proprietors Linda and Lou Browning select only the finest works available, and maintain a bridal registry. They will ship your selections back home or to other destinations. Linda, Lou and their staff are all very knowledgeable about the items featured in their shop and the artists who created them.

All Decked Out, 995-4319, is a furniture factory owned by Dale Cashman. Dale and his crew handcraft outdoor furniture and will ship anywhere in the U.S. We saw picnic tables, Adirondak chairs, benches, wooden recliners and hammocks.

Frisco Rod and Gun, 995-5366, specializes in (what else?) hunting and fishing equipment. You'll find everything you need for a hunting or fishing trip on the Outer Banks. Offshore and inshore fishing equipment, fly fishing equipment, hunting guns, ice, bait, tackle and groceries . . . it's all here. They also carry camping supplies, name brand outdoor apparel, Sperry Topsiders and T-shirts.

Hatteras Village

Seaside Shirts, 986-2257, is the place to go to design your own Outer Banks T-shirts. Lots of other themes are available too. These make great gifts for the folks back home. Stop by the **Sea Witch**, 986-2453, for gas, beach supplies, tackle, bait, auto and marine parts, silver jewelry, gifts, beach towels and hand-dipped ice cream. **Ocean Annie's**, 986-2665, has fine quality pottery and woodcrafts from all over the country plus gourmet coffee just like in their other shops located farther north on the Outer Banks. The coffee aroma

smells wonderful here, so good in fact, we can't leave this spot without some freshly ground to take home. **Village Video's**, 986-2181, fourth and final location as you head south on Hatteras Island is located here. Don't forget they also rent TVs, VCRs, camcorders and the like.

Burrus' Red & White Supermarket, 986-2333, has a full-service deli and salad bar, along with fresh cut meats. They also rent VCRs and videotapes. **Oceanside Bakery**, 986-2465, is open at 4:30 AM and closes around noon during the off season, but is open until around 4 PM in the summer. Next door is **Beach Pharmacy**, 986-2400.

Nedo Shopping Center, 986-2545, is really just one store, but it carries lots of different things you'll need for fun and sun on the beach and beyond. There are tools, small appliances, kitchen and bath supplies, books, toys, sporting goods, fishing equipment, clothes and more. At **Summer Stuff**, 986-2111, you can buy everything from clothes and shoes to toys, decoys and gifts. There's plenty to choose from here. We saw lots of name brand clothing including Jag, Jantzen, Paris Blues, Shok and more. Half of this store is devoted to clothing, accessories and shoes, the other half to gift items and knickknacks. We found the fish art particularly interesting.

Hatteras Harbor Marina Store Gift Shop, 986-2166, has jewelry, name brand quality sportswear, fishing supplies, unique gifts, deck shoes and other items. In addition, here is one of the largest charter fishing fleets on the island. Charter reservations can be made by calling

(800) 676-4939. Located adjacent to the shop is Hatteras Harbor Deli, a great place to enjoy a bite to eat while you watch the daily catch come in at around 5 PM.

Hatteras Harbor Deli, 986-2331, opens at 6 AM each day and closes around 7 PM. Breakfast and lunch are available along with daily seafood specials, homemade pasta, seafood salad and their famous shrimp pasta salad. Homemade desserts are delicious and can be enjoyed on the enclosed porch outside. The porch is a very busy place during the afternoon when the charter boats return to the marina. Steamed shrimp is available during the late afternoon hours and hand-dipped Breyers ice cream is the children's (and our) favorite. Lunches can be pre-ordered to go the next day if you need one for your fishing trip.

Lee Robinson General Store, 986-2381, opened in 1948, but the old store was replaced by a replica several years ago. We're glad they kept their old, beloved look, with a wide front porch and wooden floors. Owners Belinda and Virgil Willis have always carried everything you would usually need for a vacation at the beach. They also have something you wouldn't necessarily expect to find at a beach general store: a huge selection of fine wines. T-shirts, sweatshirts, jewelry and gifts are also worth stopping for.

Inside
Ocracoke Island

A 45-minute ferry ride across the waters of Pamlico Sound transports vacationers to Ocracoke Island. This ferry is a form of public transportation for islanders and visitors alike, and there is no fee. During the season, it departs Hatteras Village for Ocracoke every 30 minutes beginning at 5 AM. The last ferry of the day departs Hatteras at midnight, and ferry service from Hatteras Village to Ocracoke is on a first-come basis. Reservations are not accepted for this ferry ride.

If you're vacationing at points farther north on the Outer Banks and wondering whether or not to venture to the island of Ocracoke, wonder no more. Ocracoke is a world unto its own. The ferry schedule during the season makes this island a good choice for a day trip or an overnight stay. Many visitors to the Outer Banks decide to make Ocracoke their beach destination. The fact that Ocracoke can only be reached by ferry service should tell you something about this island retreat.

The gentle roll of the ferry accompanied by sea gulls in flight often provides the first-time traveler a feeling of awe — out on the water, the sight of habitable land where sky and water wash together off in the distance. You can walk around on this ferry ride, and this makes for lots of friendly exchanges among passengers. Fond memories of this quaint island destination are shared by those who have been here before, while first time visitors anticipate rolling back time a little, rolling up their sleeves and digging into some much needed rest and relaxation.

Disembarking from the ferry on Ocracoke Island releases you on a 12-mile ride along the dunes and soundside forests of cedar and pine before arriving in Ocracoke Village. (The ferry station, with a bathroom and drink machines, is the only development at this north end ferry landing.) Roll down your window, and smell the cedar mixed with salt-air. Waterfowl are plentiful here in the wide expanses of marshgrass and narrow canals. This area is a part of the National Seashore and will never be developed. Some of the most beautiful nature scenes on the Outer Banks can be seen along this stretch of land. Parking lots provided at several points along NC 12 allow for easy beach access. Miles of desolate beaches will ease you into a new adventure . . . slowing your pace . . . alone with the sea.

Ocracoke Village occupies the

western portion of the island. Life here is quite different from other Outer Banks towns and villages. Days seem longer. It would appear that a lazy island life is afforded all who live here, but residents are busy during the season earning a livelihood that must provide for them throughout the year. Many islanders live off the bounty of the sea and small island shops.

You won't find much room for vehicular traffic in the Village. The 12-mile route leading to the Village was designed for vehicular traffic, but the Village itself seems more like a neighborhood with back roads and side roads, perfect for biking and strolling in most cases. Bike rentals are popular, often replacing cars as a means of getting around.

Most of the island is still just as uninhabited as it was on a spring day in 1585, when seven English ships appeared off Ocracoke Inlet. Sir Richard Grenville, a seasoned, experienced soldier, was in command. He had about 300 troops aboard his fleet. His mission, entrusted to him by Sir Walter Raleigh and the Queen, was to establish a permanent English base in the New World. He was to fail at Roanoke Island; but that summer no one yet suspected the fate that awaited those first colonists. The Banks welcomed him in characteristic fashion, leaving his flagship, *Tiger*, hard aground on the bar. He and Ralph Lane took advantage of the delay to explore north and west in smaller vessels (see "Ocracoke Pony Pens," in this chapter — these hardy ponies may stem from stock lost from the *Tiger*). When the ship was floated and repaired, he

headed to Roanoke, leaving the island sleeping and deserted once again.

It's thought that the name "Woccocon," which was applied to the island at first, was derived from the neighboring Indian tribe the "Woccons." But its precise derivation, like that of so many Outer Banks names, is unclear, as is its subsequent degeneration through "Wococock," "Occocock," "Ocreecock," and other variations to the present "Ocracoke." Spelling held a low priority in those days. (A state to which the English tongue seems to be reverting.)

Most of the island remained in its wild state, with sheep, cattle and horses released by the early owners to graze freely. The gradual increase in colonial trade during the early 18th century led to more and more ships using the inlet, which was deeper in those days than it is now (ships were of shallower draft too). In 1715, the colony of North Carolina established Ocracoke as a port, setting aside land on the western tip of the island for the homes of pilots (for non-seagoing types, a "pilot" meets incoming ships at sea and guides them safely to shore. Pilots are generally older, brine-encrusted men who know the configurations of sand bars and channels from painful experience).

A new problem arose: pirates. They interfered with the pilots, terrorized the inhabitants of the islands, boarded and robbed ships at sea, murdered crews and passengers and made themselves generally unwelcome. John Cole, Robert Deal, Anne Bonny and dozens of others operated along the Caribbean and

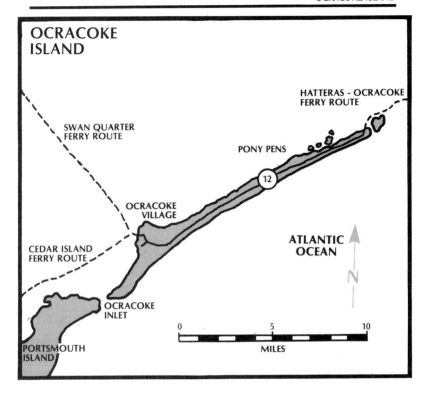

southern Atlantic coasts in the early 18th century. But, it was the notorious Blackbeard, standing out as the worst of a bad lot, who left his name stamped on the Outer Banks, and on Ocracoke, one of his lairs. Much of his early career lies somewhere between conjecture and legend. It is thought that he started as an honest English tar named Edward Drummond, born, perhaps, in Bristol.

He may have started, like many pirates, as a privateer — a sort of seagoing guerrilla. But by 1716 he had turned pirate, calling himself Edward Teach. He had found his métier, and his rise was rapid. He seems to have been a man of organizational ability, for in short order he was in command of a sizeable fleet of ships, and hundreds of men.

He also understood advertising. An evil reputation is a great thing to a terrorist, for it weakens the other side's morale and leads to quick capitulations. Blackbeard was a master in dressing for success and winning through intimidation. Tall, broad and with a bushy coal-black beard, he festooned himself with cutlasses, dirks and loaded pistols. In battle his beard was plaited with little ribbons to add a festive air.

Lighted cannon fuses dangled from under his hat, an affectation of dubious safety with primed flintlocks in his belt, but unquestionably effective in giving him the air of the very devil.

A devil with political clout: he bought Governor Eden of North Carolina and was able to move ashore to Bath with his booty in 1718. Like many men, he became bored with retirement, and before the year was up he was out raiding again part-time. Eden stayed bought and did nothing, so a few citizens went north to ask a favor of Governor Spotswood of Virginia.

Spotswood responded by sending the Royal Navy. In November of 1718, Lt. Robert Maynard left the James River, heading south in two sloops manned with sailors from British men-o'-war. Maynard must have had confidence; his two small sloops had no cannon, only small arms. The shallow-draft boats penetrated where larger warships could not go, and Maynard was able to track Blackbeard's *Adventure* to Ocracoke Inlet.

At dawn on November 22 Ocracoke Inlet resounded to the boom of pirate guns and the crackle of British musketry fire. The *Adventure* grounded, but her well-laid cannon took heavy toll of the Royal Navy men. Maynard ordered them below, then stood ready on deck as his sloop drifted down on the larger ship.

They met. Teach's men launched a volley of grenades and swarmed aboard. The sailors came up from below to begin a merciless hand-to-hand struggle. The pirate chief and the lieutenant faced each other. An exchange of pistol balls wounded the pirate, but in the next moment he had broken the officer's sword with his cutlass. Another sailor sliced the massive buccaneer in the neck, but he fought on ... then collapsed. The battle was over. The pirate's head was cut off and hung from the rigging for the trip back, showing all that could see it that Blackbeard was dead. The body was thrown overboard, where, according to island legend, it swam seven times round the ship before sinking. Most of the rest of his crew were taken to Williamsburg and given a fair trial before they were hanged. His treasure? There probably was none — he spent what little money the coasting trade yielded. But legends persist. . . .

With the pirates cleaned out, trade flourished. Most of the seaborne commerce of North Carolina, and much of that of Virginia, came through the inlet. Gradually families settled there to service the ships. There were sporadic Spanish incursions and raids in the 1740s and '50s, and at one time they even had a camp on the island. Eventually peace came between England and Spain, and the Spanish went home.

It was in 1753 that the village became a recognized town. At that time, there were only about 100 inhabitants. Most of the island remained in a wild state. The inlet was fortified in 1757. Across the water, the town of Portsmouth was also growing up, and the little port of Beacon Island Roads, as the two towns were commonly called, was doing well when the Revolution ar-

Photo: N.C. Travel and Tourism

The Ocracoke Lighthouse is a popular attraction.

rived. Much of Washington's army was supplied through Ocracoke, and coastal North Carolina trade remained intact although the British patrolled outside, landed troops and engaged in various futile retaliations.

After the war, the lighthouses were built by the new government, the first in 1798 on Shell Castle Rock, the second (the present one) in 1823. But even as they went up, the golden age of Ocracoke was drawing to an end. Hatteras and Oregon inlets opened during a storm in September of 1846, and as these were deepened by outflow, Ocracoke Inlet began to shoal. The fort was abandoned by the Confederates in 1861, and the Government sank several ships loaded with rock in the channel to seal it. By now oceangoing ships had grown much larger and deeper — Outer Banks seagoing traffic shifted to Hatteras Inlet. After the war, the village declined to 100 or so inhabitants, who subsisted as fishermen, boatmen or lifesavers. Many went to sea, and not all of them returned.

It took a war, World War II, to bring new life. Silver Lake Harbor (formerly Cockle Creek) had been dredged out in 1931, and in 1942 a naval base was established there. As cargo ships burned offshore and oil and debris and dead bodies drifted ashore, telephones and paved roads came to the villagers. The base was closed in 1945, but in the mid-'50s the National Seashore and the highway brought a new source of revenue: the tourist.

Today tourism has surpassed fishing as the island's main livelihood (though the same road service that has brought visitors also made crabbing commercially feasible). And they do come, more every year, in a two-season economy of tourists in the summer and anglers in the fall. Regret it or welcome it, the 19th century is quickly giving way to the 20th in Ocracoke Village. Electricity came in 1938, and the first paved road appeared in 1951. In the late '70s an ABC store, a doctor and a night spot arrived; in 1985, television arrived in the form of a 3½-meter dish and cable; in 1987 the first multi-story hotel and the first lakefront condo opened. Gift shops are proliferating, and so are the signs.

This year we noted a marked increase in the number of in-home businesses too. Many locals have decided to give entrepreneurship a try by expanding, renaming or starting new businesses altogether. New artisans are migrating to this island retreat as well. It is essential that you unpack your favorite pair of walking shoes and explore this island by foot if you mean to find these hidden treasures. Quiet back-road neighbor-

Insiders' Tips

Ride bikes around Ocracoke Village. It's fun and makes it easy to stop and see the sights.

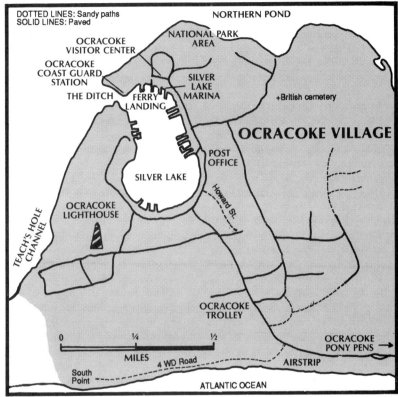

DOTTED LINES: Sandy paths
SOLID LINES: Paved

NORTHERN POND

OCRACOKE
VISITOR CENTER

NATIONAL PARK
AREA

OCRACOKE
COAST GUARD
STATION

SILVER
LAKE
MARINA

THE DITCH   FERRY
LANDING

+British cemetery

OCRACOKE VILLAGE

POST
OFFICE

SILVER LAKE

OCRACOKE
LIGHTHOUSE

Howard St.

TEACH'S HOLE CHANNEL

OCRACOKE
TROLLEY

OCRACOKE
PONY PENS

0   ¼   ½

MILES   4 WD Road   AIRSTRIP

South
Point

ATLANTIC OCEAN

hoods are transformed into gallery rows during the season, and you won't be disappointed with your finds.

A walk or a bike ride will show you that Ocracoke hasn't been spoiled yet. There's still no barber shop, no movies, no crime, not one fast-food joint. As one islander observed, "things on Ocracoke Island are changing and updating, but they aren't trying to be new." Many of the streets are only sandy paths, still unpaved and not likely ever to be. Walking them on a soft summer's night is as close to inner peace as many of us will ever get. Even some of the paved roads are so narrow and winding that

two caddies will scarcely pass abreast.

And still, to the north and east . . . Ocracoke Island stretches out unpopulated and untamed. The sea roars against the rows of dunes; the road, silent and empty, shimmers amid the beachgrass and yaupon. Toward the sound the ponies graze warily, and Ocracoke is quiet by the jealous sea.

Attractions

OCRACOKE PONY PENS

Soundside

"Ponies"? The word conjures up a picture of something small, shaggy and friendly. None of these adjectives, however, exactly fits the semi-wild Ocracoke ponies. They're not really that small, perhaps 13 or 14 hands high. They are shaggy in the winter. But they are definitely not friendly.

History, economics, and even anatomy have been used to try to explain the derivation of these hardy russet-colored animals that, in former days, roamed wild on the length of the island, as well as on Hatteras Island. A popular version goes as follows. In 1585, the vessels carrying the first colonists to Roanoke made their first landing at Ocracoke Inlet, where the flagship, *Tiger*, grounded. Sir Richard Grenville ordered the ship unloaded, and its cargo, which included a brace of horses purchased in the West Indies (then under Spanish rule), was put ashore while the *Tiger* was taken off the shoal. The usual method of getting horses ashore in those days was to let them swim; and it is thought that some escaped and began their wild existence on the Banks. Other theories say they came from Spanish shipwrecks, or, more prosaically, were introduced by the early Bankers as a ready source of horseflesh. The rugged, wild ponies have been proven of Spanish mustang descent by their number of lumbar vertebrae and of ribs. A current research effort involving genetic tracking may answer the question once and for all.

At one time there were more than 1,000 of them, roaming free, subsisting on marsh grass. As civilization came to the Banks, they were penned and sold off. When the Cape

Hatteras National Seashore was established, they were taken over by the Park Service. There are now about two dozen ponies in the herd.

The Pony Pen is located some six miles southwest of the Hatteras-Ocracoke ferry landing, on the sound side. Park Service signs will direct you to a wooden observation platform overlooking the mile-long fenced pasture. Don't count on seeing the ponies, especially in rough weather; they have shelters down near the southwest end that they retreat to. *Don't* cross the fence into the pasture. These are wild ponies, and they can bite and kick.

HAMMOCK HILLS NATURE TRAIL
Opposite Ocracoke Campground

Ocracoke isn't all sandy beaches and small town. This 3/4-mile nature trail shows us a cross-section of the island, from dune through maritime forest to salt marsh. Learn how various plants adapted to conditions of salt and stress. A pleasant walk, the trail takes about 30 minutes to complete. Bring the camera. There are some biting insects in summer and to be on the safe side you should review our notes regarding snakes in Buxton Woods Nature Trail section.

OCRACOKE ISLAND VISITOR CENTER
Near Cedar Island and
Swan Quarter Ferry Slips   928-4531

The Ocracoke Island Visitor Center is run by the National Park Service as part of the Cape Hatteras National Seashore. It's in Ocracoke Village at the very southwest end of Highway 12 on Silver Lake. To reach it from 12, just stay on the highway past the Island Inn until you reach

the Lake and a T. Turn right, and continue around the shore of the lake in a counterclockwise direction till you see the low brown building to your right. Parking is available there.

The Center has an information desk, helpful people, a small book shop and exhibits. It's also the place to make arrangements to use the Park Service docks.

It's open seasonally; Memorial Day through Labor Day, 10 AM until 5 PM. That means that things are pretty quiet during the winter, as they are in the rest of the village, but during the warm months the rangers offer a couple of dozen "Discovery Adventures," all free, presented several times each week (check at the desk for what, where and when). In the past these have included beach and sound walks, interpretations of the life and times of a pirate, day or night walking tours of the village, bird watching and history lectures. Once you've looked around the village for a couple of days you may appreciate the Park Service's thoughtfulness in arranging things for you and the kids to do.

OCRACOKE
COAST GUARD STATION

Silver Lake   (Business) 928-4731
Emergency   (SAR line) 928-3711

The southernmost of the chain of five Coast Guard stations along the Banks is Ocracoke. Its complement of 21 men maintains a 44-foot motor lifeboat and several other smaller vessels for search and rescue, law enforcement, servicing aids to navigation and environmental protection. In an average year, they

respond to 250 calls for assistance from fishermen and boaters. The station building was built in 1938 to replace an older one on the same site. The former station is now more tightly secured, but a weekly tour gives a thorough look at the station, its piers and its boats. Check at the National Park Service Visitor Center for time and dates of tours. Bona fide group tours can be arranged a week in advance by calling their business number.

OCRACOKE ISLAND MUSEUM
AND VISITOR CENTER
Silver Lake

To the east of the National Park Service parking lot in Ocracoke, you'll see a two-story white-frame building that has been recently restored. The house was built by David Williams, the first chief of the Ocracoke Coast Guard Station. In 1989 it was moved to its present location on National Park Service land. The Ocracoke Preservation Society, a group of interested local people, and the Park Service restored the building for use as a museum and visitor center. Like the restoration at Chicamacomico, this benefits both local residents and tourists.

OCRACOKE CIVIC AND
BUSINESS ASSOCIATION

24-hour answering machine   928-6711

Pat Gibson handles inquiries to the association and offers helpful advice for those visitors making Ocracoke their destination as well as for those who may just be passing through for the day on their way to destinations further south. Remember, accommodations on Ocracoke

Warm hospitality, salty ocean breezes and over 13 miles of pristine national seashore await you on Ocracoke Island. Visit Blackbeard's stomping grounds, see the rare Banker ponies and enjoy the kind of peaceful vacation that you can only find in one place–the treasure of the outer banks.

Ocracoke Island

NORTH CAROLINA
919.928.6711

are limited and advance reservations are almost always required during the summer months. Just as advance reservations are almost always required for rooms and cottages during the summer months, passage on the Cedar Island Swan Quarter Ferry should also be booked in advance. Without advance reservations, you may find yourself without accommodations on Ocracoke and unable to get to points farther north or south on the ferry. Proper planning will help you to avoid these inconveniences. You can call the association during business hours if you have specific questions about Ocracoke, or write: Civic Club Box 456, Ocracoke, N.C. 27960.

AN OCRACOKE VILLAGE WALKING TOUR
West end of Hwy. 12

You won't know Ocracoke until you park your car and walk some of the sandy lanes and paths. The little village of Ocracoke is a world of its own. Reclusive, hidden, romantic . . . these are words used by those who know the village. A haunt of writers, artists and lovers, this small lost hamlet at the world's end (or at least at the end of the highway) is unlike any of the other towns on the Banks. Things have changed since World War II and the coming of paved roads but not all that much. The roads are still narrow, the people friendly but a touch reticent, with manners and a speech of their own, distinct from mainland

North Carolina. We love Ocracoke, and you will too.

For a short walking tour of the village, park in the lot opposite the Visitor Center. Turn left out of the lot and walk down Route 12, along the shores of the Lake. The village waterfront, formerly quite sleepy, is beginning to resemble St. David's, Bermuda. You'll pass many small shops (see Ocracoke Shopping for profiles) and some large new hotels: the Anchorage, Harborside, Pirate's Quay and Princess Motel. For the tour, keep walking until, on your right, you see a small brick post office.

Opposite the post office, a sandy, narrow street angles to the left. This is Old Howard Street, one of the oldest and least changed parts of the village. Note the smallness of the old homes, the cisterns attached to them for collection of rain water and the detached kitchens. If you've been to Colonial Williamsburg you will recall seeing these detached kitchens under somewhat more monumental circumstances. Continue past Village Craftsman, unless of course you want to check out the local crafts.

After about 400 yards Howard Street debouches on School Street: turn left for the Methodist Church and public school. The church is usually open for visitors, but use discretion; there may be services in progress. (Also, please wipe your feet as you go in; the sand doesn't look good on the carpet.) If you enter, note the cross displayed behind the altar. Thereby hangs a tale, and a not so ancient one. The cross was carved from a wooden spar from an American freighter, the *Caribsea*, sunk offshore by U-boats in the dark

early months of 1942. By the strange workings of circumstance, the *Caribsea's* engineer was James Baugham Gaskill, who had been born in Ocracoke. He was killed in the sinking. Local residents will tell you another strange fact — that several days later a display case, holding, among other things, Gaskill's mate's license, washed ashore not far from his family home.

There's been a Methodist church on Ocracoke since 1828. This building was built in 1943 from lumber and pews salvaged from older buildings. A historical-sketch pamphlet is generally available in the vestibule for visitors.

If you'd like to walk to the lighthouse on the tour — it adds about another ½ mile — turn (west) and follow the road past the Island Inn about 500 yards. You will see the lighthouse towering on your right. After inspecting it (see Ocracoke Inlet Lighthouse) return to the church and school.

The next leg of the tour takes you around the north corner of the school and past the playground on a narrow boardwalk. This leads you out onto the paved road beyond it to the east. Turn left. This was the first paved road on the island, and was constructed by Seabees during WWII. Turn right after a third of a mile (first stop sign). A few minutes' walk along this narrow, tree-shaded road will bring you to the British Cemetery. You have to watch for it; it's on your right, set back a bit from the road, and shaded by live oak and yaupon. The big British flag makes it a bit easier to spot. It's not an impressive site. It's very small and un-

derstated — entirely appropriate. The *Bedfordshire* was a trawler, one of a small fleet of 24 antisubmarine vessels that Churchill loaned to the United States in April 1942 to help us against the U-boats. She was a small ship, only 170 feet long, displacing 900 tons and armed with a single four-inch deck gun. But, she was full of fight. She had no chance; she was torpedoed off Cape Lookout during the night of May 11th by U-558. Six bodies washed ashore. Four were interred here by the Navy and Coast Guard, and the little cemetery is maintained by the USCG. Each year a ceremony here commemorates their sacrifice.

To return to the Visitor Center, walk west till you reach the lakeshore, then turn right.

OCRACOKE LIGHTHOUSE

SW corner of Ocracoke Village   473-2111

This is the southernmost of the four famous lighthouses of the Banks. It's also the oldest and the shortest. It's the second oldest operational lighthouse in the United States as well. Yes, it's still "flashing" away — one long flash from a half hour before sunset to a half hour after sunrise — still warning mariners away from the ever-changing shoals offshore.

When it was built in 1823, this was a busy port. The present lighthouse replaced a still older one, the Shell Castle Rock lighthouse, which had been built in 1798 but was pretty much left behind when the inlet moved south.

The Ocracoke Inlet Lighthouse houses a 360-degree non-rotating light with a range of 14 miles. Focal plane height is 65 feet, overall height of the structure is about 75 feet. The brick walls are five feet thick at the base. That pretty, textured white surface is mortar that was hand-spread over the bricks. The two-story white house you will find nearby was originally meant for the lighthouse keeper. It underwent extensive reconstruction in the late 1980s to meet Historic Preservation standards, and it now serves as quarters for Ocracoke's ranger and the maintenance supervisor. The light itself is operated by the Coast Guard and cannot be entered.

To reach the light, turn left off Route 12 at the Island Inn, and go about 800 yards. A white picketed turnoff on the right allows you to park your auto or bike and walk the last few yards to the base of the structure. The Ocracoke Lighthouse has long been a favorite of artists and photographers.

Efforts are underway by the National Park Service to recruit volunteers to man the ground floor of the lighthouse. Volunteers will provide oral histories concerning the island and the operation of the lighthouse.

SILVER LAKE MARINA

At Visitor's Center   928-4531

Silver Lake is the Park Service-run marina in Ocracoke and is the only large marina here. You may also hear the marina referred to as the National Park Service Docks. It is run differently from a commercial marina in that there are no dockage fees and no reservations. The marina has no slips, only 400 feet of frontage on Silver Lake with tie-up facilities. The basin has been

Outer Banks Dialect Merits Study

By Nancy McWilliams

Most visitors to the Outer Banks find something special about the place, and whatever that may be they hold it dear in their hearts. The unique brogue of native Outer Bankers is no exception; for some it captures a passing interest, for others years of serious study. There is something so fascinating, so worthy of note, so *old* about the speech patterns of the natives of Ocracoke, Hatteras Island, Roanoke Island and Kitty Hawk.

Like many old-time residents of isolated coastal cultures, Outer Bankers use a varied, distinct vocabulary and dialect. Some pronunciations and phrases haven't been heard anywhere else. Many ancestral Outer Bankers speak with such a thick accent that understanding them is difficult, even in today's mixed cultural climate.

Linguistics professor Walt Wolfram of Raleigh has been spending a lot of time on Ocracoke Island listening to people talk. The recipient of a three-year, $186,000 grant from the National Science Foundation, Wolfram is studying speech patterns. Ocracoke is one of his research sites.

He finds the variety of North Carolina dialects intriguing. "There are just so many different enclaves of communities," he said. "I knew it was a rich area . . . I see it's going to keep me busy."

Ocracoke talk is distinctive due to its historic isolation, Wolfram indicated. In studying dialects, Wolfram looks at three factors: pronunciation, grammar and vocabulary. "Some things go back to historic English patterns," he said, citing the oft-quoted "hoi-toide" pronunciation heard on the Outer Banks. That way of saying "high tide" is one of the most famous speech patterns. Other words characteristic of Ocracoke are "mommick," meaning to harass, which Wolfram traced to a Shakespearean play; "knee honkey," a term for the game of hide and seek which Wolfram has not found in any other locale, and "take a skud" meaning take a drive. Grammar patterns include prefixing words with "a," as in "the storm's a-blowing." A peculiarity of grammar that Wolfram cites is the use of "weren't" following singular pronouns. "It weren't a-raining" and "She weren't at home." This also can be traced to England.

A Philadelphia native, Wolfram finds the English connection an engrossing concept. In a 40-page paper prepared for Ocracoke School, Wolfram noted that Ocracoke's rare dialect dates from 1715 and contains features of Appalachian English, New England pronunciations, Elizabethan English, Irish and a variety of Southern dialects from the mainland. He cites "complicated reasons" as to why Ocracoke residents speak as they do, one being historic settlement patterns, such as the predominant English influence here. Another is the fact that many of the island's seamen traveled the Atlantic seaboard, stopping in fisheries and shipyards to deliver goods. They returned home with bits and pieces of other accents they had picked up in their travels, which eventually mingled with traditional speech and that heard from island visitors.

"People have their identity in their dialect," Wolfram said, explaining how people still have distinct localized accents in this age constant relocation. Wolfram said the way of talking becomes an "unconscious choice" by the speaker. Even on Ocracoke, accessible only by ferry, there is television, radio and a constant stream of visitors with every kind of accent imaginable. Yet, Ocracoke speech patterns are not changing rapidly. "If you identify with a particular community, part of being a member of that community is talking like the people," Wolfram said.

It's the middle-aged men of Ocracoke, not their elders, who have the most prominent accents. "They relate strongly to the island way of life and have a tight social network," the professor explained. "They love the island and identify with it."

Of the 10 eighth graders Wolfram spent a week with at Ocracoke School, three are ancestral islanders. For homework one night, he required the youngsters to listen to old-timers and gather words for an Ocracoke dictionary. Wolfram hopes to instill respect for their language into these local kids. "If they understand and appreciate their own dialect, they'll be better able to preserve it."

As for the future, Wolfram doesn't dare to make any predictions. "It's hard to make blanket statements," he said. "Parts of the language are certainly going to die out, but parts are being retained."

"In other island communities, such as Martha's Vineyard, people get overwhelmed by outsiders and revert more to their dialect," he said.

Though he's studied dialects around the world, Wolfram finds the Ocracoke one special. "I love this dialect," he declared. "I like the Appalachian similarities and connection." Another interesting connection is the one Wolfram notes between Outer Bankers' English accents and that of the Lumbee Indians of Robeson County, North Carolina — that tribe also has the "hoi toide" speech pattern.

Wolfram plans to write a book about Ocracoke speech and is working with the local preservation society on the project. "It's our way of trying to give back to the community," he said. About half of Ocracoke's 700 residents are ancestral, and less than 25 percent of the citizens retain the historic speech patterns. Of course there are many differences among them. Wolfram interviews the islanders in casual conversations, asking particular questions and taping the interviews. "It's great fun," he said. "The community is excited about it, and they've been very responsive in the schools."

Perhaps one of the Ocracoke students summed it up best, "If everybody talked the same everywhere, it sure would be boring."

dredged to 18 feet. Renovations started in 1993 are expected to be completed in 1994. Check for water and power hookups before you arrive if these services are necessary for your comfort. Hookup fees will be imposed when these services are once again available.

Basically, the way to get dockage is to arrive here at the right time. If there's space open just pull in and tie up. The Park Service tells us that rafting is permitted only with the permission of the boat owner tied to the docks. (Rafting occurs when one boat ties up to a boat already tied to the docks.) There's a 14-day stay limit in the summertime. We've also been told that it's possible to get space there even in the summer, although it gets crowded on weekends.

If the marina should be full when you arrive, don't panic. According to the Coast Guard, it's OK to anchor out in the lake if you're careful to stay out of the channel and out of the way of ferry operations.

O'NEAL'S DOCKSIDE

Behind the Community Store   928-1111

O'Neal's is your friendly hunting and fishing center, owned by Charlie O'Neal. This is where you book your offshore fishing charters on the *Miss Kathleen, Seawalker, Bluefin* and *Outlaw,* and where you can charter trips to Portsmouth Island. They also sell a full line of supplies, boat gear and fuel.

OCRACOKE TROLLEY

Trolley Stop, Hwy. 12   928-4041

It's one thing to see Ocracoke Island through your own eyes and altogether another to see it through

the eyes of a local, someone who knows every nook and cranny of the island. The trolley is owned and operated by the O'Neal family. It seems like they have been around almost as long as the island has. The trolley runs three times a day during the week and twice on the weekends during the season and takes you past some Ocracoke history you'd never discover on your own.

The narrated tour includes the Coast Guard Station, the WWII Naval Base, several Sam Jones homes, the British Cemetery and Howard Grave Yard, a WWII Mine Control Tower, the Civil War headquarters for the Union Forces and lots more. The tour also includes a stop at the Ocracoke Lighthouse. You can't go in the lighthouse but a volunteer will be on hand to provide an oral history of the lighthouse and its role in the history of Ocracoke Island.

Reservations are required for buses or groups numbering more than 25, but for others, just show up at the Trolley Stop (you can grab a quick bite there too while you're waiting). Tours leave at 10:30 AM, 2:30 PM and 5 PM Monday through Saturday (no tours on Sundays). The Trolley is open year round, but advance reservations must be made after Labor Day. The cost is $4 per person. Senior citizens and group discounts are available.

OCRACOKE FISHING CENTER

Silver Lake   928-6661

Part of the Anchorage Inn operation, the five 200-foot piers and the new building act as a center for charter boat operations to the sound, Gulf Stream and close inshore.

There's a minimum six-foot depth alongside. Docking ($.85 per foot per day) includes a pool, telephones and other extras. Gas and diesel are available, and the boat ramp is free for guests of the marina and The Anchorage Inn. Marine supplies and a small tackle shop are conveniently located here. The Anchorage Inn is open almost year round. You may want to call ahead during December and January.

Recreation

There is no shortage of activities on Ocracoke Island, whether you want to fish, surf, rollerblade or go horseback riding. You'll want to kick off your shoes and enjoy mother nature and all she has to offer. Many folks also enjoy non-vigorous activities, and there are plenty of them too. Let Ocracoke bring out the aspiring artist in you. The docks, the harbor, the old homes, shipwrecks and sandy lanes are a delight to most who are challenged to sketch, paint or draw. Don't forget about the National Park Service programs and activities for children. Inquire at the **Visitor Center**, 928-4531.

Fishing from the surf or on a charter trip, swimming, beachcombing, clamming and walking are some of the traditional recreational choices on Ocracoke Island. Several Park Service roads access the beach for four-wheel drive vehicles. Once you're on the beach, it's possible to do all of those things and more. You can play volleyball, fly a kite and sail when the conditions are right. And if that's not enough, you can go biking, hiking or even bird watch-

ing. Bike rental places are scattered throughout the village. Try **Beach Outfitters**, located at Ocracoke Island Realty, 928-6261, (800) 242-5394 or FAX 928-1721. **Scarborough's Bicycle Rentals**, 928-4271, is located at the corner on the harbor. Another convenient spot for bike rentals is on the road next to the Island Ragpicker. A hiking trail (see Hammock Hills Nature Trail under Attractions in this chapter) is located about six miles from the village on the right as you approach from the ferry terminal. Take plenty of film for your camera. Insect repellant for most times of the year is recommended.

Ocracoke is on the eastern flyway of migrating water and land birds. Bird watchers can expect to see sandpipers, herons, willets, cardinals, indigo buntings, grosbeaks and warblers. Pelican Island is the northernmost nesting place of the brown pelican. During hatching season, Shell Castle Rock is incredibly alive with gulls, terns and their young.

Charter Boat Trips

While you're enjoying the beaches, historic sights and relaxed village atmosphere, plan to spend some time fishing too. Charter boat trips can be arranged at most inns and motels as well as at the marinas in Ocracoke. Trips are available to the Gulf Stream, Portsmouth Island and the Pamlico Sound. Offshore fishing, inshore and inlet fishing and reef fishing are all available in the waters surrounding Ocracoke. Many World War II shipwrecks in the Atlantic ocean off Ocracoke provide

popular fishing spots for many species of fish.

Offshore trips can yield tuna, dolphin, wahoo, big blues, amberjack, barracuda, king mackerel, shark, marlin and sailfish. Ocracoke Inlet and the surrounding waters offer many species of fish including pompano, spot, flounder, blue fish, gray and speckled trout, redfish, cobia and Spanish mackerel. The abundant reefs and wrecks offer a haven for schools of fish for bottom fishing including grouper, red snapper, cobia and trigger fish.

Individuals can fish by joining charter groups or by bringing their own group. Coast Guard regulations limit group sizes to six per boat, including children. Additional boats are available for larger groups. Reservations are necessary whether you stop by in person, or reserve your place by telephone or mail. Deposits are necessary. Ask about family discounts. Whole day and half day trips are available in the morning or at night. For those of you who haven't tried your hand at clamming, these trips can also be arranged. These are only some of the fishing charters available. There are lots more and they're easy to find.

Contact the following charter boat captains: Captain Woody Outlaw on *The Outlaw*, 928-4851, Captain "Mack" McLawhorn on *Mack Charters*, 928-5921, Captain David Nagel on *Drum Stick*, 928-5351, Captain Norman Miller on the *Rascal*, 928-6111 or 928-5711.

Captain R.T. "Ronnie" O'Neal, Jr., on the *Miss Kathleen*, 928-4841, is a lifelong resident of Ocracoke. Ronnie's family roots go back through many generations of Ocracokers. He has spent his entire life learning the waters and many of the fishing techniques that result in successful catches. The *Miss Kathleen* combines the appeal of a traditional wooden vessel along with modern equipment to provide a first rate fishing experience for anglers.

Captain Norman Miller has been fishing for as long as he can remember. He knows the waters off Ocracoke as well as anyone. He has lived on Ocracoke for 22 years, and he has been helping people fulfill their fishing ambitions for 20 years with his fishing charter service on the *Rascal*. He offers two types of charters: inshore and offshore fishing, specializing in red drum and wreck fish, on his 30-foot diesel power boat; and sound and inshore fishing, specializing in fly fishing and tackle fishing, on his 21-foot Catamaran. Everything you need is provided except your tackle. The *Rascal* operates Easter through Thanksgiving and is located right on Silver Lake at the Sharon Miller Realty Office. Book well in advance for your fishing excursion. Call 928-6111 for reservations.

Captain George Roberson, Sr., has been operating the *Blue Fin* charter service since 1964. It is the longest running charter service on Ocracoke Island, and it also has the distinction of being the oldest business run by its original owner on the island. Captain Roberson has been living on the *Blue Fin* since 1965.

Ocracoke Island also offers the opportunity for visitors to enjoy activities such as windsurfing, diving, kayaking, surfing, boogie boarding, horseback riding and even rollerblading around the village.

Water Sports

Guided open kayak tours are available through **Ride the Wind Surf Shop**, 928-6311. Open kayaking provides a safe, practical and efficient way to see Ocracoke's unique barrier island environment

without harming it. The shallow waters of the Pamlico Sound stretching behind the island are teeming with wildlife, and you are likely to see many species of fish, birds, crustacea, mollusks and plants within a few minutes of entering the backwaters. Ride the Wind also maintains a good inventory of kites, boogie boards and surfboards.

Ocracoke Outdoors, 928-4061, offers water sports rentals and lessons for windsurfing, kayaking and sailing. They specialize in developing intermediate skills and high-wind technique. Self-guided kayaking tours, surf kayaking and family sailing lessons are popular. You can paddle through the marshes and creeks at Springer's Point or take the long way around to Portsmouth Island. Private and group lessons are offered daily, and rates vary. Ask about family discounts. Everything you need to safely enjoy these sports is provided.

Ocracoke Divers Inc., 928-1471, is located on Oyster Creek and offers guided shallow- and deep-water diving tours on a seasonal basis. PADI-certified divers guide you to WWII and pre-WWII wrecks. Group and specialty diving tours for two or three people are available. Air, gear and accommodations can be provided. Reservations are required. A small marina has been added accessible by Pamlico Sound. Outboard motors, gasoline and beer can be purchased at the marina.

B.W.'s Surf Shop, 928-6141, will rent you a pair of rollerblades if you'd like to try rollerblading around the village. They also offer surfboard rentals to those of you who may be

Ocracoke has its own unique personality.

thinking about catching a wave or two. The waves here are especially good for beginners and boogie boarders.

Horseback Riding

Horseback riding is offered on Ocracoke Island through **Seaside Stables**, 928-3778. There's a one-hour minimum. Beach rides are popular and campfire rides can be arranged. You can reserve one to three hours for the ride. Moonlight and sunset rides are also available. All-day and evening riding can be arranged too. Reservations are required — you can call any day of the week. The stable is open March until November.

Arts and Crafts

Carol O'Brien, local artist and owner of the **Sunflower Studio/Gallery,** 928-6211, offers a School of Arts and Crafts for adults and children, January through April. Courses include oil painting, acrylics, water color, stained glass, ceramics, basketry, and glass fusing. Water color workshops will be offered during the summer months by appointment only.

Shopping

Shopping in Ocracoke is casual, interesting and easily managed on foot. Small shops are scattered throughout the village and set unobtrusively along the main street, on sandy lanes or in private homes. You'll also discover that some dockside stores take on the ambiance of general stores and carry everything you need. Ocracoke Village shops offer a variety of local crafts, artwork, quality accessories for the home, antiques, beach wear, books, music, and magazines as well as T-shirts and even a few souvenir mugs. The best part is the subtle charm of just happening upon a studio-type shop or gallery, rather than a series of stores set apart from other aspects of life in the village. You are certain to be calmed by the New Age music heard in many of the shops throughout the village.

Let's start with the **Ocracoke Variety Store**, 928-4911, on Highway 12, before you enter the village. "Hutch" and Julia Hutcherson, the owners, are most always there ready to talk about the village, their own lives and old times while you shop for groceries, beach wear, T-shirts, magazines, camping supplies, wine or beer. "Hutch" worked for A & P for many years, and the store reflects that expertise. Julia and "Hutch" are very helpful people, and they keep on hand all the menus of the cafes and restaurants of the island. So, even if you're not shopping for anything specific, stop by and take advantage of this information. They're open all year. An **ABC Store**, 928-3281, is located adjacent to the Variety Store.

The Hutchersons opened the **Ocracoke True Value Hardware Store**, 928-4288, in March 1992. As you can well imagine, this store provides a great convenience for the residents of Ocracoke. And, for all of you who just can't resist dropping by a local hardware store, remember it's the only one on the island.

A short distance down the road, is **Pirate's Chest Gifts and T-shirts,** 928-4992. This shop is filled with merchandise — you must stop in to appreciate the variety of items sold here. In case you missed them in Frisco, you'll find a wide variety of souvenirs, jewelry, craft supplies, local shells, prints baskets, books, wooden lighthouses, scrimshaw, coral, driftwood sculptures and lots more. The list just goes on and on.

Black Anchor Antiques & Collectibles, 928-6301, is an interesting place to browse and select a favorite item from yesteryear. In a far corner, you'll come upon an array of old clocks ticking away! No two are alike, and the volume of clicking-ticking reminded us to slow down, enjoy some nostalgic moments and visit with Sally and Darrell Dudley for a while. Darrell has an incredible collection of weathervanes out on the porch and perhaps the only brass moose in North Carolina. Sally's vintage jewelry, hand-shaped vases and hats and Victorian fancifuls give a nudge down memory lane. Darrell also has a selection of impressive handmade wooden model ships, old and new boats, and a collection of lighters unlike any you have ever seen before.

Island Ragpicker, 928-7571, will catch your eye with an attractive mixture of bells, baskets and rugs spilling over the porch railings and hanging from the ceiling. Started in 1985 as a place to sell their beautiful hand-loomed rugs, the owners, Mickey Baker and Carmie Prete, offer other fine quality crafts, including many by local crafters, handmade brooms, cards, decoys, pottery, dishware, jewelry and clothing. We really liked the Batik clothing and plywood sculptures made from laminated and carved birch and Lauan plywoods. Browse through selected flotsam and jetsam. Their full general book shop

features a unique selection of books and gifts. And, the soft music you hear as you browse is available on tape. This shop is closed January and part of February.

As you go along the main street in the village, you'll see the **Merchant Mariner**, 928-7611. The focus of this store changed a great deal during the past year. Fresh cut flowers, arrangements, potted plants and lots of hanging plant baskets accent this shop. Gift baskets and garden gifts are their specialty, but you will also find an eclectic assortment of children's and infant's toys, T-shirts, Bali wood carved wall hangings and gift items. No telling what they have in mind for this year. You'll just have to stop in and have a look for yourself.

No shopping experience is quite complete without a trip to the thrift store. Stop by **Cork's Closet Thrift Store**, 928-7331, for thrifty and not-so-thrifty unique island finds such as new and used clothing, housewares, collectibles, books, antiques, toys and local crafts. Cork's

Closet is located between Styron's Store and the Harbor Road.

Out back is **The Old Post Office Shop and B.W.'s Surf Shop**, 928-6141. The older part of the building was actually the Ocracoke Post Office from 1954 until 1967. Brian Waters has kept the old combination mail boxes, and they are used to display shoes and other merchandise. A boutique clothing store, B.W.'s carries a large selection of Sperry Topsiders, casual and beach active wear, outer wear, swimwear, T-shirts, sweatshirts and accessories for men and women. B. W.'s also offers rollerblade and surfboard rentals.

The **Community Store**, 928-3321, is on the waterfront and a place where you can shop all year for essential items as well as rent videos. Have you got a question about Ocracoke? Then ask it — either inside or of someone sitting on the porch — and more than likely you'll discover another piece of history. When you approach this store, you'll smile and appreciate the reminders of another era. Feet shuffle and clonk on the wood floors inside. And, as you grab an ice cream from the cooler, you won't miss the quiet groaning of the overhead fans.

David and Sherril Senseney also own **The Gathering Place**, 928-3321, across the parking lot on the Harbor. This century-old building boasts a front porch for a place to rest and look at the boats dockside. But go on in, and enjoy an eclectic collection of items including local crafts, decoys, children's play toys, artwork, North Carolina pottery, Wise Woman pottery and antique collectibles such as old records, books, shoes and kitchenware. They also display a good selection of sea glass and vintage glassware. One room upstairs is an art gallery featuring hand-painted furniture and silver jewelry by Barbara Hardy and watercolors painted by Frans van Baars. This upstairs room also offers one of the best views of Silver Lake. Treat yourself to the expansive view.

The **T-shirt Shop**, 928-3321, is right across the way, and next door is **The Fudge and Taffy Shop**, where you'll find an abundance of sweet treats, enough to please even the most discriminating palate: 15 varieties of homemade fudge, 16 flavors of taffy and fresh frozen yogurt.

Tucked away on the back side of The Fudge and Taffy Shop by the big Cypress tree is **The Hole in the Wall**, 928-6206, where you can literally shop in a hole in the wall. This shop is seven feet wide by 23 feet long. When the front door opens, it spans the width of the shop. You will find the entrance way to this shop as

unique as its merchandise. How about the hat-lined flower boxes and the ceramic cowboy-hat birdhouse! This boutique carries one-of-a-kind clothing, imported batiks, hats, accessories, jewelry and handcrafted items from Brazil, India, Egypt, Afghanistan and Guatemala. Most clothing is unisex. Batik antique coin jackets and field hats are hot selling items. Your eyes will be bombarded by bright colors here. A second location in Surf City, N.C., features multinational clothing, jewelry and hats.

Also located on the harbor next to The Fudge and Taffy Shop is **Ride the Wind Surf Shop**, 928-6311. This water sports boutique has been on the island for several years. Activewear for fit people can be found here. J. Crew and Eddie Bauer are big sellers in the fall. During the summer you'll find plenty of Rusty wear and Stussy. All the name brands are carried here for surfing and windsurfing including Hawaiian Island Creations. A good assortment of sunglasses, outer wear and kites will interest you too. Surfboards, boogie boards, and beach equipment are available for rent. Sign up for your guided open kayak trips here!

Island T-shirts & Gifts, 928-6781, is located in the heart of the village and offers three distinct rooms of merchandise including a great collection of T-shirts. The wide range of sizes and numerous designs make this shop hard to beat anywhere. You'll find beach souvenirs, books by local authors and flip flops for the entire family in a one room, while the Christmas room features a wide selection of island/beach Christmas ornaments. You won't be able to

miss the great display in the front yard of this shop where T-shirts are hung on mop and broom handles. You will have to see the rest for yourself. Rocking chairs located on the front covered porch invite weary shoppers.

Kathy's Gifts & Clothing, 928-6461, located on the waterfront, occupies the first floor space of the Princess Waterfront Suites Motel. Owner Kathy Cottrell offers lots of very well made, comfortable clothing for both men and women. She has a fine collection of classic, sophisticated clothing for women including sportswear and dressier island designs. She also has a lovely selection of accessories for the home including collectors' items with frogs, cows, rabbits, fish, shells and teddy bears. There are so many unique finds in this store, lots of handcrafted fashion jewelry in all price ranges, mobiles, gifts, cards, stationery, wrapping paper and T-shirts with unique designs. This is a shop for those of you who are looking for tasteful souvenirs for yourself or your friends and family back home.

It's not too difficult to guess that **Magnolia's**, 928-7251, is also owned by Kathy Cottrell. It is located across the street from Kathy's Clothing. Merchandising is first rate in this boutique. She carries an extensive collection of dishware sets, glassware and ceramic gifts. Antiques, cloth baskets, fish novelty items, batik women's clothing and T-shirts are also featured here.

You can never have too many T-shirts from Ocracoke, and **Tees by the Sea**, 928-3273, features T-shirts

for all ages and seems to specialize in clothing for the young. Owner Kathy Cottrell is not only in tune with what the adult shopper wants, but young people are enticed by her fashion finds as well. Parents, you will probably want to come in and take a look around for yourself.

Harborside Gifts, 928-4141, is one of the pleasant surprises for visitors to Ocracoke. The first thing you need to know about this shop is that it is newly remodeled, and it also provides the check-in and check-out locations for the Harborside Motel. The owners know about quality and carry a wide selection of sportswear for the family, as well as some gourmet foods, teas, cooking items, books and magazines. Check out their interesting T-shirts. And, above your head you'll discover the model train that runs throughout most of the store.

North Carolina crafts are in abundance at a shop owned by Philip Howard. **Village Craftsmen**, 928-5541 or (800) 648-9743 for information and catalogue sales, has become a local landmark in the past 20 years — not one easily discovered, however, unless you're willing to explore a narrow sandy lane known as Howard Street. It's a nice walk from the main street, but please use some insect repellant in warm weather! Once there, you'll discover a wide assortment of crafts, pottery, rugs, books, soaps, candles and jams. You'll also find hand-stenciled bookmarks, unique wooden children's toys, stoneware and beautiful tie-dyed T-shirts. Philip himself is an artist, and his work is sold in the shop. Outer Banks dulcimers, hand-

made on Hatteras by Adolph Caruso, will charm you. The necks of these instruments are a hand-carved duck's head or other coastal animal. Other musical instruments such as precisely tuned wind chimes, door harps, catpaws and strumsticks, will invite you to a different setting and mood in this secluded, wooded hideout on Ocracoke Island. Free mail order catalogues are kept right outside the front door of the shop when it is closed; please help yourself.

On the road leading to the British Cemetery, you'll find a handful of great places. **Over the Moon**, 928-3555, is a wonderful place filled with "celestial gifts" — well, *we* were starry eyed, especially over a huge blanket/wall hanging with a sun face on it. We were also captivated by the Beeswax impressions, porcelain ornaments, handpainted wooden music boxes hanging on the walls and the cards — all kinds of cards: Batik cards, pop up cards, pin cards and silkscreen cards. The whole earth, earth rare and constellation T-shirts were unique too. This is where you'll want to spend a long time browsing, so give yourself time.

Just down the road from Over the Moon you'll happen upon, **Island Artworks**, 928-3892. Kathleen O'Neal, the owner of this gallery-style shop, has lived on Ocracoke for 18 years. She holds a bachelor of arts degree in sculpture and has been in the jewelry business for 12 years. This gallery has a new look in keeping with the island style. The turquoise interior is finished with a flamingo-peach trim giving this shop a tropical "Bohemian" feel. Kathleen does all the copper enameling, silver smithing

and beading work herself. "Art jewelry" is an apt way to describe most of the finds in this shop. Most of the artwork displayed in this shop is provided by locals or by those who have had some connection to Ocracoke. Handcrafted cedar boxes by local artist Jack Willis can be found in unique free-form shapes. The local photography is interesting along with the mixed media pieces, paiper mâché items and handpainted furniture. We recommend this shop as a great new find on Ocracoke.

Just a stone's throw away is **The Village Bake Shop**, 928-1531, where Loni and Tony Sovern, along with their son Zack, offer up early morning sustenance that hits the spot. There's donuts, coffee cake, cinnamon buns, cookies, breads, muffins and the essential fresh-brewed hot coffee. Special occasion cakes and desserts are tempting too. They're open 5:30 AM to 6:30 PM during the season. The Soverns are announcing the opening of **Village Video**, 928-1531. You can rent videos at the same location daily until 6:30 PM.

After you've eaten your donuts (you *are* going to bike all day aren't you?!), you can head next door to **Ocracoke Island Hammocks**, 928-4387 or (800) 659-3003. You'll find a refreshing "countryesque" feeling about this shop. The suncatchers and stained glass made us feel right at home. Handmade hammocks are the Robinson's family business, and look out there's lots more in store this year. Michele and Hal Robinson are busy expanding everything — their shop, their hammock line and their gifts!

Their 100 percent handmade hammock designs are woven of du-

Photo: Mary Ellen Riddle

These Ocracoke boats are lying in wait.

rable dacron polyester rope and come in a variety of sizes. The hammock line has expanded to include three sizes, two types of porch swings, hanging chairs, and deck chairs — all with a rope back of course. Even their company name tag, found on each hammock product, is solid brass.

You can watch weaving in the shop while Hal tells you a thing or two about the business of hammocks and the history of Ocracoke. Hal Robinson does all of the woodwork, and Michele handpaints the tasteful planters and woodburnings you see. They carry other nice gifts, which include ceramic dishware, pottery, wind chimes and lots more. Mail order service is available, so give them a call or write: Ocracoke Island Hammocks, P.O. Box 207, Ocracoke, N.C. 27960. Weaving takes place year round, but the shop is usually closed from Christmas until Easter.

You can follow British Cemetery Road all the way around to find **Sunflower Studio/Gallery**, 928-6211. This art gallery is located along one of the back streets in the village known as the Back Road. It is owned by Carol O'Brien, and her husband serves as the focal point for local art. Carol offers and participates in ongoing workshops for artists. Watercolor workshops are provided during the summer months by appointment. A school of arts and crafts is offered January through April for adults and children. Classes include oil paint, acrylics, water color, stain glass, ceramics, basketry and glass fusing. Accommodations may be arranged. Shows are continuous from June throughout the summer and change biweekly.

The gallery maintains a soothing atmosphere with New Age music playing softly in the background. You won't hear the ring of a cash register, and no one will follow you around. Browsing is a personal experience, like being in someone's home. The Sunflower Studio combines contemporary and traditional arts and crafts. All of the artists are from Ocracoke, and some of the craftspeople are from other places. Only original art is featured. You will also find custom deer skin shoes, custom moccasins, fused glass, stained glass, paiper mâché and an extensive collection of handcrafted jewelry. Carol and her husband are both local jewelry makers. All jewelry pieces are unique. There are a lot of ethnic designs including items made by Navajoes, Balinese, Hopis, Europeans and Indonesians. Don't miss the local family antiques displayed around the gallery. Winter hours may be arranged by appointment.

Right across the street from the Sunflower Studio you'll find **Teach's Hole**, 928-1718, is the place to spend time if you are interested in "piratical piratephernalia." Managers George and Mickey Roberson have created a gift shop and exhibit that tell the story of Edward Teach, alias "Blackbeard the Pirate." The exhibit features a life-size re-creation of Blackbeard in full battle dress along with artifacts from the 17th and 18th centuries. Items included in the gift shop are an extensive line of pirate toys, more than 75 pirate books, maps, flags, hats, T-shirts, costumes, ship models, treasure coins, pirate music boxes and pirate movies. There is a nominal fee to view the exhibit. See our introduction to the Ocracoke section for more information on this dastardly fellow or, better yet, visit Teach's Hole and ask the experts.

Albert Styron's General Store, 928-6819, is located on the street as you approach the Ocracoke Lighthouse. Dating back to 1920, the store has recently been renovated but retains the appearance of an old general store. Some of the older fixtures remain. A wide selection of cheeses, whole coffee beans, bulk spices and other natural beans is available here. Check for daily sandwich specials. You will also find beer, wine, T-shirts, crafts and general merchandise. There is a penny candy display (now 5 cents) reminiscent of times gone by. The old-fashioned soda fountain is neat too. It was nice to notice the recycling containers outside. **Pamlico Gifts** can be found just past the lighthouse.

Inside
Restaurants

Dining out has become an integral part of nearly everyone's vacation experience, and the Outer Banks offers an excellent selection of restaurants from which to choose. Eating out is considered entertainment and recreation, in addition to just satisfying hunger. While seafood has been the mainstay of Outer Banks restaurants for a long time, lately we've noticed an interesting trend toward more ethnic, less traditional food here. The competition increases — more than 20 new restaurants opened on the Outer Banks this past year. Sam McGann, acting president of the Outer Banks Culinary Association (and co-owner and chef of the Blue Point), said, "What we're seeing is young, excited owner/operators. Many smaller restaurants are trying to make a niche for themselves by creating their own style." This means we're now seeing smaller, more personal eateries catering to sophisticated palates.

"And it's not just seafood," McGann commented. "It's ethnic, which we sorely lacked." Today, you'll find Italian, Mexican, Tex-Mex, Chinese and Thai restaurants on the Outer Banks. This variety is good for the area. "The more diversity we have, the broader the clientele of vacationer we're going to

draw," McGann said. Another trend is toward lighter, healthier cooking — clean, simple and natural are popular now. Outer Banks restaurants can please nearly every diner, offering as wide a variety as Bubba's BBQ to Penguin Isle. "They all add to a better experience for vacationers," McGann added.

When visiting the seashore, you expect fresh, top-quality seafood, and those expectations are definitely fulfilled here. From the inshore and offshore waters, many species of fish are available on menus as catches-of-the-day or traditional entrees.

Select from broiled, grilled or fried fish or culinary delights with special butters and sauces. Lately, many restaurants offer raw and steam bars, a casual dining concept that really fits the beach lifestyle. Here you'll find fresh oysters and clams, along with delicious steamed shrimp, crab and vegetables. Some restaurants have seafood trios, small portions of several fish filets. Others serve seafood or shellfish stuffed with crabmeat.

Speaking of crabmeat, Outer Banks She Crab soup, chowders and crabcakes are standard fare at most area restaurants. Soft shell crabs are the rage in spring. Crabmeat cocktails are plentiful in the appetizer section of most menus.

If you're into picking your own crabs, more than likely you'll do it at your own cottage, on an outdoor picnic table. Buy them already steamed or freshly caught to steam them in your own kettle. Restaurants on the Outer Banks have phased out the all-you-can-eat-steamed crabs affairs, where butcher paper, mallets and knives were the only table-dressing. But local seafood stores carry steamers with racks, seasonings and know-how for these great American feasts of summer.

Oysters and clams provide additional temptation when you're visiting the Outer Banks. Raw bars are noted at many restaurants. The same for scallops. They are plentiful and served in a number of ways: fried, sauteed and broiled. Shrimp are plentiful, and prices are very good at local stores for buying them by the pound for a quick steam. You can order shrimp in restaurants in creole dishes, stuffed with crabmeat or simply sauteed or broiled.

Check out the restaurants in several villages, buy from local stores or catch your own. Seafood is plentiful on the Outer Banks, and a well-prepared seafood dinner is about the best cap to a day on the beach.

OUTER BANKS-STYLE CLAM CHOWDER

Every seafaring area takes its clam chowder seriously. Chowders come in three basic varieties. Manhattan Clam Chowder has a tomato base and may be on the spicy side with hints of Tabasco, thyme, basil and oregano. New England Clam Chowder usually has a milk base and has

salt pork, onion and potatoes. The Outer Banks variety (call it Hatteras-style, Wanchese-style or whatever) uses neither tomato or milk, but features the clams in their own broth or liquor. Other ingredients may include diced potatoes, chopped onions, celery, parsley and the chef's choice of spices that enhance the clam flavor. Chowder will sour very easily if it is not handled properly, especially if made in big batches. Chowder chefs agree that the cover on a pot of chowder should never be left on while it is cooling because the condensation will spoil it. A chowder should never go into the refrigerator until it has completely cooled to room temperature. Any skin that forms on the top of a cooled chowder should be carefully skimmed off. A chowder always tastes better on the second, or even third, day if it doesn't ferment first! Chowder is not easy to make and even harder to keep. It is little wonder that chowder chefs are so sensitive and proud of their vulnerable creations.

It is very possible that no two Outer Banks clam chowders are the same. Perhaps they are not even the same at the same restaurant from one day to the next. It is the challenge and delight of the would-be chowder gourmet to sample the field and declare his or her own preferences.

HUSHPUPPIES

Many seafood restaurants on the Outer Banks serve up a basket of hushpuppies with their entrees. Hushpuppies are a traditional Southern deep-fried corn meal bread. The corn meal, flour, baking powder,

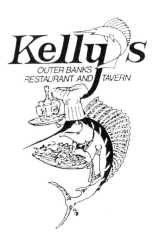

Kelly's, the Outer Banks' favorite gathering place, features items such as fresh caught gulf stream fish, North Carolina seafood, and Iowa beef.

2316 South Croatan Hwy, MP 10 1/2 Bypass
Nags Head · 919-441-4116 · Open Year Round
Dinner 5 pm 'til 10 pm
Tavern open 4:30 pm 'til 2 am

Enjoy the beautiful sunset on the Sound as you dine on beef, poultry and North Carolina Seafood at Penguin Isle.

6708 South Croatan Hwy, MP 16 Bypass,
Nags Head · 919-441-2637 · Open Year
Round · Dinner 5:30 pm 'til 10 pm
Gazebo Deck open 5:30 pm 'til 2 am

PENGUIN ISLE

SOUNDSIDE GRILL & BAR

salt, sugar, egg and milk batter is dropped by the spoonful into deep hot fat and allowed to fry until it is golden brown.

In some Southern areas, finely chopped onion is added to their mix and the hushpuppy is fried in the same oil used to fry the fish. But the quintessential Outer Banks hushpuppy cook eschews the onion and the fishy hint to his or her creations in favor of a sweet, almost cake-like quality that is achieved by increasing the flour and sugar ratio and frying in oils reserved just for hushpuppies.

Hushpuppies can vary in diameter. Some cooks believe that the size of the round crispy breads is the secret to their texture and taste. Others guard their batter recipes in the conviction that they have discovered the perfect hushpuppy formula. Many restaurants on the Banks have loyal followers who are convinced their hushpuppies are the best. To tell the truth, few restaurants make hushpuppies from scratch anymore. There are excellent commercial mixes that get "doctored" so that the cook can claim it as his or her own. The quantitative and qualitative difference may actually be very small.

By legend, and this is perhaps a true one, hushpuppies got their name as Southern cooks prepared the evening meal. Hungry hunting dogs would hang around the kitchen and bark for their share of the meal being prepared. The harried cooks, trying to get a meal completed for a waiting family, attempted to appease and quiet the dogs with bits of corn bread batter dropped into the hot frying fat. The little fried dough balls were thrown out the kitchen door with the admonishment, "hush puppy!"

PLANNING & PRICING

The restaurant competition on the Outer Banks is keen. The prime vacation months account for a large percentage of a restaurant's income, so the good business person cannot afford to be outmaneuvered by menu pricing. Competitive enterprise seems to be working here to the consumer's benefit.

We see a basic uniformity of entree pricing for the most popular items. For example, a flounder filet stuffed with crabmeat, presented in restaurants of equal ambiance and kitchen quality, will cost about the same price. For your convenience we have established four categories as a guide to menu prices. The costs are based on dinner for two persons which includes appetizers, entrees, two vegetables or side dishes, desserts and coffee. Specials and other factors can lower the basic check total just as cocktails, wine and flaming tableside desserts can increase it. For restaurants that don't serve dinner, the guideline is based on relative expense.

Restauranteurs with pocket calculators can easily challenge our best intentions in offering these guidelines. Personal choices and menu changes will prove us wrong in some cases. But we hope you'll bear in mind that these are only meant to be guides and adopt our dining-out attitude: Enjoy your favorite offerings on the menu and be prepared to pay the bill. Here are the guidelines that are reflected in the restaurant profiles to follow:

A basic meal for two less than $25	$
A check for two of $26 to $40	$$
A check for two of $41 to $55	$$$
More than $55 for two	$$$$

These guides do not reflect the 6 percent state sales tax or the gratuity, which should be at least 15 percent for good service. Some restaurants offer discounts and specials for early evening dining in order to encourage their patrons to avoid the peak dining hours. It is no secret that in season, and on shoulder season weekends, the waiting lines at popular restaurants are long. Few restaurants will accept reservations except for large parties. We list a season of operation for each restaurant. But please note: while we make every effort to get accurate information, in a competitive, active market like the Outer Banks, even the best-laid plans can get scrapped mid-season. If you're visiting off season, it's best to call ahead before you make dinner plans.

Be aware that ABC licenses are available only in Nags Head, Kill Devil Hills, Kitty Hawk and Duck. In those areas you'll find full bar service, with beer, wine, mixed drinks and hard liquor. At restaurants on Roanoke, Hatteras and Ocracoke islands and Corolla, you'll usually find beer and wine, with a few places allowing "brown bagging" where you bring your own booze and mix it with house setups.

The restaurants profiled in this guide are arranged by mile marker, north to south, Corolla to Ocracoke.

Northern Beaches

Corolla

The phenomenal growth in Corolla is reflected in the local restaurant scene. Just a few years ago, The Sanderling Inn was the only place to dine on the northern beaches. These days there are more restaurants from which to choose, though they are generally smaller and don't have the large spacious dining rooms that you find in Nags Head or other Outer Banks villages. The atmosphere is casual; the food is good; and there are some wonderful surprises.

NICOLETTA'S ITALIAN CAFE

Corolla Light Village Shops   453-4004
$$-$$$ MC, VISA

Since this small Italian cafe opened three years ago, it has earned a fine reputation for a wide variety of well-prepared foods by Chef Kevin Layton, a graduate of New York Tech for the Culinary Arts. Nicoletta's is owned by a very enterprising local couple, Bernie and Fran Mancuso. Fran handles the day-to-day management of the restaurant, and her personal touches are very apparent. This classy little bistro features tables covered in white linen. Each is adorned with a single, long-stemmed red rose. Waiters whisk about dressed in crisp black and white uniforms and a thick burgundy floral carpet softens their step. The cafe is a short walk from the red brick Currituck Lighthouse, which can be viewed from the restaurant.

Nicoletta's is open for dinner only, serving from 5 PM to 10 PM seven days a week in season. The menu features fresh seafood, veal, filet mignon and chicken garnished with fresh vegetables, and the sauces are homemade. Note that not all of the Italian sauces here are red ones. There is a select wine list and homemade desserts. Try the chocolate mousse with a cup of espresso or cappuccino — a great way to end the evening.

Black and white photographs of Ol' Blue Eyes, Frank Sinatra, hang from the walls, and you're likely to hear his tunes in the background. A separate room is available for private parties. Nicoletta's highly recommends reservations. Dress is casual, and children are welcome; there's a special menu to suit their appetites.

COSMO'S PIZZERIA
Corolla Light Village Shops   453-4666
$ MC, VISA

Cosmo's Pizzeria is open for lunch and dinner; it's the place for authentic New York-style pizza hand tossed right before your eyes. The

decor is black and white, accented with old family photos from Italy. Pizza, calzones, stromboli and other Italian dishes are all homemade and delicious! In addition, an assortment of cold and hot subs and salads is on the menu. You can eat in or take out. It's open seven days a week during the season, from 11 AM until 10 PM, and beer and wine are served.

HORSESHOE CAFE
Corolla Light Village Shops   453-8463
$$ MC, VISA, AMEX

Horseshoe Cafe brought Southwestern cuisine and Tex-Mex to the northern Outer Banks, where Chef Chris Mack, a graduate of Baltimore Institute Culinary College, offers his skills in the kitchen. You'll find plenty of good seafood, steaks, chicken and barbecue. Desserts are homemade. Horseshoe serves breakfast, lunch and dinner, with dinner entrees ranging from $8.95 to $16.95. A children's menu is available. Daily specials are offered for adults and children. You'll feel right at home in their Southwestern decor — they even have cacti. Beer and wine are served. Hours are 8 AM until 10 PM; dinner is served from 5:30 PM until 10 PM. Be sure to check out their great "siesta" T-shirts!

SUSAN'S CALYPSO CAFE
Monteray Plaza   453-8833
$$ MC, VISA

Susan's Calypso Cafe maintains one of the boldest decors on the Outer Banks. The entrance is on the southeast side of the plaza, but you won't miss it because it's surrounded by an iron picket fence. Outside dining is available in this area on iron tables and chairs. Once inside, you'll feel you're in a cafe in the Caribbean. The walls are art — covered with murals of palm trees, vines and other island scenes. Everything is decorated in shades of green, purple and ecru. The upholstered booths are just the right shade of purple, and the light oak tables provide a great contrast to the colorful interior. The "back porch" area of the dining room accommodates larger parties and is set against a backdrop of the Caribbean house next door — painted Caribbean green with pink shutters. The music is reggae and island tunes, naturally. The bar area is small with five or six bar stools.

Susan and Ron Nicoletta (yes, they started Nicoletta's) serve lunch and dinner in the island style. Dinner entrees start at $11.95. Lunch hours are from 11 AM until 2 PM, and dinner is served at 5:30 PM. Try the Havana BBQ ribs, the St. Croix London broil, the duck, grouper, coconut-battered shrimp or the jerk marinated shrimp. The calimari, conch fritters and Calypso Caesar Salad are house specialties. Draft beer and wine are available. A children's menu is offered.

TOMATO PATCH PIZZERIA

| Monteray Plaza | 453-4500 |
| $ | MC, VISA |

The owners of Kitty Hawk Pizza are now offering the northern beaches the same great homestyle cooking featured in Kitty Hawk. This restaurant features big open spaces that can handle large crowds. Greek foods, from family recipes, are offered along with great pizzas and pasta specials. Menu items include gourmet and white pizzas with bacon and fresh garlic, Gyros, Greek salads, spaghetti and lots more. Desserts of French silk pie, Snickers pie or baklava will tempt you. Beer and wine are available. Children are not only welcome, they are anticipated (lots of high chairs are on hand), and they will love the Tomato Patch cartoon character. Hours are 11 AM to 11 PM from March to October. Tomato Patch offers a breakfast buffet in July and August. Call for hours.

SMOKEY'S ORIGINAL FRIED CHICKEN, BBQ AND RIBS

| Monteray Plaza | 453-4050 |
| $ | MC, VISA |

The specialties here are fried chicken, barbecue and ribs. Eat-in or takeout is available. You'll enjoy all the trimmings such as cole slaw, baked beans, fried sweet potatoes, baked sweet potatoes, onion rings and french fries. The menu is extensive. Choices include fried jalapeno peppers and chicken wings for starters and then sandwiches, salads, seafood and good ole North Carolina barbecue. The chicken dinners are really the rage. Children's plates are available. Look for daily lunch specials and frozen yogurt for dessert. Hours are from 11 AM until 8 PM, seven days a week during the summer.

STEAMER'S RESTAURANT & RAW BAR

| TimBuck II | 453-3344 |
| $$ | MC, VISA, AMEX, DISC |

This brand new 50-seat restaurant and raw bar offers something new — a place to pick up packaged steamer meals to go, pot included. Take home lobster, blue crabs, shrimp, oysters clams and mussels with all the trimmings. Or, stay at Steamer's, where lunch and dinner are served seven days a week from March to December. Enjoy the waterside view in this upscale but casual restaurant with 28-foot vaulted ceilings. You'll wear a "patron pager" and stroll through TimBuck II while waiting for your table. Once seated, enjoy fresh, local seafood and live Maine lobsters, sandwiches and steamed items. Hours are 11:30 AM to 1:30 AM. Oh . . . this is the first restaurant on the northern beaches to offer Weeping Radish beer (made in Manteo) on draft, and they have Black and Tans also. Wine is served too.

FINELY RON'S

TimBuck II   453-4077
$$$ MC, VISA, AMEX, DISC

Ron and Jean Davidson have been lavishing their expertise on diners in Kill Devil Hills for several years, and now have relocated to Corolla. Good for Corolla visitors but sad for the folks in Kill Devil Hills. The new location is more casual and fun, but the food is just as good. With more than 20 years of restaurant experience, the Davidsons offer a variety of interesting choices. Dinner entrees feature fresh fish, duck, lamb and veal. Try the "Baked Oysters Down East" for a real treat or the wild mushroom strudel. A children's menu is offered. Lunch features a chalkboard menu with daily specials of sandwiches, soups, salads and light entrees. Reservations are recommended for dinner. Enjoy beer and

wine at the bar while waiting; you'll discover an extensive wine list, with as many as a dozen varietals by the glass.

Duck

SANDERLING INN RESTAURANT

Sanderling, north of Duck   261-3021
$$$$ MC, VISA, DISC

Located within the Sanderling Resort, the restored lifesaving station, Caffey's Inlet Station No. 5, is home to one of the Outer Banks most wonderful restaurants. Multiple dining rooms enhanced with rich woods and brass offer ocean and sound views for intimate or group dining. This is the home of Chef Connell's Progressive Southern Regional Cuisine. Start the morning with Pumpkin Nut Bread stuffed with cinnamon cream cheese and brown sugar. At midday, enjoy Carolina pork barbecue pizza topped with red onion and smoked gouda cheese. A memorable evening meal is fresh pasta, hickory grilled local seafood or the Sanderling's famous pan fried crab and scallop cake. Whichever you choose, you're "inn" for a treat! Full beverage service includes fabulous California wine selections. A fun children's menu is offered. Reservations are welcome. Breakfast is served from 8 AM to 10 AM, lunch from noon to 2 PM and dinner from 5 PM to 10 PM daily.

BARRIER ISLAND INN AND TAVERN

Duck Rd.
Duck Village   261-3901
$ MC, VISA, AMEX, DISC

Barrier Island Inn is situated on

the Currituck Sound and was Duck's first restaurant. Right away you know you'll have some activity to watch while you dine here. You'll find yourself spying on wild ospreys, ducks and windsurfers testing their sails on the Currituck Sound. The bar offers locals and visitors a chance to mix by sharing a game on the shuffleboard table. In the summer, you'll find live entertainment nightly.

Outer Banks seafood specialties along with pasta, steaks and chicken are featured. A light fare, including homemade pizza, is available in the tavern. Lunch and dinner are served year round, and breakfast is offered during the summer months. Breakfast hours are from 8 AM to 11:30 AM; lunch is served from 11:30 AM until 3 PM; and dinner is served nightly from 5 PM until 10 PM. The tavern is open until 2 AM. In summer, outdoor dining is available. Early bird discounts are offered between 5 and 6 PM, and children's menus are available.

Elizabeth's Cafe & Winery

Scarborough Faire   *261-6145*
$$-$$$ *MC, VISA, DISC*

Elizabeth's Cafe is known for its wine, earning international recognition from *The Wine Spectator* magazine for their wine list and wine offerings in 1991, 1992 and 1993. This past year, they were one of only five restaurants in the entire state that won "best of the award of excellence." Elizabeth's is a delight; the ambiance is warm and casual. A fireplace is lighted on chilly evenings. Service is excellent, and the waiters are knowledgeable about wines, which is a plus for those who are just learning. New things are stirring at Elizabeth's this year, including "prix fixe" dinners five nights a week. Serving up to 12 people at one long table ($75 per person), the diners will enjoy a six-course meal and accompanying wines. You must call ahead well in advance for reservations, where discussions of food and wine promise to be as much fun as eating and drinking. You'll learn a lot about wine and even enjoy tableside flambé. Also new this year are wine tastings outdoors in the garden from 6 PM to 8 PM nightly except Friday and Sunday. For about $30, you'll try six to eight wines and accompanying appetizers and heavy hors' d'oeuvres. Reservations are not required for the wine tastings. Fridays will feature a 6 PM wine seminar in the garden, with tickets sold in advance. At Elizabeth's, the menu changes continually, with country French and California eclectic foods at the forefront. Fresh ingredients and classic dishes with fresh seafood like Norwegian salmon offer some of the best dining on the Outer

Grab a soft-shell crab sandwich — an Outer Banks specialty — during the molting season.

Insiders' Tips

Banks. Desserts are homemade; Elizabeth's Craving is sinfully delicious.

It's a small place with seating for 60 people. In summer, there is some outdoor dining on the deck. The restaurant closes between lunch and dinner, but gourmet snacks and beer and wine are available outside, weather permitting. One of our favorite things about Elizabeth's, besides the food, wine and ambiance, is the strict no-smoking policy. Hours are 11:30 AM to 2:30 PM for lunch and 5:30 PM to 10 PM for dinner from Easter to December.

BLUE POINT BAR AND GRILL

The Waterfront Shops   261-8090
$$$ *MC, VISA*

The Blue Point is one of the most popular places on the Outer Banks. Those Two Guys, John Power and Sam McGann, have hit on a good thing with their classic, 1940-style diner on the soundfront. The small bar is a welcome place to have a cocktail, or eat lunch or dinner. The menu is creatively nouvelle and always changing. The homemade soups, unusual seafood dishes, or steak and potatoes, and great salads tempt your palate. And, while the regular food is anything but regular, the desserts have gone out-of-sight. The pecan pie topped with whipped cream and an ample sprinkling of cinnamon makes you feel almost guilty. We won't mention the chocolate concoction with almond crust, dribbled with Chambourd (raspberry) sauce. . . .

Dining at Blue Point, or the Point as it's called by locals, is hard to match. Never mind the noise or that the tables are close together on the inside. The outdoor eating, a real enclosure of the deck, is sometimes noisy, too. If it's not the ducks and geese, it's all those people enjoying good food, good conversation — letting the good times roll. A stop here is a must. Locals are happy that this place is open for lunch and dinner all year. Dinner reservations are highly recommended. Lunch is served from 11:30 AM to 3 PM and dinner from 5 PM to 10 PM. During the winter, the Point closes on Mondays.

Kitty Hawk

FAST EDDIE'S

The Marketplace
Rt. 158, MP 1
Southern Shores   261-8585
$-$$ *MC, VISA*

Fast Eddie's offers a different concept in casual dining combining a butcher, bakery and ice cream shop all under one roof. Owned by the Miller family, its decor is bright and informal with wooden floors and tables. Your food order is placed at the counter; tableside service is not available here. The hamburgers are the greatest, featuring beef freshly ground by the butcher and cooked the way you want them. The crabcakes are worth standing in line for, and they've added steamed shrimp and crabs. Ice cream is homemade, and delicious breads are baked on the premises. You can eat in or take out. Fast Eddie's opens at 11 AM and closes whenever. You'll find a good selection of foreign and domestic beer, and wine is served too.

RUNDOWN CAFE

Beach Rd., MP 1   255-0026
$-$$ MC, VISA

The owners of Tortuga's Shellfish Bar and Grill in Nags Head opened the Rundown last year, and it has been a big hit for the folks on the northern end of the beach. Rundown offers even more of a Caribbean-style menu than is available at Tortuga's. By the way, Rundown is the name of a traditional Jamaican stew, and to tie it all together, there's a batik of turtles hatching and running down to the water. In the owners' words, "There is something here for everyone." Foods maintain traditional island flavors heavily influenced by Caribbean preparations with African and Indian accents. Try the Creole crawdads or conch chowder for an appetizer. Depending on which night you're there, specials might be such delights as blackened pork tenderloin, spinach and feta stuffed chicken with roasted red pepper sauce or fresh-grilled tuna topped with sesame-ginger vinaigrette. You'll find a nice, laid back night life here too. Look for daily lunch and dinner specials. Hours are 11:30 AM till 1 AM in the winter and till 2 AM in the summer. New for 1994, the Rundown is offering a delicious, traditional Southern breakfast, served from 7 AM to 10:30 AM seven days a week.

KEEPER'S GALLEY RESTAURANT

Rt. 158, MP 4½   261-4000
$$ MC, VISA

R.V. Owens has a reputation on the beach for good food, and Keeper's Galley certainly supports it. You'll be more than satisfied with the choices here. The restaurant is open for breakfast, lunch and dinner all year except in the late winter months. The nautical decor, polished wood and seafaring nets make this a great place for families as well as intimate dining. A children's menu and full bar are available. As a matter of fact, you can eat at the bar if you like. It's located next to the Holiday Inn Express on the east side of the highway.

BLACK PELICAN SEAFOOD COMPANY

Beach Rd., MP 4½   261-3171
$-$$ MC, VISA, AMEX

This restaurant can be found where Station Six used to be. The focus of the interior of this building is still on the old Coast Guard Station but new additions make the inside interesting and conducive to casual dining. The oceanside deck is a great place to relax and enjoy great ocean views and sunsets. One section of the deck is under an awning for those of you who want to escape the sun during the day. A screened porch offers a chance to enjoy the ocean breeze. There's plenty of room for dining, and the ocean views are just as good from the inside. The bar is situated on the second level of this tri-level building and offers seating for 26 people. TV fans will marvel at the 12 TVs located above the bar. Hardwood floors, tongue and groove finishes, light gray accents, burgundy carpet and black bentwood chairs round out the decor of this new eatery.

Gourmet pizzas, cooked in plain view in a wood hearth oven, will be one signature item along with steamed shellfish of all kinds from the raw bar. Lunch and dinner are served, and the menu offers an extensive selection of appetizers — made from scratch. Pasta and seafood specials are available for dinner along with Prime Rib on Friday night. You won't find much fried food, but fish is grilled and blackened to your satisfaction. Children's portions are also available. Remember, everything is casual here. Occasionally, live music is played. The Black Pelican is open 11:30 AM until . . . year round and is closed on Tuesdays in the winter.

FRISCO'S RESTAURANT
Rt. 158, MP 4½   *261-7833*
$$ *MC, VISA, AMEX*

Enjoy the ocean view while dining in a relaxed atmosphere at Frisco's. The chefs create distinctive entrees using only fresh local seafood, choice beef, poultry and pasta. Specialty entrees include traditional Outer Banks seafood, and they're famous for their blackened prime rib and delicious lunch and dinner specials. Desserts are homemade, and they change all the time. You'll always find a great selection of homemade cheesecakes — some of Chef Mark Dough's favorites. The dining room is light, almost porchlike, with greenery throughout. Lunch and dinner are served, and the crabcakes are great. Hours are from 11:30 AM until . . . seven days a week during the season, and it's open year round. A children's menu is available, and a full bar awaits you in a separate section of the restaurant. An early bird menu is offered between 5 and 6 PM, but you must be seated by 6 PM.

VITI'S PIZZA & PASTA PARLOR
Rt. 158, MP 4½   *255-0611*
$ *MC, VISA*

Viti's is newly relocated to Kitty Hawk, having come to the beach from Manteo. Look for them near the Crafters' Gallery. The Italian food is well prepared, yet very affordable. The lasagna is from an old family recipe. Shrimp scampi is popular too. A children's menu is available. Beer and wine are served. Service is friendly and quick. A lunch buffet of pastas, pizza, soups runs $3.95. They're open all year, serving lunch and dinner. Hours are 11:30 AM to 9 PM in the winter and closing time is 10 PM in the summer.

JOHN'S DRIVE-IN
Beach Rd., MP 4½   *261-2916*
$

John's has been an institution on the Beach Road for years. The fresh fish sandwiches (dolphin, trout, tuna etc.) or creamy ice cream shakes and sundaes are worth driving miles to reach. Locals can't get enough of the good food here, for takeout or to eat at one of the picnic tables set on either side of the building. There are some interesting stories-in-pictures facing the glass enclosure to keep you occupied while you wait for your order. Call ahead for carry-outs. The decor is as good as any seafood shack in the world. They are closed on Wednesday.

CAPT'N FRANKS
Rt. 158, MP 4½   *261-9923*
$

If it's been a while since you tried a real Southern hot dog, Capt'n Franks is a must stop. The Hess fam-

ily has been serving hot dogs to the Outer Banks for over 20 years. Just walk up to the place and there's an assault on your senses you won't forget. The assortment of toppings for hot dogs stretches the imagination and the French fries with cheese are a different twist. Steamed shrimp is available by the pound during the evening and the grilled tuna dinners with hushpuppies and coleslaw are popular too. Capt'n Franks has picnic tables outside and carry out service. Call ahead for carry-outs whenever possible at this busy place. It's open all year except Sundays in the winter. Hours are from 10 AM until 9 PM during the season and 10 AM until 3 PM during the off season.

KITTY HAWK PIZZA
Rt. 158, MP 4½   *261-3933*
$

One of the best places to eat on the beach is Kitty Hawk Pizza. You'll keep coming back for good homestyle cooking. Locals and vacationers love the pizza and other treats made from family recipes on the menu. The low prices are attractive too. The emphasis on Greek food, seldom found on the Outer Banks, is a nice surprise. Gyros and their famous Greek salad are two favorites. But there's plenty of pizza, spaghetti and lasagna too. The booths and recently added Mediterranean Room accommodate large crowds or couples. It's comfortable, has some of the friendliest people on the beach and has incredible plants . . . if you find the beginning or the end of the philodendron, it'll be worth the trip. Beer and wine are served. Look for their second location in Corolla where they are situated in front of the Monteray Plaza. You'll find them called Tomato Patch Pizzeria up there.

TRADEWINDS
Rt. 158, MP 4½   *261-3502*
$-$$ *Most major credit cards*

If you're in the mood for Chinese food, Tradewinds is a good choice and one of the few restaurants that doesn't specialize in fresh seafood. Tradewinds is located in a strip shopping center on the east side of the highway, yet it stands alone when it comes to Mandarin-style dishes. They're willing to cook dishes to your specification — whether you prefer lightly steamed vegetables without a sauce — or a variation on the good food they always serve. Carry out is popular here, but the generous portions of perfectly cooked Chinese dishes are served best in this dimly lit restaurant. They're open for lunch and dinner all year. Hours are from 11 AM until 10 PM during the summer and from 11 AM until 9:30 PM during the winter.

LA FOGATA MEXICAN RESTAURANT
Rt. 158, MP 4½   255-0934
$ MC, VISA

OK, so your first question is what does the name mean? It's Spanish for "campfire," which co-owner Jose Moncaba said was selected because of its beautiful sound. This new restaurant has met with huge success, with people waiting in line to get in, even in March! The reason for the success is twofold: the food is good, and the prices are reasonable. Owners, wait staff, cooks are all natives of Mexico. They had a Mexican restaurant in Virginia Beach, and when customers from the Outer Banks said they should relocate, they took the advice. The place is large (if you recall, it used to house Pizza Inn, then Barter's steak house) and can accommodate groups in a separate room. Specialties are Texas Fajitas, Carne Azada (roast beef), Tacos de Carne Azada, enchiladas and chile

rellenos. If you want spicy food, you'll be accommodated, and if you like it mild, that's OK too. There's a full bar service, including a good selection of Mexican beer. You'll enjoy lunch for about $5 or less and can choose from 36 dinner selections, many for about $6. Spanish-style music sets the mood, and the service is quick and pleasant. La Fogata is open year round, seven days a week. Lunch is served from 11 AM to 2:30 PM and dinner from 5 PM to 10 PM Monday through Friday. Saturday hours are noon to 10 PM and Sunday, noon to 9 PM.

Kill Devil Hills

STACK 'EM HIGH
Rt. 158, MP 4½   261-8221
MP 9   441-7064
$-$$ No credit cards

These two popular breakfast eateries — one in Kitty Hawk and the other in Kill Devil Hills — will get you started on any vacation morning. Their specialties are good pancakes, good service and convenience to both ends of the beach. The owners, Kiki and Perry Kiousis, opened their Kill Devil Hills restaurant more than 10 years ago, and they know how to fix breakfast. Several varieties of pancakes are available as well as English muffins, Danish pastries and cereal; there are also ordinary eggs, bacon and sausage for diehards. There's a limited lunch menu available until 1 PM. Both locations are open from early spring through Thanksgiving. The Kill Devil Hills restaurant will be open 24 hours on weekends during the summer, of-

Now Open

Best Fajitas On The Beach!!

OPEN YEAR ROUND 441-6600

Seagate North MP5.5 K.D.H.

The Coastal-Cactus™

...Affordable Southwestern Dining

fering a breakfast menu and some sandwiches.

THE COASTAL CACTUS
Seagate North Shopping Center   441-6600
$ *MC, VISA, DISC*

Mexican food hit the Outer Banks full force this past fall and winter, with several new restaurants offering it exclusively. Jim Curcio opened Coastal Cactus in October, coming to the area with experience in a Mexican restaurant in northern Virginia. The cook has studied under Eddie Cabrera of the famed Tortilla Factory restaurant in Herndon, Virginia and learned the authentic Sonoran style of cooking. This is a place with family atmosphere, open year round, with good food and very affordable prices. $9.95 is about the most you'll pay for a dinner entree here, and that's for the Tequila-Lime Shrimp. Chimichangas, burritos and enchiladas run $5 to $6. Try the fajitas, served sizzling in a skillet with chicken, steak or shrimp and all the fixings; you put what you want into flour tortillas. Desserts are tempting, with Oreo ice cream pie, apple crumb, coco-caramel flan and chocolate rum parfait. There's a full bar service. The decor of peach and teal is accented with Southwestern pottery, wicker, pinatas and blankets. Get in on the hottest food trend — the Southwestern rage, and enjoy lunch or dinner at the Cactus. Open Tuesday through Saturday from 11:30 AM to 9 PM in the winter and

Clamming on Bodie Island makes for good eating.

Insiders' Tips

seven days a week May to December from 11:30 AM until.

CHILLI PEPPERS

Rt. 158, MP 5½	441-8081
$$	VISA, MC

"Gourmex Fiery Foods" are the words used to describe the hot new restaurant Chilli Peppers. Bryan Oroson and Jim Douglas have been on the Outer Banks restaurant scene quite some time. When both became very interested in spicy foods, the result was Chilli Peppers. You never know what will show up on the menu here; the dinner specials could be anything, depending on what's fresh, from scallops to steak to quail. "There's no telling," Bryan said, but you can bet it will be bold and spicy! Running the kitchen is Chef Damon Krasauskas, a graduate of the Baltimore International Culinary College. "The talent we have in the kitchen is such that I am confident we can produce something new and exciting on a daily basis," Bryan stated. There's a full bar offering

fresh fruit margaritas and a nice wine selection. Try the fresh fruit (nonalcoholic) smoothies too. This extremely progressive restaurant is open year round seven days a week from 11:30 AM to 11 PM. The bar is open till 2 AM, and there's a special late night menu. Chilli Peppers has a small, cozy feel about it. It proved very popular with locals during the fall and winter, having opened for business in August 1993. Ask about Chilli Peppers original line of sauces to take home with you — there's hot sauce, barbecue sauce and steak marinade.

AWFUL ARTHUR'S

Beach Rd., MP 6	441-5955
$$	MC, VISA, AMEX

This is a very popular spot on the Beach Road across from Avalon Pier. It expanded a few years ago and even with a second floor lounge is still crowded. It's casual, and folks at the beach love this place, especially for their steamed seafood — our publisher will travel all the way up

Full Menu Featuring the Finest in Seafood
Steak • Chicken • Sandwiches • Soups • Salads • BBQ

AWFUL ARTHUR'S
OYSTER BAR
Home of the Happy Oyster

Be sure to get one of our
World Famous T-Shirts

Open
Daily
(All Year)

Daily
Lunch and
Dinner
Specials

MP 6 - Beach Road • Kill Devil Hills, NC (Across from Avalon Pier)
441-5955 • All ABC Permits

from Manteo (a 40-mile round trip, mind you) just to pig out on the Alaskan crab legs . . . oh, OK, for the Bass Ale on tap, too). The seafood is great, the atmosphere is real "salty," and the local people pack in here all year. Monday is locals night in the off season, with live music. Awful Arthur's T-shirts are famous all over the world. Awful Arthur's is open 11 AM until. . . .

JOLLY ROGER RESTAURANT
Beach Rd., MP 7   441-6530
$$ MC, VISA, AMEX

Jolly Roger's is a locals' favorite and is open 365 days a year for breakfast, starting at 6 AM Monday through Saturday and 7 AM on Sun-

day. Lunch is served until 3 PM, and dinner hours are 4 PM until 10 PM daily. Food is available in the lounge until 1 AM. The food is good, portions ample, and you'll have a "jolly time" here. The menu proudly presents homestyle Italian dishes, local seafood and steaks. Breakfasts are enormously popular, and you will not walk away hungry. The in-house bakery provides homemade muffins, sticky buns and other delicious goodies in the display case as you walk in the door. All of the desserts on the menu are fresh baked too, and they're happy to accept special orders for cakes and things to go. The lounge is separate from the dining area and is a popular place for locals. Interactive TV is now available, and live entertainment is offered most nights during the summer. Steamed spiced shrimp is offered in the bar between 3:30 PM and 5:30 PM.

TOP OF THE DUNES
DINING ROOM AND LOUNGE
Beach Rd.
Sea Ranch Hotel, MP 7   441-7126
$$ *All major credit cards*

Top of the Dunes offers one of the few true oceanfront dining rooms on the Outer Banks. The menu features traditional Outer Banks seafood, baby back spare ribs, nightly specials and more. Entrees range in price from $10.95 to $14.95, and a limited children's menu is available. Top of the Dunes also features a popular Sunday buffet including their famous crabcakes. Dinner is served 5:30 PM until 9:30 PM nightly. Breakfast hours are 7 AM until 11 AM daily, and the Sunday buffet is 7 AM until 1 PM. Reservations for dinner are accepted.

GOOMBAYS GRILLE & RAW BAR
Beach Rd., MP 7½   441-6001
$$ *MC, VISA, DISC*

Goombays is on the Beach Road where the old Whaling Station used to be. Owner John Kirchmier is a 12-year veteran of Outer Banks restaurants and bars — owning or managing several popular places like Quagmire's and Horsefeathers. Goombays offers great appetizers, fresh-made pastas, fresh seafood, burgers and sandwiches for lunch and dinner. The bar is fun and colorful. Caribbean casual reflects John's acquaintance with that area

where white provides a nice contrast to tropical colors. Goombays T-shirts are cleverly-designed originals.

John offers great food with soft shell crabs (in season), fresh fish and seafood leading the way. These entrees, plus the long list of appetizers are moderately priced. It's open all year from 11:30 AM until 10 PM. The raw bar is open until 1 AM nightly serving steamed shrimp, steamed vegetables and other raw bar favorites. The bar is open until 2 AM.

PAPAGAYO'S
Beach Rd., MP 7½   441-7232
$$ *MC, VISA*

The old Croatan Inn is a landmark on the beach, but now it's dressed in a sort of rustic, Mexican decor with interesting, tasteful cuisine. If you look closely, though, you'll see remnants of the old Inn, especially upstairs in the lounge or on the oceanfront deck. The view from one area of the dining room along the ocean is great, the food and friendliness superb. The dining here is fun and sometimes gets a bit noisy with large groups and hot, spicy foods. Outer Banks seafood, Cajun-style fish, Mexican favorites such as enchiladas and chimichangas highlight the menu. A local hangout, Papagayo's is open from the spring through Thanksgiving. There's live entertainment in the lounge, and the margaritas are the best on the beach.

PORT O' CALL
Beach Rd., MP 8   441-7484
$$$ *MC, VISA, AMEX, DISC*

The menu at this Outer Banks

GOOMBAYS grille & raw bar

Tropical Taste
Casual Place
Maximum Fun

WAY COOL SPOT
To Meet & Greet

Open Daily, Year Round, 11:30 am - 2 am Milepost 7 1/2 on the beach road.

For Take Out Call 441-6001

landmark restaurant boasts a continental cuisine with entrees such as broiled shrimp stuffed with crabmeat, a whole array of seafood entrees, veal, chicken, pasta, beef and good soups and chowders. Fresh fruit and salads complement your dinner choice, and the desserts are excellent. A children's menu is offered.

Frank Gajar opened this restaurant in the mid '70s and his collection of Victorian furnishings in the Gaslight Saloon or the upper balcony offers a romantic touch for quiet dinner. Not at all typical of the Outer Banks, it's a great place, and its popularity brings people back time and time again.

A Sunday Buffet is a must while you're at the beach, and hours are from 9:30 AM until 1:30 PM. The Thanksgiving buffet is a highlight of a quieter time at the beach. A variety of live entertainment is on and off the small stage in the Gaslight Saloon. Last but not least, the gift shop/art gallery are attractions on their own.

Overall, the service and ambiance of Port O' Call reflect the sophistication of the Victorian era without diminishing the casual lifestyle for folks on vacation. Hanging painted glass lamps, window treatments of a fine hotel-restaurant and brass accents are used throughout, adding a touch of elegance. The restaurant is open from mid-March through December. Check out the early-bird specials, 12 selections for around $10 served from 5 PM to 6:30 PM.

THAI ROOM

Beach Rd., MP 8½
Oceanside Plaza   441-1180
$$ MC, VISA, AMEX

This Beach Road restaurant opened about seven years ago and is a very popular place for locals. When the owner returns from his annual trip to Thailand, it doesn't take long for word of mouth to spread the excitement throughout the area that "Jimmy is back in town," and the Thai Room is open again. The wide choices of excellent cuisine are not the ordinary for Oriental tastes. If you're ready to try something different, you'll be glad you chose the Thai Room. The menu notes the level of spicipness, so when you decide on your main entree, whether it's Thai Beef Curry or spicy chicken with noodles, or one of the many variations of shrimp, lobster and fish, let the waiter know how you like your spicy — hot, medium or with a light touch. The soups and spring egg rolls are delightful, and let us recommend Spicy Thai Noodles, a house specialty. Desserts (American style) are plentiful and delicious.

The decor takes you away from typical beach nautical to Thailand, and the Thai family who staffs the restaurant will happily offer suggestions. Carry-out is available. They're open for lunch from 11:30 AM until 2:30 PM, and dinner hours are from 5 PM until 9:30 PM during the season. There's full bar service, and a small bar where you can wait for a table.

BOB'S GRILL

Rt. 158, MP 9   441-0707
$ No credit cards

Bob's opened in March, offering a good, basic meal and some spicy Cajun delights. You'll most likely find owner Bobby McCoy behind the grill in the open kitchen. The staff is friendly and the food fast. Bob's opens at 6 AM and serves breakfast until 3 PM — that's hard to find. He also serves lunch and dinner. Try the breakfast omelets, hamburgers, tuna or blackened steak. Dinner offerings include steaks, Cajun beer-battered shrimp

and fresh mahi mahi. There's a good selection of salads. Save room for the hot fudge brownie dessert. Carry-out is available. Beer and wine are served. Bob's is open year round.

CHARDOS

Rt. 158, MP 9   441-0276
$$$ Most major credit cards

Chardo's is a fine Italian restaurant specializing in seafood and meats with regional Italian flavors. Their pastas are wonderful, and fresh sauteed or steamed vegetables accompany entrees. Salads, prepared with originality and flair, are an interesting combination of vegetables, and flavorful homemade dressings. Their tableside Caesar salads are absolutely delicious.

Chardo's offers a steak and pasta special on Tuesday, Thursday and Sunday priced at $9.95. A pasta bar is also available during the winter months for $7.95. Service is provided by a well-trained staff. The bar is away from the main dining area, which is nice, and several smaller rooms offer an intimate atmosphere for a special occasion. A favorite of local diners, it will appeal to vacationers who have been on the beach all day and want to go out for a nice dinner. They make their desserts daily. Give into temptation, and try their Cannoli, Tiramisu or Napoleon. You can linger without feeling rushed — in fact, make an evening of it. It's a good idea to call for reservations. Children can be served half-portions at half price. The wine list features the top California and Italian wines. They're open all year. Summer hours are from 4:30 PM

Chardo's

Italian Ristorante

1106 S. Croatan Highway, MP 9 on Bypass
Kill Devil Hills, NC 27948

(919) 441-0276

⁊ Reservations accepted
⁊ Open all year 4:30 pm to 10:30 pm daily.

until 10:30 PM, and the coffee bar including espresso and is available from 4:30 PM until midnight in the summer. Call for winter hours.

ETHERIDGE SEAFOOD RESTAURANT
Rt. 158, MP 9½ 441-2645
$$ MC, VISA, DISC

The Etheridge family is an Outer Banks tradition when it comes to dining on fresh seafood. This restaurant opened in 1986 offering the fresh seafood caught by the Etheridge fishing fleet over in Wanchese. The decor is nautical, of course, but a round dining room provides a different ambiance, especially in the semiprivate corners labeled "Stamtisch," which is German for meeting place.

Etheridge is a popular place for locals and visitors alike. This is a real family style restaurant. The seafood is fresh, the fried platters are great, and you'll be pleased with a decision to dine here. A children's menu is offered along with some non-seafood dishes. It's open for lunch and

dinner seven days a week, from March through December. Capt. Will's lounge offers a full-service bar.

PIGMAN'S BARBEQUE
Rt. 158, MP 9½ 441-6803
$-$$ MC, VISA

Pigman's rib-man Bill Shaver (you'll recognize him from his cornball cable TV commercials) owns this fabulous rib restaurant. You might wonder if you're at a pet shop when you meet "Joker," Bill's blue and gold macaw, and his pet pigs "Auggie" and "Piggy Lou" — who manage to keep their good dispositions despite the bill of fare that draws rib-lovers from all over. If it's barbecue you're hungry for, try beef, pork, turkey or tuna served with super cole slaw and fries. The red and white exterior is attractive and the aroma is irresistible. This is a very casual place, where you order at the counter, get your own drinks and eat on disposable plates. It's open from 11 AM until around 8 PM during the off season, but during the vacation season they're open until 9:30 PM.

MILLER'S SEAFOOD & STEAK HOUSE
Beach Rd., MP 9½   441-7674
$$ MC, VISA, DISC

The Miller family has restaurants all over the Outer Banks. Diners on a budget, but accustomed to good food and friendly service, will like this restaurant. A family restaurant where all-you-can-eat dinners are a favorite, Miller's fits the bill for informal dining near the beach. Seafood is served fried, broiled and sauteed. The menu offers prime rib and filet mignon along with beef kabob and surf and turf combination. There's a separate raw bar with an oyster shucker, and the steamed shellfish is a treat. Full bar service is available, and the homemade desserts are wonderful.

The restaurant also offers breakfast, has a moderately priced children's menu and is open from March to midwinter. Lunch is not served here, but breakfast hours are from 7 AM until 12 PM. Dinner is served from 4:30 until. Check for off season hours.

MADELINE'S RESTAURANT
Beach Rd., MP 9½
Holiday Inn   441-6333
$$ All major credit cards

Madeline's at the Holiday Inn specializes in Cajun creole cuisine and traditional Outer Banks seafood. You can expect casual family dining and two-for-one dinner specials throughout the year. It is apparent that the focus is on the family here because children under 12 eat for free when accompanied by an adult ordering

an entree. Children must order from the children's menu though. Lunch is not offered, but breakfast and dinner are served daily. Breakfast is standard fare and is served from 7 AM until 12 PM. Dinner hours are from 5:30 PM until 9:30 PM.

PEPPERCORNS
Beach Rd., MP 9½
Ramada Inn   441-2151
$$ All major credit cards

You'll find Peppercorns nestled above the dunes in the Ramada Inn. This restaurant serves great food beside an expansive ocean view. Customers can relax here and enjoy spectacular sunrises and sunsets. The atmosphere is beach casual with earth-toned decor and hanging plants.

The menu showcases the culinary talents of Mark Tate, one of three certified working chefs on the Outer Banks. In addition to seafood, beef, chicken and pasta favorites, the staff prepares nightly dinner specials sure to please and delight. You can expect good food at reasonable prices, with lots of salads and sandwiches to choose from too. A children's menu is available. Enjoy live guitar music from 8 PM to midnight in the restaurant. Peppercorns is open year round for breakfast and dinner. From Memorial Day to Labor Day, lunch is also served, and the gazebo deck bar is open daily, offering sandwiches and a full line of summer beverages. Especially popular are the tropical frozen drinks.

IMPACCIATORE'S
Sea Holly Square   441-1533
$$ MC, VISA

Maxine and Tom Rossman, owners of Papagayo's, branched out this winter to open a quaint little Italian restaurant in honor of Maxine's Italian heritage. Never mind that this establishment is located inside a former clothing store in a shopping center; once inside you won't know that. The pink, feminine and cozy decor makes you feel like you're in an intimate living room. This is a great place to sit and talk over dinner while enjoying Italian wines or champagne. Chef Steve Duffy is a good one for dreaming up concoctions such as chicken breast stuffed with ricotta or veal and beef roulettes. Everything here is homemade, including the fantastic bread and desserts. Creative and delicious lunch specials are available for less than $5. Impacciatore's is open for lunch and dinner year round. In the winter, they serve lunch Monday through Friday and dinner Wednesday through Saturday. Summertime lunch is served Monday through Saturday and dinner seven nights a week. Call for hours; reservations are strongly recommended.

OSPREY ISLAND GRILLE
Rt. 158, MP 10   441-6894
$$ MC, VISA, AMEX, DISC

This attractive restaurant boasts some bold bright colors outside; you can't miss it when driving by.

The Grille is a favorite with local diners. Owner Chuck Voigt has mastered the art of well-prepared, inexpensive healthy lunches and dinners, and Chef Billy Short deserves a lot of the credit for the menu offerings. The menu is varied, and the flavors run the gamut from Italian to Mexican to Caribbean. Seafood and

Cajun seasoning are used in some dishes, and Jamaican Jerk Chicken is a regular menu item. The portions are ample, and the quality of food is good. Daily specials are offered and include lots of fresh fish. A nice salad bar is also featured. The desserts are all homemade, and the Key lime pie is a favorite. A children's menu is available. Hours are from 11:30 AM until 9 or 10 PM, Monday through Saturday. Only dinner is served on Sunday, starting at 5 PM. It's open all year with full bar service.

SHIP'S WHEEL
Beach Rd., MP 10   441-2906
$-$$ MC, VISA

The Van Curen family has a reputation for great food at reasonable prices here on the Outer Banks. Breakfast at the beach is a tradition — you won't be disappointed here. The big plates (almost as big as cafeteria trays) are loaded with a variety of items including good pancakes, French toast, eggs and omelets. Seafood and steaks are the mainstay for dinner, and all dinners include the fresh salad bar. Lunch is not served. Breakfast hours are from 6 AM until 12 PM, and dinner is served from 5 PM until 9 PM. They're open seven days a week, March through October.

WAFFLES ETC.
Beach Rd., MP 10   441-1005
$ MC, VISA

Here's another Miller family restaurant, this one catering to breakfast lovers. Open from 7 AM to noon, Waffles Etc. serves breakfast only, and of course it wouldn't be named for waffles if they weren't a specialty — there are plain ones, pecan, blueberry or strawberry. Looking for a really big breakfast? Try country ham and eggs or delicious omelets. Prices range from 79 cents to $6.95. It's small, cute and cozy, and ready for kids too. Waffles Etc. is open March to November.

Colington

COLINGTON CAFE
1029 Colington Rd.
One mile west of Rt. 158   480-1123
$$ MC, VISA

Step back in time at this intimate Victorian cafe situated among the trees on Colington Road. This is definitely one of the most popular spots for dining on the Outer Banks. The renovated older home contains three small dining rooms in which well-prepared cuisine is offered for dinner only. You can enjoy a glass of wine or a beer upstairs while waiting for your table. A small but select wine menu is available. Homemade crab bisque and hot crab dip are two terrific appetizers. Daily specials include excellent pasta dishes and a mixed grill with hollandaise. The mixed-grill changes daily to include the freshest seafood. Salads are a la carte. Owner Carlen Pearl's French heritage proudly shines through in this restaurant's delicious cream sauces and use of fresh herbs. Carlen makes all the desserts, and you'll surely have a tough time deciding between the blackberry cobbler, the chocolate torte and the creme brulee. Desserts change, so you can try something new each time you

visit. They're open from 5 PM until 9:30 PM daily. In the summer, they're open till 10. Reservations are required.

BRIDGES SEAFOOD RESTAURANT
Colington Rd.
Two miles west of Rt. 158   441-6398
$ MC, VISA

Sure there are lots of bridges on Colington Road, but this delightful restaurant (the site of the original Colington Cafe) is named for the owner, Kristina Bridges. It's located in a small frame house as you drive down Colington Road. According to Chef Kevin Walsh, Bridges has expanded its traditional menu to include foods with a French and Italian flair. Diners will find New American cuisine featured here and can choose from seven to nine nightly dinner specials in addition to regular menu items. Specials are inventive with some great pasta entrees offered. There is a children's menu. You'll enjoy the variety of steaks, chicken and seafood dishes while appreciating the nautical decor. Beer and wine are offered. They're open from April through November, seven days a week, and dinner is served from 5 PM until 9:30 PM. We suggest giving them a try, for old favorites or new ones.

ZANZIBAR
1085 Colington Rd.   480-3116
$$ MC, VISA

After Trish Krolick visited a fondue restaurant in Raleigh, she decided this was definitely something the Outer Banks would take to. "It's a place for adults to sit and talk," Trish said of Zanzibar, located on

Outer Banks Dictionary

While some of these words and expressions are long forgotten, you will hear others regularly among ancestral natives of the barrier islands and Roanoke Island.

A-gal-lin : a date with a girl.

Borl : bile.

Berlaskin : ailing, crippled.

Call the mail over : distribute the mail.

Calm of day : dawn.

Chunk : throw.

Country : mainland North Carolina.

Dingbatter : an outsider who moves to this area.

Disremember : to forget.

Down-belower : resident of south end of Hatteras Village.

Fatbacks : menhaden, a type of fish.

Findings : salvage from a shipwreck.

Found : to give birth.

Frap : to hit.

Going to lee'urd or going to sea : death.

Haint : ghost.

Hattris : the natives' way of saying Hatteras (rhymes with mattress).

Hit's : it's.

Holp : help.

Hoi toide : high tide.

Memorize : remember.

Miz : Mrs.

Mommick : beat up, hassled, annoyed.

Moy : my or mine.

Oiland : island.

Pizzer : porch.

Poke sack : a bag.

Quamish : feeling bad.

Sot : set.

Studiments : lessons, studies.

Swarp : kill.

Timid : sensitive.

Wampus cat : a fictitious cat, referring to a rascally person.

Woide : wade.

Winard : windward, moving into the wind.

Wind : air.

water's edge in Colington. The view is fantastic, especially at sunset. It has a quiet, intimate atmosphere, and it offers something different — the concept of dinner being cooked at your table. Fondue pots sit right in the middle of each dining table. You'll dip fried or herb bouillon-cooked beef, chicken, seafood and fresh vegetables into Swiss or cheddar cheese and other tasty sauces. Trish and her partners bring lots of restaurant experience to Zanzibar and promise to deliver "a dining event" to customers. Beer, wine and cappuccino are offered. After dipping your entrees in sauces, you'll have to try the chocolate fondue desserts, in which you dip fruit, cake or marshmallows into milk, dark or white chocolate. Yum! Ask about the special "dinner for two." Drop in for dinner, dessert or just an appetizer. This is a small place, seating only 50, but you can relax on the front porch and enjoy the view if you have to wait for a table. It's open year round for dinner only from 5 PM until. By the way, the name Zanzibar came from a place on the African coast famous for its exotic spices.

Nags Head

SWEETWATERS
Rt. 158, MP 10½   441-3427
$-$$ MC, VISA, AMEX

Celebrating its 10th anniversary this year, Sweetwaters is open for lunch and dinner in the spring, summer and fall. This summer will find Sweetwaters offering breakfast from 7 AM to 11 AM, with delicious items such as eggs Benedict and omelets.

Located conveniently next door to the Cineplex 4 theater, Sweetwaters is the perfect spot for a meal before or after a movie. Lots of greenery and light natural wood reflect a casual ambiance. The menu offers many choices from great burgers, pasta dishes and salads to grilled seafood, chicken and steak. There is a full-service bar, and the lounge is a popular place for meeting friends and generating a lively evening. You must try the desserts: Key lime pie, carrot cake, apple pie or hot fudge cake. Hours are from 11:30 AM to 10 PM in season. There is a children's menu as well as daily lunch and dinner specials. Full-bar service is offered in the dining room or in a separate lounge area.

KELLY'S RESTAURANT & TAVERN
Rt. 158, MP 10½   441-4116
$$$ MC, VISA, AMEX, DISC

Kelly's is an Outer Banks tradition. The proprietor, Mike Kelly, always gives his personal attention to every aspect, so the service and friendliness of this special place are always evident. This is a large restaurant and a busy place. From the moment you walk in the door, you'll enjoy the decor that reflects the maritime-rich environmental history and wildlife focus of the area with mounted fish, birds and other memorabilia from the Outer Banks. Dinner is served in several rooms upstairs and downstairs. Dinner in the widow's watch, three levels up, offers a quiet romantic evening for special occasions. There's always a crowd at Kelly's, but diners can enjoy cocktails in the lounge while waiting. On chilly evenings, it's nice

to be next to the fireplace. The lounge is a great place to go for after-dinner entertainment. Kelly's is open for dinner only and is one of the most popular places for locals and Outer Banks visitors alike.

The menu at Kelly's offers many seafood dishes, as well as chicken, beef and pastas. There's a raw bar for those who like to feast on oysters (in season) and steamed shellfish. An assortment of delicious home-made breads accompanies dinner. Kelly's is well known for the sweet potato biscuits. Desserts are always good after a leisurely meal. A children's menu is available. We've found the wait staff to be very accommodating with children, bringing out crayons and special placemats for little ones. Kelly's is open all year from 5 PM to 10 PM. The lounge is open from 4:30 PM to 2 AM. Kelly's is also famous for hosting private parties and for an outstanding catering service.

CAROLINIAN RESTAURANT
at the Carolinian Hotel
Beach Rd., MP 10½   441-7171
$ *MC, VISA*

Serving Outer Banks guests since 1946, the Carolinian serves continental breakfast and dinner daily during the season. Fresh seafood is popular for dinner along with nightly specials. Families can take advantage of early dining discounts, and a children's menu is available. Large groups are easily accommodated here — family reunions or conferences are no problem. This is an oceanfront dining room, but views are limited. The outdoor tiki hut bar is enjoyed by many during the summer. Breakfast hours are from 8:30 AM until 10:00 AM, and dinner is served from 5:30 until. . . .

MULLIGAN'S OCEANFRONT GRILLE
Beach Rd., MP 10 ½   480-2000
$-$$ *MC, VISA*

Mulligan's has been an Elizabeth City tradition for years. Now Nags Head has its own Mulligan's, which opened in June 1993. Chuck Powell has been told all his life that he ought to own his own restaurant, and now he does. Serving steaks, filet mignon and an array of pasta dishes, Mulligan's is a great place for lunch or dinner. Located in the old 1949 Miller's Pharmacy, the building is a "national landmark," according to Powell, who used to frequent the soda fountain when he was a vacationer here. While Powell updated the building in a beautiful fashion, with the feel of the "Cheers" TV show bar, he kept the integrity of the building intact and decorated it with lots of old local photographs. "People would rather eat in a saloon than drink in a restaurant," is Powell's motto, and his place has already developed quite a following. Start your evening with the excellent Oysters Christopher appetizer and move on to the crabcakes, teriyaki chicken or scallop roumaki. An unusual touch here is that Mulligan's offers single or double meals, the single for the smaller appetite or the double for heartier eaters. Dinner includes soft bread sticks, salad and potato or rice. Save room for cheesecake or carrot cake. Mulligan's is open seven days a week from 11 AM to 2 AM.

It's Prime Only

Beach Rd., MP 10½   480-1400
$$$$ MC, VISA, AMEX

This steak restaurant opened its doors New Year's Eve, 1994 — an appropriate occasion to celebrate a beginning. Owner Russell Poland said ever since JK's burned, the Outer Banks has needed a good steak place, so he combined that need with the atmosphere that was missing since A Restaurant By George closed its doors. It's Prime Only is located in a building vacated by an office supply store, but you wouldn't know it. The den-style lounge is a beautifully furnished, elegant place to sip a glass of brandy or coffee after enjoying your meal. Comfortable couches and armchairs are arranged near a fireplace. In the dining area, tiny white lights dot green plants, and the tables are brightened with candle lamps. It's Prime offers a lovely atmosphere, yet there's no strict dress code. (You won't fit in here in a bikini top and cutoffs, though.) There's complete bar service. Of course, the mainstay here is beef, from the petite filet to the porterhouse, served sizzling hot on a 450-degree platter. The food is literally crackling when it reaches the table. Other selections include chicken, pasta, tuna and salmon. Something we really like about this place is its "no split fee," allowing parties with light appetites to share a meal without the extra plate charge most restaurants impose. Also, side dishes such as broccoli, creamed spinach, mushrooms and mashed potatoes are served family style so that everyone can share. Children's offerings are hamburgers or pasta. It's Prime is open year round for dinner only, seven days a week from 5 PM to 11 PM.

CW's

Rt. 158, MP 11   441-5917
$ Most major credit cards

CW's has been serving food to the Outer Banks for 20 years. Since 1982, Wayne Blackbird has been

running the show, offering traditional seafood and steaks in this plantation-style building. CW's is known for its crab soup, seafood and baby back ribs. They serve breakfast all year from 7 AM to noon and dinner in the season from 4:30 PM till 1 AM. There's full bar service and completely separate smoking and non-smoking rooms — a rare find on the Outer Banks. The coffee is great, and breakfast starts at $1.50. Enjoy the original art on loan from Seaside Art Gallery that adorns the walls.

TORTUGA'S LIE

Beach Rd., MP 11   441-RAWW
$-$$ MC, VISA

If you didn't know about Tortuga's, you might not stumble into this small, turquoise and white building on the Beach Road. But, you do know, because we're telling you — this is one of the most fun restaurants on the beach. The laid-back island atmosphere is coupled with friendly owners (who are almost always there . . . we can't figure

out when they sleep!) and delightfully prepared food. You can choose from a menu that features everything from Gator Bites (yep, the real thing) to sandwiches and fresh seafood cooked in imaginative and delicious ways. And, while you typically wouldn't point out French fries as a high point of a restaurant, theirs are the best we've ever had.

While you're waiting for your food, you can amuse yourself by reading all the license tags nailed to the ceiling, or talking with other diners — it's a small place that promotes congeniality. Locals also frequent this spot for their Black and Tans — a combination of Bass Ale and Guiness Stout that goes down like smooth cream. If you're a beer lover and haven't discovered them yet, make a point to while you're here. Locals pack in here during the off season for Sushi night — it's one of our favorite places to be on a Wednesday night! Out back there are volleyball games, and on the front porch you can relax and enjoy a bucket of beer. Tortuga's is open seven days a week from 11:30 AM to 2 PM.

WOODY'S GOOD TIME BAR & GRILL
Pirate's Quay
Rt. 158, MP 11   441-4881
$-$$ *All major credit cards*

Woody's is a popular place for locals. One menu is available throughout the day, and selections include steamed and smoked seafood, burgers, seafood platters, salads and more. The hot wings are very tasty, and the chocolate decadence is to die for. There's no dinner entree here more than $7.95, and children's items are available. Hours are from 11 AM until midnight. Something new this year is that Woody's is serving breakfast in the summer season from 7 AM to 11:30 AM.

PIER HOUSE RESTAURANT
Beach Rd., MP 11½   441-5141
$ *MC, VISA*

Since you're at the beach, you might as well enjoy an ocean view, which you can do at the Pier House. You'll practically feel like you're in the ocean the view's so good. You can sit on the screened porch and enjoy the breeze or dine in air-conditioned comfort in the dining area. This is a great place to eat an early breakfast (as early as 6:30 AM) or to have fresh seafood for lunch or dinner. The ambiance is casual; it's the

place where local firemen and rescue personnel have lunch. It's not a fancy place, but the folks are friendly, and the food is good. All-you-can-eat nightly specials are popular, and fresh seafood, cole slaw, hush puppies and daily specials top the menu. Seafood is fried, grilled, broiled and steamed — any way you like it! For a small fee, you can stroll the pier after your meal to watch the fishermen and surfers.

THE WHARF
Beach Rd., MP 11½   441-7457
$$ *MC, VISA*

You can't miss this popular beach establishment on the Beach Road — it's the one with the long, long line of people out front. The line forms early, moving along while you visit with friends or meet new ones. There is a menu, but the ever-popular "all you can eat" seafood buffet is the main target for folks who get hungry around 6:30 in the evening. You'll find steamed items, fried shrimp, chowder, broiled catch of the day, clam strips, barbecue, prime rib, loads of vegetables and desserts. The buffet is $13.95 per person. You better come hungry to the Wharf! New this year are scallops and homemade yeast rolls. The service is efficient in a friendly atmosphere of beach informality. You'll not be disappointed unless you're looking for

North Carolina law requires you to turn your headlights on when using your windshield wipers.

Insiders' Tips

a setting for a romantic dinner for two! A new children's buffet ($4.95) offers hamburgers, hot dogs, PBJ's, pizza, chicken tenders and all-you-can-eat dessert served on a souvenir Frisbee. Kids 3 and under eat free! They're open from Easter through October. Hours are from 4 PM until . . . during the summer and 5 PM until . . . during the off season. The Wharf is closed on Sundays. No alcoholic beverages are served here.

THE SNOWBIRD
Beach Rd., MP 12   480-0467
$ No credit cards

The gleaming white building on the Beach Road has been an Outer Banks tradition for 35 years. It's gone through several changes in those years, but has always offered delicious ice cream. New owner Kent Copeland comes to the Outer Banks from Wilson where he ran a 200-seat barbecue restaurant. In addition to the ice cream and drinks the Snowbird is known for, Kent now offers delectable hamburgers and dolphin.

There are oyster, shrimp and rib eye steak sandwiches, and oyster or scallop boats. The yummy onion rings will add to your meal. There's outdoor seating, or you can call ahead and take your selections home. The Snowbird is open every day in season from 11 AM to 9 or 10 PM, depending on the time of year. Be sure to try the ice cream sundaes and flurries.

MIDGETTS SEAFOOD RESTAURANT
Rt. 158, MP 13   480-0810
$$ MC, VISA, DISC

Midgett is a legendary name on the Outer Banks. The menu here features family recipes from the 1920s. The 100-seat restaurant opened four years ago and was built by a father-and-son team. The atmosphere is quiet and nautical without being pretentious, and there's a definite family feel to the place.

Jeffrey Wade Midgett put away his tools after helping his dad, Jeffrey Gray Midgett, build the place. He's now making a good impression as chef. The menu features a bounty

of seafood entrees, as well as ribs, chicken and beef. Seafood entrees are fried, broiled or grilled. The desserts are all homemade — you'll love the Key lime pie. Midgett's offers a separate early bird menu from 4 PM to 6 PM and a senior citizens' menu is available too. There's a big porch and a nice gazebo in case you have to wait for seating. Overall, Midgett's has a fine atmosphere and excellent food. There's full bar service. They're located just south of Jockey's Ridge. Reservations are not accepted, and they're open for dinner seven days a week during the season, from 4 PM until.

DAIRY MART
Beach Rd., MP 13   441-6730
$

Soft ice cream came on like gangbusters in the '60s, and here you'll find a holdover from those times. It's a drive-in where you order and eat at picnic tables adorned with umbrellas for a spot of shade during summer. In addition to the deli-

cious ice cream and variations on the same, owners Ron and Carol Rodrigues serve excellent quick sandwiches, fries and onion rings. The "Big Daddy Burger" or "Little Mamma" are favorites. (Make sure you have a big appetite before tackling a "Big Daddy.") For some, the ice cream is the main meal on hot summer days. Be sure to try the "Crunchy Cougar" or any other of their 17 fantastic original sundaes. They're open from May to October and closed Wednesdays.

SEAFARE RESTAURANT
Rt. 158, MP 13½   441-5555
$-$$ All major credit cards

The Seafare Restaurant is recognized by many as, "the place to eat," on the Outer Banks. This is a family-owned and operated business, and it all began in Nags Head in 1959. The Seafare has been nationally known for their she-crab soup for about 50 years, and they now offer blue claw crab soup. Chef and owner Michael Hayman oversees this

nightly seafood buffet (smorgasbord). It features a 40-item salad bar, just for starters, four homemade soups, 12 vegetables, 15 types of seafood, four types of meat, homemade cobbler, chocolate chip cookies (made from scratch) and ice cream. In addition to all of this, wonderful steamed items are available including shrimp, crabs, mussels, clams and scallops. The snow crab legs are popular, and the homemade rum rolls are a family tradition. All of the breads are homemade. A full menu selection is also available if you're just not up to the heartier fare. The Seafare has a small bar with complete service.

Dinner is served nightly from 4 PM until. From June 15 to Labor Day, the Seafare opens at 3 PM. Call for off season hours. Reservations are not accepted. Inquire about senior citizens and children's discounts. All major credit cards are accepted including Discover, Diner's Club and Carte Blanche. The Seafare, in appealing to families with children,

added a splendid outdoor play-yard last summer, to the delight of parents and kids. This certainly makes waiting for a table a lot more fun.

LANCE'S

Rt. 158, MP 14   *441-7501*
$$ *MC, VISA, DISC, AMEX*

Lance's is the shocking-pink restaurant on the bypass in Nags Head. It's been around since 1985 as an eatery; before that it was a sporting goods shop, which even now is reflected in the decor. You'll see lots of Outer Banks memorabilia — decoys, trophy mounts of billfish and a 735-pound blue marlin. Lance's is well-liked by the locals; during NFL season you can hardly squeeze in here. 1994 finds Lance's offering a totally new menu of fresh gamefish, crab imperial and a steam bar. Enjoy oysters, clams, hard and snow crabs, shrimp, prime rib, steak or Lance's famous lobster. There's a menu for kids, and Lance's is open for lunch and dinner from 11 AM to 2 AM in the summer. Open year round, Lance's only serves dinner in the off season. They have complete bar service.

THE LINKS ROOM

At Nags Head Golf Links   441-8076
$ VISA, MC

You'll appreciate the splendid sound view from the Links Room, located in the golf clubhouse at the Village at Nags Head resort. This spacious dining room is open year round, but for lunch only. There's a nice fireplace; this is a place for hungry golfers or just about anyone looking for a quiet, classy lunch spot. Daily specials feature such items as pasta, Reubens or steak. There's a full bar.

PENGUIN ISLE SOUNDSIDE GRILLE

Rt. 158, MP 16   441-2637
$$-$$$ Most major credit cards

As night falls, a variety of wildlife can be spotted in the low-lying marshlands of Roanoke Sound, right outside the windows of this popular restaurant. Windsurfers in the distance cruise by with colorful sails, and brilliant sunsets abound. But, no penguins in these parts! The menu carries the story of the restaurant's name.

Residents and visitors to the beach come to this restaurant for outstanding dinners featuring contemporary American cuisine. The decor is tasteful and creative with displays of local art, hand-carved decoys, lighted authentic ship models and, interestingly enough, wine bottle exhibits. You see, wine is like art here, and there's good reason for this.

Penguin Isle is not only the place to go for a diner's treat, it's also very much a wine destination too. The staff is very knowledgeable, and manager and wine buyer, George Price, has a lot to do with this. The thinking here is that great food should be complemented with great wine. The much heralded *Wine Spectator's*, "Award of Excellence," identifies their wine list as, "one of the best in the world," in 1992 and 1993. So, you can see why wine is art at Penguin Isle. Seasonal wine dinners are also offered by reservation only. If you would like to be on their mailing list just call or write: P.O. Box 1898, Nags Head, NC 27959.

The dining room and gazebo lounge offer views of the water from almost every table. There's also a deck, and it's a great place to enjoy a cocktail or wine before dinner. Acoustic music is offered in the lounge or outside on the deck from Thursday through Saturday during the summer. A full bar in the Gazebo and the gazebo menu awaits you. Owners Mike Kelly and Doug Tutwiler combine their talents to create a truly distinctive restaurant. Kelly is also the owner of Kelly's in Nags Head. (You can never get too much of a good thing.) Chef Lee Miller is currently one of only three certified working chefs on the Outer Banks.

Penguin Isle serves a nouvelle cuisine with a New Orleans touch, featuring fresh local seafood, handmade pasta, Iowa beef, chicken, duck, fresh baked breads and much more. Creative food pairings, or fusion cookery, is the chef's specialty, but the trio platter featuring fresh fish, shrimp and scallops is hard to beat too. We'll let you in on a secret: the seafood gumbo and bean cakes

The SNOWBIRD

- Fresh Seafood
- Dolphin Boats
- Oyster Sandwiches
- Shrimp Burgers
- Fresh Hamburgers
- Soft serve ice cream
- Flurries - Sundaes
- **OUTSIDE TABLES**

call 480-0467 for orders to go
MP 12 Beach Road

are delicious for starters.

Residents come time and time again. Visitors will love it too. It's a great place for private parties, wedding receptions and on-site catering, offering a sort of casual elegance. Penguin Isle is open for dinner nightly, from 5 PM until 10 PM through most of the year. A children's menu is available, and early dining specials are offered from 5 PM until 6:30 PM. You must be seated before 6:30. Penguin Isle is the recipient of the AAA, Three Diamond Award.

WINDMILL POINT

Rt. 158, MP 16½   441-1535
$$$ *MC, VISA, AMEX*

Magnificent views of the sound at sunset, dotted with colorful sails of windsurfers, delight diners here. Famous for the memorabilia from the S.S. *United States*, this restaurant provides excellent cuisine to match the views. There are two dining areas, tastefully furnished down to the table cloths, napkins and chairs that

hug rather than hold you. Service is fast and unobtrusive. The upstairs lounge, which features the authentic kidney-shaped bar from the ship, is a pleasant place to await your call to dinner. Again, the views from "up on deck" are great.

Favorites from the menu are the seafood trio, lightly poached or grilled with a nice sauce or a seafood pasta entree of scallops and light seasonings. Chef Vanischak's creations get better every year. A children's menu is available. The lounge opens at 4:30 PM, and dinner is served from 5 PM until 10 PM daily throughout the year.

THE ISLAND'S EYE

Beach Rd., MP 16   480-1993
$-$$ *MC, VISA*

This family owned and operated restaurant opened in May of '92. Kerstin and Wayne Everhart have been in the restaurant business a long time and have put their expertise to work. The atmosphere is soothing and warm with pink, mauve

and blue accents, and there's greenery everywhere. The Island's Eye is
open for dinner only. Selections include seafood broiled, pan fried,
blackened or baked and combination platters of beef, poultry and
pasta. The barbecue shrimp is great
for starters. Some of Wayne's family
recipes are treats too. It's family oriented, and a children's menu is available. There are $6.95 early dining
specials offered from 4:30 PM to 6
PM. A full bar is conveniently located here for your enjoyment —
but a bar crowd is not encouraged.

MILLER'S WATERFRONT RESTAURANT
Rt. 158, MP 16   441-6151
$ MC, VISA

This Miller's Restaurant is located
soundside in Nags Head with a gorgeous view and moderately priced
dinners. They offer fried, broiled,
steamed and sauteed seafood and
steaks. The desserts are homemade,
and a children's menu is offered.
The lower deck seating is near the
water. Dinners start at $7.95. Full
bar service is offered, and there's a
separate lounge for those waiting
for dinner. Miller's is open March to
November from 4:30 PM until
(opening at 5 PM in the shoulder
seasons).

THE DUNES
Rt. 158, MP 16½   441-1600
$ MC, VISA

When a large crowd or a big family is gathering for a meal, this restaurant will accommodate all with
its three huge dining rooms and
plenty of parking. Breakfast at The
Dunes is a favorite, and they have
everything in every combination

you'd imagine in addition to a very
popular breakfast bar. Large portions hold true for lunches, which
offer great burgers, fries and cole
slaw or crunchy clam strips and other
seafood. The rib-eye steak sandwich
is a good choice if you've gone without breakfast or if your beach appetite has grown.

Dinners feature local, well-prepared seafood at moderate prices to
go along with a huge salad bar. They
offer a children's menu and provide
fast, friendly service. It's open daily,
from 6 AM until 12 noon for breakfast, from 11 AM until 2 PM for
lunch, and from 4:30 PM until . . . for
dinner. The breakfast bar is available only on weekends until Father's
Day; then it's available seven days a
week through Labor Day. The Dunes
is open from Valentine's Day
through Thanksgiving.

OWENS RESTAURANT
Beach Rd., MP 16½   441-7309
$$-$$$ MC, VISA, AMEX, DISC

Owens is an Outer Banks legend
serving wonderfully fresh local seafood meals. The architectural style
is that of an old Nags Head lifesaving
station. Inside, take a step back in
time while surveying the museum-
quality original memorabilia and
historic artifacts from the early lifesaving stations on the Outer Banks.
People have returned time and time
again during the more than 48 years
the Owens and Shannon families
have been serving dinner. The legend of the restaurant's quality meals,
friendly service and casual atmosphere is well known on the Outer
Banks. They have several large dining rooms, and the Station Keepers

Lounge is a nice place to start the evening.

Let's talk about dinner here: Seafood, and lots of it, comes fresh and delicious in favorites like coconut shrimp, "Miss O" crabcakes and shrimp and surrey pasta. The seafood platter is out of this world. There's a mixed grill for those who appreciate prime beef with their seafood. Owens serves the finest Iowa beef and is well known for the live Maine lobsters (you pick from the tank). Appetizers are very good, especially the homemade soups, which include lobster bisque and Outer Banks clam chowder. Desserts are wonderful, if you have room after managing the more than ample portions of dinner. Just go ahead and finish it off; don't leave wondering if you've missed something. You might choose to retire to the Station Keepers Lounge and top the evening off with an espresso or cappuccino. Service matches the quality of food — excellent. Owens is rich in the tradition of Southern hospitality. The restaurant is casual; after all this is the beach, and families are always welcome. Owens is open from March through the late fall for dinner only, serving from 5 PM to 10 PM in season and 5:30 to 9:30 in the spring and fall.

SAM & OMIE'S

Beach Rd.
at Whalebone Jct.   441-7366
$$ MC, VISA

Sam & Omie's probably should be listed as an attraction in our guide due to its longtime popularity, but we'll take space here to brag about this place, which has been around for more than a half-century. This weather-beaten building situated at the "official end" of the beach road is the scene of people enjoying good, moderately priced food, story-telling, fresh oysters in season, drinks or a game of pool on the billiard table in the back room. The walls are adorned with sports mania and photographs include some long ago Redskin football greats. There are nautical treasures as well to keep you busy looking around while waiting for dinner.

Here you'll find breakfast a time to get caught up in local lore and good food. Some folks hang around for lunch, which features salads and sandwiches. Try their soft crab sandwich and iced tea for lunch. All meals are priced lower than most places. It's open almost all year, from 7 AM until 10 PM. Please note that they have thoughtfully added a nice new handicapped ramp and handicapped-accessible rest rooms.

Watch the hang gliders and fly a stunt kite on Jockey's Ridge.

Insiders' Tips

R.V.'s

Nags Head-Manteo Causeway   441-4963
$-$$ MC, VISA

R.V.'s is without a doubt one of the most popular places for lunch and dinner — just check the parking lot if you doubt that. Owner R.V. Owens also has Keepers' Galley (see the Kitty Hawk section of this chapter).

If you want to eat at the bar, OK. Another option is to be seated on the enclosed porch for a lunch or dinner which, of course, features traditional Outer Banks seafood. Local folks pack in here during the week and on weekends; the gazebo raw bar, located on an attached deck overlooking the water, takes on a life of its own and stays open late. Some menu favorites are discovered right up front in the appetizers, which are big enough for a good feed. Prices are reasonable, the ambiance is light and lots of fun. They're open from Valentine's weekend until Thanksgiving for lunch and dinner.

TALE OF THE WHALE

Nags Head-Manteo Causeway   441-7332
$$ Most major credit cards

This fine family restaurant is a step above some of the other seafood restaurants around the beach. The ambiance is friendly, and the service is good. The decor is nautical and dark, cooling after those long days in the sun.

The specials feature everything from mixed grills to broiled shellfish. Combination platters can be served fried or broiled. Desserts are wonderfully cool and tasty, if you have room! During the summer, live acoustic entertainment is featured regularly on Friday and Saturday evenings on the gazebo deck outside along with a beautiful view across the marshlands and waters. Diners can enjoy cocktails while they wait or just stop by to see the sunset here. Tale of the Whale is open from mid-April until October for dinner only. Hours are from 5 PM until. . . .

DANIELS' RESTAURANT

Nags Head-Manteo Causeway   441-5405
$$ MC, VISA

Daniels' is another Miller family enterprise. The restaurant is really known for its family atmosphere and moderately priced fried, broiled, sauteed and steamed seafood. Portions are generous, and entrees include the salad bar. All-you-can-eat dinner specials start at $7.95, and the homemade cheesecakes are delicious. A children's menu is available. Dinner is served seven days a week from 4:30 PM until . . . and they're open March to November. There are outstanding soundside views and full bar service.

THE OASIS

Nags Head-Manteo Causeway   441-7721
$-$$ MC, VISA

The Oasis was built in the 1940s, which qualifies it as one of the oldest restaurants on the beach. Bought from the original owner by Violet Kellam in 1950, it became the home of the "barefoot college coeds," whose portraits now fill the lobby. It served a time as The Dock restaurant during the early '80s. Several years ago, Violet's grandchildren — Mike, Mark and Kellam France — took the place over, spruced it up,

Tale of the Whale

Specializing in Seafood
Steaks & Prime Rib
Home of the Peanut Pie
Manteo/Nags Head Causeway
Nags Head, NC 27959

Phone: 441-7332

and renamed it The Oasis. Now, the barefoot girls are just a memory. The Oasis is open for breakfast, lunch and dinner and features a truly beautiful, panoramic view of the sound. You're so close to the water you can almost get your feet wet. Breakfast is traditional fare beginning at 8 AM. Lunch hours are 11:30 AM until around 4:30 PM and, besides fresh seafood, the lunch menu offers good Southern homestyle specials daily. Dinner starts at 4:30 PM and continues until at least 9:30 PM (later if there's a need for it). Dinner entrees include peppered salmon, blackened tuna, prime rib and T-bone steaks. New this year is a steam bar with oysters, shrimp, clams and vegetables. Also new is the 100-foot dock you are welcome to stroll upon; boaters can arrive via water now. This is a pleasant place, where a full dinner and drinks won't cost you an arm and a leg. A children's menu is available. There is full bar service.

Roanoke Island

Manteo

CLARA'S SEAFOOD
GRILL AND STEAM BAR

On the Waterfront   473-1727
$-$$$ MC, VISA, AMEX, DISC

Clara's combines the Owens' family tradition for excellence with expansive waterfront views across Shallowbag Bay to bring you a wonderful dining experience. You can watch the boats sail in and out of the marina and waterfowl diving for fish while your food is being prepared, or perhaps just have a friendly conversation. Just across the way, the *Elizabeth II* is visible. The ambiance is comfortable and casual, just as you would expect to find in a neighborhood cafe.

Some changes have been made at Clara's, making this restaurant appealing to most everyone's taste and budget. There's an emphasis on one menu, all day, offering local favorites, creative specialties and traditional Outer Banks seafood prepared any way you like it. Daily specials offer plenty of what you hope for at a fine Outer Banks eatery. Sandwiches, of all kinds, are available, including wholesome clubs, a beef bleu cheese sub, burgers and more. The spinach salad with hot bacon dressing is delicious. Selections also include entrees such as their famous tuna kabobs, black beans and rice and filet mignon with three-flavor peppercorn sauce. So you see, there really is something for everyone at Clara's.

A Sunday brunch here is a great way to start the day. The buffet offers a traditional breakfast fare and omelettes made to order. You can enjoy mimosas, and bloody Mary setups are provided. Call for more details.

The steam bar showcases waterfront nostalgia, waterfowl decoys and a functional nautical look. You'll be reminded of what the waterfront was like in times past. There's no doubt about it, this is a great meeting place for locals and visitors. (The steam bar is described in detail in the Nightlife chapter.) Live entertainment is featured on Friday evenings along with happy hour specials on items such as steamed spiced shrimp. Of course, you can order off the menu in the steam bar too.

Clara's is much more than just a place to meet; it remains a perfect place for special occasion dinners, plus, they're only seven minutes away from *The Lost Colony*, making it a great place to enjoy an early dinner before the show. Beer, wine and champagne are available, and brown bagging is allowed. A children's menu is provided. Hours during the season are from 11:30 AM until 9:30 PM. It closes at 9 PM during the off season.

DARWIN'S CAFE

On the Waterfront   473-6113
$ *MC, VISA*

This popular small cafe specializes in fine natural foods of an eclectic nature. There's an assortment of homemade soups, salads, pizzas and deli sandwiches, along with Mexican, chicken and seafood dishes. They also have homemade desserts and fresh-baked muffins, specialty subs and delicious black beans. There's a nice wine and beer selection too. The dinner menu changes nightly, offering fine seafood and wonderful salads. Everything is made fresh on the premises. Inventive daily specials are offered — be sure to check the blackboard. A light fare breakfast can be enjoyed during the season beginning at 8:30 AM. Hours are from 8:30 AM until 9 PM, seven days a week during the season. Darwin's is open for lunch year round. Check for off season hours. (Ask here about canoe rentals.)

1587

At the Tranquil House Inn
Queen Elizabeth St.   473-1587
$$$$ *VISA, MC, AMEX, DISC*

While it's difficult to write about a restaurant that's brand new, we couldn't leave out 1587, located at the charming Tranquil House in downtown Manteo. Serving breakfast and dinner, 1587 (named after the year the English colonists tried to settle Roanoke Island) brings a new dimension in dining to the Outer Banks. Here the owner Don Just promises you'll discover "a new world" of food and atmosphere. The menu features such delicacies as seared sesame crusted tuna with wasabi vinaigrette and shitake mushrooms, roasted jerk pork tenderloin with mango rum salsa, free range veal chop with chanterelle mushroom fricasee, lacquered duck with orange and tamarind glaze. Fresh berry summer pudding with raspberry coulis or red currant tart with lemon zabaglione highlight the dessert menu. For breakfast, there's salmon benedict or chef Paul Keevil's specialty "Devil's Mess," an Indian curried omelet. A native Londoner, Keevil adds curry to several of his signature dishes.

At 1587, freshness is the keyword. Keevil, who made a huge splash in Richmond, Virginia., with the small gourmet diner Millie's, promises the same near-perfect presentation of food that is artistic, pleasant and offers "unparalleled quality" in fresh herbs, vegetables and meat. Of course, there's a lovely selection of wine. Brown bagging is OK. The chefs are visible to diners as they work in the open kitchen of this romantic, elegant setting. There's a soft glow of intimate lighting and tastefully decorated surroundings. A copper-top bar and cozy waiting area greet arrivals to the 80-seat restaurant. Polished wood and mirrors reflect the lights of boats harbored in Shallowbag Bay, and the graceful outline of the *Elizabeth II* adds to the ambiance. This should truly be a gourmet dining experience that you will long remember. Reservations are not accepted. Hours are 7:30 to 10:30 AM for breakfast and 5 to 10 PM for dinner.

DUCHESS OF DARE
Budleigh St.   473-2215
$$ *MC, VISA*

This is a favorite gathering place for locals, and it's situated in the heart of downtown Manteo. Locals get here early for breakfast and enjoy the Walker family's cooking at lunch and dinner too. When was the last time you ate at a counter? Try it here and listen in on the latest talk around town. Sunday breakfast buffet from 6:30 AM to noon draws a good crowd and is the only meal offered on Sunday. At other times the good seafood, vegetables and salads satisfy your hunger pangs. All desserts are homemade. The price is right for family dining. It's open all year. In the summer, a breakfast buffet is served daily. Also, there's a nightly seafood buffet. Beer and wine are available.

POOR RICHARD'S
On the Waterfront   473-3333
$ *No credit cards*

Richard Brown owns and operates this cheery and convenient sandwich shop overlooking the sound and the *Elizabeth II.* It has become a Manteo "thing" at lunch when, it seems, every local within easy walking distance descends on the place between noon and 2 PM. They come for good reason. Richard serves up a great selection of made-to-order sandwiches. His tuna salad and all the grilled sandwiches are especially good. Soups, meatless chili, salad plates and ice cream are also available. Enjoy inside dining or take your meal out the back porch and enjoy the fresh air and water's view.

Poor Richard's is open all year. During the busier months it opens early for breakfast with scrambled egg and bacon sandwiches, bagels with cream cheese and other light breakfast options. Summer hours are 8 AM to 8 PM Monday through Friday, 8 AM to 4 PM on Saturday and closed on Sundays. Winter hours vary.

BUTCH'S HOTDOGS

On the Waterfront   473-3663
$ *No credit cards*

If you're a dog lover — and we don't mean the kind that slobbers and wags its tail — you'll want to mosey into Butch's. You can get regular or foot longs, smothered with all the fixins, just the way you like them. Or, try their cooked-fresh-daily turkey salad or turkey breast sandwiches, Polish sausage and barbecue. Cookies are baked fresh daily, and some of our favorites are chocolate chip, pecan and macadamia nut with white chocolate chunks. The old-fashioned milk shakes, malts and hand-dipped ice cream are treats everyone will enjoy. And, shoot, go ahead and take Fido something . . . he's probably hungry, too.

THE WEEPING RADISH
BREWERY & BAVARIAN RESTAURANT

Main Hwy. 64   473-1157
$$ *MC, VISA, DISC*

You'll see the Bavarian-style res-taurant through the trees on the Main Highway, adjacent to the Christmas Shop. The shade of pine trees and gardens make this a delightful place to relax before a meal. The name, Weeping Radish, comes from the radish served in Bavaria as an accompaniment to beer. Cut in a spiral, the radish is sprinkled with salt and packed back together. The salt draws out the moisture and gives the appearance of a "weeping radish."

An authentic German atmosphere prevails, and guests are tempted by a variety of German dishes such as veal, sauerbraten and sausages. Homemade noodles, or spaetzle, and cooked red cabbage are two of the side dishes served here. Traditional American food is served, too. New this year is seating in the "Gingerbread House," open air dining in the outdoor beer garden. There's also a children's playground!

A brewery that opened in 1986 offers a pure, fresh malt brew of German tradition, without chemical additives. This "nectar of the gods" is a big reason why this is a favorite spot with locals and visitors alike. Relax and enjoy a brew in the outdoor beer garden. The Weeping Radish is open all year.

GARDEN PIZZERIA

Main Hwy. 64   473-6888
$ *No credit cards*

This is a delightful, small eatery shaded by those wonderful Manteo pines and offering some of the best pizza we've tasted anywhere. You can order for takeout, eat inside or out on the small deck. The White Pizza is topped with ricotta, mozza-

rella, provolone and romano cheeses, broccoli, pepperoni and minced garlic — with no tomato sauce. Have you ever? Before we tasted it, we might have wondered, but now we have to have our "White Pizza Fix" on a regular basis. Don't miss out on the good food here; try the mouth-watering Philly cheese steak sandwiches, burgers or the wide assortment of deli sandwiches, homemade salads and antipasto salads. The fresh tuna and chicken salad plates are just right for a lighter lunch or dinner. Garden Pizzeria will make up party platters, vegetable or cold cut varieties for take out. Don't forget, we're talking authentic NY-style pizza here made from homemade dough and fresh fixings. The soups are fresh, and the desserts are homemade. They're located on Highway 64, across the street from McDonald's. They offer free evening delivery to Roanoke Island and Pirate's Cove on Thursday, Friday and Saturday. Ask about full-service catering. Hours are 11 AM to 8 PM Monday through Thursday and 11 AM to 10 PM Friday and Saturday, closed Sunday.

DARRELL'S

Main Hwy. 64   473-5366
$-$$ MC, VISA

Darrell's started as an ice cream stand more than 30 years ago and since the late 1970s has been a good family-style restaurant that appeals to locals and visitors. The daily lunch specials such as popcorn shrimp accompanied by salad and vegetable are real bargains. Darrell's fried oysters are the best we've had anywhere, consistently tender and tasty. Try them! Steamed seafood is available too, and the hot fudge cake is a must — sinfully delicious and worth it. A children's menu is available, and Darrell's is conveniently located for dinner — especially if you're planning to attend the performance of *The Lost Colony*. They're open from 11 AM until 9 PM all year and closed on Sunday. Beer and wine are served.

THE CRAB DOCK

Main Hwy. 64   473-6845
$-$$ MC, VISA

This is a relatively new addition to the Manteo restaurant scene, having opened several years ago. The Crab Dock has picked up on the current "steam bar" craze and serves crabs, shrimp, mussels, snow crab legs and clams along with soups and sandwiches. They shed their own soft crabs too. A full menu is available featuring fresh local seafood, and there's a kid's menu in case yours haven't yet developed their culinary tastes buds to accommodate the seafood — that's fine, more for you. One of the nicest things about this spot is the huge deck out back overlooking the sound. You're literally on top of the water, which means there's usually some sort of breeze to keep things cool, and the nautical, laid back mood is all the more enhanced. Crockett's Seafood Market is right next door, so it would be hard to get any fresher fish. They serve lunch and dinner from 11 AM until 9 PM during the season; they also serve beer and wine.

DOUG SAUL'S BAR-B-Q
AND FAMILY BUFFET

U.S. Hwy. 64   473-6464
$

Some say the barbeque here is the best on the Outer Banks. Look for this tiny cafe along the Main Highway behind Island Pharmacy. The buffet also features fried chicken, cole slaw and other vegetables.

The ambiance is friendly and centered around the conversations of the local crowd that likes the ribs, barbeque sandwiches, the buffet and the casual atmosphere. Eat in or call for takeout. Saul's Bar-B-Q also specializes in the catering of off-site pig pickin's and family barbecues.

THE ELIZABETHAN RESTAURANT
at the Elizabethan Inn
Main Hwy. 64   473-2101
$-$$ MC, VISA, AMEX, Diner's

Recognized by locals for practicing seacoast cookery, this family restaurant delivers good food at a great value. Their special recipe for Outer Banks style clam chowder is a longtime favorite, and they guarantee you'll find no better cup of coffee anywhere.

Of special note are the all-you-can-eat buffets with wide varieties of well-prepared food at nominal prices — weekend breakfast buffets, weekday lunch buffets and evening seafood buffets during the summer feature big shrimp. We enjoy the variety of country-cooked vegetables included in the buffets too.

The Elizabethan Restaurant serves breakfast, lunch and dinner every day and offers seniors' discounts, nonsmoking sections and carry-out. Children are welcome. No alcohol is served. Banquet rooms are available for private parties. Call for prices. Casual dress and an easygoing atmosphere make this restaurant a family favorite, and they're open year round. Summer hours are 6:30 AM to 2 PM for breakfast and lunch and 5 PM to 9 PM for dinner.

PIRATE'S COVE
RESTAURANT & RAW BAR

Manteo-Nags Head Causeway   473-2266
$$-$$$ MC, VISA

Dine here on the water, where

the masts, booms and bridges of fishing boats are at ease, dockside. The views from this second floor restaurant, above the Ship's Store, are beautiful. You can enjoy lunch or dinner as the fleet returns. Bring your camera. Lunch items include sandwiches, seafood salads, soups and burgers. (If you're an onion ring lover, don't miss them here.) Popular dinner selections are the mixed grill and broiled seafood platter. A children's menu is available. Beer and wine are served, and brown bagging is allowed. Hours are from 11:30 AM until . . . during the season. Check for winter hours.

Wanchese

QUEEN ANNE'S REVENGE
Old Wharf Rd.   *473-5466*
$$ *MC, VISA, DISC, AMEX*
Named after one of Blackbeard's famous pirate ships that terrorized sea travelers off the Carolina Coast during the early 1700s, this restaurant continues to be a favorite on the Outer Banks. Well-hidden off the beaten path in Wanchese, Wayne Gray and Jimmy and Donald Beach have operated this restaurant since 1978. Some were skeptical about its success, since it's in Wanchese on a dead-end road, but their intent to serve only the finest seafood and beef in this pleasant setting has cast aside all doubt. Many return to dine here, and it's known as a place where recipes are exchanged, new ones are tested and a lot of time is spent in food preparation, with quality ingredients. The grounds are delightful. Once inside you'll enjoy dinner in one of three dining rooms; on chilly evenings, the one with the fireplace is especially nice.

There's a fine selection of appetizers, including Bouillabaisse and Black Bean and She Crab soups. The seafood here is excellent, featuring Blackbeard's Raving and the Wanchese Seafood Platter. There's Chateaubriand for Two carved at your table. The seafood varies according to weather and fishing conditions, but it is only the best, the freshest and always excellent. The desserts are homemade and served in generous portions. Beer and wine are served.

Entrees begin at $13.95. They're open seven days a week, June through September for dinner and closed on Tuesday during the winter.

FISHERMAN'S WHARF
Near the end of Hwy. 345   *473-5205*
$$ *MC, VISA*
Located at Mill Landing overlooking the fishing port of Wanchese, the dining room of this family-owned

---

Dolphins travel up and down the beach daily and can often be seen from the shore.

Insiders' Tips

restaurant is rather ordinary and situated over the dock where fresh fish is unloaded from the fleet. But, this view assures diners, almost better than at any other Banks restaurant, that the fish they'll be served is as fresh and local as it gets.

The Daniels family of Wanchese fishing-history operates this restaurant for lunch and dinner from April through October. Seafood plates, complete with homemade hushpuppies and good cole slaw, are the best selections from a variety of items on the menu. Save room for the homemade desserts. A children's menu is available. Lunch hours are from noon until 3 PM, and dinner is served from 3 PM until 9 PM daily.

Hatteras Island

Down Under
Restaurant & Lounge

Rodanthe Pier   987-2277
$-$$ *MC, VISA, AMEX*

Ocean views are spectacular at this popular oceanfront restaurant that's been newly remodeled. Breakfast, lunch and dinner are served. Crabmeat and Western omelettes are good breakfast fare, and lunch specialties include the Great Australian Bite. This is similar to an Aussie Burger made with a hamburger, fried egg, grilled onions, cheese and bacon. Spicy fish burgers and real marinaded chicken sandwiches are good too. Dinner selections include their famous "Down Under Shrimp." The shrimp are stuffed with jalapenos and cream cheese and wrapped in bacon. It's fairly obvious that the owners of this restaurant know something about the Australian way of doing things.

Happy Hour is offered at the bar between 3 PM and 6 PM daily during the season. Steamed, spiced shrimp are 10 cents apiece. Down Under opens at 7 AM after Memorial Day, and lunch is served at 11:30 AM. Dinner begins at 5 PM, but the lunch menu is available for dinner as well. Parents will appreciate the children's

Serving: Breakfast Lunch & Dinner

Spectacular Oceanview Dining — Happy Hour 3-6 PM daily featuring 10¢ spiced shrimp

RODANTHE PIER • HATTERAS ISLAND • PHONE 987-2277

menu, and Down Under is open April to Thanksgiving.

WAVES EDGE RESTAURANT

Waves   987-2100, 441-0494
$-$$$ MC, VISA

At Waves Edge, you can enjoy spectacular sunsets over the Pamlico Sound while dining on fresh local seafood and delicious baby back ribs, beef and chicken dishes — all seasoned with fresh herbs from their soundfront organic garden. Mesquite grilling is very popular here, and their homemade hushpuppies, wheat rolls and desserts are savory.

Waves Edge also offers a Sunday Brunch Buffet featuring soup, fruit, eggs Benedict, fried chicken, creamed chip beef, broiled fish and more. Mimosas are available after 1 PM. A good wine and beer list is yours for the asking. This restaurant is located 15 minutes south of the Oregon Inlet Bridge. They're open for dinner at 4 PM nightly during the season, seven day a week, and the Sunday Brunch Buffet is available 10

AM until 2 PM. Waves Edge is open from April through October.

THE FROGGY DOG

Avon, NC 12   995-4106
$-$$ MC, VISA, DISC

This is a real comfortable place to eat, where the natural wood finishes, a touch of nautical decor and plants provide the right ambiance for all meals. Froggy Dog is open seven days a week, all year. Children's and senior citizens' portions are available.

Breakfast is a combination of good food and local lore. Portions are big enough, and everything is homemade. Lunches are great with salads and sandwiches. Dinner offers several entrees from broiled, fried or sauteed seafood to steaks and chicken. You won't be disappointed in the meals served by the folks at Froggy Dog. Early bird specials are offered from 5 to 6 PM. This has been a favorite place for 12 years, and they're open year round. Don't forget to check out the Lily Pad

Lounge, a very popular nightlife destination on Hatteras Island. (See the Nightlife chapter for more information — there's a lot happening here in the lounge late night.)

PIER BAR & GRILL

Avon Pier   995-6160
$ MC, VISA

The restaurant at the Avon Pier has been completely renovated and remodeled. Plenty of outside decking is available where you can enjoy watching sunrises and sunsets at this oceanfront location. The dining room is accented with natural wood trim, and you'll find the light oak tables and chairs a nice contrast to the black and white tile floors.

Breakfast offers a standard fare beginning at 6:30 AM. Lunch hours are 11 AM to 5 PM, and fish baskets, sandwiches and burgers top the menu. Dinner selections include seafood and vegetable platters, and the hours are 5 PM to 10 PM. Senior citizens receive a 15 percent discount, and there are daily specials for everyone.

SEA ROBIN RESTAURANT

Waterside at Avon   995-5931
$-$$ MC, VISA

Sea Robin has enlarged its seating capacity, attesting to its popularity as a good place with good food. The restaurant is situated on the sound side of Avon, and the views are wonderful. It's off the road and quiet.

They're open for breakfast from 7 AM to 11:30 AM with eggs Benedict or steak and eggs for top choices. At dinner, the menu features a full list of entrees from the Sea Robin Seafood Platter and surf 'n turf to Cajun fish and crabmeat saute. Dinner

hours are from 5 PM until 9 PM, and a children's menu is provided. The Sea Robin serves beer and wine.

THE MAD CRABBER RESTAURANT & SHELLFISH BAR

Avon   995-5959
$-$$ MC, VISA

Don't you just love this name!? The Mad Crabber is a lively place, offering dinner nightly. They're not fancy, but they have good, fresh seafood. Steamed crabs and shrimp lead the way. You'll find blue crabs, Dungeness from the pacific northwest and snow crabs. Fried hard crabs and scallops on the shell are available too. If you're set on something else, try their good hot dogs. "Fat Tuesday" and "Wide Wednesday" offer all-you-can-eat specials with $1 drafts. Wine and draft beer are served, and children's items are available. There's a separate game room for your enjoyment where you'll find two pool tables and low-key fun. Dinner hours are from 5 PM until 10 PM, seven days a week, and they're open April until November 30.

BIG WAVE DINER

Avon
Hwy. 12   995-4966
$-$$ MC, VISA

This restaurant is the place to go around here for casual dining and tasty food. Their back deck, overlooking a pretty pond, is a perfect place to relax and enjoy the sunset. They specialize in charcoal grill items and vegetarian entrees. Avon locals think they have one of the best burgers in town. Their sandwiches (all sorts), pasta entrees and homemade desserts are very good too.

The Froggy Dog
RESTAURANT
& Lilly Pad Lounge
in Avon, NC

The traditional place to go on Hatteras Island for breakfast, lunch and dinner 7 days a week. Live entertainment nightly 10 pm - 2 am in the Lillypad Lounge 10¢ steamed shrimp daily from 3-6 pm.
Late Night Menu

Salads are fresh and delicious. Beer and wine are served. The dinner menu is available after 5 PM and sandwiches, etc. can be ordered throughout the day. Big Wave is open mid-March to mid-December.

DIAMOND SHOALS RESTAURANT
Buxton
Hwy. 12   995-5217
$-$$ MC, VISA

A popular place with the locals, visitors also enjoy the big servings of good food and come back often. It's within walking distance of several motels in Buxton, which means you can walk it off if you've eaten too much! They're open for breakfast and dinner all year, and the service is friendly and efficient. Breakfasts are big, and the all-you-can-eat dinners with plenty of seafood choices top the list in the evening. Dinners feature fried and broiled seafood. Breakfast hours are from 6 AM until 11:30 PM, and dinner is served from 5 PM until 9:30 PM.

TIDES RESTAURANT
Buxton
Off Hwy. 12   995-5988
$-$$ MC, VISA

If you're not careful you may miss the turn off to the Tides, which is located across the street from the entrance to the lighthouse. It's a family style restaurant and a favorite place for breakfast and dinner. Traditional breakfast fare is served, and we really enjoyed the homemade biscuits and both the blueberry and pecan pancakes. Dinner selections always include the fresh catch of the day, and other items such as steaks, chicken and ham are offered too. The stuffed potatoes are as good as they get, and sandwiches and burgers are also served for dinner. The portions are large, and the service is good. Beer and wine are available, and brown bagging is allowed. Tides is a popular spot that is open for breakfast from 6 AM to 11:30 AM and for dinner from 5:30 to 9:30 PM.

THE GREAT
SALT MARSH RESTAURANT

Hwy. 12
Buxton   995-6200
$$-$$$ MC, VISA, AMEX, DISC

This unique California-style grill is located in front of the Osprey Shopping Center, just south of Natural Art Surf Shop. The contemporary decor is accented with black and white tile floors and black laminated tables. This was a first for Hatteras Island, and we must say it offers a nice dining alternative. The owners of this fine restaurant have found their niche, and the people just keep coming back. Lunch items include French dip and crabcake sandwiches, oversized burgers and delicious crabmeat and guacamole omelettes. Their famous pan-sauteed crabcakes are served for dinner and Soft Shells a la Salt Marsh is a wonderful signature dish. Soft shells are sauteed and served on a bed of garlic-laced spinach. Fried Oysters Parmesan is a new entree this year, and it's fast becoming popular in addition to prime rib and pasta entrees. For dessert, try their homemade Mile High Pies, either Key lime or lemon — scrumptious! A select wine list awaits you, and beer is available too. Reservations are welcome for dinner. Lunch hours are from 11 AM until 2:30 PM, and dinner is served from 5PM until. . . . They're closed on Sunday.

BILLY'S FISH HOUSE
RESTAURANT

Hwy. 12
Buxton   995-5151
$-$$ MC, VISA

There's nothing real fancy here, but the ambiance is busy, and you're on-location, so to speak, where the onetime fish house has kept the evidence. Concrete floors with a slant for an easy wash and run off and picnic tables with a view of the water set the casual mood. And, in good weather, you can eat right on the dock.

Billy and Chalaron May turned their fish house into a restaurant, and it captured an easygoing crowd which, surprisingly enough, enjoys some of the best seafood served anywhere, even when eaten on plastic table service. The tile fish is always popular, and we highly recommend their homemade crabcakes. Entrees are served with your choice of vegetables and hushpuppies. Foods are lightly fried with peanut oil, and the owners are introducing alternative entrees as well. The pasta dinners featuring fresh seafood seem to entice a lot of folks. Lunch hours are from 11 AM until 3 PM, and dinner is served from 5 PM until 9 PM. Billy's is open from Easter through mid-November.

THE PILOT HOUSE

Buxton   995-5664
$$$ MC, VISA

This soundside restaurant is designed to capture the spectacular views across the sky and water. There is a lounge upstairs that also has a view of the ocean — well worth the climb.

Although the building is rather new, the Pilot House has been a longtime favorite — before the original restaurant burned down and since rebuilding. The decor is soft and on the nautical side, but not overpowering. Fresh seafood is well-prepared and served in several com-

Bubba's Bar-B-Q

RIBS·CHICKEN· SLICED PORK ·TURKEY BEEF

All cooked on an open pit with hickory wood

Call The Hog Line - 995-5421 in Frisco
6 Miles South of Hatteras Light House

or 995-4385 in Avon
Located next to Food Lion
Try Bubba's Original Recipe Fried Chicken. Avon Store Only.

binations or as the fresh catch of the day. Soups are homemade, and you'll want to try the seafood bisque. The Pilot House is open from mid-April through late fall, seven days a week for dinner only.

FRISCO SANDWICH SHOP

NC 12, Frisco 995-5535
$ *MC, VISA*

You won't miss the colorful sign out front, so stop in for breakfast, lunch or dinner. They're open seven days a week during the summer, and they're closed on Sunday the rest of the year. Owner Stan Lawrence and his staff know how to make great deli-style sandwiches, and it has kept them going for over 16 years now. They've grown from the original drive-in sandwich shop to a restaurant complete with places to sit down and enjoy the company of locals and visitors. Breakfast is traditional fare and is served from 7 AM until 11 AM. The rest of their menu is available until whenever.

The Sandwich Shop is home to the best hamburger on Hatteras Island. Homemade pizza is served during the season too. Live bands are featured on the weekends during the summer, and food is available until.... This is the home of the Diamond Shoals Band, and bluegrass is pretty popular too. Beer and wine are available.

BUBBA'S BAR-B-Q

NC 12
Frisco 995-5421
Avon Shopping Center 995-4385
$ *MC, VISA, DISC*

When you get serious about barbecue, Bubba's is the right place to eat. The pork, chicken, beef, ribs and turkey plus all the trimmings can't be beat. If it's takeout or eat in, you will chew on the world's best, as far as we're concerned. Owner Larry Schauer (Bubba) and his wife (Mrs. Bubba) left their farm in West Virginia and came to the beach to do their cooking. Lucky for us! All their meats are cooked right before your eyes on an open pit with hickory wood. We're talking original recipe barbecue here, nothing but the best. The homemade cole slaw, beans, red-skinned potato salad, cornbread and French fries are good too! Homemade pies such as Sweet Potato and Coconut Custard are the favorites. Cobblers and other goodies will tempt you. Try the Double Devil Chocolate Cake, a "major cake" that has become an attraction in itself. A children's menu is available. Bubba's opens at 11 AM, seven days a week during the season; check for off season hours. Bubba's Too, in Avon, is open year round at the shopping center with Food Lion. Bubba's fans are pleased to know that this year, Bubba's Sauce is now being marketed throughout the area. This traditional Carolina sauce with a vinegar base is being sold in grocery stores and specialty shops.

GARY'S RESTAURANT
NC 12
Hatteras   986-2349
$-$$ *MC, VISA, DISC*

Gary's has grown up from a fast-food style restaurant to a small cafe, where relaxing over a cup of coffee and great breakfast or enjoying a nice lunch (including homemade soups), or a cozy dinner will satisfy your appetite. Shades of blue and white accent the decor, with tables nicely arranged throughout the dining room. The dinner menu features a list of surf-side and land-side entrees such as the Commodore's Choice Platter of oysters, scallops, shrimp and fish, and a New York Strip or Delmonico steak. The seafood is fresh, and the steaks are cut by the local butcher. Breakfast hours

are from 6 AM until 11 AM, and lunch is served from 11 AM until 2 PM. Dinner is from 5 PM until 9 PM on Friday, Saturday and Sunday only. Gary's is closed on Tuesday; check for winter hours. Beer and wine are sold, and carry-out is available.

THE CHANNEL BASS
Hwy. 12
Hatteras Village   986-2250
$$ *MC, VISA*

Situated on the slash off the sound, this family owned restaurant has been here forever — well, almost. The Harrisons are a famous fishing family, and you'll notice all the trophies in the foyer that belong to Shelby (Mrs. Harrison)! They've been serving fresh seafood, some of which was caught aboard *Miss Channel Bass*, for about 30 years.

The menu is loaded with seafood platters, either broiled or fried — they even have broiled crabcakes that are just as good as the fried ones but a lot better for your diet — along with a steamed seafood platter, veal and charbroiled steaks. Salad dressings are homemade. They cut their own beef, and they rely on an old family recipe for their great hushpuppies. The homemade coconut, Key lime and chocolate cream pies are out of this world. You'll enjoy all the food served here as well as the local chatter about the big fish caught from the big boats at nearby Hatteras Harbor.

The Captain Gran Room overlooks the water, and a private dining room is available. Large groups are welcome. Early bird discounts are provided, and you'll always find nightly specials. Beer and wine are served. Brown bagging is allowed, and there's a children's menu. Dinner hours are from 5:30 PM until 10 PM, Monday through Saturday and from 5 PM until 10 PM on Sunday.

BREAKWATER ISLAND RESTAURANT
Hatteras Village   986-2733
$$ Most major credit cards

This family owned restaurant is the latest undertaking by the Odens of Hatteras Village. Things started out fairly simple years ago when Donald Oden just took care of his fishing business at Oden's Dock. Now they run the Hatteras Harbor Motel and a very nice restaurant located on the dock. The views are wonderful, and so is the food. Dinner selections feature fresh local seafood, prime rib, veal and pasta entrees. Entrees are accompanied by a vegetable, salad and fresh-baked breads. Live acoustic entertainment is offered outside on the deck Sunday evenings from 6 PM until 9 PM during the summer. Dinner is served from 5:30 PM until . . . seven days a week during the season. Beer and wine are served. Children's items are available. Check for winter hours.

LIGHTSHIP RESTAURANT
NC 12
Hatteras Village   986-2031
$-$$ MC, VISA

This new restaurant opened in August 1993, just in time for the arrival of Hurricane Emily. Wanchese native Bret Daniels is owner and operator. The Lightship is open year round, serving a traditional breakfast, along with steaks and local seafood. Wine and beer are offered. Hours are 7 AM to 11 AM for breakfast, noon to 2 PM for lunch and 5 PM to 9 PM for dinner. A separate lounge offers live music on summer weekends.

Ocracoke

THE PELICAN RESTAURANT
NC 12   928-7431
$$ MC, VISA

In the heart of Ocracoke Village, The Pelican Restaurant gives you the choice of dining inside in one of two rooms or being seated on the porch for a delightful breakfast, lunch or dinner. The old cottage, refurbished for the restaurant, is situated near the activity of Ocracoke Village, but trees and shrubs offer lots of privacy. The linen table cloths and fresh flowers add to its casual, relaxed atmosphere. A treat here is also the outdoor Tiki Bar. Beer, wine and special frozen fruit drinks make waiting for a table anything but a bother.

The menu offers a wide variety of seafood cooked the way you like it. The blackened fish prepared with Pelican's special sauce is diner's favorite as is the wonderfully prepared quiche. For breakfast, you can't miss with their omeletes and crabcake Benedict. Lunch includes sandwiches, soups and salads, and the dinner entrees are varied too. Expect to find prime rib, chicken and combination platters. This restaurant is open seasonally. Breakfast hours are from 7 AM until 11 AM. Lunch is served from 11:15 AM to 3 PM. Dinner is served from 5:30 PM until 9:30 PM.

PONY ISLAND RESTAURANT

NC 12   928-5701
$-$$ MC, VISA

A good casual restaurant, Pony Island serves more than adequate portions of a variety of well-prepared foods for breakfast and dinner. Some delightful surprises await you. Nightly specials might present an unusual treat, such as a Chinese dinner or something with a flavor from the Southwest. Or, you will get to choose from fresh seafood prepared in a variety of ways. If you've had a good day fishing, bring it in, they'll cook it for you, but be sure to clean it first. Homemade desserts are a great finishing touch to their fine meals.

The Pony Island Restaurant is adjacent to the Pony Island Motel and located less than a block off the highway. They're open from Easter until late fall and are one of a few places on Ocracoke that serves breakfast. If you're up around 6:30 AM for a day at the beach or going out to sea, take advantage of their big breakfast biscuits, hotcakes, eggs and omelettes. We go just to get their "Pony Potatoes," which are hash browns covered with cheese, sour cream and salsa . . . yum . . . a meal in themselves. Dinner hours are from 5 PM until 9 PM nightly.

MARIA'S

NC 12   928-6891
$$ MC, VISA

Maria's offers very good Italian food — a nice change of pace from seafood — but the seafood is well-prepared too. Homemade pasta dishes, pizza, soups and salads are other popular menu selections. Soup and salad bar is included with all entrees.

Located some distance away from the hustle and bustle of the village on the main road, it's perhaps not a recommended casual stroll, but then again, however you get there, the food is good and the hospitality welcoming. Open year round, Maria's serves dinner from 3 PM to 10 PM. Beer and wine are sold.

THE BACK PORCH

Country Rd. 1324   928-6401
$$-$$$ MC, VISA

Whether your dinner is served on the screened porch, in the small nooks or the open dining room of this well-known Ocracoke restaurant, you'll find it a most pleasant experience. The service is friendly and portions pleasing. John and Debbie Wells renovated this older building and refurbished it to blend with the many trees on the property. Its location off the main road adds to its appeal as a place for quiet dining. And that appeal is great . . . overall, it's one of our favorite restaurants on the whole Outer Banks.

The menu is loaded with as many fresh items as possible. All sauces, dressings, breads and desserts are made right in their kitchen, and they hand-cut their meats. Nearly everyone asks to have one of their secret recipes — they are that good. Outer Banks seafood is plentiful in original and unusual dishes, such as crab cakes with red pepper sauce, or their appetizers of smoked bluefish or crab beignets. Non-seafood dishes are a tasty option as well, our favorite being the Cuban black bean and Monterey jack cheese casserole. Be prepared for some pleasant surprises, one of which is the freshly ground coffee. There are reduced prices and smaller portions for children and senior adults. The wine selections and imported beers are well-matched with the menu. *The Back Porch Cookbook*, authored by Debbie, is available at the restaurant . . . so now you can try your hand at some of those secret recipes! Hours are 5 PM to 9:30 PM seven days a week in season.

CAP'T. BEN'S

NC 12   928-4741
$$ MC, VISA, AMEX

Since 1970, Cap't. Ben's has been a favorite restaurant for locals and visitors on Ocracoke Island. Located on the main road, before you enter the village, this casual restaurant beckons you to come on in and enjoy a good meal.

Ben Mugford is owner and chef. For more than 23 years he has perfected some house specials. He combines Southern tradition with gourmet foods to achieve a well-balanced menu. Ben is really noted for his crabmeat, prime rib and seafood entrees and offers some of the best freshly cooked seafood on the island. Lunch is served from noon until 4 PM and dinner from 4 to 9 PM. For a special lunch, try the shrimp salad sandwich or plate or Cap't. Ben's own crabcake sandwich. Lunch sandwiches are served with chips or fries and dinners with soup and salad. Those with a hearty appetite at midday can request dinner entrees then. A large variety of domestic and imported beers is available, and the wine list is quite adequate for the menu.

The decor is nautical and friendly, and the lounge is a comfortable place to relax, should you have to wait for a table. Cap't. Ben's is open from April through November, every day for lunch and dinner.

ISLAND INN RESTAURANT

Lighthouse Rd.   928-7821
$$ MC, VISA, DISC

This family-owned and operated restaurant is located at the Island Inn. In the main dining area and the Garden Room you'll find a nautical decor accented with black and white checked tablecloths and interesting curios displayed throughout. Fresh flowers are set on every table. The Garden Room is lined with windows and is a perfect place to enjoy a meal any time of the day. The restaurant is family oriented but couples will be able to enjoy a romantic dinner here as well. Inquire about private parties.

Breakfast, lunch and dinner are served, and the owners want to make sure you know that everyone is welcome, not just guests of the Inn. Breakfast hours are from 7 AM until 11 AM. A traditional fare is provided with specialty items like oyster and shrimp omelets available too. Lunch items include fresh fruit salads, marinaded grilled chicken, crabcake, oyster and homemade pimento cheese sandwiches and burgers. The pimento cheese sandwich originated from a family recipe. Lunch is be served from 11 AM until 3 PM. Seafood entrees are grilled, fried or broiled to your liking for dinner. Pasta entrees featuring fresh local seafood are a hit, and the vegetarian

casserole is a nice alternative too. Dinner hours are 5 PM to 9 PM. Beer and wine are served, including a house wine with the Island Inn label. Desserts are all homemade and include carrot cake, chocolate cake and Ocracoke Fig Cake when available. Children's menus are offered. Arrangements for groups or tour buses should be made in advance. Check for off season hours.

HOWARD'S PUB & RAW BAR

NC 12   928-4441
$ MC, VISA

Howard's has been on the scene for some time in Ocracoke and is a fun, friendly place to go for a meal, beer and conversation. In fact, it's the only place open year round for late night snacks, and it's the late night hangout too. The knotty pine walls are adorned with important notices — whatever people want to tack up. An interesting array of college pennants, photos of parties held here and other items lend a note of

familiarity for those who visit. There's a wide-screen TV, free popcorn and live music at night in season and on weekends in the off season. Entertainment generally begins around 10 PM. There's even room for dancing later in the evening. You'll find plenty of board games on hand to help you pass the time, and darts are popular too. There's one game, "Ring Toss," that can't be played without a beer in hand.

Buffy and Ann Warner are from West Virginia where he was a senator and she worked for the governor as director of economic development. Their lifestyles have changed a bit, and you can tell they love it.

In addition to a great raw bar, appetizers, subs, burgers, fish sandwiches and other foods are featured, and the daily special might be chicken wings, Polish sausage or steamed shrimp. Lunch and dinner are served daily, from 11 AM until 2 AM, 365 days a year. Families are welcome; don't hesitate to bring your children — they can't hurt anything here.

It's the only raw bar on the island, and the T-shirts attest to the popularity of their "oyster shooter," which you'll just love if you're a raw oyster and Tabasco fan. This is a place you can't, and shouldn't, miss as you drive into the village. Beer and wine are served. We never go to Ocracoke without a stop at Howard's Pub.

CAFE ATLANTIC

NC 12   928-4861
$$ MC, VISA, DISC

Located off to the side of the main highway, this traditional beach-style building was opened a few years ago by Bob and Ruth Toth. The views from the dining room look out across the marsh grass and dunes. The gallery-like effect of the rooms is created by hand-colored photographs by local photographer, Ann Ehringhaus. There's a nonsmoking dining room upstairs and a smoking section downstairs, a consideration we appreciate. For those hot summer days, you'll be glad to know that Cafe Atlantic is air-conditioned.

The Toths make all their soups, dressings, sauces and desserts from scratch. Lunches feature a variety of soups, sandwiches and salads. Dinner features mostly sauteed or grilled seafood. However, if it's fried seafood you desire, you can order that as well. Many of the pasta dishes, sandwiches and seafood choices are available to carry out. A children's menu is available too.

Cafe Atlantic is open from early March through October and has a nice wine and beer selection. Inquire about on and off site catering. Lunch hours in season are from 11 AM until 3:30 PM, and dinner is served from 5:30 PM until 9:30 PM.

Inside
Nightlife

If the beach, water sports, fishing, shopping and sight-seeing on the Outer Banks don't wear you out, you'll find a few nightspots where live music and dancing will finish you off!

The Outer Banks lifestyle is a bit different than what you might expect from other resort beaches. It was established a long time ago, at least among some the people on the Outer Banks, that if you get to bed early, then you won't be late getting up the next day for a fishing expedition to the Gulf Stream or to a hard-earned job. We won't, however, include the mass of college-age "kids" in this, who stay up partying until who knows when yet *still* manage to be at their 6 AM shift . . . aah, youth!

There are plenty of ways to entertain the whole family in the evening hours. Miniature golf, amusement parks and rides, water slides, movies etc. are listed in the Recreation sections by town or village.

But if what you want to do is unwind, there are places waiting for you, and we've included some of them here. Drinks are available at most lounges until around 2 AM, and some serve food after midnight. Local entertainment guru Linda McBreen operates a call-in service listing all the entertainment happenings. Call her

recorded message at 480-CLUB (2582) for updates on which bands are playing at what clubs.

Duck

BARRIER ISLAND INN RESTAURANT AND TAVERN
Duck Village   261-8700

This is a soundside favorite in Duck Village where folks enjoy fabulous sunsets overlooking Currituck Sound and indoor recreation including a pool table, dart board and tabletop shuffleboard. Live entertainment can be heard most summer nights. Locals gather here and newcomers are likely to get caught up in the fun. There's food and beverage service until whenever, and the tavern menu offers appetizers, sandwiches, pizza and steamed shrimp. Summer brings a comedy club — call for a schedule. This nightspot is open year round, which is a good thing because it gets pretty quiet on the north beaches during the winter months.

Kitty Hawk

RUNDOWN CAFE
Beach Rd., MP 1   255-0026

The same friendly owners of

Tortuga's Lie Shellfish Bar and Grill in Nags Head have decided it's time to offer the folks on the north end of the beach a great alternative nightspot. The Rundown is your summertime blues and jazz connection, with live music on Thursdays. In case you're wondering about the origination of the name, Rundown is a traditional Jamaican stew, and the decor here is very Caribbean. So relax and enjoy this nightspot; it's a fun place to meet people and the kind of place you don't mind stopping by on your own.

FRISCO'S
Rt. 158, MP 4   *261-7833*

A popular hangout for locals, this refurbished restaurant is a crowd pleaser and well known as a friendly gathering place. The lounge is a busy place during lunch, and a light fare menu is available during the evening. Lounge specials are offered daily, and it's also a great place for karaoke. Karaoke is even more fun when you bring your own group of singing stars. Call for schedule. The U-shaped bar is the perfect place to relax, and small tables let you stretch out in the lounge. Frisco's is open all year.

Kill Devil Hills

AWFUL ARTHUR'S
Beach Rd., MP 6   *441-5955*

It's loud, packed with people and as popular as it gets. There's occasional live entertainment here, but the real draw just seems to be the atmosphere and the raw bar. You'll see table after table of youngish patrons having a good time at the

beach. Monday night is locals night during the off season.

TOP OF THE DUNES LOUNGE
AT THE SEA RANCH
Beach Rd., MP 7   *441-7126*

There's live entertainment most nights at the Top of the Dunes Lounge, open from 5 PM to 2 AM year round. The dance floor is perfect for nightly dancing, and the large screen TV attracts its share of patrons. The atmosphere is subdued and attracts a mature crowd.

JOLLY ROGER RESTAURANT
Beach Rd., MP 7   *441-6530*

The lounge is separate from the dining area in this favorite locals' hangout. You'll find live entertainment most nights during the summer and a variety of local talent. Steamed spiced shrimp is offered in the lounge between 3:30 PM and 5:30 PM. Interactive TV has been a real hit; big prizes can be won. You can play every night. Tuesday is trivia night.

PARADISE BILLIARDS
The Dare Center, MP 7   *441-9225*

Indoor table recreation is here with two foosball tables and six pool tables. This is a popular place, so you may have to wait for a table. The 50-inch big screen TV will help entertain you along with dart boards and Interactive Trivia — a computerized trivia game. Paradise is open noon until 2 AM, serving beer and wine. Hot dogs and barbecue sandwiches are available until midnight. Persons under 18 must be accompanied by an adult until 7 PM, and you must be 18 years or older after 7 PM.

GOOMBAY'S GRILLE AND RAW BAR
Beach Rd., MP 7½   441-6001

This popular nightspot is located where The Whaling Station used to be, on the Beach Road. The bar is fun and colorful, and the bartenders are local characters. Caribbean casual reflects owner, John Kirchmier's, acquaintance with that area. Goombay's is centrally located near First Street in Kill Devil Hills and becomes a destination for lots of folks at one time or another during the evening. It's a kind of hangout where you're sure to feel right at home. The bar is set off to the side from the dining area, so you can lounge in the bar area or have a seat nearby after the dining room closes at 10 PM. The bar is open until 2 AM, and you can get steamed shrimp and steamed veggies from the raw bar after the restaurant closes.

PAPAGAYO'S CANTINA
Beach Rd., MP 7½   441-7232

Let the ocean breezes lift your spirits from this second floor, ocean-front lounge and deck. It's a great place to enjoy a cocktail at the end of a sun-filled day, and there's live music during the season most nights, and sometimes on weekends during the off season. It's a popular place for locals and visitors who like Mexican food and margaritas.

PORT O'CALL GASLIGHT SALOON
Beach Rd., MP 8½   441-7484

The Gaslight Saloon is a favorite place of Victorian style, featuring dark wood panelling and a long mahogany bar. Antique furnishings surround a small dance floor. Live entertainment is offered seven nights a week in season, and every weekend while they're open, mid-March through December. Port O' Call has become a popular destination for all those seeking live music, but since the lounge is quite large, upstairs and down, lots of people can fit comfortably here. Expect a cover charge for bands.

SHUCKER'S PUB AND BILLIARDS
Oceanside Plaza, MP 8½   480-1010

A pub and billiard room are featured here. There are five billiard tables and plenty of TV for sports fans. Hours during the season are 12 PM until 2 AM, seven days a week. Beer and wine will quench your thirst, while steamed shrimp, pizza and subs will satisfy your appetite. You must be 21 or older after 10 PM.

TOPSIDE RAW BAR AND PUB AT THE OCEAN REEF MOTEL
Beach Rd., MP 8½   441-4080

Nightlife at this small lounge and eatery is definitely a well-kept secret by locals. It's small, and it's quiet. Everybody knows everybody else, and you basically bring your own fun. Jimmy Buffet can be heard in the background while you try your hand at a game or two of backgammon or checkers. Beer and wine are served, along with frozen yogurt, pizza, deli food and shrimp. There are video games and darts also. Topside is open 11 AM until 2 AM.

MADELINE'S AT THE HOLIDAY INN
Beach Rd., MP 9½   *441-6333*

A popular place for the local population, Madeline's features beach music or a DJ for top-40 music. It's open all year for dancing or meeting friends, and there's no cover charge. The lounge is usually open 9 PM until 2 AM. Expect a mature crowd. It's a convenient location for guests of the hotel, of course.

PEPPERCORN'S AT THE RAMADA INN
Beach Rd., MP 9½   *441-2151*

Enjoy the breathtaking ocean view while visiting with friends and listening to acoustic guitar or duos at the new expanded lounge area in Peppercorn's. They're open from 8 PM to midnight Memorial Day to Labor Day. This is a nice place to relax, chat and enjoy a drink.

Nags Head

SWEETWATERS
Rt. 158, MP 10 ½   *441-3427*

This restaurant offers a separate bar area with booths, tables and service at the bar. The restaurant and bar open at 11:30 daily, and the bar closes whenever. Live acoustic and keyboard entertainment is featured during the week and two TVs are available for your viewing enjoyment. The complete menu is available in the bar until 10 PM, and a light menu is available after that time.

THE COMEDY CLUB AT THE CAROLINIAN LOUNGE
Beach Rd., MP 10½   *441-7171*

Listen to good, live comedy six nights a week at the oldest summer comedy club in the country. In its 11th year, the club at the Carolinian Lounge features nationally-known comedians. We suggest you make reservations for your night of laughter . . . this form of entertainment is popular! You can also enjoy your favorite beverages at the outside, oceanfront bar during the summer; it's a great place to relax. Live music is featured periodically, call for a schedule of events. The Comedy Club begins at 10 PM, Monday through Saturday during the season, and the doors open at 9 PM. During the off season, the Comedy Club is offered on weekends.

KELLY'S
Rt. 158, MP 10½   *441-4116*

A great restaurant and tavern, Kelly's has become synonymous with good times on the Outer Banks. Live music is featured all year. There's a packed house almost every night. This is definitely one of the most popular nightspots on the Outer Banks throughout the year. There's a dance floor that's always hopping, and booths surround the dance area if you're looking for a little quieter, or at least less active, location. The lounge area has expanded again to include a separate area for a dart board. The elongated U-shaped bar

Photo: Baum Center

Seniors enjoy an evening of bowling and relaxation.

is a favorite place to sit and watch the band. A lounge menu is available, and tables are located in the lounge for your comfort and convenience, but move fast because they're usually occupied with fun-loving folks.

WOODY'S GOOD TIME BAR AND GRILL

Rt. 158, MP 11   441-4881
at Pirate's Quay

This bar and grill is becoming one of the more popular places on the beach. There's lots of good food downstairs in the dining room ranging from prime rib to good seafood. The hot wings are great. Entertainment at Woody's offers a varied line up of rock 'n' roll, reggae and funk. From June through August Woody's features reggae weekends. Shows usually begin at 10 PM, and you can use your receipt from dinner for free cover for the lounge upstairs (special shows are an exception).

Expect a cover for bands. A full menu is served until midnight.

TORTUGA'S LIE SHELLFISH BAR AND GRILL

The Beach Rd., MP 11   441-7299

This is another local favorite, and it's considered a great alternative nightspot for folks at this end of the beach. You won't find live entertainment, but you will find plenty of conversation. Tortuga's Lie is affectionately known as Tortuga's, and you should know that it's one of the few places on the beach where you can find a half-and-half on draft — that's right, they have Guiness and Bass Ale on tap. Enjoy live acoustical music on weekends, and relax on the porch with a bucket of beer. For the more energetic types, Tortuga's is known for its backyard volleyball games. What fun! Hours are 11:30 AM until 2 AM.

LANCE'S SEAFOOD BAR AND MARKET
Rt. 158, MP 14   441-7501

Lance's is a great place to relax and enjoy local seafood in an unpretentious atmosphere. The folks here are down to earth, and the locals like to hang out. You can have a seat at the bar or at one of the many wooden tables in the combined dining and lounge area. The tables even have holes in the center of them allowing for convenient throw away of seafood shells. Carved decoys and such line the walls, and there's no shortage of interesting things to look at. The lobster tank always catches the eye.

STATION KEEPERS LOUNGE AT OWENS' RESTAURANT
Beach Rd., MP 16½   441-7309

Station Keepers Lounge, upstairs at Owens' Restaurant, is an intimate setting where you can actually *talk* to companions. The natural wood and brass accented by Tiffany lights create a cozy ambiance. Station Keepers Lounge features a light menu. If steamed seafood is your pleasure — this is the place to be. The lounge is one of the few places on the beach where you can enjoy espresso, cappucino or specialty coffee drinks. Enjoy the sweet life with the incredible homemade desserts. You will definitely enjoy a relaxing evening. Open from 5 PM until. . . .

Roanoke Island

CLARA'S SEAFOOD GRILL AND STEAM BAR
Manteo Waterfront   473-1727

Clara's steam bar overlooks the Roanoke Sound and offers a casual meeting place for locals and vacationers alike. The functional nautical decor featuring waterfront nostalgia and waterfowl decoys helps to tell the story of how life once was here on the downtown waterfront. A full menu is available, and you can enjoy happy hour, Monday through Friday, 4 PM until 7 PM. Special prices are offered on steamed local seafood including clams, oysters, crab legs and shrimp. The topped oysters and clams are just delicious. Beer, wine and champagne are sold here, and brown bagging is allowed — setups are provided. You can look forward to live entertainment every Friday night during the season with guitar and vocal background music. Steam bar hours are 11:30 AM until 9:30 PM during the season and 11:30 AM until 9 PM during the off season.

Hatteras Island

DOWN UNDER RESTAURANT AND LOUNGE
Rodanthe Pier   987-2277
Rodanthe

Down Under stays open until

What's prettier than a coastal sunset?

around midnight and is a great place to go for a night out on Hatteras Island. Surfers, windsurfers and just plain beachgoers like to hang out here. They've added a sunset deck and have the only cold, frosty (almost ice-caked) mugs on the island that we've found. Food is served until 10 PM. Ocean views are splendid.

Lily Pad Lounge at The Froggy Dog Restaurant
Hwy. 12
Avon   995-4106

The Lily Pad Lounge is open seven nights a week year round. You'll find live acoustic and duo music nightly Sunday through Thursday from 9:30 PM to 1:30 AM, with no cover charge. On Friday and Saturday from 10 PM to 2 AM, the big band sound hits the floor, and cover charge is $3 to $5.

Lounge hours are from 3 PM until 2 AM. From Easter to Labor Day, they open at noon and serve lunch in the bar. A late night menu is available. Between 3 PM and 6 PM you can take advantage of the 10-cent shrimp special. The band schedule can be found in the *Hatteras Monitor* and the *Island Breeze.*

Ocracoke

3/4-Time Dance Hall & Saloon
NC 12, Main Rd.   928-1221

When you get here, you'll have to shift gears to get into the flow of this more traditional dance hall. There's plenty of fun on the dance floor and great music from the stage. It's a surprising place on an otherwise remote, quiet island. There's something for everyone, and local bands are scheduled most weekends during the summer. The music varies from country to Top 40. Acoustic music can be heard here during the week without a cover charge. Cover charges range from $2 to $5. Dances on the weekend are a lot of fun along with Karaoke, pool tables, darts, foosball and Ping Pong. Beer and wine are available, and the kitchen offers pizza from 6 PM until 1 AM.

HOWARD'S PUB & RAW BAR

NC 12, Main Rd. 928-4441

Howard's Pub & Raw Bar is the place to go for late night entertainment, and they're open all year. There's a deck for sunning or stargazing, and the huge screened porches have comfortable Adirondack rocking chairs for relaxing. There's a wide screen TV for sports fans, dart board, backgammon, checkers, Trivial Pursuit, Barrel of Monkeys and card games. You'll even find horseshoes out back. They serve food until 2 AM, and the weekend music ranges from bluegrass to jazz ensembles to open mike or Karaoke. The cover charge is never more than $2. Beer and wine are available, and there's free chili on Monday night while you watch football. Pub hours are 11 AM until 2 AM. (Don't forget about their an-nual Halloween costume party.) And, for those times when the power fails Ocracoke completely, Howard's is equipped with a generator and can keep on cooking (and keep the beer cold too).

TIKI LOUNGE AT THE PELICAN RESTAURANT

Ocracoke Village 928-7431

The Tiki Lounge is an outdoor lounge featuring live entertainment periodically during the summer. You can enjoy your favorite frozen drinks in a relaxing tropical atmosphere. The lounge is located in the side yard of the Pelican Restaurant. It's one of only two outside bars that we know of on Ocracoke Island. Sit back, relax and enjoy!

JOLLY ROGER

Ocracoke Village 928-3703

This eatery overlooks the Jolly Roger Marina and Silver Lake Harbor; it's across the street from the Silver Lake Motel on NC 12. The local acoustic group, "Martin and Friends," can be heard playing on the deck here on Thursday evenings until dark. Beer and wine and a full menu are available, and there is no cover charge.

Photo: Dare County Tourist Bureau

Many hang gliders come to Pea Island to soar over the dune line.

Inside
Cottage and Long-term Rentals

On the Outer Banks, from Carova to Ocracoke, you'll find an unusual assortment and a wide variety of rental properties and choices for lodging. These properties include hotel and motel rooms, efficiency apartments, condos, cottages and homes. Your selection of accommodations is determined by the time of year you want to visit, how far ahead you plan, the length of your stay and your desired location. Weekend, partial-weeks, weekly, monthly, seasonal and long-term rentals are available throughout most of the Outer Banks.

Certain types of rentals are more readily available than others; week to week rentals are the most popular, followed by seasonal and monthly rentals. Weekend, partial-weeks and long-term rentals are less plentiful. Since vacation planning is a primary use of this guide, we've made this a comprehensive chapter, covering cottages and hotel/motel rooms, short-term and long-term rentals, and information on reservations, rental companies, equipment rental companies, regulations, and hints for successfully planning your stay on the Outer Banks.

Vacation Cottages

The Outer Banks is a family resort, and there is a wide range of accommodations available for families. When you rent a home or cottage, your options are greater. Eating arrangements, periods of rest and relaxation and elbow room are important considerations.

Competition for rentals of cottages and condos (and often even hotel/motel rooms) depends greatly on the area in which you are trying to locate. Demand and price for rentals vary, in most cases, according to the proximity of the property to the oceanfront, amenities offered and the time of year during which you plan to stay. Traditionally, oceanfront properties book first. Semi-oceanfront properties, those properties located oceanside, and properties located between the highways (Route 158 and the Beach Road) in the central areas of the beach typically book up next. Properties located soundfront, soundside, or generally west of the Route 158 tend to book at a slower rate due simply to the fact that they are located farther from the ocean.

DESCRIPTION OF LOCATIONS

Oceanfront properties are in great demand every year and, of course, these rental properties command higher prices as a result of their location. There are generally no intervening homes or lots between the cottage and the ocean, although the distance from the ocean varies. Semi-oceanfront properties are usually located one lot behind the oceanfront lot or oceanfront house. Again, distance to the ocean varies.

Oceanside properties are those from which you can walk to the beach without having to cross a major street or road. There will be other rows of houses along roads or lanes between your cottage and the ocean.

Cottages from Kitty Hawk to Nags Head are often located between the highways. What this means is that the house is located between the Beach Road (in some places marked as N.C. Highway 12 or Virginia Dare Trail) and Route 158. The Beach Road is two lanes (one in each direction) and not difficult to cross most of the time. Traffic travels at a slow pace. The pavement gets hot, though, so plan to wear shoes when walking from a cottage between the highways to the ocean.

Soundfront, soundside or west side locations generally mean facing the waters of the sound, near the sound without crossing a major road, or not very close to the water of the sound, but on the west side of the bypass.

By reading the location descriptions in this book, you will be able to choose the area of the beach you'd prefer to visit . . . each has its own personality. Then, call the rental companies located in that area and request a brochure. Most of these

companies offer toll free numbers, and they are happy to send their brochure to you. Rental brochures are sophisticated marketing tools and locations are described in great detail. If the property is not located on the oceanfront, descriptions often indicate how far a walk it is to the beach. Read the cottage and location descriptions carefully so that you'll know exactly what you're renting.

RESERVATIONS

Rental managers tell us that the best time to reserve a cottage is as soon as you have determined when you will visit the Outer Banks and as soon as you are able to provide monies to secure your reservation. These monies are known as advanced rents. Mailings of rental brochures occur between Thanksgiving and mid-January, in plenty of time for you to make informed choices about accommodations. There is a wide variety of accommodations available ranging from basic beach box-style cottages to luxurious homes.

Traditionally, most reservations are received by March or April. If, however, you are unable to book as early as you would like, or you decide at the last minute that you need an Outer Banks getaway, don't be discouraged. Rental managers say that reservations were available last year for just that sort of thing. So, go ahead, give them a call. They'll be happy to try to accommodate you, even on major holidays.

There is a tremendous inventory of rental properties, and it's a good idea to make several choices before calling to make a reservation. In

many cases you'll have to ask about nonsmoking cottages and cottages equipped for handicapped persons. For those who rent a property one year, most companies will offer the option of reserving vacation time in the same property for the following year. It is not uncommon for visitors to rent the same cottage year after year.

MINIMUM STAYS

During the off season some options exist for partial weeks and weekend rentals in cottages. During the season, it's practically impossible to rent for less than a full week, which in this market runs either Saturday to Saturday or Sunday to Sunday. Hotels and motels are more flexible. Measure the difference in cost.

CANCELLATIONS

Cancellation policies are spelled out in rental brochures and lease agreements, and you can expect few exceptions. Most cancellations or transfers of any confirmed reserva-tions are required in writing. You will probably lose all or part of your deposit if the property is not re-rented. Forfeiting money is a difficult experience. Make sure you read the small print and that you know what the policy is on cancellations.

THE RATE SEASONS

Rates change with the season and vary from company to company. Early spring and fall months offer some great bargains for the beach. More people are considering these "shoulder seasons" and have discovered a very enjoyable vacation time. During the fall months, locals sit back and breathe a little easier, the sun is still shining, the weather is warm, and the beaches are less crowded. For the most part, families have returned home to get the kids off to school.

Spring months usher in an end to winter's hibernation, and the prices have not yet returned to peak season levels. These months some-time bring with them less predictable weather, but locals abound with renewed energy and anticipation of the summer weather and all those beach-related activities.

Winter rentals are available at significant savings. The supply of properties is smaller, oceanfront cottages in particular, because many owners "winterize" their properties and don't reopen them until the warmer months return. Older cottages may not be insulated, making them unavailable for occupancy during the winter months.

You must check each rental company for specific rate/date changes, but here's a general idea of what to expect.

In season is from mid-June through Labor Day. During this time you'll pay the most expensive rates.

Mid-season is from just after Labor Day through Thanksgiving and from Easter until mid-June.

Off season is from around December 1 through pre-Easter week.

Mid-season rates are as much as 20-30 percent less than in-season rates, and off season rates can be as much as 50 percent less than in-season rates. In some cases off season rates are effective beginning late September, so visitors can expect significant discounts during October and November as well. And, as we said, it is a wonderful time to visit the Banks.

ADVANCE RENTS

Money paid in advance is no longer considered a deposit; it's now called advance payment or advance rent. The transaction is governed by the laws of the North Carolina Real Estate Commission involving renting or leasing property.

Details, explanations and rules are spelled out in rental brochures and again in your lease. Read the fine print, and save yourself a potential headache. Personal checks are usually accepted for these advance rents, and some rental companies allow credit card transactions. In most cases, rent balances, taxes and other applicable fees and deposits are due 30 days prior to arrival. Final payments made upon check-in are usually required in the form of certified checks, travelers' checks or cash. Personal checks are not accepted at check-in.

SECURITY DEPOSIT

This is another fee often included in the total amount you will pay for the use of someone else's cottage on the beach. It's exactly what it implies. Most security deposits range from $50 to $250, and they can be higher. This fee is returnable upon a satisfactory inspection of the cottage after you vacate. If there is damage, expect a smaller refund or no refund at all, if the situation war-

Photo: N.C. Travel and Tourism

The beach is a great place for families to play together.

rants it. The rental company has the final word on this, as a part of the business transaction for the homeowner.

HURRICANE EVACUATION REFUND POLICIES

Your rental contract addresses refunds for hurricane evacuations, but be advised that policies vary. You need to check your rental agreement to determine the specific provisions.

In many cases, partial or complete refunds are provided when a mandatory evacuation has been issued by the Dare County Emergency Management Control Group. Adjustments to your bill are made in the form of prorations from the number of days you were unable to occupy the property due to mandatory evacuation. Most rental managers we spoke to said that prorations are not provided for any amount of time you do not occupy the property once

reentry has been permitted.

Hurricane evacuation refund policies for Hatteras and Ocracoke Islands include provisions for refunds due to mandatory evacuation as well. Provisions are also made for interrupted ferry service to Ocracoke, since it is impossible to access this area without this service. Check your rental contracts for the specifics; these policies vary too.

HANDLING AND INSPECTION FEES

In almost all cases the rental company charges a handling and inspection fee. In most instances this fee is $20. It covers paperwork, the processing of your reservation, mailing and any miscellaneous expenditures. This is a nonrefundable fee.

TAXES

All fees are taxable. Rental charges and handling fees are taxable. If cleaning, pet, or extermination fees are applicable, they are taxable as well. Deposits are not taxable as they are returnable funds. The N.C. State tax (use tax) rate is 6 percent, and the local/county lodging tax rate is 4 percent. Thus, combined tax rate is 10 percent on your rental charges and fees.

PET RULES AND FEES

Some rental cottages are available for bringing along the family pet. Don't be surprised, however, at the additional charges for spraying or for the use of growth regulators to inhibit the growth of fleas. Each company has a complete policy for your protection, your pet's protection and for the protection of the homeowner who allows you to bring the important member of the family! These fees are not deposits, so are not refundable.

CHECK-IN, CHECK-OUT TIMES

Check-in times vary from company to company with most occurring between 3 PM and 6 PM. You check-in at the rental company before taking occupancy of the cottage. Be prompt, but don't be early as the cleanup crews need sufficient time to get your cottage in tip-top shape. Rental managers urge you not to try to occupy the cottage before it is ready. They understand your eagerness to settle into your cottage, in many cases after a long drive, but they simply are unable to let you do so.

Most checkouts occur between 9 AM and 11 AM. Again, it is important to check out on time to allow for necessary maintenance. Late fees may be imposed if you stay too long. Don't forget to return your keys or you may lose your key deposit.

OCCUPANCY

Each rental cottage is governed by rules and regulations that are spelled out in the rental brochure from which you select your place at the beach. Please do not exceed the advertised occupancy limits. Most cottage owners and rental companies on the Outer Banks discourage large groups of young adults or college students who, instead, can select their accommodations from some motels and hotels on the beach. Groups who try to get around the rules governing occupancy stand to lose their money and risk eviction.

WHAT'S FURNISHED

A rental cottage is a fully-furnished home, in most instances. The rental brochures will list the furnishings, like small appliances, TVs, VCRs, stereos, toasters, microwaves, etc., and note other items provided such as beach chairs, beach umbrellas, hammocks and outdoor grills.

Insiders' Tips

Touches of a paste made of boric acid and sweetened condensed milk are sure to drive away cockroaches. (Make sure the paste is placed where kids and pets can't get to it!).

Most of the time, all you bring are your sheets and towels, paper products, detergents, and personal toiletries. However, most rental companies will rent sheets and towels. If it's important to keep track of the time, bring a clock or radio; otherwise, judge time by the sun and relax!

MAIL AND PHONE SERVICE

Rental companies are a service business, and the people who speak with you on the phone to assist with the details of your personal vacation will go the extra mile and take phone calls and mail if it's required while you're here. But you can make it easier on everyone by taking care of things like this before you arrive. Obtain the phone number of the cottage you will be renting, and leave this number with close friends or relatives in case of emergencies.

Some older cottages don't have telephones, so be sure you check this out. In any event, long distance charges are the responsibility of the renter. Rules are spelled out in detail in most rental brochures and in your cottage upon check-in.

RECYCLING

Citizens of Dare County take recycling seriously. In fact, you'll often find that volunteers at the recycling center also work in shops and rental offices of businesses on the Outer Banks. The North Carolina legislature set guidelines for compliance for all its counties, and the permanent residents know what it means to keep the beaches clean and lighten the load of trash to area landfills.

Guests are encouraged to recycle, too. Rental companies have appropriate information about recycling centers located from Corolla to Ocracoke, and there's information on the locations and operating hours of recycling centers for each town in our Service Directory. Thanks for doing your part to protect this beautiful environment.

EQUIPMENT RENTALS

If you prefer not to bring everything from home, equipment rental companies can make life a lot easier. Strollers with large wheels for easy movement in the sand, beach chairs, umbrellas, bikes, videos, VCRs, camcorders, cribs, high-chairs, cots ...you name it and you can probably rent it! For those of you who are looking for a little adventure during your Outer Banks vacation, we have also included contact information for companies that rent boats, water vehicles, jet skis, canoes, all-terrain vehicles and dune buggies. For additional information on renting recreational or water sports vehicles and equipment, check the Recreation chapter. We've listed the following rental companies for your convenience.

Ocean Atlantic Rentals: (800) 635-9559. Locations in Corolla, at the Village Shops, 453-2440; Duck, at Scarborough Faire, 261-4346; Nags Head/Kill Devil Hills at MP 10, 441-7823; Waves at 987-2492; and Avon, at 995-5868. Write: P.O. Box 1030, Nags Head, N.C. 27959. Delivery is offered from each location for those with prepaid advance reservations only, in most cases. Fees depend on the amount of equipment

The Outer Banks provide a wealth of opportunities for sailing enthusiasts.

Photo: Mike Booher/DCTB

delivered to each location.

Money'$ Worth Beach Home Equipment Rentals, (800) 833-5233, is located in Kitty Hawk, 261-6999; and Coinjock, 453-4566. It's mailing address is P.O. Box 1256, Kitty Hawk, N.C. 27949. All items are delivered to your vacation home on your check-in day and picked up after you check-out. This company is the only one that services the real estate companies directly. You do not have to be present for delivery or pickup service. A minimum rental order of $20 is required for delivery and pickup service. Money'$ Worth also notes that TV reception is very poor on the Outer Banks without cable hook up. Please check with your property manager to confirm that your unit has cable service.

Lifesaver Rent-Alls, (800) 635-2764, is located in Kill Devil Hills, Lifesaver Shops, 441-6048; and in Kitty Hawk (in season) at MP 1, Three Winks Shopping Center, 261-1344. Write: P.O. Box 1164, Kill Devil Hills, N.C. 27948. This company has been renting beach equipment for years on the Outer Banks and has a good reputation.

Metro Rentals, 480-3535, is located in Kill Devil Hills at the corner of Route 158 and Colington Road (the first stoplight after the Wright Brothers Memorial). They specialize in party supplies; everything from tents to punch bowls including folding chairs, tables, table cloths, glassware and more. You will also find construction equipment for all your home-improvement projects, and beachcombing equipment for those of you who enjoy finding treasures in the sand. If you have a decorative flag and wonder how you are going to find a pole to fly it, Metro Rentals also manufactures quality flagpoles.

For a free brochure write: P.O. Box 77, Kill Devil Hills, N.C., 27948

Water Works, is located in Duck, 261-7245; Whalebone Junction at MP 16, 441-8875; and on the Nags Head/Manteo Causeway, 441-6822. Write: P.O. Box 1134, Nags Head, N.C. 27959. This water sports destination offers parasailing at their Route 158 location in Nags Head. Canoes, kayaks, water vehicles, jet skis and tour boats are rented at each of their locations. Airboat rentals are also available at the causeway location. Sails for Yamaha water vehicles and Sea Doos can be rented along with beach equipment. Waterworks also sells and services Yamaha equipment. It offers pickup service only.

Shoreline Recreation & Wetsports is located on Highway 64 South in Manteo next to Manteo Marine, 473-1231. Write: P.O. Box 2265, Manteo, N.C. 27954. It offers daily rentals of recreational vehicles, all-terrain vehicles, canoes and water scooters. Sailboats and water skis are for sale only. It has pickup service only.

Beach Outfitters, (at Ocracoke Island Realty office, P.O. Box 238, Ocracoke, N.C. 27960) 928-6261 or (800) 242-5394, accepts VISA, MC. Reservations are requested. Open all year, this rental company offers discounted packaged items for full weeks only. Other discounts are also available depending on the dollar amount rented. Free delivery and pickup is available with full-week rental and prepayment (Ocracoke Island only). Write for a free brochure.

Island Rentals, is located in Ocracoke, 928-5480. Write: P.O. Box 369, Ocracoke, N.C. 27960. Affiliated with Sharon Miller Realty, they've branched off and expanded. Rentals include a 16-foot Southern Skimmer, beach equipment, croquet sets, Nintendo and cottage equipment.

Rental Companies

We've listed some rental companies, their locations and contact information on the Outer Banks for your convenience. We have also listed the areas where the rental companies' properties are located in case you are looking for a cottage in a specific area.

Atlantic Realty, 261-2154 or (800) 334-8401 (out-of-state), is located on Route 158, MP 2½. Its mailing address is 4729 North Croatan Highway, Kitty Hawk, N.C. 27949. It manages rental properties from Corolla to South Nags Head.

B&B on the Beach, 453-3033, 473-5555, or (800) 962-0201 (out-of-state), is located in the Brindley & Brindley Realty & Development Building in Corolla Light. Write: P.O. Box 564, Corolla, N.C. 27927. It manages rental properties from Carova to the Pine Island development in the north beaches.

Bodie Island Rentals, 441-2558, is located at the Bodie Island Beach Club Timeshare Resort, MP 17 on the Beach Road in Nags Head. Write: P.O. Box 331, Nags Head, N.C. 27959. It manages timeshares in the Bodie Island Resort.

Britt Real Estate, 261-3566 or (800) 334-6315 (out-of-state) is located north of Duck Village on Duck Road. Write: 1316 Duck Road, Kitty

Hawk, N.C. 27949. Britt Real Estate manages rental properties from Corolla to Southern Shores.

Cove Realty, 441-6391 or (800) 635-7007, is located between the Beach Road and Route 158, MP 14. Write: P.O. Box 967, Nags Head, N.C. 27959. Cove Realty manages rental properties in Old Nags Head Cove, Nags Head and South Nags Head.

Dolphin Realty, 986-2241 or (800) 338-4775, is located in Hatteras. Write: P.O. Box 387, Hatteras, N.C. 27943. It manages rentals on Hatteras Island.

ERA Ocean Country Realty, 995-6700, located on Highway 12 in Avon, manages rentals on Hatteras Island. Write: P.O. Box 806, Avon, N.C., 27915.

Gardner Realty, 441-8985 or (800) 468-4066 (out-of-state), is located on the Beach Road, MP 16. Write: 2600 Virginia Dare Trail, Nags Head, N.C. 27959. Gardner Realty manages rental properties mainly in South Nags Head.

Hatteras Realty, 995-5466 or (800) Hattera, is located on N.C. Highway 12, Avon. Write: P.O. Box 249, Avon, N.C. 27915. It manages rental properties on Hatteras Island.

Karichele Realty, 453-4400 or (800) 453-2377, is located in the Tim Buck II Shopping Village in Corolla. Write: P.O. Box 100, Corolla, N.C. 27927. Managing rental properties from Carova to Pine Island.

Kitty Dunes Realty, 261-2171 in Kitty Hawk; 453-Dune in Corolla; (800) 334-Dune for catalogue information; reservation hotline 261-2326; and Canadian representative (514) 376-4382. Write: P.O. Box 275, Kitty Hawk, N.C. 27949. Managing

rental properties from Carova to the Oregon Inlet Bridge.

Kitty Hawk Rentals/Beach Realty & Construction, 441-7166 or (800) 635-1559 (out-of-state), is located on Route 158, MP 6. Write: P.O. Box 69, Kill Devil Hills, N.C. 27948. There is also a location in Duck 261-6605 or (800) 849-Duck (out-of-state). Write: 1450 Duck Road, Duck, N.C. 27949. Their newest location is in Corolla at the Tim Buck II Shopping Village, 453-4111. Write: 790 B. Ocean Trail, Corolla, N.C. 27927. This company manages rental properties from Ocean Hill to South Nags Head.

Joe Lamb, Jr. & Associates, 261-4444 or (800) 552-6257 (out-of-state), is located on Route 158, MP 2. Write: P.O. Box 986, Kitty Hawk, N.C. 27949. This company manages rental properties from Whalehead to South Nags Head.

Midgett Realty, 986-2841 or (800) 527-2903 (out-of-state), manages rental properties from Rodanthe to Hatteras Village. Write: P.O. Box 250, Hatteras, N.C. 27943.

Sharon Miller Realty, 928-5711 or (800) 553-9962 (out-of-state), is located on Ocracoke. Write: P.O. Box 264, Ocracoke, 27960. Sharon Miller Realty manages Ocracoke Island rental properties.

Nags Head Realty, 441-4315 or (800) 222-1531, is located at 2300 South Croatan Highway. Write: P.O. Box 130, Nags Head, N.C. 27959. It manages rental properties from the Crown Point development in the north beaches to South Nags Head.

Ocracoke Island Realty, Inc., 928-6261, 928-7411 or (800) 242-5394 (out-of-state), manages Ocracoke

The beach is a perfect place to relax and get away from it all.

Island rental properties. Write: P.O. Box 238, Ocracoke, N.C. 27960.

Outer Banks, Ltd., 441-5000 or (800) 624-7651 (out-of-state), is located on Route 158, MP 10. Write: P.O. Box 129, Nags Head, N.C. 27959. It manages rental properties from Duck to South Nags Head.

Outer Beaches Realty, 995-4477 in Avon and 987-2771 in Waves, manages rental properties from Rodanthe to Hatteras Village. Write: P.O. Box 280, Avon, N.C. 27915.

Pirate's Cove Realty, 473-6800 or (800) 537-7245 (toll free), manages rental properties in the development of Pirate's Cove. Mailing address P.O. Box 1879, Manteo, N.C. 27954.

R & R Resort Rental Properties, Inc., 261-1136 or (800) 433-8805 (out-of-state), is located in Duck Village. Write: 1184 Duck Rd., Duck, N.C. 27949. It manages rental properties from Corolla to Southern Shores.

Real Escapes Properties, 261-

3211 or ((800) 831-3211 for brochure requests only), is located in Duck. Write: 1183 Duck Road, Duck, N.C. 27949. An office is also located in Corolla at Whalehead Landing, 453-3777. It manages rental properties from Corolla to Duck.

Remax Ocean Realty, 441-3127 or (800) 548-2033 (out-of-state), is located at Seagate Station in Kill Devil Hills. Write: P.O. Box 8, Kill Devil Hills, N.C. 27948. It manages rental properties from Duck to Nags Head.

Resort Central, Inc., 261-8861 or (800) 334-4749 (toll free), is located on Route 158, MP 2½. Write: P.O. Box 767, Kitty Hawk, N.C. 27949. It manages rental properties in the areas of Duck south to Nags Head. (This company does not handle general real estate sales, rentals only.)

Resort Realty, 261-8383 or (800) 458-3830 (out-of-state), is located in Kitty Hawk. Write: P.O. Box 1008,

Kitty Hawk, N.C. 27949. There is also an office in Duck, (800) 545-3908; and Corolla, (800) 633-1630. This company manages rental properties from Corolla to South Nags Head.

Salvo Real Estate, 987-2343, is located on N.C. 12 in Salvo. Write: P.O. Box 56, Salvo, N.C. 27972. It manages rental properties in Rodanthe, Salvo and Waves.

Seaside Realty, 261-5500 and (800) 395-2525 (out-of-state), is located on Route 158, MP 3½ in Kitty Hawk. Write: 4425 North Croatan Highway, Kitty Hawk, N.C. 27949. It represents rental properties from Corolla to South Nags Head.

Southern Shores Realty, 261-2111 or (800) 334-1000, is located on N.C. 12, #5 Ocean Boulevard, Southern Shores. Write: P.O. Box 150, Kitty Hawk, N.C. 27949. It manages rental properties in Southern Shores and Duck.

Sun Realty, 441-7033 or (800) 346-9593 (out-of-state), is located on Route 158, MP 9 in Kill Devil Hills. Write: P.O. Box 1630, Kill Devil Hills, N.C. 27948. This Kill Devil Hills location is the booking headquarters for rentals at each of Sun Realty's other locations on the Outer Banks. Satellite offices include: Corolla, Duck, Kitty Hawk, Avon and Salvo. Sun Realty offers the largest inventory of rental properties on the Outer Banks, managing rental properties from Corolla to Avon.

Surf or Sound Realty, 995-5801 or (800) 237-1138 (toll free), is located on N.C. 12. Write: P.O. Box 100, Avon, N.C. 27915. It manages rental properties on Hatteras Island.

Mercedes Tabano Ltd., 987-2711,

is located in Rodanthe. Write: P.O. Box 188, Rodanthe, N.C. 27968. It manages rental properties in Rodanthe, Salvo and Waves.

Twiddy & Company Realty, 261-3521 in Duck and 453-3341 in Corolla, manages rental properties from Carova to Southern Shores. Write: 1181 Duck Rd., Duck, N.C. 27949.

Village Realty, 480-2224 or (800) 548-9688 (out-of-state), is located on Route 158, MP 15 in Nags Head. Write: P.O. Box 1807, Nags Head, N.C. 27959. It manages rental properties in the development of the Village at Nags Head and other Nags Head properties.

Water Side Realty, Inc., 995-6001 or (800) 530-0022, is located in Buxton. Write: P.O. Box 1088, Buxton, N.C. 27920. It manages rentals from Avon to Hatteras Village.

Stan White Realty, 441-1515 or (800) 338-3233 is located on Route 158, MP 10½, Nags Head. Write: P.O. Drawer 1447, Nags Head, N.C. 27959. It manages rental properties from Kitty Hawk to South Nags Head.

White Duck's Real Estate, 261-4614 or (800) 992-2976 (out-of-state), is located on Duck Road. Write: 1232 Duck Rd., Duck, N.C. 27949. This is a division of Stan White Realty, managing rental properties from Corolla to Southern Shores.

Wright Property Management, 261-2186, is located at MP 4 3/4, Route 158, Kitty Hawk. Write: 3630 N. Croatan Highway, Kitty Hawk, N.C. 27949. Managing rental properties from Ocean Sands to South Nags Head.

The Young People, 441-5544 or (800) 334-6436, is located on Beach

Road, MP 6. Write: P.O. Box 285, Kill Devil Hills, N.C. 27948. It manages rental properties from Corolla to South Nags Head.

Long-term/ Resident Rentals

We decided to include a section on long-term rentals in the guide because not all rental companies offer long-term leases. Most companies, in fact, manage only weekly rentals. We realize that there are a lot of visitors to the Outer Banks who either need or want to stay for extended periods of time. We could have titled this section employee rentals because most longer-term leases serve those seeking transitory employment in this area. Summer rentals are necessary to accommodate the large numbers of seasonal employees needed to fill service positions.

For our purposes, long-term rentals refer to all rentals exceeding a one-week time period. Definitions for long-term rentals vary from company to company, but all agree that these include all rentals (or leases) other than those occurring on a week-to-week basis. These include monthly, summer and winter leases and six to 12 month leases.

The inventory of long-term rentals includes cottages, condos, apartments, duplexes, triplexes and mobile homes. Most rental properties are available in areas from Duck south to Nags Head and on Roanoke Island. These areas are proximate to where most of the seasonal and year-round jobs are available on the Outer

Banks.

Soundfront is generally the only waterfront location available for long-term rental. There is an extremely limited inventory of oceanfront properties as most are closed for the winter. The majority of long-term rentals are located west of the Route 158 and between the highways in the central areas of the beach (Kitty Hawk, Kill Devil Hills, Colington Island and Nags Head).

INVENTORY OF LONG-TERM RENTALS

Inventories of long-term rentals vary tremendously from company to company. Property managers may manage as few as 10 properties or as many as 100. Do not expect inventories to be extensive, but those companies specializing only in long-term rentals often have more properties available for lease. There seems to be increasing interest in these rentals as companies such as KMart and Wal-Mart move into the area and offer year-round employment opportunities.

LEASE AND OCCUPANCY REQUIREMENTS

Check with the rental company to determine specific occupancy rules regarding rental rates, deposits, pets and issues of that nature. Most companies do require the first month's rent, a security deposit equalling one month's rent, and, sometimes, references from previous employers and landlords.

Windsurfers find excellent conditions for the sport along the Outer Banks.

LONG-TERM/RESIDENT RENTAL COMPANIES

We've listed some rental companies, their locations and contact information for your convenience. You will find only the phone numbers in cases where contact information has already appeared in this chapter. We have also listed the areas where the properties are located in case you are looking for a rental in a specific place.

Atlantic Realty, 261-2154, manages long-term rentals in Colington, Kill Devil Hills and Kitty Hawk.

Baer's Cottages, 441-2237, is located in Kill Devil Hills. Write: P.O. Box 426, Kill Devil Hills, N.C. 27948. This company has more than 100 long-term rental properties in its inventory. It manages rentals from Duck to Roanoke Island.

The D.A.R.E. Company, 441-1521, is located in Kill Devil Hills. Write: P.O. Box 2598, Kill Devil Hills,

N.C. 27948. It manages long-term commercial and residential rentals from Corolla to South Nags Head.

Kitty Dunes Realty, 261-2171, specializes in long-term properties in Colington Harbour through the Colington Realty office. It also manages properties in Kill Devil Hills and Kitty Hawk.

Kitty Hawk Rentals/Beach Realty & Construction, 441-7166 or (800) 635-1559, manages long-term rentals in Duck, west of Route 158, and between the highways in the central areas of the beach.

Joe Lamb, Jr. & Associates, 261-4444, manages rental properties on the beach, Kitty Hawk to Nags Head.

Nags Head Realty, 441-4315 or (800) 222-1531, manages long-term rental properties in the central beach, Kitty Hawk to South Nags Head.

Outer Banks Long-Term Rentals, Inc., 261-1727, is located at the

Landmark Professional Building in Kitty Hawk. Write: P.O. Box 287, Kitty Hawk, N.C. 27949. It specializes in the leasing of units at Sandpiper Cay Condominiums and properties in Southern Shores and Kitty Hawk (six to 12 month leases only).

Jim Perry & Company, 441-3051 or (800) 222-6135 (toll free), is located in Kill Devil Hills. Write: P.O. Box 1876, Kill Devil Hills, N.C. 27948. It manages year-round rentals only (no weekly rentals) in the central beach areas from Southern Shores to South Nags Head.

Remax Ocean Realty, 441-3127 or (800) 548-2033, manages long-term rental properties from Kitty Hawk to Nags Head, including areas between the highways and west of the Route 158.

Resort Central, Inc., 261-8861 or (800) 334-4749, manages six-to 12-month leases from Kitty Hawk to Nags Head. Properties are also available in Manteo.

Seaside Realty, 261-5500, manages long-term rental properties from Kitty Hawk to Nags Head.

Southern Shores Realty, 261-2111 or (800) 334-1000, manages long-term rentals in Southern Shores.

Sun Realty, 261-1152 or (800) 346-9593, manages long-term rentals from Kitty Hawk to Nags Head.

Water Side Realty, Inc., 995-6001 or (800) 530-0022, manages long-term rentals on Hatteras Island.

Stan White Realty & Construction, Inc., 441-1515 or (800) 338-3233, manages long-term rentals from Kitty Hawk to Nags Head.

The **Young People Realty**, 441-5544, manages long-term rental properties from Kitty Hawk to Nags Head.

Hotel and Motel
Accommodations

The Motel Market

The familiar concept of a resort hotel or motel on more cosmopolitan beaches is a rare find on the Outer Banks. Most commercial properties here don't offer room service, assistance with luggage or other such "big city" services. But, the comfortable ambiance more than makes up for these things. Hotels and motels are almost always filled to capacity.

Outer Banks accommodations include family-owned and-operated motels, bed and breakfasts, inns and larger hotels. Rooms vary in decor, furnishings and amenities such as phones and TVs. Many older beachfront motels are most suitable for anglers or families who vacation on a low budget. They're comfortable, favorite meeting places for family reunions or group fishing trips and often are not fancy enough to worry about getting sand everywhere — in other words, perfect for the beach. Rates will vary from one area to another on the Outer Banks.

Hopefully, reading this book will make it easier for you to choose suitable accommodations. We have noted the availability of nonsmoking rooms and other information such as access to dining establishments and swimming pools.

IN-SEASON RATE GUIDELINES

Motel accommodations come in several basic categories. We've indicated the in-season cost for a one night-stay for two, with two double beds or double occupancy:

$40 to $52	$
$53 to $75	$$
$76 to $95	$$$
$100 and up	$$$$

The rates do not include local and state taxes. Rates are based on proximity to the ocean, view and amenities. The locations are indicated by mile posts or beach town and sometimes both.

RATE SEASONS

Commercial motels and hotels adjust their rates similarly to rental companies. Make sure you get confirmations on dates and accommodations as well as rates. In season begins in mid-June and continues through Labor Day.

Mid-season or off-season rates, of course, are lower. Vacations taken the last weeks before each season begins could present some cost savings. Again, it's important to take notes and ask for confirmations on all reservations.

EXTRA PERSONS

Children under 12 or staying in

the same room as two adults are often allowed without an additional charge. Ask about the specific policy when you call for reservations.

Extra adults are not often allowed in rooms when they will exceed the bed capacity of that room. Again, ask and get confirmation of a charge, even though it's sometimes small.

DEPOSITS

All motels and hotels require deposits to confirm your reservations. Policies vary from one property to another, but the average is 25 percent to 33 percent of the total reservation costs, or one night's rate. The policy regarding payment of deposits or refunds of deposits varies from company to company. Get clear information on this when reserving your place at the beach.

CHECK-IN, CHECK-OUT TIMES

Check-in times vary from around 2 PM until late arrival, when so specified or requested. Checkout times are generally at 11 AM for beach motels, hotels and inns. Times will be posted and, of course, you will be informed when making your reservations. If you plan to drive to the beach and take occupancy for a vacation, it's wise to know an exact check-in time. If you arrive early, there are public beach access points along the beach road that allow you to park and walk out onto the beach.

PAYING THE BILL

Many hotels and motels expect the balance of the reservation paid upon arrival. Personal checks are seldom honored for this final payment. Be prepared with travelers' checks or a credit card. Expect to include in your final payment the state and local taxes, which should be quoted to you when you reserve space. Although many banks here have automatic teller machines, don't rely on last minute transactions to cover cash requirements. Plan ahead.

MINIMUM STAYS

Protecting prime time has become a way of business for motels and hotels. For that reason it's sometimes difficult to get a one-night stay. Established minimums are the rule. Week-long reservations are accepted, of course, and in some instances partial weeks are as well. Don't expect a refund on reservations not fulfilled. In other words, if you reserve a week, but for some reason can't stay the week, you're apt to pay anyway, except in dire circumstances. Make definite plans, and know the details for your pleasure and convenience.

COTS AND CRIBS

Infants usually stay free of charge if you bring a small crib. The motel or hotel might provide a crib for a fee. Cots also carry a cost and are added to the room fee. Since these items may be in short supply, reserve them early if you know you'll need them.

PARKING

Motels and hotels provide free parking for at least one car per reservation. Keep valuables with you and not in the car, which is sometimes exposed to excessive heat and sunlight. The responsibility for your car and whatever you leave in it is yours.

OFF-SEASON PACKAGES

Many motels and hotels remain open all year, and the off season can be a wonderful time to be on the Outer Banks. Though not always hot and sunny, the Outer Banks attracts sport-fishing enthusiasts in the fall and early winter. Others are drawn to quiet, deserted beaches and mild winters. Some businesses offer short-stay packages, sometimes including discounts for meals at a variety of restaurants.

WEEKLY RATES

There's no way to note here an average weekly rate. Prices depend on proximity to the beach and amenities, yet some do allow a discount for a week's rental. Some offer one night free of charge. Our best advice is to ask when you're making your reservation.

MOTEL LOCATIONS

Any property that uses the term oceanfront must have rooms that face the ocean. These rooms may have balconies and views. Some, located on ground level or behind the dunes, may not have a view of the ocean, even though they face the ocean. Ask what's available and clarify which location you prefer. It would be disappointing to be told you have an oceanfront room and upon arrival discover the oceanfront room is behind the dune. (It's the voice of experience, speaking!)

PERSONAL CHECK CASHING

Since you'll need a credit card, travelers checks or cash to settle the remainder of your accommodations bill, we thought a word about these matters would be smart. Unless you have established prior credit or have an automatic teller card, there are only a few local banks that will cash your check. Cash advances on credit cards are handled without question. *Banks on the Outer Banks are not open on Saturdays or Sundays.* Banking hours are 9 AM to 5 PM Monday through Thursday and 9 AM to 6 PM on Friday.

GOLF AND TENNIS PRIVILEGES

Most any commercial motel/hotel property can offer these two amenities because several local golf courses and an indoor tennis center are open to the public. It's important to ask where the facilities are located in proximity to where your reservations are being made, if convenience is a factor. Ask about free passes and discount green fees.

GUARDED BEACHES

Nags Head Ocean Rescue and the Lifeguard Beach Service provide lifeguard service on our beaches from Nags Head to Kitty Hawk. Some areas are not guarded, so be aware if that's a concern to you. Many areas are red-flagged when stormy seas prohibit safe swimming. Pay attention to these flags! Lifeguard stands are located in front of many motel properties and at public beach accesses with adequate parking to ensure a crowd. The areas between the lifeguard stands are patrolled by a four-wheel drive vehicle equipped for rescue. Ask, when you make your reservations, if your particular hotel/motel has a guarded beach if this is important to you.

Members of the Lifeguard Beach Service and Ocean Rescue are specially trained in ocean rescue and are equipped with surfboards and life rings. Listen to their advice: if they say stay out of the water, they have good reason to say so. Believe us, they've seen too many vacations ruined because swimmers thought they could outsmart—and outswim—this Outer Banks surf. See the chapter on Ocean Swimming for more information. Remember, lifeguard service will not be provided by the National Park Service on the Cape Hatteras National Seashore in 1994.

Northern Beaches

When you're vacationing on the northern beaches you're in an area without hotels, motels, or efficiencies and apartments as known on others parts of the Outer Banks. Plans are in the works for a hotel or inn to be developed as part of the Pine Island resort but it could be several years before construction begins.

Visitors to this area are offered an incredible variety of privately-owned homes which we often refer to as vacation cottages. They are almost always leased through real estate property management companies. However, there's the old adage about "an exception to everything" and Sanderling Inn Resort is that exception.

**SANDERLING INN RESORT
AND CONFERENCE CENTER**
NC 12, 1461 Duck Rd.   261-4111
                              (800) 701-4111
$$$$ MC, VISA, DISC

The Sanderling Inn Resort is situated on 12 acres of oceanside wilderness just five miles north of Duck Village. The heavy strands of beach grass, sea oats, pines, fragrant olives and live oaks provide a natural setting for a luxurious vacation. It is one of the most beautiful areas on the Outer Banks. The Inn is built in the style of the old Nags Head beach homes with wood siding, cedar shake accents, dormers and porches on each side. If it has been a while since you've spent time in a rocking chair, on a porch overlooking the ocean or sound, be forewarned—it's been known to cause instant relaxation!

All of the rooms at Sanderling welcome you to comfort and understated elegance. Lounging robes, Caswell Massey soaps and toiletries, complimentary fruit, wine and cheese are provided for guests. A continental breakfast and afternoon tea are also complimentary to guests.

The main lobby and gallery of Sanderling Inn provides a warm welcome to travelers. This area boasts an English country decor mixed with contemporary finishes accented by the mellow tone of polished wood floors and wainscotting. The Inn's main building has 28 rooms complete with kitchenettes in every guest room. Audubon Prints and artwork line the walls of each of the rooms. There are another 32 rooms located in Sanderling Inn North, and rooms here are decorated in beach pastel with wicker furniture. Each of the rooms in the North Inn has a refrigerator and wet bar. All rooms at Sanderling have remote color cable TV, telephones, and some even have complete kitchens. Accommodations are designed for the comfort and privacy of two guests per room, but sleeper sofas and cribs are available at an additional charge throughout the year.

A separate building also houses a variety of excellent conference and meeting facilities including the Presidential Suite, complete with Jacuzzi bath, steam shower and two decks — one overlooking the ocean and the other the sound.

This is a complete resort with lovely beaches as well as a health club with two exercise rooms, indoor pool, separate whirlpool room, locker rooms, saunas, outdoor pool, tennis courts and a natural walking or jogging trail. The nearby Audubon Wildlife Sanctuary and Pine Island Indoor Tennis and Racquet Club provide a wide range of choices for fitness and recreation.

Full package deals are available including New Year's Eve, Valentine's Day, Honeymoons and Winter Escapes. Packages generally include a meal or meals at the Sanderling Inn Restaurant, full use of the health club and indoor pool, welcome gifts and other extras. Some seasonal discounts are available, and no pets are allowed. Wheelchair access is provided to all buildings on the property, and handicapped-accessible rooms are available. The Sanderling Inn is open year round.

The Sanderling Inn Restaurant (covered in detail in our section about North Beach Restaurants) is

housed on the property in a turn-of-the-century lifesaving station, which is open year round.

Kitty Hawk

SEA KOVE MOTEL

Beach Rd., MP 3   261-4722
$$-$$$ No credit cards

Sea Kove is a family-owned-and-operated establishment located on the west side of the beach. Twenty efficiency apartments comprise this older property including 10, one-bedroom efficiencies and 10 two-bedroom efficiencies. Units are basically furnished with full-size kitchens, TVs and air conditioning units, and they rent on a weekly basis. Fisherpersons enjoy staying here during the fall months. Amenities include a playground and in-ground swimming pool. Sea Kove is open April through November.

BEACH HAVEN MOTEL

Beach Rd., MP 4   261-4785
$-$$ MC, VISA

A small motel, right across from its private beach on the beach road, the Beach Haven has five semi-efficiencies located in two buildings that offer a practical, homey atmosphere — something a little bit different than your standard motel room. Items like coffee makers, refrigerators, microwaves, hair dryers and porch chairs are provided. Telephones are not provided in the rooms. Accommodations sleep one to four comfortably, depending on the unit, and the decor reflects a contemporary beach look with rattan furniture and pastel colors. A grill and picnic table are located on the premises, and children

are welcome to play in the yard. Owners Joe and Janet Verscharen live on site to help make your stay here most pleasant. Guests of the motel have referred to it as an, "oasis." Beach Haven is AAA-approved with a three diamond rating. Inquire about off season rates; open April through October.

HOLIDAY INN EXPRESS
Rt. 158	261-4888
MP 4½	(800)836-2753
$$	Most major credit cards

This property is located between the highway and the beach road. It's a short walk to the guarded Kitty Hawk beach, and it has its own outdoor swimming pool. The 98 large rooms provide color cable TV and telephones, and some have couches, microwaves and refrigerators. Most offer queen-size beds and are attractively furnished in a soft beach decor. Nonsmoking rooms and handicapped-accessible rooms are available. The rates are very reasonable, and children under 17 stay free if accompanied by their parents. It is close to shopping and several restaurants. Keeper's Galley is a favorite local restaurant and is on the premises. Meeting rooms are not available. Group rates may apply at this year round resort.

BUCCANEER MOTEL AND BEACH SUITES
Beach Rd., MP 5¼	261-2030
	(800)442-4412
$$	MC, VISA

The Buccaneer is an older, well-maintained, oceanside, family motel. The present owner, Keith Byers, has been here more than 10 years, and the pride of an on-site owner/operator is obvious. Fresh paint, colorful flowers, and a neat, well-cared-for appearance are reinforced by the friendly management style.

While one- and two-bedroom regular motel rooms are offered for the overnight traveler, efficiency apartments from one to four bedrooms are available for those who wish to stay longer. Handicapped-accessible rooms are also offered. Ten percent discounts are offered on all weekly stays. AARP and other discounts are available during the off season. As with many of the older properties, there are no phones in the rooms, but pay phones are on the premises. All rooms are air conditioned with color cable TV and refrigerators.

While the Buccaneer is across the highway from the beach, there are no other buildings between it and the water; you only have to go over a small sand dune and you're at the water's edge. A dune-top deck and private beach access make enjoying the ocean almost as easy as if it were oceanfront. Other things you'll enjoy about this gem of a motel are a large, outdoor, swimming pool with adjoining deck, a children's playground, charcoal grills and a fish cleaning station. The motel is open March through November.

3 SEASONS GUEST HOUSE

Seascape Golf Course	261-4791
	(800)847-3373
$$$	MC, VISA

3 Seasons Guest House is a bed and breakfast tucked away in the Seascape Golf Course on the west side of Route 158 in Kitty Hawk. For golf enthusiasts and fanatics, (you know who we mean) this location is ideal. The putting green is found in front of the property, and the ninth hole is located behind it—a golfer's dream come true.

3 Seasons is located 2½ blocks from the ocean and sits on a hill, so ocean views can be enjoyed by guests. Make no mistake, not all of their guests come here to play golf, many

just come to do what most of us enjoy doing on the Outer Banks — relax!

Susie and Tommy Gardner have been operating 3 Seasons as a bed and breakfast since 1992. This is a five-bedroom house, and four of the rooms are available for double occupancy. Each guest room has a private bath and TV. The decor takes you back home again, it's comfortable and gives you a feeling of being at the beach.

Guests will enjoy the common area with a fireplace, and the Jacuzzi on the deck creates a big splash. Complimentary cocktails are served during the afternoon on the enclosed patio. Guests will also enjoy a full breakfast cooked to order daily between 8 AM and 10 AM. Bicycles are available for a ride to the beach or through trails nearby.

Pets aren't allowed here, and 3 Seasons is not equipped to accommodate children under 18. 3 Seasons is open March through November.

Kill Devil Hills

The town of Kill Devil Hills is centrally located and offers quick access to more shopping facilities and services than any other area on the beach. It appeals to the entire family as a vacation destination. According to the latest Census, Kill Devil Hills also boasts the largest number of year-round residents on the Banks. Family vacationers are attracted to the area in many cases simply because there are so many alternatives for accommodations, shopping and recreation. There is also a wide variety of eateries ranging from fine dining establishments

to fast food chains. Public beaches and sound accesses are plentiful, but keep in mind that they are popular. Getting around may be take a little more time.

THE FIGUREHEAD BED & BREAKFAST
417 Helga St., MP 5½
West of 158   261-2326
$$$$ *MC, VISA*

The Figurehead Bed & Breakfast opened in 1988 and overlooks the sound. Situated on a dune, the three-story house has accommodations on the second and third levels. The Keeping Room provides a common living area and has a fireplace that is perfect for chilly evenings in the off season. The wide porch is a great place to sit comfortably in a rocking chair and watch the sun go down.

A view of the sound awaits guests from the Osprey Watch, a loft room upstairs, which has a private sun deck and Jacuzzi. Sea One, with a private bath, offers privacy for couples or business persons. It is also a partially equipped handicap

room. Smoking is permitted outside only on the decks. The owner of this property does have a cat, but pets are not allowed.

A picnic area for outdoor cooking and dining, complimentary newspapers and soundside access are all part of the charm of this cozy home. Owner Ann Ianni serves a continental breakfast. Soft colors, natural woods and a blend of old and new furniture are used to capture the spirit of seaside living. We consider The Figurehead an excellent option for accommodations, located less than ½ mile from the ocean. Be sure to inquire about off season rates; they're really quite reasonable. Nightly and weekly rentals are available. Some holidays require minimum stays, and it's open year round.

TANARAMA MOTEL APARTMENTS
Beach Rd., MP 6   441-7315
$$$ *MC, VISA, AMEX*

The Tanarama offers 33, one- and two-bedroom efficiencies and two regular motel rooms. This is not a modern motel, but it is very popular with families. Most of the units are oceanfront with ocean views, but there are some located on the west side of the Beach Road. Some of the efficiencies offer two beds and a complete kitchen in one room, while oceanfront efficiencies offer a complete kitchen, living area and a separate bedroom with three double beds. Phones are not provided in any of the units. Guests are invited to use the outdoor, in-ground pool and the Avalon Fishing Pier is on the north side of the motel. It's open March through Thanksgiving.

DAYS INN MARINER MOTEL

Beach Rd. 441-2021
MP 7 (800)325-2525
$$$ Most major credit cards

There are 70 units in this oceanfront property, and 58 of them are located on the ocean. Thirty-three of the rooms offer two double beds, and 37 units are one- and two-bedroom apartments. All have refrigerators, color cable TV and telephones, and each of the rooms has been refurbished in a fresh, contemporary, beach look. Nonsmoking rooms are available. About five years ago, eight one-bedroom efficiency apartments and four motel rooms were built across the road. There's easy ocean access, and the units are big and offer flexible living arrangements for families or groups. The recreation area has facilities for volleyball, and the outdoor swimming pool and showers are right on the ocean. All Days Inn programs are honored, and AARP discounts are available. The Mariner is open mid-February through the end of November.

QUALITY INN SEA RANCH HOTEL

Beach Rd. 441-7126
MP 7 (800)334-4737
$$$ All major credit cards

The Sea Ranch was one of the first resort properties on the Outer Banks to include recreational amenities, a restaurant, lounge and retail shops. This nice oceanfront destination is a family-owned and operated Quality Inn property. A five-story oceanfront tower and a two-story building with 50 motel-style rooms and 28 luxury condominiums compose this hotel. All rooms have color cable TV with HBO, refrigerators, microwaves and phones. Room service is available, which is a rare amenity on the Outer Banks. The apartments have glass-enclosed oceanfront balconies, two bedrooms and two baths. They tend to rent weekly but can be rented nightly, depending on occupancy. Approximately 25 of the hotel rooms are oceanfront with views. Rooms in the west wing do not offer ocean views. Nonsmoking rooms are available.

Amenities include The Top of the Dunes Dining Room and Lounge. The view overlooks the ocean; this is one of the few oceanfront dining rooms on the Outer Banks. (Look for more details in the chapters on restaurants and night spots.) The lounge provides a dance floor and nightly entertainment. And, if you're in the mood for exercise, you'll find a year-round, indoor pool is also located on the premises for your enjoyment. The Nautilus Fitness Center is very popular with locals and visitors. Alice's Looking Glass, a women's boutique, and Shear Genius Hair Salon round out the retail shops. Inquire about duck hunting packages. Its open all year, and the rates are reasonable.

THE CHART HOUSE MOTEL

Beach Rd., MP 7   *441-7418*
$ *MC, VISA*

David and Kristin Clark live in the large brick Colonial oceanfront property and offer a personal touch to their roles as hosts for the 18-unit motel. The Chart House, built in 1966, has become a legend on the Outer Banks and boasts six efficiencies and 12 regular rooms. All rooms offer two double beds, color TV, refrigerators and coffeemakers. The one-room efficiencies have fully-equipped kitchens, and five of them connect to regular motel rooms to accommodate larger groups and families. Nonsmoking rooms are available.

The motel sits perpendicular to the ocean, therefore direct ocean views are not available. A small pool and patio away from the road help to make your stay here enjoyable.

The Chart House is open mid-March through November.

NETTLEWOOD MOTEL

Beach Rd., MP 7   *441-5039*
$-$$ *VISA, MC, Choice*

Locally-owned and operated for nearly 20 years, the Nettlewood is a favorite of the older set who like to come to the beach in small groups and prefer a small, clean motel without extras. There are 22 rooms with one or two double beds and 16 efficiencies with two double beds and complete kitchens located on the west side of the Beach Road. All rooms have remote control, color cable TV and refrigerators. In 1991, the Evanhoffs built four large (1,500-square-foot) condos on the oceanfront across the street that are very popular, offering three bedrooms and two baths, sleeping up to eight. The condos rent weekly, and rates for all units vary seasonally. There is a large in-ground swimming pool on the premises, and they're open year round.

• **367**

HAMPTON INN

Beach Rd.   441-0411
MP 7 3/4   (800)338-7761
$$-$$$ All major credit cards

New ownership of this 97 room, four-story property has produced some fresh upgrades to both the exterior building and guest room areas. The property has exterior and interior corridors with guest-room views ranging from the ocean to panoramic sights of the area including the Wright Brothers National Memorial and Museum.

All guest rooms have microwaves and refrigerators, remote control color TVs, free HBO and private balconies or patios. Twelve of the first floor guest rooms open directly onto the outdoor courtyard and pool. Room choices include single, double and king rooms. Nonsmoking and rooms equipped for the physically challenged are available upon request.

A complimentary continental breakfast is offered daily in the lobby, 6 AM until 10 AM. The meal consists of cereals, pastries, juices, coffee, tea and fresh fruits. Discounts are available to AARP members, and children 18 and under stay free in parent's room. The Hampton Inn is open all year.

COMFORT INN NORTH

Beach Rd.   480-2600
MP 8   (800)854-5286
$$$-$$$$ All major credit cards

One of the newer oceanfront motels on the beachfront, this three-story property has 120 motel rooms in the Comfort Inn style. Some rooms offer refrigerators and microwaves and all have full baths, color cable TV with HBO, phones and a coffeemaker. Nonsmoking and handicapped-accessible rooms are available upon request. Exterior corridors lead you to your room.

The units are filled with light and offer mauve and teal finishes. The building is T-shaped, and not all rooms maintain ocean views. However, oceanfront rooms do offer private balconies.

Guests will enjoy the oceanfront pool, and a hospitality room is available for meetings. Other amenities include a game room and coin-operated laundry. A complimentary breakfast is provided. The Comfort Inn North is AAA-approved, and AARP discounts apply. It's open all year.

CHEROKEE INN BED & BREAKFAST

Beach Rd., MP 8   441-6127
                         (800)554-2764
$$-$$$ MC, VISA, AMEX

The Cherokee Inn Bed and Breakfast is owned by Kaye and Bob Combs. The property was originally operated as a hunting and fishing lodge. We can still picture the feasts that must have taken place here around a grand table near the end of a day almost 50 years ago. It was operated as an Inn during the past 17 years and most recently as a bed and breakfast during the past seven years. Guests will enjoy learning more about the history of this establishment from its proprietors who are second generation surrounded by four generations of family just a short distance away. Six guest rooms are available on the second floor of this three-story building. White wicker and pickled wicker furniture help create a bright homey atmosphere in the rooms and floral accents create a

nice finishing touch. Rooms include private baths, remote color TVs and ceiling fans. Five of the rooms offer a double bed, and one room offers a double and a twin bed. Central heat and air is provided.

The common area is located on the first floor, and guests really enjoy the wraparound porch in the summertime. A continental breakfast is provided, and bicycles are available for your use along with an outdoor shower. The picnic area is popular too. The Cherokee Inn is located on the west side of the Beach Road and is open April through October.

TANGLEWOOD MOTEL
Beach Rd., MP 8¼   *441-7208*
$$$-$$$$ *MC, VISA*

Tanglewood is a small oceanfront motel where the 11 units, on upper and lower levels, are referred to as vacation apartments. Rooms located on the upper level all offer ocean views, while rooms on the lower level are tucked behind the dunes. Each

unit is unique, but all offer a complete kitchen with microwave, refrigerator, color cable TV and a full bath. Rooms do not have phones, but a phone booth is located on the premises. Most units sleep five or six people, and one unit accommodates up to 10. Linens are provided, and maid service is offered midweek for weekly rentals.

Guests will enjoy an outdoor swimming pool, the boardwalk to the ocean with a deck for lounging and an enclosed, outdoor bath house with hot and cold water for relaxing showers after a day at the beach. Other amenities include a fish-cleaning table and picnic tables. Inquire about weekly, daily and off-season rates. The Tanglewood is open March through December.

CAVALIER MOTEL
Beach Rd., MP 8½   *441-5584*
$$-$$$ *MC, VISA*

A variety of rooms is available at this courtyard motel on the oceanfront. Three one-story wings enclose the two swimming pools, volleyball court, children's play area and shuffleboard courts. There are 40 rooms with doubles and singles and six, one-room efficiencies with two double beds and kitchenettes on the oceanfront. Some units offer full baths, while others have just showers. Some of the units have full kitchenettes, but all have refrigerators, microwaves, color cable TV and phones. In addition to these units, there are also 13 cottages that rent weekly; inquire about rates. Pets are allowed in the cottages.

Parking is outside each room, and the covered porch with outdoor furniture is just right for relaxation. An observation deck sits atop the oceanfront section. It's a well-maintained, family-oriented property and is reasonably priced. Port O'Call, a well-known restaurant and lounge on the beach, is opposite the motel and the Wright Brothers Memorial is nearby. The Cavalier Motel is open year round.

Days Inn Oceanfront Wilbur & Orville Wright

Beach Rd., MP 8½   441-7211
Nags Head Beach   (800)329-7466
$$$ *Most major credit cards*

An oceanfront property situated on a wide area of the beach, this Days Inn offers a lot of history from its beginning in 1948. Originally built to resemble an old mountain lodge, it boasts an inviting lobby decorated with the nostalgia of Old Nags Head where guests can read the paper and have coffee. Oriental rugs cover a large portion of the polished hardwood floors, and the fireplace is large enough to take away the chill of cold mornings at the beach in the off

season. Visitors enjoy balconies with old-time furniture and nice views. A shipwreck is located just north of the building, attracting off-the-beach divers or snorkelers.

All 52 rooms have been renovated and brought to 1990s decor. There are singles, doubles, kings, king suites and efficiency suites for six with a living room, adjoining bedroom and complete kitchen. All rooms have telephones, color cable TV and refrigerators. Oceanfront rooms also have microwaves. Nonsmoking rooms are available. There are interior and exterior corridors, and suites have interior and exterior entrances.

A complimentary continental breakfast is available throughout the year. Hot cider and popcorn are served around the fireplace during the winter months, and lemonade and cookies are served in the summer. This Days Inn has a large, outdoor, seasonal pool and sun deck, volleyball court, barbecue pit for cookouts and a boardwalk to the beach. The Days Inn is centrally located, and it's open year round.

Ocean Reef - Best Western Hotel

Beach Rd.   441-1611
MP 8½   (800)528-1234
$$$$ *Most major credit cards*

The 70 one-bedroom suites of this newer oceanfront hotel are decorated and arranged like luxury apartments with a contemporary beach decor. The views are great, and you'll find everything you need for a truly luxurious vacation at the beach. Each room has color cable TV, phones and a fully equipped galley-style kitchen. There's even a

double vanity in the bath area. Non-smoking rooms and handicapped-accessible rooms are available.

Upper-floor rooms have private balconies overlooking the ocean. Some first floor units open onto the oceanfront pool and courtyard, while others offer a private patio. One of the few properties on the beach to have one, the penthouse suite boasts a private Jacuzzi and rooftop deck. There is a heated, seasonal outdoor pool and a whirlpool located in the courtyard. The exercise room has the latest equipment and a sauna. You'll also find a laundry facility on the premises. During the summer season, bar and food service is available in the deli, which features sandwiches, salads, a raw bar, checkers and a dart board. Ocean Reef is open all year.

COLONY IV MOTEL

Beach Rd.	441-5581
MP 9	(800)848-3728
$$$	Most major credit cards

This modern family-owned and operated beach motel is very well maintained and offers lots of amenities. Managers Cindy and Tom Kingsbury, of the Neal family's second generation, provide a good deal of hospitality for moderate prices on the oceanfront here in Kill Devil Hills. Amenities include an outdoor pool and patio, nine-hole miniature golf course, two picnic areas with grills, a children's playground, a dune-top gazebo, game room, horseshoes and other outdoor game areas. A complimentary continental breakfast is served every morning. Laundry facilities are also available for your convenience.

There are 87 units, and 14 of the rooms are efficiencies. All of the units offer two double beds, (one has a king-size bed), phones, refrigerators and microwaves. Some rooms have direct access to the beach, while others have a small balcony overlooking the beach. The efficiencies have an eating area and, when combined with adjoining rooms, they create a good arrangement for family vacationers. The motel is open February through November.

BUDGET HOST INN

Rt. 158   441-2503
MP 9   (800)Bud-Host
$$-$$$$ All major credit cards

This motel is located on Route 158 rather than the Beach Road. The two blocks to the ocean are manageable, and the 40 rooms are all well-furnished and maintained. Rooms have either king-size beds or extra-length double beds, color cable TV, phones and tub/showers. Refrigerators and microwaves are not available in the rooms, but there is a staff refrigerator and a microwave located in the lobby. Nonsmoking rooms and handicapped-accessible rooms are available. The motel also offers two "Family Rooms" that sleep six to eight people comfortably. A conference room accommodates up to 30 people. The property maintains an indoor heated pool for year-round use, and a small picnic area is under construction to the south of the motel. Pets are accepted, and cribs are free. Inquire about discounts; it's open year round.

RAMADA INN HOTEL

Beach Rd.   441-2151
MP 9½   (800)635-1824
$$$-$$$$ All major credit cards

This five-story, 172-room hotel was built in 1985 and is located on the oceanfront. A resort hotel/convention center, it is very popular for tour groups and small meetings. Most rooms have been refurbished, are standard with air conditioning/heat and are nicely furnished. All have a balcony or patio, color cable TV with pay-per-view movies, a small

refrigerator and microwave. A rare thing on the Outer Banks, room service and help with the luggage are both available. Nonsmoking and handicapped-accessible rooms are available too.

Meeting facilities are centrally located on the third floor overlooking the ocean. Several meeting rooms or suites are available to fit a variety of needs.

For guests, the enclosed swimming pool is located just off the second floor, atop the dunes and surrounded by a large sun deck. A flight of steps takes you onto the beach where volleyball is popular. Guests will also enjoy the heated whirlpool and an oceanfront gazebo. Food and beverage service is available at the Gazebo Deck bar, adjacent to the pool.

"Peppercorns" is the name of the hotel's fine oceanview restaurant that serves breakfast and dinner year round and offers lunch on the deck during the summer. If you enjoy hotel accommodations rather than motels or rental cottages, you'll enjoy the Ramada Inn year round.

HOLIDAY INN

Beach Rd.   441-6333
MP 9½   (800)843-1249
$$$$ All major credit cards

Located on the oceanfront, the 105 rooms of this resort property have been recently remodeled, and you'll enjoy a visit here. The ocean views are spectacular. The banquet and conference facilities have been expanded and can accommodate 10 to 300 people. You'll want to take advantage of the seasonal, outdoor pool and Jacuzzi, and outdoor, oceanfront bar. All rooms offer re-mote-color cable TV and phones, and some offer microwave/refrig-erators. This Holiday Inn has a non-smoking floor. Madeline's, the full-service restaurant and lounge, of-fers Top-40 and Beach Music. The restaurant specializes in traditional Outer Banks seafood, and the lounge is usually open 9 PM to 2 AM. There's no cover for the mature crowd in the lounge. You'll find this a good place to stay. It's open all year.

TANYA'S OCEAN HOUSE MOTEL

Beach Rd., MP 9½   441-2900
$$ Most major credit cards

Tanya's is an Outer Banks leg-end with its unique, individually designed rooms called "Carolina Collection Rooms." The story goes that Tanya Young and a designer friend decided to do a theme room at the motel, and it got out of hand, resulting in a different design for each room. There's Carolina Party Room, Jonathan Seagull's Nest, and so on. No two rooms are alike. There are 43 rooms including a few "nor-mal" rooms, if you prefer. One room has a waterbed. All are ocean side and have a refrigerator and color cable TV with HBO. They tend to be small but very clean. All oceanfront rooms offer microwave/refrigera-tors. Some ocean views are avail-able, but they aren't panoramic be-cause of the high dunes. There aren't any balconies. Vacationers will be sure to enjoy the outdoor pool sur-rounded by picnic tables with um-brellas. The pool is 40 feet long and faces the sun all day. Tanya's is open April through mid-October.

QUALITY INN
JOHN YANCEY MOTOR HOTEL

Beach Rd.   441-7141
MP 10   (800)367-5941
$$$-$$$$ Most major credit cards

This is a nice family hotel conve-niently located on a wide beach that is guarded by the Beach Life-guard service during the summer months. Shuffleboard courts, an outdoor pool and a playground are located on the premises. Affiliated with Quality Inns, it is an older motor hotel, but the main building has been stripped, rebuilt and re-decorated within the past few years. The owners used teal, pink and beige to achieve the contemporary beach look that is so popular now. Renovations continue, and guests of this property will be sure to no-tice the exterior work too. The ex-terior face-lift includes white stucco with teal trim on the entire prop-erty.

There are 107 rooms housed in three buildings, and most of these are doubles. Nonsmoking rooms are available, and they have one handicapped-accessible room. The standard rooms have color cable TV, pay-per-view in-room movies, small refrigerators and telephones. Ten rooms offer microwaves. Five units have fully equipped kitchens, and three rooms include hot tubs. Surf fishing enthusiasts enjoy stay-ing here because of the wide beach. This is a family oriented establish-ment, and children under 12 stay free. You can rent roll-away beds to accommodate extra children. In-quire about package deals. The property is open all year.

Nags Head

The entire Nags Head area is accentuated with rental properties including older, Nags Head-style cottages, timeshare condos, standard motel-style rooms, efficiencies and delightful new beach homes. (We've listed the rental companies that handle rentals of these fine cottages in the Outer Banks Rentals chapter.) The town of Nags Head is not as commercially developed as Kill Devil Hills, and residential development is more spread out. Nonetheless, there are lots of wide beaches just waiting for your enjoyment. A great variety of shopping facilities, restaurants, attractions and recreation is also available here.

CAROLINIAN OCEANFRONT HOTEL
Beach Rd.   441-7171
MP 10½   (800)852-0756
$$-$$$ MC, VISA, AMEX

This is one of the most nostalgic hotels on the Outer Banks. Eighty-eight rooms compose this older oceanfront hotel. The large lobby is reminiscent of the Old Nags Head style with knotty pine panelling and rattan furniture. There are two dining rooms serving breakfast and dinner on the lobby level. Rooms are small and comfortable. All units have phones, color cable TV and air conditioning.

Guests will enjoy the outdoor pool and kiddie pool located on the south side of the hotel. The outdoor oceanfront deck bar is very popular and open daily during the season. The beach around the Carolinian is wide, and you may even stumble upon a volleyball game or two. We recommend this hotel to those of you who are looking for a little nostalgia and basic accommodations without any extras. We can't forget about the Comedy Club, open Monday through Saturday during the season with shows offered nightly. Inquire about packages and weekly rates. The Carolinian is open Easter Weekend through Thanksgiving.

OCEAN VERANDA MOTEL
Beach Rd.   441-5858
MP 10½   (800)582-3224
$$ MC, VISA, AMEX, DISC

A well-maintained oceanfront property, Ocean Veranda offers 16 standard rooms, 14 efficiencies and one honeymoon suite with a king-size, canopy waterbed. Standard rooms are large and have two double beds, AC, refrigerators and color cable TV. Efficiencies have complete kitchens, some with microwaves and can adjoin other rooms to accommodate larger families of up to five people. Rollaways and cribs are available for a small charge. Children younger than age 6 stay free. A small charge for extra persons in the rooms is applicable. All rooms on the second level offer partial ocean views.

Complimentary coffee is offered in the office between 8 and 9 AM. Amenities include an outdoor pool and two gazebos providing comfortable gatherings, a children's playground, picnic area and barbecue. Ocean Veranda is in the midst of everything on the beach and is open January through November.

BEACON MOTOR LODGE

Beach Rd.   441-5501
MP 10 3/4   (800)441-4804
$$ *Most major credit cards*

Quite a few options are available at this oceanfront property for visitors who have a variety of needs while on vacation, whether it's a weekend in spring or fall or a week in the summer. The James' family has owned the Beacon Motor Lodge since 1970. They're oriented towards accommodating families, with one-, two- and three-room combinations ranging from motel-type rooms to efficiencies. There are 47 rooms in all (and two cottages). Nonsmoking rooms are available. Finishes are mauve, turquoise and peach. All rooms are equipped with small refrigerators, phones and color cable TV with remote controls. Many units also have microwaves.

The oceanfront patio accommodates all guests, and the oceanfront rooms open onto a large, walled terrace affording wonderful views of the ocean from early morning until moonrise. Amenities include two children's pools, a large fenced-in, elevated, outdoor pool with tables and umbrellas, a playground, patios with grills, an electronic game room and laundromat. Some provisions have been made for the handicapped, and there is oceanfront ramp access. Inquire about discounts and weekly rentals, and note that credit cards are not accepted for some discounts. AAA and Mobile Travel Guide approved, the Beacon Motor Lodge is open Easter through October.

NAGS HEAD INN

Beach Rd.   441-0454
MP 14   (800)327-8881
$$$$ *Most major credit cards*

This sparkling white stucco building with blue accents and plush, Bermuda lawns is a relatively new addition to the Nags Head motels. It is operated as a family destination and designed for family enjoyment. It is a tasteful contrast to the older Nags Head style cottages nearby. Sunshine radiates through the glass panels of the lobby, and greenery thrives here. The lobby is located on the ground level along with offices and covered parking for guests.

Five-stories high, guest rooms begin on the second floor, and all rooms located oceanside afford panoramic ocean views from private balconies. Rooms located street side do not offer balconies, but the view of the sound from the fifth floor rooms is notable. All rooms have a small refrigerator, color Supercable TV with HBO, phones, individual heaters and a private, full bath. Nonsmoking rooms are available, and there are handicapped-accessible rooms on each floor. The Nags Head Inn also features one suite with adjoining sitting room, wet bar and Jacuzzi. This room makes a perfect honeymoon suite and is very tastefully decorated.

A small conference room with adjoining kitchen/sitting area can accommodate about 30 people comfortably. The heated, all-weather swimming pool is located on the second floor with a deck overlooking the ocean. During the summer months, the glass doors are removed providing a completely wide open lounging and sitting area for your enjoyment. Of course it's nice and toasty in the pool area in the winter months, so don't forget to pack your family's bathing suits; the kids will love you for it. Tour groups are welcome, and rates are seasonal. They're open all year.

SILVER SANDS MOTEL

Beach Rd., MP 14   441-7354
$-$$ MC, VISA

This is one of the few motels not located on the ocean side of the beach road, but it's directly across from beach access. It's a small motel and all 26 rooms have been renovated. Rooms have color cable TV with HBO, refrigerators and air conditioning. Guests are offered either two double beds or one queen-size bed. One handicapped-accessible room is available. The walls are rustic pine, and most of the rooms are furnished with Crate furniture, offering a simple, basic decor. Rooms do not have telephones.

There is also a newer two-story building offering balconies with ocean views from the upper floor. The main building offers 16 units near the outdoor swimming pool. Complimentary coffee is provided for guests. For the location, you can't beat the price. It's open Easter through November.

SURF SIDE MOTEL

Beach Rd.   441-2105
MP 16   (800)552-7873
$$-$$$$ Most major credit cards

This attractive five-story motel is situated right on the oceanfront, and all rooms face north, south and east for ocean views. Some rooms have views of the sound as well. All oceanfront rooms have private balconies and are attractively decorated in soft muted beach tones. Refrigerators, air conditioning, color cable TV and phones are standard, and the honeymoon suites feature king-size beds and private Jacuzzis. Of course, there's an elevator for easy access and handicapped-accessible rooms are available.

The folks are very friendly and can also accommodate you in an adjacent three-story building that offers rooms and efficiencies with either ocean or sound views. If you're in your room for any length of time, you'll be very comfortable.

Complimentary coffee and sweets are provided for early morning convenience, and a friendly afternoon wine and cheese social hour is held for guests. You can choose between an indoor pool and Jacuzzi that is open all year and an outdoor pool for swimming in warm weather. The Surf Side is open all year.

The *Surf Side* boat is available for charter fishing expeditions at the Oregon Inlet Fishing Center. Call Oregon Inlet for reservation information.

FIRST COLONY INN

Rt. 158   441-2343
MP 16   (800)368-9390
$$$$ Most major credit cards

This refurbished landmark hotel of another era has become a favorite for those who like the ambiance of a quiet inn. Its history dates to 1932, when it was known as Leroy's Seaside Inn. The old Nags Head-style architecture of this inn, resplendent

under an overhanging roof and wide porches, has been preserved and now is listed in the National Register of Historic Places. This is as close as you'll come to what it must have been like 61 years ago when the little hotel first opened.

It was during the spring of 1988 that efforts began to save the dilapidated building from demolition. The Lawrence family, with deep roots in the area, felt that the inn was too valuable for the community to lose. The building was sawed into three sections for the move from its oceanfront location to the present site, four miles south, between the highways. It took three years of rehabilitation to return the inn to its original appearance. The interior was completely renovated and now contains 26 rooms, all with traditional furnishings and modern comforts.

The sunny breakfast room is where you will enjoy a complimentary, deluxe continental breakfast and afternoon tea. Upstairs there's an elegant but cozy library with books, games and an old pump organ — a favorite place to read the paper or meet other guests. A great selection of jazz music can also be heard at times throughout the reception area.

Each room is individually appointed in English antique furniture. Special touches such as tiled baths, heated towel bars, English toiletries, telephones, TVs, individual climate control and refrigerators are standard. Some rooms offer wet bars, kitchenettes, Jacuzzis, VCRs and private balconies. Some rooms also have an additional trundle bed or day bed for an extra person. The first floor is wheelchair accessible, and one room is designed for use by the handicapped. Smoking is not permitted in the inn.

Guests are invited to relax at the 50-foot swimming pool and sun deck located behind the inn or to follow the private boardwalk across the street to the oceanfront gazebo. Discounts and group rates apply under certain conditions, and there is a

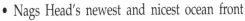

policy of one night free for stays of five week nights or longer. This magnificent inn provides easy access to the ocean and is centrally located to many shops and restaurants in Nags Head. It is open year round.

ISLANDER MOTEL
Beach Rd., MP 16   441-6229
$$$ MC, VISA, AMEX

The Islander is a small, popular oceanfront property. The attractive landscaping and well-maintained rooms help explain its popularity. Most rooms have an ocean view, and some have private patios or balconies. Some of the first floor units do not offer ocean views because they are tucked behind the dunes. The rooms are large and frequently refurbished. All have sitting areas and refrigerators. Some first floor units offer kitchenettes.

Guests will enjoy the pool and private dune walk to the ocean. This property is conveniently located for access to all restaurants, shops, recreational outlets and Nags Head attractions. You'll find the comforts of this attractive motel more than adequate. The Islander is open April through October.

BLUE HERON MOTEL
Beach Rd., MP 16   441-7447
$$$ MC, VISA

This family owned motel provides reasonably priced, oceanfront rooms, a year-round indoor swimming pool, a spa and an outdoor pool. It's considered one of the best kept secrets of the small motels in the area. The Gladden family lives on the premises and gives careful attention to the management of the property. It's conveniently located in the midst of fine Nags Head restaurants and offers plenty of beach to those who come here to relax.

Nineteen rooms offer doubles or kings, and 11 efficiencies provide full kitchens that comfortably sleep up to four. All units are air conditioned and heated. All have refrigerators, coffee pots, color cable TV, phones and shower/tub combinations. One handicapped-accessible room is available. Second and third floor rooms offer private balconies. Weekly rates are offered. The Blue Heron Motel is open all year.

OWENS' MOTEL
Beach Rd., MP 16   441-6361
$$ MC, VISA, AMEX

The Owens family has owned and operated this attractive, historic motel for more than 40 years. It was one of the first motels on the beach. Adjacent to their famous restaurant, this property is well-maintained with care given to maintain its family atmosphere.

A newer three-story oceanfront addition was built about 10 years ago. All oceanfront accommodations are efficiencies with large, private balconies. Each room has two double beds, a tile bath and shower and a kitchen. Air conditioning and color cable TV are also standard in the guest rooms.

The motel swimming pool on the west side of this property offers guests an alternative to the ocean. Easy access to Jennette's Fishing Pier and a comfortable oceanfront pavilion with rocking chairs will also entice you. Owens' Motel is open April through October.

SEA FOAM MOTEL
Beach Rd., MP 16 1/2   441-7320
$$-$$$ MC, VISA, AMEX

Twenty-nine rooms, 18 efficiencies and two cottages make up this attractive oceanfront motel. Efficiencies accommodate two to four people, and cottages sleep up to six comfortably. The efficiencies and cottages rent weekly; inquire about rates. Rooms are tastefully decorated in mauve and green, with some washed oak furniture. All rooms have color cable TV with HBO, refrigerators, microwaves and phones. All are air conditioned, and some have recently been refurbished and have king-size beds. Each of the units has a balcony or porch with comfortable furniture. The one- and two-story buildings provide some units with oceanfront and poolside views.

Children are welcome, and they will enjoy the playground. A large outdoor pool, children's pool, sun deck and shuffleboard are other recreational options. A gazebo is located on the beach for guests' pleasure. Sea Foam Motel is within walking distance of restaurants and Jennette's Fishing Pier. Free coffee is provided until 11:00 AM, and under the Family Plan, children under 12 stay free with parents. Sea Foam Motel is open March through mid-December.

QUALITY INN SEA OATEL

Beach Rd.   441-7191
MP 16½   (800)441-4386
$$$-$$$$ *Most major credit cards*

This year-round Quality Inn has an excellent oceanfront location near restaurants, recreation, shops and Nags Head attractions. Each of the 111 rooms has been completely renovated. The exterior reflects major renovation, and the blue roof is easy to identify. Nonsmoking and handicapped-accessible rooms are available.

It's one of the nicest places on the south end of Nags Head. The front desk is open 24 hours a day, and all rooms conform to the standards of Quality Inn. Color cable TV with HBO and phones are standard. You'll also find a coin-operated laundry, snacks and ice. A sheltered gazebo is located on the beach for your enjoyment. Inquire about Lost Colony packages and other package options. It's open all year.

South Nags Head

We can't forget South Nags Head; this area most closely resembles what the Outer Banks used to be like not so long ago in the north-of-Oregon Inlet region. The area remains more remote because of its location. Families still enjoy vacationing here because, with the exception of a motel or two, there really isn't any commercial development in South Nags Head. But everything you need to make your stay at the beach more enjoyable is only minutes away.

COMFORT INN SOUTH

Beach Rd.   441-6315
MP 16½   (800)334-3302
$$$$ *All major credit cards*

The Comfort Inn South is a seven-story hotel located on the oceanfront in South Nags Head. It is one of the only hotels in this area and is in a residential neighborhood.

Exterior and interior renovations were completed in 1992 when the Comfort Inn acquired this property, and tremendous changes have occurred since then to make guests more comfortable. The exterior consists of a light peach concrete finish with aqua-teal trim giving this hotel a clean, contemporary beach look. The interiors include new carpet, wall coverings and window treatments in each of the 105 rooms. Deluxe oceanfront rooms, oceanside rooms and street-side rooms are available. Oceanfront rooms have magnificent views from private balconies. All rooms have remote color cable TV and phones. Rooms with refrigerators and microwaves are also available. Nonsmoking rooms are offered too. A honeymoon suite with Jacuzzi is popular as are rooms with kings and connecting rooms. Corporate meeting rooms can accommodate groups with up to 450 people.

The hotel is away from busy areas of the beach and affords guests more than typical privacy while staying here. The in-season guest lounge and the outdoor, oceanfront pool and deck are favorite gathering places. Deckside (alcoholic) beverage service is featured during the summer months. Other amenities include a children's pool, game room and playground.

In other words, this oceanfront property holds strong appeal for families and business groups. A deluxe continental breakfast is offered in the lobby. Jennette's Fishing Pier is only a block away. The Comfort Inn South is open all year.

FIN 'N FEATHER MOTEL

Nags Head-Manteo Causeway
Hwy. 64   *441-5353*
$-$$ *MC, VISA*

A favorite small motel along the edge of the water, Fin 'N Feather has 10 units, two of which are efficiencies with fully equipped kitchens that rent by the day or week. It is popular with those who come to the Outer Banks to fish or hunt. If you're planning to come in the fall or spring, make your reservations well ahead of time. Its location, near the Pirate's Cove Fishing Center, will please anyone headed out for a day on the open seas. There's a boat ramp here, too.

The rooms are clean and comfortable with blue and white decor. Large windows open onto the water from either side and afford stunning views. Most of the rooms have two double beds, and there are no phones or microwaves. Rooms do have heat/air, and most are equipped with refrigerators. It's open April through October.

Roanoke Island

Roanoke Island's accommodations are conveniently located for the enjoyment of all the island has to offer. None of the motels or inns is considered to be out-of-the-way, but some of them do require a walk or a bike ride to popular waterfront destinations. The inns are all notable, and there are standard motel-style rooms too. Rental cottages are not really in demand here because Roanoke Island is more typical of a year-round community. In any case, you will be sure to enjoy historical attractions, shopping, a variety of restaurants, live theatrical performances and more — lots more!

THE ELIZABETHAN INN

Hwy. 64   *473-2101*
(800)346-2466
$-$$$ *Most major credit cards*

The Elizabethan Inn is a full-resort facility on the main highway in Manteo with spacious shaded grounds, and it's only seven miles from the beach. Roanoke Island is the only spot in America that has a historic tie to that great Elizabethan age of Queen Elizabeth I, Sir Walter Raleigh, Shakespeare and their legendary peers. This inn honors that heritage with its quasi-Tudor architecture and country manor charm.

Contained within four distinct buildings of this comfortable hotel, are 100 rooms, efficiencies and apartments, conference facilities, a restaurant, a health club and a gift shop. Nonsmoking and handicapped-accessible rooms are available. All rooms have color cable TV with HBO, refrigerators and direct-dial phones. Rooms are available with a king-sized or two queens as well as standard double beds. Two deluxe rooms have Jacuzzi baths. Though the rooms in the original building are smaller than those in the Center Court, Elizabethan Manor or Nautics Hall sections, all are com-

fortable and well suited for a quiet, Roanoke Island-style vacation.

There's a restaurant on the premises, specializing in Seacoast Cookery that serves three meals daily. The restaurant offers a full menu, buffets and banquet facilities for small and large groups. The registration lobby is filled with interesting antiques, and a friendly staff welcomes you to the historic ambiance of Manteo and the inn. A small gift shop offers a selection of fine gifts plus local books, souvenirs and sundry personal needs.

The Nautics Hall Fitness Center, located here, is the largest and most complete health club in the area and is available for guests of the Inn.

As you might expect, it's a big draw. There are two pools — one outside and the other, competition-size and heated, located indoors. A full range of equipment for intense workouts awaits you. For a more detailed description of the health club facility, see the write up under Recreation for Roanoke Island. Inquire about special packages. The inn is open all year.

ROANOKE ISLAND INN
305 Fernando St.   473-5511
$$$ Most major credit cards

This white clapboard building offers the atmosphere of a gracious, restored home with the comforts of a small, well-designed inn. The furnishings are homey yet handsome and reflect genuine care by the inn-keeper. The ambiance is laid back and friendly. There's an eight-room addition that was designed for the privacy of the guests. Each room has its own private entrance, private bath, TV and phones, and there are bikes for touring. There's an inter-esting collection of books and art-work related to the Outer Banks in the lobby, and a light breakfast is offered in the butler's pantry.

The grounds, situated on the wa-terfront in downtown Manteo, are private and comfortable adorned gardenia and fig bushes and other native plants. The pond out back provides "nature's music" to soothe and relax guests. You'll enjoy a stay here. The inn opens sometime in the spring, usually around Easter, and closes when they get tired.

SCARBOROUGH INN

Hwy. 64   473-3979
$-$$ Most major credit cards

Located across from the Christ-mas Shop, this small inn is a delight-ful, friendly place to stay. A native of Manteo, owner Sally Scarborough long dreamt that she would have an inn someday. When her husband, Phil, a native of Wanchese and former Coast Guard officer, retired, her vision became a reality. With the help of designer-architect John Wil-son, IV (who, by the way, owns and designed the beautiful Roanoke Is-land Inn), Sally modeled her two-story inn after a turn-of-the-century inn. Each of the guest rooms is filled with Victorian and pre-Victorian an-tiques, not reproductions, and other furnishings. Most furnishings were

refinished by Sally, and a good num-ber of them were family heirlooms.

There's a story behind every room and its eclectic mix of fur-nishings. Sally creates a casual, com-fortable atmosphere with these sto-ries, and the attention to detail in each of the rooms can't go without mention. Antique sewing machines, expertly refinished, serve as TV stands. Some doors have been sal-vaged from an old church, and the king-size beds with lace canopies are beautiful. Each of the six rooms at the inn is located away from the street and has two double beds, color cable TV, phones, private baths, small refrigerators and cof-fee pots. Donuts are delivered to your room in the morning. You will find little extras like tile baths, ce-dar in the closets and marble-top dressers. Each of the rooms located in the two-story building of the inn opens onto a covered porch, and all rooms have exterior entrances. The four rooms in the Annex provide two suites with two separate rooms and two smaller rooms, all of which are tastefully furnished. One of these is handicapped-accessible. The Barn offers guests two king rooms that are light and airy. Each of these six rooms offers wet bars, double vanities and a small storage space for kitchen utensils and mis-cellaneous items.

Complimentary bicycles are available, and there's a glider swing in the back yard. Travelers will ap-preciate the care and attention given by the owners. Your stay here will be most pleasant. It's open year round.

DUKE OF DARE MOTOR LODGE

Hwy. 64 473-2175
$ *MC, VISA*

Located on the main street, but only a few blocks from the Manteo waterfront, this small motel provides the essentials for basic accommodations. The L-shaped motor inn has clean rooms and standard features, including full baths, color cable TV and phones. Most rooms have double beds. Handicapped-accessible rooms are available. An outdoor pool is located on the property for your family's enjoyment.

The Creef family has owned and managed the motel for almost a quarter of a century. Shopping is close by. This is an inexpensive, family-oriented motel. It is open all year.

TRANQUIL HOUSE INN

On The Waterfront 473-1404
(800)458-7069
$$$$ *All major credit cards*

This 25 room country inn is located on Shallowbag Bay. A visit here will accommodate your desire for privacy and comfort. It's modeled after an old hotel that stood in about this same place from just after the Civil War until the 1950s. Rooms are on three floors, and all are individually decorated in a charming inn style. Although the inn looks authentically turn-of-the-century, it is only six years old, so all modern conveniences are included: TV with HBO, telephones and private baths. Two of the 25 rooms are one-bedroom suites on the second floor that feature a queen bed, a separate sitting room with a sleeper sofa, two TVs and a kitchenette. Large rooms on the third floor are loft rooms with high ceilings. Nonsmoking rooms are available, and there is one handicapped-equipped room. A ramp to the first floor makes rooms on that level accessible to all. You'll feel welcomed by the hospitality and fine surroundings.

The spacious second-floor deck facing east to the bay opens to sights of waterfowl and the *Elizabeth II* sailing ship that docks across the way.

• **385**

Shops along the Waterfront are only a few steps away. A marina is located just out the back for those who would prefer to arrive by boat.

A unique breakfast and dinner restaurant, 1587, is new to the inn and offers gourmet delights and an extensive selection of wines. Another feature is a fully appointed conference facility available for groups on an hourly or daily basis. Bicycles are free for guests of the inn, available on a first-come, first-serve basis. Inquire about special packages. Tranquil House Inn is open all year.

DARE HAVEN MOTEL

Hwy. 64   473-2322
$ MC, VISA, AMEX

This small motel located toward the north end of Roanoke Island is a favorite place for fishing enthusiasts and families. If you plan a charter from the waterfront, Wanchese or Pirate's Cove, there's enough room here to park your own boat and trailer. Families planning on attending the Lost Colony or visiting any of the other Roanoke Island attractions and historic sites of Fort Raleigh will also find this location very convenient. The motel is close to the beaches and other Outer Banks attractions.

The 26 motel-style rooms have telephones, heat and air. Accommodations are very basic, clean and comfortable. Most are decorated in the traditional Outer Banks style with paneled walls, and porches extend all the way around the building. All rooms are located on the first floor. This is a small, economical, family owned and operated motel. It is open all year.

Wanchese

C.W. PUGH'S
BED AND BREAKFAST

Old Wharf Rd.
Wanchese   473-5466
$$ MC, VISA, DISC

This charming house is more than 100 years old and is situated next door to Queen Anne's Revenge (reviewed in the section on Restau-

rants). It's in the process of being completely restored. There are four rooms, three of which are ready for use. There are baths on the first and second floors, a parlor and a seating area for a complimentary full breakfast. Antique furniture and some reproductions are used throughout. One of the rooms will accommodate three people, two adults and a child.

The spacious lawn is appealing for those who like some elbow room, and the winding lanes of Wanchese are perfect for bicycle rides. It's situated near the end of the road where, at one time, Mr. Pugh was a lighthouse keeper, at Marshes Light, a house built on pilings out on the water. His duty was to help keep the channel waters open for passing ships in an area where shifting sands and numerous vessels came into the harbor. Now there is an electric light out on the sound these days. Nancy Gray, whose husband Wayne Gray is one of the operators of Queen Anne's Revenge restaurant next door, has managed the bed and

breakfast accommodations here for six years. Jim and Don Beach, the other restaurant owners, continue their work in restoration.

In a country setting, not far from historic Manteo or the beach, this is a good choice for those whose number one requirement is quiet and relaxation. It's open Easter through Thanksgiving.

Hatteras Island

Accommodations on Hatteras Island offer vacationers clean, well-kept rooms, efficiencies and, more recently, bed and breakfasts. The need for luxurious accommodations can be filled mostly with rentals of upscale vacation cottages. Make no mistake, there are plenty of luxurious oceanfront cottages for rent on Hatteras Island, but motel-style accommodations tend to appeal to those who are trying to get back to the basics—a great stay at the beach without a lot of extras or frills. Generally, rooms are clean and simply

furnished, but that doesn't mean that refurbishing doesn't take place on a regular basis or that rooms aren't decorated in a contemporary beach look. You'll find a lot of "moms and pops" but we find them quite appealing. "Independents" work hard to attract the kind of repeat business they've achieved on Hatteras Island.

Swimming pools are common amenities, but you won't find an array of other amenities because, for one thing, people who visit this part of the beach seem to want just that — the beach. Many are avid fishing enthusiasts or enjoy surfing, windsurfing, sailing, beachcombing or just relaxing at the ocean.

Rodanthe

HATTERAS ISLAND RESORT

Rodanthe	987-2345
	(800)331-6541
$$	MC, VISA, AMEX

This is a large oceanfront resort in a two-story building that includes 28 motel-type rooms with two double beds, dressing rooms and showers and 14 efficiencies featuring queen beds with full kitchens. Each of the eight oceanfront rooms and efficiencies offer ocean views. A second building behind the dune offers ten motel-type rooms as well.

The 25-acre oceanside property also has 35 two-, three-, and four-bedroom cottages arranged in clusters. Cottages rent weekly; inquire about rates. All units have color cable TV and are comfortably furnished. Phones are not available in the rooms, but pay phones are conveniently located on the premises.

Families will enjoy the outdoor, oceanfront swimming pool, kiddie pool, large patio area, volleyball and basketball. The Hatteras Island Fishing Pier is right out front on the Atlantic, and it draws a lot of people to the resort. The motel is open April through November.

AN OCEANFRONT INN

- *Indoor swimming pool • Jacuzzi*
- *Private oceanfront balconies*
- *Restaurant on premises*

P.O. Box 557 • Avon, NC 27915 • Telephone (800) 845-6070

Avon

THE CASTAWAYS

Avon	995-4444
	(800)845-6070
$$-$$$	MC, VISA, AMEX

Bea and Chappy Chaplin took over ownership here a couple of years ago. The 68 rooms occupy five floors. All rooms have wet bars, refrigerators and private balconies. Microwaves are available upon request. Only first floor rooms do not offer ocean views because they are tucked behind the dunes. Nonsmoking and handicapped-accessible rooms are available. Meeting and conference facilities accommodate up to 200 people.

Amenities here include a heated, indoor, competition-size swimming pool and Jacuzzi. The wide, unspoiled beaches at the Castaways are beautiful and perfect for swimming, sunbathing and beach recreation. A boarded walkway leads you across the dunes and onto the beach, where you will enjoy this retreat at the sea.

The restaurant is attractively decorated in a tropical island motif. The ambiance works here and makes it easy to get into a real vacation mind set. The pace is leisurely, and the restaurant offers a popular breakfast buffet that attracts visitors and locals. It's open 7 to 11 AM in the spring and closes in December. Inquire about packages. The Castaways is open year round.

Buxton

CAPE HATTERAS MOTEL

Buxton	995-5611
$$$-$$$$	MC, VISA, AMEX

When you arrive in Buxton, you'll see the Cape Hatteras Motel situated on both sides of the road. Owners Carol and Dave Dawson have maintained this motel, some parts of which have been here for more than 30 years. After the storms of '91 and '92, we happily report that at least six of the dune motel rooms will be available for occupancy this year. The 30 efficiency units have great appeal for those who love to

• **389**

fish, surf, windsurf and just enjoy the beach on Hatteras Island.

Efficiencies sleep up to six comfortably. They offer doubles as well as queens and kings. All of them have full kitchens. Some newer and more modern townhouses and efficiencies are located on the ocean. These units attract windsurfers who enjoy some of the best conditions on the east coast at nearby Canadian Hole. Guests also enjoy an outdoor swimming pool with spa. Efficiencies rent weekly, but nightly rentals may be available depending on supply. The owners of Cape Hatteras Motel know what guests need to make their stay enjoyable, and they try to provide just that. Restaurants are close by, making this a very popular place in season. Book reservations early; Cape Hatteras Motel is open year round.

OUTER BANKS MOTEL

| Buxton | 995-5601 |
| $-$$ | MC, VISA, AMEX |

Located next door to the Cape Hatteras Motel, this motel offers 11 motel-style rooms, six efficiency units and 17 two- and three-bedroom cottages. Units accommodate anywhere from one to nine persons comfortably. Eighty percent of the units provide an ocean view. Rooms and efficiencies offer enclosed, sliding window porches with screens, perfect for evenings outside listening to the ocean. The motel-style rooms are pine paneled and offer full, tile baths, phones, microwaves, toasters and small refrigerators. Efficiencies have fully-equipped kitchens. All units offer air conditioning and color cable TVs. Phones are not provided in the efficiencies or the cottages.

The Dillons also have 14 additional cottages in the village of Buxton, one mile from the ocean in the area of Connor's Market. Because these units are not oceanfront, rental rates are lower. These cottages are clean and simply furnished, and they provide the basics for accommodating family vacationers.

There's a coin-operated laundry, fish-cleaning station and a guest freezer for storage of that big catch. If you enjoy soundside crabbing, there are several row boats for your use without charge. There's even a library in the office in case you want to grab a good book on your way to the beach!

With the particularly wide beaches in Buxton, this motel is always filled with satisfied guests. This is a good choice, but be sure to book early. It's open year round.

LIGHTHOUSE VIEW MOTEL

Buxton	995-5680
	(800)225-7651
$$-$$$	MC, VISA

Lighthouse View is located on the curve in the road in Buxton. The 69 units include a choice of motel rooms, efficiencies, duplexes, villa units and cottages. Most units are oceanfront, and all are oceanside. (The rate guideline above pertains to motel rooms.) Rooms offer color, cable TV, phones, full baths, air conditioning and daily maid service. Efficiencies accommodate three to six people and are equipped with complete kitchens. The oceanfront villas of-

fer private balconies on the oceanside and on the soundside, so you can enjoy sunrises and sunsets. The six new oceanview duplexes offer two decks and sleep up to six people each. Efficiencies and villas rent on a weekly basis but, supply permitting, they can be rented nightly. Cottages are rented by the week only. Efficiencies, duplexes, villas and cottages are fully furnished and have linen service — linens can be exchanged, but daily maid service is not provided. Handicapped-accessible rooms are available.

The Hooper family has been serving vacationing families for more than 35 years. With all this in mind, it's safe to say that the variety offered here will turn up something to meet your needs. An outdoor pool and hot tub are also contained in this well-maintained complex. Lighthouse View Motel is open all year and very convenient for surfers, windsurfers and fishing enthusiasts.

FALCON MOTEL

Buxton	995-5968
	(800)635-6911
$-$$	*MC, VISA*

We've looked at many motels and, in our opinion, The Falcon offers some of the best-priced accommodations on the Outer Banks, if you're looking for traditional Outer Banks-style rooms. This motel appeals to quiet, family oriented guests who appreciate moderate prices, accommodations with character and the peaceful environment of Hatteras Island. The style is reminiscent of some older beach motels along the coast, and that means sturdy, light-colored brick, white trim and larger-than-average rooms with adjoining baths and a wide, covered porch with wooden deck chairs for relaxing. Rooms here are all on one level.

The motel includes 35 units with 30 rooms and five fully equipped apartments. Nonsmoking rooms are available. (The rate guideline above pertains to the rooms because the apartments rent mostly on a weekly basis.) Rooms have a light-airy feel; they're well maintained. Color cable TV with HBO and heat and air are standard, and many rooms have refrigerators and microwaves. Parking is right outside your door.

You'll find a shaded picnic area with barbecue grills amidst mature oak trees away from the road. They've added martin-houses, blue bird houses and have planted shrubs and flowers that attract the local bird population. There is a swimming pool and boat ramp on the premises as well. An osprey platform is located on the soundside area beyond the trees. Falcon Motel is owned by Doug and Anne Meekins. Anne exudes friendliness to everyone, especially those in search of family lodging who have an interest in birding and the overall environment of Hatteras.

The Falcon Motel is located in the heart of Buxton within easy walking distance to several restaurants and shops; Diamond Shoals Restaurant is right across the street. The beach is only a short walk away. You'll enjoy your stay here. It's open March through mid-December.

COMFORT INN

NC 12   995-6100
Buxton   (800)432-1441
$$$ All major credit cards

The Comfort Inn is the newest hotel on Hatteras Island. It is located in the heart of Buxton, close to the beach and shops. The 60 units with exterior access include standard motel-style rooms and mini-efficiencies — no suites. All rooms have color cable TV with HBO, refrigerators and direct-dial phones.

Mini-efficiencies offer microwaves as well. Rooms are finished in soft, beach colors. Nonsmoking and handicapped-accessible rooms make this property attractive to visitors of the island.

The management and staff welcome their guests to this comfortable motel and give attention to all the details of your visit. A complimentary continental breakfast is served in the greeting room or lobby. Guests will enjoy the heated swimming pool. The gazebo and the three-story watch tower provide panoramic views of the ocean, the sound and nearby Cape Hatteras Lighthouse.

Comfort Inn of Hatteras Island offers special vacation packages, has ample parking for boats and campers and is open year round.

TOWER CIRCLE

Old Lighthouse Rd.   995-5353
$ No credit cards

This small motel is located on Old Lighthouse Road off Highway 12. It's the closest motel to the Cape Hatteras Lighthouse. There are 30 units including 13 rooms with two double beds and 17 apartments. Accommodations sleep anywhere from one to six people comfortably. It's an older brick veneer property that has juniper paneling in its modestly furnished rooms. Color cable TV and heat and air conditioning are offered in all of the units, and each unit opens onto the porch. Motel-style rooms do not offer microwaves or refrigerators, and there are no phones in any of the units. Apartments all have complete kitchens; some have two bedrooms; some are

two-room efficiency apartments. All linens are furnished for the apartments, and fresh linens can be delivered.

You'll enjoy your visit here. The Grays have owned the motel for 21 years and treat their guests like old friends, which many of them are. Many people return here. Guests sit on the porch, swap stories and enjoy the homey atmosphere.

Tower Circle is open April through November, and it's just a short walk over the dune to the beach. We think it's an ideal place to stay if you're into surf fishing.

SURF MOTEL

Old Lighthouse Rd.   995-5785
$-$$$ MC, VISA

It's only a 1 1/2-block walk to the ocean from this motel managed by Bea and Jack Goldman. The Surf Motel is popular with surfers (of course), windsurfers, anglers and family vacationers. Four motel-style rooms, eight efficiencies and one apartment are located here. The

rooms offer doubles and singles; the efficiencies sleep two or four comfortably and have full kitchens; and the apartments, featuring two separate bedrooms and 1½ baths, are popular with families up to six people. Rooms were newly carpeted last year, and the decor is a traditional Outer Banks style with wood-tone panelling.

Amenities include an outdoor, enclosed hot and cold shower, horseshoe pit, barbecue grills, fish-cleaning stations and a freezer for your daily catch. There is a handicap ramp. Daily maid service is provided. The Surf Motel is open March through December.

CAPE HATTERAS
BED AND BREAKFAST

Old Lighthouse Rd.   995-4511
                                 (800)252-3316
$$ MC, VISA

This bed and breakfast opened in April of 1992 and is popular with windsurfers, surfers and couples who just want to get away. The owners are

both windsurfing enthusiasts — they can't get enough of the Outer Banks. The two-story building houses five rooms. All are nonsmoking rooms located on the first floor, and each has its own entrance opening onto a covered porch that runs the entire length of the building. Two of the rooms offer two double beds; two rooms have one queen-size bed; and there is one efficiency unit. All rooms have color, cable TV and private baths. Refrigerators, microwaves and phones are not provided. However, the efficiency does provide a small separate bedroom with a double bed and double sleep sofa, range oven, refrigerator, eat-in area and a full kitchen. It sleeps two to four people comfortably. You'll find the beach decor combined with traditional furnishings makes these rooms comfortable and interesting.

Amenities include a common dining and living area upstairs where a complimentary full breakfast is served, color cable TV, VCR, stereo and a small library. Outdoor showers appeal to guests. Beach gear, bicycles, sailboards and lockable storage is available. Daily maid service is provided, and weekly rentals are available. It's open year round, but we recommend that you call after November to be sure.

CAPE PINES MOTEL

Buxton   995-5666
$ MC, VISA, DISC, Diners Club

Steve and Hazen Totton have owned this property since 1988, and, along with their daughter and son-in-law, they rolled up their sleeves and put a fresh face on this motel. Cape Pines is located ½ mile south of the Cape Hatteras Lighthouse in the center of Buxton. It maintains a strong appeal for those who favor traditional, one-story motels with private, exterior entry to each room.

The 26 motel rooms offer AC/heat, color cable TV and full baths. Most of the rooms have been refurbished and feature new furniture for a contemporary beach look. Microwaves are available for rent.

Guests will also find three apartments offering separate bedrooms, living room and full kitchens. The apartments rent on a weekly basis only during the summer season.

Stretch out and relax around the pool and the lawn. You'll also find picnic tables and charcoal grills. Fish-cleaning tables are nearby, and there's a pay phone on the premises. The grounds are very well maintained, and parking is convenient. Cape Pines Motel is open year round.

Hatteras Village

DURANT STATION MOTEL

Hatteras Village   986-2244
$$$-$$$$ MC, VISA

Durant Lifesaving Station is tucked just behind the dunes near the ocean and serves as a focal point for this condo motel. This property offers one motel room and 29 apartments, which are individually owned and furnished. The one-, two- and three-bedroom apartments rent weekly or nightly depending on availability. Each of the apartments is comfortably furnished. The motel room rents nightly only. Linen service is provided; towels are exchanged daily; and linens are available upon request.

The Lifesaving Station has been refurbished, but some trappings of those early times have been retained. The lookout room, several flights up, offers a glimpse of what it must have been like to live here and be a part of the lifesaving service. This large building has three interconnecting apartments with ample privacy for individual guests, or they can be used for a large family reunion. The motel caters to families during the summer season and to fishing parties in the off season. Partial handicap facilities are available. Durant Station is open early spring through November.

SEA GULL MOTEL

Hatteras Village   986-2550
$$ MC, VISA

This is a well-maintained motel situated about 125 yards from the ocean. The high dunes, while protective, prevent direct ocean views. Guests will find a variety of accommodations including 35 motel-style rooms, six apartments and four efficiencies offering fully equipped kitchens. Handicapped-accessible rooms are available upon request. The motel rooms rent nightly, and the apartments and efficiencies rent weekly with three-day minimums. Rooms are large and comfortable and offer one double, two doubles or two twins. Color cable TV and AC/heat will make your stay more enjoyable, but you won't find phones, refrigerators or microwaves.

Most nights you can just raise the window and catch the ocean breezes! If the beach isn't enough, amenities include an outdoor pool, a wading pool for the children, picnic tables, grills and fish-cleaning tables. A few shops are within walking distance, and Gary's restaurant is just across the street serving three meals daily. One of the nicest things about this motel is its spacious grounds and walkway to the beach. The atmosphere is friendly. Sea Gull Motel is open March through November.

GENERAL MITCHELL MOTEL

Hatteras Village   986-2444
                       (800)832-0139
$-$$ MC, VISA, DISC

Named for Billy Mitchell, of the U.S. Air Service who directed the sinking of two retired battle ships off Hatteras to prove the potential of air power, this 30-year-old motel is typical of smaller motels built to accommodate fisherpersons who don't need a lot of extras. The rooms are clean and comfortable and do not face the ocean. The two buildings house 33 motel-style rooms and 15 efficiencies. The motel rooms offer color cable TV, AC/heat and two double beds. You won't find phones, refrigerators or microwaves. The efficiencies provide full kitchens, and some have mini-kitchens. There is a two-day-minimum rental period for the efficiencies.

Amenities include an outdoor pool and Jacuzzi, and a short walk brings you to the beach. Avid anglers will appreciate the freezer for the storage of surf catch. This motel caters to the fishing and hunting crowd and is located on the left as you enter Hatteras Village from the north. General Mitchell Motel is closed January and February.

ATLANTIC VIEW MOTEL

Hatteras Village   986-2323
$$ Most major credit cards

The office of Atlantic View is close to the main road, but the motel itself is located down a paved lane. The beach is just a few minutes away. Twenty motel rooms and eight efficiencies await you and your family. The rooms are larger than most standard size rooms, and accommodations are fully carpeted providing two double beds, color cable TV and AC/heat. Efficiencies have fully-equipped kitchens for your convenience. Handicapped-accessible rooms are available upon request. Phones are located near the office. High dunes prevent ocean views.

This is a particularly nice place for families. Guests and their children will enjoy the play area, in-ground swimming pool, smaller kiddie pool, volleyball nets, basketball goal and free bikes. Shankie and Donna Peele own the Atlantic View. They cater to small families, but some rooms connect to accommodate larger groups. For a family on a tight budget, this motel is a good choice. The Atlantic View is open year round.

HATTERAS MARLIN MOTEL

Hatteras Village   986-2141
$-$$ MC, VISA

Hatteras Marlin Motel is owned and operated by the Midgett family and located within sight of the harbor fishing fleet, restaurants and shops. The 40 units are located in three buildings and consist of standard motel rooms and one- and two-bedroom efficiencies. Two new two-bedroom suites, which have been built near the back of the property and away from the road, offer a combined living, kitchen and dining area. (The older buildings near the road share parking with Midgett's gas station and convenience store.)

The newest building is situated along a canal. You'll often see ducks waddling around in the grassy areas of the yard. All rooms are well-maintained and have color cable TV and air conditioning. Only the two new suites have phones. Accommodations sleep one to six persons comfortably and rent weekly or nightly depending upon demand. There's an in-ground swimming pool and sun deck awaiting you. Hatteras Marlin Motel is open all year.

Ocracoke

Ocracoke's accommodations include motel rooms, efficiencies, inns and cottages that range from basic, clean and comfortable to some of the most luxurious nightly accommodations found anywhere on the Outer Banks. We think no trip to the Outer Banks is complete without a trip to this quaint and charming island. It was of particular interest to discover that proprietors here have been able to successfully provide visitors, both individuals and families, with wonderfully updated accommodations while still maintaining the subtle charm this island retreat is known for.

BERKLEY CENTER

Ocracoke   928-5911
$$-$$$ No credit cards

Two buildings, situated on three acres, house this nine-room bed and breakfast on the Ocracoke Harbor. The Manor House, originally built in 1860, was remodeled in 1950. The Ranch House dates from the mid-'50s, but the architecture and cedar exterior create an impression of age and quality. Both buildings are furnished in reproduction antiques. All interior walls, floors and ceilings of the Manor House are made of hand-carved wood panels of redwood, pine, cypress and cedar.

Berkley Center is adjacent to the Park Service and Ferry Dock but away from the congestion that one might anticipate from seasonal visitors. The grounds are comfortably surrounded by trees. A complimentary continental breakfast, consisting of fresh breads, fruits, preserves and coffee, is available in the breakfast room of the Manor House. A guest lounge is also located here and offers the only television you'll find; this a real opportunity to get away from the hustle and bustle of everyday life. It's also not uncommon for guests to relax and enjoy the company of owners Ruth and Wesley Egan, Sr. He is better known as "Colonel," having retired from the United States Air Force.

All rooms are spacious and have been furnished in classic fashion, most with private baths, double sinks and a large closet. Two sets of two rooms share a large bath, ideal for a family. Phones are not provided in the rooms. Berkley Center is open April through October.

PRINCESS WATERFRONT MOTEL

Ocracoke   928-6461
$$$ MC, VISA

Situated on the edge of Silver Lake, the Princess Waterfront Motel is an older building, but very typical in appearance of Ocracoke Village. The first floor of the building features retail shops, and the second offers spacious efficiency apartments for adults.

Opened in 1988 and owned by Scott and Kathy Cottrell, the six units are equipped with a full kitchen, phone, remote-control, color cable TV with Showtime and modern furnishings. Since the building sits perpendicular to the waterfront, not all rooms have a full view of the harbor. The private dock is at the end of the parking lot. Guests have pool privileges at The Anchorage Inn across the street. It's open year round.

ANCHORAGE INN AND MARINA

Ocracoke   928-1101
$$$-$$$$ MC, VISA

The Anchorage Inn overlooks Silver Lake and the village; it's really like a small resort offering accommodations, a marina and fishing center, recreational amenities and gift shops nearby. An attractive red brick building with white trim, it was expanded from its original three floors to five in recent years. An elevator provides access to each floor.

If you arrive in Ocracoke via the Cedar Island Ferry, the Anchorage Inn is visible amidst the booms, masts and lines of the ships in the harbor. Entering the village from the main road, it's situated on Silver Lake one block before you reach the ferry terminals.

Accommodations here offer some of the highest views available of the harbor and Ocracoke Village and are especially nice from all upper floor rooms. All rooms have some view of Silver Lake Harbor. The fourth floor is a nonsmoking floor, and each of the rooms has a king-size bed. The motel-style rooms offer full baths, direct dial phones, AC/heat, and color cable TV with the Movie Channel.

The Anchorage Inn offers complimentary continental breakfast. A private pool with a sun deck is situated on the harbor and is available for all guests. You will also enjoy the gazebo out over Silver Lake for watching early evening sunsets. A boat dock and ramp are located on the premises for the convenience of boating enthusiasts. Most guests are able to walk to restaurants, shops and the historical sights on Ocracoke Island. Bike rentals are available. Windsurfing equipment can be rented and fishing charters, which depart from the dock across the street, can be booked from the Inn receptionist or from your room. The motel is open year round.

PONY ISLAND MOTEL

Ocracoke   928-4411
$$ MC, VISA

Located at the edge of Ocracoke Village and away from the Silver Lake Harbor, the Pony Island Motel offers 31 rooms, nine efficiency units and five cottages in a quiet setting. The grounds are spacious, and for nearly 20 years owners David and Jen Esham have been hosts to families and couples in search of solitude. The Pony Island Motel is more than 30 years old but offers comfortable, air conditioned and heated accommodations that sleep one to five people with ease. Each room has color cable TV with Showtime, and efficiencies provide fully-equipped kitchens. Rooms are constantly being refurbished but do maintain a more traditional decor with paneled walls.

The motel is within walking distance of the Ocracoke Lighthouse and other island attractions. Bike rentals are available. The large pool, deck, picnic tables and lawn offer plenty of elbow room for family activities. The Pony Island Restaurant, a locals' favorite, is right next door. The motel is open March through November.

EDWARDS MOTEL

Ocracoke   928-4801
$ MC, VISA

This older motel, located away from the center of Ocracoke and off the main route, near The Back Porch Restaurant, consists of eight motel rooms, three efficiencies and two cottages all in one area. The 13 units have screened porches, AC/heat and color cable TV, and some open onto a veranda. Phones are not available in any of the units. The cottages rent weekly, and the efficiencies require a three day minimum. The rate guideline above pertains to the nightly rentals of the motel rooms only.

The Edwards Motel has been in the same family for 25 years. Ruth and David Sams bought it from Ruth's sister Mary and her husband Bernie Edwards. They offer inexpensive accommodations in a familial setting with a carefully landscaped green lawn, flower beds and pine trees. The motel is open Easter through mid-November.

BLUFF SHOAL MOTEL

Ocracoke   928-4301
                               (800)292-2304
$$ MC, VISA, DISC

This small, seven-room motel is located on the main street of the village. All rooms are comfortable and have private baths and small refrigerators. The rooms have been refurbished with new carpet and paneling; every room opens onto a long porch. All rooms have color cable TV with Showtime. Bluff Shoal Motel is close to everything and across the street from The Pelican Restaurant. The post office, community store and many shops in the village are within walking distance. Owners Mike and Kay Riddick keep their property open all year.

PIRATE'S QUAY

Ocracoke   928-1921
$$$$ MC, VISA

Jo Everhart manages this extraordinary hotel that sits directly on Silver Lake across from the Coast Guard Station. One of the newer properties, it opened in 1987 and may provide some of the most luxurious accommodations available on a nightly basis anywhere on the Outer Banks. The hotel is made up of six individually owned condo suites, each with living room, dining room, full kitchen, two bedrooms and a bath-and-a-half. Units on the top floor have cathedral ceilings. Two decks off each suite, a waterfront gazebo and docking facilities make the most of the harborfront location.

Each condo suite accommodates four adults and children and has a Jacuzzi, color cable TV with Showtime and central air conditioning. All are beautifully furnished, and kitchens are completely stocked with all the dishes and cookware and gadgets you need. Each unit's decor is based on the taste of the owner.

An additional feature is the laundry, right on the property and available for your use. Pirate Quay's proximity to the village makes walking or biking manageable, and it's open year round.

THE ISLAND INN

Ocracoke   928-4351
$$-$$$ MC, VISA

The Island Inn, owned by Cee and Bob Touhey since just before the 1990 season, provides a variety of accommodations for adults and families with children. Originally built as an Odd Fellows Lodge in 1901, the main building has served as a school, a private residence and naval officers' quarters. It was restored by former owners and has been recognized in *Country Inns of the Old South*, and *County Inns, Lodges and Historic Hotels of the South*.

The owners had their first date on Ocracoke Island and vacationed here for many years. They have returned to live and work, and the refurbishing of many of the 35 rooms reflects their preferences in the style of this romantic, country inn. There are rooms and suites located in the main building. All are furnished as a separate guest room in a private home with antiques and quilts, providing a restful ambiance for guests.

The rooms and suites for adults only accommodate a wide range of needs.

Across the street, a much newer 19-unit, double-decked structure includes two honeymoon rooms with king-size beds and bay windows affording views of beautiful sunsets over Silver Lake. Families with children will find the casualness of the accommodations a welcome retreat. The inn also has a two-bedroom cottage for rent and a swimming pool that stays open as long as weather permits. Color cable TV with free Showtime is available in every room. The inn is open all year.

OSCAR'S HOUSE

Ocracoke   928-1311
$$ MC, VISA

Oscar's House was built in 1940 by the Ocracoke lighthouse keeper and was first occupied by the World War II Naval Commander for the Ocracoke Naval Base. Stories abound about Oscar, who lived and worked for many years on the island as a fisherman and hunting guide.

This four-room bed and breakfast guest house is located on the main road and is managed by Ann Ehringhaus, a local fine art photographer and the author of *Ocracoke Portrait.*

The house retains the original beaded-board walls. An upstairs bedroom and loft create a comfortable setting for guests. All rooms are delightfully furnished. You won't find private baths, but sharing is easily managed. The large kitchen with a big table is available to guests; however, the stove is off limits. Ann serves a complimentary full breakfast to all guests and will gladly adhere to special preferences for vegetarian or macrobiotic meals. Smoking is allowed on the back deck only.

In addition, Oscar's house offers an outdoor shower, dressing room and a deck area complete with barbecue grills. Meals can be eaten outdoors. Oscar's House is within walking distance of all shops and restaurants in the village, and bicycles are free for guests. Ann will also gladly transport guests to and from the Ocracoke Airport, which is open to single and twin engine planes. This bed and breakfast is open April to October.

motel-style rooms. Rocking chairs line the wide upper and lower decks fronting all rooms and provide nice places to read and relax. The lobby accommodates a comfortable reading area as well and offers the visitor a house selection of books to borrow. Guests will enjoy the coffee bar with complimentary coffee in the mornings.

Each room has a private bath and remote color cable TV with Showtime, and some of the rooms have a refrigerator. Ten of the rooms have two double beds, and the other two offer one double bed. The 12 units located on the first floor have ramp access, and wheelchairs will fit through the doors to the rooms. Improvements are always being made here to assure that guests are comfortable.

A sun deck at the back of Boyette House is perfect for sunbathing. If you'd like to be picked up at the boat docks or the airport, this can be arranged, free of charge. The motel is open most of the year, but its best to call ahead during the winter months just to make sure. It is within walking distance of Silver Lake and the restaurants in Ocracoke. Look for 12 new units in 1995.

BOYETTE HOUSE
Ocracoke   928-4261
$$ MC, VISA

Lanie Boyette-Wynn and her son, who is third generation on Ocracoke, preside over this very pleasant motel that opened over 14 years ago. The atmosphere is one of a quaint bed and breakfast, although the 12-unit, two-story wood structure is a comfortable motel offering

SILVER LAKE MOTEL
Ocracoke   928-5721
$$ MC, VISA

Silver Lake Motel is situated in a grove of trees along the main street of Ocracoke Village. The Wrobleski family built the two-story, 20-room motel in 1983 and have added another building since then. The wooden structure, with long porches and rooms paneled in California redwoods, has become well-known for its rustic appeal and comfort. Most of the furniture in the older rooms was built by the owners, and the rooms have wooden shutters, pine floors and wallpapered baths that create an informal, restful atmosphere. New curtains and bedspreads update the look of these units.

In the newer building, there are 12 suites with private porches overlooking the lake and hammocks and wicker furniture. A variety of accommodations is available. Rooms adjacent to these suites can be opened to allow for larger families. Suites offer living rooms and full kitchens. They also have wood floors and wallpapered baths, and Victorian furnishings and wall coverings provide a very tasteful decor. End units have their own seven-foot-across Jacuzzi, designed for relaxation while looking out over Silver Lake. Handicapped-accessible rooms are available. All of the rooms have color cable TV with Showtime and are heated and air conditioned. A common area located on the second floor of the main building, serves as a dining room and lounge.

The Silver Lake Motel offers families comfortable and attractive rooms, and for those who arrive by boat, a deep water dock is provided. It is open year round.

HARBORSIDE MOTEL
Ocracoke   928-3111
$$ MC, VISA, AMEX

This charming motel is located across from Silver Lake Harbor on the main street of the village. Its 18 rooms are well-kept and comfort-

able. There are four efficiencies available. All rooms have color cable TV, and guests can use the waterfront sun deck, docks and boat ramp across the street. Nonsmoking rooms are available.

Harborside has its own newly remodeled gift shop with a wide selection of clothing, books, gourmet foods and small gifts. Other shops and restaurants of Ocracoke Village are within walking distance. The Swan Quarter and Cedar Island ferry docks are close by as well. This property has been owned by the same family since 1965, and its hospitality and service are well-established. All rooms are refurbished on a regular basis, which is the true mark of caring for the comfort of guests.

A complimentary breakfast of homemade muffins, coffee, juice and tea is provided. They also have bikes with baby seats for your pleasure. Harborside is open Easter through mid-November.

BLACKBEARD'S LODGE
Ocracoke   928-3421
                    (800)892-5314
$-$$$$ MC,VISA

Barbara Martin and her family have owned and operated Blackbeard's Lodge for 12 years now. This two-story motel is located on the Back Road right across the street from The Back Porch Restaurant.

This is a family-oriented property with a wide variety of accommodations to suit almost anyone's needs. There are 36 units which accommodate anywhere from two to 10 people, and all of the units feature private baths, air conditioning units and color cable TV with

THE HARBORSIDE MOTEL
"On Ocracoke Harbor"

Motel Rooms & Efficiencies * Continental Breakfast * Cable T.V.
Showtime * AAA, AARP, and Senior Discounts * Boat Ramp, Docks,
Large Sundeck overlooking Harbor * Refrigerators all rooms* Bike
Rentals * In the heart of the Village * Close to Cedar Island and
Swanquarter Ferries*

Harborside Motel– P.O. Box 116, Ocracoke, N.C. 27960
(919) 928-3111 or (919) 928-4141

 # THE HARBORSIDE SHOP

While on Ocracoke visit The Harborside Shop which features *
Unisex Sportswear for adults & children * Quality Gifts * Ladies
Apparel & Accessories * Gourmet Foods * Cards & Books

Showtime. Linen service is provided for each of the 36 units, and maid service is daily. Ten of the units are efficiency apartments, some offer adjoining rooms. All of the apartments offer fully equipped kitchens (no microwaves). The remainder of the 26 rooms include suites, a room with a waterbed and a refrigerator and rooms with Jacuzzi bathtubs, king-size beds and wetbars.

Some units may require a minimum stay of three nights. Units rent nightly and weekly. Amenities include a seven-foot deep above-the-ground pool and bicycle rentals. Pets are not allowed. Ask about group rates and special rates for school trips. Blackbeard's Lodge is open April through October.

EUGENIA'S BED AND BREAKFAST
Ocracoke   928-1411
$$ *MC, VISA*

Proprietor Jean Fletcher lived in Swan Quarter for about 20 years before retiring from teaching and relocating to Ocracoke. Jean, or Eugenia, moved to Ocracoke five years ago and has been operating her bed and breakfast for three years now. This establishment is furnished with antiques and collectibles and offers three guest rooms. Two of the rooms offer double beds, and one room offers two three-quarter beds. Each of the rooms has a private bath, and the house is equipped with central heat and air conditioning.

Guests will enjoy a full breakfast including homemade breads, jams and casseroles. Breakfast is served daily at 8:30 AM. The lounge attracts guests who like to relax or watch television. The porch swing and rocking chairs are the perfect places to reflect upon your Ocracoke vacation. Eugenia's is located on the southside of Cafe Atlantic as you enter town. The airport is only ½ mile away and the shuttle/van service is free. Eugenia's is open March through October.

SHIPS TIMBERS

Ocracoke   928-4061
$$ MC, VISA

This small but historical bed and breakfast is located in the center of Ocracoke Village on an oyster-shell lane just off the main road across the street from The Community Store. The house is more than 75 years old and was built of timber from the *Ida Lawrence*, a ship that washed ashore on Ocracoke beach in 1902. It is included in the National Register of Historic Places.

Owner Erik Mattsson, who is well-known in these parts for his special interest in water sports, caters to guests who enjoy kayaking, sailing and windsurfing. The three air-conditioned rooms and a shared bath and a half are a popular place for families. The hospitality on and around its large porch and yard make this bed and breakfast more lively. Weekly rentals are available.

A full, healthy breakfast is served. Package rates are available. Ships Timbers is open April through October.

Inside
Camping

The Outer Banks is an ideal place to camp out under the stars and listen to the ocean all night long. Long ago, there were campgrounds up and down the islands, and this simple, unencumbered way of "life at the beach" was very popular. However, some sites have closed, and much land has been developed since then. Camping is available in Kitty Hawk, Colington Island, Manteo, along the Cape Hatteras National Seashore, in the villages of Hatteras Island and on Ocracoke Island. A few campgrounds do have permanent residents, but they also offer some convenient spaces for transient campers. The campground facilities are either managed by the National Park Service or are privately owned. Owners and managers of the campgrounds all agree, it is best to reserve in advance for campsites during the summer months, especially July and August!

All National Park Service campgrounds on the Outer Banks operate under a common policy and charge the same fees, except for the Ocracoke campground that is on the "Mistix" Reservation System between Memorial Day and Labor Day each year. (See Ocracoke campground for details.) Each of the other NPS campgrounds accepts cash only upon entrance to the camping area. Reservations are not accepted; entry is handled on a first come, first served basis. You can call the NPS, 473-2111, for information on any of their campgrounds located on the Outer Banks. We suggest that you call for opening and closing dates too, because they change from year to year. The National Park Service Campgrounds are scheduled to open one week before Memorial Day weekend this year, and they will close immediately after Labor Day weekend.

The National Park Service will be unable to open one of their campgrounds in 1994 due to budget cuts. Salvo Campground and Frisco Campground will be closed to all campers during 1994. Oregon Inlet, Frisco, Cape Point and Ocracoke Campgrounds will be open May 20 through September 6 during the 1994 season.

The National Park Service would also like to inform visitors to the Cape Hatteras National Seashore that they will not be able to provide guarded beaches in this area. Please note this change for you and your family's safety.

Photo: N.C. Travel and Toursim

Tons of folks come to camp on the Outer Banks.

North of Oregon Inlet

COLINGTON PARK CAMPGROUND
Colington Island   441-6128
No Credit Cards

Colington Island is close to the beach but is more closely related to the quiet, calm waters of the sound. This campground is heavily wooded, and summer camping is very pleasant. It was originally designed as a tent camp. You will still find more tent sites than RV sites, but the sites have been converted to accommodate recreational vehicles too. There are 55 sites, all with water, power and picnic tables. Hot showers, toilets, a laundry, grocery and playground are on the property as well. Rates begin at $15 per night for one camper or one tent with two people. A $2 per night additional fee for air conditioning is imposed. Lots of fishing and crabbing opportunities are nearby.

The campground is open year round and is located on Colington Road past Billy's Seafood Market.

JOE & KAY'S CAMPGROUND
Colington Island   441-5468
No Credit Cards

The 70 sites here are rented on a yearly basis, but there are also 18 tent sites and two additional sites with water and electric hookups available for transient use. The rates average $10 to $15 a night with a $2 a night charge for electricity and water, and $2 a night for extra people. Entrance to this campground is on a first-come, first-served basis. Joe & Kay's offers a reasonably priced, cool shady site — a nice place for family camping. Crabbing is nearby. Joe & Kay's is located on the left side of Colington Road just before you cross the first bridge. This campground is open April through November.

OREGON INLET CAMPGROUND (NPS)

Bodie Island   473-2111

Several National Park Service camping areas are located along the Outer Banks and Oregon Inlet offers 120 sites. The sites are along the flat, sandy, windswept shores of the island. Turn east before you cross the Bonner Bridge. This is close to primitive camping. You won't find utility connections, but water, cold showers, modern toilets, picnic tables and charcoal grills are available. Dumping stations are located nearby. The NPS recommends that campers bring awnings or other materials for shade. You may need mosquito netting and long tent stakes for this sandy area. Fees begin at $11 per night. Oregon Inlet is open from mid-spring till mid-fall on a first-come basis. Call for opening and closing dates.

Manteo

CYPRESS COVE CAMPGROUND

US 64   473-5231
                              MC, VISA, DISC

An in-town campground, Cypress Cove is located behind Hardee's Restaurant on the edge of town. This is a year-round, family-vacation campground. Amenities include a playground, basketball court, horseshoes, nature trail and a stocked fishing pond (bass, brim and catfish); no fishing license is required. Hot showers and rest rooms are conveniently located. The campground is wooded, so there's plenty of shade from the afternoon sun. There are a total of 60 sites; 27 are tent sites; and 33 accommodate RVs. Rates are sea-

sonal. Tent sites begin at $15 a night and RV sites at $17 a night. Additional charges apply for cable, $1 a night, and sewer hookups, $2 a night. Six fully furnished trailers or "Kamper Kabins" are available for rent; in season rates begin at $35 a night for one or two people. And, if that's not enough to choose from, there are 12, two- and three-bedroom "mobile home efficiencies" that sleep four to six people. Rates begin at $65 a night for a two-bedroom and $75 a night for a three-bedroom.

Hatteras

The campgrounds here are spacious and offer some of the best out-under-the-stars living along the East Coast. If you are a tent or trailer camper you'll love Hatteras Island.

Some Hatteras Island campgrounds are located on the oceanside where there is abundant open space, flat sand, plenty of sun and wind and no shade. Sunscreen and long stakes are essential. Other campgrounds are located in the middle or on the soundside of the island amidst stands of pine and live oaks. These sites offer firmer ground, more shade and less wind. Mosquito control is being well-managed, but you'll find them (or they'll find you) in warm weather along the soundside wooded areas. Know your pesky critters such as chiggers, ticks and mosquitoes, and decide if their presence will put a damper on your mood. If you're a veteran camper, you'll know how to deal with them!

CAMP HATTERAS

Waves   987-2777
                         MC, VISA, AMEX, DISC

This 50-acre, world-class campground is a complete camping facility. It has nightly and yearly campsites with full hookups, concrete pads and paved roads. A natural area is available for tents and everything else you'll need while camping. With 1,000 feet of ocean frontage and 1,000 feet of sound frontage, three swimming pools, a club house, a pavilion, a marina, fishing, two tennis courts, a nine-hole miniature golf course, volleyball, basketball, shuffleboard, picnic tables and grills, there is no need to go any farther for family recreation. The grounds are extraordinarily well-kept and more organized than most campgrounds. Its sports and camping areas are separated. If you're looking for a top-notch camping experience under the wide open skies and close to other Outer Banks attractions, this one comes highly recommended. During the course of the year, rates for full hookups range from $19 per night to $31 per night, and rates for tents range from $17 per night to $24 per night.

CAPE HATTERAS KOA

Rodanthe   987-2307
                                    MC, VISA

This large campground offers 269 sites with water and power and 66 sites with sewer connections. It's located 14 miles south of the Bonner Bridge across Oregon Inlet.

You'll find lots of amenities here: a dump station, laundry, two pools, Jacuzzi, playground, game room, restaurant, "Kamping Kabins," a well-stocked general store and a full time recreation director in the summer. The ocean is just over the dunes for fishing and swimming. The 200-foot soundside pier is perfect for fishing, crabbing or just sitting and enjoying evening sunsets. A soundside swimming area is also nice for smaller folks. Rates vary according to the time of year, but in-season rates for two people begin at $25 per night for water, $27 per night for water and electric and $30 per night for a full hookup. In-season rates for "Kamping Kabins" begin at $37.50 per night for a one-room cabin and $47.50 per night for two rooms. These are not fully furnished; they come with beds only. Cape Hatteras KOA is open March 15 through November.

NORTH BEACH CAMPGROUND

Rodanthe   987-2378
                 Most major credit cards accepted

North Beach is in the village and right on the ocean. The 110 sites, all with water and power, offer ideal camping facilities. Hot showers, toilets, picnic tables, a laundry and a grocery store are all here, and the sea just over the dunes. Rates begin at $14.50 a night for tents and $16.50 a night for full hookups. This campground is south of Chicamacomico Lifesaving Station. The Rodanthe Fishing Pier is only ¼ of a mile up the road, so the location is ideal for all you fisherpersons! This campground is open March through November.

OCEAN WAVES CAMPGROUND

Waves   987-2556
                                    MC, VISA

Families have been camping in Waves, at Clyde and Carolyn

Every once in a while it's necessary to rinse off the sand.

Bullock's place, since 1985. This campground is located oceanside and offers 64 spaces with full hook-ups, 25 of the sites are concrete paved. Conveniences include three bathhouses, hot showers and a laundromat. Guests will enjoy the game room, picnic tables and an outdoor pool. Rates for a family of four (two children under 12), begin at $16.50 per night for a full hookup and $11.50 per night for a tent site. The cost for cable is $2 per night. Plenty of ocean fishing and swimming nearby will keep the entire family happy. Ocean Waves is open March 15 through November and is located off of NC 12 in Waves.

SALVO CAMPGROUND (NPS)
Salvo   473-2111

Salvo Campground will be closed to all campers in 1994 due to budget cuts.

Salvo Campground is a very large, flat soundside camping area with 90 sites. It is the only soundfront campground on the Outer Banks run by the NPS. The fee is $10 a night. You'll find rest rooms, potable water, cold showers, grills and picnic tables. For windsurfers, sound access adjacent to this area is available for day use. Plan on dealing with mosquitoes. Remember, reservations are not accepted.

KINNAKEET CAMPGROUND
Avon   995-5211
                                          MC, VISA

Avon is another small village on Hatteras Island that has seen enormous growth in the past few years — they've added a traffic light and a supermarket! The soundside campground is off NC 12 and is geared toward trailers and mobile homes. It has 53 full-hookup sites and 15 tent sites. Every site has a picnic table, access to hot showers, toilets and electricity. Rates for two people begin at $12 a night year round for full hookups and $10 a night for tents. The cost for additional persons is $5 a night. A dump site is available. Reservations are recommended.

SANDS OF TIME
Avon   995-5596
Off NC 12 on Harbour Rd. and N. End Rd.

In its second year of operation, this Avon campground is open year round and maintains 15 full hookups, 56 trailer sites with sewer and electric, 36 sites with water and 20 tent sites. You will also find a pay phone, flush toilets, hot showers, laundry facilities and dump sites. Pets with leashes are allowed, and families will enjoy volleyball, horseshoes and picnic tables. Rates for tent sites are $15 a night in season and $13.50 a night during the off-season. Rates for full hookups are $18 a night in season and $16 a night during the off season. The cost for cable is an additional $2 a night.

CAPE WOODS CAMPER PARK
Buxton   995-5850
Back Rd.   MC, VISA

One hundred twenty five camping sites are located here on the southern side of Buxton: 25 are tent sites; 30 sites have electric and water; and 70 sites come complete with full hookups. This is a good example

of the forested camping areas located in the middle of the island. Most sites have shade as there are tall stands of poplar, pine and live oak trees. Cape Woods offers freshwater fishing in a series of canals running around the perimeter of the campground. Ocean fishing is nearby. Amenities include an outdoor swimming pool, playground, volleyball site, horseshoe pit, basketball court, picnic tables and two bathhouses, one of which is handicapped equipped. In season rates for a family of four begin at $14 a night for tents, $16 a night for water and electric and $20 a night for full hookups. The charge for cable is $2 a night. Inquire about monthly and seasonal rates. Cape Woods is open March through December 15.

STOWE-A-WAY
Buxton   995-5970
Back Rd.   MC, VISA

This is one of the smaller campgrounds on Hatteras Island. There are 30 campsites with full hookups and 10 tent sites. You'll find a bathhouse with hot showers and flush toilet. There's a picnic table at every site. Fishing for bass and blue gill is permitted in the freshwater pond. Rates for two people begin at $15 a night for full hookups and $13 a night for tents. The campground is located on Buxton's back road, just around the corner from the Centura Bank. Stowe-A-Way is open year round, weather permitting.

CAPE POINT CAMPGROUND (NPS)
Cape Hatteras   473-2111

Cape Point is the largest of the Park Service's campgrounds on the Outer Banks. It's also one of the wildest! Utility connections are not available, but there are flush toilets, cold showers, drinking water, charcoal grills and picnic tables. The 203 sites are located behind the dunes on the southwest face of The Point. Paved access to the site is provided. It's a short walk to the ocean, and for surfers, this campground is located about two miles from the best surfing spot on the Atlantic, the Buxton Lighthouse. Bring netting to fend off mosquitoes, awnings for shade and long tent stakes for the sand. The fee is $11 a night, and like most other NPS campgrounds, it's generally open from mid-spring to mid-fall on a non-reservation basis, but call for dates. A handicapped area is also available and dumping stations are located nearby.

FRISCO WOODS CAMPGROUND, INC.
Frisco   995-5208
                                   MC, VISA

This 30-acre campground is one of the best, and it is located in Frisco Woods. Developed by Ward and Betty Barnett, the soundside property boasts abundant forest and marshland beauty. There are at least 300 sites: 90 are tent sites; 150 offer electricity and water; and 35 are full hookups. An in-ground swimming pool, picnic tables, hot showers, small country store, propane gas and

public phones are all available for your fun and convenience.

Frisco Woods is a favorite amongst campers because of its natural setting. You'll enjoy good crabbing and soundside fishing and virgin forest for long walks. If you like semi-wild, basic camping, this is the place. It's also very popular with the windsurfing crowd because you can sail right off the site. In season rates for two people begin at $16 a night for tent sites, $16 a night for electric and water and $21 a night for full hookups. Cable is $2 a night. The cost for each additional person is $3 a night, and pets are welcome. Frisco Woods is open March through November.

FRISCO CAMPGROUND (NPS)
Frisco   473-2111

Another National Park Service campground, this one is located on the southern side of the island about four miles past Buxton on Highway 12. It's on the beach and is open Memorial Day to Labor Day. There are 127 no-frills sites. It's one of the more isolated campgrounds and definitely for those who like their camping away from civilization! A 14-day limit is imposed, and the fee is $11 a night payable at the entrance on a first-come basis. For your use are flush toilets, cold water outdoor showers, drinking water, charcoal grills and picnic tables. Frisco Campground can accommodate about 800 people.

HATTERAS SANDS CAMPING RESORT
Hatteras Village   986-2422
                                   MC, VISA

This well-maintained campground is located close to the ferry

Photo: Mary Ellen Riddle

A red-winged blackbird takes in the view.

dock on the back road in Hatteras Village, and it's a 10-minute walk from the ocean. There are 62 sites with water and electricity, 41 sites with full hookups and 15 tent sites. Three camping condos furnished with beds (water and electricity available outside), and some pull-through sites are also available. The two, full-facility bath houses have received the highest rating *Trailer Life* has to offer, a 10/10. Needless to say, these are some clean bath-houses!

An Olympic-size pool, game room and mini mart will surely meet your needs. A canal winding through the resort provides crabbing and fishing for the family. Hatteras Sands is also within easy walking distance of the village shops and restaurants. In season rates for two people begin at $21.50 per night for tents, $25 per night for water and electricity and

$28 per night for full hookups. Camper condos range from $30 per night to $45 per night depending upon the season. Some special rates and a 10 percent discount are available for Good Sam Park. Hatteras Sands is open March through November.

Ocracoke

TEETER'S CAMPGROUND

Ocracoke   *928-3511, 928-5880*

Teeter's is located near the heart of Ocracoke Village, next to the British Cemetery. There are nine full hookup sites, 16 with electricity and water and 10 tent sites. Year-round rates for two people begin at $12 a night for tents, $15 a night for electric and water and $20 a night for full hookups. Campers will appreciate the trees and lush, green grass at this campground. Hot showers are available, and a picnic table is located at every site. Self-contained units are welcome year round, but as soon as it gets cold enough for water to freeze, the grounds are closed to others.

BEACHCOMBER
Ocracoke   *928-4031*
                            MC, VISA

The newest campground in Ocracoke, Beachcomber is located less than a mile from Silver Lake and the nearest beach access. The campground has 29 sites with electricity and water and six tent sites. Rates for two people begin at $12 a night for tents and $15 a night for electric and water. Hot showers and fully-equipped bathrooms are available. Pets are required to be on a leash. Beachcomber is open April through October, depending on the weather. Reservations for May through August are recommended.

OCRACOKE CAMPGROUND (NPS)
NC 12, east of town

This campground is composed of 136 campsites on the oceanside of Ocracoke Island. No utility hookups are available, but there are cold showers, a dumping station, drinking water, charcoal grills and flush toilets. A 14-day limit on stays is imposed at this campground.

We suggest bringing awnings,

netting and long tent stakes for use in the sand to provide strong grounding against the high winds that sometimes blow across this area. In fact, out here on the island, there is almost always a breeze, but there are insects too, especially in summer months. The campground is sparsely vegetated and only three miles from the village.

Ocracoke is the sole NPS campground on the "Mistix" reservation system. From Memorial Day weekend to Labor Day you must either write Mistix Corporation at P.O. Box 85705, San Diego, CA 92186-5705, and include a check or money order, or call (800) 365-CAMP. Be prepared to provide the operator with your campground request. MC, VISA and DISC are accepted. Always be sure to verify your reservations. The rate is $12 per night between Memorial Day and Labor Day. During the off season, reservations are not available. Entry to the campground is on a first-come, first-served basis, and the rate is reduced to $11 a night.

Camping out on an island is often included in our dreams of getting away from it all. Camping out *here* gets right to the heart of the matter. This campground offers the most penetrating isolation of the Outer Banks!

Happy Camping!

THE ONLY COUNTRY ON THE BEACH
CAROLINA 92 FM

WNHW, the only station on the Outer Banks offering a mix of modern, traditional and cross-over country music, with CNN and local news, sports, weather, fishing information, beach conditions, community promotions, tourist information, and daily updates of what's happening on the Outer Banks and surrounding areas. Located at 92.5 on the FM dial, Carolina Ninety-Two serves Northeastern North Carolina with offices in Nags Head. Stay informed and entertained with the only country at the beach, WNHW, Carolina Ninety-Two!

Inside
Real Estate

Real estate remains a good investment on the Outer Banks despite the current economy. For the most part, it's a buyers' market. For those who have a dream of owning a place at the beach, lower interest rates have given additional incentive to prospective purchasers. And, while there's not much land on the Outer Banks, compared with other resort areas, there are many different ways to own your place by the sea. There is a good deal of new construction here, and it's particularly noticeable in the north beach areas. However, one thing to keep in mind is the high cost of building materials here on the Outer Banks. Prices for lumber have skyrocketed, and even though the cost of vacant land stabilized, providing an incentive to build on your own, you may find it makes better sense to purchase improved properties. Plan your strategy carefully!

While there are homes for sale all over the Banks, there seems to be a concentration of them in the central areas, particularly west of Route 158. Whether you're interested in rental income-producing investment properties, second homes or primary residences, there's an avenue for just about everyone to own property on the Outer Banks.

Most of the resort development of the '80s was planned with appreciation in mind, but that investor-driven phenomenon is gone for now. Today the values of lots and homes have stabilized and more than likely will remain so. Investor incentives have changed. Realtors suggest that "end users," or those who purchase a property intending to make use of it, will gain the most in this market. Tailor your purchases to your needs. You will probably not see dramatic price fluctuations like you would in more metropolitan areas because sellers here are motivated for different reasons. Generally, you can expect to see less erosion of prices with increasing rental incomes for investment properties. Occupancy levels have been increasing on average of 10 percent every year according to the Chamber of Commerce occupancy tax figures. Bear in mind though, that while certainly the number of visitors increases every year, so do the number of available properties!

Following the slowdown nationally, and locally, of the real estate market, the industry as a whole here seems to be getting a closer evaluation than it did during the last 10 or so boom years. This, in our opinion, benefits the buyer especially. The overall quality of construction, planning and development are getting a closer look, creating a higher degree of stability. During the real estate boom of the '80s, builders were frantic just trying to keep pace with the demand for new construction. In slower times, most builders have too much at risk not to do quality work. Land use and planning are constantly reviewed. Town planners and building code authorities generally have support for strong enforcement of codes and regulations. Continuing concern for coastal development will partially dictate future building. Water resources and water quality have come under careful scrutiny more recently. Yet development and environmental concerns don't have to be divisive. One supports the other over the long haul. Many of the developers involved with real estate projects on the north beaches (where so much of the building is occurring now) make it a point to balance their vision with a great concern for maintaining as much of the integrity of the natural environment as possible.

Perhaps the only thing that could interrupt this focus on careful planning and development, other than a slow economy, is a powerful storm. In a few areas, the oceanfront is not currently buildable, so be sure you've researched your pending property purchase well. The integrity of some soundfront properties was challenged by the "storm of the century" in March 1993. Keep in mind that flood maps have been revised so be sure to reference your property carefully.

If you're looking to buy a timeshare, townhouse, single-family home or lot, select a real estate firm, ask intelligent questions, listen for specific answers and make wise decisions. Here are some of the questions you should ask yourself: What type of property do you want? How much is affordable? Will it be rented? Where will the usual services such as water, sewer and electricity come from? What area will offer the highest appreciation, lowest taxes, insurance and the best services? Where are the flood plains? What about fire and rescue services? Is the proximity of schools and churches a consideration? Medical facilities? Business opportunity? What about a nice, quiet get-away-from-it-all fishing retreat vs. a luxury mansion? What about a bulkheaded boat dock?

We've provided you with a rundown here of whole ownership and timeshare properties. Included here are some of the brightest and best developments in the area, a rundown on real estate firms, architects and builders and designers. If you're in pursuit of the second American dream — a home at the beach — then this chapter will certainly get you started.

Residential Resort Communities/Developments

We've listed most of the newer and more established oceanside and soundside residential communities to give you an idea of what's here on the Outer Banks; starting as far north as you can go and still be on the Outer Banks and continuing south to the southern banks of Hatteras Island. These communities include resorts that offer recreational amenities and easy access to the ocean and sound, those that provide a mixture of seasonal and year-round living and neighborhoods with more of a year-round lifestyle. Most developments have strict architectural guidelines to ensure quality development. It should also be noted that there are many one-road (dead-end streets) subdivisions on the east side of Duck Road located between Southern Shores and Corolla. These subdivisions offer private roads and private ocean accesses. In most cases, you will see entrance signs to these smaller subdivisions as you are driving on Duck Road. These neighborhoods offer great rental opportunities but with fewer amenities. Call your local Realtor for more information about sales or rentals.

The information in this section should be helpful to those of you who are interested in owning or renting an Outer Banks property. If you are a potential purchaser, don't forget to inquire about homeowner fees. These are costs in addition to your monthly mortgage payments. They can be assessed on a monthly or annual basis.

Carova Beach: North Swan Beach, Swan Beach, Seagull and Pennys Hill Subdivisions

---

Off the paved road   *453-3111 or*
Corolla   *(800) 654-5224*

Access to these subdivisions is by four-wheel drive vehicle. Enter the beach at the ramp in Ocean Hill. (Be sure to read the rules of the road.) You are now in Fruitville Beach Township. Enjoy a 12-mile ride out to the northernmost subdivision, Carova Beach. You'll be riding on some of the widest beaches anywhere, but it's recommended you drive at low tide. (It's debatable whether or not there will ever be a paved road through these areas.) Most of the time it's just you and nature. (Driving into Virginia is no longer permitted, and there's a posted area and gate to prevent crossing the border.) Watch for the herds of wild Spanish Mustangs!

Carova Beach is bordered on the north by Virginia's False Cape State Park. It is bordered on the south by North Swan Beach, and as you continue south you come to Swan Beach, Seagull and Pennys Hill subdivisions. Development began in Carova in 1967, followed by development in North Swan Beach and Swan Beach. Carova is the largest subdivision off the paved road. There was a planned road through this area when development began but, ironically, the road came up from the south from Duck to Ocean Hill instead.

Carova consists of approximately 2,000 lots. Resales are available in most areas. If you're wondering how many cottages have been built in this 12-mile stretch, there are approximately 400 improved lots from Ocean Hill to the Virginia line and 2,500 property owners. There are 75 registered voters indicating there aren't many year-round residents. The Seagull and Pennys Hill subdivisions are much smaller.

These subdivisions offer lots fronting the canals, sandy trails and open water between Currituck

Sound and the Atlantic Ocean. Basic amenities are offered including electricity, telephone and water/sewage by individual well and septic. Cable is not offered in this area, but we've been told that television reception is excellent. Carova's volunteer fire department has just been enlarged. Riggs Realty knows this area better than most, and they are the most active realty company as far as off-road beach sales go, so give them a call and find out more about the area some call "Heaven."

THE VILLAGES AT OCEAN HILL

Ocean Trail (NC 12)   453-4455
Corolla   (800) 662-3229

On the northern end of the Outer Banks, in the quaint village of Corolla, at the very end of the paved road lies Ocean Hill. This unique resort community covers 153 acres, including lakefront and oceanfront to soundfront lots. There are 300 single family homesites assuring lots of wide open space. This second-home neighborhood-type project is still very much available to the buying public. There are no year-round residents at this time, but many of the owners plan to retire here. Amenities include oceanfront and lakefront pools, tennis courts and a freshwater lake. Very wide, white, sandy beaches are also part of the package. There are strict architectural guidelines to ensure quality development. Call Twiddy Realty for sales information and your local Duck or Corolla Realtor for rental information.

THE WHALEHEAD CLUB

Ocean Trail (NC 12)
Corolla   232-2075

In November 1992, the Currituck County Board of Commissioners signed documents that will forever preserve the historic Whalehead Club for the public. The main reason for the purchase was to preserve the county's history and heritage. The property will be used as a "destination" beach for the public. It will also provide ocean access, as the property is located adjacent to the State of North Carolina Wildlife Resource Commission property.

The State WRC property encompasses the Currituck Beach Lighthouse property and already has a handicapped-accessible pier that winds its way through the marsh to beautiful views of the sound and the Whalehead Club property. A new entrance to the Whalehead Club property will be built across from the Currituck Beach Light.

The Whalehead property includes a boat ramp, numerous protected boat slips in the harbor and expansive grounds with beautiful sound frontage and natural vegetation. These facilities grandly accomplish Currituck's longtime goal of providing adequate water access for the public.

COROLLA LIGHT RESORT VILLAGE

Ocean Trail (NC 12)   453-3000
Corolla

More than 200 acres comprise this northern Outer Banks resort. Construction began in 1985 and some very large, luxury homes are located here as well as luxury three-bedroom condos and four-bedroom villas. Sizes range from 1,300 square feet to 3,600 square feet. When it all began, Corolla Village was a sleepy, well-hidden oceanside community with a lighthouse, post office and a Winks store. The developer, Richard A. Brindley, and the marketing and sales team at Brindley & Brindley Realty, have created a beautiful ocean-to-sound resort that boasts two oceanfront pool complexes, tennis courts scattered throughout the resort, a soundside pool and water sports center and most recently an indoor sports center that houses a competition-size indoor pool, tennis courts, racquetball courts and exercise rooms. Two miniature golf courses complete the recreational amenities. The resort has its own water treatment facility. There are strict architectural guidelines to ensure quality development. Corolla Light Village Shops are also located in the heart of this development. Contact Brindley & Brindley for sales information and your local Corolla Realtor for rental information.

MONTERAY SHORES

Ocean Trail (NC 12)   453-4343
Corolla   473-1030

Monteray Shores, located on the soundside of this northern Outer Banks area, features magnificent homes with a unique Caribbean style. The red tile roofs, arched verandas, spacious decks and abundance of windows make these homes a popular option to the wooden structures found in most Outer Banks residential communities. But if you prefer Outer Banks-style homes, these are also available. This community features single-family residences and

offers sound or ocean views from every homesite. While there are no oceanfront lots, the soundside clubhouse, junior Olympic swimming pool, hot tub, four tennis courts, jogging trails, stocked fishing ponds, boat launching ramps and other recreational amenities provide a dash of sophistication and luxury to this area of the northern Outer Banks. Phase I of the Monteray Shores Shopping Plaza is complete. The plaza includes a Food Lion grocery store, specialty shops and eateries including Susan's Calypso Cafe and Smokey's. These services provide a tremendous convenience for visitors and residents of the northern Outer Banks. Contact Bob DeGabrielle & Associates for sales information. They have an exclusive listing in this resort. Contact Kitty Dunes Realty for rental information. You can call or write for more information: 4100 Monteray Shores, Corolla, N.C. 27927.

BUCK ISLAND

Ocean Trail, (NC 12)   453-4343
Corolla   (800) 964-2825

In a small section of the northern Outer Banks lies the exclusive community of Buck Island. This development is located just south of Monteray Shores on N.C. 12 (or 10 miles north of Duck). It is an oceanfront and oceanside development. There are 78 single-family homesites and 41 townhome sites. Property is still very much available to the buying public. Buck Island is reminiscent of the nautical seaside villages of Kiawah and Nantucket and boasts timeless Charleston-style architecture along a promenade of hardwood trees and turn-of-the-century street lights. A guarded entrance, pristine ocean beach, beach cabana, pool and tennis courts complement the commitment to full service and excellence that has become the hallmark of developer Buck Thornton. Homesites, custom homes and Charleston-style townhomes offer a wide variety of opportunities if you wish to own a retreat in the north beaches.

Phase I of the TimBuck II Shopping Center includes a 16,000-square-foot building that 13 merchants call home. The shopping center features ground-level covered parking, public rest rooms and the signature seaside village architecture found throughout Buck Island resort. Phase II is underway. You can call or write for more information: P.O. Box 4502, Corolla, N.C. 27927-4502.

CROWN POINT

| Ocean Trail (NC 12) | 453-2105 |
| Corolla | 441-7181 |

Crown Point is located one mile north of Ocean Sands. This is a single-family subdivision (no multifamily units) with oceanfront and oceanside properties. It is completely separate from the Ocean Sands subdivision. There are approximately 90 homes here with a third of the project remaining for single-family development. Crown Point is a very popular resort for weekly rentals. Amenities include a swimming pool, tennis courts and private beach access. Contact Coastland Realty for sales information and your local Duck or Corolla Realtor for rentals.

OCEAN SANDS

| Ocean Trail (NC 12) | 453-2105 |
| | 441-7181 |

Ocean Sands is located nine miles north of Duck. It is an oceanside and oceanfront development. This planned unit development, or PUD, is considered to be a model of coastal development by land use planners, government officials and environmentalists alike. The Ocean Sands concept is centered around clusters of homes that form small colonies, buffered by open space. This design eliminates through-traffic while increasing privacy and open vistas. Clusters are devoted to single-family dwellings, multifamily dwellings and some to appropriate commercial usage. Many of the approximately 450 residences at Ocean Sands are placed in rental programs. Amenities include tennis courts, an Olympic-plus size swimming pool, nature trails and a fishing lake stocked with bass. You will also enjoy private roads guarded by a security force. Ocean Sands is a family oriented community buffered on the east by the Atlantic Ocean and on the west by vast acres of wildlife preserve. A section consisting of 166 lots is now offered for sale. Contact Coastland Realty for sales information and your local Duck or Corolla Realtor for rentals.

PINE ISLAND

| Ocean Trail (NC 12) | 453-4216 |
| | 473-6511 |

Pine Island resort is situated on 385 acres, with 300 single-family homesites, and 3½ miles of oceanfront. This planned oceanfront and oceanside community is bordered on the east by the Atlantic Ocean and on the west by the 5,000 acres of marsh, islands and uplands preserved in perpetuity as the National Audubon Society Pine Island Sanctuary. Homesites are generous, and there are strict architectural guidelines. Central water and sewer and underground utilities are available. A tennis court and swimming pool will be built for Phase I owners. As development continues there will be additional tennis courts, swimming pools, a bath house, jogging paths and more. Property owners will also have access to a private landing strip for touchdowns. These Pine Island homesites are but a portion of the Pine Island master plan, which includes the Pine Island Racquet Club and the proposed Pine Island Hotel, Villa and Beach Club. For those of you who are familiar with Sanderling, Pine Island will function much like that resort except on a larger scale — everything will be private. Contact Bob DeGabrielle & Associates for sales information. They have an exclusive listing in this resort. Contact any Duck or Corolla Realtor for rental information.

SANDERLING
Duck Rd.   Sales, 261-2181
Duck   Rentals, 261-3211

This ocean-to-sound community of nearly 300 homes and lots is one of the most desirable residential communities on the Outer Banks. The heavy vegetation, winding lanes and abundant wildlife offer the most seclusion of any resort community on the beach. The developers have

taken care to leave as much natural growth as possible, and there are strict building requirements to ensure privacy and value. The Sanderling Inn Resort is located just north of the residential area. The homeowners have their own recreational amenities and access to the resort's facilities as well. Contact any Duck or Corolla Realtor for sales and rental information.

PORT TRINITIE
Duck Rd. (NC 12)
North of the Duck Village
Homeowners Association   261-7315

Located two miles north of Duck, Port Trinitie is situated on 23 acres of oceanfront/oceanside property that stretches across Duck Road to offer some gorgeous views on the soundfront. Amenities include two swimming pools, two tennis courts, soundside pier and gazebo and an oceanfront gazebo. This development began with condominiums, which are co-ownership properties, but Port Trinitie now offers a 50/50 mixture of whole ownership single-family dwellings (cottages and townhomes) and co-owned condos. This family oriented resort is primarily built out, but resales are available through your local Realtor. You can contact the homeowner association for rental information.

NORTHPOINT
Duck Rd. (NC 12)   480-2700
North of Duck Village

Fractional ownership is popular here at NorthPoint though some lots remain for individual ownership and development. There is an enclosed swimming pool, tennis and basketball courts and a long soundfront pier for fishing, crabbing and small boat dockage. One of the first fractional ownership developments on the northern Outer Banks, it has enjoyed good values on resales.

SHIP'S WATCH
Duck Rd. (NC 12)
1251 Duck Rd.   261-2231
Duck   (800) 688-1295

Portrayed by *Mid-Atlantic Country* magazine as the "Palm Beach of the Outer Banks," Ships Watch is a year-round community of luxurious seaside homes in the village of Duck. Pampered vacationers, complete service and maintenance and attention to details are characteristics of this resort. Carefully placed on high rolling dunes, the homes offer spectacular views of either the ocean, the Currituck Sound or both. An Olympic-sized pool, tennis courts, jogging trail, soundside pier and boat ramp, golf privileges and weekly socials offer entertainment for the whole family. This resort provides rentals, fractional and whole ownership. Parlayed as a high-end property, developer Buck Thornton and his associates have experienced great success with this resort. Contact Ships Watch for sales and rental information.

SCHOONER RIDGE BEACH CLUB
Duck Rd. (NC 12)
Duck   261-3563

Schooner Ridge is located in the heart of Duck Village, but its ocean-front/oceanside homes are well hidden from the hustle and bustle of the village proper. The high sandy hills fronting the Atlantic Ocean are perfect for the large single-family homes with lots of windows and decks. Britt Real Estate handles lot sales and resales for Schooner Ridge. The community offers indoor and outdoor recreational amenities. Bike paths wind through the area, and all the shops in the village are within walking distance.

NANTUCKET VILLAGE
Duck Rd. (NC 12)
Just south of Duck

This private resort consists of 36 townhouse units developed on Currituck Sound. This is a year-round development offering an indoor pool and an outdoor tennis court. The sandy, soundside beach is free of marsh grasses and is an ideal place for wading and enjoying water vehicles. Most units are available for rentals. Contact your local Duck Realtor for sales and rental information.

OCEAN CREST
Duck Rd. (NC 12)
Located near Nantucket Village   261-2000

This is an ocean-to-sound resort consisting of 54 lots that hit the market in August 1992. Lots are 15,000 square feet or better and are zoned for single-family dwellings. This is an upscale neighborhood with very strict architectural guidelines. Homes must be 2,000 square feet or larger. Amenities include a swimming pool, tennis courts and private ocean access. Expect good water views. Contact Southern Shores Realty for sales information. They have an exclusive listing in this subdivision.

CHICAHAUK

Ocean Blvd.-Duck Rd.
Southern Shores

Southern Shores is a unique 2,600-acre incorporated town with its own government and police force. Although there is a shopping center on its western boundary, commercial zoning/development is not allowed elsewhere. This town has heavy maritime forests along the soundside fringe, wide open sand hills in the middle and beachfront property. Recently, the post office has officially recognized Southern Shores as a town, so folks who reside here no longer use Kitty Hawk for mailing purposes. The heavy year-round population attests to the popularity of Southern Shores. Development has been carefully paced through the years, and there are still many lots that remain undeveloped. It is considered one of the most desirable places to live on the Outer Banks.

MARTIN'S POINT

Rt. 158
Kitty Hawk   261-4183

Martin's Point is an exclusive waterfront community of magnificent custom homes and homesites. There are stringent building requirements, a guarded entry and some of the most beautiful maritime forest found anywhere. Homes range from 1,200 square feet to 13,000 square feet. This is primarily a year-round neighborhood composed of both young families and retired folks. Rentals are available on a very limited basis. Owners here have easy access to schools, shopping and golf.

When you arrive on the Outer Banks via the Wright Memorial Bridge, the entrance to Martin's Point is on your immediate left at MP 0. The community is closed to drive-through inspections, but if you're considering a permanent move to the Outer Banks, it's an area you'll want to look over.

KITTY HAWK LANDING

West Kitty Hawk Rd.
Kitty Hawk

This is a residential community of mostly year-round residents. It's located on the far western edges of Kitty Hawk. To get there you turn at MP 4 on West Kitty Hawk Road and just keep driving until you see the signs. The community borders Currituck Sound. It has deep water canals, tall pines and gorgeous sunsets.

SANDPIPER CAY CONDOMINIUMS

West side of Rt. 158
Kitty Hawk   261-2188

This resort community consists of 280 condominium units and is located near Seascape Golf Course. One hundred fifty-five of the units are second homes, and 40 percent of the units are either long-term rentals or primary residences, making this a year-round resort. Only 5 percent of the units are available for short term or weekly leases. All of the original inventory is sold, though some resales are available. All are priced under $100,000. There are two-story townhouses and single-story garden units. Amenities include a large outdoor pool, clubhouse and tennis court. Homeowner fees apply. Contact Sandpiper Cay for more information.

FIRST FLIGHT VILLAGE
West side of Rt. 158
Kill Devil Hills

This is one of the Outer Banks' most popular year-round neighborhoods in the central area of the beach comprised of Kitty Hawk, Kill Devil Hills and Nags Head. Generally, there aren't many truly year-round areas available here, making First Flight especially attractive to many. The entrance to First Flight Village is located at First Street, on the west side of the Route 158. This is a family oriented neighborhood, so, if you are considering a permanent move to the Outer Banks and you have a family, you will want to consider this community. There are quite a few long-term rentals available in this area as well. First Flight Village real estate is considered moderately priced. Contact your local beach Realtor for sales and rental information.

COLINGTON HARBOUR
Colington Rd.
Kill Devil Hills   441-5886

Development began more than 20 years ago on this big island. It is located about four miles west of the Wright Brothers Memorial. In other words, you will drive four miles once you've left Route 158 to access Colington. This is a deep-water community with some 12 miles of bulkheaded canal and soundfront lots. Access to Albemarle Sound and the Atlantic Ocean is through Oregon Inlet, which is approximately 25 miles by boat to the south of Colington Island. There are a large number of luxury homes, complete with boat docks, but there are also

many average size homes. This community combines year-round residents with seasonal and weekly renters. The picnic area, playground, sandy beach on Kitty Hawk Bay, boat launching ramp, boat slips for rent and fuel dock are available to all residents, including year-round renters. Clubhouse activities, the Olympic-sized swimming pool, children's pool and tennis court are available to club members. What makes Colington Harbour popular is its remoteness, private entry and the many canals that offer waterfront living to most residents.

COLINGTON HEIGHTS
Colington Harbour
Kill Devil Hills
Beach Realty   261-3815

This is the last developable subdivision within Colington Harbour. There are 23 lots on approximately 35 acres. The inventory includes wooded interior lots, waterview lots and waterfront properties. Essentially, this is a maritime forest development. Large lot sizes contribute to the privacy of the area. Roads are private, and private beach access is provided on Albemarle Sound. Architectural controls are in effect, and all of the water impact fees have been paid by the developer, making the real estate even more attractive.

BAY CLIFF
Williams Dr., Colington Island
Kill Devil Hills

Bay Cliff is about four years old and not yet heavily populated. It is a planned unit development with a homeowners' association. It is carved out of an incredible maritime forest, and there are restrictions on clearing land. The initial development was done with preservation in mind. The community has its own central sewage system, which means there's no need for septic systems here, as is the case in most beach development. There are 72 lots, some of which are already built out. The focal point of the community — in addition to the nature trails and woods — is its large soundfront clubhouse (the Claw Club) with pool, bar, game room and lounge. There are boat slips at the clubhouse as no bulkheading is allowed for individual lot owners. The marsh grass and wetlands are protected, and rightly so. Once you've seen the sunsets and heard the sounds of nature in the forest and along the water's edge, you'll appreciate the careful planning and development. This community consists of a mixture of year-round residences and investment properties.

SOUTH RIDGE

West side of Rt. 158, MP 13   441-2800
Nags Head   441-2450

This new subdivision is located on the hill behind the Nags Head Post Office. There will be 150 homes in this neighborhood consisting of second homes, investment properties and year-round residences. Owners and renters can enjoy the ocean and sound views. Contact Remax Ocean Realty for additional information. They have an exclusive sales listing in this development.

THE VILLAGE AT NAGS HEAD

Rt. 158   Sales, 441-8533
Nags Head   Rentals, 480-2224
                    (800) 548-9688

Development began about seven years ago at the Village, and this community has become one of the best sellers on the Outer Banks. The golf course, with a beautiful clubhouse and popular restaurant, and the oceanfront recreational complex, with tennis, swimming and a restaurant, make this attractive residential community most desirable. Single-family homes, townhomes and condos provide something for everyone. The Ammons Corporation developed this large community, which spans the highway, around MP 15. The oceanfront homes are some of the largest and most luxurious anywhere. There's lots to do when you live or vacation here. It's an excellent choice for beach living, vacation rentals, or investment.

PIRATE'S COVE

Manteo-Nags Head Causeway
Manteo   Sales, 473-1451
                    Rentals, 473-6800
                    (800) 762-0245

Pirate's Cove is a distinctive residential-marina-resort community. Hundreds of acres of protected wildlife preserve border Pirate's Cove on one side, while the peaceful waters of Roanoke Sound are on the other. Deep-water canals provide each owner with a dock at the door, and the centrally located marina is home to many large yachts and fishing boats. Pirate's Cove offers homesites, homes, condominiums and even dockominiums fronting deep-water canals. There's always activity here. Fishing tournaments seem as important as sleeping to many of the residents, and locals and visitors can get in on the fun. Other recreational amenities include lighted tennis courts, swimming pools, Jacuzzi, sauna and a beautifully appointed clubhouse. Scheduled recreational activities for all ages are available, or enjoy waters ports including waverunners and boat rentals. One of the prettiest settings on the Outer Banks enhances the Victorian-nautical design of these homes.

HERITAGE POINT
Hwy. 64 West
Manteo 473-1450
This new year-round resort community is subdivided into 111 lots and located on a historic site on Pearce Road next to Ft. Raleigh National Historic Site. Site improvements and restrictive covenants are in place. Interior, soundview and soundfront lots overlooking Croatan and Albemarle sounds are available. Lot sizes range from ½ acre to 3½ acres. Two tennis courts are proposed along with a 111-slip boat basin. A parking area and common beach area will be provided for homeowners. Homeowner association fees apply. Contact Heritage Realty for more information. They have an exclusive sales listing in this development.

RESORT RODANTHE
NC 12
Rodanthe 987-2914
This resort consists of 20 condominium units located diagonally to the oceanfront in Rodanthe. All units have ocean and sound views. The condos are for sale, but the owners do rent them. Amenities include a swimming pool and private ocean access. Couples or small families would be happy here as only one- and two-bedroom units are available. Contact Resort Realty for sales information and either Resort or Sun Realty for rentals.

MIRLO BEACH
NC 12
Rodanthe 987-2350
This sound-to-oceanfront resort community is located 12 miles south of the Oregon Inlet Bridge, adjacent to the wildlife preserve. There are approximately 10 large oceanfront cottages in Mirlo Beach, each sleeping an average of 12 people comfortably. Amenities include tennis courts and private beach and sound accesses. This resort has a very good rental history. Contact Midgett Realty for sales and rental information.

ST. WAVES
NC 12
Waves 995-4600
This subdivision, developed during the '80s, consists of approximately 55 lots and 20 houses. Homes and homesites are available for sale. These properties offer ocean views, sound views and lake views. The homes are upscale, and all have been built within the last five years. Architectural controls are in tact. Amenities include a swimming pool, tennis court and a centrally located lake. St. Waves maintains an excellent rental history. The rental term seems

to be longer on Hatteras Island than it is in areas north of the island because of the popularity of the area for fishermen during the shoulder seasons. Contact Hatteras Realty for more information.

KINNAKEET SHORES

NC 12
Avon   *995-5821*

The name comes from the first settlers of the area back in the late 1500s. Once a desolate stretch of narrow land between the Atlantic Ocean and Pamlico Sound, Kinnakeet Shores is a residential community that is being carefully developed. It consists of 500 acres under wide open skies, beautiful marshlands and one of the best windsurfing areas in the world. Recreational amenities include a planned clubhouse, swimming pools, tennis courts and a fitness center. This is the largest development on Hatteras Island and the homes tend to be quite big, reminding us of the northern beaches. This is primarily a second-home development, offering one of the most popular rental programs on the island. A small shopping plaza is conveniently located in Avon with a Food Lion grocery store. Restaurants are also located in Avon, and if those don't suit you, you're only a five-mile drive from the village of Buxton. Contact Sun Realty for additional sales and rental information.

HATTERAS PINES

NC 12
Buxton   *995-4600*

This 150-acre subdivision is nestled in a maritime forest in the heart of Buxton. Consisting of 114 lots rolling along the dunes and ridges, it may be one of the safest places on the island to build a year-round home because of the shelter of the woods. The roads for this development are intact, along with protective covenants. A pool and tennis court are planned. Contact Hatteras Realty for more information.

HATTERAS BY THE SEA

NC 12
Hatteras   *986-2841*

This rather small community of 36 lots on 25 acres is one of the last oceanfront areas available for residential living. There's not much land on the southern end of the Outer Banks, and a good portion is preserved by the National Seashore designation. A large pool and some carefully designed nature paths will be included here. Sunrise and sunset are unobstructed for homeowners. Contact Midgett Realty for more information.

Fractional Ownership and Timesharing

Fractional Ownership

Fractional ownership, formerly called co-ownership, is very close to the same concept as timesharing. Here you share ownership of a building/house with other owners. Most fractional ownership properties are divided into five-week segments for 10 owners with two weeks reserved for maintenance each year. The weeks of ownership are spread throughout the year with some weeks in prime time, others in the off season. At some resorts the weeks rotate through the years, which means everyone is assigned the most favorable season at some point.

Fractional ownership can offer some of the tax benefits of vacation home ownership, depending on whether you occupy the property for the five weeks or rent it out. Appreciation is generally not as great on fractional ownership interests as on single-family homes, but some of the more popular fractional ownership resorts on the northern Outer Banks have been quite profitable in resales.

This type of ownership is a comparatively inexpensive way to own a piece of the beach. The homes are luxurious and often include recreational amenities in addition to prime oceanfront or oceanside locations.

The resorts described in this section start on the north beaches and continue south.

PORT TRINITIE
Duck Rd. (NC 12)
North of Duck Village   261-3922

Port Trinitie, situated on 23 acres of oceanfront/oceanside property, stretches across Duck Road and offers some gorgeous soundfront views. It is located two miles north of Duck. Amenities include two swimming pools, two tennis courts, a soundside pier and gazebo and an oceanfront gazebo. This development began with condominiums, which are co-ownership properties, but Port Trinitie now offers a 50/50 mixture of whole ownership single-family dwellings (cottages and townhomes) and co-owned condos. This family oriented resort is primarily built out, but resales are available through your local Realtor. You can contact the homeowners association for rental information.

Timesharing

Timesharing is a deeded transaction under the jurisdiction of the North Carolina Real Estate Commission. A deeded share is 1/52 of the unit property being purchased. This deed grants the right to use the property in perpetuity. Always ask if the property you're inspecting is deeded timeshare because there is such a thing as undeeded timeshare, which is the right to use a property, but the property reverts to the developer in the end. What you are buying is the right to use a specific piece of real estate for a week per share. The weeks are either fixed at the time of sale, or they rotate yearly.

Insiders' Tips

Drive through the Audubon's Pine Island Sanctuary just north of Sanderling.

Some disadvantages of being locked into a time and place have been partly removed by RCI (Resort Condominiums, Inc.), a timeshare bank. There are other similar operations. Members trade their weeks to get different time slots at a variety of locations around the world.

Qualifying for the purchase of a timeshare unit can be no more difficult than qualifying for a credit card, but be aware of financing charges which are higher than regular mortgages.

Most timeshare resorts on the Outer Banks are multifamily construction with recreational amenities that vary from minimal to luxurious and sometimes include the services of a recreational director. Timeshare units usually come furnished and carry a monthly maintenance fee. Tax advantages for ownership and financing are not available to the purchaser of a timeshare, so investigate from this angle.

Many offer "free weekends" — you agree to a sales pitch and tour of the facilities in exchange for accommodations. Listen, ask questions and stay in control of your money and your particular situation. If you get swept away, you'll only have five days to change your mind, if you so desire, according to North Carolina Time Share Act, which governs the sale of timeshares. But, if you can afford it, a relatively small amount of money to cover your vacation lodgings for years to come, along with the option of trading for another location, make timesharing a rather hassle-free and attractive option for many people.

Timeshare sales people are li-censed, which is to everyone's advantage, and they earn commissions. Some very good arrangements are out there, some not so good. Check thoroughly before you buy. We recommend contacting Marvin Beard, the Supervising Broker of **Outer Banks Resort Rentals**, 441-2134. Marvin and his wife sell and rent timeshare (units) exclusively. They do not sell or rent any other kinds of properties. This company is the only one on the Outer Banks that rents and resells timeshare for owners of the 15 timeshare resorts located on the Outer Banks. Mr. Beard is also the selling broker for the developers of the following three resorts: Ocean Villas, Ocean Villas II and The WindJammer. Units there have been previously unsold or sold one time and foreclosed upon. It is best to keep the purchase of timeshares in proper perspective; your deeded share only enables you to vacation in that property during a designated time period each year for as long as you own that share. This makes timeshare very different from other potential investments. All real estate investment decisions require thorough research and planning, and timeshare is no exception. The rental of timeshare units should not really be of any special concern to you because a rental in any case is a one time deal — just like renting a motel room or a cottage for a week — you're not being asked to buy anything.

Duck Village
Duck   261-3525
    Barrier Island, one of the largest

timeshare resorts on the Outer Banks, is situated on a high dune area of ocean to sound property. These are multifamily units of wood construction. There is an attractive, full-service restaurant and bar with a soundside sailing center in addition to the beach. A full-time recreation director is on board here for a variety of planned activities and events. Indoor swimming, tennis courts and other recreational facilities provide a full amenities package. This is a popular resort in a popular seaside village.

SEA SCAPE BEACH AND GOLF VILLAS
Rt. 158, MP 2
Kitty Hawk   261-3881

There's plenty of recreation here. Tennis courts, two swimming pools, an indoor recreation facility, weight room, game room and a lovely golf course await you at Sea Scape. The multifamily units are of wood construction, and they are located on the west side of Route 158. Sea Scape provides a shuttle to the beach. Some of the two-bedroom, two-bath villas have ocean views and access to a host of other amenities. Reduced rates for golf are available to guests. Resales are being actively sold. Sea Scape offers a unique opportunity for timeshare ownership with a rent-to-own offer.

OUTER BANKS BEACH CLUB
Beach Rd., MP 9
Kill Devil Hills   441-7036

The round, wooden buildings of the Outer Banks Beach Club were the first timesharing opportunities built and sold here. There are 160 units including oceanfront, oceanside and clubhouse units across the street proximate to the clubhouse/indoor pool. There are also two outdoor pools in great oceanfront locations. One-, two-and three-bedroom units also have access to whirlpools, tennis courts and a playground. There is a full-time recreation director for a variety of activities and games.

DUNES SOUTH BEACH AND RACQUET CLUB
Beach Rd., MP 18
Nags Head   441-4090

Townhome timesharing at this resort features two- and three-bedroom units with fireplaces, washers and dryers, Jacuzzis and hot tubs. There are 20 units, and most are oceanfront. All of the units are oceanside. A pool, tennis court, putting green and playground make up the recreational amenities.

Realtors/Real Estate Sales Companies

Visitors to the Outer Banks may stumble upon their dream home, but your best bet is to contact local Realtors. Remember, real estate agents and brokers are not necessarily Realtors. Brokers and their agents must join the Board of Realtors to become members, but Realtors subscribe to a strict code of ethics that help protect buyers and sellers. They help to ensure fair treatment for both parties.

Realtors can offer information such as property values, appreciation, history of sales and resales and neighborhood analyses. They can tell you whether or not a neighborhood is composed of year-round or seasonal residents, and they can render an opinion as to whether or not you'll be satisfied with the area you're considering.

Boards of Realtors are your best resource for answers about major developments and fair market prices. They supervise the Multiple Listing Service. Only brokers and their agents who are Realtors have access to MLS information. For any of your real-estate related questions, we've listed the addresses and telephone numbers for the state and county Board of Realtors:

North Carolina Association of Realtors, (NCAR), 2901 Seawell Rd., P.O. Box 7918, Greensboro, N.C. 27417-0918, (919) 294-1415.

Dare County Board of Realtors, Inc., P.O. Drawer G, 110 W. Oregon Ave., Kill Devil Hills, N.C. 27948, (919) 441-4036.

Also, below are some Outer Banks real estate sales companies, their locations and contact information. While this list is not inclusive, it is representative of reputable real estate sales companies on the Outer Banks. Most, if not all, of these companies are members of the Board of Realtors. Call the Dare County Board of Realtors to be sure.

20/20 Realty, Ltd., 473-2020, is located at 516 South Main highway, Manteo. Write P.O. Box 2020, Manteo, N.C. 27954. It represents Roanoke Island and the Outer Banks.

Atlantic Realty, 261-2154 or (800)-334-8401 (out-of-state), is located at MP 2½, Route 158 in Kitty Hawk. Write 4729 North Croatan Highway, Kitty Hawk, N.C. 27949. It represents the area from Corolla to South Nags Head.

BC Realty & Construction, Inc., 261-5050 or (800) 238-4044, is located at 4713 North Croatan Highway, Kitty Hawk, N.C. 27949. It represents the area from Carova to South Nags Head and Roanoke Island. It offers construction, full turnkey service and sales only, no rentals.

Beach Realty & Construction/ Kitty Hawk Rentals, 261-3815, is in Kitty Hawk. This office handles real estate sales, rentals and construction. It's located at MP 2¼, Route 158. Write 4826 North Croatan Highway, Kitty Hawk, N.C. 27949. It is located in Duck on Duck Road near Sanderling, 261-6600; call (800) 849-3825. Write 1450 Duck Road, Duck, N.C. 27949. Also located in Kill Devil Hills at 2901 North Croatan Hwy., 441-1106 or (800) 635-1559. Write P.O. Box 69, Kill Devil Hills, N.C. 27948. It represents the area from Ocean Hill to Nags Head.

Brindley & Brindley Realty & Development, Inc., 473-5555 or 453-3000, is located at 1023 Ocean Trail in the Brindley Building at Corolla Light. Write P.O. Box 453, Corolla, N.C. 27927. It represents the area from Carova Beach to Southern Shores.

Britt Real Estate, 261-3566 or (800) 334-6315 (out-of-state), is located on Duck Road north of the village. Write 1316 Duck Road, Duck, N.C. 27949. Represents the area from Corolla to Southern Shores.

Century 21 At The Beach, 261-

2855 or (800) 245-0021, is located at The Dunes Shops, 4½ MP, Kitty Hawk. Write P.O. Box 987, Kitty Hawk, N.C. 27949. It represents the area from Carova Beach to the Oregon Inlet.

Christi Real Estate and Construction, 261-6400, (800) 282-6401, is located (and receives mail) at 4628 N. Croatan Highway, Kitty Hawk. This office handles sales and construction from Corolla to Nags Head.

Coastland Realty, 441-7181 or 453-2105, is located on Ocean Trail, 10 miles north of Duck. Write 694 Ocean Trail, Corolla, N.C. 27927. It offers real estate sales only and represents the northern Outer Banks and specifically Ocean Sands and Crown Point.

Cove Realty, 441-6391 or (800) 635-7007 (out-of-state), is located between the Beach Road and Route 158, MP 14. Write P.O. Box 967, Nags Head, N.C. 27959. It represents Nags Head and South Nags Head and specializes in Old Nags Head Cove.

The D.A.R.E. Company, 441-1521, is located at the 8 ½ MP, Kill Devil Hills on Route 158. Write P.O. Box 2598, Kill Devil Hills, N.C. 27948. It represents Dare and Currituck counties.

Dolphin Realty, 986-2241 or (800) 338-4775, is located in Hatteras Village. Write P.O. Box 387, Hatteras, N.C. 27943. It represents properties on Hatteras Island.

Duck's Real Estate, 261-2224 or (800) 992-2976, is located on Duck Road. Write 1232 Duck Road, Duck, N.C. 27949. It represents the area from Carova to the Oregon Inlet.

ERA Ocean Country Realty, 995-6700, is located in Avon and represents Hatteras Island properties.

Gardner Realty, 441-8985 or (800) 468-4066, is located on the Beach Road at MP 11, Nags Head. Write 2600 Virginia Dare Trail, Nags Head, N.C. 27959. It represents the areas of Kitty Hawk, Kill Devil Hills and Nags Head but specializes in the area of South Nags Head.

Hatteras Realty, 995-4600, is located on NC Hwy 12 in Avon. Write P.O. Box 249, Avon, N.C. 27915. It represents Hatteras Island.

Heritage Realty Group, Inc., 473-1707, is located at 405 Queen Elizabeth Street, Manteo. Write: P.O. Box 1718, Manteo, N.C. 27954. It represents Roanoke Island and the Heritage Point development.

Kitty Dunes Realty, 261-2173 is in Kitty Hawk. Write P.O. Box 275, Kitty Hawk, N.C. 27949. Another location is at 1180 Ocean Trail in Corolla at the Whalehead Landing Shops, 453-Dune. This company is also located in Colington (Colington Realty), 441-3863. Write 2141 Colington Road, Colington Island, N.C. 27948. Residents of Canada should contact the Canadian Representative, (514) 376-4382. It represents the area from Carova to the Oregon Inlet Bridge.

Joe Lamb, Jr. & Associates, Realtors, 261-4444, is located at Route 158, MP 2 in Kitty Hawk. Write P.O. Box 986, Kitty Hawk, N.C. 27949. It represents the Kitty Hawk, Kill Devil Hills, Nags Head and some northern Outer Banks properties.

Midgett Realty can be reached at 986-2841 or (800) 527-2903 for the Hatteras Village location. Call 995-5333 for the Avon location and 987-

2350 for the office in Rodanthe. Write P.O. Box 250, Hatteras, N.C. 27943. It represents the southern end of the Banks.

Sharon Miller Realty, 928-5711 or 928-5731, and (800) 553-9962, is located on Ocracoke Island. Write P.O. Box 264, Ocracoke, 27960. It represents Ocracoke Island properties.

Nags Head Realty, 441-4311 or (800) 222-1531, is located at 2300 South Croatan Highway. Write P.O. Box 130, Nags Head, N.C. 27959. It represents the area from Carova to Oregon Inlet.

Ocracoke Island Realty, Inc., 928-6261 or (800) 242-5394 (out-of-state), is located on Ocracoke Island. Write P.O. Box 238, Ocracoke, N.C. 27960. It represents Ocracoke Island properties.

Outer Banks, Ltd., 441-7156, is located on Route 158, Nags Head. Write P.O. Box 129, Nags Head, N.C. 27959. It represents the area from Corolla to Nags Head and Roanoke Island.

Outer Banks Resort Rentals, Marvin Beard, 441-2134, is located at Central Square Shops in Nags Head. Write P.O. Box 1166, Nags Head, N.C. 27959. It represents the sales of timeshares only.

Outer Beaches Realty, 995-4477 in Avon and 987-2771 in Waves, is located on NC Highway 12 in Avon and Waves. Write P.O. Box 280, Avon, N.C. 27915. It represents Hatteras Island.

Jim Perry & Company, 441-3051 and (800) 222-6135, is located at the Jim Perry Building on Route 158, Kill Devil Hills. Write P.O. Box 1876, Kill Devil Hills, N.C. 27948. It repre-sents the Outer Banks.

Pirate's Cove, 473-1451 and (800) 762-0245 (toll free), is located on Highway 64/264 Nags Head Causeway. Write P.O. Box 1929, Nags Head, N.C. 27959. It represents properties in Pirate's Cove.

Real Escapes Properties, 261-2181, is located four miles north of Duck at Sanderling Resort. Write 1183 Duck Road, Kitty Hawk, N.C. 27949. It represents Sanderling.

Remax Ocean Realty, 441-2450 and (800) 729-1051, is located at Seagate Station on Route 158, Kill Devil Hills. Write P.O. Box 8, Kill Devil Hills, N.C. 27948. It represents the area from Corolla to Hatteras Village.

Resort Realty, 261-8282 is in Kitty Hawk, located in the Resort Realty Building on Route 158. Write P.O. Box 1008, Kitty Hawk, N.C. 27949. For its Duck location call 261-8686. Write P.O. Box 8147, Kitty Hawk, N.C. 27949. For its Corolla location call 453-3700. Write P.O. Box 545, Corolla, N.C. 27927. It's also located in Rodanthe, 987-2725. Write P.O. Box 126, Rodanthe, N.C. 27968. It represents the Outer Banks.

Riggs Realty, 453-3111 and (800) 654-5224, is located in the Austin Building, N.C. 12 at 1152 Ocean Trail. Write P.O. Box 400, Corolla, N.C. 27927. It specializes in the Northern Beaches and has the larg-est selection of four-wheel-drive ac-cessible houses on the Outer Banks. This company is involved with sales only, no rentals.

Salvo Real Estate, 987-2343, is located on NC Hwy 12 in Salvo. Write P.O. Box 56, Salvo, N.C. 27972. It represents Hatteras Island.

Seaside Realty, 261-5500 and (800) 395-2525 (out-of-state), is located on Route 158, MP 3½, Kitty Hawk. Write 4425 North Croatan Highway, Kitty Hawk, N.C. 27949. It represents the area from Corolla to South Nags Head.

Southern Shores Realty, 261-2000 and (800) 334-1000, is located on NC Hwy 12 in Southern Shores. Write P.O. Box 150, Southern Shores, N.C. 27949. It represents the area from Corolla to Nags Head.

Sun Realty, 441-8011, on Route 158 in Kill Devil Hills, has locations from Corolla to Avon. Call 453-8811 in Corolla, 261-4183 in Duck, 261-3892 in Kitty Hawk, 967-2755 in Salvo and 995-5821 in Avon. It represents the Outer Banks.

Surf or Sound Realty, 995-6052, is located on NC Hwy. 12 , Avon. Write P.O. Box 100, Avon, N.C. 27915. It represents Hatteras Island.

Mercedes Tabano, 987-2711, is located on NC Hwy. 12, Rodanthe. Write P.O. Box 188, Rodanthe, N.C. 27968. It represents Hatteras Island.

Twiddy & Company Realty, 261-8311, is in Duck. Write 1181 Duck Road, Duck, N.C. 27949. In Corolla call 453-2135. Write P.O. Box 368, Corolla, N.C. 27927.

The Villages at Ocean Hill, 453-Hill and (800) 662-3229, represents the area from Carova Beach to Southern Shores.

Village Realty, 441-8533, is located at the Village at Nags Head. Write P.O. Box 1807, Nags Head, N.C. 27959. It represents the Village at Nags Head.

Water Side Realty, Inc., 995-6001 and (800) 530-0022, is located in Buxton. Write P.O. Box 1088, Buxton, N.C. 27920. It represents Hatteras Island.

Stan White Realty & Construction, Inc., 441-1515 and (800) 338-3233, is located on Route 158, MP 11. Write P.O. Drawer 1447, Nags Head, N.C. 27959. It represents the area from Duck to Hatteras Village.

Woodard Realty & Construction, Inc., 261-1962 and (800) 782-2118 (out-of-state), represents the Outer Banks and Currituck for construction and the area from Corolla to Oregon Inlet for sales. Write P.O. Box 2347, Kitty Hawk, N.C. 27949.

The Young People, 441-4816, is located on the Beach Road, MP 6, Kill Devil Hills. Write P.O. Box 285, Kill Devil Hills, N.C. 27948. A branch office is now open in the office building in front of Sandpiper Cay Condominiums. It represents the Outer Banks and especially the central beach areas.

Building Homes on the Outer Banks

Buying a lot and building a house at the beach is pretty close to nirvana for a lot of people. North Carolina law requires that building contractors have a license, helping to assure that you maintain a pleasant state of mind. Some still get around the laws, so check qualifications and reputation before signing on the dotted line. You can contact the **Outer Banks Homebuilders Association** for information about local builders and building services. Members subscribe to a code of ethics that help protect your interests. You can call them at 441-8600, or write to them for their free brochure at P.O. Box 398, Kitty Hawk, N.C. 27949. Get in touch with owners of local homes to query them about their experience with their builder. Ask lenders. If you're itching to buy a lot or home, going to the real estate company first is fine, but you can reverse the situation and go to a lender first instead. They'll also know the reputable sales and construction companies all over the Outer Banks.

It's a good idea to contact an architect too. Building on sand requires particular knowledge; these folks will know what's required in the engineering and design of your new house.

Building a home in a coastal environment exposes you to more than a trifling of codes and restrictions. Send for informative pamphlets. Regulations set by the North Carolina Coastal Management Authority are in place to protect the environment. Use them to protect yourself as well. CAMA will become a familiar acronym to you here as you go through the building process.

Local building codes and restrictions vary with each area of the beach. Try to meet with local planning boards. Although the builder obtains permits, it's always good for you to know how it's done and what's required.

Before you buy, before you build, do lots of homework. The best real estate agents have lots of general information; some have specific information, which is what you need. Get educated with specific, printed information. The best builders know

the ropes, too. Again, get enough information to know the process of building your home. Questions that come up "after the fact" can drive you up a wall if you live out of town and the builder is out on the construction site driving nails and not in the office answering the phone.

A road tour of the Banks will reveal a wide variety of homes. It can get tough to choose what you want. And what about furnishings? Does that wall space allow for a proper-size bed or couch? What can be used on the windows?

We've listed designers, architects, builders and interior decorators for your use. We're not saying this list is inclusive, just that these are folks whose good reputations has been tested over time.

General Contractors

Bateman & Associates
Kill Devil Hills   441-1702

B.C. Realty & Construction, Inc.
Kitty Hawk   261-5050

Beach Realty and Construction
Kitty Hawk   261-3815

Brumfield Construction, Inc.
Kill Devil Hills   441-2130

Carolina Beach Builders
Kill Devil Hills   441-5598

Cartwright Builder & General Contractor
Kill Devil Hills   441-6341

Christi Real Estate & Construction
Kitty Hawk   261-6400

Creef Construction Company
Southern Shores   261-8234

Dean P. Edwards, Inc.
Kitty Hawk Village   261-7858

Dixon & Meekins, General Contractors
Kill Devil Hills   441-2100

Dog Point Builders
Frisco   995-6340
Colington   441-6311

Farrow Builders
Frisco   995-5452

Olin Finch & Co.
Duck   261-8710

Fulcher Homes
Kitty Hawk   261-3316

Hoffman Builders, Inc.
Nags Head   441-5331

Allen Huddleston
Southern Shores   261-2134

Landmark, A Design Build Company
Kill Devil Hills   441-8400

Magnacorp Design & Construction
Duck   261-4447

Mancuso Development
Corolla   453-8921

Midgett Realty
Hatteras Village   986-2841

Newcomb Builders, Inc.
Kitty Hawk   441-1803

Newman Homes Construction, Inc.
Kitty Hawk   261-3844

Outer Banks Homes
Kill Devil Hills   441-8254

Real Escapes Ltd.
Sanderling   261-3474

Sandalwood Construction Company, Inc.
Kitty Hawk   261-3258

The Shotton Company
Port Trinitie   261-5555

Snearer Construction Co. Inc.
Kitty Hawk   261-2228

Stormont & Company
Kitty Hawk   261-8724

Bo Taylor Fine Homes, Inc.
Nags Head   441-8544

Technique Designs & Construction
Southern Shores   261-8897

Thornton Construction Ltd.
Corolla   491-8711

Lee Tugwell, General Contractors, Inc.
Manteo   473-3620

Waldt Construction Company
Duck   261-3721

Bobby Ware
Roanoke Island   473-6338

Stan White Realty and Construction, Inc.
Nags Head   441-1515

Woodard Realty & Construction Co. Inc.
Kitty Hawk   261-1962

Designers and Architects

Benjamin Cahoon Architect
Nags Head   441-0271

Carolina Beach Builders
Kill Devil Hills   441-5598

Dare Drafting & Design
Kill Devil Hills   441-5704

Design Associates II
Southern Shores   261-8498

Dixon Design Associates, Inc.
Corolla   453-4279

Alex Engart, AIA	
Duck	261-4473
Mike Florez & Associates	
Kitty Hawk	261-7127
Landmark, A Design Build Company	
Kill Devil Hills	441-8400
Magnacorp Design & Construction	
Duck	261-4447
Lester Powell Building Designs	
Nags Head	480-3888, 473-5529
Real Escapes Ltd.	
Sanderling	261-7447
Sandcastle Design Group	
Southern Shores	261-2766
Technique Designs & Construction	
Southern Shores	261-8897
Thornton Construction, Ltd.	491-8711
Corolla	473-6500
John F. Wilson, IV	
Manteo	473-3282

Interior Design/Decorating

A&B Carpets	
Manteo, Kitty Hawk,	
Hatteras area	473-3219

Ambrose Furniture	
Kitty Hawk	261-4836
Decor by the Shore	
Kitty Hawk	261-6222
Designer's Market	
Kitty Hawk	261-6090
Interior Techniques	
Kitty Hawk	261-4925
Interiors	
Kitty Hawk	261-4105
Island Design	
Southern Shores	261-7822
Manteo Furniture	473-2131
Manteo	
Mary Isaacs Interiors	
Manteo	473-1043
Outer Banks Textiles	
Kill Devil Hills	441-7563
Phelps Drapery & Interiors, Ltd.	
Kitty Hawk	261-6644
Village Home Furnishings	
Nags Head	441-6868
Viking Furniture	441-6444
Kill Devil Hills	

POWERBOAT RENTALS

◆ Experience the thrill of taking the helm of one of our 20 foot luxury Powerboats, and fish, ski or cruise the beautiful waters of North Carolina's Outer Banks.

◆ Fishing equipment available to rent.

◆ Ski packages available for rent.

◆ All boats equipped with VHF Radio and complete Coast Guard approved safety kits.

RESERVATIONS SUGGESTED

CLUB NAUTICO OF MANTEO MARINE
at Pirate's Cove Marina
Manteo Causeway
Manteo, NC 27954
473-5633
1•800•367•4728
NON-MEMBERS WELCOME

Licencees of Adventurent, Inc.
© Adventurent, Inc. 1992. All rights reserved.

Inside
Fishing

Fishing is, beyond any doubt, the number one participant and spectator sport of the Outer Banks. In its various forms — surf fishing, sound fishing, pier fishing and full-scale Gulf Stream billfishing — it is available for most of the year, with temporary but fierce booms when the season arrives and the big ones begin to bite. It's available from Corolla down to Portsmouth, and on to Cape Lookout, but Hatteras Island is the true mecca of anglers. Off Cape Point, beyond the lighthouse and Diamond Shoals, is the point where the warm blue waters of the Gulf Stream collide with the cooler, food-rich Labrador Current — a combination that provides a long fishing season and a variety of species matched by few other places in the world.

Hatteras Island's heavy dependence and concentration on sport fishing, along with its relative isolation, have made it the testing ground for many of the rigs and ideas that are now common in salt water fishing. Probably 60 to 65 percent of the terminal gear used in North Carolina has traditionally been made by various small subcontractors on the Outer Banks, that sit around in the off season and manufacture when they can't fish. This has, in turn, led

to the development of specialized rigs for the different types of fishing found on the Banks.

Fishing columnist, tackle shop owner (and fisherman) Damon Tatem of Nags Head says there are three types of fishing on the Outer Banks: the people who come with their kids in tow ready to catch pan fish from the piers, the anglers who don't mind chunking down $1,000 or more to charter a boat, and the "serious" fall and spring fishermen who are determined to catch the big bluefish or speckled trout from mid-September to December. Of course, there is always the summer vacation fishing crowd, from Memorial Day to Labor Day — folks who enjoy fishing as a relaxing hobby and make it part of their annual trip to the coast.

The main word to describe Outer Banks fishing is variety! "We get everything," Tatem declares. "We get the Florida fish, the northern fish; we virtually get a complete spectrum of fish."

In today's climate of environmental awareness, size and bag limits are getting stricter, Tatem emphasizes. "The regulations have to be there," he says. "Twenty years ago the catches were unlimited for striped bass in the sound. Now there are bag limits and size limits. This is an example of complete spectrum management. That's the way it is, and that's the way it's going to be."

A trend becoming more popular with fishermen is catch and release. "People in the '70s would catch bluefish and fill their truck and dump them out," Tatem recalls. "Now people eat more fish, and they also realize they're not an inexhaustible resource. They're a public trust — a resource that belongs to everyone, and everyone's got to take care of it."

It was fishing that enticed Tatem to move to Nags Head in 1970. For him the striped bass is his favorite fish to catch, while the spot is the preferred fish for his dinner table.

Beginners who desire to learn fishing on the Banks should talk to tackle shop staff and ask a lot of questions, Tatem advises. Go out and watch others fish too. "This is a good place to learn," he says. "The summertime fishing is easy. All you've got to do is put bait on a line and catch a fish."

The bluefish craze exists here because it's possible to put on a lure and catch a 15-pound fish. "That's why fall fishing is so big," Tatem says. "It's almost guaranteed, provided that we're not having a 75-mph gale."

Surf and Pier Fishing

Surf fishing is a sport and an art form all its own. Much of the time it involves the use of four-wheel-drive vehicles. Armed with specialized gear and up to seven rods apiece, the hard core surf fisherman spends September through December roving the Dare County beaches at low tide

to read the configuration of the sand bars. "Where is it shallow?" they ask themselves, and every other fisherman they meet. Where are the bars? Where are there offshore holes at high water, where the fish will lurk?

On the Banks, the surf fisherman will find distinct species of fish at different times of the year. Surf fishing really begins in early to mid-March, for those migratory fish (such as croakers and trout) that move offshore in winter and then move inshore and head north in the spring.

The next class is perhaps the most sought after: the drum family, or channel bass, as the largest are called. (To clarify: a *Sciaenops ocellata* weighing, say, one pound, is known on the Banks as a puppy drum. A little older, a little bigger, and it becomes a yearling drum. One from 35 to about 70 pounds will be called a red drum, or sometimes an old drum. The really big ones, and it takes from 40 to 60 *years* out there for them to attain this seniority, are 'channel bass,' for which the world's record is 94 pounds, caught off Avon in 1984). The drum and channel bass have two seasons: mid-March to mid-May, as they move north, and then again mid-October to early December, as they return south.

Another popular surf and pier fish is the blue, or bluefish, a vicious, toothy little fellow who's found at his best around here from mid-October to late November. These jumbo blues, along with drum, are the most popular fish available to the serious surf or pier fisherman. By the end of May surf fishing begins to taper off. In May to July about all

the surf holds is one-pound blues, sea mullet and Spanish mackerel in about the same size range. There are some summer fish, available mainly from the piers, and good for fun; spot, croaker, grey trout — nice pan fish. Also, there are cobia and king mackerels weighing from 15 to 50 pounds; the Spanish mackerel have been good the past three years or so also. Pompano, up to four pounds, are available in late summer and fall and make a very tasty catch. And then there are the miscellanea: skate, blowfish, dogfish, rays, tarpon in late summer, and assorted sharks — none all that common, but don't be surprised if one shows up on your hook.

Most fishing from piers and in the surf is done with casting lures or rigs using a sinker that will anchor in the sand and one or two hooks arranged to keep the bait away from the bottom. Hooks are usually size 4 to 6 for the smaller species and 6/0 to 9/0 for the larger. Bait is generally cutbait, cut mullet, shrimp, bloodworms, squid or flounder and shark belly. Trout are commonly caught on a medium to large plastic lure; mackerel and large bluefish on metal casting lures; channel bass on mullet, cut menhaden or spot. As far as tide and time, low and incoming tides are often more productive than high water. Trout are best taken near dawn in clear water, while smaller drum are most likely found in the morning or evening in rough, murky water.

To try for the really big fish, you've got to haunt the ends of the piers, with a long rod (most often custom made), live-lining bluefish or spot with a large float and a four-foot wire leader.

Sounds too complex for you? Novices *can* catch fish on the Banks, if they use their heads. The tackle shops listed at the end of this section are stocked up not only with equipment but with information. All too often the visiting fisherman brings equipment that is too light and not suited to unique Banks conditions. It can make sense to leave your stuff at home and buy equipment here — it will certainly be better suited to conditions, and may (since it's made here) be cheaper as well. There are bait and tackle shops scattered in every village and on every pier. And, believe it or not, fishing gear is also sold in drug stores, department stores and even some gas stations that serve as general stores.

A second option is renting. Most Banks tackle shops and piers rent rod, reel, terminal gear and sometimes even foul weather gear and waders. Most can direct you to a local guide service.

Frank Merillat is a local guide who specializes in surf fishing. He has 30 years of fishing under his belt, the last 15 or so in Hatteras. Here are his surf fishing tips. "The first thing you have to realize is that all these fish are transitory. It's not like inland fishing where they hang around a tree or a rock. Off Hatteras it changes from tide to tide. This makes for more risky fishing, in terms of getting a predictable catch.

"It also means you have to work a little — study the habits, or patterns, of the fish. The hard part is not catching them, it's finding 'em. Very few surf fish are difficult to catch.

Right Hook

Rt. 1, Box 980, Manteo, NC 27954
1•800•79R•HOOK

Oregon Inlet Fishing Center
1• 800•272•5199

Let's hope he has a plentiful catch at the end of the day.

They bite readily at a variety of bait. Again, it's not like freshwater fishing, where you have to feed them the proper fly, place it just right, etc. Blues and drum are aggressive eaters and will readily bite.

"To find the fish — the hard part — you've got to learn to read the water to understand what the bottom looks like; where the bars and sloughs are . . . .

"The point is that this structure is rapidly changing, day to day. So, if you fish at the Point, for example, all the time — just because it's been written about so much — you may not get consistent catches.

"How do you read the water? Look at it. At low tide you can see the distinguishing marks: breaking waves, smooth water where the channels run. So it's very important to do your homework.

"Also, if you want to catch fish at

Hatteras you need to spend time actively fishing. Not sitting in your motel room, not watching from your truck. You have to stand out there with a bait in the water. It's no mystery: These fish pass in migratory groups, and if you have a bait in the water when they're there you'll catch one.

"It's also important to vary your methods. If you're not catching anything with mullet, you might try a lure or shrimp. Fish are changeable characters! Fish far out; fish close in. Jiggle the bait, vary the speed and motion of your retrieve. Hold your rod, then you can feel a bite. When the rod's in the rod holder you may be missing fish.

"Much of the time you catch nothing. You wait. Then suddenly there's a burst of action. You just got to be ready.

"Don't depend on the tackle shop

people for *all* of your information. They talk to hundreds of people a day, so even when they give you a good spot it'll be crowded. A guide obviously can aid a fisherman. If you want to learn about gear, methods, habits, places to fish, then a guide's the way to go. Somebody who knows all this stuff doesn't need one, or if it's not important to you to catch a fish. It's important to me to catch fish, and I'm a good fisherman. But if I went to Florida, I'd hire a guide. I don't like to waste the money and time. There's no way in the world a guide can guarantee you a fish, but I can guarantee you'll be better prepared to fish on your own afterward.

"Another subject. The time is here that fishermen need to be aware of our impact on the beach. If you drive on the dunes, or leave trash, you're ruining the island. Throw back fish you don't want. And if you do catch a beautiful 40-pound drum, use it! Eat it, or give it to some old-timer on the island. There are lots of people who'll take a nice fish off your hands. Don't throw it in the dumpster. If I came to your home town and treated it the way some people treat this island, I'd be thrown in jail. If we don't conserve and behave thoughtfully, we'll lose these beaches and our sport with them."

Fly Fishing

Fishing columnist Ford Reid says saltwater fly fishing has been making a bit of a splash here in the past few years. While fly rods are still pretty rare, there are times (in the spring when big bluefish and red drum move into Pamlico Sound)

that fly fishing is entirely appropriate. "You are in for some fun and some very big fish on very light tackle," he says. He advises those who want to try it to carry their equipment with them just in case conditions are right: the fish are close, the winds light and the seas fairly calm. Dawn is usually the best time for those conditions. Remember to clean your fly rod after using it in the ocean because of the saltwater's corrosive effect.

Head Boats

An excellent intermediate choice between pier fishing and chartering a big boat yourself is the head boat, so called because it takes all comers on a regular schedule and charges a set amount "a head" (usually from $15 to $20 per person for a half-day, morning or afternoon). A lot of experienced fishermen enjoy head boating, but beginners especially love it. There's no pressure to bring home a big one, though certainly you can, and there's lots of fun and camaraderie for a small amount of cash.

Outer Banks head boats generally cruise the sounds and inlets. In the spring and fall, however, they often head out to sea. Croaker, flounder, spot and sea trout are the mainstays, depending of course on the season and your luck. Head boats generally provide fishing tackle, ice, bait, snack facilities, rest rooms and soft drinks, and the crew will help you bait your hook and deal with the fish once it's aboard, if you really aren't sure how it's done.

Oregon Inlet Fishing Center, Hatteras Harbor Marina, Pirate's

Cove and several other locations on the Banks run head boats, especially during the season.

FRESH WATER FISHING

The fresh water fishing on the Outer Banks isn't nearly as well known as the salt water fishing, but it's there. Kitty Hawk Bay and Currituck Sound offer bass fishing, and there are white and yellow perch and some nice catfish in the brackish sounds. Numerous bass clubs fish this area. In early spring, use crank and spinner baits, and use worms in the summer. Of course, go back to spinner and crank baits in the fall. For Kitty Hawk Bay, the public boat ramp west of the bypass opposite Avalon Pier offers the easiest access.

Don't say we didn't warn you that fresh water licenses are required. North Carolina has carefully drawn lines between prominent points, and state fish and wildlife commission patrols will catch *you* if you fish inside them or north of the Wright Memorial Bridge. Licenses are available at Tatem's Tackle Box and Tackle Express in Nags Head, or TW's Bait and Tackle in Kitty Hawk.

Boat Fishing: The Sounds

Pamlico, Albemarle, Roanoke sounds — the small boater excels in these broad, shallow, brackish waters between the banks and the mainland. The sounds in summer are crammed with 14 to 24-footers after the hordes of gray trout, croakers, spot, flounder and tarpon, and at night even channel bass. Another popular fish in the sounds is cobia, which seems to hit its peak in late May and early June; this is a dramatic fish, a hard fighter, and good eating as well.

Lately, there have been good catches of striped bass in the Croatan, Albemarle and Roanoke sounds in the fall and winter, and even into spring.

In general, sound fishing is a more relaxed, family type of recreation than either surf or ocean fishing. You can hire a guide and a boat or just set out on your own from a handy ramp in your own rig — A long, carefree day of summer fishing in the calm sound, maybe a cooler of beer and a picnic lunch . . . who needs to fight a marlin?

Ocean Fishing

The ocean fisherman revels in the Hemingwayesque challenge of a big, fighting billfish. And they're out there . . . big ones; in 1974 the IGFA all-tackle record blue marlin, 1,142 pounds, was taken off Oregon Inlet, and that was no fluke . . . hundreds are regularly taken off

Insiders' Tips

When the bluefish "blitz" in the spring and fall, the water can turn almost white with feeding fish. You never know when blitzes are going to happen, so be prepared!

Photo: Mary Ellen Riddle

Some people take surf fishing literally.

Hatteras during the summer months. Read our interview with Captain Ernal Foster of the *Albatross* who started the Gulf Stream charter business in Hatteras in 1938.

Most of the Gulf Stream charter boats operate out of Oregon and Hatteras inlets. A couple work out of Ocracoke and Roanoke Island. The Gulf Stream lies a couple of hours out, depending on where you depart, some 25 to 40 miles offshore. This is the closest the Gulf Stream comes to the coast north of Florida. Blue and white marlin, dolphin, tuna and wahoo are taken primarily by trolling. The blue marlin begin to show in mid-April, and peak in June; during July and August they taper off, but they're still there. By then the white marlin is getting plentiful, with a normal catch being one per boat per day. September is a good month for sailfish.

Wreck fishing off the coast is de-veloping into a fun sport. The *Country Girl* or the *Sea Fox* take anglers to the artificial reefs caused by boat and bridge debris. What's being caught? Sea bass, snapper and grouper, pretty much year round. The *Liberty* and the *Zane Grey* wrecks southeast of the Inlet are good sites to try. Certainly there are enough wrecks for those who want to try this method of fishing.

An excellent introduction to Gulf Stream fishing is the annual Sport Fishing School, held in Hatteras every year since 1950. This five-day course (usually held the end of May or first part of June) takes groups into the Gulf Stream for some exciting fishing, teaching how to catch blue marlin, white marlin, tuna, wahoo and dolphin. Most "students" are retirees or professional people, including families, who regard it as a vacation. Cost is $800, lodging not included. For a brochure write North

Carolina State University, Division for Lifelong Education, Box 7401, Raleigh N.C., 27695-7401.

Handicapped anglers who want to fish the Gulf Stream may contact Captain Bob Sumners at 441-8998 or (800)633-8998. He is moored at Pirate's Cove. His *For Play'N* is the area's only handicapped-accessible sport fishing boat. Equipped with a special "Geezer Gadget," invented by Capt. Sumners, the boat has proven successful for all kinds of fishermen, including quadriplegics.

Autumn and Winter Fishing

Most Banks fishermen look forward to autumn. As the water cools in September, the larger fish begin to come inshore once again. The bluefish reappear, in larger sizes; Spanish mackerel show from four up to possibly nine pounds; puppy drum arrive in the surf. The return of the bluefish, now fat at 10 to 15 pounds, begins in November. There is generally a terrific run of spot in September and October, averaging around a pound apiece, but copious, easy to catch and tasty. As autumn goes on, the "pier jockeys" begin to pull in channel bass again.

November is the most looked-for month in terms of both quality and quantity of fishing, with Thanksgiving traditionally the peak (channel bass, jumbo bluefish, loads of two to five-pound flounder). This may continue into December if the weather is warm. Recreational fishermen are happy that Nags Head has instituted a net-free zone from November 1 to

December 15, a time when commercial fishing gear is prohibited for the area from Gulfstream Street north to Eighth Street.

Tournaments are prevalent beginning in June and lasting through November. Pirate's Cove, located just over the bridge on the way to Manteo, has become the base for many of these, but others are held in Nags Head and Hatteras. See Annual Events for more information about tournaments.

The winter brings a lull. It's very cold, so there is little fishing from mid-December to mid-March, except for striped bass fishing in the sounds. There is also year-round offshore fishing for yellowfin tuna, with catches being made nearly every day in the 15 to 20-pound range. A popular spot is offshore Avon. The fish are in the ocean even when the fishermen are home keeping warm; big trout, croakers and bluefish. As it gets colder the fish move offshore, to 80 to 100 feet of water. The commercial fishermen net them there, and many charter captains turn to commercial fishing in the winter. Few sport anglers can muster much enthusiasm for the local winter weather.

All in all, the Banks offer the best year-round saltwater fishing to be found for a long way up or down the Atlantic coast.

New Regulations

Just this spring, new fishing regulations went into effect, allowing sport fishermen better access and limiting commercial activities dur-

ing heavily populated times.

IT IS NOW UNLAWFUL:
• To use seines Wednesday through Saturday during the Nags Head Surf Fishing Tournament and from November 1 through December 15 from Gulf Stream Street north to Eighth Street in Nags Head.

• To use commercial gear within 750 feet of public fishing piers.

•To use commercial fishing gear within a half mile of Cape Point from the Friday before Easter to December 31.

• To use commercial gear within ¼ mile of the beach from National Park Service ramp #4 to the northern terminus of the Bonner Bridge from the Friday before Easter to December 31.

• To use commercial gear in the pond northeast of the terminus of the Bonner Bridge.

Off-Road Vehicles

The use of Off-Road Vehicles (ORVs) on the beaches of Hatteras, Ocracoke and Bodie Island has been limited. A "zone" concept governs beach driving now, with these zones being opened or closed by National Park Service officials depending on erosion, nesting season, high visitor use areas, etc.

Though no permit is currently required to drive on the beach in the park area, it is smartest to check with a ranger before you venture out to make sure you understand their guidelines and assure you are not entering a closed zone. Not knowing is no excuse, especially if you've wound up in some ecologically sensitive area.

One tip: there is *no* beach driving allowed on the Pea Island National Refuge. In Nags Head, ORV permits are $25 per season (October 1 to April 30). Kill Devil Hills has the same driving season but requires no permit. You cannot drive on the beaches of Kitty Hawk and Southern Shores. Other spots where ORVs are not allowed on beaches are swimming areas at the Cape Hatteras Lighthouse, Coquina Beach and Avon.

Once you're safely and legally on the beach, having reached it *only* by using one of the clearly marked and numbered ramps, you should remain on the portion of the beach between the water and the foot of the dunes. In other words, *do not* drive on the dunes. Access points in the National Seashore Park areas are marked by a light-brown sign with a white jeep icon. An "X" or "/" through a jeep means "no access" by four-wheel drive vehicle. The same goes for sound side driving: you should stay on the marked routes only. Your speed should be reasonable and prudent. And please pick up your trash — not just to be a nice person, but to avoid the access-limit laws that have closed much of Cape Cod, for example, to any four-wheel drive traffic at all. Vehicles must be state registered and street legal; the driver must also be licensed.

For current information on open zones and guidelines, you may contact the Headquarters, National Park Service, Cape Hatteras Group, 473-2111, any National Park Service visitor contact facility, or you may write to: Cape Hatteras National Seashore, Route 1, Box 675, Manteo, N.C. 27954.

Each township on the Banks has its own requirements for beach driving during certain times of the year. To get information or permits, contact the town administrative offices.

Citations and Tournaments

The Official North Carolina Saltwater Fishing Tournament is held annually to recognize outstanding angling achievement. The Department of Commerce, Travel and Tourism Division, awards citations for eligible species caught at or above certain minimum weights. Regulations on eligibility and boundaries may be obtained at these locations, which are also weighing stations for fish presented for citation:

Avalon Fishing Pier	Kill Devil Hills
Avon Fishing Pier	Avon
Bob's Bait & Tackle	Duck
Cape Hatteras Fishing Pier	Frisco
Dillon's Corner	Buxton
The Fishin' Hole	Salvo
Frisco Rod & Gun Club	Frisco
Hatteras Fishing Center	Hatteras Village
Hatteras Harbor Marina	Hatteras Village
Hatteras Marlin Club	Hatteras Village
Hatteras Tackle Shop	Hatteras Village
Hatteras Island Fishing Pier	Rodanthe
Island Marina	Manteo
Jennette's Pier	Nags Head
Kitty Hawk Fishing Pier	Kitty Hawk
Nags Head Fishing Pier	Nags Head
Nags Head Ice & Cold Storage	Nags Head
O'Neal's Dockside	Ocracoke
Oregon Inlet Fishing Center	Oregon Inlet
Outer Banks Pier and Fishing Center	South Nags Head

Home of the World's Best Charter Fleet

☆ **YACHT CLUB** ☆

MANTEO, NC

Offshore Gulfstream charters ☆ Inshore Inlet trips ☆ Half-day tower trips ☆ Marlin, Sailfish, Tuna, Dolphin, Blues, Mackeral, Cobia and Amberjack ☆ MAKE-UP TRIPS AVAILABLE

Pirate's Cove ships store has fine sportswear for the outdoorsman ☆ Casual resort wear for the ladies ☆ Nautical gifts ☆ One of a kind 14 carat gold and sterling silver

We invite you to come down each afternoon around 4:30 and watch the charter boats unload their catch. Don't forget your camera.

Located on the Manteo/Nags Head Causeway
P.O. Box 1997 • Manteo, NC 27954
(919) 473-3906   (800) 367-4728

Pelican's Roost — Hatteras Village

Pirate's Cove — Manteo-Nags Head Causeway

The Red Drum Tackle Shop — Buxton

Salty Dawg Marina — Manteo

Tatem's Tackle Box — Nags Head

TW's Bait & Tackle Shops — Duck and Kitty Hawk

Teach's Lair Marina — Hatteras Village

Tradewinds Tackle Shop — Ocracoke

Village Marina — Hatteras Village

Whalebone Tackle Shop — Nags Head

Willis Boat Landing — Hatteras Village

ELIGIBLE SPECIES AND MINIMUM WEIGHTS FOR CITATIONS, 1994

Amberjack 50 pounds, or 50 inches w/ release
Barracuda — 20 pounds
Bass, Black Sea — 4 pounds
Bluefish — 17 pounds
Cobia 40 pounds or 33 inches with release
Croaker — 3 pounds
Dolphin — 35 pounds
Drum, Black — 40 pounds
Drum Red — 45 pounds or 40 inches with release
Flounder — 5 pounds
Grouper (any) — 20 pounds
Jack, Crevalle — 20 pounds
Mackerel, King 30 pounds or 50 inches with release
Mackerel, Spanish — 6 pounds
Marlin, Blue — 400 pounds*
Marlin, White — 50 pounds*
Mullet, Sea — 1 1/2 pounds
Pompano — 2 pounds
Porgy (Silver Snapper) — 4 pounds
Sailfish — 30 pounds*
Shark (any) — 150 pounds
Sheepshead — 10 pounds
Snapper, Red — 10 pounds
Spot — 1 pound
Tarpon — 30 pounds*
Tautog — 8 pounds
Triggerfish — 7 pounds
Trout, Gray — 6 pounds
Trout, Speckled — 4 pounds
Tuna, Bigeye — 100 pounds
Tuna, Bluefin — 80 pounds
Tuna, Yellowfin — 70 pounds
Wahoo — 40 pounds
*CITATION FOR RELEASE REGARDLESS OF SIZE

Current All-Tackle N.C. Saltwater Game Fish Records

Fish	Weight	Location	Date
Amberjack	125	Off Cape Lookout	1973
Barracuda	67-7	Cape Lookout	1985
Bass, Black Sea	8	Off Oregon Inlet	1979
Bluefish	31-12*	Off Hatteras Island	1972
Cobia	103	Off Emerald Isle	1988
Croaker	5	Oregon Inlet	1981
Dolphin	77	Cape Hatteras	1973
Drum, Black	87	Off Cape Lookout	1990
Drum, Red	94	Hatteras Island	1984
Flounder	20-8	Carolina Beach	1980
Grouper, Warsaw	245	Wrightsville Beach	1967
Mackerel, King	79	Off Cape Lookout	1985
Mackerel, Span.	13	Ocracoke Inlet	1987
Marlin, Blue	1142	Oregon Inlet	1974
Marlin, White	118-8	Oregon Inlet	1976
Mullet, Sea	3-8	Bogue Banks' Pier	1971
Pompano	7-13	New River Inlet	1981
Porgy, Saucereye	13-2	Off Cape Lookout	1987
Sailfish	100	Off Ocean Isle	1987
Shark, Tiger	1150	Yaupon Beach	1966
Sheepshead	18-7	Off Carolina Beach	1982
Snapper, Red	40	Cape Lookout	1970
Spot	1-13	Manns Harbor	1979
Tarpon	164	Indian Beach Pier	1978
Tautog	19	Off Oregon Inlet	1992
Triggerfish	11-4	Off Wrightsville Beach	1990
Trout, Gray	14-14	Nags Head	1980
Trout, Speckled	12-4	Wrightsville Beach	1961
Tuna, Bigeye	300	Off Oregon Inlet	1989
Tuna, Bluefin	732-8	Off Cape Hatteras	1979
Tuna, Yellowfin	237	Atlantic Ocean	1979
Wahoo	127	Off Oregon Inlet	1973

*World All-tackle record

To make application for all-tackle record recognition, write Dale Ward, Coordinator, N.C. Division of Marine Fisheries, P.O. Box 769, Morehead City, N.C. 28557. A good photograph is needed for proof.

Call (800) 682-2632 for information or to report violations.

Inside
Surfing, Windsurfing
Ocean Swimming and
Kayaking

Surfing

Surfing has been around on the Banks since Bob Holland first began coming down from Virginia Beach in the late '50s. Holland opened the area's first surf shop. Since then, word of the good surf has spread; the East Coast Surfing Championships started here in the late '70s, and in 1978 and 1982 the U.S. Championships were held here.

"The best spot is at the lighthouse," says Scott Busbey, a resident pro and owner of the Natural Art surf shop. "Waves there usually break from the left, and the three jetties they built for erosion control formed a good sand bar."

Local surfers look forward to the hurricane season, from about the first of June to the end of November. This is when they begin to watch weather reports, hoping for the big northern swells. Waves get up to eight feet, and sometimes larger, but more than about eight feet tends to be "victory at sea."

Cape Hatteras (not just the lighthouse beach) is always a popular spot. It has the advantage of having two beaches, facing different directions; one faces south, the other east

by southeast. When wind and swells are unsuitable at one, the other may be surfable. But when the wind comes from the southeast, which it often does in midsummer, be prepared to go swimming; surfing is poor. Two to three feet tends to be summer average. There's no channel at the Cape, which means you've got to muscle your way out there in heavy weather. Beware of the current when the waves come up; it's often two knots or more to the south along the beach, faster than you can swim, though on a board you might fight it. Wet suits are a must until about the first of June; after that skin is OK till late October, or even later, depending on how long the summer lasts.

The lighthouse is usually the best, but not the only good break. The sandbars off the Banks are constantly shifting and changing, and there's a continual migration of surfers along them to find the best spots. Surf along the Banks is where you find it. Places to check: Ramp 41; Frisco pier (off Billy Mitchell Airport stay at least 400 feet from the pier itself); and Kitty Hawk Pier, south of Coquina Beach. But, you can always find a crowd at the lighthouse.

Some people go out on a charter boat and don't even put a line in the water.

Learning to Surf

A lot of people, many of them from far inland, have learned to surf at Hatteras. If you've never done it, but you suspect that riding those big Atlantic waves in to the Cape Point break might be your kind of thrill, here are some tips to help you get started.

First, a bit of traditional surfer lore: the younger you are, the easier it is to start. If you're old enough to swim, and feel confident 100 yards off the beach, you can surf. Here's how.

You can't surf without a board. (Body surfing doesn't count.) You can rent one, or borrow one if you can convince a surfer to let go of his custom-made. Fortunately, any of the surf shops will rent you one for around $10 or so a day, a reasonable price, we think. (There will also be a deposit.) If you rent yours, be sure to ask if it's been waxed; if it hasn't, you'll be sliding all over, and then off, the board.

Second, you've got to find a break. We suggest not starting off where all the others are surfing. Get off by yourself, so that you won't be in the way of the more skilled. The break won't be as good, but then, neither are you. Right?

Item number three. To surf, you've got to learn to paddle the board. Find your balance position. Your chest should go about at the thickest part of the surfboard. This is important, so try paddling about till you feel comfortable. Watch how the others do it up the beach.

Now paddle out to sea.

To surf, you must realize that the wave is moving toward the beach at some speed, while the shallowing water forces it to crest. You won't be picked up by it unless you're moving in the same direction at almost the same speed. (This is why paddling is so important.) This is the hardest part of learning — getting your timing down, learning to watch and catch the wave at that exactly correct fraction of a second.

Once the wave has you, you'll know it. You'll be carried forward fast and effortlessly as part of the sea in motion. It's a thrill.

Finally, to get up: just stand up — just as if you were doing a push-up from the speeding board. Don't get to your knees first. Just stand up naturally. Place one or the other foot forward about a shoulder-width apart. (Most people do it left foot forward, but there's no shame in being a "goofy-foot.")

If you can stand up and ride a wave into the beach that way once, you've done pretty well for your first day; don't stay out forever and agonize with sunburn tomorrow. The rest, the turning, and the other advanced maneuvers, will come with practice.

When you feel more confident, when you want to try the good breaks with the others, remember your manners. Stay out of the way if someone's already on a wave. You'll find, after hanging around for a while, that most surfers are friendly, and with time you'll fit in with the others just fine. Also, please help keep litter off the beaches; a clean beach provides a better surf experience. And, show respect for private property as you make your way to your favorite surfing spots. The Outer Banks is lucky to have a very active Surfrider Foundation, a non-profit organization dedicated to pro-

tection, enhancement and enjoyment of the world's oceans and coastal resources. If interested, call 441-0216.

"Awoo!"

Windsurfing

Windsurfing, or board sailing, is almost as popular in this area as surfing . . . some would argue more so, and they could be right. Some days when the wind is up, the sound is so colorful with the sails of windsurfing boards it looks like a floating carnival. It's well known that the entire Outer Banks and, some think, especially Hatteras, is the best windsurfing location on the Atlantic coast. To be even more specific, the Canadian Hole, located soundside just before you get into Buxton, is considered the best of the best spots. But there are plenty of other great places — wherever you can get out onto the shallow, wind swept waters.

Ted James came to Hatteras in '72 from Florida to surf and fish, "looking for what Florida lost years ago." He runs a commercial fishing boat in the winter, and has been making his Fox boards here and in Florida since 1968. James was one of the first to put sailboards in big surf here, and he was instrumental in improving the boards and rigs to their present state of excellence. He was busy shaping a racing board in his Buxton workshop when we asked him to tell us a little about windsurfing.

"It's real simple why Hatteras is so popular for windsurfers. People have been cussin' the wind here since there was wind. But with sailboards, the more wind the better.

"The equipment you use is a board and a rig. The heart of the system is a 'universal' that swivels and pivots in every direction. That allows you to position the mast, boom and sail, and determine your direction. Basically, to sail cross wind, the mast is up and down. To sail downwind, tip the mast forward, and that turns the front of the board downwind. Mast back turns the board upwind.

"Now, that sounds complicated, and that's why I recommend lessons. What we do is spend 2½ hours — the first lesson — on teaching people to sail short distances. The second lesson we practice, increasing sail area, smaller boards, switching rigs — whatever challenges the individual. We also teach self-rescue and rigging in the second lesson. Self-rescue's important in case the wind dies, or something breaks. People are recreationally proficient after two lessons.

"Now, that's not experienced surfers; that's people who walk in the door. You don't have to be athletic. Though it's easier to teach people who sail, in a way, because they know the wind. Surfing is not as big an advantage. No, you don't have to know how to swim. We put a jacket on them.

"It's not easy — you have to pay attention — but we've had people uncoordinated, overweight, and they catch on. For a lot of them, it's the first athletic success they've ever had. And it means a lot to me to help them succeed. Our students range from 12 to 60. We've taught more than 1,000 people in the last three years and only had one person who couldn't do it. It's neat — sometimes you get teenaged sons, and Dad outshines them. They kind of laugh a little bit then."

Ralph Buxton, owner of Kitty Hawk Sports, started teaching windsurfing in 1980 in the Nags Head area. He is well known for his participation in and promotion of the sport. He explains that while the Canadian Hole is certainly a great place to sail, windsurfers also enjoy the many upper Banks windsurfing areas because the wind conditions are just as good, and there are many other attractions available to them if the wind isn't cooperating. Kitty Hawk Sports' Sailing Site in Nags Head is an ideal place to learn because of its shallow and sheltered water.

The basic sailboarding season is year round. December to March is slow, though, simply because it's cold. (There's plenty of wind out there, however, if you want it.) James runs competitive events, the Hatteras Wave Classic in October and the Pro-Am in the spring. Kitty Hawk

Sports runs the Easter Dash for Cash, the August Watermelon Regatta and the Thanksgiving Classic Regatta. The magazine *Windsurfing the Outer Banks* sponsors a windsurfing competition in the third week of April. The first Saturday in October is the date for the magazine's windsurfing event that benefits local water rescue squads. There's a raffle, swap meet and race at Camp Hatteras in Waves. These are as much fun to watch as they are to participate in.

Windsurfing the Outer Banks is a great guide giving detailed information (who, what, where, when and how) about this sport. This annual publication is for sale up and down the Banks. For more information, refer to our write up in Hatteras Island Recreation.

Hard-core windsurfers are excited about the new speed reef installed in the sound at Avon. This 200-meter vinyl-coated artificial reef softens choppy waves, flattens water and gives speed sailors a choice new location. Check with Windsurfing Hatteras for upcoming Hatteras Speed Reef events. Watching these competitions should be great fun too.

Windsurfing and Surf Shops

There are plenty of surf shops on the Banks, scattered north and south. For a 24-Hour surf report, call 995-4646.

WINDSURFING HATTERAS
Avon   995-4970

HATTERAS ISLAND SURF SHOP
Waves   987-2296

WAVE RIDING VEHICLES
Kitty Hawk   261-7952

KITTY HAWK SPORTS
Nags Head   441-6800 and 441-2756
Avon   995-5000
Duck   261-8770

SECRET SPOT SURF SHOP
Nags Head   441-4030

VITAMIN SEA SURF SHOP
Kill Devil Hills   441-7512

BW'S SURF SHOP
Ocracoke   928-6141

BERT'S SURF SHOP
Kitty Hawk   261-7584
Nags Head   441-1939

CAVALIER SURF SHOP
Nags Head   441-7349

CHICAMACOMICO WATERSPORTS
Rodanthe   987-2296

NATURAL ART SURF SHOP
Buxton   995-5682

NEW SUN SURF SHOP
Nags Head   441-3994

RODANTHE SURF SHOP
Rodanthe   987-2412

17TH ST. SURF SHOP
Kill Devil Hills   441-1797

WHALEBONE SURF SHOP
Nags Head   441-6747
Kitty Hawk   261-8737

FOX WATER SPORTS
Buxton   995-4102

Umbrellas dot the shore on warm, sunny summer days.

RIDE THE WIND
Ocracoke   928-7451

OCRACOKE OUTDOORS
Ocracoke   928-4061

Kayaking the Sounds

Kayaking is a growing recreational pastime on the Outer Banks. "Eco-tours" are taking customers into the marshes, sounds and sloughs, where they explore hidden channels and play in the inlets. Kayaking in sounds is very easy to learn, and offers an excellent chance to observe the local flora and fauna quietly and unobtrusively. There are thousands of square miles of sheltered sounds to explore. Several guided trips are offered, with the two and four-hour excursions being the most popular. For those who want more, overnight camping trips are also available. You can ex-

plore shallow sound waters near Corolla, Kitty Hawk, Wanchese, Nags Head, Manteo, Alligator River National Wildlife Refuge or Ocracoke. Having mastered kayaking in the sounds, advanced kayakers will want to try paddling in the ocean. For information, contact Kitty Hawk Sports 441-6800, or Kitty Hawk Kites 441-4124, both in Nags Head. In Ocracoke contact Ride the Wind, 928-7451; or Ocracoke Outdoors, 928-4061.

Ocean Swimming

If you've grown up around the sea, sailing as a kid, spending long days on surfboards, you probably know that Mother Ocean can sometimes be dangerous. It's important to know that the Outer Banks surf can, at times, be especially treacherous. We feel it is a good idea, especially if you have children, to only swim in areas that are guarded. And, if the red flags are flying, warning swimmers to stay out of the ocean, *please* pay attention to them. Sometimes they fly when the weather seems fine, but the average person can't judge when the water is safe. Trust those flags!

Here are a few tips to make you better acquainted with the ocean.

RIPS

Rip currents can carry a child or a wader out into rough water in seconds. They generally move along the shore and then straight out toward sea. They often occur when there's a break in a submerged sandbar. You can see a rip; it's choppy, turbulent, often discolored water that looks deeper than the water around it. If you are caught in a rip, don't panic, and don't try to struggle straight back to shore against its force. Remember that rip currents are narrow. Very few are wider than 30 feet across. So simply swim parallel to the beach until you're out of it, or let it carry you seaward till it peters out. Then move to one side or the other of it and swim back.

UNDERTOW

When a wave comes up on the beach and breaks, the water must run back down to the sea. This is undertow. It sucks at your ankles from small waves, but in heavy surf undertow can knock you off your feet and carry you out. If you're carried out, don't resist. Let the under-tow take you out till it stops. It will only be a few yards. The next wave will help push you shoreward again.

LOSING CONTROL IN WAVES

If a wave crashes down on you while you are surfing or swimming, and you find yourself being tumbled in bubbles and sand like a sheet in a washing machine, don't try to struggle to the surface against it. Curl into a ball, or just go limp and float. The wave will take you to the beach or else you can swim to the surface when it passes.

PRECAUTIONS AND TIPS

Never swim alone.

Observe the surf before going in the water.

Look for currents.

Stay out of the water if you can't swim.

Stay off the beach during electrical storms.

Swim in areas with on-duty lifeguards.

Observe warning flags near public accesses. If they're red, don't go in.

Protect yourself from the sun. Sunburns don't turn into tans. They peel off.

Keep non-swimming children well above the marks of the highest waves. Keep an eye on children at all times, and teach them never to turn their back on the waves while they play at water's edge.

Don't swim near fishermen or deployed fishing lines.

Stay 300 feet away from fishing piers.

Watch out for surfers.

N.C. Travel and Tourism

Windsurfing is a popular sport on the Outer Banks.

Public Beaches with Lifeguards

COROLLA
Currituck Beach Light
Shad Street
Bonito Street

DUCK
Ocean Pines
North Snow Geese Drive
Barrier Island
Plover Drive

SOUTHERN SHORES
13th Street (parking permit required)

KITTY HAWK
Public bath house at Kitty Hawk Rd.
Kill Devil Hills
Helga Street
Hayman Street
5th Street
3rd Street at the Sea Ranch
2nd Street
1st Street
Ashville Drive

Woodmere Avenue
Raleigh Street
Sutton Avenue at the Comfort Inn
Ocean Bay Boulevard
Oregon Street
Cavalier Motel
Clark Street
Outer Banks Beach Club
Atlantic Street
Holiday Inn
Ramada Inn
John Yancey Motel

NAGS HEAD
Bonnett Street
Epstein Street at the Windjammer
Hargrove Street

ROANOKE ISLAND
Old Swimming Hole on Croatan Sound at Dare
County Regional Airport

CAPE HATTERAS NATIONAL SEASHORE
There are no lifeguard stations provided by the
National Park Service at this time, including
Hatteras and Ocracoke island public beaches.

Inside
Scuba Diving

Many people aren't aware that scuba diving on the Outer Banks is an adventure of some importance. While the waters off the Florida Keys, Caribbean islands and south seas are full of colorful fish and vegetation, the Outer Banks has shipwrecks.

These waters are for the serious divers who are tough and willing to brave cold water and little visibility in some cases. The changeable weather off the Outer Banks is another consideration. The Banks' shifting sands uncover new wrecks almost every year, and area divers keep busy discovering them. Check local shops for the latest information on what's being picked up and where. Enjoy the opportunity to explore the sea and its sometimes ancient treasures.

Dive Destinations

LST 471, a ship sunk in 1949. About ¼ mile north of Rodanthe Fishing Pier, 100 yards offshore in 15 feet of water.

Oriental (Boiler Wreck) thought to be a Federal Transport that sank in 1862. About four miles south of Oregon Inlet. The boiler of the ship is visible in the surf.

Marore Tanker, off Rodanthe. Approximately 22 miles SE of Or-

egon Inlet, 12 miles offshore. Torpedoed on February 26, 1942, 100 feet deep.

Tug, identification unknown. Kill Devil Hills. Approximately 300 yards south of Avalon Pier, 75 yards offshore, in 20 feet of water.

Metropolis Freighter, Corolla (Horsehead Wreck). Three miles south of Currituck Beach Lighthouse, 100 yards offshore in breakers. About 15 feet deep. Went down in 1878, 85 lives were lost. Was carrying 500 tons of iron rails and 200 tons of stones. Was formerly the Federal Gunboat, *Stars and Stripes*. Good off season wreck. Accessible by four-wheel drive only.

Triangle Wrecks, *Josephine* (lost 1915), *Kyzickes* (1927), *Carl Gerhard* (1929). Off Milepost 7 at Kill Devil Hills about 100 yards out and 200 yards south of the Sea Ranch. Depth about 20 feet.

USS Huron, Federal screw steamer lost off Nags Head in 1877. Now in 26 feet of water. Many artifacts.

Liberty Ship, *(Zane Grey)* about one mile south of Oregon Inlet at 80 feet.

U-85, German sub sunk in 1942. Northeast of Oregon Inlet in 100 feet of water. Boat needed. (See Bodie Island Section.)

York, Benson, Buarque Freight-

ers and tankers sunk by the U-boats during Operation Paukenschlag in 1942. They lie offshore but within dive boat range, in 100 to 120 feet of water. Good, challenging dives.

Beach Diving — There are more than 12 wrecks in shallow water between Duck and Hatteras. Great for free diving (without scuba gear) and spear fishing. Ask local divers for locations.

Sound Diving — If you don't mind shallow, murky water, you may enjoy groping around north and west of Roanoke Island. Old Civil War forts lie submerged, and local divers have found cannonballs, bottles and relics with metal detectors.

Important Numbers

Oregon Inlet USCG Station	987-2311
Ocean Rescue Squad (helicopter available)	911
Diver Alert Network (DAN)	684-8111

Shops and Facilities

NAGS HEAD PRO DIVE CENTER
Kitty Hawk Connection, MP 13½
Nags Head   441-7594

This is the oldest dive facility on the Outer Banks offering a full line of services. Located across from Jockey's Ridge, they sell and rent equipment, airfills to 5,000 psi and offer PADI instruction. The Nags Head Divers also run their 50-foot dive board, the *Sea Fox*, out of the Manteo waterfront to the historic wrecks off the Outer Banks. They're open seven days a week from 10 AM to 5 PM during the season. Call for information.

SEA SCAN DIVE CENTRE
Beach Rd., MP 10 ½
Nags Head   480-3467

This Nags Head dive center is a full dive, full service NAUI Pro Facility offering sales, rentals, repairs, instruction and charters. Sea Scan also offers personal guide service to the wrecks for a fee. Near shore and offshore trips are available on their boat, *Diving Blues Make It So*. Snorkeling lessons are fun for the entire family. Sea Scan is open year round.

HATTERAS DIVERS
Hatteras Village   986-2557

Located just west of Hatteras Harbor Motel on the waterfront, this shop is owned by Donny Lang, who plans charter trips to Tarpon, Abrams, Dixie Arrow, Proteus, BoxCar reefs and other popular destinations. From June to October the hours are 9 AM to 6 PM Monday through Saturday. They can arrange charters, fill your air tanks and offer rental gear. For information call or write: P.O. Box 213, Hatteras, NC 27943.

OCRACOKE DIVERS INC.
Oyster Creek Rd.
Ocracoke Village   928-1471

This Ocracoke dive company is now a full-service marina offering guided shallow- and deep-water diving tours. PADI-certified divers guide you to WWII and pre-WWII wrecks. Group and specialty diving tours for two or three people are available. Air, gear, gas and accommodations can be provided. Reservations are required.

Inside
Ferry Schedules

Hatteras Inlet (Ocracoke) Ferry

Hatteras Village   986-2353

This free state-run ferry service links Hatteras and Ocracoke Island with an enjoyable 40-minute trip. During this trip you cross the county line — so there's a point that's neither Hyde nor Dare (couldn't resist that one). The ferries accommodate cars and even large camping vehicles and are scheduled often enough during the summer so that your wait will not be too long. Reservations are not required, as they are for the Cedar Island and Swan Quarter ferries from Ocracoke Village. Yes, there are (small) bathrooms on the ferry. The summer schedule is as follows:

SUMMER SCHEDULE
MAY 26 THROUGH OCTOBER 16

Leave Hatteras	Leave Ocracoke
5:00 AM	5:00 AM
6:00 AM	6:00 AM
7:00 AM	7:00 AM
7:30 AM	8:00 AM
Then every 30 minutes until	
6:30 PM	7:30 PM
8:00 PM	9:00 PM
10:00 PM	11:00 PM
Midnight	

WINTER SCHEDULE
OCTOBER 17 THROUGH MAY 25

Leave Hatteras every hour on the hour from 5 AM to 6 PM, and at 8 PM, 10 PM, and midnight.

Leave Ocracoke every hour on the hour from 5 AM to 7 PM, then at 9 PM and 11 PM.

From Ocracoke: Swan Quarter and Cedar Island

RESERVATIONS

To avoid possible delay in boarding the Cedar Island-Ocracoke Toll Ferry and the Swan Quarter-Ocracoke Toll Ferry, reservations are recommended. These may be made in person at the departure terminal or by telephone. For departures from Ocracoke, call 928-3841; for departures from Cedar Island, call 225-3551; and for reservations for departures from Swan Quarter, call 926-1111. (Office hours 6 AM to 6 PM, later in summer.)

Reservations may be made up to 30 days in advance of departure date and are not transferable. These reservations must be claimed at least

30 minutes prior to departure time. The name of the driver and the vehicle license number are required when making reservations.

Ocracoke-Swan Quarter Toll Ferry

Crossing Time: Approximately 2½ hours.
Capacity: approximately 30 Cars

This 2½-hour ferry ride connects Ocracoke with Swan Quarter in Hyde County, on the mainland. You'll go through Swan Quarter National Wildlife Refuge and connect with Highway 264 with its gracious old cedars lining the way.

YEAR-ROUND SCHEDULE

Leave Ocracoke	Leave Swan Quarter
6:30 AM	9:30 AM
12:30 PM	4:00 PM

One-way fares and rates applicable are listed at right.

Ocracoke — Cedar Island Toll Ferry

Ocracoke Village   928-3841
Crossing Time Approximately: 2½ hours.
Capacity Approximately 30 Cars

Though it takes 2½ hours, this is a popular path for those going south from Ocracoke. (The alternative is to drive back to Nags Head and get on Highway 264 South or to take the ferry to Swan Quarter.) This ferry will take you across the Pamlico Sound to Cedar Island. From Cedar Island, those going south can take Highway 70 to Morehead City. Take a good book and a basket of snacks. Relax, and enjoy the view from the ferry.

SUMMER SCHEDULE
May 26 through October 15

Leave Cedar Island	Leave Ocracoke
7:00 AM	7:00 AM
8:15 AM	9:30 AM
9:30 AM	10:45 AM
12:00 PM	12:00 PM
1:15 PM	3:00 PM
3:00 PM	4:15 PM
6:00 PM	6:00 PM
8:30 PM	8:30 PM

SPRING AND FALL SCHEDULES
May 11 through May 25
October 3 through October 30

Leave Cedar Island	Leave Ocracoke
7:00 AM	7:00 AM
9:30 AM	9:30 AM
12:00 PM	12:00 PM
3:00 PM	3:00 PM
6:00 PM	6:00 PM
8:30 PM	8:30 PM

WINTER SCHEDULE
October 31 through May 10

7:00 AM	7:00 AM
10:00 AM	10:00 AM
1:00 PM	1:00 PM
4:00 PM	4:00 PM

Insiders' Tips

Dave Poyer's *Hatteras Blue*, a terrific underwater adventure set on the Outer Banks, makes for great reading.

Photo: N.C. Travel and Tourism

A pelican perched on a piling makes an appealing picture.

Fares and Rates (One Way)

A. Pedestrian — $1

B. Bicycle and Rider — $2

C. Single vehicle or combination 20' or less in length and motorcycles (minimum fare for licensed vehicle) — $10

D. Vehicles or combinations from 20' to 40' in length — $20

E. All vehicles or combinations 40 to 55 feet in length having a maximum width of 8 feet and height of 13 feet 6 inches — $30

For further information about ferry schedules, call (800)BYFERRY (293-3779)

Vehicle Gross Load Limits

All Crossings:
Any axle — 13,000 pounds
Two axles (single vehicle) — 24,000 pounds

Three or more axles — 36,000 pounds (single or combination vehicle)

More information may be obtained from Director, Ferry Division, Morehead City, N.C. 28557, or by calling 726-6446 or 726-6413.

Inside
Medical Care

Since there is no hospital on the Outer Banks, a growing number of emergency care centers have been developed. Community health care clinics have sprung up along with these centers. The facilities are supported by ambulance and helicopter evacuation to the nearest hospitals in the event such transportation is necessary.

Emergency Numbers

Emergency service in Dare and Currituck counties   911

Ocean rescue   911

Northern and southern regions of the Outer Banks fire and rescue service   911

Outer Banks areas Coast Guard (emergency only)   995-6410

Ocracoke Island Coast Guard   928-3711

Medical Centers and Clinics

CHESAPEAKE MEDICAL SPECIALISTS
Marketplace, Rt. 158
Southern Shores   261-5800
An affiliate of Chesapeake General Hospital, this center staffs 12 specialists and takes appointments Monday through Friday from 9 AM

to 5 PM. Available are cardiologists, rheumatologists, dermatologists, a vascular surgeon, orthopedic and plastic surgeons, ear, nose and throat specialists, allergy specialists and a gastroenterologist.

NORTH BEACH MEDICAL CENTER
Juniper Trail
Southern Shores   261-4187
Here you can obtain psychological counseling (261-5190), audiology services, speech and language, occupational and physical therapy (261-9049).

FIRST FLIGHT FAMILY PRACTICE
Rt. 158, MP 10½   441-3177
Nags Head
This clinic is open from Monday through Thursday for medical appointments. Dr. Charles Davidson provides general medical care. X-ray is available. Hours are from 9 AM to 5:30 PM Monday through Thursday.

VIRGINIA DARE WOMEN'S CENTER
Rt. 158, MP 10½
Nags Head   441-2144
Appointments are available for women-centered medical care. Patty Johnson is a certified nurse-midwife and family nurse practitioner. Maternity care, baby care and pap smears are offered along with generalized care. Hours are Monday,

Tuesday and Thursday from 9 AM to 1 PM and 2 to 5 PM.

OUTER BANKS MEDICAL AND EMERGENCY CARE

West of Rt. 158, MP 10½
W. Barnes St.
Nags Head 441-7111

This is the only 24-hour medical facility on the beach. Walk-ins are welcome, and there is an X-ray laboratory on the premises. Appointments for family medical care are accepted.

MACDOWELL FAMILY HEALTH CENTER

Hwy. 64, Main Rd.
Manteo 473-2500

Dr. Brian MacDowell provides complete family medical care at this office. X-ray is available, as well as psychological counseling services provided by Debra MacDowell, MA, NCC. Counseling hours are on Thursday from 8:30 AM to 12:30 PM. Call for appointments. Hours are 8:30 AM to 5 PM Monday, Tuesday, Wednesday and Friday.

DARE MEDICAL ASSOCIATES

Hwy. 64, Main Rd.
Manteo 473-3478

Dr. Walter Holton provides family service and acute care from this office. X-ray is available. Hours are 8 AM to 5 PM. Monday through Friday.

HATTERAS ISLAND MEDICAL CENTER

Hwy. 12
Buxton 986-2756

Dr. Seaborn Blair, III and Katie Williams, FNP, combine their knowledge and skills to form a solid medical care and services center on the lower end of Hatteras Island. X-ray is available. They maintain 24-hour emergency call coverage and have office hours on weekdays from 8:30 AM to 5 PM except Wednesday and Saturday. Wednesday hours are from 9 AM to 5 PM, and Saturday hours are 9 AM to 1 PM.

BUXTON MEDICAL CENTER

Hwy. 12
Buxton 995-4455

Dr. J. Whit Dunkle and Katie Williams, FNP offer comprehensive family medical care and operate a 24-hour emergency on-call service. Their hours are Monday, Wednesday and Friday from 1:30 PM to 5:30 PM.

OCRACOKE HEALTH CENTER

Ocracoke 928-1511
Past the firehouse

Graham Evans, P.S., provides general medical care for all ages in this small island clinic. Hours are Monday, Tuesday, Wednesday and Friday from 8:30 AM to noon and 1 PM to 5 PM; Thursday from 8:30 AM to noon. If necessary, call the rescue squad at 911.

Regional Medical Center

Rt. 158, MP 1 1/2
5200 N. Croatan Hwy.
Kitty Hawk 261-9000

The communities of the Outer Banks rely on this medical center for convenient and competent health care whether it is routine or specialized. The separate units are thoughtfully arranged in order to provide quick access to the appropriate diagnostic and health care center.

In addition, preventive and educational programs are offered here.

This medical complex consists of:

URGENT CARE/FAMILY MEDICINE
261-4187

Physicians from Beach Medical Care staff this center that provides urgent care and family medicine for scheduled and walk-in patients seven days a week. Off season hours are Monday through Sunday 9 AM to 9 PM. Summer season extended hours are 8 AM to 10 PM.

RMS SURGERY & PROCEDURE CENTER
261-9009

This is an outpatient surgery center. Procedures such as breast biopsy, hernia repair, laparoscopy, D and C, tonsillectomy, adenoidectomy, oral surgery, cosmetic plastic surgery, and tendon repair are performed here.

MEDICAL SPECIALISTS
261-9000

Approximately 30 medical specialists rotate through this facility. A directory of the physicians and specialities can be obtained by calling the above number. Roche Biomedical Laboratory is located here where blood tests are handled quickly for complete diagnosis.

RADIOLOGY AND IMAGING
261-4311

Outer Banks Radiology provides routine as well as diagnostic services such as mammograms, ultrasounds, fluoroscopy etc.

Dentists

Though not a complete list of the dentists located on the Outer

An ounce of prevention is worth a pound of cure.

Banks, the following listing includes those who have indicated they're available for emergency care.

BUDDE & BUEKER, DDS
Rt. 158, MP 5½
Executive Center, Kill Devil Hills   441-5811

FRANK AUSBAND, DDS
Rt. 158, MP 11
Nags Head   441-0437

JEFFREY JACOBSON, DDS
Colington Rd.
Colington   441-8882

MICHAEL MORGAN, DDS
Juniper Trail
Southern Shores   261-2358

Chiropractic Care

WELLNESS CENTER OF THE OUTER BANKS
The Marketplace
Southern Shores   261-5424

Daniel Goldberg, DC, offers a

full range of chiropractic services and nutrition management. Massage therapist Kim Conners is also available for appointments.

DARE CHIROPRACTIC
Rt. 158, MP 5
Kitty Hawk   *261-8885*

Burt Rubin, DC, Allan S. Kroland, DC, and B.L. Ackley, DC, have the largest full-service chiropractic clinic on the beach. Nutritional counseling and stress management support are available. They have a new location in Kitty Hawk. Holly King, CMT is available for massage. Call for an appointment.

OUTER BANKS CHIROPRACTIC CLINIC
Rt. 158, MP 10
Nags Head   *441-1585*

Craig Gibson, DC, has office hours by appointment.

Other Services

Ask-A-Nurse: Call (800) 832-8836 for a free service from Albemarle Hospital. This number gives you access to 24-hour phone consultations with specially-trained nurses. This is a good alternative when faced with a medical question when you're not sure what to do.

Dare Vision Center is located on the beach on the Route 158 at MP 9, Kill Devil Hills, 441-4872, and in Manteo on Highway 64 near McDonald's, 473-2155.

Outer Banks Hotline, 473-3366, north of Oregon Inlet or call collect south of the inlet, is a 24-hour crisis counseling service that also provides shelter to victims of abuse. They operate a thrift shop in Manteo and conduct regular public-awareness seminars and trainings.

Atlantic Counseling Services, 441-1372, Route 158, in Nags Head is run by Robin Craven, MA, certified professional counselor. He offers individual and family counseling as well as psychotherapy. Call for appointment.

Alcoholics Anonymous is available. Call 261-1681, 441-6020 or 473-5389. In Hatteras call 995-4240 or 995-4283.

Inside
Service and
Information Directory

Important Numbers

COAST GUARD

Buxton Village	995-5881
Hatteras Island	987-2311
Hatteras Village	986-2175
N. of Oregon Inlet	987-2311
Ocracoke	928-3711, 995-6452*

Call goes through Hatteras and is more reliable according to Coast Guard.

COUNTY SHERIFF
FOR EMERGENCIES CALL 911

Hatteras Island (Dare County)	986-2146
N. of Oregon Inlet (Dare County)	473-3481
Northern Outer Banks (Currituck County)	232-2216
Ocracoke Island (Hyde County)	926-3171

FIRE DEPARTMENT
FOR EMERGENCIES CALL 911

Avon Village	995-5021
Buxton Village	995-5241
Carova Beach	453-8690
Chicamacomico	987-2347
Colington	441-6234
Corolla	453-3242
Duck	261-3929
Frisco	995-5522
Hatteras Village	986-2356
Kill Devil Hills	480-4060
Kitty Hawk	261-2666
Manteo	473-2300
Nags Head	441-5853
Ocracoke	928-4831

Salvo Village	987-2411
Southern Shores	261-2394
Wanchese	473-5454

Most homes and cottages are provided with a fire extinguisher. If you need service, your rental property manager will take care of this. However, if you own a home, or for any reason need service, call Fire Defense Center, 261-1314 or 491-2478. They will pick up and deliver refills and new products.

POLICE DEPARTMENT
FOR EMERGENCIES CALL 911

(If there is no listing for a particular community, call the Sheriff's Department.)

Hatteras Village	995-4412
Kill Devil Hills	480-4020
Kitty Hawk	261-3895
Manteo	473-2069
Nags Head	441-6386
Southern Shores	261-3331
Duck	261-3185

NATIONAL PARK SERVICE OFFICES

North of Oregon Inlet	473-2111
	441-6644
South of Oregon Inlet	995-4474
Ocracoke Island	928-4531

CRISIS HOTLINE

Outer Banks Hotline offers con-

THOUSANDS DIE EACH YEAR . . .

YOU CAN MAKE THE DIFFERENCE!

Many animals are abandoned annually in Dare County . . . left to wander in search of a home . . . food . . . water.

The sad fact is that most of them don't find homes. They die as a result of starvation, injury, abuse or neglect.

We're working to change this. And you can make a difference.

PLEASE HELP US HELP THEM!

Send your tax-deductible contributions to:

Outer Banks S.P.C.A.
P. O. Box 3006
Kill Devil Hills, NC 27948
473-1101 ext. 250 or 473-5918

fidential counseling and information for any crisis, and a shelter for battered women and their children.

| North of Oregon Inlet | 473-3366 |
| South of Oregon Inlet | Call collect |

Animal Services

VETERINARIANS

Kitty Hawk, Nags Head, Manteo and Hatteras Island all have established veterinary clinics. Check the Yellow Pages under Veterinarians for a complete listing.

| Dare County Animal Shelter | 473-2143 |

Kennels

WATER OAK KENNEL
| Buxton Village | 995-5663 |

ANIMAL HOSPITAL OF NAGS HEAD
| 158 Bypass | 441-8611 |

SALTY DOG
GROOMING & BOARDING
| Colington | 441-6501 |

NORTH RIVER KENNEL
| Powells Point | 491-2284 |

COASTAL ANIMAL HOSPITAL
| Kitty Hawk | 261-3960 |

SITE SITTERS, INC.
| | 441-5030 |

On site house and pet sitting service is available.

Automotive Services

The Outer Banks automotive services and parts stores have improved through the years. It's a good idea to get your automobile serviced before vacation time rolls around. However, if you are here and need service, here's a handy listing of some businesses we've had good experiences with.

R.D. SAWYER FORD,
| Manteo | 473-2141 |

COASTAL AUTO MART
| Kitty Hawk | 261-5900 |

OUTER BANKS
CHRYSLER/PLYMOUTH/DODGE/JEEP
| Kill Devil Hills | 441-1146 |

Other recommended auto services and towing:

KITTY HAWK EXXON
| Kitty Hawk | 261-2720 |

SETO'S TEXACO (AAA)
| Kitty Hawk | 261-3138 |

BAYSIDE TOWING
| Kill Devil Hills | 441-2985 |

KILL DEVIL HILLS
AMOCO AUTO REPAIR
| Kill Devil Hills | 441-7283 |

BERRY AUTOMOTIVE
| Manteo | 473-6111 |

AUTOTECH
| Nags Head | 441-5293 |

MANTEO WRECKER SERVICE (AAA)
| Manteo | 473-5654 |

FARROW BROTHERS AUTOMOTIVE
| Avon | 995-5944 |

BALLANCE GULF & OIL
| Hatteras Village | 986-2424 |

Car Rentals

Car rentals are available at the Dare County Airport in Manteo and at a few other places on the Outer Banks.

NATIONAL CAR RENTAL
(Kill Devil Hills Amoco)   441-5488

B & R RENT-A-CAR
Dare County Airport   473-2600

R.D. SAWYER FORD
Manteo   473-2141

OUTER BANKS CHRYSLER/PLYMOUTH
Kill Devil Hills   441-1146

Child Care

BETTER BEGINNINGS
Kitty Hawk   261-2833

This owner-operated, year-round service provides day care for families on the Outer Banks. They take children 6 weeks to 12 years old, provide lunch and two snacks daily and are state licensed.

SUNSATIONAL SITTERS
441-TOTS

This service sends mature, trained sitters directly to your hotel, motel or cottage, allowing you some free time while on vacation. Sitters are bonded and insured, trained in CPR and first-aid and have passed extensive reference, background and police checks. Service is available 24-hours a day, seven days a week. Early reservations are recommended.

AUPAIRCARE
(800)288-7786

AuPairCare provides live-in European au pairs on yearly cultural visas, providing affordable, long-term, live-in child care. Host families choose from well-qualified, English-speaking applicants between the ages of 18 and 25. Unlike employees, au pairs function much like family members, sharing meals and social occasions. Local community counselors are close at hand to provide guidance and support. This is a great way to share the world with your children.

Fishing Report

WOBR Radio	473-3373
Red Drum Tackle Shop Hatteras	995-5414
Oregon Inlet Fishing Center For their boats	441-6301
Kitty Hawk Fishing Pier	261-2772
Nags Head Fishing Pier	441-5141
Hatteras Island Fishing Pier Rodanthe	987-2323
Frisco Pier	986-2533
O'Neals' Dockside Ocracoke	928-1111

Liquor Laws & ABC Stores

Most restaurants in Duck, Kitty Hawk, Kill Devil Hills and Nags Head serve mixed drinks. Areas where you are allowed to "brown-bag" your own liquor are found in Corolla, Manteo, Wanchese and the beaches south of Oregon Inlet.

Some restaurants serve only beer and wine, which can be purchased at most convenience stores and grocery stores. Liquor by the bottle is available only in ABC stores, as follows:

Corolla
Ocean Trail, Currituck Co.   453-2895

Kitty Hawk
MP 1, Rt. 158   261-2477

Duck Village, Wee Winks Square
                                      261-6981

Nags Head
MP 10, Rt. 158   441-5121

Manteo
Rt. 64   473-3557

Buxton, NC 12
Osprey Shopping Center   995-5532

Ocracoke Island,
Next to Variety Store   928-3281

ABC Store hours are generally 10 AM till 9 PM Monday through Saturday. No personal checks or credit cards are accepted. Maximum purchase is one gallon and legal age for admittance to a store is 21 years.

Libraries

The main Dare County Library, 473-2372, is located in Manteo on Highway 64/264 across from the Manteo Elementary School. Bookmobile service is provided through the county. Call for schedule.

The Kill Devil Hills branch, 441-4331, is located off Route 158 between the Baum Center and the water treatment center near Colington Road.

The Hatteras branch of the Dare County Library, 986-2385, is located in the county recreation building across from Burrus' Red & White store.

The Ocracoke Library is located behind the Fire hall. The hours are posted on the door.

Media Information

NEWSPAPERS

The Outer Banks has a local paper, *The Coastland Times*, which is published on Sundays, Tuesdays and Thursdays. The office is located in Manteo (473-2105) and in Kill Devil Hills (441-2223).

The *Daily Advance* is a newspaper published in Elizabeth City and can be obtained at some newsstands on the beach.

Stores throughout the Outer Banks carry a wide range of papers during the week and on Sunday.

The *Carolina Coast*, part of the *Virginian Pilot*, is produced weekly and is available throughout the Outer Banks.

Look for your copy of the *Washington Post*, *The New York Times*, *The Wall Street Journal*, *The Virginian Pilot-Ledger Star*, *The Richmond Times Herald*, *The Raleigh News & Observer* and others — costs are a bit inflated for some papers due to the distribution to this remote area.

A favorite local newspaper with strong appeal is the *North Beach Sun*. The friendly folks at Gulfstream Publishing offer a popular tabloid, filled with personal and local news of the northern Outer Banks. It is published four times a year and distributed to boxholders, convenience stores, real estate offices and other businesses along the beach from Kitty Hawk to Corolla.

Another special newspaper on the scene is *The Hatteras Monitor*, published 11 times a year. It covers items of interest on Hatteras and Ocracoke islands only, so is a great source for more detailed information to that part of the Banks. Operations are based in the Spaceship in Frisco. You can call at 995-5378.

Another Hatteras and Ocracoke area-based newspaper, which recently won five statewide journalism awards, is *The Island Breeze*, put out under the leadership of Tony McGowan (for some of your *real* Outer Banks fans, you may remember that he was the founding general manager of *The Outer Banks Current*, a general newspaper that many of us were quite sad to see leave). This paper is published monthly. Call 986-2421 for information.

TELEVISION

Falcon Cable TV supplies cable connection service for the Outer Banks (Corolla to Hatteras Village, not Ocracoke). Most motels, hotels and cottages have cable connections. Some add special features such as HBO, Showtime, Cinemax, The Movie Channel or the Disney Channel.

Channel 12 features Outer Banks Panorama, an informative program on communities, shopping, restaurants, real estate, recreation and attractions of the Banks. Falcon also offers six channels of Pay-Per-View

movies, events and concerts. (You'll need a Tocom converter from the cable office to access these.) Channel 19 provides a continuous preview of all programming carried on channels 2 (PBS) through 51. Most newspapers also carry a listing, however the Channel 19 listings are most convenient.

RADIO

The Banks' first native radio station was WOBR, Wanchese, FM 95 stereo, and it is still owned by the same person who began it. The station plays adult contemporary and has a great Sunday morning jazz show from 10 to noon. They stay in tune with what a majority of Outer Bankers want to hear.

WOBR leases their AM (1530) station to the Outer Banks Worship Center for Christian programming.

WRSF Dixie 105.7 plays "today's hottest country."

WVOD FM 99.3, "The Voices of Dare," Manteo, is a locally owned station that began broadcasting in the spring of 86. They offer a lot of different sounds and a varied format centering around adult contemporary. Sunday listeners are in for some special programming, starting with Sunday Classics, playing classical music all morning, then, in the afternoon, a beach music show. This station is also very community-minded, offering air space and the support of their personnel to local groups with worthy causes. A great source for information on local school closings, road conditions, etc.

WNHW FM 92, "Carolina 92" plays a huge variety of country music, including contemporary, cross-over, traditional, folk and rockabilly. Carolina 92 also airs music features like a weekly countdown on Sunday afternoons. They also air CNN news and sports, local news and weather, and fishing and beach reports. Catch the popular Winston Cup Today racing update daily at 5:30 PM. WNHW's Ken Mann has long been associated with quality broadcasting in this area.

WCXL 104.1 FM is a 100,000-watt station based in Elizabeth City. It does a nice job of covering the Outer Banks with an adult contemporary and beach music mix.

Postal Service and Package Shipment

Post Offices

Corolla	
Next to Winks Store	453-2552
Kitty Hawk	
MP 4, Rt. 158	261-2211
Kill Devil Hills	
MP 8, Rt. 158	441-5666
Nags Head	
MP 13, Rt. 158	441-7387
Manteo	
Downtown	473-2534
Wanchese	
Rt. 345	473-3551
Rodanthe	
NC 12, south of Joe Bob's	987-2273
Avon, NC 12	
Near Avon Shopping Center	995-5991
Buxton	
NC 12, past Buxton Books	995-5755
Hatteras	
NC 12, one mile before ferry	986-2318

Ocracoke	
NC 12, in the village	928-4771

Hours vary at these island post offices, so if you have a particular need, call first.

Package Shipment

Outer Banks Transit, 441-7090, Route 158, MP 9 in Kill Devil Hills, is centrally located on the Banks and serves as a UPS and Postal Service pickup point. They sell packaging materials and will lend a friendly hand to accommodate your needs. Package delivery service to the Norfolk area, Xerox copies, FAX service and money orders are available here.

UPS has a service center on Roanoke Island and several drop boxes throughout the area. They accept packages for shipment weekdays from 3:30 PM to 5:45 PM at their Manteo location. There are some size limitations. They offer overnight shipment to many locations in the U.S. For information call (800) 662-7506.

Federal Express has several drop box locations all around the Outer Banks. Large self-service drop boxes are located near Surfside Books at the Seagate North Shopping Center in Kill Devil Hills as well as in Manteo at Chesley Mall and in front of Manteo Booksellers. Call (800) 238-5355 for information or door pickup in most areas. (If you're in a rental cottage, make sure you know the house number and street, in order to give exact directions. The villages of the Outer Banks are fairly well-known for their lack of specific street numbers and names!)

OUTER BANKS

After more than 10 years of helping individuals and families in crisis on the Outer Banks, Hotline is facing a crisis of its own. Now, we need your help.

The Problem - - Hotline's building is no longer safe.
Hotline's building has worked very hard over the years. It has provided a safe haven, upon demand, by domestic violence victims, law enforcement, the medical centers, social services, mental health or other community agencies and to those defined as "homeless." It has housed an extensive thrift shop operation which provides a substantial portion of Hotline's funding as well as low cost clothing and goods to those in need. It has also provided space for Hotline's paid staff and volunteers to operate the Crisis Line, the Sexual Assault Program, the Legal Advocacy Program, and the numerous other programs Hotline offers in aid.

The solution is at hand - - all we need is your help!
A new building is currently under construction. But we need additional funding to complete and furnish it adequately. If you would like to help Hotline mail your tax deductible donation to:

The Outer Banks Hotline, Inc.
PO Box 1417, Manteo, NC 27954,
or call (919) 473-5121

Rental Services

Please refer to our Rentals section. This information merits a chapter unto itself.

Self Service Launderettes

Superette Launderette
Rt. 158, MP 6, Kill Devil Hills

Wash 'N Dry
Meadowlark St., MP 8½

P & G Wash & Dry
Outer Banks Mall, MP 15, Nags Head

Speed Wash
Rt. 158, MP 16½, Nags Head

Mr. Clean Laundromat
Chesley Mall, Manteo

The Wash Basket
off NC 12, Buxton

Frisco Launderette
Rt. 12, across from Scotch Bonnet, Frisco

Hatteras Harbor Marina
Rt. 12, Hatteras Village

There are no self-service laundry centers on Ocracoke Island.

Recycling at the Beach

Dare County has a dedicated population when it comes to recycling. The recycling centers on the Outer Banks are conveniently located in each town. A well-organized group of volunteers stands by to receive your recyclables. The schedules vary from town to village.

Give recycling your attention while you're at the beach. Basically, the items accepted are all kinds of paper, corrugated cardboard, aluminum cans (beverage cans only, flattened to save space), steel cans, glass — green, brown and clear jars and bottles with lids removed — milk and water jugs with lids removed, plastic bottles and jars with marking on the bottoms with a 1 or 2 in the recycle logo. Be as organized as possible, and have newspapers flat in brown bags or tied. Here's a list of recycling centers:

Carova Beach — permanent bin north of Swan Beach subdivision;

Corolla — Door-to-door collection. (They're way ahead of the rest of the Banks on this one!);

Duck — Duck Fire Station, 8 AM to noon Fridays in winter and 8 AM to 5 PM daily in summer;

Southern Shores — Behind the Fire Station on Dogwood Trail across from Kitty Hawk Elementary School. Tuesday and Saturday from 9 AM till noon;

Kitty Hawk — Please use Dare County drop-off site in Kill Devil Hills;

Kill Devil Hills, 480-4044. Dare County Public Works Complex off Colington Road, behind the Wright Memorial grounds. Monday through Friday 10 AM to 4 PM, Saturday 10 AM to 2 PM;

Nags Head, 441-1122 — Public Works building behind the Food Lion at MP 10, 7 AM to 3:30 PM Monday through Friday. Town Hall on Saturday 9 AM till noon, June through August weekends 8 AM to 4 PM. On Meekins Avenue behind Village Furniture 9 AM to sunset,

Tuesdays. Nags Head Cove at the clubhouse 9 AM to sunset, Wednesdays. North Ridge behind the Mormon Church 9 AM to sunset, Thursdays. Village at Nags Head beach access 9 AM to sunset, Fridays. South Nags Head, behind the old fire station 9 AM to sunset, Mondays;

Manteo, 473-1583 — Behind the Duke of Dare Motel on Fernando Street. Tuesday and Saturday, 8 AM to noon;

Dare County-Manteo, 473-1101, Ext. 156 — Manteo Transfer Station, Bowsertown Road: Monday through Saturday, 8 AM to 5 PM;

Buxton — behind Centura Bank Monday through Saturday, 10 AM to 4:30 PM;

Rodanthe/Salvo/Waves — Chicamacomico Volunteer Fire Station, daylight hours, daily;

Ocracoke — Hyde County Jail has a permanent bin.

Some centers have telephone numbers. Please call as designated to determine any changes in hours of operation.

Storm and Hurricane Procedures

June through November is hurricane season in the Outer Banks. All of the southeastern U.S. is prone to hurricanes but the Banks, due to their low elevation, frontage on the ocean and lack of shelter, are particularly vulnerable. A hurricane strikes the Banks about every nine years; a major one every 42 years; a tropical cyclone about every five years. The Dare County Civil Preparedness Agency promulgates the following Hurricane Safety Rules:

1. Enter each hurricane season prepared. Every June through November, recheck your supply of boards, tools, batteries, nonperishable foods and the other equipment you will need when a hurricane strikes your area.

2. When you hear the first tropical cyclone advisory, listen for future messages; this will prepare you for a hurricane emergency well in advance of the issuance of watches and warnings.

3. When your area is covered by a hurricane watch, continue normal activities, but stay tuned to the local stations (see Media in this Service Directory), or the National Weather Service Station at Buxton for advisories. Remember, a hurricane watch means possible danger within 24 hours; if the danger materializes, a hurricane warning will be issued. Meanwhile, keep alert. Ignore rumors.

4. When your area receives a hurricane warning:

Plan your time before the storm arrives, and avoid the last-minute hurry that might leave you marooned or unprepared.

Keep calm until the emergency has ended.

Leave low lying areas that may be swept by high tides or storm waves.

Leave mobile homes for more substantial shelter. They are particularly vulnerable to overturning during strong winds. Damage can be minimized by securing mobile homes with heavy cables anchored in concrete footings. Moor your boat securely before the storm arrives, or evacuate it to a designated safe area.

When your boat is moored, leave it, and don't return once the wind and waves are up.

Board up windows, or protect them with storm shutters or tape. Danger to small windows is mainly from wind-driven debris. Larger windows may be broken by wind pressure.

Secure outdoor objects that might be blown away or uprooted. Garbage cans, garden tools, toys, signs, porch furniture and a number of other harmless items become missiles of destruction in hurricane winds. Anchor them, or store them inside before the storm strikes.

Store drinking water in clean bathtubs, jugs, bottles and cooking utensils; your water supply may be contaminated by flooding or damaged by hurricane floods.

Check your battery-powered equipment. Your radio may be your only link with the world outside the hurricane, and emergency cooking facilities, lights and flashlights will be essential if utilities are interrupted.

Keep your car fueled. Service stations may be inoperable for several days after the storm strikes, due to flooding or interrupted electrical power.

Remain indoors during the hurricane. Travel is extremely dangerous when winds and tides are whipping through your area.

Monitor the storm's position through National Weather Service advisories.

5. When the hurricane has passed:

Seek necessary medical care at the nearest Red Cross disaster station or health center.

Stay out of disaster areas. Unless you are qualified to help, your presence might hamper first-aid and rescue work.

Do not travel until advised by the proper authorities.

If you must drive, do so carefully along debris-filled streets and highways. Roads may be undermined and may collapse under the weight of a car. Slides along cuts are also a hazard.

Avoid loose or dangling wires, and report them immediately to your power company or the nearest law enforcement officer.

Report broken sewer or water mains to the water department.

Prevent fires. Lowered water pressure may make fire-fighting difficult.

Check refrigerated food for spoilage if power has been off during the storm.

Remember that hurricanes moving inland can cause severe flooding. Stay away from river banks and streams.

Tornadoes spawned by hurricanes are among the storm's worst killers. When a hurricane approaches, listen for tornado watches and warnings. A tornado watch means tornadoes are expected to develop. A tornado warning means a tornado has actually been sighted. When your area receives a tornado warning, seek inside shelter immediately, preferably below ground level. If a tornado catches you outside, move away from its path at a right angle. If there is no time to escape, lie flat in the nearest depression, such as a ditch or ravine.

During the summer season visitors may be notified of hurricane watches or hurricane warnings. The hurricane watch means that a hurricane could threaten the area within 24 hours. Evacuation is not necessary at that point, but you should be alert and check on the storm's progress from time to time via radio. If a hurricane warning is promulgated, visitors should leave the Banks and head inland using Rt. 64/264 or U.S. 158, following the recently installed "Hurricane Evacuation Route" signs, which are green and white, as well as heeding the instructions of local authorities.

Surf Report

Wave Riding Vehicles for surfers, 261-3332.

Beach Service, through Nags Head Volunteer Fire Dept., 441-5853.

Natural Art Surf Shop, in the Hatteras area, 995-4646.

Tours, Limos and Taxi Service

Kitty Hawk Aero Tours, 441-4460, offers light-plane tours over the Outer Banks. This is a good way to become familiar with the geography of these barrier islands. They fly several times a day depending on weather and demand.

Wright Brothers Air Tours, 441-6235, offers flights leaving the airstrip adjacent to the Wright Brothers Memorial. Flights are several times a day, depending on weather conditions and demand, over the ocean and islands.

Burrus Flying Service, 986-2679, takes off from Billy Mitchell Airfield in Frisco, for tours over the lower Hatteras Island, Pamlico Sound and Portsmouth Island.

Pamlico Air Service, 928-1661, take off from Ocracoke for a sightseeing tour or service to Norfolk. Rates vary.

Historically Speaking offers step-on tour guiding and receptive tours for motor coach travelers, complete with historical commentary on Roanoke Island and the Outer Banks. Call for your personalized tour reservation, 473-5783.

Island Limo offers shuttle service between Norfolk International Airport and the Outer Banks, Memorial Day through Labor Day, along with morning, evening and weekend shuttle service. They also have a stretch limo for nights-out around the beach. Regular taxi service and four-wheel drive off-road excursions, to Hatteras, Oregon Inlet or Carova Beach are also offered. Call 441-LIMO (5466) or (800)828-LIMO.

Outer Banks Limousine Service offers 24-hour taxi and limousine service on the Outer Banks and to and from Norfolk International Airport by appointment. Deliveries are also accommodated. Call 261-3133.

Outer Banks Transit provides scheduled trips to Norfolk International Airport and other Norfolk destinations. Package delivery and pickup are also accommodated. Call for a schedule at 441-7090.

Beach Cab offers 24-hour service and airport service. Call 441-2500.

Bayside Cab is based at Kill Devil Hills Amoco, MP 6 and offers point to point service, on call. Call 480-1300.

The **Beach Bus** is new this year, but sure to be noticed — these double decker, English-style tour buses are bright red! Owners David and Diane Hoare will provide sightseeing adventures from the northern Outer Banks near Wright Brothers National Memorial to Roanoke Island. Day and week passes are available. Some buses are open air on the top, and all will have a conductor to provide commentary. Evenings, the Beach Bus will offer a restaurant crawl or a Lost Colony ride. Call 255-0550.

Ticks, Chiggers and Other Pests

Whenever you're in the woods or scrub anywhere on the Outer Banks in warm weather, it's possible to pick up ticks. Ticks are small, hard-shelled black or brown insects endemic to the South. Check yourself all over carefully within three or four hours after the walk. The ticks bury their heads beneath the skin and gorge themselves on your blood. They head instinctively for hairy, warm areas.

The Outer Banks Medical Center advises tick removal with tweezers, using slow, steady traction to make them release. Or, put a little alcohol on them: that often makes them back out on their own. There are other folk remedies you hear, too. If the head breaks off and is left in the skin, just leave it. It's not alive and the area will gradually heal.

If within two to 14 days after a tick bites you have headaches, flu symptoms and a rash, see a doctor. Some ticks carry Rocky Mountain Spotted Fever. It's treated with antibiotics. A recently identified scourge carried by ticks is Lyme Disease.

Chiggers are tiny reddish insects that live in dirt or fallen pine needles, as on a trail. To avoid them, spray your socks, shoes and pants with a chigger-specific repellent before your walk. Don't sit down. Chiggers, once on you, will migrate to where your clothes are tight and start biting. Locals use clear fingernail polish over the bites. Calamine or Benadryl lotions work for the itching. (Don't scratch!)

Watch out for poison ivy and poison oak in the Banks woods, as well. For any severe or extensive tick, chigger or poisonous plant symptoms, see a doctor.

Weather Report

Call 473-5665 (a local call) to hear a recording of the latest weather report, provided by WOBR-FM, 95.3.

Western Union

You can send cables or telegrams or get information by calling toll-free: (800) 325-6000. There are three Outer Banks locations where you can pick up or send messages and money: Outer Banks Transit, Rt. 158, MP 9, Kill Devil Hills, 441-7090.

Island Pharmacy, Highway 64, Manteo, 473-5801.

Provisions for the Disabled

North Carolina businesses are required to provide at least one handicapped parking space nearest buildings and entryways. Please reserve these spaces, marked with wheelchair signs, for those licensed to use them.

Violators are subject to fines.

Outer Bankers are becoming more aware of the needs of those with disabilities. Some very special services are available, such as a modern wooden ramp that extends into Jockey's Ridge State Park. Available with it are tapes for the visually impaired, made and donated by the Girl Scouts. Ocean Atlantic Rentals now has a special wheelchair with huge sand tires for getting the handicapped down to the water. There are also unique accommodations for handicapped fishermen. Visit a local library to see a copy of "Access North Carolina," a detailed guide to the state's handicapped accessible vacation spots, including many on the Outer Banks. This guide tells about parking, ramps, rest rooms, campgrounds and programs. Obtain a free copy in advance of your vacation by calling (800) VISIT NC.

Inside
Places of Worship

Fifteen years ago when we started Insiders' Guide, it was possible for us to list all the churches on the Banks! As with so many other aspects of life here, the number of worship centers has grown so much that printing them all is impractical. So, we're compromising and giving you information on some of the churches in most of the denominations represented here. We'd suggest you pick up a copy of the Sunday edition of the *Coastland Times* where you'll find a comprehensive list of all services available.

Assembly of God

WORSHIP CENTER ARK
Rt. 158 ,
MP 11½   441-5182

MANTEO ASSEMBLY OF GOD
Wingina Ave.
Manteo   473-5646

WANCHESE ASSEMBLY OF GOD
Hwy. 345
Wanchese   473-3767

AVON ASSEMBLY OF GOD
                                    995-5911

Baptist

FIRST BAPTIST CHURCH
Rt. 158, MP 4½
Kitty Hawk   261-3516

MANTEO BAPTIST CHURCH
Hwy. 64
Manteo   473-2840

CAPE HATTERAS BAPTIST
Buxton   995-5159

NAGS HEAD BAPTIST CHURCH
Rt. 158, MP 12
Nags Head   441-7548

Catholic

HOLY REDEEMER
Rt. 158, MP 7
Kill Devil Hills   441-7220

HOLY TRINITY
Whalebone Junction
Nags Head   441-7650

OUR LADY OF THE SEAS
Buxton   995-6370

ANNUNCIATION CATHOLIC
Ocracoke Fire Hall
Services are held June 15 through Labor Day.

Christian Science Society

Meets at the Ramada Inn, Kill Devil Hills, 261-3973

Church of Christ

ROANOKE ACRES
Manteo   473-5584

Church of Jesus Christ of Latter Day Saints

Windjammer Dr.
Nags Head   473-5710

Episcopal

ST. ANDREW'S BY THE SEA
Beach Rd., MP 13
Nags Head   441-5382

Full Gospel

LIBERTY CHRISTIAN FELLOWSHIP
Williams Dr.
Colington   441-6592

ROCK CHURCH
Rt. 158 Bypass, MP 4
Kitty Hawk   261-3500

Lutheran

GRACE LUTHERAN
Rt. 158 Bypass, MP 13
Nags Head   441-1530

Methodist

DUCK UNITED METHODIST
Duck   261-1525

COLINGTON UNITED METHODIST
Colington Rd.
Colington   441-6195

KITTY HAWK UNITED METHODIST
803 Kitty Hawk Village Rd.
Kitty Hawk   261-2062

BETHANY UNITED METHODIST
Wanchese   473-5254

MT. OLIVET UNITED METHODIST
Ananias Dare St.
Manteo   473-2089

BUXTON UNITED METHODIST
Buxton   995-4306

Presbyterian

OUTER BANKS PRESBYTERIAN CHURCH
Rt. 158, MP 8½
Kill Devil Hills   441-5897

ROANOKE ISLAND PRESBYTERIAN FELLOWSHIP
Wingina & Harriott
Manteo   473-6356

Unitarian

UNITARIAN UNIVERSALIST CONGREGATION OF THE OUTER BANKS
Intersection of W. Kitty Hawk and Herbert Perry roads, ½ mile from intersection of Rt. 158 and Kitty Hawk Rd.   261-2801

Inside
The Arts

Appreciation and support for the arts have increased tremendously on the Outer Banks during the past four years. Diverse cultural programs are provided through the agendas of three groups organized to promote the arts in Dare County: the Dare County Arts Council, the Outer Banks Forum and the Theatre of Dare. Even though the three groups function independently, they maintain a common goal: to offer all forms of cultural arts to broad-based audiences. A great deal of creative talent has migrated to the Outer Banks and audiences can expect first-rate programs. Events do tend to be scheduled during the off season simply because of the demands a seasonal economy places on its residents. Look for most scheduled events to occur between the months of September and May.

Organizations

DARE COUNTY ARTS COUNCIL
261-5868

This is a very visible and active arts organization that recognizes the importance of artists and their work throughout the Outer Banks. The Arts Council is the local branch of the North Carolina Arts Council, a non-profit organization. It is a "presenting" organization for the Arts, that provides quality programs throughout the community. It is extensively involved in the schools. Their mission is, "to nurture, support, and encourage excellence in all of the arts in Dare County." The thrust of this organization has been the visual arts, but their affiliation with the N.C. Arts Council has caused the local branch to actively promote all areas of the arts, including the performing arts, entertaining arts and the culinary arts. Membership brochures are available in the local art galleries. Fees vary, and special membership rates are available for seniors, students and practicing artists.

Events are held throughout the year, including sponsorship of the Frank Stick Memorial Art Show at the Ghost Fleet Gallery in Nags Head. This event has become a very popular social and cultural event for residents of the Outer Banks. It is held each year in February. Call 261-5868 for more information.

This year marks the third year of the Dare County Arts Council Writer's Group Literary Readings. Members of the group hold evenings of readings in conjunction with the Frank Stick Show in February and on a monthly basis throughout the year.

Photo: Mike Booher/DCTB

Many artists call the Outer Banks home.

OUTER BANKS FORUM
261-1998

The Forum is an organization of more than 400 members that has successfully offered various programs of the lively arts for more than 11 seasons. These programs provide entertainment that would otherwise be unavailable to the Outer Banks, including orchestral music, choral music, operas, drama, dance, theater and storytellers. The thrust of this group is the performing arts. The Forum offers a six-performance subscription series on an annual basis. The annual subscription fee entitles one to admission to each of the six performances. The Forum offers open membership, all performances are open to the public through admission at the door. Children under 12 accompanied by an adult are admitted free. The season runs October through April each year, and all performances are held at the Kitty Hawk Elementary School. Performances begin at 7:30 PM.

THEATRE OF DARE
441-6609

The community theatre is a non-profit, volunteer group. It offers a three show season beginning in September and ending in May. Performances are staged and directed by talented and experienced locals. This organization does not have a permanent home, so it's best to call for performance locations. There is a fee for admission. Donations are accepted, and everyone is welcome. Interested individuals meet monthly.

THE LOST COLONY
473-3414

This work is a continuing outdoor drama, written by Pulitzer Prize-winner Paul Green and performed during the summer only, at an outdoor theatre, Waterside Theatre, on the grounds adjacent to the Fort Raleigh National Historic Site on Roanoke Island. *The Lost Colony* is reviewed in the section on Attractions, Roanoke Island.

Galleries

JOHN DE LA VEGA GALLERY
Corolla Village   261-4964

DOLPHIN WATCH GALLERY
Corolla Village   453-2592

DUCK BLIND LTD.
Duck Village   261-2009

MORALES ART GALLERY
Gallery Row, Nags Head   441-6484

Scarborough Faire, Duck   261-7190

WOODEN FEATHER
Seagate North, Rt. 158
Kill Devil Hills   480-3066

PORT O'CALL
RESTAURANT & GALLERY
Beach Rd., Kill Devil Hills   441-8001

TERRA COTTA GALLERY
Sea Holly Square, Beach Rd.
Kill Devil Hills   480-2323

GLENN EURE'S GHOST FLEET
GALLERY OF FINE ART
Driftwood St. , Nags Head   441-6584

JEWELRY BY GAIL
Driftwood St., Nags Head   441-5387

IPSO FACTO GALLERY
Gallery Row, Nags Head   480-2793

GREENLEAF GALLERY
Rt. 158, Nags Head   480-3555

SEASIDE ART GALLERY
Tim Buck II, NC 12, Corolla

Beach Rd., Nags Head   441-5418

ANNA GARTRELL'S ART &
PHOTOGRAPHY GALLERY BY THE SEA
Beach Rd. , Nags Head   480-0578

YELLOWHOUSE GALLERY & ANNEX
Beach Rd. , Nags Head   441-6928

ISLAND ART GALLERY
CHRISTMAS SHOP
Main Rd., Manteo   473-2838

ISLAND TRADING CO.
Waterfront, Manteo   473-3365

GASKINS GALLERY
NC 12, Avon   995-6617

BROWNING ARTWORKS
NC 12, Buxton   995-5538

SUNFLOWER STUDIO
Back Rd., Ocracoke   928-6211

VILLAGE CRAFTSMEN
Howard St., Ocracoke   928-5541

ISLAND ARTWORKS
British Cemetery Rd., Ocracoke 928-3892

Inside
Annual Events

This listing of annual events reflects those occurring during the 1994 calendar year. But, since this book is published each June, some of you will be referencing events in the winter and spring of 1995. Most events are held on the same weekends and days each year. Each year new and exciting events take place on the Outer Banks reflecting the dynamic and diverse interests of those who visit this area regularly and of those who have chosen to make this truly unique barrier island our home.

JANUARY

Old Christmas Celebration at Rodanthe Community Center includes dancing, an oyster roast and the appearance of Old Buck the Christmas bull.

Annual Frank Stick Memorial Art Show at Glenn Eure's Ghost Fleet Gallery, Nags Head, is sponsored by the Dare County Arts Council, 261-5868.

Annual Beaux Arts Ball is a fundraiser sponsored by the Dare County Arts Council. Write: P.O. Box 2518, Kill Devil Hills, N.C. 27948, or call 261-5868.

FEBRUARY

The Dare County Arts Council Writers' Original Literary Readings at the Ghost Fleet Gallery, Nags Head, meets monthly for readings. Dare County Arts Council, 261-5868.

MARCH

Taste of the Beach — Local restaurants and beverage distributors provide the public with a taste of their best Outer Banks treats. Enjoy steamed shrimp, oysters, tuna bites, fine wines and beers and a whole lot more. There is an admission fee. For information, call Kelly's Restaurant, 441-4116.

Annual Kelly's-Beach 95 St. Patrick's Day Parade begins at Nags Head Pier, (9½ MP) and proceeds north to the 10½ MP on the Beach Road. This is always a fun time for the whole family. Free hot dogs and sodas are provided by Kelly's Restaurant, 441-4116.

Call (800) 334-4777 for information about the **Annual Kitty Hawk Kites Hang Gliding Camp**.

Call 441-5620 for information about the **Annual Craft Show** at the Outer Banks Mall in Nags Head.

The **Annual Spring Arts and Crafts Fair**, at Baum Senior Center, Kill Devil Hills, is sponsored by the Outer Banks Women's Club, 261-2406.

APRIL

Outer Banks' **Homebuilder's Association's Parade of Homes** will open homes to the public from Corolla to South Nags Head. There is a fee. Write: P.O. Box 398, Kitty Hawk, NC 27949, or call 441-8600.

Annual Small Business Expo, is sponsored by the Outer Banks Chamber of Commerce. Write: P.O. Box 1757, Kill Devil Hills, N.C. 27948 or call 441-8144 or 995-4213.

Call (800)-334-4777 for information about the **Annual Kitty Hawk Kites Hang Gliding Camp**.

Call 441-6800 for information about the Annual **BIC Windfest and Kitty Hawk Sports One Hour Winduro**.

SpringFest takes place at the Weeping Radish Restaurant and Brewery in Manteo on Easter Weekend. It offers a German menu, Bavarian-style foods, special SpringFest beer, free children's entertainment, a German oompah band, and folk dancers. Call 473-1157.

Outer Banks **SilverArts Competition** takes place at the Thomas A. Baum Senior Center in Kill Devil Hills. This is the art section of the NC Senior Games featuring an exhibition of talent and craftsmanship of all of the visual arts. Call 441-1181.

At the **Blues Fishing Tournament and Music Festival**, Highway 12, Rodanthe, Hatteras Island restaurants provide concessions: hot dogs, hamburgers, smoked fish, chicken, and more. There is blues music throughout the festival. There are lots of children's activities including an adult/child surf fishing tournament and distance casting tournament. Call JoBob's at 987-2201.

The Outer Banks **Senior Games Competition** includes shuffleboard, billiards, horseshoes, table tennis and lots more. Dare County seniors age 55 and up are eligible to compete. All are welcome to watch and cheer for your favorite seniors. Contact the Baum Center for information, 441-1181.

Call 441-6800 for information about the Annual Kitty Hawk Sports **Windsurfing Camps**.

Call The Island Inn, 928-4351, on Ocracoke for information about the **Surf Fishing Invitational Tournament.**

MAY

The **Annual Hang Gliding Spectacular** takes place at Jockey's Ridge State Park in Nags Head on Mother's Day Weekend every year. It's the oldest continuous hang gliding competition in the country and draws pilots and spectators from all over the U.S. Both novice and experienced pilots compete in a variety of flying maneuvers. The event features spectacular flying, an outdoor street dance, fine arts show and an awards ceremony with guest Francis Rogallo, "father of hang gliding." Call Kitty Hawk Kites, (800) 334-4777.

The **Annual Kitty Hawk Kites and Outer Banks Outdoors Sea Kayaking Jamboree** takes place at Route 64, Manteo-Nags Head Causeway at the Waterworks Tower. There are free demonstrations of sea kayaks all day. Tour the historic Manteo waterfront or paddle through the Hatteras Island National Seashore. Beginners to advanced are welcome. It's fun for the entire family. Call Kitty Hawk Kites, (800) 334-4777.

British Cemetery Ceremony in Ocracoke is an official memorial ceremony for English sailors who died there. An English official is sent to Ocracoke each year to attend this Coast Guard service. Call the Ocracoke Civic Club, 928-6711.

To participate in the **Nags Head Woods 5K Run** at the Nags Head Woods Preserve, write: 701 West Ocean Acres Drive, Kill Devil Hills, NC 27948, or call 441-2525.

The **Annual Memorial Day Weekend Arts & Crafts Fair**, Ramada Inn, Kill Devil Hills, is sponsored by the Outer Banks Women's Club, 261-2406.

For information about **The Sport Fishing School** in Hatteras, write: Box 7401, Raleigh, N.C. 27695 or call 515-2261.

World Championship Striking Fish Tournament is sponsored by Tournaments Unlimited at Hatteras Harbor Marina weigh-in station. Call (800) 676-4939 or (800) 551-5289.

Call 441-6800 for information about **Kitty Hawk Sports/North One Hour Winduro** in Nags Head.

Call (800) 334-4777 for information about the **Annual Kitty Hawk Kites Hang Gliding Camp**.

Call 441-5620 for information about the **Annual Craft Show** at the Outer Banks Mall, Nags Head.

Virginia Bluewater Game Fish Association Tournament takes place at Pirate's Cove Yacht Club. Call 473-3906 or 473-3700.

JUNE

Kitty Hawk Kites provides free daily workshops during June, July, and August. **Kid's Day** is every Wednesday at the Nags Head location. Call for a free calendar, (800) 334-4777.

Competitors in all age categories are encouraged to register for the **Annual Outer Banks Body Board Contest**. Winners and participants will receive prizes. There is an entry fee. Preregister at Kitty Hawk Sports' Nags Head store. This event takes place on the beach near the Ramada Inn. Write: P.O. Box 939, Nags Head, NC 27959, or call 441-6800.

Dare Days Street Festival in Manteo is always the first Saturday of June. It features arts and crafts, food, musical entertainment and a concert. It's sponsored by the town of Manteo. Write: Box 1000, Manteo, NC 27954 or call 473-1101, ext. 319.

Annual Rogallo Kite Festival, Jockey's Ridge, is a "family fun fly" that celebrates kite flying's beauty. It is open to kite enthusiasts of all ages and features stunt kites, homebuilts and kids' competitions. A free kite-making workshop for children adds to the fun and enjoyment. Kite buggy racing events will be included in this year's festival. Call Kitty Hawk Kites at (800) 334-4777.

Annual Ships Watch/Buck Island Beach Music Festival is organized each year by Tim and Buck Thornton to benefit The Nature Conservancy, a private, nonprofit conservation organization. This gala festival will feature music by Bill Deal and Ammon Tharp, the original Rhondels, as well as the Coolin' Out Band. A great meal will be catered by famous Kelly's Outer Banks Restaurant. For information call Ships Watch, 261-2231.

Hatteras Marlin Fishing Tournament is sponsored by the Hatteras Marlin Club. Write Box 218, Hatteras, N.C. 27943, or call 986-2454.

Living history takes place aboard the *Elizabeth II*, downtown Manteo. Meet 16th-century mariners, soldiers and adventurers (Tuesday through Saturday). Write: Elizabeth II State Historic Site, P.O. Box 155, Manteo, N.C. 27954, or call 473-1144.

The National Park Service offers **free educational activities and programs** at Fort Raleigh, Wright Memorial and Cape Hatteras National Seashore. Write: National Park Service, Route 1, Box 675, Manteo, N.C. 27954, or call 473-2111.

The Lost Colony Outdoor Drama takes place on Roanoke Island, three miles northwest of Manteo. Pulitzer Prize-winning playwright Paul Green's rousing spectacle of song, dance and drama depicts the story of America's first English settlement and its mysterious disappearance. It's in its 53rd production season and occurs nightly except Sundays. For a listing of special performances or more information call 473-3414 or (800) 488-5012.

Call 986-2166 or (800) 676-4939 for information about the **Annual Blue Water Open Billfish Tournament** at Hatteras Harbor Marina.

Wil-Bear's Festival of Fun takes place at Kitty Hawk Connection, Nags Head. The star of the day is Wil-Bear Wright, the colorful Kitty Hawk Kites mascot. Children of all ages are thrilled with action-packed workshops on kite-flying, kite making, paper airplane making and T-shirt painting. Face painting, juggling, yo-yo and toy demonstrations will also be part of the special entertainment. Call Kitty Hawk Kites (800) 334-4777.

The **Annual Craft Show** takes place at the Outer Banks Mall, Nags

Head, N.C. For information, call 441-5620.

Contact the Outer Banks Chamber of Commerce, 441-8144 for information about the **Annual Seafood Festival in Wanchese, Blessing of the Fleet**.

Call (800) 334-4777 for information about the **Annual Kitty Hawk Kites Hang Gliding Camp**.

Sunset Festival at Pirate's Cove and Arts on the Dock occurs every Wednesday, 4 PM to sunset at Pirate's Cove Yacht Club, 473-1451.

JULY

Write P.O. Box 491, Ocracoke, N.C. 27960, or call 928-6711 for information about the **Independence Day Parade** in Ocracoke, July 4, Ocracoke Preservation Society.

Sand Sculpture Contest at the Ocracoke Lifeguard Station takes place on July 4 and is sponsored by the National Park Service, 473-2111.

Take part in the **Annual Independence Day Celebration** at the Manteo Waterfront on July 4. Activities include children's games, food, concessions, arts and crafts, musical entertainment and a street dance. A fireworks display begins at 9 PM. Call 473-1101.

Fireworks in Hatteras Village occur on July 4. Spectators can sit on the beach and watch the largest display of fireworks on the island. This event is very popular with vacationers and residents and is sponsored by the Hatteras Village Civic Association and Volunteer Fire Department.

The **Annual Fireworks Festival and Fair** at the historic Whalehead Hunt Club in Corolla takes place on

July 4. The Currituck County Board of Commissioners and the Corolla Business Association host this event, and proceeds will be donated to the Whalehead Preservation Trust Fund and Currituck Wildlife Museum. The event includes plans for an old-fashioned picnic atmosphere complete with live music, food, crafts, pony rides, art displays and a variety of other activities. The highlight of the celebration will be a fireworks display over the Currituck Sound.

Annual Youth Fishing Tournament includes pier fishing or surf fishing. Register at piers from Kitty Hawk to South Nags Head. Ages up to 16 are welcome. It is jointly sponsored by the Nags Head Surf Fishing Club, the NC Beach Buggy Association and the NC Sea Hags. Write Box 626, Kill Devil Hills, N.C. 27948, or call 441-5723.

Write: P.O. Box 1997, Manteo, N.C. 27954, or call 473-3906 or (800) 367-4728 for information about the **Seamark Foods/Oscar Mayer Children's Tournament at Pirate's Cove Yacht Club**. (NC Special Olympic athletes invited.)

Annual Kitty Hawk Sports Skim Jam Competition is held on the beach near the Ramada Inn. Skim board riders compete on skim at the break of the wave. Preregister at Kitty Hawk Sports, 441-6800.

Annual Wright Kite Festival at the Wright Memorial is a fun family event. Kite flying for all ages includes free kite making workshops and boomerang clinics for the kids. Wil-Bear Wright will be on hand too. The event is sponsored by Kitty Hawk Kites and the National Park Service. Call Kitty Hawk Kites (800) 334-4777.

AUGUST

The **Annual Wacky Watermelon Weekend and Watermelon Winduro** is at Kitty Hawk Connection and Kitty Hawk Sports sailing site. This watermelon-centered event begins with a parade led by the state's Watermelon Queen and includes an Olympic watermelon toss, big league watermelon bowling, carving, long distance seed spitting and watermelon consumption. The most charged event of the day is the Kamikaze Watermelon Drop. Sailors of all skill levels are invited to the winduro to compete for awards and prizes. Register at Kitty Hawk Sports' Nags Head store, 441-6800.

Annual Rolling Rock Volley by the Sea takes place in Nags Head. A volleyball tournament is open to men and women. Doubles are played on Saturday, and triple coed competition occurs on Sunday. Prizes and cash are part of the event. Call Ray Pugh at 441-2639 or 473-2418.

Local seniors provide the crafts for the **Annual Senior Adults Craft Fair** at Thomas A. Baum Center, Kill Devil Hills. Proceeds go to seniors. It's a community project sponsored by the Outer Banks Women's Club, 261-5388.

Annual Alice Kelly Memorial Ladies Only Billfish Tournament, takes place at Pirate's Cove Yacht Club, 473-3906 or (800) 367-4728.

Forty-sixth Anniversary of Rogallo Wing Invention at Kitty Hawk Kites in Nags Head is a ceremony that honors Francis M. Rogallo, inventor of the flexible wing and "father of hang gliding." You will learn about the history of kites and gliders, enjoy refreshments and have a chance to meet Mr. Rogallo himself, (800) 334-4777.

Annual Pirate's Cove Billfish Tournament occurs at Pirate's Cove Yacht Club (Member NC Governor's Cup Billfish Series). Call 473-3906 or (800) 367-4728.

Annual New World Festival of the Arts is coordinated by Edward Louis Greene of the Christmas Shop. Write Box 994, Manteo, N.C. 27954, or call 473-2838.

Virginia Dare Day Celebration at Fort Raleigh National Historic Site Visitors Center is a celebration of the birth of Virginia Dare, the first English child born into the new world. Programs, singing and dancing are featured. Call the National Park Service, 473-5772.

Annual Corolla Seafood Festival Fund Raiser, is sponsored by the Corolla Volunteer Fire Department. Write the fire department in Corolla, N.C. 27927 or call 453-3242.

Nags Head Woods Benefit Auction is held at The Sanderling Inn in Duck. Call 441-2525.

The **Annual Herbert Hoover Birthday Celebration**, takes place at Manteo Booksellers. Write: P.O. Box 1520, Manteo, N.C. 27954, or call 473-1221.

Write Route 1, Box 675, Manteo, NC 27954, or call 441-7430 for information about the **Observance of National Aviation Day** at the Wright Memorial.

SEPTEMBER

Eastern Surfing Championships take place in Buxton. (Competition open to association members only.) Write Box 400 AD, Buxton, N.C. 27920, or call 995-5785.

Hatteras Village Invitational Surf Tournament, is sponsored by the Hatteras Village Civic Association; call 986-2579.

Carolina 92-Pirate's Cove Annual Small Boat Fishing Tournament, takes place at Pirate's Cove Yacht Club, 473-3906 or (800) 367-4728.

Annual Labor Day Arts & Crafts Show at the Ramada Inn, Kill Devil Hills is sponsored by the Outer Banks Women's Club, 261-2406.

"The Allison" Crippled Children's White Marlin Release Tournament occurs at Pirate's Cove Yacht Club, 473-3906 or (800) 367-4728.

Enter the Annual **Outer Banks Triathalon on Roanoke Island**. Dare Volunteer Action Center. Write: P.O. Box 293, Manteo, N.C. 27954 or call 473-2400.

North Beach Sun Trash Festival, includes Operation Beach Sweep and an afternoon festival in Duck. Beach Sweep participants receive a ticket to the festival for live music and a North Carolina barbecue dinner. Call the *North Beach Sun*, 480-2787.

"Octoberfest" is celebrated at the Weeping Radish Restaurant and Brewery in Manteo. It features live music, food and entertainment — Bavarian style. Call 473-1157.

Annual Flying Wheels Rollerblade Spectacular takes place at Monteray Shores, Corolla. The best bladers and beginners roll through the streets to compete for gift certificates and prizes. Money raised is donated to the Corolla Wildhorse Fund. The 1K rally is lots of fun for those 12 and under. Contact Kitty Hawk Kites, (800) 334-4777.

Annual Hotline Small Boat Fishing Tournament, occurs at Pirate's

Cove Yacht Club. Call 473-3906 or (800) 367-4728.

Annual Outer Banks Volleyball Championships swing into action on the beach at the Pebble Beach Motel. Write P.O. Box 1209, Nags Head, N.C. 27957, or call 441-5111.

Write P.O. Box 3232, Kill Devil Hills, N.C. 27948, or call 441-8772 for information about the **Albemarle Challenge Cup Regatta**, Roanoke Island Yacht Club, Colington Harbor Clubhouse. There is an entry fee.

Annual Craft Show occurs at the Outer Banks Mall, Nags Head. For more information, call 441-5620.

Call (800) 334-4777 for information about the **Annual Kitty Hawk Kites Hang Gliding Camp**.

Place your bids at the **Annual Chamber of Commerce Auction** at the Ramada Inn, Kill Devil Hills. There will be hors d'oeuvres and open bar from 5:30 to 7:30 PM. The auction begins at 7 PM. There is a fee. Contact the Outer Banks Chamber of Commerce at 441-8144 or 995-4213.

OCTOBER

Annual Artrageous Weekend is a community paint-in and art auction sponsored by the Dare County Arts Council and the Youth Center Inc. It is a day of fun and color for everyone. Children and adults are invited to spend the day painting. Children love participating in this event. All art supplies are provided by the Arts Council. "People in uniform," local politicians and dignitaries are also invited to step out and be creative. Collaborative paintings by professional artists and children are auctioned. All proceeds benefit the Arts Council, and the proposed

Dare County Youth Center. Write: P.O. Box 2518, Kill Devil Hills, N.C. 27948, or call 441-9150.

Nags Head Woods Oyster Roast and Pig Picking is a fund raising event for the Nags Head Woods Preserve, 441-2525.

Write Box 626, Kill Devil Hills, N.C. 27948, or call 441-5723 for information about the **Nags Head Surf Fishing Club Invitational Tournament**.

Annual Outer Banks Stunt Kite Competition, at Jockey's Ridge features novices, intermediates and experts competing in this serious kite flyers' competition. A variety of events include compulsory maneuvers, freestyles and individual and team ballet. The "Power Challenge" — when flyers pit their strength into the wind — is sure to be a favorite. You'll see the best and the latest in the kiting world. Contact Kitty Hawk Kites, (800) 334-4777.

Annual Vision Classic at Jockey's Ridge State Park is a gliding event cosponsored by Pacific Airwave, a west coast manufacturer, and Kitty Hawk Kites. Come see hang gliding pilots try the latest in equipment. Call (800) 334-4777.

Autumnfest '94, is an end of the season festival featuring live music, food, children's games, arts and crafts. It is sponsored by the Outer Banks Chamber of Commerce. Call 441-8144 or 995-4213.

The KMA-sponsored **King Mackerel Tournament** is held in Hatteras Village. Proceeds support Graveyard of the Atlantic Museum. Call 986-2579.

Outer Banks King Mackerel Festival (sanctioned by the Southern

King Fish Association, Inc. and King Masters Association) is held at Pirate's Cove Yacht Club, 473-3906 or (800) 367-4728.

Annual Hatteras Island Adult Care Inc., Charity Golf Tournament at the Ocean Edge Golf Course, Frisco is held on Columbus Day Weekend each year. Proceeds benefit the Adult Care Program that provides funds for meals for home-bound adults on Hatteras Island. Entry fees are tax deductible. This tournament is held in conjunction with the **Kiwanis Club Craft Fair** and **Live Lobster Sale and Bake Sale**. Both events are held at the Cape Hatteras School. Contact the Ocean Edge Golf Course for information, 995-4100.

Annual Octoberfest is held at Frisco Woods Campground, Frisco. The day's events include a pig pickin' (with all the trimmings), live music, crafts, a bake sale and rummage sale. This event is sponsored by Ocean Edge Golf Course, Frisco Woods Campground and Bubba's Bar-B-Que. Call 995-5208.

First Flight and Kitty Hawk Elementary Fall Carnival takes place on Halloween or a date close to it from 10 AM until 4 PM. Booths and stations for children and adults, including games and face painting, concessions, a bake sale, raffle and silent auction. Proceeds benefit both elementary schools, 261-2313.

Halloween Carnival at Ocracoke School takes place on the Friday night before Halloween. The carnival kicks off at 3 PM with a children's costume parade. See the spook house for a small fee and special auction of local contributions (unusual finds). It's the biggest fund-

raiser for Ocracoke School and popular with everyone, 928-6271.

Call 441-5620 for information about the **Halloween Carnival for The Little Kids** at Outer Banks Mall, Nags Head.

Annual Craft Show is held at the Outer Banks Mall, Nags Head. For more information, call 441-5620.

Autumn Festival at Cape Hatteras School, Buxton is held on a Saturday close to Halloween. It's a fun day for children. Proceeds will benefit the school. Call 995-5730.

NOVEMBER

Annual Celebrity-Waiter Heart Fund Dinner at Kelly's Restaurant, Nags Head includes great food and a lot of fun. Proceeds benefit the American Heart Fund. Call 441-4116.

North Beach Seafood Festival at the Barrier Island Inn, Duck is held from 10 AM until 8 PM. The event includes a seafood buffet, live music and crafts. Call 261-3901.

Invitation Inter-Club Surf Fishing Tournament and Open Invitation Tournament, in Buxton is sponsored by the Cape Hatteras Anglers Club. Write Box 145, Buxton, N.C. 27960, or call 995-4253.

North Carolina Ducks Unlimited Championship King Mackerel Tournament, takes place at Pirate's Cove Yacht Club, 473-3906 or (800) 367-4728.

Turkey Trot Fund Raiser for the Corolla Wild Horse Fund is sponsored by the Corolla Volunteer Fire Department, Corolla, NC 27927 or call 453-3242.

A **Christmas Arts and Crafts Show** is held at Cape Hatteras School, Buxton. Call 987-2416.

For information about the **An-**

nual **Craft Show** in the Outer Banks Mall, Nags Head, call 441-5620.

Stop by the **Annual Christmas Arts & Crafts Show** at the Ramada Inn, Kill Devil Hills. The show is sponsored by the Outer Banks Women's Club, 261-2406.

DECEMBER

Write Box 967, Manteo, N.C. 27954, or call 473-3494 for information about North Carolina Aquarium/Roanoke Island, **Christmas at the Aquarium**, Roanoke Island.

Outer Banks **Hotline's Annual Festival of Trees** invites local businesses and individuals to donate fully decorated Christmas trees that are auctioned and delivered to buyers. Proceeds benefit Hotline's Crisis Intervention Program and needy families in the area, 473-5121.

Annual Holiday Ball at the Hatteras Civic Center features live music and hors d'oeuvres. It's a BYOB affair. Proceeds benefit development of the Graveyard of the Atlantic Museum in Hatteras Village. Write P.O. Box 191, Hatteras, N.C. 27943.

Christmas Parade & Christmas on The Waterfront, Manteo is always the first Saturday of the month. The event includes food, Christmas crafts, enter-tainment and Santa and is sponsored by the town of Manteo, 473-2774.

Elizabeth II **Christmas Open House** is held at the Elizabeth II Historic Site, Manteo. The event features tours by costumed guides, refreshments, entertainment and singing. Call 473-1144.

Write First Flight Society, Box 1903, Kill Devil Hills, N.C. 27948, or call Al Jones 441-2424 for information about the **"Man Will Never Fly" Memorial Society International Annual Seminar and Awards Program**.

Write First Flight Society, Box 1903, Kitty Hawk, N.C. 27949, or call 441-7430 for information about **First Flight Commemoration** at the Wright Brothers National Memorial, Kill Devil Hills.

Annual Christmas Parade in Hatteras Village includes lots of local participants, but anyone may join in the fun. The event features floats, a bike decorating contest and prizes for the best decorated home and business as well as refreshment and caroling at the Community Center. Contact Dale Burrus at Burrus Red & White Supermarket, 986-2333.

Call 441-5620 for information about the **Annual Christmas Craft Fair** at the Outer Banks Mall, Nags Head.

Inside
Portsmouth Island

Southwest of Ocracoke —

It's deserted now, except for its "ghosts" in Park Service uniforms. Empty. If you've never had that eerie feeling . . . then maybe you'll want to take the trip that most Banks visitors never make, to quiet, roadless, unpopulated Portsmouth Island.

It wasn't always that way. Portsmouth, which was a planned community authorized by the Colonial Assembly in 1753, was for many years the largest (actually, the only) town on the Banks and was a major shipping center for nearly 100 years. The slow changes of geology and economics have left it behind, however, and now it is a quaint, uninhabited island that is part of Cape Lookout National Seashore. The village itself is a historic district.

There is no bridge to Portsmouth from Ocracoke. There isn't even a vehicle ferry. The only way to get there, unless you brought a boat with you, is to make an arrangement with one of the authorized licensed operators in Ocracoke. They are: Dave McLawhorn (928-5921) and Rudy Austin, 928-4361/4281. You can contact them or the NPS for rate and schedule information; you'll probably pay about $40, depending on how many are in your party.

As you cross the inlet, if you decide to go, reflect on the fact that this was once the channel for much of the trade of Virginia and North Carolina. Throughout the 1700s and up to the mid-19th century, Ocracoke channel was deeper than it is now. And of course ships were of shallower draft then, too. Seagoing ships could enter the inlet, moor or anchor near the southwest side and offload their cargo into smaller coasters. Then cargo was taken up the sound to such early ports as New Bern and Bath. Portsmouth Village was established to facilitate this trade by providing piers, warehouses, other port facilities and labor.

The new town grew rapidly. The British raided Portsmouth during the Revolutionary War; a steady flow of supplies moved through it to General Washington's embattled armies. The British captured the town again during the War of 1812. But this again was only a temporary interruption, and the town continued to grow. At its peak, just before the Civil War, it handled more than 1,400 ships a year and had a total population of almost 600 — no Boston, but definitely the largest town on the outer islands.

Two things doomed Portsmouth: war and weather. In September of

Photo: Mary Ellen Riddle

Portsmouth Island is quiet, roadless and now uninhabited.

1846, a terrific storm opened two new inlets (named Hatteras and Oregon), and these gradually deepened as Ocracoke Inlet began to shoal. The Federals didn't help matters by sinking several ships laden with rock in Ocracoke channel, but war merely hastened Portsmouth's end. Such seagoing traffic as was left to the Banks shifted to Hatteras Inlet, and the backcountry trade was carried more and more by the new railroads. After that it was only a question of time. Few villagers returned after the war ended, even when a fish-processing plant was built, and the population steadily declined. Its last male resident, Henry Piggott, died in 1971, and with that Portsmouth's last two residents, Elma Dixon and Marian Babb, finally left.

Except for National Park Service volunteer caretakers who spend much of the year there, only mos-

quitoes inhabit the village.

As you debark, at a newly-built dock at Haulover Point, you'll be able to look over the harbor from whence wharves, warehouses and lighters once served the merchant ships anchored inside the Inlet. For a short tour, proceed southeast down the road. The first house on the right is the Salter-Dixon House, built around 1900. Part of this house is open as a visitor center, regularly in the summer months and intermittently in the spring and fall. Displays and more information, as well as rest rooms and drinking water, are available inside. Down the main road you'll see a fence on the right and then a collapsed house. This is the Henry Babb house, built before 1875.

The small white building south of the Salter-Dixon house is the former Post Office. This was more or less the center of the village in its day. About 40 yards west of it is the community cemetery, the largest in the village, with about 40 graves.

From the crossroads, follow the footpath south across the marsh to the former schoolhouse. Miss Mary Dixon taught classes in this one-room building until 1947. Now go back to the post office and proceed down the main road eastward. If you stop on the first little bridge and look to the north across the creek you will see a (now) yellow-painted cottage formerly owned by Henry Piggott, mentioned above. Continue across the second little bridge. To your left you will see the Methodist Church. You may go in. (There used to be a collection plate for the public to leave donations to aid the Park Service in the upkeep of the church, but the plate was removed because its use conflicts with federal regulations regarding the safeguarding of public funds.) The rope operating the church bell, formerly functional, has been disconnected due to excessive use. Do not try to play the organ either. Behind the church is the Babb, Dixon plot where Mr. Piggott is buried.

Continuing east from the church, beyond the last houses you'll enter a stretch of open road. Beyond this lies the landing strip, the old Coast Guard station, watch tower and outbuildings. Surf rescue boats were kept in the large building, as at Chicamacomico. The station was closed in 1937, though it was briefly reactivated for WWII.

About 100 meters south of the station is the cistern of the old marine hospital, which was built in 1846 to serve sick and/or quarantined seamen. The Park Service has cut back the vegetation that threatened at one point to overwhelm it. The hospital proper burned down in 1894 and was not replaced.

To get to the Atlantic beach and the Wallace Channel Dock, walk on past the station; it's about another mile. If a northerly wind is blowing, there may be a few inches of water to wade through on the way.

A few notes of caution are in order. Prepare for mosquitoes in the summer. There's no mosquito control any more on the island, and they get fierce. (Imagine what it was like living here before window screens and insect repellent were invented.) Wear sunscreen, too. Don't go inside any of the buildings other than the Salter-Dixon house and the church. They belong to the Park Service and are off-limits.

A note to anglers: Portsmouth Island has great surf fishing, and you don't have to share it with hordes of other people. Don Morris, in Atlantic, NC, has a car ferry that can take a limited number of four wheel drive vehicles over. He's at 225-4261. NPS permits are required for all vehicles on Cape Lookout and Portsmouth Island; as of this writing there is no fee for permits, which are available from the concessionaire and from any Cape Lookout Ranger Station.

Camping is allowed on the island — not in the village, though, and you'd really have to be prepared for mosquitoes to try this!

Even if you're not up for such a hardy venture as a campout on the deserted island, a day trip is definitely a pleasure worth the trouble.

Inside
Nearby Attractions

MERCHANTS MILLPOND STATE PARK
Gatesville, N.C.   *357-1191*

Located off Route 158, NC 32 and NC 37, this state park is approximately 30 miles from Elizabeth City, North Carolina and Suffolk, Virginia. It is one of North Carolina's rarest ecological communities. Overnight tent camping is available, and campsites contain a picnic table and grill. Drinking water and washhouse facilities are available. Primitive camping facilities include a canoe-in campground for fishermen. Reserve in advance during the spring, summer and fall. Canoes can be rented inexpensively ($2.50 an hour) for use in the millpond and Lassiter Swamp, and "paths" in the water are well marked with colored buoys. Renting a canoe is a great way to see the swamp, and to enjoy one of its most attractive features — the quiet serenity it offers.

Fishing is a popular activity, and the millpond has largemouth bass, bluegill, chain pickerel and black crappie just waiting to bite your hook. A North Carolina fishing license is required. Hiking, photography, picnicking and nature study are popular activities as well.

We discovered the beautiful 2,700-acre state park on a side trip to the Dismal Swamp. Actually, the Dismal Swamp we observed from Highway 17 is a minor natural wonder compared to Merchants Millpond State Park. The Dismal Swamp canals along the road are picturesque and provide shaded picnic areas. On the other side, off Highway 32, there are no signs directing one to the Great Dismal Swamp. Only when we stopped in Sunbury were we told that the Dismal Swamp is all but dried up — the same as the Florida Everglades — and that the Millpond State Park canoe area provides a more in-depth study of a swamp. We discovered helpful, friendly people on our day-long "safari," but that's another story in itself. North Carolinians are easygoing and hospitable wherever we meet!

Towering bald cypress and tupelo gum trees draped in Spanish moss dominate the 760-acre millpond. At its upper end is Lassiter Swamp, an ecological wonderland containing remnants of an ancient bald cypress forest and the eerie "enchanted forest" of tupelo gum whose trunks and branches have been distorted into fantastic shapes by mistletoe.

More than 190 species of birds have been recorded in the park. Spring and fall bring migrations of warblers and other species. In winter, a variety of waterfowl stop by on their journey south. Reptiles, amphibians and mammals such as beaver, mink and river otter make their homes in the park. We observed a great blue heron standing in the shallow water near the dock. Later a beautiful mallard duck glided over to observe us enjoying a picnic. Turtles lined up in rows to sun themselves on logs.

There is sufficient warning about ticks and other pests that infest the woods. Proper clothing and hats are recommended, in addition to careful inspection after a trek through this beautiful habitat. On a breezy spring day, we observed several people launch their canoes and kayaks loaded with camping gear and supplies for a weekend of camping in one of the canoe-in camp sites.

An outstanding state park close to the Outer Banks, it is worth the almost two-hour drive to reach, especially for veteran campers, boaters and anglers who enjoy getting away from everything man-made to a truly beautiful environment.

MUSEUM OF THE ALBEMARLE
Elizabeth City, N.C.   *335-1453*
This museum is a part of the North Carolina Archives and History and reflects the story of the people who have lived in the Albemarle region, from the native American tribes to early English-speaking colonists, adventurers, farmers and fishermen. The interpretive exhibits change occasionally, but a variety of handmade quilts and other crafts, carved waterfowl, early farming equipment and English porcelain figurines allows a look back in

time to the days when early Virginia settlers began making their way to the Carolinas.

The geography of the region is displayed by maps. The history of the people and their livelihoods is depicted in the array of tools and equipment used in early times. There are guided tours, lectures and audiovisual programs available for groups or individuals, with two weeks notice. There is also a small gift shop on the premises.

Admission is free. The museum is accessible for the handicapped and is open Tuesday through Saturday 9 AM till 5 PM; and Sunday 2 PM till 5 PM It's closed Mondays and holidays. Call for program reservations or inquiries.

To reach the Museum of the Albemarle drive north from Kitty Hawk on Route 158 through Camden, across the Pasquotank River and through Elizabeth City to Route 17 south. It's located a few miles west of the city on the right side of the road. Distance from Kitty Hawk is about 47 miles.

THE NEWBOLD-WHITE HOUSE
Hertford, N.C.   *426-7567*
As you leave Elizabeth City and drive southwest towards Hertford and Edenton on Route 17, follow the signs to the Newbold-White House. You'll turn left at a large intersection in Hertford (State Route 1336). The distance from Kitty Hawk is about 60 miles.

The Newbold-White House sits on the left, back off the road about 1 mile. This late 17-century house was built by Joseph and Mary Scott who were Quakers. Joseph became a mag-

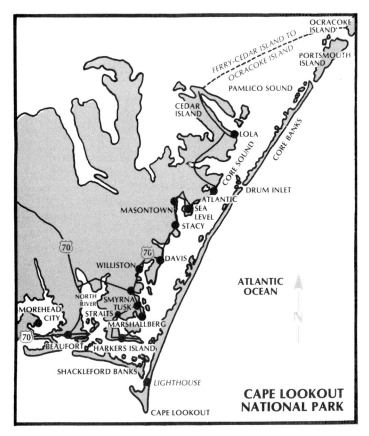

CAPE LOOKOUT
NATIONAL PARK

istrate and legislator. In colonial times, permanent settlers came from Virginia by way of the Perquimans River to a territory that became known as the Carolinas. This house is the first one in North Carolina.

Scott patented more than 600 acres on the river banks and was believed to have built this house about 1685. (The Newbold-White family later owned it.) Tobacco farming was the primary work here. The use of tobacco as a form of payment (cash) was prevalent during the late years of the 17th century. Many years

later cotton and peanuts were farmed.

A tour of the restored home is worth your while. It features large fireplaces with great wooden mantels, pine woodwork and a winding corner staircase. The leaded casement windows with diamond-shaped glass panes were restored with authentic glass made in Germany, copying a piece of glass found on the premises before the start of restoration several years ago. The bricks were handmade and laid in original English bond on the lower portion of the house and Flemish bond higher up. The history behind the use of the house as a public meeting place represents the formative years of the proprietary government and courts of North Carolina. The Visitor Center offers an audiovisual journey to those times and a look at how life was lived. The house is open March 1 till December 22, 10 AM till 4:30 PM, Monday through Saturday. Admission is $2 for adults and 50 cents for children and students.

Historic Hertford

The older part of Hertford lies to the right of the intersection of Route 17 and State Route 1336. Hertford is one of the oldest towns in North Carolina and was incorporated in 1758, primarily to serve as the county seat and commercial center for Perquimans County.

About 50 19th-century buildings stand on the tree-lined streets of the downtown. These magnificent homes and yards recreate a sense of the early life of people who lived by farming, fishing, lumbering and later cloth manufacturing. Drive time from Kitty Hawk is about an hour.

Albemarle Plantation

426-5555
Hertford, N.C.   (800)535-0704

Albemarle Plantation is not the name of an 18th- or 19th-century home or plantation but is a golfing and boating community whose golf course is open to the public. The Dan Maples golf links, which opened several years ago, is the sporting challenge here. It's our understanding that the course is in great shape and

offers an option to those who enjoy the sport while they're on vacation. While we're not advertising the real estate sales, the golf course is close enough to the Outer Banks to mention. For tee-times call the toll-free number. Follow Route 17 from Elizabeth City to Hertford. Drive time from Kitty Hawk is just over an hour.

Historic Edenton

One of the oldest towns in America, Edenton was settled about 1660 along the shores of Edenton Bay and Albemarle Sound. To reach Edenton, continue on Route 17 from Hertford. Edenton is in Chowan County, one of the first four counties of North Carolina (Perquimans, Pasquotank and Currituck are the other three).

Edenton had its own Tea Party in 1774 when 51 women gathered at the home of Mrs. Elizabeth King and vowed to support the American cause. The town is quaint and steeped in history. The aforementioned discovery about the Edenton Tea Party encouraged a closer look!

A journey through the history of the town reveals the restored homes of several prominent North Carolinians. James Iredell served as Attorney General during the Revolution and was a Justice of the Supreme Court from 1790 to 1799. Samuel Johnston was a government leader and senator during Revolutionary times. Dr. Hugh Williamson signed the Constitution; Joseph Hewed signed the Declaration of Independence. Thomas Barker was a North Carolina agent to England and a reputed leader of the Edenton Tea Party.

The Chowan County Courthouse, the Barker House, St. Paul's Episcopal Church and Iredell House are just a few of the area's 18th-century buildings, representing the finest in colonial architecture. A walk along King Street will reveal a remarkable collection of Georgian, Federal and Greek revival homes nestled among gardens and trees.

Edenton was a prosperous port town, and between 1771 and 1776 more than 800 ships served business and commerce with links to Europe and the West Indies. Blackbeard the pirate sailed into Edenton Bay on numerous occasions.

Barker House serves as a Visitor Center. Guided tours of the town begin at Barker House on Edenton Bay. An audiovisual presentation is available here as well. Hours are Monday through Saturday from 10 till 4:30 PM November through May; from 9 AM till 4:30 PM June through October, and on Sundays from 2 PM till 5 PM all year. For group tour reservations and further information call 482-2637.

There are a number of fine restaurants and bed and breakfast accommodations in Edenton.

Caroline's opens early with homemade breads, pastries and rolls in addition to traditional breakfast. Boswell's is known for its fine seafood and ethnic creations. Bob and Sharon's Bar-be-que on Route 32 is an attractive cafe with good eats.

The Lords Proprietors' Inn, 482-3641, Granville Queen Inn, 482-5296 and The Governor Eden Inn, 482-2072 are very good choices for accommodations. All are beautifully restored and maintained older homes that operate as bed-and-breakfast type inns. Call for rates and reservations.

Edenton can be reached from Roanoke Island and Manteo via Route 64/264 by driving 40 miles west until you come to Route 32 that will take you, after a right turn, toward Edenton. Just follow the signs from there.

MULBERRY HILL PLANTATION

Edenton, N.C.   482-8077

Mulberry Hill Plantation is off Route 32, approximately 8 miles from Edenton. Tom and Janie Wood have restored the house, which was built around 1800, and welcome guests who appreciate the simplicity of a bed and breakfast. Most of the acreage of the original plantation is being developed as golf course-homesites, but when you drive through the small gate to this grand old home, the spacious lawn and mature trees take you back in time. The view of Albemarle Sound is magnificent. There are four guest rooms and three baths. A plantation breakfast is served. Golf and tennis privileges are available to guests. If you're looking for a place away from it all, try Mulberry Hill Plantation. Weddings and other social occasions are sometimes held here. Call for rates and reservations.

SOMERSET PLACE

Pettigrew State Park   797-4560

We don't know who wrote the site press release, but its opening paragraph is worth quoting: "Passion, splendor and grim reality are all found in the epic story of Lake Phelps and the vast plantations carved from the haunting and mysterious coastal swamps on its banks by two extraordinary families. Here among majestic cypress and sycamore trees stands the elegant early 19th century home of Josiah Collins, III that once hosted the cultivated elite of North Carolina's planter aristocracy. Nearby, beneath sheltering limbs of great oaks, Charles Pettigrew, the state's first Episcopal bishop-elect, his congressman son and Confederate brigadier general grandson lie in eternal slumber beside rich, fertile farmland wrested from primeval nature by that potent combination of African slave labor and English immigrant ambition that has become the most enduring symbol of the 'Old South.'"

That's a hard act to follow, but let's try. The plantation was one of the four biggest in North Carolina, with more than 300 slaves growing corn and rice. The mansion, a 2½-story frame building with 14 rooms, was built in Greek Revival style circa 1830. It has been fully restored, with period furnishings. Six original outbuildings remain. The lawns and gardens alongside nearby Phelps Lake are especially beautiful in summer. A historically important collection of the plantation's slave records is open for genealogical research. A state historic site now, Somerset Place is open on the following schedule. From April to October it's open Monday through Saturday 9 AM to 5 PM and Sunday 1 to 5 PM. From November to March it's open Tuesday through Saturday 10 AM to 4 PM, Sunday 1 PM to 4 PM, and it's closed Mondays. Admission is free, but groups planning to visit should

write Box 215, Creswell, N.C., 27928 to make reservations. To reach it take Route 64/264 west across the Croatan Sound from Manteo, and follow it west for about 40 miles. Turn left at the little town of Creswell and another five miles will bring you to Pettigrew State Park and Somerset Place.

CAPE LOOKOUT NATIONAL SEASHORE

Low, unpopulated, almost forgotten even by North Carolinians, more barrier islands stretch southwestward for 55 miles from Ocracoke Inlet. North Core Banks with Portsmouth Village, South Core Banks, Cape Lookout and Shackleford Banks were incorporated into the Cape Lookout National Seashore in 1966.

These low, sandy islands have been untouched by either development or by stabilization. (Remember that the Outer Banks were stabilized by the CCC in the 1930s with dunes and plantings.) As a relatively recent NPS acquisition, and a remote one, there are few facilities available for the visitor. But if you don't mind roughing it a little bit (deer ticks, chiggers, deerflies, mosquitoes, gnats, squalls, hurricanes, rip currents, sharks, and jellyfish), these islands are a great place for primitive camping, fishing, boating and bird watching. A no-kidder: gnats may annoy you, but really stay alert for storms, as there is little shelter on most of these islands. You can call Coast Guard weather at 726-7550 for a forecast before you leave the mainland. Here's some helpful information for you "naturalists":

1) Two concessions operate out of

Davis and Atlantic, NC, offering primitive cabins for overnight lodging.

2) There are no established campgrounds but primitive (back pack style) camping is allowed.

3) There are no paved roads but four-wheel drive vehicles can operate on the beach front.

4) Water is available from pitcher pumps in the Cape Point area.

At Cape Lookout itself are located the lighthouse, erected in 1859, and a small Coast Guard Station, no longer active.

Access: if you have your own boat, you will find launching ramps at marinas throughout Carteret County, though the easiest access to Cape Point is from Shell Point on Harkers Island. Concession ferry services (privately run, federally overseen) are available from Harkers Island to the Cape Lookout Light area, from Davis to Shingle Point, from Atlantic to an area north of Drum Inlet, and from Ocracoke to Portsmouth Village. For current rates and more information, write or call the Park Service, Cape Lookout National Seashore, 3601 Bridges Street, Suite F, Morehead City, N.C. 28557-2913; 240-1409 or Harkers Island Station, 728-2250.

For complete information about the Cape Lookout area, get a copy of *The Insiders' Guide to the Crystal Coast and New Bern*, available at bookstores or through our handy order form in the back of this book.

HOPE PLANTATION
Windsor, N.C. 794-3140

Hope Plantation began as a grant from the Lord Proprietors of the Carolina Colony to the Hobson family in the 1720s. David Stone, a delegate to the North Carolina Constitutional Convention of 1789 and later judge, representative, senator, and governor (1808-1810), built an impressive home on the site circa 1800. The Hope Mansion is an outstanding Federal Period residence and is reminiscent in some ways of Monticello and in other ways of Scarlett O'Hara's Tara. Historic Hope Foundation acquired the mansion and land in 1966. Now restored, it and two smaller houses (the King-Bazemore and the Samuel Cox Houses) are open to the public as a furnished house-museum. There are also restored 18th-century gardens. Hope is on the National Register of Historic Places.

Hope Plantation is outside of the town of Windsor, roughly a two-hour drive west of Manteo. Take 64 out of Roanoke Island west to its intersection with 13; go north on 13; Hope is on NC 308, four miles west of US 13 bypass. The plantation is open March 1 through December 23, Mondays through Saturdays from 10 AM to 4 PM; Sundays 2 PM to 5 PM; it's closed January and February. Adult admission is $5 for both houses. Picnic facilities are available.

Index of Advertisers

Index

ORDER FORM
Fast and Simple!

Mail to:	Or:
Insiders Guides®, Inc.	**for VISA or**
P.O. Drawer 2057	**Mastercard orders call**
Manteo, NC 27954	**1-800-765-BOOK**

Name _____

Address _____

City/State/Zip _____

Qty.	Title/Price	Shipping	Amount
	Insiders' Guide to Richmond/$12.95	$2.50	
	Insiders' Guide to Williamsburg/$12.95	$2.50	
	Insiders' Guide to Virginia's Blue Ridge/$12.95	$2.50	
	Insiders' Guide to Virginia's Chesapeake Bay/$12.95	$2.50	
	Insiders' Guide to Washington, DC/$12.95	$2.50	
	Insiders' Guide to Charlotte/$14.95	$2.50	
	Insiders' Guide to North Carolina's Triangle/$14.95	$2.50	
	Insiders' Guide to North Carolina's Outer Banks/$12.95	$2.50	
	Insiders' Guide to Wilmington, NC/$12.95	$2.50	
	Insiders' Guide to North Carolina's Crystal Coast/$12.95	$2.50	
	Insiders' Guide to Charleston, SC/$12.95	$2.50	
	Insiders' Guide to Myrtle Beach/$12.95	$2.50	
	Insiders' Guide to Mississippi/$12.95 (8/94)	$2.50	
	Insiders' Guide to Orlando/$12.95	$2.50	
	Insiders' Guide to Sarasota/Bradenton/$12.95 (8/94)	$2.50	
	Insiders' Guide to Northwest Florida/$12.95 (7/94)	$2.50	
	Insiders' Guide to Lexington, KY/$12.95	$2.50	
	Insiders' Guide to Louisville/$12.95 (12/94)	$2.50	
	Insiders' Guide to the Twin Cities/$12.95 (12/94)	$2.50	
	Insiders' Guide to Boulder/$12.95 (11/94)	$2.50	
	Insiders' Guide to Denver/$12.95 (11/94)	$2.50	
	Insiders' Guide to The Civil War (Eastern Theater)/$12.95	$2.50	
	Insiders' Guide to Western North Carolina/$12.95 (2/95)	$2.50	
	Insiders' Guide to Atlanta/$12.95 (2/95)	$2.50	

Payment in full(check or money order)
must accompany this order form.
Please allow 2 weeks for delivery.

N.C. residents add 6% sales tax _____

Total _____